Steve Fuschi

Understanding Human Relations

Exam

Know /Power
Freud / Ego /super Ego etc
~~Mazlows hier~~
Starts from Mazlows theory. up to
present.

38 multiple choice

SECOND EDITION

Understanding Human Relations
A Practical Guide to People at Work

Robert A. Baron
Rensselaer Polytechnic Institute

Paul B. Paulus
University of Texas at Arlington

Allyn and Bacon
Boston • London • Toronto • Sydney • Tokyo • Singapore

Executive Editor • *Susan Badger*
Series Editorial Assistant • *Dana Lamothe*
Production Administrator • *Susan McIntyre*
Editorial-Production Service • *York Production Services*
Photo Research • *Susie Howard*
Cover Administrator • *Linda Dickinson*
Composition Buyer • *Linda Cox*
Manufacturing Buyer • *Louise Richardson*

Baron, Robert A.
    Understanding human relations : a practical guide to people at
work / Robert A. Baron, Paul B. Paulus. — 2nd ed.
      p. cm.
    Includes indexes.
    ISBN 0-205-12798-3
    1. Group relations training. 2. Interpersonal relations.
I. Paulus, Paul B. II. Title.
HF5549.5.G73B37 1991
650.1′3—dc20
                                    90-48394
                                      CIP

Printed in the United States of America
10 9 8 7 6 5 4 3 2 1   95 94 93 92 91 90

Photo Credits

The photo credits are continued on page 495 which should be considered an extension of the copyright page.

p. 8, © Mary Kate Denny/PhotoEdit; p. 10, Courtesy of the AT&T Archives; p. 16 (left), The Bettmann Archive; p. 16 (right), NASA; p. 18, Courtesy of the authors; p. 36, E. Richter/H. Armstrong Roberts; p. 38, © Raymond Depardon/Magnum Photos,

To
Jessica, my little ray of sunshine. RAB
and
Christopher and Leigh, my constant sources of joy and
pride. PBP

Contents

 # Preface

The Benefits of Feedback

Judging from the feedback provided by both students and colleagues, the first edition of **Understanding Human Relations** was a success. They cited its coverage, readability, emphasis on both research and application, and special features designed to increase student interest and involvement. In the second edition we have tried to maintain these positive features while updating and expanding the coverage significantly. In this process we were greatly aided by the feedback provided by a number of reviewers who responded to a variety of questions about features of the first edition. We tried to accommodate as many of their suggestions as possible.

Changes in Content

New Chapters. One major change involves the addition of two new chapters. These chapters cover major topics that are central to understanding human relations—*interpersonal relations* and *group behavior.* The new chapter on groups covers the various ways in which groups influence individual behavior. This includes a discussion of responsibility diffusion in groups, deindividuation, group task performance, group decision-making, group socialization and development, and brainstorming. The second chapter deals with interpersonal relations. Topics covered in this chapter are affiliation, social comparison, friendship, love, the development of relationships, and romantic relationships in the workplace.

Revisions and New Topics. All of the other chapters have been significantly updated and revised in light of new developments and reviewer feedback. Among some of the new topics covered in this edition are:

The Case Method of Research
Contrast Effects in Social Perception
Similarity Effects in Social Perception
ERG Theory
Work-related Motives

Leadership Motive Pattern
Dissonance and Attitude Change
Substitutes for Leadership
Situational Leadership Theory
Charismatic Leaders
Communication and Cooperation
Arbitration, Mediation, and Integrative Agreements
Daily Hassles and Stress
Individual Differences in Stress Resistance
Career Changes over The Lifetime
Optimism and Pessimism and Stress
Career Development and Lifestyles
Phases in Organizational Socialization
Effective Organizational Socialization
Sensitivity Training
Team Building
Quality Circles
Sexual Harassment

Special Features

Most of the special inserts included in the first edition were positively received. Reviewers were particularly pleased with the "Human Relations in Action" sections. These provide a number of exercises that require students to assess themselves or others in various ways. The exercises are designed to involve students in understanding some of the basic principles of human relations. We have provided many new versions of this type of insert. We have also completely revised the "Case-in-Point" sections. These present various human relations scenarios that allow students to apply many of the concepts presented in the chapters. At the end of each chapter we present additional cases and exercises to further aid students in applying the concepts that they have learned.

Reviewers of the Second Edition

Eve McClure
Highline Community College

James Wilson
Pan American University

Ursula White
El Paso Community College

Esther Hamilton
Pepperdine University

Jacqueline Vines
Davenport College of Business

Reviewers of the previous edition

Merle Ace
University of British Columbia

Bonnie Bailey Allen
Warner Pacific College

Patricia Baxter
Pensacola Junior College

Joseph Benson
New Mexico State University

Jerry Goddard
Aims Community College

William Ickes
University of Texas

Leo Kiesewetter
Illinois Central College

Vaughn Luckadoo
Central Piedmont Community College

David Nakamoejo
Kapiolani Community College

Illustrations

Illustrations and flow charts can be very helpful in facilitating understanding of the major findings and conceptual frameworks. We have increased their use in this edition.

Resource Materials for Students

A Student Study Guide. This guide has been prepared to assist students in learning and reviewing the information presented in the text. It includes learning objectives, definitions of key terms, review quizzes, and a fill-in-the-blanks guided review.

Resource Materials for Instructors

An instructor's manual is available that includes test items, discussion questions, and ready-to-duplicate materials for exercises.

A Concluding Comment

We have made significant efforts to make this edition even better than the first one. In our view, the changes in content, inserts, illustrations, and pedagogical aids have helped us to achieve this goal. However, in the final analysis, it is the judgement of our students and colleagues that is most important in determining whether this is really so. To help us determine where we have succeeded or where improvement is still needed, we need your input. We would appreciate feedback on any feature of this text. We promise that we will take your suggestions seriously. We look forward to hearing from you.

Robert A. Baron
Department of Managerial Policy and Organization
and Department of Psychology
Rensselaer Polytechnic Institute
Troy, New York 12180-3590

Paul B. Paulus
Department of Psychology
University of Texas at Arlington
Arlington, Texas 76019-0528

CHAPTER 1

Understanding Human Relations: An Introduction

Learning Objectives

After reading this chapter,
you should be able to:

1. Define the field of human relations.

2. Know the characteristics of scientific
   management.

3. Describe the major events and
   developments that led to the emergence
   of an independent field of human
   relations.

4. Discuss the major features of human
   relations in the 1990s.

5. Explain key methods of research in
   human relations (e.g., systematic
   observation, experimentation).

6. Explain the central role of theory in
   human relations research.

irk Copeland and Susan Grimes were both starting their jobs at Al's Hamburgers, one of the most popular hamburger restaurants in town. They had been there often as customers, but now they were on the other side of the counter. The pay wasn't too great, but the hours were nicely flexible. Kirk was assigned to the kitchen to help prepare food while Susan was being trained to handle customer orders. Fortunately, it was a fairly slow day, so their manager, Jim Miller, had plenty of time to train them. He was quite friendly and seemed to have a personal interest in his employees. But he was also very demanding. He stressed the importance of being on time and the need to work fast during the busy periods. Kirk wasn't sure he was going to like the assistant manager as well. She seemed to be concerned mostly about getting the job done. She was not very friendly and would hardly even look at Kirk when she spoke. Susan was a different story though. Kirk thought she was kind of cute. He never met her before, but maybe he would ask her for a date when they got to know each other a little better.

"Hey Kirk, get moving!" came a voice from behind.

Kirk looked around and saw this was one of the veteran employees, Jeff Hyland.

"We're getting behind. Let's get with the program!"

There was now a long line of customers, and all of a sudden there was no time for fantasy. Kirk picked up his pace and he noticed that Susan was doing the same. *Boy, we're already under pressure the first day on the job*, he thought. *Well, at least it won't be boring working here.*

Our lives are constantly changing. We change jobs, relationships, and schools, constantly encountering new people and new challenges. To some extent this can be quite exciting and pleasant. There can, however, also be some drawbacks. Kirk discovered this as he spent his first day on the job. Although he had favorable reactions to the manager and to Susan, the other new employee, he was not sure about the assistant manager and Jeff. Although the hours at the job were flexible, the pay was rather low. Whether the work situation and relations would be positive would depend on how well the various group members got along.

Human relations is concerned with the factors that help and hinder effective relationships in the work environment. Indeed, one of the most basic assumptions of human relations is as follows: In *order* to have an effective organization, we must provide for effective, satisfying relations between the people in it. Consistent with this point of view, human relations generally concentrates on two major goals: (1) increasing our understanding of interactions between individuals, and (2) developing practical techniques for enhancing such relations.

As you already know from your own experience, human beings can interact with one another in an almost endless number of ways—everything from helping and cooperation on the one hand through conflict and aggression on the other.[1] It is not at all surprising, then, that human relations is a highly diverse field. This breadth is readily apparent in the following list, which contains a small sample of the many questions our field currently addresses:

1. Does setting specific goals increase work-related motivation?
2. How can we discover the true intentions of other persons?
3. What are the best techniques for persuading others?
4. When is conflict constructive and when is it destructive within an organization?
5. What type of leaders are best?
6. How can groups function most effectively?
7. What are the best strategies for bargaining with others?
8. Is the "grapevine" really a reliable source of information?
9. How can individuals best handle stress?
10. What steps can be taken to reduce prejudice and discrimination in work settings?

In the remaining chapters we will examine all of these questions and many others. Before turning to these intriguing topics, though, it will be useful to consider some background information—facts you will find useful in understanding later parts of this book.

First, a working definition of the field of human relations will be presented. The reason for beginning in this manner is simple: such a definition will help you understand what human relations is, what it is not, and what it seeks to accomplish. Second, the origins of the human relations approach—where it came from and how it developed—will be briefly outlined. Third, the manner in which our field attempts to discover new facts about relations between people, and to put such knowledge to practical use, will be described. Finally, several features of this text and its overall organization will be called to your attention. Armed with this information, you will be ready for what then follows: a survey of many fascinating aspects of human relations in work and life settings.

HUMAN RELATIONS: A WORKING DEFINITION

Earlier it was noted that human relations seeks two major goals: increased understanding of interpersonal relations and the practical application of such knowledge to work settings. At first glance these goals may seem to provide a useful definition of the field. In fact, they *do* come close to meeting this need. There is one complicating factor, though, that should not be ignored. This involves the fact that human relationships are extremely varied in scope. Indeed, their full range is perhaps best captured by the phrase, "from love to hate, and everything in between." This great diversity, in turn, raises an important question: Does the field of human relations seek greater understanding of *all* forms of interpersonal behavior, or does it focus primarily on certain key, work-related aspects of such relationships? The answer, unfortunately, is something of a mixed bag. On the one hand, human relations is certainly not restricted in its scope. It does seek knowledge about a wide range of human behavior. And given the varied nature of interactions between people in work settings, this is fully appropriate. On the other hand, human relations is *applications-oriented;* helping to solve practical problems is its stock-in-trade. Consistent with this orientation, then, it tends to direct much of its attention to certain aspects of human relationships—aspects most directly related to the attainment of important organizational and individual goals. Human relations thus tends to focus on topics such as motivation, communication, conflict, leadership, and persuasion. In contrast, it devotes somewhat less attention to other topics, such as mental health and aggression. This is not because these latter aspects of human relations are perceived as being less interesting or important than those listed in the first group. Far from it! But they are viewed as being somewhat less directly related to behavior in work settings and receive less attention for this reason.

Our working definition of the field of human relations, then, is as follows: *Human relations seeks to understand those aspects of interpersonal relations most directly linked to attainment of organizational and individual goals in work settings.* Further, it seeks to apply such knowledge to the enhancement of these goals. In short, it is concerned with determining how individuals can work together most effectively and with developing practical techniques for maximizing such effectiveness (see Figure 1.1).

Human Relations: Myth versus Reality

Now that we have seen what human relations is, it is equally important to see what it is not. The reason this is important is as follows: Many persons taking their first course in human relations, or reading a book like this one, seem to begin with false ideas about the nature of the field. Indeed, they seem to believe that it offers both more or less than is actually the case. Basically, there appear to be three major "myths" about human relations. Each of these is described (and refuted) below.

Human relations will provide you with a sure-fire formula for success. A reasonable reaction to this idea might be "Ah—if only that were true!" Unfortunately, many factors operate, and the ways in which they function in combination varies greatly from person to person and situation to situation. For these reasons there can be no simple answers, and no perfect formula for success. Thus, although the field of human relations can shed much light on the causes of both success and happiness, it cannot solve all of our problems in this respect.

Human relations tells you how to manipulate other people—how to get them to do what you want, and to share your views. Here, too, popular belief is wrong. First, although many techniques for influencing others exist and are of interest to human relations, none are perfect. In fact, most can readily be resisted. Second, even if such super-effective tactics for controlling others existed, teaching people to use them would hardly be a major goal of human relations. On the contrary,

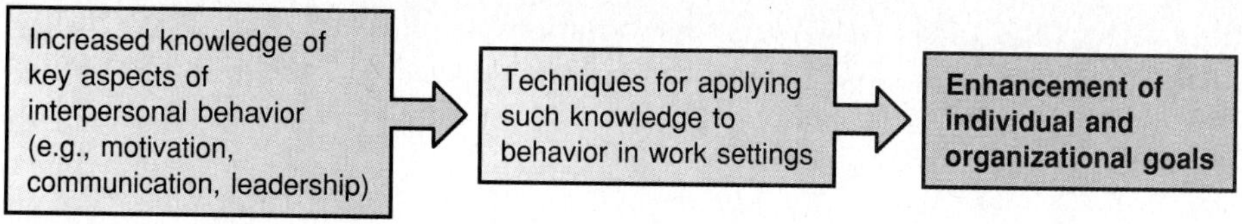

Increased knowledge of key aspects of interpersonal behavior (e.g., motivation, communication, leadership) → Techniques for applying such knowledge to behavior in work settings → **Enhancement of individual and organizational goals**

FIGURE 1.1 Human Relations: Knowledge and Application
Human relations seeks increased understanding of key aspects of interpersonal behavior. It then applies such knowledge to the enhancement of both individual and organizational goals.

as a field concerned with maximizing individual satisfaction as well as organizational effectiveness, such steps would be contrary to its basic orientation. Thus, if you expect your first contact with human relations to equip you with tactics for manipulating or using others, forget it; you've come to the wrong place!

Human relations is just a lot of common sense. In some ways, this is the most dangerous myth of all. It suggests that everything you will encounter in this text and in your course is "common knowledge"—information you knew before exposure to human relations. Certainly, we do learn valuable lessons from our experiences (see Figure 1.2). However, we have learned that many popular ideas about human beings and human behavior are inaccurate. In fact, many of these ideas are often downright misleading. If you believe that human relations is merely common sense, then prepare for some surprises—they are sure to follow. (For further proof of the inaccuracy of common sense as a guide to understanding human behavior, see the **Human Relations in Action** on page 6.)

In sum, human relations will not offer you a "yellow brick road" to success; nor will it teach you how to manipulate or control others. What it *will* do is increase your understanding of the people around you, your relationships with them, and yourself. This knowledge will, in turn, help you understand what is happening in many situations in the world of work and how to cope with problems

FIGURE 1.2 Common Sense: Sometimes Useful; Often Not
Although we can learn a lot from our experiences, we need to be aware that many of our common sense ideas are not supported by behavioral science research. (Cathy © 1989 Universal Press Syndicate. Reprinted with permission. All rights reserved.)

more effectively. In short, while human relations cannot guarantee personal happiness or success (and makes no promises in this respect), it can help you to cope with a complex and everchanging social world. In this manner, its practical usefulness can hardly be exaggerated.

HUMAN RELATIONS: A CAPSULE MEMOIR

In the 1990s the notion that the "human side of work" is important is far from surprising. Most people both inside and outside of business realize that communication, motivation, and other aspects of human relations play a key role in the successful functioning of organizations. You may be surprised to learn, though, that this idea is relatively new. It took form only during the present century and did not gain widespread acceptance among managers until recent

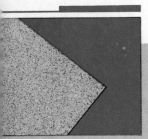

HUMAN RELATIONS IN ACTION

Common Sense: An Unreliable Guide to Human Behavior

Common sense, it was noted earlier, is often wrong. In many cases, it offers ideas or beliefs about human behavior that turn out to be false. You can readily demonstrate this fact for yourself in the following manner. Simply ask several of your friends who have not taken a course in human relations to answer the questions below. (It's also best to select friends who have not had any exposure to psychology.) Because common sense suggests a ready answer to each, your friends will probably respond quickly and confidently. After they are done, compare their answers with the ones given on page 31, which are based on the findings of systematic research. You will probably discover that your friends have done quite poorly.

You may also want to take this quiz yourself before looking at the answers. It may also be interesting to take it twice: right now and again at the end of this course. You will certainly do much better after reading this text and attending lectures than you do today.

Indicate whether you think each of the following statements is true or false by placing a *T* or *F* in the space provided.

____ F **1.** When people are paid or rewarded in some way for doing things they enjoy, they come to like them even more.

____ F **2.** Once the persons involved in a conflict realize that they have nothing to gain by continuing their dispute, they will quickly resolve their difference.

decades. Why did it take so long to develop? And where, finally, did it come from? It is on these and related questions that we now focus.

Scientific Management: The Beginnings

How can productivity be improved? This basic question has puzzled and enticed managers since ancient times. In one sense the modern field of human relations can also be traced to this issue. To understand why this is so, we must return to the closing decades of the nineteenth century—a period of rapid industrial growth and technological advance. The prevailing view of work was then much as it had been throughout history. The tasks being performed were what really mattered; the people who performed them were of much less importance. In accordance with this perspective, engineers worked long and hard to design the most efficient machinery possible. As they proceeded with this task, however, they gradually came to a new conclusion: While machines and equipment are important, they are only a part of the total picture. The people who run them must also be considered. Efforts to take into account this basic idea soon led to

___I___ 3. When going on a job interview, it is best to groom yourself as neatly as possible, and to demonstrate a high level of friendliness toward the interviewer.

___I___ 4. If a leader discovers that she or he is wrong, it is better for that person to admit the error and change position rather than to "stick to her/his guns."

___I___ 5. When people work together with others in a group, they tend to put out more effort than they do when they work on the same task alone.

___F___ 6. In general, males work harder for a male supervisor, while females work harder for a female supervisor.

___F___ 7. When we evaluate the performance of others on some job, we usually assign equal weight or importance to their ability and to the amount of effort they have expended.

___F___ 8. Groups tend to make more cautious and conservative decisions than individuals do.

___F___ 9. The best way to stop a rumor is to present evidence that refutes it.

___F___ 10. The very top executives in most large companies are extremely competitive, hard-driving types.

(Answers: see p. 31.)

time and motion studies—attempts to design jobs so they could be performed in the most efficient manner possible.

This new concern with the human side of work soon paved the way for the emergence of a major new approach—**scientific management.** Although it was practiced by many persons, its most noted advocate was Frederick W. Taylor. In a famous book entitled *The Principles of Scientific Management,* Taylor outlined the key features of this new approach.[2] In general, it, too, was concerned with maximizing efficiency and getting the most work possible out of employees. Thus scientific management emphasized the importance of effective *job design*—planning work tasks in a systematic manner. In addition, though, it contained two new features that, taken together, focused attention on employees as well as on their work.

First, Taylor suggested that workers be carefully selected and trained for their jobs. In this regard, he broke with the traditional view holding that employees are basically interchangeable cogs who can be readily shuffled from job to job. Second, Taylor recognized the importance of motivation in work settings. Indeed, he firmly believed that efforts to raise worker motivation might well result in major gains in productivity (see Figure 1.3). His view concerning the basis of such motivation was, by modern standards, quite naive. Briefly, he assumed that work motivation stems mainly from the desire for gain—that is, the desire for money. Today, in contrast, it is realized that people actually seek many goals through their work, such as approval from others and enhanced status. But al-

important

FIGURE 1.3 Work Motivation: A Major Concern of Scientific Management
One of the major problems in work settings is employee motivation. *Scientific management advocated developing procedures to increase worker motivation.*

though Taylor was mistaken about the nature of motivation in work settings, he did grasp the importance of this key factor. This, as we shall see, was a major step forward.

To repeat: scientific management was primarily concerned with raising efficiency and output—*not* with enhancing worker satisfaction or morale. But it did begin to recognize the importance of considering people in work settings, especially their abilities, training, and motivation. In this way, it opened the door to further study of the "human side of work" and contributed to the development of modern human relations.

Human Relations Emerges: Work Settings as Social Systems

As we have just noted, scientific management did direct some attention to the importance of human behavior at work. Yet, it is also obvious that it did not go far enough in this respect. Good job design and high motivation are indeed important factors, but they are only part of the total picture. Performance in work settings is also strongly affected by many other conditions, including the nature of the relations among employees, communication between them, their attitudes toward work, and the effectiveness of their leaders. Today, this fact seems obvious and easy to grasp. In the past, though, this was not so. In fact, it actually took some dramatic research findings to call the social nature of work settings to the attention of practicing managers. The research that accomplished this important task—and so stimulated the emergence of human relations—is usually termed the **Hawthorne studies.** Given its importance in the development of the modern perspective, this research is worth considering here.

The Hawthorne Studies: A Brief Description   In the mid-1920s a series of fairly typical scientific management studies were begun at the Hawthorne plant of the Western Electric Company, a manufacturing plant outside Chicago (see Figure 1.4). The purpose of the research was simple: to determine the impact of level of illumination on worker productivity. Several female employees took part in the study. One group worked in a control room where the level of lighting was held constant; another group worked in a test room where brightness of lighting was varied in a systematic manner. Results were quite baffling: Productivity increased in both the test and control rooms. Further, there seemed to be no orderly link between level of lighting and productivity. For example, output remained high in the test room even when illumination was reduced to that of moonlight— a level so dim that workers could barely see what they were doing!

Puzzled by these findings, officials of Western Electric called in a team of experts headed by Elton Mayo. The findings they uncovered proved to have a major impact on management and on the developing field of human relations.[3] In an initial series of studies (known as the *Relay Room Experiments*), Mayo and his colleagues examined the impact of thirteen different factors on productivity. These included length of rest pauses, length of work day and work week, method of payment, place of work, and even a free mid-morning lunch. Subjects were again female employees who worked in a special test room. Once more, results were quite mysterious: Productivity increased with almost every change in work

FIGURE 1.4 The Hawthorne Studies: An Important Milestone
Research at the Hawthorne plant played an important role in stimulating the emergence of the field of human relations.

conditions (see Figure 1.5). Indeed, even when subjects were returned to the initial, standard conditions that existed at the start of the research, productivity continued to rise. What did these results mean? Why did productivity improve in this totally unexpected manner? These were among the questions faced by Mayo and his colleagues.

As if such findings were not puzzling enough, additional studies soon added to the confusion. For example, in one investigation (known as the *Bank Wiring Room Study*) male members of an existing work group were carefully observed by members of the research team. No attempts were made to alter the conditions under which they labored, but they were interviewed by another investigator during nonwork periods. Here, results were quite distinct from those in the earlier studies. Productivity did not rise continuously. On the contrary, it soon became apparent that workers were deliberately restricting their output. This was revealed both by observations of their work behavior (e.g., all men stopped work well before quitting time) and by interviews (almost all admitted that they could easily do more if they wished). Why was this the case? Why did these workers consciously restrict their output, while those in the Relay Room experiments did not? Gradually Mayo and his colleagues arrived at the answer. On the basis of the findings already described and through interviews with as many as 20,000 workers, they reached the following conclusion: *Work places are actually complex social systems.* Thus, in order to comprehend behavior in them, it is necessary to understand work attitudes, social relations, communication, and a host of other factors.

Armed with this insight, Mayo and his associates were soon able to interpret the puzzling findings obtained in their research. First, with respect to the Relay Room Experiments, it was clear that productivity rose continuously because subjects reacted favorably to the special attention they received and to the relatively free supervisory climate in the test room. In short, they knew they were being observed; and because they experienced positive feelings about this attention, their motivation—and productivity—rose. In contrast, output was held low in the Bank Wiring Room Study because of other factors. The men in that group feared "working themselves out of a job" and raising the amount they were expected to complete each day if their productivity was too high. To avoid such outcomes, they established informal but powerful rules about behavior on the job—rules that tended to hold production down to low levels. Indeed, even punishments for "rate busters" (men who worked too hard) were established.

FIGURE 1.5 The Hawthorne Studies: Some Puzzling Results
In one part of the Hawthorne studies, female employees were exposed to several changes in work conditions. Surprisingly, almost every one of these alterations produced an increase in productivity. (*Source:* Based on data from Roethlisberger & Dickson, 1939, Note 3.)

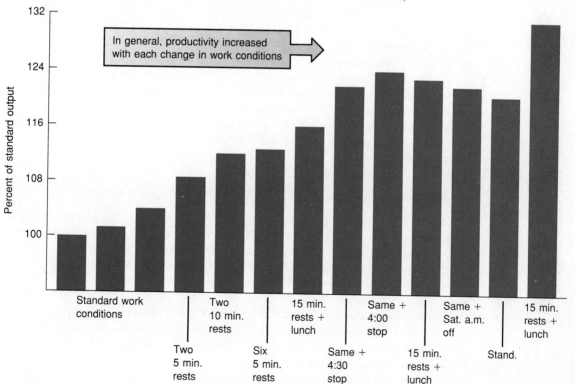

Such rules, present in virtually task-performing or social group, are generally known as **norms.** They specify how group members *should* or *ought to* behave. In this way, they often play a key role in shaping group functioning.

In short, Mayo and his colleagues concluded that social variables such as group pressure, relations between employees and management, relations among employees themselves, and various group norms all played a role in producing the results of both sets of studies. In one case, these factors operated to enhance productivity. In the other, they acted to restrain it. In both instances, however, insight into on-the-job performance could be gained from attention to key aspects of human behavior.

The Hawthorne Studies: Their Lasting Impact At this point it is important to note that the Hawthorne studies were, by modern research standards, quite flawed.[4] For example, essential control groups were missing, subjects knew that they were being carefully studied, and no attempt was made to ensure that they were generally representative of all workers. This last condition is necessary if results are to be extended to large groups of employees.

Despite these drawbacks, though, the Hawthorne studies had an impressive overall effect. The findings of these studies called attention to the fact that work settings are actually complex social situations. They also indicated that full understanding of behavior in them requires knowledge of many factors ignored by scientific management. As this basic principle gained recognition, a new perspective known as the **human relations approach** took shape.[5] This perspective devoted far more attention to human needs, motives, and relationships than had previously been the case. In addition, it recognized the fact that lasting gains in productivity and morale can be achieved only through appropriate changes in these and related factors. In this manner, it served as the foundation for modern human relations. And since this field, in turn, has exerted a major impact upon modern organizations and many practices within them, one fact is clear: The workers in that long-vanished plant outside Chicago probably had greater and more lasting effects upon the entire world of work than most of them would ever have dreamed possible!

Human Relations in the 1990s: Some Major Features

Modern human relations is a diverse field; the topics it studies and the practical techniques it develops are as varied in nature as human behavior and the problems people encounter at work. Basically, though, it seems to possess several major features that identify and set human relations apart from other fields or approaches. These are described below.

Human Relations and the Human Resources Model Suppose you approached a large number of managers and asked each to describe his or her basic view of human nature. What type of answers do you think you would receive? Unfortunately, even today, many of the replies would be somewhat negative in tone. Some of the persons questioned might suggest that human beings are basically lazy and either unwilling or unable to accept much responsibility. Further, they might note that the role of the manager is mainly that of giving such persons direction—keeping them on the "straight and narrow," so to speak. This traditional view, often known as **Theory X,** has prevailed for centuries. Do you think the boss in Figure 1.6 takes this view?

In contrast, other persons you question might report a more positive view of human beings and human behavior. These managers reject the notion that most persons are basically lazy and shiftless. Instead, they contend that under appropriate conditions people are just as capable of working hard and accepting responsibility as they are of "goofing off." Indeed, they might add that for many individuals, work serves as a primary source of satisfaction. According to this newer perspective—known as the **human resources model** or simply as **Theory Y**—it is the manager's task to identify the conditions that encourage such favorable outcomes and to ensure that they exist.[6]

Which of these contrasting perspectives is adopted by human relations? As you can readily guess, the second. Most practitioners of human relations assume that people *can* demonstrate many desirable behaviors at work, provided appropriate conditions exist. But please note: The human resources model does *not* assume that employees are always responsible or productive. It simply suggests that they react to conditions around them. If these are favorable (e.g., they are treated with respect and enjoy good relations with coworkers), they may work hard, accept responsibility, and show many other desirable actions. However, if conditions are negative (e.g., they feel exploited and do not have confidence in their leaders), they may adopt far less positive patterns. In short, modern human relations does not view the world of work through rose-colored glasses. At the same time, though, it does assume that there are no built-in reasons why work cannot be pleasant or satisfying, or why employees cannot be encouraged to show constructive actions on the job. In this respect, certainly, it is more optimistic than the older and more traditional view represented by Theory X.

FIGURE 1.6 Theory X: One Example

Theory X bosses assume that people are basically lazy and need constant direction. Do you think Mr. Dithers fits into this category? (Reprinted with special permission of King Features Syndicate.)

Human Relations and the Contingency Approach: Realizing That There Are No Simple Answers   What style of leadership is best? What is the most effective means of motivating employees? What is the best technique for reaching complex decisions? At first glance, these questions may strike you as being both intriguing and reasonable; indeed, you might assume that they are close to the core of modern human relations. In fact, however, there is one basic problem with all of them: They seem to imply the existence of simple, unitary answers. In other words, they suggest that there is indeed *one* best style of leadership, one best technique for enhancing motivation, or one best procedure for reaching decisions. It is a basic assumption of modern human relations that such an approach is both inaccurate and simplistic. Where behavior in work settings is concerned, there are—alas!—no simple answers. The processes involved are far too complex and are affected by far too many factors to permit us this luxury. Recognition of this fact is often known as the **contingency approach,** and is a hallmark of human relations as we enter the 1990s (see Figure 1.7).[7]

Because of its awareness of such complexity, the answers offered by human relations often include such phrases as "under some conditions" or "all other factors being equal." Some persons, hoping for simple "cookbook" formulas for dealing with organizational behavior, find such replies disappointing. Indeed, they often grumble about the inability of human relations to offer "straight answers." While we understand the reasons behind such complaints, we do not view them as justified. People and organizations are complex, so expecting simple answers about them is unfair and a bit naive. Even more important, accuracy—*not* simplicity—is the ultimate goal of our attempts to understand the human side of work. In the chapters that follow, therefore, we will reflect the approach prevailing in our field. We will do our best to avoid superfluous complexity, but we will also steer clear of conclusions that are misleading because, in the quest for simplicity, they overlook much.

FIGURE 1.7   The Contingency Approach: An Overview
The *contingency approach* calls attention to the fact that behavior in organizations is a complex function of many interacting factors, processes, and conditions. Because of this fact, there are usually no straightforward or simple answers to many of the questions investigated by human relations.

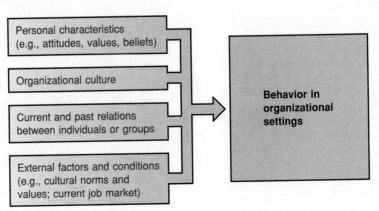

Human Relations: An Integrative Field Another major feature of modern human relations involves its *integrative nature*. As we have already seen, a major goal of human relations is that of understanding many aspects of interpersonal behavior. In order to accomplish this task, human relations draws heavily upon the principles and findings of several behavioral sciences, notably psychology, sociology, and organizational theory. From psychology, it acquires information about basic individual processes such as learning, perception, and motivation. From social psychology and sociology, it gains knowledge about group processes such as leadership, cooperation, and communication. And from organizational theory, it obtains information about the impact of organizational structure and the external environment upon individual employees.

But human relations does much more than simply "borrow" from these fields. It also attempts to combine information about individuals, groups, and organizations in a comprehensive framework for understanding human relations at work. In this respect, it is somewhat unique. Generally, each of the fields named above tends to focus on only a single level of analysis—individuals, groups, or organizations as a whole. Human relations seeks to overcome these restrictions and boundaries by combining information from many different sources. Its working rule of thumb is simply this: If knowledge from another field of study is helpful in understanding some aspect of interpersonal behavior, by all means use it. This flexible, integrative approach may yield a better and more accurate picture of human behavior in work settings than could otherwise be obtained.

Human Relations and the International Perspective In recent years, human relations has adopted an *international perspective*.[8] This shift has involved efforts to understand differences between work settings in various nations and the effects these have on both employees and organizations. In addition, it has also included sophisticated attempts to understand how these differences relate to the culture and history of different societies. One well-known example of the latter approach is provided by Ouchi's influential book, *Theory Z*.[9] Ouchi described several major differences between Japanese and American corporations—differences he felt were related to contrasting levels of productivity in these organizations. Some examples: guarantees of long-term employment are more common in Japanese than in American companies; decision making is more likely to be by consensus in Japanese companies; and performance is evaluated over longer periods of time in Japanese than in American companies. Ouchi related these differences to various cultural and historical factors, such as the fact that Japanese industry emerged, suddenly, out of an essentially feudal society, while American industry developed gradually, in the context of markedly different social conditions. Although strong support for his conclusions does not yet exist, Ouchi has stimulated many human relations experts to focus more attention on the role of cultural factors in human relations effectiveness.[10]

Human Relations: Application as a Guiding Principle When Edison wired a portion of lower Manhattan for electric lights in 1880, physicists still had little understanding of what happened in those wires when the current was switched on. Yet this lack of theoretical knowledge did not prevent thousands of people

is a field of study derived from psychology

why is organization important?

from using the new invention or benefiting from it. In contrast, when the Viking lander touched down on the surface of Mars in 1976, its safe arrival depended on full scientific knowledge of the physical forces that had affected its long journey across space (see Figure 1.8). Together, these two incidents illustrate an important point: Sometimes it is possible to attain progress and practical benefits in a given area without full scientific knowledge about it, and sometimes it is not. But which of these principles applies to human relations in work settings? Can we go ahead and produce beneficial changes in such settings even in the absence of full scientific knowledge about human behavior in them? Or must we wait for such information before proceeding? Most practitioners of human relations strongly support the former approach. They believe that we can intervene in work environments and produce beneficial changes, even in the absence of complete knowledge about the complex processes occurring in them. In short, they believe that it is possible for us to do some good right now, even though we do not understand precisely how such positive outcomes are produced or what specific factors play a role in their occurrence.

FIGURE 1.8 Progress: Does It Always Require Full Scientific Knowledge?
Sometimes, progress in a given area is possible even in the absence of complete scientific knowledge. This was so with respect to the use of electric lighting. In other instances, fairly complete scientific knowledge is needed before certain achievements are possible. This was the case for the Viking mission to Mars.

Fortunately, existing evidence tends to support this optimistic point of view. And the word "fortunately" is fully appropriate. At the moment, no complete theory of human behavior in work settings exists, and none seems likely to be developed during the next few years. Thus the fact that we can produce positive changes even in the absence of such theory is advantageous, to say the least. In any case, because of this general orientation, human relations as a field is deeply committed to applying the knowledge it obtains. It not only seeks to understand work settings and the behavior in them but also attempts to change these settings in ways that will enhance the outcomes of both individuals and organizations. This is a major theme of human relations—perhaps *the* major theme—and one you will find emphasized throughout the remainder of this book.

Human Relations as Producer: Knowledge from Applied Research Common sense, we have already seen, is not very reliable as a guide to human behavior. Indeed, it can often lead us into serious errors in our efforts to understand the persons around us. How, then, can we hope to uncover important facts around human relations in the world of work? How can we gain valuable insights into the way people interact with one another in work settings and organizations? Many possible answers to these questions exist, but most practitioners of human relations agree that two strategies are probably most useful. These involve (1) the adaptation, generalization, and application of knowledge acquired by related fields, and (2) original research focused on key aspects of human relations. As you will soon see, most of the information presented throughout this book was obtained by means of these methods.

Since human relations uncovers many intriguing facts about people and their behavior at work through research of its own, it is important to have some basic knowledge about this process. There are two basic reasons why human relations specialists decide to proceed in this manner. First, the information they require about some aspect of interpersonal relations may not be available elsewhere. Researchers in other fields may simply not have investigated the precise topic or question in which they are interested. Second, as we have already indicated, human relations experts always cast an eye toward application. They wish to use the knowledge at their disposal to enhance the attainment of both individual and organizational goals. Since the fields on which human relations draws are often less concerned with application, additional research may be needed to determine the best ways of putting knowledge to use. For both reasons, human relations experts do conduct research projects designed to add to our understanding of behavior in the world of work.

But, you may be wondering, how do they carry out such projects? The answer is fairly simple: by means of two techniques used in many other fields concerned with human behavior—**experimentation** and **systematic observation**.[11] Of course, you may not wish to become a researcher or to conduct such projects yourself. But since much of the information presented later in this book is based on studies using these techniques, it seems worthwhile to take a brief look at their major features.

Experimentation: Knowledge through Intervention

Suppose a human relations expert became interested in the following question: When individuals go on a job interview, how should they dress? (You may notice that this is similar to one of the questions on the quiz about common sense.) Further, imagine that no firm evidence on this question exists. How could our human relations expert go about finding out? One possibility is as follows: She could conduct an appropriate *experiment* (see Figure 1.9).

Unfortunately, many people seem to feel that experimentation is a complex and mysterious process—one well beyond their grasp. In fact, its basic logic is surprisingly simple and involves only two major steps: (1) some factor believed to affect behavior is systematically varied, in either its presence or strength, and (2) the effects of such variation upon some aspect of behavior are studied. The logic behind these procedures is as follows: If the factor varied actually affects behavior, persons exposed to different levels or amounts of it should also show differences in the way they act. For example, exposure to a small amount of the factor in question should result in one level of behavior; exposure to a larger amount should result in a different level, and so on.

Please note: *This reasoning is correct only if all other factors that might also affect the behavior under study are held constant.* If additional factors are allowed to vary freely, it is impossible to tell just why any difference in behavior occurs.

FIGURE 1.9 Laboratory Experiments: Useful Sources of Information
Laboratory experiments can provide much useful information about human relations. Here a group of students are involved in a brainstorming experiment (see Chapter 9).

The factor varied systematically is usually termed the *independent variable,* while the aspect of behavior studied is known as the *dependent variable.*

Now let's return to the example above, and see how a human relations specialist might conduct an experiment concerned with the impact of style of dress on the outcome of job interviews. One way to do this would be to arrange for a number of personnel managers to interview a job applicant. In reality, the job applicant would be an assistant of the researcher. To keep matters simple, let's assume only one person—a female—plays this role. The applicant then dresses in one of three distinct styles when reporting for each interview: (1) a very *informal* manner (old pants and a rumpled shirt), (2) a neat but *traditionally feminine* manner (a frilly blouse with dangling jewelry), or (3) a neat and *professional* manner (a tailored suit and simple jewelry). After each interview, the personnel manager would rate the applicant on a number of dimensions, such as suitability for employment and motivation for success, and would indicate whether she should be hired.

The ratings assigned to the applicant when dressed informally, in a feminine style, or in a professional manner would then be compared. If style of dress does affect ratings in a job interview, it would be expected that the ratings would differ under the three conditions. For example, as shown in Figure 1.10, the applicant might receive higher ratings when dressed in a neat but feminine manner than when dressed informally. She might receive the highest ratings when "dressed for success."[12] If such results were obtained, it could be concluded (at least tentatively) that the way people dress when going on a job interview *does* matter—a finding of practical importance to both interviewers (who may be unduly influenced by this factor) and to applicants (who want to load the dice in their own favor).

Of course, the study could have turned out in some other way. For example, the applicant might receive similar ratings when dressed in a traditionally feminine or professional manner. Regardless of the precise results, though, the basic purpose of the research would remain the same. In order to determine whether a particular factor (independent variable) affects some aspect of work-related behavior, two basic steps are followed: (1) this factor is varied in some manner, and (2) the impact of such variations on subjects' behavior is carefully observed.

You should realize, by the way, that the experiment described here is the simplest type that can be performed. Only one factor was varied in order to examine its effects upon behavior. In many cases, researchers seek to study the impact of several independent variables at once. They do so because in most real-life situations behavior is affected by many factors and conditions at once. Thus, in the example above, the way the job applicant behaved during the inverview might also have been varied. For example, she could have pretended to be shy in one condition and confident in another. Or her level of friendliness toward the interviewer might have been made an independent variable, so that she smiled at this person a lot in one condition, a moderate amount in another condition, and not at all in a third. By varying several factors at once, it is often possible to obtain more information about work-related behavior than it is by varying only one. Also, the experimental situation can sometimes be made somewhat more realistic than would otherwise be the case. Regardless of the number of independent variables studied, though, the basic strategy remains the same: System-

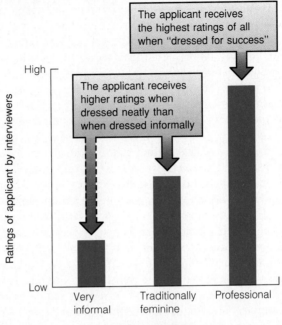

FIGURE 1.10 Experimentation: A Simple Example
In the imaginary experiment shown here, a job applicant dressed in one of the three different styles when reporting for an interview. Results indicated that the applicant received highest ratings from the personnel managers who interviewed her when she dressed in a professional style.

atically vary each of these factors in order to determine whether, and to what degree, such changes affect some important aspect of behavior.

A final note of caution: This discussion has not considered several basic issues that arise when actual experiments are performed (for example, are the persons who participate in a study representative of a larger group to whom the results are to be extended?) Because of such matters, conducting experiments is often more difficult than suggested here. Despite these complications, though, experimentation remains a basic tool of human relations, and for good reason: The results it yields can greatly increase our knowledge of behavior in work settings.

The Correlational Method: Knowledge through Systematic Observation

As we have seen, experimentation is an important technique for uncovering new facts about human relations. Unfortunately, though, there are many situations in which it cannot be used. Practical or ethical constraints may simply make it impossible for researchers to perform an appropriate experiment. For example, imagine that a human relations specialist has reason to suspect that certain styles of leadership are more effective in inducing high productivity among employees than others. Could he persuade the top executives in a large company to alter their "style" in specific ways, or even replace these executives at will, in order to vary this factor? Probably not. Similarly, imagine that a researcher believes certain types of stress lead to heart attacks among employees. Could he expose individuals to low, moderate, and high levels of such conditions in order to determine if such changes affect the number of employees who collapse on the job? Obviously not. In these and countless other cases, the use of experimentation is not feasible because of practical or ethical restrictions.

Fortunately, it is not necessary for researchers to throw up their hands in despair in these instances. They can turn to an alternative approach known as the **correlational method.** Briefly, this technique involves careful observation of two or more variables in order to determine if they are related in any manner. If changes in one are found to be consistently associated with changes in the other (for instance, if, as one rises, so does the other), evidence for a link between them is obtained. Please note: in contrast to experimentation, *no attempt is made to vary one of the factors in order to observe its effect upon the other.* Instead, naturally occurring variations in both are observed in order to learn whether they tend to occur together in some way.

To see how the correlational method can be applied to the study of behavior in work settings, let's return to the topic examined above: the impact of a job applicant's style of dress on the outcome of a job interview. Basic procedures would be relatively simple. The researcher interested in this question would arrange to visit the employment offices of many different companies. There she would observe the style of dress of each female job applicant; that is, she would classify each applicant as dressed in an informal, traditionally feminine, or professional manner. (Probably, the researcher would try to make these observations in a discreet way, so that applicants would not notice her presence.) Then she would also obtain the ratings assigned to each person by the personnel managers who interviewed them. In a final step, she would compare these two variables—applicants' style of dress and the ratings they received—in order to determine whether they are related in any manner. Note once again that the researcher would not attempt to vary applicants' style of dress to determine the impact of such changes on their ratings, nor would she attempt to intervene in the situation in any other way. Rather, she would simply *observe* whether changes in style of dress are related to job interview ratings.

As you can probably see, the correlational method offers several key advantages. It can readily be employed to study behavior in many different settings, including those involving work. Similarly, it can be applied to topics and issues that, for ethical or practical reasons, cannot be studied by direct experimentation. And often it permits researchers to uncover important relationships without affecting the organizations or the persons involved. (In contrast, of course, experimentation requires some kind of intervention or change.)

Given all these advantages, you might now be wondering why human relations specialists and other researchers ever prefer to use experimentation. Doesn't it involve a lot of extra work for very little gain? The answer, in fact, is quite simple.

Despite its many "pluses," the correlation method suffers one major drawback: It is usually not very effective in establishing cause-and-effect relationships. Specifically, the fact that changes in one variable are accompanied by changes in another does *not* guarantee that changes in the first *caused* changes in the second. The opposite may be true, or—even worse—changes in both may actually be caused by changes in some other factor not carefully observed. For example, imagine that systematic observation reveals that the greater the hair loss of male executives, the higher their salaries. One interpretation of this result is that hair loss causes promotions—not a very reasonable suggestion, to say the least. Another interpretation is that promotions, with all the extra worry and pressures they involve, cause hair loss. This is a bit more convincing, but not much. There is yet another possibility: Both hair loss and promotions stem from another factor—increasing job experience and age. In short, there is no direct link between these two variables; instead, both are affected by another factor.

In this case it is easy to see that the third alternative is the most likely one. But in many other instances such a choice is more difficult, and it is precisely this type of ambiguity that leads many researchers to prefer experimentation. In any case, the moral for researchers—and for consumers of research findings—is clear. Always be on guard against interpreting even a strong correlation between two variables as evidence of a direct causal link between them. There are also two somewhat more limited methods that are sometimes used in human relations research that need to be briefly mentioned.

Natural Observations: Simple but Useful

The simplest, and in some ways most intuitively obvious, technique for acquiring information about human relations is **natural observation.** As this phrase suggests, this approach involves spending time in an organization and simply observing the events and processes that take place. For example, suppose that an investigator wanted to determine how employees react to a forthcoming merger with another company. Information about this issue could be obtained by visiting the organization in question and observing what such persons say and do in the days or weeks prior to the merger. Further, their behavior could be compared to behavior during some baseline period, before news of the merger was announced. In a variation on this basic theme, known as *participant observation*, an investigator could actually be hired by the organization and could then observe it from the inside, as an actual member.[13]

Direct observation of organizational behavior offers several obvious advantages. It is applied to actual work settings, and can be used without disrupting normal routines. Further, almost anyone—including persons already employed by the organization—can be trained to use it. On the other hand, it suffers from several limitations. Being so close to the daily functioning of the organization may make it difficult for observers to remain impartial; they may become friendly with several persons and be strongly affected by such relationships. Similarly, since most of what takes place in organizations is fairly dull and routine, there is a natural tendency to focus on unusual or unexpected events—with the result that observers' conclusions can be distorted by such occurrences. Finally, as we shall see in Chapter 2, all human beings—even the keenest and most observant—have limited capacity to notice, process, and store incoming information. Accordingly, observers may miss much that is important and reach conclusions that are biased by their selective sample of information. For these reasons, natural observation is not generally viewed as a basic method for acquiring scientific knowledge about behavior in work settings. Rather, it is seen as a starting point in this process—a basic for insights and ideas that may then be studied by more systematic means.

The Case Method: Generalizing from the Unique

Suppose that in the study of mergers noted above, an investigator decided that she would not simply observe employees in the days or weeks prior to a merger. Instead, she would interview them, focus on specific potential changes (e.g., a rise in experienced levels of stress, the initiation of wild rumors), and in general, use a more detailed and systematic approach. To the extent she chose to proceed in this manner, she would be using a second approach known as the **case method.** The basic idea behind this strategy is as follows: By studying one organization in depth, we can learn much about processes occurring in many others, and so increase our knowledge of human relations. The case method, too, rests on observation of ongoing events and processes. In contrast to natural observation, however, it involves active questioning of employees and other procedures for gaining information about them, their reactions, and their company.

The case method does generally provide more detailed and systematic information than natural observation, and it was widely used in human relations in its early decades. However, it suffers from some of the same drawbacks as natural observation (e.g., investigators may become so involved with a particular organization that they lose some of their objectivity). Further, since each organization is, in some ways, unique, it is not clear that findings and principles can be generalized to others, which may differ in important respects. For these reasons, the case method, too, is often viewed as the beginning—not the end—of the research endeavor. In short, it can provide intriguing hypotheses and insights that are then subjected to test through other, more systematic methods.

Theory: An Essential Guide to Human Research

By this point, you should have a good grasp of the basic methods of research used in human relations research. You may still be wondering, though, about a related issue: Where do the ideas for the specific research projects come from? Actually, there are several answers to this question. On some occasions, the idea for a study is suggested by informal observation of organizations and the activities within them. On others, it is suggested by the findings of previous research, which yielded puzzling or unexpected results. Perhaps the most important source of research ideas, though, can be stated in a single word: **theory.** Briefly, theory represents attempts by scientists to answer the question "Why?" It involves efforts to understand precisely *why* certain events occur as they do, or *why* various processes unfold in a specific manner. Thus theory goes beyond mere description: It seeks explanation. The formulation of comprehensive, accurate theories is a major goal of all fields of science, and human relations is no exception. Thus a great deal of research in our field is concerned with efforts to construct, refine, and test such frameworks. But what, exactly, are theories? And what is their value to human relations? Perhaps the best means of answering both questions is through a concrete example.

Imagine that we observe the following: When individuals are given concrete goals, their performance on many tasks improves. (We'll return to this finding, and research on *goal setting*, in Chapter 4.) This observation is certainly useful by itself. After all, it allows us to predict what will happen when goals are introduced (performance will increase), and it suggests a useful means for improving performance in a wide range of settings. These two accomplishments— *prediction* and *intervention* (control) are major goals of science. Yet, the fact that concrete goals enhance performance does not explain *why* this is the case. It is at this point that theory enters the picture.

A theory designed to explain the impact of goals on performance might read as follows: When individuals are given concrete goals, they know just what they are supposed to accomplish. This increases their motivation and helps them to choose the best strategies for reaching the goal. As a result, performance increases. Note that this theory, like all others, consists of two major parts: several basic concepts (goals, motivation, task strategies), and assertions concerning the relationships between these concepts.

Once a theory has been formulated, a crucial process begins. First, predictions are derived from the theory. These are developed in accordance with basic principles of logic and are known as *hypotheses*. Next, these predictions are tested in actual research. If they are confirmed, confidence in the accuracy of the theory is increased. If, instead, they are disconfirmed, confidence in the theory may be weakened. Then, the theory may be altered so as to generate new predictions, and these, in turn, are tested. In short, the process is a continuous one, involving the free flow of information between a theory, predictions derived from it, and the findings of ongoing research. Figure 1.11 summarizes this process.

We will have reason to consider many different theories in later portions of this book. As each is presented, try to keep these two points in mind: (1) such theories are designed to explain key aspects of human relations behavior, and (2) they should be accepted as valid only to the extent that predictions from them are confirmed in careful research.

USING THIS BOOK: A DISPLACED (BUT NOT MISPLACED) PREFACE

When was the last time you read a preface? If you are like most readers, your answer is probably something like, "Who remembers?" or even, "Preface— what's a preface?" This is unfortunate, for prefaces often contain useful information—facts that can help you make more effective use of a given book. For this reason, several features of this text will be described here, in a spot where (it is hoped) you are more likely to read them.

First, a few words about overall structure. This book begins with a consideration of basic processes that underlie behavior in work settings, such as motivation, perception, and communication. Then it turns to several important forms of interpersonal behavior often encountered in the world of work (e.g., cooperation, influence, and leadership). It then examines special problems or challenges in human relations, such as stress, burnout, and prejudice and discrimination. Finally, it concludes with a discussion of how human relations principles and findings can be applied to your own career.

You should note in particular certain features of this book that are designed to make it easier and more convenient for you to use. Each chapter is preceded by an outline and a list of specific learning objectives. All chapters end with a summary of major points. Key terms are printed in bold type (**like this**) and are defined in a list at the end of the chapter. Many graphs and charts are also included. All are designed to help you understand concepts and facts presented, and all contain special labels that call attention to the major points being made. Finally, two distinct types of special sections are presented: The first is labeled *Human Relations in Action*, which offers exercises or demonstrations you can perform to gain firsthand experience with the principles or facts covered (see p.

FIGURE 1.11 Theory: An Important Guide to Research in Human Relations
Once a theory has been formulated, predictions derived from it are tested through direct research. If these predictions are confirmed, confidence in the theory's accuracy is increased. If they are disconfirmed, confidence in the theory's accuracy is reduced. The theory may then be modified in order to generate new predictions or, ultimately, to be rejected.

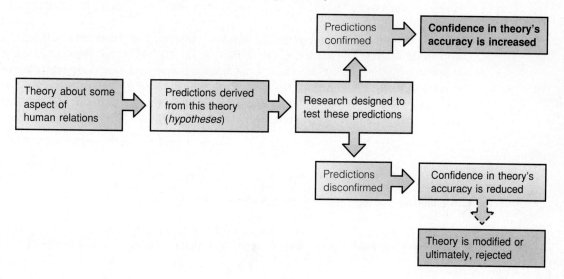

6). The second type, called *Case in Point*, presents human relations problems that exemplify important principles discussed in the chapter. Additional exercises and cases are presented at the end of each chapter.

To conclude: All the features just described are designed to make this book easier to read and more convenient to use. They can only go so far, though, and what you gain from them ultimately depends on how much effort you invest in reading and understanding each chapter. Given the fascinating nature of human behavior and its importance in the world of work, there is every reason to expect that you will find it a positive and worthwhile experience.

SUMMARY

Human relations, as a field, seeks two major goals: (1) increased understanding of interpersonal relations in work settings, and (2) the application of such knowledge to the attainment of both individual and organizational goals. Its roots can be traced, in part, to **scientific management.** While this approach was concerned mainly with enhancing productivity, it did direct some attention to the proper training of employees and to their motivation. In these ways it showed more concern with the "human side of work" than did older, traditional views. It was not until the completion of the famous **Hawthorne studies,** however, that widespread recognition of the social nature of work developed. These investigations pointed to the conclusion that behavior on the job is affected by many of the same factors that influence behavior in other contexts (e.g., motivation, attitudes, communication).

Modern human relations generally adopts the **human resources** model—a view contending that under appropriate conditions, employees will show many positive forms of work-related behavior. It is an integrative field, drawing heavily on findings and principles from other areas. Its major thrust, however, is application—using such knowledge to enhance the attainment of individual and organizational goals.

While human relations readily "imports" information from related fields, it also adds to our knowledge about behavior in work settings through original research. In their quest for such knowledge, human relations experts employ several different techniques. The most important of these are (1) **experimentation** and (2) **systematic observation. Natural observation** of behavior can also be very informative. Much of our search is guided by theory.

KEY TERMS

case method: A method of research in which one organization is studied in detail in order to establish general principles about organizational behavior or organizational processes.

contingency approach: A perspective suggesting that organizational behavior is affected by a very large number of interacting factors.

correlational method: A basic method of research in which two or more variables are carefully studied in order to determine whether changes in one are associated with changes in the other.

experimentation: A basic method of research in which one or more factors (independent variables) are varied systematically to determine if such changes exert any impact upon one or more aspects of behavior (dependent variables).

Hawthorne studies: A classic series of investigations that, taken together, demonstrate the impact of many social factors on behavior in work settings.

human relations: The field that seeks to understand work-related aspects of interpersonal relations in order to apply such knowledge to enhancing the attainment of organizational and individual goals.

human relations approach: An approach to work settings which pays attention to human needs, motives, and relationships.

human resources model: A view of behavior in work settings suggesting that under appropriate circumstances employees can show many positive forms of behavior.

natural observation: A method of research in which an investigator simply observes events and processes occurring in an organization. The observer makes every effort possible to avoid affecting these events or processes by his or her presence.

norms: Rules, in task-performing or social groups, that indicate how members of these groups should behave.

scientific management: An early approach to management and behavior in work settings that emphasized the importance of good job design. In addition, it also directed some attention to employee motivation and to the importance of selecting and training employees for their jobs.

systematic observation: see correlational method.

theory: Efforts, by scientists, to explain why various processes or events occur in the way that they do. Theories consist of two major parts: basic concepts and assertions regarding the relationship between them.

Theory X: A traditional view of behavior in work settings. According to this approach, most persons are lazy and irresponsible. Thus the major task of managers is that of providing them with direction and discipline.

Theory Y: *See* Human resources model.

hypothisis:

NOTES

1. Baron, R.A., & Byrne, D. (1991). *Social Psychology: Understanding Human Interaction,* 6th ed. Boston: Allyn and Bacon.

2. Taylor, F.W. (1911). *The Principles of Scientific Management.* New York: Harper & Brothers.

3. Roethlisberger, F.J., & Dickson, W.J. (1939). *Management and the Worker.* Cambridge: Harvard University Press.

4. Franke, R., & Kaul, J. (1978). "The Hawthorne Experiments: First Statistical Interpretations." *American Sociological Review,* 623–43.

5. McGregor, D. (1960). *The Human Side of Enterprise.* New York: McGraw-Hill.

6. Tosi, H.L., & Carroll, S. J. (1982). *Management,* 2d ed. New York: Wiley.

7. Lawrence, P.R., & Lorsch, J.W. (1967). *Organization and Environment.* Homewood, Ill.: Irwin.

8. Steers, R.M., & Miller, E.L. (1988). "Management in the 1990's: The International Challenge." *Academy of Management Executive, 2,* 21–22.

9. Ouchi, W.G. (1981). *Theory Z: How American Business Can Meet the Japanese Challenge*. Reading, Mass.: Addison-Wesley.

10. Sullivan, J.J. (1983). "A Critique of Theory Z." *Academy of Management Review,* *8,* 132–142.

11. Aronson, E., Ellsworth, P.C., Carlsmith, J.M., & Gonzales, M.H. (1990). *Methods of Research in Social Psychology*. New York: McGraw-Hill.

12. Cash, T.F. (1985). "The Impact of Grooming Style on the Evaluation of Women in Management." In M. Solomon, eds., *The Psychology of Fashion*, pp. 343–55. Lexington, Mass.: Lexington Press.

13. Mintzberg, H. (1973). *The Nature of Managerial Work*. New York: Harper and Row.

ADDITIONAL CASES AND EXERCISES: APPLYING WHAT YOU'VE LEARNED

The Job Interview

Don H. Hockenbury
Psychology Instructor
Tulsa Junior College

Sandra E. Hockenbury
Adjunct Instructor
Tulsa Junior College

Bonnie tossed and turned in her bed, glancing again at the digital clock on the night stand. The glowing red numerals said 2:15 A.M. Although she wanted to sleep, her mind kept rehashing conversations she'd had during the last several days. It had been a week since the personnel office of a large corporation had called her to schedule the job interview. The interview was scheduled for 9:00 A.M. tomorrow morning, less than seven hours from the time displayed on the digital clock.

The description of the job in the newspaper sounded perfect—very close to what she wanted to be doing, definitely challenging, and with opportunities for advancement. Plus, she had heard that the company was an excellent place to work. Her next-door neighbor knew someone whose son worked in the design department, and she said he really liked it there.

Bonnie was anxious to make a good first impression and to do well in the interview, so earlier in the week she had turned to several of her friends for advice, especially Karen and Judy, who had both recently changed jobs. Karen had spent two months looking for her job, Judy three. They were both pleased with the jobs they had landed, and each felt that she had a lot of insight into the interviewing process.

First, there was the seemingly simple matter of clothes. "It's worse to overdress than to underdress," said Karen.

Judy disagreed. "Dress for the job you want, not the job you're applying for," she suggested. Bonnie had read in a recent newspaper article that business suits are out—a more feminine look shows you're secure and don't need to dress like a man.

"Just try to look nice, dear, and pin your hair back," said Bonnie's mother.

Her boyfriend Mike was no help at all. "Hey, Bonnie, you always look great to me, but to tell you the truth, I prefer you in blue jeans and a T-shirt."

How was she supposed to act? At least everyone seemed to agree on one thing: greet the interviewer with a firm handshake and a warm smile. But after that, everyone had a different opinion.

Karen said, "Whatever you do, don't make the mistake of talking too much. Let them do most of the talking—and don't volunteer anything. Just answer their questions. Be dignified and reserved," she continued, "You don't want to seem too eager. And whatever you do, don't be too cocky! After I was hired, they told me that they had turned down another candidate who was just as qualified as I was because she had acted like she already knew it all. Most companies want a team player, someone who knows she's the new kid on the block. I made it clear that I knew I had a lot to learn."

But Judy had completely opposite advice. "You have to be assertive, Bonnie. Don't be afraid to ask questions—make sure you take the lead at some point in the interview. They wouldn't be interviewing you if they didn't think you were qualified for the job. I bet they're looking for someone with a lot of initiative and self-confidence. Be confident—act as if you've already gotten the job and make it clear that you know you deserve it. Hey—it worked for me!"

"Just be yourself, dear," Mom advised.

And her boyfriend Mike said, "You've got such a great personality—everyone says so. Whattaya worried about?"

And what about the salary? The salary range wasn't listed in the newspaper ad, and the personnel office manager hadn't mentioned anything about it when she called Bonnie to schedule the interview. The ad had simply said, "Excellent benefits—salary commensurate with experience." Bonnie knew what kind of salary she wanted, but she didn't know what to expect. Once again, everyone had a different theory.

Judy said, "Don't settle for less than you're worth. Ask for what you want. And never, never accept their first offer."

But Karen said, "Be careful not to ask for too much, or you'll price yourself right out of the job. My new manager told me that they eliminated candidates who expected too much money to start."

"Just make sure that you can pay your rent, dear," said Mom.

"If you make more than I do, I can quit my job and stay home to watch 'Wheel of Fortune,' " joked Mike.

And then there was the matter of simply arriving for the interview. "Never show up more than five minutes before the interview," Judy said authoritatively. "If you get there any earlier it'll look like you're overly anxious about getting the job. Wait in your car if you have to, but don't walk in the door more than five minutes ahead of time."

"Always get there at least fifteen minutes early," Karen suggested. "It makes you look responsible and gives you time to think about your interview strategy."

"Just remember to set your alarm clock, honey," said Mom.

"Nine o'clock!" Mike said, clearly startled. "You mean, like nine in the morning? You must have misunderstood. Nobody does anything at nine in the morning."

Bonnie turned over again. The clock said 2:23 a.m. Both Karen and Judy had ended up with great jobs, she thought to herself. But who should she listen to? What should she do in the morning?

Questions

1. Bonnie had at least a week to investigate the company and the job she was applying for. Can you see any problems with the strategy she used for obtaining help? Are Bonnie's sources of advice and information reliable? What additional resources could she have consulted?

2. What limitations do you see in the advice that Judy and Karen offered? What about the information the next-door neighbor shared with her?

3. Is it possible to use the experimental method to study whether arriving early, late, or on time for a job interview has any effect on the interviewer's perceptions of the person applying for the job? If so, briefly describe how such an experiment could be designed.

4. Briefly describe how the correlational method could be used to investigate whether job applicants are rated more favorably if they talk a lot or only respond minimally in a job interview.

5. If Bonnie had asked for your advice in this situation, what would you have said to her?

6. Have you ever found yourself in a similar situation? What did you do to prepare for the job interview? What was the outcome? Is there anything you would have done differently? Why or why not?

Answers to Questions on pp. 6–7.
Every statement is false.

Perception: Making Sense of the World Around Us

Learning Objectives

After reading this chapter,
you should be able to:

1. Define *perception* and explain why it is an
active process.

2. Define *social perception* and indicate its
relevance to human relations.

3. Explain how we employ *attribution* to
understand the causes of others' behavior.

4. Explain such causes of error in social
perception as the *self-serving bias, contrast
effects, stereotypes,* and *fundamental
attribution error.*

5. Indicate how social perception can affect
job interviews.

erri and David Larkin need to hire a new secretary for their small telephone company. They had interviewed quite a few candidates and were trying to decide between two of the most qualified. They were both good typists and had good work records.

"I like Jane better," said David. "She made a really good impression. She was dressed neatly, well-spoken, and looked you straight in the eye."

"Yeah, I'm sure you liked that," laughed Merri. "She is quite cute!"

"That's right, but isn't that good for public relations purposes?" mumbled David somewhat unconvincingly.

"Which one did you like best? I thought Janna was really impressive. She's from a good family and went to Lamar High School. It's one of the best schools in town."

"Well just because she's from a good family and good school doesn't mean she'll be a good secretary," argued David. "Besides she seemed a little too casual to me. So how are we going to decide? Shall we just flip a coin?"

"No, maybe we should look at some more candidates, until we find one we both can agree on," proposed Merri.

"O.K. but I still think we're not going to find anyone better than Jane," said David.

One of the basic truths of human relations is that we all see the world and the people in it a little differently. David and Merri had different perceptions of the job applicants. They had formed differing impressions on the basis of the same information. The impressions we make on others are, of course, very important in our success in being hired or promoted. We will discuss some of the factors that go into making impressions as well as those that explain why we often have different impressions of the same people or situations.

Such differences, which can be quite large, point to a key fact: Contrary to what common sense may suggest, we do not know the world around us in a simple or direct manner.[1] Rather, we construct a "picture" of it through an active and complete process. This process through which we select, organize, and interpret information brought to us by our senses is termed **perception,** and it plays a key role in behavior.

Indeed, in most situations, how people act is largely a function of how they view their environment. For example, in the situation described above Merri and David were exposed to identical (or very similar) information about two job candidates. Yet they constructed rather different impressions of these persons. And then, on the basis of these contrasting perceptions, they reached opposite conclusions about which one should be hired. In this and almost every other situation we could describe, perceptions play a key role in shaping overt behavior.

In the discussion of perception that follows, we will first focus on this process as it applies to the physical world—how it helps us make sense out of the input brought to us by our eyes, ears, nose, mouth, and skin. We will then examine **social perception,** the process through which we seek to understand other persons. As will soon be apparent, a working knowledge of both types of perception is essential to understanding many aspects of interpersonal relations in work settings.

PERCEIVING THE PHYSICAL WORLD

At any moment in time, we are literally flooded with input from our senses. Our eyes respond to many wavelengths of light, our ears react to many pitches of sounds, and so on. Yet we do not perceive the world as a random collection of such sensations. Rather, we recognize specific objects and orderly patterns of events. The basic reason for this lies in the fact that perception is an active process—one that imposes order and meaning on the vast array of sensations we receive. Generally, this process is so automatic we are not even aware of its existence. But careful study reveals that it involves strong tendencies toward selectivity and organization.

Attention: Perception Is Selective

If you've ever attended a noisy party, you are already familiar with the fact that perception is highly selective in nature. At such times, you can easily screen out all of the voices around you except that of the person with whom you are conversing. While the words of this individual stand out and make sense, those of all the others blend into a single background buzz. But if for some reason you decide that you wish to listen to what someone else is saying, you can readily shift your attention to *this* person. Indeed, you can even do this while continuing to look the first person in the eye—thus convincing him that he is still the center of your interest! In such cases attention is obviously a conscious process. We decide where to direct it and then do so. In many others, though, attention seems to follow a course of its own choosing. Indeed, sometimes (e.g., during a dull lecture) we cannot seem to force it to remain where we want even for a few minutes! In such cases, factors other than our own will seem to play a crucial role. But what are they? What factors lead us to pay attention to certain events or stimuli, while ignoring others? In general, they seem to fall into two major categories: factors that are *internal* and factors that are *external* in nature.

Internal Factors Affecting Attention: Motivation and Past Experience

The role of one internal factor that strongly affects attention can be readily illustrated. Imagine you are attending a business meeting. What stimuli or events will you notice? The answer: It depends, in part, on your current motivational state. If it is close to lunch time and you are hungry, you may focus on the delicious smell of food entering the room from a nearby restaurant. If, instead, you are deeply concerned about your upcoming promotion, you may direct your total attention to the words and actions of your boss—the person who must "go to bat" for you to ensure your success. And if you are worried about getting a ticket because the time on the parking meter has run out, you may listen for, and notice, the sound of the small scooter on which your local meter attendant rides. In short, where we direct our attention—and what stimuli we perceive—is often strongly affected by our current motives (see Figure 2.1).

But motivation is not the only internal factor that affects attention. Another is our past experience. This fact, too, is easy to notice—once your attention has been drawn to it! Imagine that three people watch a demonstration of a new computer at a local shopping mall. One is an engineer, another an accountant, and the third a teenage boy, famous locally for his success in playing Pac-Man. What will they notice? In all probability, very different things. The engineer's attention may be drawn to the advanced technology used in the new equipment. The accountant may focus on the excellent software—special programs she can use in her recordkeeping. And the teenager may notice the brightness of the colors on the screen, and how much fun it will be to play various games on this computer. In short, each person's attention will be drawn to different aspects of

FIGURE 2.1 Selectivity in Perception: What We See Depends on What We Want or Need
What would you notice as you walked down a street like this one? To a large degree, it would depend on your current motivational state.

the same item because past experience (or training) orients him or her in these directions.

Such differences in attention or perspective are common in many settings, including organizations. For example, in examining a competitor's product, marketing people may concentrate on the materials used in the product, or clever aspects of its manufacture. And again, engineers may notice its technical features. Unfortunately, differences of this type can often lead to a serious "communication gap" between such persons: After all, they seem to see different things when examining the same object. An important task for managers, then, is noticing such differences and making sure that they do not cause unnecessary friction between the persons involved.

External Factors Affecting Attention: Salience and Vividness

In addition to the internal factors just mentioned, attention is often affected by external factors—various aspects of stimuli themselves. That is, certain features of objects or events in the world around us determine whether they are more or less likely to be noticed. Among the most important of these are salience and vividness.

Salience refers to the extent to which a stimulus stands out from the others around it. The greater its salience, the more it tends to be noticed. For example, you would probably be more likely to notice a topless female bather on a beach where all other females are more modestly dressed than on a beach where every other woman is also topless. More generally, salience—and attention—is enhanced by intensity, large size, motion, and novelty. Experts in marketing are well aware of these principles, and they often use them in planning effective advertisements.

In contrast, **vividness** refers to the emotion-provoking properties of a stimulus. For example, a sign warning about the danger of misusing some equipment in a factory might be fairly low in vividness. If it were accompanied by a photo of a worker badly injured through such carelessness, its vividness might be enhanced. In general, the more vivid a stimulus is, the more it attracts our attention.

Attention: A Word on Its Effects

Attention, of course, is the crucial first step in perception. We cannot respond to or interpret any event or stimulus unless we notice it first. Thus attention acts as a kind of filter with respect to perception. Only what passes through can have any impact on our understanding of the world around us. We have just considered several of the factors that determine what passes through. We should also note, though, that attention has other effects as well. In many cases, stimuli that succeed in capturing our attention tend to be viewed as more important than ones that do not. For example, they are more likely to be seen as the cause of later events.[2] This applies to people too: Persons we notice most in a group tend to be viewed as being the most influential.[3] In short, stimuli that capture our attention seem to become "larger than life" in several important ways. In this respect, attention is indeed a crucial process.

Organization: Perception Is Structured

As noted earlier, we are rarely aware of single, isolated sensations. Rather we tend to organize the information brought by our senses into meaningful patterns. Such organization generally seems to follow several basic principles.

Perceptual Grouping First, we tend to group stimuli together in certain ways. Specifically, we tend to perceive separate stimuli as related to the extent that they are near one another (*proximity*) or similar in some manner (*similarity*). We also tend to complete incomplete patterns. That is, we tend to "fill in the gaps" and perceive incomplete stimuli or patterns as complete ones (*closure*). All of these principles are illustrated in Figure 2.2, and, as you can see, their effects are very strong. In fact, it is almost impossible *not* to perceive the world around us in accordance with these principles. Experts on perception are not yet certain why it is so, but some believe that these tendencies are innate and that they reflect basic ways in which our perceptual systems (or our minds) operate.[4]

FIGURE 2.2 An Example of Perceptual Grouping
Can you see how the principles of proximity, similarity, and closure are combined in this situation to produce a complete pattern from distinct stimuli?

It should be noted that the principles just described do not apply solely to simple stimuli such as the ones shown in Figure 2.2. Actually, they are quite general in nature. For example, if several persons work near each other in an office, or are similar in some manner, they may be perceived as a group or unit by their manager, even if there is no actual basis for drawing this conclusion. Similarly, when various issues are discussed, there is often a strong tendency to perceive everyone involved as being "pro" or "anti", despite the fact that many different views or positions exist. These and many similar errors occur because, in interpreting the world around us, we seem to act like "perceptual misers." Our basic rule of thumb seems to be as follows: Find—and then use—the simplest structure or organization possible.

Figure-ground Another basic organization principle in perception is related to our tendency to perceive any scene or event as consisting of **figure-ground**— objects (*figure*) and the space between them, or background (*ground*). For example, as you read this page, you do not perceive a random mixture of black marks and white space. This tendency to divide the world into figure and ground, too, seems to be innate. When persons blind from birth recover their sight suddenly through an operation, they demonstrate the distinction between figure and ground almost at once.[5]

Intriguing illustrations of our tendency to divide the world into figure and ground are provided by *ambiguous figures,* visual patterns in which figure and ground can be readily reversed. One of these is shown in Figure 2.3. When you first look at this drawing, you will probably see a white vase surrounded by a

FIGURE 2.3 Ambiguous Figures: Figure Versus Ground
Look at this drawing. When you concentrate on the white part, what do you see? Now try concentrating on the black spaces. What do you see now? The sudden shift in perception you probably experienced provides a clear demonstration of our tendency to organize the world into *figure* and *ground*.

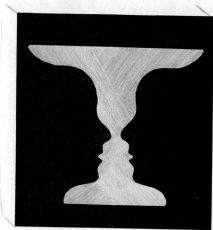

black space. Next, concentrate on the black area, and try to make *this* stand out as figure. When you do, you will form an entirely different perception. Drawings such as this call attention to the basic point underlying this entire discussion: The physical world presents us with a complex array of sensations. The pattern we perceive in these stimuli are largely of our own making.

SOCIAL PERCEPTION: PERCEIVING OTHERS

Why do people act the way they do? What are their major traits? Motives? Goals? These are only a few of the questions we ask about the persons around us. And the answers we obtain (or formulate) are of great practical importance. Indeed, they strongly shape our relations with bosses, co-workers, subordinates, friends, spouses, and lovers—just about everyone with whom we have contact. How, then, we go about performing these answers involves the process of **social perception.** As is the case with respect to the physical world, we actively combine, integrate, and then interpret information about other people. And through this active process, we form a useful picture of them—a basic understanding of what they are like, and what makes them tick.

Since human beings are extremely complex, social perception, too, is a complicated affair. For this reason, we could not possibly examine all its features here. What we can do, though, is focus on two key aspects of such perception: **attribution**—the process through which we seek to understand the causes of others' behavior, and **impression formation**—the way we combine varied information about them into a unified impression.[6,7] In addition, we will examine several sources of error in social perception—tendencies or biases that lead us to false conclusions about others.

Attribution: Understanding the Causes of Others' Behavior

In our efforts to know other persons, we draw on several sources of information. For example, we pay close attention to their physical appearance, because such factors as age, style of dress, and attractiveness can all yield useful clues about their major traits. By far the most important source on which we draw, though, is behavior. We observe the overt actions of individuals, and then try to infer their traits, motives, or goals from this source (see Figure 2.4).

Unfortunately, our efforts in this regard are complicated by two facts. First, other persons often seek to mislead us about their underlying traits or motives. If they are hostile or lazy, they try to conceal these facts as best they can. And if they are trying to take over our job, they may attempt to conceal *this* fact for as long as possible. Second, and even more important, others' actions often stem from external factors beyond their control, *not* from their lasting traits or goals. For example, imagine that you observe an employee at a large company working furiously as hard as she can. Does this mean she is a highly motivated person, well deserving of a promotion? Not necessarily. It may simply be that her supervisor is standing just out of view, carefully watching her every move. Or the supervisor may have warned her, just a few minutes earlier, that she is on dangerously thin ice where her job is concerned. To the extent that an individual's behavior stems from external factors such as these, it tells us little about lasting traits or motives. After all, under other conditions, the worker just described might strongly prefer to goof off in a flagrant manner.

One question we ask repeatedly about other persons is "Why?" Why did your boss decide to call a meeting at 4:30 P.M. on Friday? Why did one of your suppliers fail to deliver a major order on time? Why does Randi Helson in accounting always wait twenty-four hours before returning your calls? In short, one thing we frequently want to know about others is why they have acted in certain ways (see Figure 2.4). On closer examination, this question breaks down into two major parts: (1) We want to know what others are *really* like—in other words, what major traits or characteristics they possess; and (2) we want to know whether their actions stemmed primarily from *internal* causes (their own traits, motives, values), or primarily from *external* causes (factors relating to the situation in which they operate). Research findings suggest that we attempt to answer these questions in somewhat different ways.

From Acts to Dispositions: Using Others' Behavior As a Guide to Their Traits
Understanding others' major traits can often be very useful. For example, knowing that your opponent in a negotiating session has a reputation for being scrupulously honest can be a big "plus" in bargaining with him or her. Similarly, knowing that one of your subordinates is a true workaholic can assist you in scheduling vacations: You can leave this person for last, since she won't care anyway! But how, precisely, do we go about identifying the traits of other persons? The answer seems to be as follows: In general, we do so by observing their behavior and then *inferring* their traits from this information.

At first glance, this might seem to be an easy task. Other people are always doing *something,* so we have a rich source of evidence on which to draw. Un-

FIGURE 2.4 Attribution: The Answer to the Question Why
Attribution is the process of figuring out the reasons for the actions of ourselves and others. This often requires some careful mental effort. (Reprinted by permission Tribune Media Services.)

FIGURE 2.5 Socially Undesirable Behavior: Can Be Quite Informative
How confident can we be that this person's behavior reflects an internal trait? Since this behavior is *socially undesirable,* we can be fairly confident that it reflects a trait such as exhibitionism.

fortunately, though, there are complications to consider. Perhaps the most important of these involves the fact that others sometimes attempt to conceal their major traits, especially if they are traits generally viewed as undesirable. Thus employees who are careless, lazy, and unprincipled do their best to hide these facts from view and will demonstrate them only under conditions where they feel it is safe to do so, or when their "social guard" is down.

Despite such difficulties, however, there are several techniques we can use to help cut through efforts by others to conceal some of their major traits.[8] First, we can focus on actions by these persons that are low in *social desirability*— actions that are not widely approved in a given situation and which most persons would not choose to perform (see Figure 2.5). For example, imagine that one of the rising young stars in your company announced, suddenly, that she had just accepted a position with another firm; she was leaving at the end of the day. Clearly, this action would be viewed as inappropriate by most persons. The fact that she performed it provides a strong basis for assuming that she possesses several negative traits (for example, she is irresponsible, ungrateful, lacking in concern for others).

Second, we can pay careful attention to actions by others that produce what are termed *noncommon effects*—outcomes that would not be produced by other, different actions. Since such behaviors yield highly distinctive effects, they often reveal much about the motives or traits of the persons involved. For instance, following up on the case of the "sudden quitter," suppose that you learned that the job she had accepted was in an isolated and unattractive town, that the work she would be doing was much duller than her work at her present company, but that her salary had more than doubled. Would this information reveal anything more about her major traits? It would. In fact, you could now infer (and with a high degree of confidence) that she is a very mercenary person—money is more important to her than good working conditions, interesting work, or the friendship of former co-workers. Finally, in our efforts to understand others' major traits, we also focus on behaviors that they have freely chosen to perform. Behaviors that were somehow forced upon them by role obligations, inflexible company rules, or circumstances beyond their control are relatively uninformative—they tell us little about the traits possessed by such persons.

In sum, by focusing on certain aspects of others' behavior we often can attain accurate knowledge of their major traits and characteristics. (See Figure 2.6 for a summary of this aspect of attribution.) Yet we often have more information about a person than just their actions at one point in time. We may observe them over a period of time in a variety of situations. We may also be aware how other people act in these situations. All of this information can help us in determining the extent to which a person's behavior is likely to be the result of internal or external factors.[9] In doing this, we focus mainly on three factors: (1) the extent

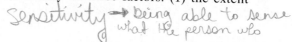
Sensitivity → being able to sense what the person who

FIGURE 2.6 Inferring Others' Traits
In order to identify others' major traits, we often focus on the aspects of their behavior shown here.

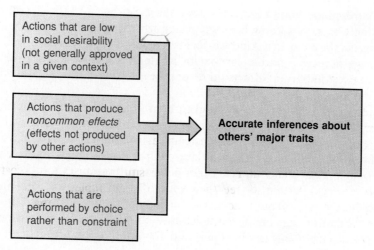

Actions that are low in social desirability (not generally approved in a given context)

Actions that produce *noncommon effects* (effects not produced by other actions)

Actions that are performed by choice rather than constraint

Accurate inferences about others' major traits

to which other persons behave in the same manner as the individual in question (*consensus*); (2) the extent to which this person behaves in the same manner on other occasions (*consistency*); and (3) the extent to which this person acts in the same manner in other situations (*distinctiveness*). Information about these three factors is then combined, and forms the basis for our decision as to whether another person's behavior has stemmed mainly from internal or external causes. But what combinations lead us to one or another of these conclusions? Research evidence suggests that if consensus, consistency, and distinctiveness are all high, we tend to attribute others' behavior to *external* causes (for example, luck, actions by their boss or by co-workers). In contrast, if consensus and distinctiveness are low, but consistency is high, we attribute their behavior to *internal* causes (for example, their own skill, effort, or personality).

Admittedly, our comments up to this point are somewhat abstract. Perhaps the nature of this process can be clarified by a concrete example. Imagine that during a weekly staff meeting, another member of your department continuously interrupts the proceedings. She asks one question after another, makes silly jokes, and generally slows things down. Is her behavior due to internal or external causes? The answer depends largely on the three factors mentioned above. First, imagine that (1) no one else acts in this manner (consensus is low); (2) you have seen her act this way at other staff meetings (consistency is high); and (3) you have seen her act in a similar manner in other situations (distinctiveness is low). You would probably thus conclude that her behavior stems from internal causes: She likes (or needs) to be the center of attention, or simply enjoys long meetings.

Now, in contrast, assume these conditions exist: (1) Several other persons act in the same manner during the meeting (consensus is high); (2) you have seen her act this way at other staff meetings (consistency, too, is high); and (3) you have seen this person act differently in other situations (distinctiveness is high). In this case, you would probably decide that her actions stem from external causes (see Figure 2.7). That is, you conclude there is something about this particular meeting that induces such behavior from the people attending. (Perhaps it is so dull that some persons interrupt just to break the monotony.)

Causal Attribution: Some Implications for Work Settings "O.K.," you may now be thinking, "so now I know how we decide whether other people act in certain ways because they are that kind of person, or because they have to. So what?" Whether we perceive another's behavior as stemming from internal or external causes can exert important effects on several key aspects of interpersonal behavior in work settings.

First, and most generally, we tend to hold others responsible for any effects produced by their actions if these behaviors stemmed from their own traits or motives (i.e., internal causes). If, instead, their actions seem to have derived mainly from external causes beyond their control, we do not assign such responsibility. Imagine that someone in another department promises to have some work done for you by a certain date. When you go to get the work, you find that it is not ready. Do you blame this person for failing to keep his word? It depends. If you learn that he was unable to finish the job because of a serious equipment failure, you realize it was not his fault, and may "forgive and forget." If, instead,

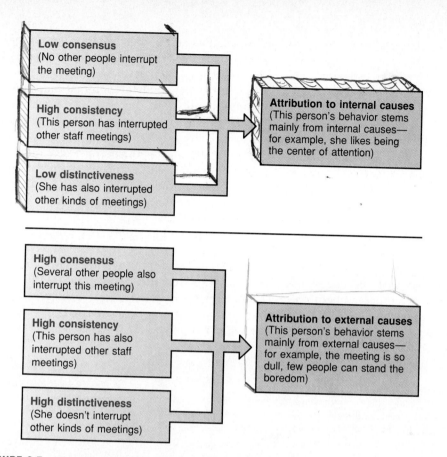

FIGURE 2.7 How We Answer the Question "Why?" About Others' Behavior
In deciding whether another person's behavior stems mainly from internal or external causes, we take into account three factors: *consensus, consistency,* and *distinctiveness.*

you find that your job is not ready because he has been goofing off, you will probably react with anger and resentment. In this and many other instances, the apparent causes behind others' behavior play a crucial role in our relations with them.

Second, and perhaps even more important, conclusions about the causes of others' behavior can strongly affect our evaluations of their performance. To see why this is so, consider the following situation. You are asked to evaluate the performance of two persons, both up for promotion. When you examine the records, you find both individuals are about equal. But you also know they have attained these similar results in different ways. One individual is highly talented, but is coasting along, putting little effort into his work. The other is lower in ability, but has worked very hard to attain success. To whom would you assign the higher rating? Probably, to the hard worker of modest ability. In any case, whatever your decision, you would take into account the causes behind each person's behavior, as well as his or her actual performance.

Actually, research findings indicate that when we evaluate others' performance (or our own), we pay close attention to many factors relating to the potential causes of this behavior. Among the most important of these seem to be *effort, ability, luck,* and *task difficulty*.[10] Both effort and ability are internal causes, while luck and task difficulty are external ones. However, ability and task difficulty tend to be quite stable across time, while effort and luck are variable and may change greatly from one moment to the next. Thus two key dimensions seem to be involved in our attempts to understand (and evaluate) the performance of others: the internal-external dimension discussed earlier, and a dimension involving stability across time (the lasting causes-temporary causes illustrated in Figure 2.8). Apparently, we take both dimensions into account when judging others' performance. The way we do so, however, is somewhat complex. First, consider successful performance on some task. It is evaluated more positively when perceived as stemming from internal causes (high ability or effort) rather than external causes (an easy task, good luck). This makes excellent sense; after all, individuals who succeed because of talent or hard work seem to deserve more credit than those who succeed because of a lucky break. In contrast, poor task performance is evaluated more harshly when it is seen as stemming from internal causes rather than external ones. Again, this is quite reasonable. If workers fail because of

FIGURE 2.8 Attribution and Evaluations of Others' Performance: Two Key Dimensions
In evaluating others' performance, we tend to use two dimensions: one ranging from internal to external causes of behavior and another ranging from lasting to temporary causes. The major causes of others' behavior—ability, effort, luck, task difficulty—occupy different points along these dimensions.

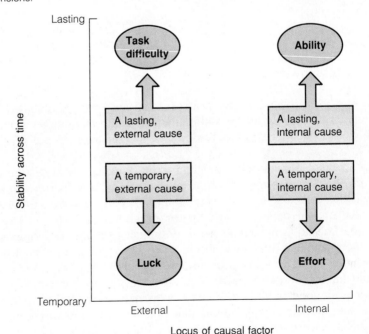

factors outside their control (e.g., bad luck), we may excuse their poor showing. If they fail because of laziness, however, we have less reason to be charitable.

In addition to these effects, we also seem to give a special edge to high effort. Thus, if two people perform at a similar level, the one who seems to be working harder often receives higher ratings.[11] There is a practical message in this fact for your own career: If you want to attain high evaluations from your supervisors, be sure to keep your effort at visibly high levels. If you do not, and appear to be coasting, even good performance may fail to yield high ratings.

FORMING IMPRESSIONS OF OTHERS: PUTTING IT ALL TOGETHER

According to common belief, first impressions are very important. Supposedly, the way in which you "come across" to others the first time you meet exerts a lasting impact upon their feelings or thoughts about you. Is this really true? Since we've found that "common sense" is often wrong about such matters (recall our discussion of this issue in Chapter 1), you might guess that it is incorrect here, too. In this instance, though it actually seems to be on the right track. First impressions do matter; in fact, they appear to matter greatly. Since they do, it is useful to know something about them. Specifically, it is helpful to know just how they are formed, and what factors affect them. It is on these issues that we will now focus.

First Impressions: How They Are Formed

When we meet another person for the first time, we are literally flooded with new information. Almost at once, we notice his appearance, style of dress, and manner of speech. Further, as we listen to what he has to say and observe the things he does, we begin to form some idea of this person's major traits or motives through the attribution process described above. As you know from your own experience, though, we do not merely gather these separate pieces of information. Instead, we go further and combine them into a unified picture. In short, we form an overall impression of each person we meet—an impression that can range from very favorable through very unfavorable. But how, precisely, do we perform this task? How do we combine so much varied information into a distinct first impression with such lightning speed? A great deal of research has been performed on this question, and the results point to the following answer: We perform this task through a special type of averaging.[12]

Expressed very simply, our impressions of others seem to represent a *weighted average* of all available information about them. That is, they reflect a process in which all information at our disposal about others is averaged together—but with some "facts" or input receiving greater weight than others. As you can readily see, this makes good sense. After all, in forming an impression of a new boss you would probably be influenced to a much greater degree by the way this person gives you orders (respectfully versus arrogantly) than by the color of his or her eyes. The fact that not all information about other persons affect our impressions of them to the same extent, though, raises an important question: Just what kinds of input receive the greatest weight? Again, research provides some revealing answers.

First Impressions: What Input Matters Most

In forming impressions of others, we take into account many kinds of information. The importance assigned to each of these, of course, varies from situation to situation and from context to context. In general, though, we attach greatest weight to five distinct types.

First, as you might expect, we seem to pay more attention to information relating to others' lasting traits or characteristics than to information about more temporary factors. For example, if you perceive that a person working under your direction is very high in ability, this will probably have a stronger and more lasting impact upon your impression of her than noticing that she seems quite tired and rundown this morning.

Second, when we receive information about others second-hand, rather than from a direct face-to-face meeting with them, we are much more strongly affected by such input when it comes from a source we view as credible or reliable than when it comes from a source whose reliability we doubt. For example, if the office gossip, who is well known to exaggerate, tells you that the new accountant keeps whips and chains in her locker, you may doubt this tale and reserve judgment. If, instead, you hear the same report from a friend you know to be very cautious and reserved, you may be more likely to believe it—and to change your impression of the new employee.

Third, the information that we acquire first about others often seems to exert a stronger impact on our impressions than information that we receive somewhat later. Such *primacy effects*, as they are usually termed, help explain why it is often so hard to alter a first impression; once individuals attain initial information about others and form impressions of them, they pay little attention to new facts— even ones that refute their initial view.

Fourth, we seem to assign much greater weight to negative information about others than to positive information about them.[13] In short, we seem to base our impressions of others more on their worst traits or behaviors than on their best.

Fifth, we attach greater weight or importance to information relating to extreme behavior by others (either very positive or very negative) than to information about more moderate actions.[14] For example, if you learn that another person left his last job because he refused to become involved in illegal dumping of toxic chemical wastes, you may form a strongly positive impression of him. If, instead, you learn that he left his last job because he didn't like commuting for more than an hour, your impression may be less strongly affected by such information. (See Figure 2.9 for a summary of this discussion.)

To conclude: Existing evidence suggests that our overall impressions of others are not formed in a random manner. Rather, they seem to stem from an orderly—

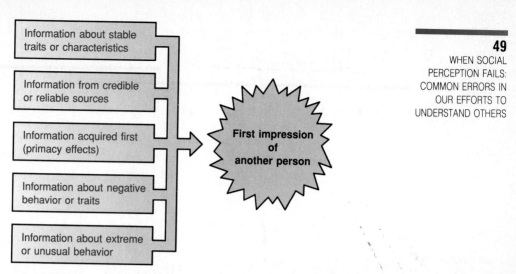

FIGURE 2.9 Forming Impressions of Others: Some Key Types of Information
In forming impressions of others, we seem to assign extra weight or importance to the types of information shown here.

if largely unconscious—process involving a special type of averaging. To compare your own first impressions with that of others, complete the **Human Relations in Action** on page 50.

WHEN SOCIAL PERCEPTION FAILS: COMMON ERRORS IN OUR EFFORTS TO UNDERSTAND OTHERS

Given the complexity of other persons, it is only reasonable to expect that we make errors in our perception of them. In fact, this is definitely the case. There are a number of different ways in which our perceptions of people around us can fail and lead us to misunderstand them. Since being aware of these potential errors may help you recognize and combat them, several will now be described.

Overestimating the Role of Internal Causes: The Fundamental Attribution Error

Suppose, while standing in a checkout line in a store, you witness the following scene: The clerk on duty shouts angrily at a customer, telling him to take his business elsewhere. How would you account for this rude behavior? Your first reply might be "I wouldn't try," or "It's impossible to tell." In fact, though, research findings point to another answer: The chances are quite good that you would conclude (tentatively, of course) that the clerk is a hostile person, best avoided. This simple example illustrates what is perhaps the most common form of bias in attribution: A strong tendency to view others' actions as stemming mainly from internal rather than external factors.[15] (It is so common, it is often termed the **fundamental attribution error**.) In short, we generally perceive others as behaving as they do because they are "that kind of person." The many external factors that may also have affected their actions tend to be ignored or downplayed.

As you can probably see, this is a serious type of error. Because of it, we may expect others to behave more consistently than is justified. For example, if you see your boss act in a forgiving manner toward an employee who has made a serious error, you may jump to the conclusion that he is kindhearted. In fact, though, he may have been forgiving because of external factors (e.g., the employee in question is a distant relative, or the son of an old friend), *not* because he is a

HUMAN RELATIONS IN ACTION

Forming First Impressions: What's in a Face?

We often form impressions of people based on very limited information about how they look, talk, or dress. To check on the impressions you have of four different people, we have provided photographs of four young men. From these pictures we would like you to give your impressions on the items provided below. Simply indicate the extent to which you think the person has the characteristic listed by circling the number that best represents your feeling. For example, if you think the person is very intelligent, circle the "1;" if you think he is very unintelligent, circle the "7;" if you think he is average in intelligence, you would circle "4."

| Person A | Person B | Person C | Person D |

Rating Scales

Person A

Intelligent	1	2	3	4	5	6	7	Unintelligent
Honest	1	2	3	4	5	6	7	Dishonest
Warm	1	2	3	4	5	6	7	Cold

forgiving soul. Because you overlook such possibilities, though, you are shocked (and hurt) when he fails to be kind to you when you make the same type of error. After all, you may reason, aren't kindhearted people usually forgiving? In this and many other situations, our tendency to attribute the behavior of other persons to internal causes can lead us to false conclusions about them.

The Actor-Observer Effect: You Tripped; I Was Pushed

A second and closely related type of error in attribution can be readily illustrated. Imagine that while walking along the street you see a woman trip and fall. How would you explain this behavior? As noted above, the chances are good

Person B

Intelligent	1	2	3	4	5	6	7	Unintelligent
Honest	1	2	3	4	5	6	7	Dishonest
Warm	1	2	3	4	5	6	7	Cold

Person C

Intelligent	1	2	3	4	5	6	7	Unintelligent
Honest	1	2	3	4	5	6	7	Dishonest
Warm	1	2	3	4	5	6	7	Cold

Person D

Intelligent	1	2	3	4	5	6	7	Unintelligent
Honest	1	2	3	4	5	6	7	Dishonest
Warm	1	2	3	4	5	6	7	Cold

Now compare your ratings with those obtained from another class of students provided on p. 65. Do your general impressions agree with those of this group? If they do, why do you think this is so? If there are some major discrepancies, how do you interpret these? On which trait is there the most agreement? Why is there more agreement for this trait than for the others? You might ask your teacher to collect the ratings of all of the members of your class so that the class scores can be obtained and be used as another basis for discussion. Whatever the exact results, you will most likely find considerable agreement on one or two of the traits. If this occurs by simply looking at pictures, just think how much more powerful this is likely to be in everyday interactions where we are provided with even more information on which to form initial impressions. By the way, it should be noted that the ranking on exam scores for these four students did not match that of their ranking in rated intelligence. This reflects the fact that these ratings are "snap" judgments and not indications of actual characteristics of these individuals based on careful study.

that you will attribute it to traits of this individual—for example you may conclude that she is a clumsy oaf. Would you explain your own behavior in the same way? Probably not. Instead, you may assume you tripped because of external causes—broken pavement, slippery soles on your shoes, and so on.

This tendency to attribute our own behavior to external causes but that of others to internal ones is generally termed the **actor-observer effect,** and it is quite common.[16] It seems to derive from the fact that while we are quite aware of the many situational factors affecting our own behavior, we are less aware of the impact of these factors upon the actions of other persons. Thus we tend to perceive our actions as stemming largely from situational causes, but that of others as deriving from their own traits.

This error in social perception, too, can have serious consequences. Specifically, because of it, we may often overlook important inconsistencies in our own behavior or feelings. As a result, we may fail to obtain fuller understanding of our own traits or motives. For example, consider the case of a young man who gets into repeated arguments with his supervisors and so loses one job after another. Because of the actor-observer effect, he may perceive that these incidents stem from external causes; bad luck or the built-in hostility of managers. Actually, though, his difficulties stem from his own traits—stubbornness and abrasiveness. Because of the actor-observer bias, though, he may never realize this key fact. Research has confirmed that supervisors do tend to attribute subordinate performance to internal factors (e.g., ability, effort) while subordinates tend to attribute performance to external factors such as co-workers and supervisors.[17]

The Self-Serving Bias: Taking Credit for Success, Avoiding Blame for Failure

While our tendency to perceive our own behavior as stemming mainly from situational factors and that of other persons as deriving mainly from internal factors is quite general, it is sometimes overridden by another error: the **self-serving bias.**[18] Briefly, this refers to our strong tendency to take credit for good outcomes (i.e., success), while denying responsibility for negative ones (i.e., failure). Both of these tendencies are easy to spot. For example, suppose you write a report for your boss and she likes it very much. How would you account for this result? Probably, you would assume that it stemmed from such factors as your hard work, high level of intelligence, and innate talent. But now, instead, imagine that she rejects the report, and criticizes it harshly. How would you explain this result? The chances are good that you would view it as stemming from external factors—her unreasonably high standards, the lack of clear instructions about what was needed, and so on. (For another example, see Figure 2.10.) In short, we seem to be all too ready to take full credit for success but to deny personal responsibility for failure, even in work situations.

Basically, there are two reasons behind this bias or error. First, it allows us to protect or enhance our own self-esteem—the way that we feel about ourselves. Second, it permits us to present a positive public image—to appear favorably in the eyes of others.[19] Regardless of its precise origins, though, the self-serving bias, too, can get us into deep trouble. Imagine what happens when two persons work on a task together, a common situation in work settings. Each may perceive any success attained as stemming mainly from his or her own contributions. However, each will perceive failure as mainly the fault of the other person. Needless to say, this can lead to a great deal of friction between the persons involved. For this reason, the self-serving bias, too, is a type of error to be carefully avoided.

Stereotypes: "They're All Alike, Aren't They?"

Another type of error in social perception is, in some ways, the most disturbing we will consider. It refers to the belief—almost always false—that all members of a given group possess certain traits or show certain kinds of behavior. Such beliefs are known as **stereotypes,** and they are all too common. Indeed, distinct stereotypes exist for racial and ethnic minorities, religious groups, the elderly, various occupations or professions, and even for blondes and redheads! You can demonstrate this fact for yourself quite simply: Just try to list the major traits shared by "all" lawyers, accountants, coal miners, and redheads. The chances are good that you can come up with several for each of these groups, even though you know very well that the people in them are all unique individuals.

Why do stereotypes exist? Several factors seem to play a role. First, it appears that as human beings, we possess a basic tendency to divide the world into two social categories: *us* and *them.* Further, persons we perceive as outside our own group are viewed as being more similar to one another than persons in our own group. In other words, because we have less information about them, we tend to lump them all together, and see them as quite homogeneous.[20] Second, stereotypes seem to come from our tendency to do as little cognitive work as possible in thinking about other persons.[21] By assigning people to particular groups, we can assume that we know much about them (their major traits, how they tend to act), and we save the tedious work of understanding them as individuals.

FIGURE 2.10 Self-Serving Bias: One Way of Avoiding Blame
Cathy's friend fits with the expectations of the *self-serving bias* since he is attributing his weight related problems to external factors. Cathy on the other hand, shows no *self-serving bias* since she blames her problems on her own characteristics. (Cathy © 1990 Universal Press Syndicate. Reprinted with permission. All rights reserved.)

In most cases, stereotypes carry a distinctly negative tinge; many of the traits or behaviors they include are far from flattering. But they are dangerous in other ways, as well. Most important, they often show an unsettling self-fulfilling nature.[22] When people perceive all members of a group as having certain traits, they tend to treat them as if they exhibit those traits. As a consequence, the target of such treatment may respond by fulfilling portions of the stereotype. For example, many people seem to believe that older workers (those in their sixties) lack energy, are old-fashioned, and cannot perform many tasks as well as younger workers. Because of such beliefs, they treat employees in this age group as persons needing special help and as unable to handle difficult jobs. Faced with such treatment, older workers may begin to doubt their own abilities and so come to confirm these false beliefs. In this and other ways, stereotypes can be a very damaging type of error in social perception. Indeed, they represent a case of perception shaping reality rather than reflecting it.

Halo Effects: How Overall Impressions Shape Social Judgments

Have you ever heard the phrase, "Love is blind"? If so, you are already familiar with a final type of error in social perceptions: **halo effects.** This type of error refers to the fact that once we form an overall impression of another person, this global impression tends to exert strong effects on our judgments of his or her specific traits.[23] Unfortunately, halo effects are both common and powerful. For example, most organizations contain one or more "superstars"—people who have acquired the reputation for being exceptionally talented and competent. Once they have gained such a "halo," everything they do is evaluated favorably. Ideas that would be perceived as mediocre if suggested by someone else are seen as creative and brilliant when proposed by these persons. And actions that might be viewed as risky or foolish if undertaken by others are seen as daring and bold when performed by these "chosen" men and women. On the other side of the coin, some people acquire a "rusty halo"—a reputation for being unable to do anything right. This global impression then spills over onto all their traits or behaviors, so that whatever they do or suggest is perceived in a negative light.

As you can readily see, halo effects, too, carry high costs. They may lead some persons to develop an overblown view of their own merits or worth, while crushing the egos of others who are equally deserving. Further, by assigning undue influence to persons who are not ready to receive it, and by blocking recognition of hidden pools of talent, they can harm organizations as well as individuals. Clearly, then, it is important to recognize the existence and impact of halo effects; only then can their harmful effects be avoided.

Similar-to-Me Effects

It is a well-established principle that we tend to like individuals who are similar to ourselves better than we like those who are dissimilar. So it probably will not surprise you to know that this fact—often termed the **similar-to-me-effect**—is another source of bias in work settings. It has been found that the higer the perceived similarity between supervisors and their subordinates, the higher the performance ratings they assign to one another.[24]

Of course, people in work settings perceive similarities along a number of different dimensions. They may perceive similarity in outlook or values, standards of performance, and background or personal characteristics (e.g., education or age). The greater the perceived similarities between supervisors and their subordinates are, the higher the satisfaction and performance of the subordinates.[25]

These findings suggest that subordinates who are similar to their supervisors in several respects may have an unfair edge over those who are not. Correspondingly, supervisors who are perceived as similar by their subordinates may also gain an advantage. However, it may also be the case that the perception of similarity helps produce a positive relationship between people in a work group. It is possible that this factor, not merely perceptual bias, accounts for the higher evaluations assigned by supervisors to similar subordinates (see Figure 2.11). In sum, while it is important to guard against similar-to-me effects when they operate to distort accurate evaluations of performance, increasing perceived similarity between supervisors and their subordinates may yield actual benefits that should not be overlooked.

Contrast Effects: The Impact of Prior Events or Experiences on Current Perceptions and Judgments

Consider the following situation. A young woman with moderately good qualifications applies for a job with two different firms. At the first, she is interviewed by a personnel director who has just finished speaking with two other applicants. Both were at the top of their college classes and possess all the skills and training sought by the company. At the second company, she is interviewed by a personnel director who has just seen two other applicants, neither of whom is at all suitable for the job in question. From which interviewer will she receive higher ratings? The answer seems obvious: from the second. She will be perceived much more

FIGURE 2.11 Potential Benefits of Perceived Similarity
Supervisors often rate subordinates they perceive as similar to themselves more favorably than subordinates they perceive as dissimilar. This may reflect the impact of one form of bias (the *similar-to-me effect*), or, as shown here, the positive effects of perceived similarity on supervisor-subordinate relationships.

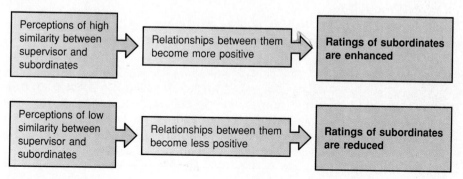

favorably by this person because, in contrast to the two other persons he has just seen, she will "shine." She will receive lower ratings from the first interviewer because compared to the two persons he has just interviewed, she will appear quite mediocre.

This incident illustrates the potential impact of **contrast effects,** another common source of error in social perception.[26] These effects reflect the fact that our reaction to a given stimulus (or person) is often influenced by other stimuli (people) we have recently encountered. The impact of contrast effects is, perhaps, most obvious in the context of interviews. However, they can also operate in other organizational contexts as well. For example, in situations where several individuals deliver reports in succession, reactions to each will probably be influenced by the quality of the presentations that preceded it. If the first individual does an outstanding job, the ones who follow may appear quite ordinary; if the first person "bombs," whoever follows may benefit from this fact and appear to be better than he or she actually is. Many persons are aware of such effects and thus attempt to make sure that when they make presentations, they do not immediately follow star performers. Stars are indeed tough acts to follow, and the costs of doing so with respect to one's own performance evaluations can be high.

For an example that involves many of social perception principles we have discussed, please see the **Case in Point** below.

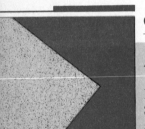

CASE IN POINT

A Good Impression and a Bad Impression

It was time for the six-month evaluation of new employees at Serve Rite Food Services Corporation. Serve Rite handles food services for a variety of companies and colleges and hires a broad range of employees, from food service clerks to managers. Susan Link, the regional manager, was discussing her feelings about some of her managers with Bob Olds, the personnel manager.

"I really like Ryan Dalton. He is bright and highly motivated. He came highly recommended, and he certainly has not disappointed us. I have very few problems with people in his district."

Bob nodded in agreement. "He sure was a lot better than the one he replaced. We were always getting complaints about him."

"Unfortunately, not all of our people seem to be working out," continued Susan. "I have heard some complaints about Vicky Hans. "She has turned a lot of people off with her interpersonal style. Apparently, she really wanted to show them who was boss, and as a result she has a morale problem. We are having a tough time keeping her locations staffed."

The Hans case was somewhat of a puzzle to Bob. Vicky seemed to be quite personable in the interviews and had done well in her prior management positions.

SOCIAL PERCEPTION AT WORK: BIAS IN JOB INTERVIEWS

As you've been reading this chapter, it has probably become evident to you that many of the biases discussed played an important role in the workplace. One specific area in which they may have a significant impact is the *job interview*.

Bias in Job Interviews   Job interviews are still widely used by companies for selecting employees.[27] Since this involves first meetings with strangers, it would seem very susceptible to the type of biases we have been discussing. The interviewer is trying to form impressions about traits of the potential employee from the conversations and interactions that take place during this short period of time. So first impressions are likely to play an important role and the interviewer will be tempted to make snap judgments about the suitability of the applicants. What affects these judgments? Obviously practically everything related to the interview—the person's dress, the quality of the answers, personality, and various nonverbal cues. It is pretty hard to control your personality, but it is possible to maximize your chance for making a good impression by dressing well and appropriately and by finding out what kind of answers the interviewer is anticipating. But what about nonverbal cues? Apparently, one can use positive nonverbal cues

"Susan, do you think there might be something about that district other than Vicky's style that could be responsible? In my discussions with Vicky she has mentioned that there are some key people who seem to resent working for a female manager. Maybe if we gave her a chance in another district, she might do quite well."

Susan shook her head in disagreement. "Bob, I think she is just using her female status as an excuse for her failure. I just don't think she has the people skills to be a good manager."

Questions

1. How many of the principles discussed in the section on forming impressions can you find in this example?

2. How confident are you that Susan has an accurate impression of these two employees? What would you suggest as ways for her to develop more accurate or soundly based impressions?

3. What could Vicky have done to develop a more positive impression with her boss?

such as smiling and having eye contact to generate a good impression.[28] However, this does not work when the interviewer has considerable information about the applicant's qualifications.[29,30] Further, when applicants with poor credentials emit many nonverbal cues, they seem to be down-rated relative to applicants who do not engage in such behavior.[31] Perhaps this is due to the fact that interviewers attribute such actions to efforts by these applicants to shift attention away from their poor qualifications. Whatever the reason, it is clear that emitting a high level of positive nonverbal cues can sometimes backfire and produce effects opposite to the ones intended. The best strategy to follow, therefore, seems to be this: By all means, practice effective nonverbal behavior, and try to use it to your advantage during an interview. But for best results, combine it with clear evidence of competence and excellent qualifications.

Stereotypes   We noted earlier that stereotypes can exert strong effects on our perceptions of others. Do these cognitive frameworks also play a role in job interviews? Again, growing evidence suggests that they do. While several different stereotypes have been studied in this regard, the ones usually viewed as most important, and which have received most attention, are those related to sex: *sex-role stereotypes*.

Such stereotypes suggest that members of the two sexes possess different characteristics. For example, according to these stereotypes, males tend to be forceful, assertive, and decisive, while females tend to be passive, emotional, and indecisive. We should hasten to note that such stereotypes have, by and large, been found to be false: Differences between the sexes in such traits are nonexistent, or at least much smaller, than sex-role stereotypes suggest.[32] This does not prevent them from affecting social perception, however. Several studies have found that under conditions where limited information about job applicants is available, interviewers tend to assign lower ratings to females than to males.[33]

While such results are disturbing, we should note again that they have usually been reported in situations where interviewers have little information about applicants. Fortunately, in many real contexts, this is not the case. Interviewers receive a considerable amount of information about applicants' previous experience, training, and background. Are the biasing effects of sex-role stereotypes weaker under these conditions? Apparently they are.[34] In this more realistic situation, sex of applicants may have little if any effect on such ratings, and the interviewers' decisions are influenced by other factors considered, such as perceived similarity, objective qualifications, and subjective qualifications (e.g., ability to express ideas and to motivate). In fact, the overall pattern of findings suggested the following process. *Perceived similarity, liking,* and *objective qualifications* all affect interview outcomes through their impact on subjective qualifications; sex of subject had no effect on this factor. In sum, Graves and Powell's results suggest that while the outcome of job interviews may be affected by several forms of bias (e.g., the similar-to-me effect, liking for specific applicants), they are not strongly determined by applicant sex. Whether this is due to recent changes in society (e.g., growing awareness of sex bias) or to the specific context of the study (interviews on a college campus) cannot be determined at this point. Still, it appears that at least one important type of interview is less subject to this damaging type of bias than might be feared.

So the general recommendation we can make is that it is possible to do some things to help make a good impression and it is foolish not to do so. Yet, the most important fact appears to be one's objective qualifications and the personal characteristics—such as initiative, pleasant interaction in style, and ability to express ideas—that are seen as important for success.

As we have just seen, there are many ways in which social perception can fail—many ways in which it can lead us to false conclusions about others. Such errors have important implications for human relations in work settings. Because of the "slants" or tendencies discussed earlier, we often misunderstand other persons, reach false conclusions about their behavior, or assume that they possess certain traits when they do not. Such errors, in turn, can exert adverse effects upon our relations with them, and so upon the morale and productivity of the organization. For these reasons, it is important for everyone—managers and employees alike—to be aware of these potential errors and to take active steps to combat them. The effort involved in this regard can be fairly high. But the benefits, too, can be substantial.

SUMMARY

Contrary to common sense, we do not know the world around us in a simple or direct manner. Rather, we construct a picture of it through an active and complex process of **perception.** Perception is selective—we pay more attention to certain stimuli or events than to others. In addition, perception is organized—we impose order on the formation brought to us by our senses.

Social perception involves our attempts to understand the persons around us. One key aspect of such perception is **attribution**—the process through which we seek knowledge of the causes behind others' behavior. A basic task in attribution is that of deciding whether other persons act the way they do because of internal or external causes. Our decision in this respect can exert important effects upon our evaluation of others' performance. Impressions of others seem to be formed through a process in which we average all available information about these persons. In forming such impressions, however, certain types of information are assigned greater weight or importance than others.

Social perception is subject to a number of errors. First, we tend to overestimate the importance of internal factors in shaping others' behavior (the **fundamental attribution error**). Second, we tend to perceive our own behavior as stemming mainly from situational factors, but that of others as deriving mainly from their own traits (the **actor-observer effect**). Third, we tend to take credit for success but to avoid the blame for failure (the **self-serving bias**). Another common error in social perception involves the acceptance of **stereotypes**—the belief that all members of some social groups share the same traits and behaviors. Social perception is also subject to **halo effects.** Here, our overall impression of another person (usually favorable) affects or distorts our evaluations of his or her specific traits or actions. We also tend to like, and evaluate more positively, persons who are similar to ourselves (the **similar-to-me effect**). Our evaluation of a particular person is also affected by other people we have recently encountered—the **contrast effect.**

Errors in social perception are important, for they can lead us to false conclusions about others, and so can reduce both morale and productivity in work settings. For example, it affects the outcomes of job interviews, where the ratings assigned to applicants are often influenced by such factors as the nonverbal cues they emit and by various stereotypes (e.g., sex-role stereotypes).

KEY TERMS

actor-observer effect: A tendency to attribute our own actions to situational causes but those of others to internal causes.

attribution: The process through which we seek to determine the causes behind the actions of others or ourselves.

contrast effects: An evaluation of a given person on some dimension that has been affected by prior contact with another person who is rated considerably higher or lower than this individual on this dimension.

figure-ground: A tendency to perceive scenes or events as consisting of objects standing out against a background.

fundamental attribution error: A tendency to overemphasize the importance of internal causes in the behavior of others.

halo effect: An overall impression of someone that influences our evaluations of his or her specific traits or behaviors.

impression formation: The process through which we combine diverse information about other persons into unified "pictures" of them.

perception: The active process through which we interpret and organize information provided by our senses. It is through perception that we construct a representation of the world around us.

salience: The extent to which a given stimulus stands out from other stimuli around it.

self-serving bias: A tendency to take credit for positive outcomes while attributing negative ones to external causes (e.g., other persons).

similar-to-me effect: The tendency of raters to assign higher evaluations to ratees who are similar to themselves in various respects (e.g., in terms of attitudes, demographic factors).

social perception: The process through which we come to know and understand other persons.

stereotypes: Beliefs suggesting that all members of a given social group possess the same traits (often negative) or show similar behaviors.

vividness: The emotion-provoking properties of a given stimulus. The greater the ability of a stimulus to induce emotional reactions among the persons exposed to it, the higher its vividness.

NOTES

1. Sekuler, R., & Blake, R. (1985). *Perception.* New York: Random House.
2. Harvey, J.H., Yarkin, K.L., Lightner, J., & Town, J.P. (1980). "Unsolicited Inter-

pretation and Recall of Interpersonal Events." *Journal of Personality and Social Psychology*, *38*, 551–68.

3. Fiske, S.T., & Taylor, S.E. (1984). *Social Cognition*. Reading, Mass.: Addison-Wesley.

4. Roedigner, H.L. III, Ruston, J.P., Capaldi, E.D., & Paris, S.G. (1984). *Psychology*. Boston: Little Brown.

5. von Seden, M. (1960). *Space and Sight: The Perception of Space and Shape in the Congenitally Blind Before and After Operation*. New York: Free Press.

6. Ross, M., & Fletcher, G.J.O. (1985). "Attribution and Social Perception." In G. Lindzey & E. Aronson, eds., *Handbook of social psychology*, 2d ed. New York: Random House.

7. Kleinke, C.L. (1986). *Meeting and Understanding People*. New York: Freeman.

8. *See* Note 6.

9. Kelley, H.H., & Michaela, J.L. (1980). "Attribution Theory and Research." *Annual Review of Psychology*, *31*, 457–501.

10. Wong, P., & Weiner, B. (1981). "When People Ask "Why" Questions, and the Heuristics of Attributional Search." *Journal of Personality and Social Psychology*, *40*, 650–63.

11. Knowlton, W.A. Jr., & Mitchell, T.R. (1980). "Effects of Causal Attributions on a Supervisor's Evaluation of Subordinate Performance." *Journal of Applied Psychology*, *65*, 459–66.

12. Anderson, N.H. (1981). "Integration theory applied to cognitive responses and attitudes." In R.E. Petty, T.M. Ostrom, and T.C. Brock, eds., *Cognitive Responses in Persuasion*. Hillsdale, N.J.: Erlbaum.

13. Hamilton, D.L., & Zanna, M.P. (1972). "Differential Weighting of Favorable and Unfavorable Attributes in Impressions of Personality." *Journal of Experimental Research in Personality*, *6*, 204–12.

14. Fiske, S.T. (1980). "Attention and Weight in Person Perception: The Impact of Extreme and Negative Behavior." *Journal of Personality and Social Psychology*, *38*, 889–906.

15. Johnson, J.T., Jemmott, J.B. III, & Pettigrew, T.F. (1984). "Causal Attribution and Dispositional Inference: Evidence of Inconsistent Judgments." *Journal of Experimental Social Psychology*, *20*, 567–85.

16. Jones, E.E., & Nisbett, R.E. (1972). "The Actor and the Observer: Divergent Perceptions of the Causes of Behavior." In E.E. Jones et al. eds., *Attribution: Perceiving the Causes of Behavior*. Morrison, N.J.: General Learning Press.

17. Gioia, D.A., & Sims, H.P. Jr. (1985). "Self-Serving Bias and Actor-Observer Differences: An Empirical Analysis." *Journal of Applied Social Psychology*, *15*, 547–63.

18. Mullen, B., & Riordan, C.A. (1988). "Self-serving Attributions for Performance in Naturalistic Settings: A Meta-Analytic Review." *Journal of Applied Social Psychology*, *18*, 3–22.

19. Greenberg, J., Pyszczynski, T., & Solomon S. (1982). "The Self-Serving Attributional Bias: Beyond Self-Presentation." *Journal of Experimental Social Psychology*, *18*, 56–67.

20. Linville, P.W. (1982). "The Complexity-Extremity Effect and Age-Based Stereotyping." *Journal of Personality and Social Psychology*, *42*, 183–211.

21. *See* Note 14.

22. Skrypnek, B.J., & Snyder, M. (1982). "On the Self-Perpetuating Nature of Stereotypes About Women and Men." *Journal of Experimental Social Psychology*, *18*, 277–91.

23. Fisicaro, S.A. (1988). "A Reexamination of the Relation Between Halo Error and Accuracy." *Journal of Applied Social Psychology*, *73*, 239–44.

24. Pulakos, E.D., & Wexley, K.N. (1983). The relationship among perceptual similarity, sex, and performance ratings in manager-subordinate dyads. *Academy of Management Journal*, *26*, 129–39.

25. Turban, D.B., & Jones, A.P. (1988). Supervisor-Subordinate Similarity: Types, Effects, and Mechanisms. *Journal of Applied Psychology*, *73*, 228–34.

26. *See* Note 24.

27. Arvey, R.D., & Campion, J.E. (1982). "The Employment Interview: A Summary and Review of Recent Research." *Personnel Psychology*, *35*, 281–322.

28. Imada, A.S., & Hakel, M.D. (1977). "Influence of Nonverbal Communication and Rater Proximity on Impressions and Decisions in Simulated Employment Interviews." *Journal of Applied Psychology*, *62*, 295–300.

29. Rasmussen, K.G. Jr. (1984). "Nonverbal Behavior, Verbal Behavior, Resume Credentials, and Selection Interview Outcomes." *Journal of Applied Psychology*, *69*, 551–56.

30. Riggio, R.E., & Throckmorton, B. (1988). "The Relative Effects of Verbal and Nonverbal Behavior, Appearance, and Social Skills on Evaluations Made in Hiring Interviews." *Journal of Applied Social Psychology*, *18*, 331–48.

31. Baron, R.A. (1986). "Self-Presentation in Job Interviews: When There Can Be 'Too Much of a Good Thing.' " *Journal of Applied Social Psychology*, *16*, 16–28.

32. Parsons, J.E., Adler, T., & Meece, J.L. (1984). "Sex differences in achievement: A test of alternate theories." *Journal of Personality and Social Psychology*, *46*, 26–43.

33. Tosi, H.L., & Einbender, S.W. (1985). "The Effects of Type and Amount of Information in Sex Discrimination Research: A Meta-Analysis." *Academy of Management Journal*, *28*, 712–23.

34. Graves, L.M., & Powell, G.N. (1988). "An Investigation of Sex Discrimination in Recruiters' Evaluations of Actual Applicants." *Journal of Applied Personality*, *72*, 20–29.

ADDITIONAL CASES AND EXERCISES: APPLYING WHAT YOU'VE LEARNED

A Small Change of Perspective

William Ickes
Professor of Psychology
University of Texas at Arlington

Karen Foreman and Tim Mahoney had competed their way through the last seven years of their lives. As undergraduate business majors at the University of Pennsylvania, they had vied for the top grade in the classes they took together, and for the top honors at their graduation exercises. As candidates for the MBA at the Wharton School of Business, they had again competed for grades, recognition, and the approval of the faculty. And now, as new junior executives for rival advertising agencies, they were in an initial, head-to-head competition for a new account, a company that wanted to introduce another brand of toothpaste to the marketplace.

Karen searched for cracks in Tim's facade as he stood at the front of the boardroom, making his agency's presentation to the company's board of directors. She noticed the slight trembling of his fingers as he worked the buttons on the VCR and noted each of the small stammers and hesitations in his voice as he provided the narrative accompaniment to the videotape he displayed.

He's the kind of guy who can't keep it together under pressure, she thought, a little smugly. *He's probably not all that well-prepared to begin with. I've always suspected that "deep down" he was insecure and unsure of himself. Well, this is the acid test of what kind of person he really is. If he winds up looking a little nervous and awkward, it will send a message to the board members that he isn't the kind of person they want handling their ad campaign.*

Fifteen minutes later, Tim finished his presentation to a moderate round of applause and another twenty minutes of hard-nosed questions. Although he handled all of the questions thoughtfully and with some degree of grace, Karen still felt that the small signs of nervousness tended to undermine his overall performance. *They'll see that they're dealing with a different kind of person when it's time for me to make* my *presentation,* she thought.

And soon, almost without her realizing it, it *was* time for her presentation. Karen strode purposefully toward the front of the boardroom, a confident smile on her face. Then, as she turned to face all of the assembled board members, her self-confidence received a rude shock. She found herself confronted by a dozen pairs of eyes, boring into her appraisingly. The faces that were turned toward her were critical, and in some cases, even skeptical. She felt instantly like a person condemned to stand in front of a firing squad.

I didn't count on this, she thought to herself, as she fought to control a growing sense of panic. *I knew that this would be a stressful situation, but I had no idea that it would be* this *stressful. I just hope that I can perform half as smoothly as Tim did under the same situational pressure. Well, here goes . . .*

Questions

1. In what way(s) did Karen fall victim to the error in attribution called "the actor-observer effect"?

2. Were Karen's original attributions about Tim's performance accurate or biased? Were her original feelings of self-confidence justified or unjustified?

3. How could Karen have avoided the attributional errors associated with the actor-observer effect?

4. Were these errors likely to be costly ones for her in this situation? What other situations can you think of in which the errors associated with the actor-observer effect might be equally or even more costly?

The Case of the Lingering Doubts

A real "plum" has developed at American National Life. Dan Fredrickson, Assistant Director of Financial Services, has left suddenly to take another job. His position is a good one, and there's a logical candidate for it: Jack Conley. He has worked closely with Dan for the past two years and seems ready to step into his shoes. Although two of the people who must make the decision are in favor of this move, the third is not. In fact, Scott Premo has opposed promoting Jack strongly and consistently each time the subject has come up. In contrast, Jill Shaver and Tom Franklin feel he's totally right for the post. Right now, the three executives are going round and round on this issue once again.

"Oh come on, Scott," Jill says with some irritation. "What gives? Why are you so darned adamant about not promoting Jack?"

"I don't mean to be stubborn," Scott replies, "but I still have my doubts about him."

"But why, for heaven's sake?" asks Tom. "He's done good work. Dan recommends him. And he knows the job inside and out."

"That may all be true, but I still remember the way he flubbed that Flexi-Life scheme. He botched it good, and we still have to deal with the repercussions even now."

"But Scott, that was over two years ago, when he first came to the company. He made some mistakes, I admit, but he was green and inexperienced. His performance since then has been real consistent. Can't you take that into account?"

"I can and I can't. I usually make up my mind about someone pretty early in the game. And in this case, I put him down as a potential loser a long time ago."

"That's the trouble, right there," Tom responds. "You can't seem to shake your first impression of the guy. All his hard work since then counts for nothing. I can't figure you out, Scott. Sure, first impressions are important, but we can all make a mistake. I think you ought to reconsider."

"I'm trying, I'm trying," Scott replies. "But I just can't help having lingering doubts about this guy. . . ."

Questions

1. Why do you think Scott continues to cling to his first, negative impression of Jack Conley?

2. Do you think he is justified in retaining his doubts about Jack's competence?

3. What kind of information, if any, would be effective in re-shaping his thinking about, and evaluation of, Jack?

4. Do you think Scott's impression of Jack is accurate?

Comparative Results for Human Relations in Action on p. 51.

The people shown in the photographs received the following ratings on the three dimensions:

	Intelligent/Unintelligent	Warm/Cold	Honest/Dishonest
Person A	4.2	3.0	3.4
Person B	2.8	3.3	3.3
Person C	3.3	3.8	4.2
Person D	3.2	3.3	3.2

3

Communication: The Fine Art of Getting Your Message Across

Learning Objectives

After reading this chapter,
you should be able to:

1. Define the process of communication and describe its major forms.

2. Describe how the formal structure of an organization influences the nature of the communication that occurs within it.

3. Describe how informal patterns of communication operate within organizations.

4. Describe several personal factors that influence communication effectiveness.

5. Distinguish between messages that are best communicated in written and in spoken forms.

6. Identify and describe the most prevalent nonverbal communication cues in human relations.

7. Discuss how the way we dress and use space can be a form of communication.

8. Identify and describe measures that can be taken by individuals and by organizations to improve communication effectiveness.

he largest auditorium at Apex, Inc., a middle-sized firm specializing in a wide range of consumer products, is filled to overflowing. Robert Callahan, CEO of the company, has called a special meeting to which all managerial staff—everyone from junior assistants to senior vice presidents—has been summoned. This is a rare event; Callahan usually communicates directly only with top executives. Partly for this reason, the grapevine at Apex has been operating at a feverish pitch for the past week. Each day wild rumors have swept through company headquarters, only to be replaced by other, even wilder ones. On Monday it was widely reported that Callahan would use the meeting to announce his resignation and his move— along with many of the best people in the company—to one of Apex's strongest competitors. On Tuesday the most popular view was that Apex had just been purchased by a larger firm, and that hundreds of jobs would be lost as the new owners moved their own people into key positions. Today, the number one rumor involves reports of a disastrous drop in sales, and adoption of stringent cost-cutting measures to combat it.

But now the time for rumor is almost past, for at precisely twenty minutes after the announced time of the meeting, Callahan strides into the room and steps up to the podium. After a few opening comments, he gets quickly to the point. For once, it appears, all rumors have been wrong. The purpose of the meeting is that of announcing good news—not a corporate disaster. Rather than being bought by another company, Apex has just done some buying of its own: It has purchased a moderate-sized chain of retail stores. These will serve as prime outlets for many of the company's products, and should add substantially to future earnings. As Callahan outlines the many benefits that will stem from this purchase, audible sighs of relief can be heard throughout the room. He finishes speaking, and then holds a brief question-and-answer session. After this, the meeting adjourns.

That afternoon, three close friends—Joe Barton, Kim Fleming, and Lou Wallace—meet to compare reactions.

"Well," Lou asks the others, "what do you think?"

"I was surprised," Kim answers. "The grapevine really blew this one. Not a single rumor was even close."

"That's right," Joe agrees. "But you know, I don't think he told us the whole story. I have a feeling that there's more to it than this."

"Why do you feel that way, Joe?" Lou asks.

"Remember when Hal Boldman asked him what this meant in terms of our ability to hold future mergers? He answered quickly enough, and said that it would strengthen our position. But it seemed to me that he kind of flinched. Also, his voice went up a notch or two after that. That's usually a sign that someone is lying, or at least holding something back."

"Gee," Kim remarks, shaking her head. "I can't believe he'd lie at this kind of meeting. And you know his reputation for being up-front."

"Yeah, I do," Joe answers, "but remember: The stakes are pretty high in this case, so who knows what he's got up his sleeve."

"Hm . . . ," Lou adds, stroking his chin, "what could he be up to? Hey! I've got it! I heard a while back that Consolidated was real interested in buying us, but wanted to beef up our distribution system. This could be just what they wanted. Maybe Callahan's making us more attractive for a really big merger!"

"I think you've hit it," Joe exclaims. "In fact, I don't see what else it could be. Just wait until I tell Frank Baldocci. He's been shouting 'Merger, merger!' forever. And now it looks as though he's right."

With these words, Joe rushes off, only too eager to get this latest "fact" into the Apex rumor mill.

Suppose at some future time you hold a managerial job. What single activity do you think will occupy most of your time? While you may be tempted to answer "doing my job," "making decisions," or even "buttering up my boss," think again: The actual answer is even more basic. Recent surveys indicate in fact, that practicing managers spend about 80 percent of their time engaging in a single process: **communication.**[1] That is, they spend most of their day speaking to others, listening to them, or reading the words they have written. Unfortunately, much of this communication seems to be unsuccessful; other surveys indicate that a majority of organizational communications fail in their basic purpose—they simply do not get their message across.[2]

Despite this fact, communication in the world of work is far from a total waste of time. In fact, in one sense, it can be viewed as the cement holding organizations together. To see why this is so, simply consider what would happen if all communication with a company were blocked. Leaders would no longer be able to lead, since they would not convey their wishes to subordinates. Various departments or individuals would be unable to coordinate their activities. Decisions could not be made, or would be reached in the absence of essential information. And the organization would be unable to react to changing conditions in a unified and effective manner. In short, total chaos would soon reign supreme!

Fortunately, of course, such conditions rarely if ever occur. On the contrary, communication, however effective, is a continuous process in all work settings. Further, it takes many different forms. It can be formal and flow through channels dictated by the organizational chart. Or it can be informal and proceed through the grapevine or similar mechanisms. (Examples of both types of communication were provided in the story at the beginning of this chapter.) Communication in an organization can occur in face-to-face meetings, through written memos or reports, or even by means of the marvels of modern technology, as one computer communicates directly with another. Regardless of the precise form it takes, though, one fact about communication is clear: It is the very lifeblood of organizations, for without it they simply cannot exist.

Because communication plays such a key role in the world of work, it is essential to know something about it. In fact, without such knowledge, you will be hard-pressed to understand our later discussions of many other aspects of human relations. In this chapter, therefore, we will provide you with a basic understanding of the nature of communication. In order to do so, we will touch on several topics. First, we will offer a simple model of communication—a framework for understanding what it is and what it seeks to accomplish. Second, we will examine organizational influences on communication—aspects of organizations that shape its form and content. Third, since communication often occurs between specific individuals, we will consider some of the personal factors that can affect its nature. Finally, we will turn to several techniques for enhancing communication—tactics for facilitating the smooth and accurate flow of information between individuals or groups.

COMMUNICATION: A DEFINITION AND A MODEL

A boss praises a good job by one of her subordinates. A foreman directs the activities of a construction crew. An accountant prepares a memo on the tax aspects of a proposed business deal. A young woman smiles alluringly at a man seated at a nearby table in the company cafeteria. Probably, you will be quick to agree that all of these incidents, varied as they are, involve some form of communication. But what, precisely, does this mean? What, in short, is communication? Many definitions exist, but most agree on the following basic points: *Communication is a process in which one person or group (**the sender**) transmits some type of information to another person or group (**the receiver**).*[3] In some cases, this is all that occurs: Communication is a one-way street. This type of process is common when top executives in a large company send directives downward to their subordinates; often they do not expect any information in return, at least not immediately. But in most situations, there is another aspect to the process: The receiver responds in some manner. That is, the person or group who receives the initial message returns a message to the person or group who initiated the communication. In a word, the receiver provides some kind of *feedback* to the sender. When this occurs, communication is a two-way, reciprocal affair, involving the mutual exchange of information between two or more sides.

Actually, the definition of communication just presented implies a simple model of this process—a framework for understanding just what steps it involves. Within this model, communication begins when two conditions exist: (1) some individual or group has an idea or concept, and (2) it wishes to make this information known to someone else. At this point, a key step in communication must occur: The concept or idea must be put into a form that can be transmitted to the receiver—it must be **encoded.** This is necessary because, popular beliefs about ESP (extrasensory perception) aside, most persons cannot read the minds of others! Rather, they can learn what others are thinking only if this is made external in some way. Thus, for communication to occur, ideas and concepts must be put into words (spoken or written), into some nonverbal form (e.g., gestures, facial expressions), or perhaps entered directly into a computer. Only if this key step is performed can information be transmitted. By the way, it should be clear that our ability to encode ideas, thoughts, and feelings is far from perfect. If you have ever had difficulty describing the way you feel to someone else, you are already aware of this fact.

Once encoding is accomplished, another issue quickly arises: How can this information be transmitted to the receiver? The answer depends in part on how the message has been encoded. If it has been placed in the form of a written report, it can be transmitted by mail or, if especially urgent, by messenger. If it has been entered into computer storage, it can be sent directly to another computer over phone lines or even by satellite. And if it is expressed vocally, it can be presented directly in a face-to-face meeting or over the phone. Whatever means are chosen, though, the message must be transmitted over an appropriate channel of communication in such a way that the receiver can actually obtain it.

Let's now assume that the receiver has somehow gotten the message. What happens next? The receiving person or group must now interpret and make sense of the information received. In short, the message must be **decoded**—converted back into an idea or concept. Once again, of course, our abilities to accomplish this task are limited. If you have ever experienced difficulty in understanding what another person is saying, or in deciphering materials in one of your textbooks (not this one, of course!), you are well acquainted with this fact.

Finally, after decoding has occurred, the receiver may reverse the process and transmit information back to the original sender. Such **feedback** is common, and, as we will see at many later points in this book, it is often extremely valuable as well. It helps senders gauge the impact of their messages—whether these have been understood and whether they have produced the intended effects. Further, it allows receivers to have some input into the overall process.

Despite the apparent simplicity of the communication process, the phenomenon rarely operates flawlessly. As we will point out later in this chapter, there are many potential barriers to effective communication. The name given to factors that distort the clarity of a message is *noise*. As Figure 3.1 illustrates, noise can occur at any point along the communication process. For example, messages that are poorly encoded (e.g., written in an unclear way), or decoded (e.g., not comprehended), or channels of communication that are too noisy or full of static all may reduce communication effectiveness. These factors, and others (e.g., time pressure, organizational politics), may contribute to the distortion of information transmitted from one party to another.

To summarize, communication involves a process in which one or more persons transmit some type of information to one or more other persons who, after attempting to interpret this message, often return additional information to the sender. As will soon become clear in this and later chapters, it is this two-way flow of facts, ideas, concepts, and information that serves as the basis for most, if not all, activities carried out in work settings.

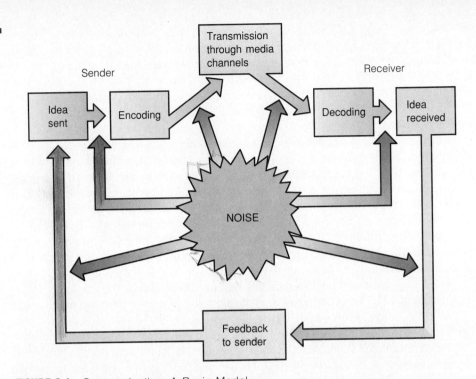

FIGURE 3.1 Communication: A Basic Model

In its most basic form, communication consists of the distinct steps shown here. First, a *sender* desires to make an idea known to a *receiver* (either of which may be an individual, a group, or an organization). The idea must be *encoded,* converted into a form that can be transmitted (e.g., the written or spoken word). This message is then sent via one or several communication channels (e.g., telephone, and/or letter) to the receiver. This receiver must then *decode* the message—convert it back into an understandable idea. This idea may then be returned to the sender in the form of *feedback.* The model also recognizes that *noise,* factors distorting or limiting the flow of information, may enter into the process at any of several points.

ORGANIZATIONAL INFLUENCES ON COMMUNICATION: WHO SHOULD (OR CAN) COMMUNICATE WITH WHOM?

Everyone communicates in organizations—this is a basic fact of life at work. It is a rare person indeed who can perform his or her job in total isolation from others. But, just as clearly, everyone does not communicate with everyone else. Production-line employees do not generally speak directly to the company president. Similarly, people in different departments often do not have the opportunity (or perhaps the desire) to communicate with one another. Thus communication within organizations, at least at the formal level, is far from a haphazard affair. Several factors relating to **organizational structure** and policy dictate who can, or who should, communicate with whom. Moreover, these same factors sometimes specify the form of such communication as well as its appropriate targets. Such organizational influences on communication are important and will be considered here. We should hasten to add, though, that where communication is concerned, they are only part of the total picture. Every work setting is also interlaced with informal networks of communication—networks having little to do with the organizational chart or formal company policy. A great deal of information is transmitted through such networks, often with amazing speed. Thus we will consider these networks as well.

73
ORGANIZATIONAL
INFLUENCES ON
COMMUNICATION:
WHO SHOULD (OR
CAN) COMMUNICATE
WITH WHOM?

Organizational Structure and Communication: The Formal Channels

Consider two organizations. One is a small high-tech company that manufactures only a few different products and operates on the very edge of expanding knowledge. The other is a giant, mature business that employs thousands of people, and produces, advertises, and sells a wide range of items. Will communication within these two companies differ? Of course it will. One major reason for this lies in the fact that the two organizations have very different structures. The small high-tech firm is likely to have very few departments. Further, it probably shows what is termed a *flat organizational structure*—very few levels of management separate top people in the company from those working in production. In fact, if the company is small enough, the CEO may personally make frequent appearances on the factory floor and talk directly to employees. In contrast, the giant corporation will probably possess many different divisions, departments, and other subunits. It will also show a much *taller organizational structure*—one in which many levels separate production workers from top executives. And it will almost certainly evidence a higher degree of *formalization*. That is, there will be many rules and policies, perhaps written down in company handbooks, governing employee behavior and outlining the responsibilities that go along with each position. In contrast, the small high-tech business may be almost totally lacking in such formal rules.

Considering these contrasts in organizational structure, it is not difficult to predict how communication in the two companies will differ. In the small firm, as we have already noted, communication between persons holding different jobs may be quite direct. Few rules governing who may talk to who will exist, and as a result, information will flow quite readily between people performing different functions. In the mature corporation, in contrast, communication will be much more rigid. Generally, it will follow the *scalar chain of command*, with people occupying given jobs communicating directly only with those at their own level, immediately above, or immediately below. For example, production-line people will communicate with one another and with their foreman. Foremen, in turn, will communicate mainly with each other, with the production-line people, and with first-line managers. These persons, in turn, will communicate mainly with foremen and with their own supervisors (e.g., division managers). And this pattern will continue throughout the organization. Similarly, communication across subunits (e.g., from marketing to production) will flow only through limited, formal channels, and will involve only specific persons designated by the organizational chart.

These differences in communication seem quite dramatic—and they are. But others exist as well. Most importantly, the direction of communication—from higher to lower levels with the organization or vice versa—will also differ sharply.[4] In a small company, communication may be very much a two-way street. While the CEO and other executives will communicate *downward* to their subordinates, their closeness to these people and to production may ensure that a good deal of communication occurs *upward* as well. That is, top people in the company may receive a great deal of feedback about their decisions, policies, and actions from subordinates—even from people on the factory floor. In contrast, in the giant corporation, communication will tend to be predominantly downward, from high levels to lower ones. Directives and orders will flow from the top and then be communicated downward through successive steps in the chain of command. Only on relatively rare occasions will this pattern be reversed, so that communication moves upward from lower to high levels (see Figure 3.2, for a summary). In fact, one classic study found that 70 percent of assembly-line workers initiated communication with their supervisors less than once a month.[5] Among managers, a recent study revealed that less than 15 percent of their total communication was directed at their superiors.[6] Research has also shown that when people do communicate upward, their conversations tend to be shorter than discussions with their peers.[7]

Perhaps more importantly, we should note that upward communication often tends to suffer from serious inaccuracies. One aspect of this problem is due to the fact that subordinates frequently feel that they must highlight their accom-

FIGURE 3.2 Upward, Downward, and Horizontal Communication: An Overview
The types of messages communicated within organizations tend to differ according to whether they are traveling upward (from lower to higher levels), downward (from higher to lower levels) or horizontally (across the same levels).

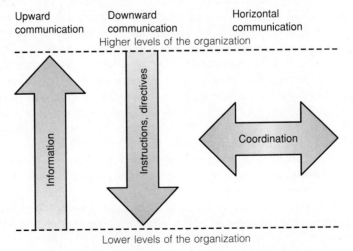

plishments and downplay their mistakes if they are to be looked upon favorably.[8] Another factor that limits upward communication is the tendency for some individuals to fear that they will be rebuked by their supervisors if they speak to them, especially when they fear their outspokenness will threaten their superiors and lessen their chances for promotion.[9] As a result of such dynamics, it is not unusual to find that upward communication tends to be quite limited. This feature of upward communication can cause quite serious problems, as you might imagine, in jobs requiring a high degree of coordination between persons. The dynamics between pilots and copilots of commercial airlines is a perfect example of this problem. Too many times copilots are reluctant to clearly assert themselves to pilots when they fear a pilot is making an error. Norms in the cockpit dictate that a senior person should not be contradicted, and so copilots are frequently much too polite to do so. Unfortunately, many fatal accidents have been directly attributed to such failures of upward communication in the cockpit.[10]

75
ORGANIZATIONAL
INFLUENCES ON
COMMUNICATION:
WHO SHOULD (OR
CAN) COMMUNICATE
WITH WHOM?

And when upward communication occurs, it may be viewed as out of order or inappropriate, even if it is positive. As you can readily see, this lack of upward communication can lead to major problems. Because of the one-way nature of communication in their companies, many high-ranking executives tend to become increasingly isolated from the day-to-day realities of their business. That this is the case is suggested by the following dramatic finding. In actual surveys, fully 95 percent of high-ranking managers report they understand their employees' problems. In contrast, only about 30 percent of their employees agree that this is so![11]

But lack of upward flow is not the only communication problem large organizations face. Another has to do with the type of feedback that is ultimately transmitted to top management. As you probably know, most people are reluctant to transmit negative information to others. One reason for this is they realize that, by doing so, they run the real risk of picking up on a negative "tinge," in a kind of guilt-by-association syndrome. This reluctance to transmit negative information to others, often known as the **MUM effect,** is especially strong with respect to one's superiors. Thus it can sometimes badly distort the flow of feedback reaching top managers within an organization.[12] In extreme cases, it can create a situation in which top people bask in the flow of uniformly positive reports from subordinates while their company teeters on the very brink of ruin! (For an example of such effects, see the **Case in Point** on page 76.)

Looking back over our comments so far, it appears we have painted a disturbingly bleak picture of communication within large organizations. Is this really accurate? Must "big" always mean "worse" where communication is concerned? Fortunately, the answer is "no." A number of techniques can prove useful in enhancing communication even within the largest organizations. Several of these will be considered in a later section. However, here we will briefly examine two: **suggestion systems** and an **open-door policy.**

Suggestion systems can take many different forms. The simplest one—and probably the least effective—is that of placing the familiar suggestion box in some prominent place. The hope, of course, is that employees will share their gripes, ideas, and suggestions with management by writing them down and placing them in the box. Unfortunately, when such boxes are opened, they often contain more gum wrappers, cigarette butts, and obscene notes than usable, useful suggestions. A much better approach is to hold regular meetings in which managers consult with employees to learn their views on various policies or procedures, and their ideas on improving the situation. Such opportunities for feedback and upward communication can prove very beneficial. In fact, in recent years, some companies have saved large amounts of money by paying attention to employees' suggestions for improving methods of production or reducing costs.

In a sense, the second tactic, adoption of an *open-door policy,* can be viewed as a logical extension of the suggestion system. When using this strategy, top managers make it known to employees that they are available at certain times for feedback and input from everyone—even persons on the lowest rungs of the corporate ladder. In principle, such systems sound promising. But in practice they often fail, and for fairly obvious reasons. First, employees wishing to walk through the supposedly open door must leave their work station or office and travel a substantial distance to appear in the manager's office. (Remember: the offices of top executives are often placed as far as possible from production lines or the

CASE IN POINT

What We Don't Know Can Hurt Us—Or the MUM Effect Strikes Again

Fred Massouh is president of Marnet, a small clothing manufacturing firm. He is looking over the monthly sales figures. The last few months have not been as good as expected. The company had introduced a number of new products and was expecting a surge in sales, but sales are about the same as last year. What can be the problem? All the feedback about the new product line had been favorable. Fred picks up the reports and walks to the office of Jane Alexander who is head of marketing.

"Jane what is going on with our sales these past few months?" he says with a rather stern tone of voice. "I thought we had such a good retailer response to our new products?"

Jane moves somewhat nervously in her chair and avoids looking Fred in the eye. "Eh, yes, I noticed it too." There is an uncomfortable pause as they both stare at the figures.

"Well, Jane, is that all you have to say?" presses Fred, staring straight at her.

With a somewhat pained look, Jane sits upright in her chair as she begins to explain her perspective on the problem. "Apparently, there has been some negative reaction to some of the new summer dresses. Although they're bright and attractive, the retailers feel we have priced them too high and they are not giving us prime selling space."

"Why haven't you told me about this before?" interrupts Fred.

"Well, I hate to say this, Mr. Massouh, but I knew how much you liked routine activities of a company.) Second, they must get past the manager's receptionist, secretary, and perhaps an assistant or two before actually getting in to see this person. Third, most employees are reluctant to bypass their immediate supervisor—to go over his or her head even by company invitation. Fourth, and perhaps most important of all, many persons do not believe the top manager really wants to see them; instead, they interpret the open-door policy as just a piece of good public relations (which all too often it really is).

For these reasons, it is usually better for an executive who genuinely seeks increased feedback to use the open door as an invitation to walk out and visit employees. If he or she merely sits inside hoping someone will appear, disappointment is likely to follow. In contrast, visits to various offices and production facilities may convince employees that the chief really is interested in their views and can encourage increased feedback. At least one top U.S. executive has found this approach quite useful. Victor Kiam, owner of Remington, Inc., a manufacturer of electric shavers, visits his production workers at regular intervals to report to them on the company's progress, and to learn of their views. The result: pro-

77
ORGANIZATIONAL
INFLUENCES ON
COMMUNICATION:
WHO SHOULD (OR
CAN) COMMUNICATE
WITH WHOM?

our new products and I did not want to upset you. I was hoping things would turn around. Besides, you're always so busy with company business. I noticed that you have been closing your door more lately just to minimize distractions. I didn't want to bother you until I was sure about the sales trends."

Fred Massouh continues to fiddle with the reports for a few minutes and then slowly rises to leave. He stops at the door and looks back at the somewhat downcast Jane.

"Jane, I realize this is not all your fault. I have been a little preoccupied with the new lines we are developing for next year. I probably need to make more of an effort to stay in touch with the rest of you who are working with this year's product. This way I can avoid some of these surprises in the future."

Questions

1. How would you characterize the communication structure at Marnet?

2. What features of organizational communication discussed so far are evident at Marnet?

3. What recommendations would you make to Fred Massouh to improve communication at Marnet?

4. What nonverbal communication signals were evident during the discussion? What do you think they meant? Compare your ideas with the results presented in the next section.

ductivity and morale at Remington are considerably higher than at competing companies.

Through these and other techniques, even giant corporations can help counter the barriers to communication sometimes erected by their sheer size. Thus, even in the largest companies, there is no reason why costly communication gaps must be allowed to persist.

The Grapevine and Rumors: Informal Channels of Communication

How do people get most of their information at work? It would be comforting to answer, "Through official channels of communication." Such a reply would be reassuring, for it would suggest that most information circulating within a given company is, in fact, accurate. Actually, though, this answer is wrong—in many cases, dead wrong. Most people working in most organizations receive more information through informal channels than through formal ones. In short, they learn more about what is happening in their company, how it is doing, what changes lie ahead, and countless other issues from friends and acquaintances than from official memos, policy statements, or announcements. Such informal networks of communication are generally known as the **grapevine,** and are based on the friendly social relations that often develop between persons who have regular contact at work.[13] Once they arise, they seem to operate at "full speed ahead" much of the time, far surpassing official channels in the volume of information they transmit.

The factors underlying development of an active grapevine are easy to discern. First, as we have already noted, they develop in a natural way of friendly social relations among employees. Exchanging the latest news or gossip with one's friends may provide a pleasant interruption to work activities. In fact, learning what's new according to the grapevine may be one of the high points of the day! Second, we all wish to understand the world around us and the events that affect our lives, and to exert some degree of control over them if we can. Thus gathering as much information as possible can be a useful course of action. Finally, the grapevine often serves as a kind of safety valve, allowing individuals to express their concerns and anxieties, and to attain reassurance from others. In short, exchanging information in this informal way may serve as a kind of simple group therapy for many individuals.

In view of these benefits, it is hardly surprising that an active grapevine exists in almost all organizations. Somewhat more surprising, though, is the fact that the information carried by such informal networks is often quite accurate. In fact, in one well-known study, approximately 80 percent of the information transmitted through the grapevine was found to be correct.[14] That remaining 20 percent, though, can often lead to serious trouble. As you probably know from your own experiences, a story can be mainly true but still be quite misleading because one essential fact is omitted or distorted. For example, the grapevine may report that someone has been promoted over another person who was more directly in line for this reward. However, it may omit the fact that the person turned down the promotion because it would require a move to a distant city, and personal factors make it impossible for her to pull up roots at the present time. In such cases, the grapevine can be correct, but still remain almost totally misleading.

This problem of inaccuracy is clearly responsible for giving the grapevine such a bad reputation. In extreme cases, information may be transmitted by messages known as **rumors**—messages with little or no basis in fact, usually unverifiable. Typically, rumors are based on speculation, an over-active imagination, and wishful thinking, rather than facts. Rumors race like wildfire throughout organizations because the information they present is so interesting and ambiguous. As such, it is open to embellishment as it passes orally from one person to the next. Before you know it, almost everyone in the organization has heard the rumor, and its inaccurate message becomes taken as fact ("It must be true since everyone knows it"). Hence, even if there was, at one point, some truth to a rumor, the message quickly becomes untrue (see Figure 3.3).

If you have ever been victimized by a rumor, you know how difficult it can be to negate and undo its effects. This is especially the case for organizations, which can also be the victims of rumors, such as commonly heard rumors about the possibility of corporate takeovers. Such rumors may not only influence the value of the company's stock but also threaten the employees' feelings of job security. A notable example of the negative effects involved a rumor about the use of worms in McDonald's hamburgers, which circulated in the Chicago area

79
ORGANIZATIONAL
INFLUENCES ON
COMMUNICATION:
WHO SHOULD (OR
CAN) COMMUNICATE
WITH WHOM?

FIGURE 3.3 Rumors: Often Unreliable
When rumors get passed from one person to another, they may at some point be taken as fact. (Reprinted by permission Tribune Media Services.)

in the late 1970s. As a result, sales dropped by as much as 30 percent in some restaurants.[15] Although McDonald's survived the rumor, such a cut in business volume, no doubt, hurt.

What, then can be done to counter the effects of rumors? Although this is a difficult question to answer, there is some research evidence available suggesting that directly refuting a rumor may *not* help counter its effects.[16] Directly refuting a rumor just serves to help spread it among those who have not already heard about it ("oh, I didn't know people thought that") and strengthen it among those who already heard it ("if it weren't true, they wouldn't be protesting so much"). What does help is directing people's attention away from the rumor, focusing instead on other things they know about the target of the rumor. For example, in research studying the rumor that McDonald's uses worms in its hamburgers, it was found that reminding people about other things they thought about McDonald's (e.g., that it is a clean, family-oriented place) helped counter the negative effects of the rumor. Keep in mind that the rumored information someone has about any target may be just part of the set of beliefs held. If you should ever become the victim of a vicious rumor, keep this in mind: Directing people's attention to other positive things they already believe about you may be a helpful way of countering its effects. Although rumors may be impossible to stop, their impact can, with some effort, be effectively managed.

It would be misleading to emphasize only the negative effects of informal communication networks. The informal flow of information from person to person can also be quite beneficial. For example, research has shown that the more involved people are in their organizations' communication networks, the more powerful and influential they become on the job.[17] Informal connections can apparently help people attain formal power.

PERSONAL INFLUENCES ON COMMUNICATION: DIFFERENT STYLES, DIFFERENT CHANNELS

As we noted earlier, everyone in organizations communicates. Receiving and transmitting information are basic parts of life at work. But as you probably know from your own experience, all people do not accomplish these functions with equal ease. Some find communication a simple or enjoyable task. They can easily transmit information to others either in person, over the phone, or through letters and reports. In contrast, other persons find communication difficult and unpleasant. Indeed, in extreme cases, they may even suffer great nervousness or anxiety when faced with such tasks as giving a speech or preparing a written report. These differences in reactions to communication and in its successful use call attention to a key point: Personal factors, too, play a major role in this process. As you might guess, many traits, abilities, and characteristics are important in this respect. However, most seem to fall under two major headings: factors relating to *personal style*, and factors relating to the use of *verbal* and *nonverbal channels of communication.*

Personal Style and Communication: Why Some People Are More Effective Communicators Than Others

When groups choose one of their members to serve as a spokesperson, they do not proceed in a random fashion. Rather, they try to select an individual who is known to be effective in communication with others. The reason for this is obvious: The better this person's communication skills, the more clearly and forcefully will he or she make the group's views known. But what factors make an individual an effective communicator? This question has been a central one in the study of *persuasion*—the process through which we attempt to change others' minds, and sway them to our own way of thinking. Since we will cover persuasion in detail in Chapter 7, we will not attempt to mention all the personal factors contributing to communication effectiveness here. Instead, we will merely call your attention to a few that seem especially important in this respect.

The first of these—whether to communicate with others in a simple or complex style—is easy to illustrate. Suppose you have to listen to two persons presenting verbal reports. One speaks in short, clear sentences consisting mainly of everyday language. The other offers involved, complex thoughts, expressed in sentences filled with jargon. Which would you prefer? Almost certainly, the former. While you will probably find the first speech easy to follow and understand, the second may leave you totally confused—or even with a splitting headache. The moral provided by this example is obvious: When attempting to communicate with others, it is usually best to follow the *K.I.S.S. principle:* Keep It Short and Simple.[18] This is true in written as well as verbal messages. (For a humorous example of this concept, see Figure 3.4). Communicators who attempt to dazzle their audiences with complex, involved messages are more likely to put them to sleep or bore them to tears than to communicate successfully with them. So, this aspect of personal style is definitely important.

The fact that individuals often respond favorably to communicators who keep their messages simple makes eminent good sense. After all, no one likes being

FIGURE 3.4 The K.I.S.S. Principle: Less Is More
In many ways, keeping it short and simple (the K.I.S.S. principle) is often the best policy. (Cathy © 1990 Universal Press Syndicate. Reprinted with permission. All rights reserved.)

confused or bewildered—at least not for long. But now prepare for a mild surprise: Research findings also suggest that while most persons prefer simplicity and clarity in communication, they are strongly impressed by speed, too.[19] In many cases, individuals who present verbal messages rapidly, at a fast rate of speech, are viewed as being more effective communicators than those who deliver their messages at a slower and more leisurely pace. Specifically, fast talkers are perceived as more knowledgeable about their subject matter, more competent, and even more sincere than slow ones. And they are not simply *viewed* as being more effective; in fact, they really are. Communicators who speak at a fast rate tend to produce more persuasion among their audience than those who talk more slowly.[20] Taken together, these facts point to a straightforward and important conclusion: If you want to be effective at interpersonal communication, by all means strive for a fast rate of delivery. Being able to present your views rapidly and without hesitation appears to be a major "plus."

Imagine the following scene: You have just heard another member of your organization argue strongly for a particular decision. She presented her views clearly and logically, and spoke in a fluent and convincing manner. How will you react? Under normal circumstances, you might well be strongly swayed by her words; at the least, you would pay careful attention to them. But let's assume for the moment that one thing stands in the way of such responses on your part: You simply don't trust her. Bitter experience has taught you that she often bends the truth for her own purposes. And you have reached the conclusion that she is interested solely in furthering her own career—the good of the company or of other people does not concern her in the least. To the extent you hold these views, you will pay little attention to what she has just said, or to any other form of communication in which she engages. The reason is simple: For you, she is not a *credible* source of information.

A great deal of evidence suggests that this factor—an individual's credibility—often plays a key role in determining success at communication.[21] If an individual is viewed as high in credibility—as someone who can be believed and trusted—he or she may be quite effective in transmitting information to others. If, instead, an individual is seen as low in credibility, effectiveness in communication will be sorely restricted. Thus, if you wish to be successful in getting your message across in a wide range of situations, you should be careful to protect your personal credibility. Once you are perceived as untrustworthy, your chances of getting others to listen, let alone change their minds, will be small indeed. Successful politicians have to take these factors seriously if they want to stay in office (see Figure 3.5).

Verbal Communication: Speaking with Words

Because you are reading this book, we know that you are familiar with verbal communication—transmitting and receiving ideas using words. Verbal communication can be either *oral,* using spoken language as in face-to-face talks, telephone conversations, and tape recordings or *written,* as in memos, letters, order blanks, and electronic mail. Because both oral and written communications involve the use of words, they fall under the heading of verbal communication.

What types of verbal communication are most effective? Research has shown that supervisors believe that communication is most effective when oral messages are followed by written ones.[22] This combination is especially preferred under certain conditions,—for example, when immediate action is required, an important policy change is being made, a praiseworthy employee is identified, or a company directive or order is announced. When the information to be communicated is of a general nature, or requires only future action, written forms are judged to be most effective.

Apparently, the oral message was useful in getting others' immediate attention, and the follow-up written portion helped make the message more permanent, something that could be referred to in the future. Oral messages also have the benefit of allowing for immediate two-way communication between parties, whereas written communiques are frequently only one-way (or take too long for a response if they are two-way). As a result, it is not surprising that researchers have found that *two-way communications* (e.g., face-to-face discussions or telephone conversations) are more commonly used in organizations than one-way communications (e.g., memos).[23] One-way, written communications tend to be reserved for more formal, official messages that need to be referred to in the future at the receiver's convenience (e.g., official announcements about position openings). Apparently, both written and spoken communication have their place in organizational communication.

It also appears that the choice of a communication media greatly depends on a very important factor—the degree of clarity or ambiguity of the message being sent. The more ambiguous the message, the more managers prefer using oral media (such as telephones or face-to-face contact); the clearer the message, the

FIGURE 3.5 Personal Style: Two Great Communicators
Success in politics seems to require having an appealing personal style. Presidents Roosevelt and Reagan were both acknowledged masters at using their personal style in communicating with their audiences.

more managers preferred using written media (such as letters or memos).[24] Apparently, most managers are sensitive to the need to use communications media that allows them to take advantage of the rich avenues for two-way oral communications when it is needed, and to use the more efficient one-way, written communications when these are adequate (see Figure 3.6).

However, some managers, identified as "media insensitive," make their media choices almost randomly. Interestingly, media sensitivity was related to a managers' job performance. It was expected that those who were media sensitive would be more effective than those who were media insensitive. Eighty-seven percent of the media sensitive managers received their company's highest per-

FIGURE 3.6 Oral or Written Communication? Matching the Medium to the Message
What type of communications medium do managers prefer using? The research findings reviewed here show that it depends on the degree of clarity or ambiguity of the message. Oral media (e.g., telephones or face-to-face contact) were preferred for ambiguous messages; written media (e.g., letters or memos) were preferred for clear messages. (*Source:* Based on data in Daft, Lengel, & Trevino (1987); see Note 24.)

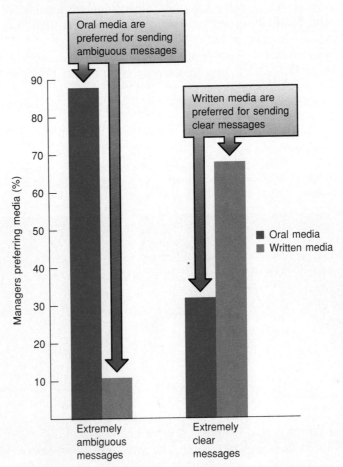

formance ratings; only forty-seven percent of the media insensitive managers received equally high evaluations. Apparently, the skill of selecting the appropriate communications medium is an important aspect of a manager's success. Although it is difficult to say whether the managers' choices of communications media were directly responsible for their success, or whether their media sensitivity was part of an overall set of managerial skills that together led to their success, these findings highlight the importance of making appropriate media choices in successful managerial communication.

It would be misleading to conclude this section with the idea that communication occurs only at the verbal level. Although words are a very important part of communication, they represent only one way of transmitting messages. A great deal of what is communicated is done in the absence of words—nonverbally.

Nonverbal Communication: Using the Unspoken Language

In a best-selling book of the 1970s, Desmond Morris referred to human beings as the "naked ape." While he had many reasons for choosing this description, a more apt one might be the "talking ape," for language—written or spoken— plays a central role in human behavior. Despite this fact, however, it is not the total story where communication is concerned. While we do transmit a great deal of information to others through words, we also communicate with them *nonverbally* through an unspoken language of gazes, expressions, and body movements[25] (see Figure 3.7). We also send them important messages through our use of physical space—how close we stand to them, or how we arrange our office.[26] Because of the existence of this silent "language," no discussion of communication can be complete without some attention to **nonverbal cues.** In this section, therefore, we will describe a number of these cues, indicating the kind of information each transmits, and how they can best be "read" or interpreted.

Unmasking the Face: Reading Facial Expressions Perhaps the most obvious nonverbal cues are provided by facial expressions. The people around us smile, frown, clench their teeth, and display many other facial actions. Research on these expressions has yielded many interesting facts, but among these, two seem most important. First, although the number of expressions individuals demonstrate seems infinite, all appear to be based on combinations of only six different emotions: happiness, sadness, surprise, fear, anger, and disgust.[27] Second, facial expressions are, by and large, universal. That is, a smile is interpreted as a sign of happiness or friendliness and a frown a sign of sadness or annoyance all over the world.

But if facial expressions are universal, and if they are based on only a few underlying emotions, why are they so often misleading? Why do they sometimes give a false impression about others' true feelings? The answer is simple: Individuals often attempt to conceal their real feelings and emotions. Thus they alter or manage their outward expressions in order to mislead others in this respect. There are many reasons for this. First, they may not wish to reveal their true feelings to others, either because this would be embarrassing or because they simply do not feel comfortable about disclosing this information. Second, concealing their actual feelings may be part of their job or role. For example, negotiators must avoid tipping their hands to their opponents, and they usually try to do this by maintaining a "poker face." Similarly, physicians generally attempt to hide worry or concern from their patients in order to avoid upsetting them. Third, many persons actually earn their living from skilled manipulation of their own facial expressions—actors, salespersons, and politicians to name a few.

While efforts to conceal or manufacture false facial expressions are often successful, there are several clues that can help you recognize when others are engaging in such actions. The most important of these are summarized in Table 3.1. We suggest that you examine them closely, for a working knowledge of these cues can help you determine whether others' facial expressions are a carefully managed mask, or a true reflection of their inner feelings.

Gazes and Stares: The Language of the Eyes   Ancient poets often described the eyes as "windows to the soul." In this respect, they were quite correct. Individuals do communicate a great deal of information through gazes, winks, stares, and other actions involving their eyes. Indeed, they can transmit everything from

FIGURE 3.7   Sign Language: An Important Form of Nonverbal Communication
A form of nonverbal communication that is used very effectively by hearing-impaired people is sign language.

TABLE 3.1
Clues that Others Are Managing Their Facial Expressions

The presence of these clues may indicate a person is trying to disguise his or her inner feelings through some type of facial deceit.

Clue	Description
Timing of facial expression	Genuine reactions are shown very quickly. If the interval between some emotion-producing event and the appearance of a corresponding facial expression is too long, deceit may be present.
Gaps in the total pattern of a facial expression	One part of the face suggests a specific emotion while another does not. (Example: the eye-brows are raised in surprise, but the mouth stays closed, rather than dropping open as it usually does during genuine surprise.)
Microexpressions	Fleeting facial expressions lasting a fraction of a second that appear before deceit can be started. These may reveal the true feelings of another person.

anger and feelings of intense dislike ("if looks could kill") through friendliness or even stronger positive reactions ("the look of love"). Systematic research of this form of nonverbal communication confirms the fact that the eyes have an eloquent language all their own.

Here is a sampling of the many messages the eyes may transmit. First, a high degree of gazing or eye contact from other persons suggests they like us, or are experiencing positive emotions in our presence. A low level of eye contact or attempts to avoid our gaze imply the opposite. Second, a high rate of blinking is a clear sign of nervousness. Watch for this cue when others are speaking. If, during some remark, they show a sudden rise in blink rate, this may be a sign they are lying. Third, one type of eye-contact is often a sign of anger or hostility: staring. Here, one person continues to gaze at another without looking away no matter what this person does.[28] In addition to communicating anger, such efforts to "stare down" another person can represent an attempt to take charge of a situation and assert dominance. In any case, if during a meeting another person begins to stare, be on guard: An unpleasant emotional storm may soon follow!

Body Language: Gestures, Movements, and Posture   Have you ever pounded your fist on a table in anger, shifted your posture so as to orient toward an important person when he or she entered the room, or held your hand out with the thumb pointing up as a sign of a positive reaction or agreement? If so, you are already familiar with the fact that individuals often communicate with one another through body language—movements or adjustments in their bodies or body parts.[29] This type of nonverbal communication is also quite common and can transmit a wide range of information. Imagine that during an interview the person being questioned moves about and fidgets a lot. What would this indicate? Probably, that he or she is nervous and ill at ease. (Keep this point in mind the next time you are interviewed.)

While fidgeting may represent an unconscious type of body language, gestures—a second form—are usually more direct. Here, we move body parts (especially our hands or arms) to communicate some specific meaning. For example, moving our index finger in a circular motion around the ear often means that some person being discussed is confused, illogical—or worse! Similarly, holding our hand with the palm toward another person means "Stop!" or "Enough!" And of course, shaking our head up and down means "Yes."

Finally, overall posture can contain an important message. When another person slumps in his or her chair during a meeting, this may be a sign of boredom or depression. If this individual sits up straight, this may signify interest or elation. Similarly, if two persons lean toward each other while holding a conversation, this is often a sign that they like one another; if they lean away, though, less favorable reactions probably exist.

Communication through Dress: Do the Clothes Make the Person?   If you have ever heard the expression, "clothes make the man (or woman)," you are probably already aware of the importance of one's *mode of dress* as a vehicle of communication. This is especially the case in organizations, where as self-styled "wardrobe engineer" John T. Malloy reminds us, what we wear communicates a great deal about our competence as employees.[30] Organizational researchers are becoming increasingly aware of the importance of style of dress as a communications vehicle[31] (see Figure 3.8).

As you might imagine, what we communicate by the clothing we wear is not a simple matter. It is important to keep in mind that we cannot make up for the absence of critical job skills by simply putting on the right clothes. People who are qualified for jobs, however, may communicate certain things about themselves via the way they dress. Clearly, one of the key messages sent by the clothes people wear is their understanding of the appropriate way of presenting themselves for the job. Generally speaking, the most positive images are communicated when dressed appropriately for the occasion. An important reason for this appears to be that people who are dressed just right for an occasion tend to feel better about themselves; they have higher levels of self-confidence. For example, in one study, student job candidates appeared for an interview wearing either their informal street clothes (e.g., t-shirts and jeans) or more formal garb (e.g., suits with shirts and ties). Those who wore the more formal clothing not only felt they made a more positive impression than those dressed less appropriately but also tended to express this more positive self-image by requesting a starting annual salary that was, on average, $4,000 higher.[32] Apparently, then, clothing may be a powerful vehicle of communication not just because of what it connotes about the wearer, but also because it changes the wearer's feelings.

Communication through Physical Space: Office Design as a Nonverbal Cue   That people communicate with others through facial expressions, gestures, eye contact, and body movements is hardly surprising. All of us have had experiences with this type of unspoken language, and we have learned to both read it and use it. Perhaps more unexpected is the fact that we also communicate with others through our use of physical space. One way we do this is by varying the distance between

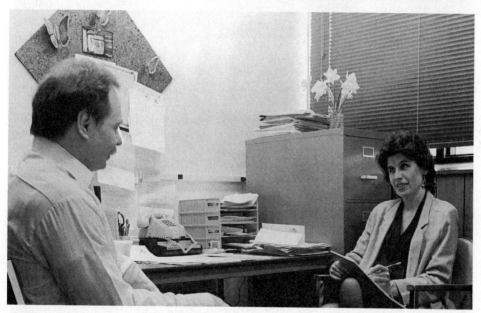

FIGURE 3.8 Dress and Job Interviews: Affects Impressions
How a person is dressed may be very influential on the impressions made during job interviews. Research suggests that the more formally dressed person is likely to make a better impression and have a more positive self-image than the informally dressed one.

us. The more we like others and the more comfortable we feel around them, the closer we tend to stand or sit to them.[33] Thus we approach friends, lovers, or members of our families much more closely than strangers, casual acquaintances, or persons we do not like. Status—one's relative standing in a group or organization—also plays a role. The general rule seems to be that higher-status persons (those with a lot of power and prestige) can approach lower-status individuals quite closely. In contrast, lower-status persons cannot do the same to high-status persons; such actions on their part are strictly forbidden.

Organizational status is also communicated by the amount of space at one's disposal. The more space a person commands, the more powerful that person is likely to be in an organization. For example, research has shown that higher status life insurance underwriters have larger desks and larger offices than lower status underwriter trainees.[34] It is not only the amount of space that communicates organizational status, but also the way that space is arranged. For example, among faculty members at a small college, it was found that more senior professors were likely to arrange their offices so as to separate themselves from visitors with their desks, whereas junior professors were less likely to impose such physical barriers.[35] These various office arrangements systematically communicated different things about the occupants. Specifically, teachers who did not distance themselves from their students by use of their desks were seen as more open and unbiased in their dealing with students than those who used their desks as a physical barrier (see Figure 3.9).

The use of space appears to have symbolic value in communicating something about group interaction. Consider who usually sits at the heads of rectangular tables. In most cases, the group leader. It is, in fact, traditional for them to do so. But, at the same time, studies have shown that people emerging as the leaders of groups tend to be the ones who just happened to be sitting at the head of the table.[36] Apparently, where one sits influences the available communication possibilities. Sitting at the head of a rectangular table enables one to see everyone else and to be seen by them. It is, therefore, not surprising that leaders tend to emerge from such positions.

It is important to note that whenever nonverbal channels of communication are used, they are also used in conjunction with verbal information. Neither is

FIGURE 3.9 Physical Space: Another Way of Communicating
The arrangement of physical space in an office can communicate status or openness to communication. What do you think the arrangement of this office tells about the characteristics of its occupant?

isolated; both work together as vehicles of communication in organizations. What we do, how we look, and what we say all matter.

Cultural Differences Studies of international negotiations have shown that persons from different cultures use various nonverbal cues in very different ways, and that such differences, in turn, can often be the source of considerable confusion.[37] In Japanese culture, a smile is perceived as a means of reducing tension and of averting unpleasantness; lowering one's eyes is a sign of respect. It is considered crucial to avoid a direct "no" at almost any cost. The result: Rather than rejecting an offer from an opponent, Japanese negotiators may simply lapse into total silence, or even get up and leave the room. Needless to say, such tactics are totally puzzling to Americans, who expect an immediate response of some kind.

South Koreans show more signs of emotion than either Americans or Japanese and often describe their reactions to various offers more bluntly. Persons from mainland China closely resemble Americans in nonverbal style, while—surprisingly—those from Taiwan are very different. And Brazilians demonstrate yet another nonverbal style: They often talk without pauses and touch one another—and their opponents—frequently. Such physical contact is virtually nonexistent in negotiations between persons from many other cultures.

The fact that persons from different cultures use nonverbal cues in contrasting ways points to the following conclusion: In order to prevent such differences from introducing needless "noise" into delicate international discussions, negotiators and others involved in international business should receive training designed to enhance their awareness of such factors. Only in this way can many needless and potentially costly problems be avoided.

Nonverbal Communication: Some Practical Uses By now you are probably convinced that individuals do communicate with one another through nonverbal cues. Further, you now realize that these cues are varied in scope and can involve facial expressions, eye contact, body language, and even the use of physical space. But what, you may be wondering, are the practical implications of all this? Growing evidence suggests that the way individuals use and interpret this silent language can have many important effects on their lives and careers.

First, it has been found that being expressive—using nonverbal cues freely and effectively—can contribute to success in several different fields. For example, in one study, clients at a large clinic who typically saw different doctors were asked to rate all of these physicians.[38] It was found that the doctors who were expressive—those who showed a high level of nonverbal communication with clients—were the most popular. Similarly, in the same investigation, a group of highly successful sales persons were studied. As you might expect, they too were found to be high in expressiveness. The message in these findings is clear: In some fields, at least, being able to communicate with others nonverbally can be a big plus.

Second, research findings indicate that skill in nonverbal communication can often yield handsome dividends during interviews.[39] Persons who are able to transmit positive cues to the interviewer may well receive higher ratings than those who do not communicate in this manner. This fact is illustrated clearly in a study in which subjects played the role of interviewer and conducted a brief job interview with another person who played the role of an applicant for an entry-level management job.[40] Actually, the individual being interviewed was an accomplice, who behaved in one of two ways. In one condition, she emitted many positive nonverbal cues. For example, she leaned forward toward the interviewer, smiled on many occasions, and showed a high level of eye contact with this person. In the other, she refrained from demonstrating these positive cues. After the interview, subjects rated the applicant on several dimensions related to her qualifications for the job and personal traits. As Figure 3.10 illustrates, the accomplice received higher ratings when she emitted many positive nonverbal cues than when she showed more neutral behavior.

These and related findings suggest that being aware of the process of nonverbal communication, and being able to use it effectively, can yield important benefits. Thus there seem to be strong reasons for attempting to develop our skills in this subtle but important area of human relations. (How expressive are you? For some

FIGURE 3.10 Positive Nonverbal Cues: A Plus in Job Interviews
When an accomplice emitted many positive nonverbal cues during a simulated job interview (e.g., smiled often, leaned forward), she received higher ratings from the interviewer than when she did not emit such cues. These findings indicate that nonverbal communication can play an important role in many work settings. (*Source:* Based on data from Baron (1986); see Note 40.)

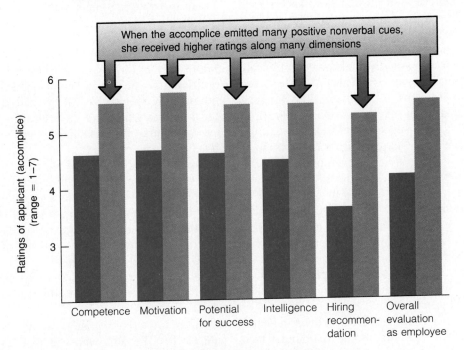

insight into this intriguing question, refer to the **Human Relations in Action** on page 94.)

ENHANCING COMMUNICATION: SOME CONCRETE, USEFUL STEPS

If the present chapter has a single theme, it is this: Communication is an essential aspect of human relations in all settings, and a key process in the world of work. Our next point follows logically from this view: Efforts to enhance communication—to improve its accuracy and effectiveness—are highly desirable. In this final section, we examine a number of steps that may prove useful in this respect.

Timing, If Not Everything, Is Important

Imagine the following scene: It is 4 P.M. on Friday, and most employees in the offices of the Big Chaw Chewing Tobacco Company are clearing their desks for the weekend. Just at this point, Elmer G. Kudd, the firm's CEO, calls a special meeting to discuss the firm's new advertising campaign. How useful do you think this meeting will be? And how effective do you think communication will be during it? The answer is obvious: Low on both counts. And the reason for this, too, is clear: If ever there was a wrong time for such a meeting, this is it! Communication and all other aspects of this gathering are sure to suffer as those present think about the upcoming weekend and repeatedly look at the clock. The moral is: When attempting to communicate with others, try to choose a time when their minds are likely to be on what you have to say, not one when they are being distracted by other factors, or deluged with other messages. Keeping these basic points in focus can definitely help you get through to your audience more successfully.

On the Virtues of Feedback

In its ideal form, communication is very much a two-way street. One person or group transmits information to another and then receives some response in return. In our informal relations with friends or family, this pattern is always present. In many work settings, though, it may be absent. Managers transmit orders or decisions downward to lower levels, and they neither invite nor receive any reactions from the persons involved. If anything can serve as the proverbial "kiss of death" to a business, this is it. In the absence of a return flow of information, it may be difficult if not impossible to gauge the impact of new policies or procedures. Thus feedback—the return flow of information—should always be part of any communications network. Building it may require the establishment of special channels for upward and horizontal communication. (Remember, most communication in organizations tends to flow from the top down.) Given the informative nature of feedback and the negative results that may occur in its absence, though, the effort required is almost certain to prove worthwhile.

Listening: The Other Side of the Coin

Have you ever had the following experience: You are introduced to someone at a party or meeting. You speak with her for a few minutes and then another person joins you. You are about to introduce your new acquaintance when you discover—much to your chagrin—that you have already forgotten her name! Why does this occur? It would be comforting to be able to blame it on the frailty of human memory, but in fact, the reason is even simpler: Often, we just don't listen.[42] Instead of paying careful attention to what others say, we allow our minds to wander. We daydream, we think about what we are going to say when it is our turn to talk, or we mentally argue with the speaker, and so fail to follow all his or her remarks. Obviously, if we do not listen carefully to what others say, communication with them must suffer (see Figure 3.11). In fact, in extreme cases, where we have managed to totally tune another person out, it may cease altogether. For this reason, learning to be a good listener is essential to being an effective communicator.

In this respect, a few simple guidelines can help. First, try hard to concentrate on what the other person says. This is going to be more difficult with some speakers than others, but if you care about communicating with this person, you have no choice—you must pay attention. Second, ask questions. This will clarify points

HUMAN RELATIONS IN ACTION

Measuring Your Own Expressiveness: A Short Self-Assessment

As we noted earlier, a high level of expressiveness—the emission of many clear nonverbal cues—can often come in handy. This is more likely to be the case in some jobs than in others, but in general it can be a useful skill to possess. As you probably already realize, though, individuals differ greatly in terms of expressiveness. Some are very high on this dimension, others are very low, and most fall somewhere in between. Where do you stand in this respect? Are you relatively expressive or relatively lacking in this trait? In order to find out, answer each of the questions listed below.

To what extent is each of the following statements true or false about you? Indicate your answer by writing a number from 1 (not at all true of you) to 9 (very true of you) in the space next to each statement.

_____ **1.** When I hear good dance music, I can hardly keep still.

_____ **2.** My laugh is soft and subdued.

_____ **3.** I can easily express emotion over the telephone.

_____ **4.** I often touch friends during conversations.

_____ **5.** I dislike being watched by a large group of people.

_____ **6.** I usually have a neutral facial expression.

_____ **7.** People tell me that I would make a good actor or actress.

FIGURE 3.11 Listening: A Key to Effective Communication
Careful listening is essential for effective communication. Obviously Zero is a little deficient in this area. (Reprinted with special permission of King Features Syndicate.)

about which you are confused and will get you actively involved in the process. Third, avoid jumping to conclusions or making evaluations. Instead, try to hear the other person out before deciding whether you agree or disagree. Fourth, listen for the main points. Some people tend to wander verbally when communicating, so it may not be important to try to understand everything they say. But do try

———— 8. I like to remain unnoticed in a crowd.

———— 9. I am shy among strangers.

———— 10. I am able to give a seductive glance if I want to.

———— 11. I am terrible at pantomime and in games like charades.

———— 12. At small parties, I am the center of attention.

———— 13. I show that I like someone by hugging or touching that person.

You have just completed the Affective Communication Test (ACT),[41] a questionnaire designed to measure individual differences in expressiveness. In order to obtain your score, proceed as follows: (1) Add your answers from items 1, 3, 4, 7, 10, 12, and 13. (2) Reverse the scores of items 2, 5, 6, 8, 9, and 11. For example, if you entered 3 for item 2, now enter 6; if you entered 9, now enter 1. (3) Add the numbers you obtained in (1) and (2). This is your total score.

If you obtained a total score of 87 or greater, you are quite expressive; most people fall below this level. If, instead, you obtained a score of 54 or lower, you are fairly low on this dimension. Research findings indicate that persons scoring high in expressiveness are more likely to have had certain types of experiences than persons scoring low in expressiveness. For example, they are more likely to have held an elected office, or to have given a lecture to a group. Can you remember any experiences you have had that are consistent with your own level of expressiveness?

to identify the main points and keep them in mind. Finally, listen for the hidden as well as the overt message. What people do not say may often be as informative as their actual words. Further, there may be important information in the nonverbal cues that accompany their statements. If you practice these simple skills, you will become a good listener and this, in turn, may greatly improve your ability to communicate overall.

Getting Your Message Across: Say It Again in a Different Way

Suppose that you follow all of the principles described so far in this chapter. You cultivate a high level of credibility, become skilled at using nonverbal cues, learn to listen, and time your communications so they are likely to have the most punch. Does this mean you are guaranteed to succeed—guaranteed to get your message across to others? Not at all. Even under the best of conditions, communication is an "iffy" proposition. Too many factors enter into the picture for it to ever be perfect. But there is one additional principle that can prove helpful in many cases: redundancy. What this involves is transmitting your message several times, in different forms or through different channels. For example, a message delivered in person one day could be reinforced with a written memo the next. Similarly, telephone conversations can be followed up with letters. And when communicating face-to-face with others, appropriate nonverbal cues can be employed to emphasize—and drive home—your point. Of course, when using redundancy, it is important to be careful about slipping into mere repetition, and passing the point where you begin to bore or annoy receivers. The last thing you want to do is watch their eyes glaze over from hearing your "pitch" still once more. With broad limits, though, redundancy can indeed be a valuable technique.

To conclude: By means of effective listening, good timing, redundancy, adequate feedback, and other techniques, you can greatly improve your communication skills. The costs involved in implementing some of these steps are high; much effort is involved. But the rewards are substantial. Not only can effective communication contribute to your own career; it can also lead to enhanced coordination with others, improved morale, exercise of effective leadership, and improvements in overall productivity within your work group. Given these rewards, it is hard to imagine a process more deserving of our close attention.

SUMMARY

Communication is a process in which one person or group (the sender) transmits some type of information to another person or group (the receiver). It involves the encoding of ideas or concepts by the sender, and the decoding of this information by the receiver.

Within an organization, communication often proceeds through formal channels dictated by the organizational chart. Such communication tends to be mainly downward in direction, from higher to lower levels of the company. In addition to such formal channels, all organizations also possess informal networks of communication, known collectively as the **grapevine.** Communication within these systems can be quite accurate and rapid. However, the grapevine often transmits rumors—information based solely on speculation or imagination.

A number of personal factors influence communication in work settings. Individuals who present information in as simple a manner as possible, who speak rapidly, and who are viewed as being high in credibility tend to be more effective as communicators than those who do not demonstrate these characteristics.

In addition to communicating verbally through spoken or written language, we also transmit much information to one another nonverbally. Such communication involves facial expressions, eye contact, and body movements. Our use of physical space can sometimes send important messages to others. For example, persons who choose an open office arrangement are generally perceived as friendlier and more helpful than those who select a closed office arrangement.

Several steps can prove useful in facilitating communication. These include timing communications carefully so they don't compete with other messages, seeking and providing feedback, learning to listen effectively, and employing redundancy (repeating one's message through another channel or in a different form).

KEY TERMS

communication: The process through which one person or group transmits some type of information to another person or group.

decoding: One of the key aspects of communication, in which information is converted from the form in which it was transmitted back into ideas or concepts.

encoding: One of the key aspects of communication, during which ideas and concepts are converted into a form of information that can be transmitted over existing communication channels.

feedback: In communication, information returned to the initial sender by the initial receiver. It is the presence of feedback that makes communication a two-way process.

grapevine: Informal channels of communication based on social relations among employees.

MUM effect: The reluctance of most persons to transmit negative information to others; the effect seems to be most pronounced with respect to the transmission of negative information upward with an organization.

nonverbal cues: Cues involving facial expression, eye contact, body movements, or the physical use of space that serve as a silent form of communication between individuals.

open-door policy: A strategy for enhancing communication within an organization in which managers make themselves available for feedback from employees. In an effective variation of this procedure, managers seek out employees and invite feedback from them.

organizational structure: The way in which an organization is "put together"—its departments, formal lines of communication, chain of command, and so on.

receiver: The individual toward whom communication is directed.

rumor: Information transmitted through the grapevine that has little if any basis in fact.

sender: The individual who initiates communication by transmitting information to one or more other person.

suggestion system: A technique for enhancing upward communication within an organization. In such a system, some provision is made for input and suggestions from employees.

NOTES

98

CHAPTER 3

COMMUNICATION:
THE FINE ART OF
GETTING YOUR
MESSAGE ACROSS

1. Roberts, K.H. (1984). *Communicating in Organizations*. Chicago: Science Research Associates.

2. Reber, R.W., & Terry, G.E. (1975). *Behavioral Insight for Supervision*. Englewood Cliffs, NJ: Prentice-Hall.

3. See Note 1.

4. Hawkins, B.L., & Preston, P. (1981). *Managerial Communication*. Santa Monica, Calif.: Goodyear.

5. Walker, C.R., & Guest, R.H. (1952). *The Man on the Assembly Line*. Cambridge, Mass: Harvard University Press.

6. Luthans, F., & Larsen, J.K. (1986). "How Managers Really Communicate." *Human Relations*, *39*, 161–178.

7. Kirmeyer, S.L., & Lin, T. (1987). "Social Support: Its Relationship to Observed Communication with Peers and Superiors." *Academy of Management Journal*, *30*, 138–151.

8. Read, W. (1962). "Upward Communication in Industrial Hierarchies." *Human Relations*, *15*, 3–16.

9. Glauser, M.J. (1984). "Upward Information Flow in Organizations: Review and Conceptual Analysis." *Human Relations*, *37*, 613–43.

10. Foushee, H.C. (1984). "Dyads and Triads at 35,000 Feet: Factors Affecting Group Processes and Aircrew Performance." *American Psychologist*, *39*, 885–93.

11. Likert, R. (1959). "Motivational approach to management development." *Harvard Business Review* (July–August): 75–82.

12. Rosen, S., Grandison, R.J., & Stewart, J.E., III (1974). "Discriminatory Buck-Passing: Delegating Transmission of Bad News." *Organizational Behavior and Human Performance*, *12*, 249–63.

13. Baskin, O.W., & Aronoff, C.E. (1989). *Interpersonal Communication in Organizations*. Santa Monica, Calif.: Goodyear.

14. Walton, E. (1961). "How Efficient Is the Grapevine?" *Personnel*, *28*, 45–49.

15. Thibaut, A.M., Calder, B.J., & Sternthal, B. (1981). "Using Information Processing Theory to Design Marketing Strategies." *Journal of Marketing Research*, *18*, 73–79.

16. See Note 15.

17. Brass, D.J. (1985). "Men's and Women's Networks: A Study of Interaction Patterns and Influence in an Organization." *Academy of Management Journal*, *28*, 327–43.

18. Borman, E. (1982). *Interpersonal Communication in the Modern Organization*, 2d ed. Englewood Cliffs, N.J.: Prentice-Hall.

19. Miller, N., Maruyama, G., Beaber, R.J., & Valone, K. (1976). "Speed of Speech and Persuasion." *Journal of Personality and Social Psychology*, *34*, 615–24.

20. Maclachlan, J. (1979). "What People Really Think of Fast Talkers." *Psychology Today*, *13161*, 113–14, 116–17.

21. Rajecki, D.W. (1990). *Attitudes: Themes and Advances*. Sunderland, Mass.: Sinauer Associates.

22. Level, D.A. (1972). "Communication Effectiveness: Methods and Situation." *Journal of Business Communication*, *10*, 19–25.

23. Klauss, R., & Bass, B.M. (1982). *International Communication in Organizations*. New York: Academic Press.

24. Daft, R.L., Lengel, R.H., & Trevino, L.K. (1987). "Message Equivocality, Media Selection, and Manager Performance: Implications for Information Systems." *MIS Quarterly*, *11*, 355–66.

25. Buck, R. (1984). *Nonverbal Behavior and the Communication of Affect.* New York: Guilford Press.

26. Morrow, P.C., & McElroy, J.C. (1981). "Interior Office Design and Visitor Response: A Constructive Replication." *Journal of Applied Psychology*, 66, 640–50.

27. See Note 25.

28. Ellsworth, P.C., & Langer, E.J. (1976). "Staring and Approach: An Interpretation of the Stare as a Nonspecific Activator." *Journal of Personality and Social Psychology*, 33, 117–22.

29. Ekman, P. (1977). "Biological and Cultural Contributions to Body and Facial Movement." In J. Blacking, ed., *The Anthropology of the Body.* A.S.A. Monograph 15. London: Academic Press.

30. Malloy, J.T. (1975). *Dress for Success.* New York: Warner Books.

31. Forsythe, S., Drake, M.F., & Cox, C.E. (1985), "Influence of Applicant's Dress on Interviewer's Selection Decisions." *Journal of Applied Psychology*, 70, 374–78.

32. Solomon, M.R. (1986). "Dress for effect." *Psychology Today* (April): 20–28.

33. Hayduk, L.A. (1983). "Personal Space: Where We Now Stand." *Psychological Bulletin*, 94, 293–335.

34. Greenberg, J. (1988). "Equity and Workplace Status: A Field Experiment." *Journal of Applied Psychology*, 73, 606–613.

35. Zweigenhaft, R.L. (1976). "Personal Space in the Faculty Office: Desk Placement and Student-Faculty Interaction." *Journal of Applied Psychology*, 61, 529–32.

36. Greenberg, J. (1976). "The Role of Seating Position in Group Interaction: A Review, with Applications for Group Trainers." *Group and Organization Studies*, 1, 310–27.

37. See Note 6.

38. Friedman, H.A., Prince, L.M., Riggio, R.E., & DiMatteo, M.R. (1980). "Understanding and Assessing Nonverbal Expressiveness: The Affective Communication Test." *Journal of Personality and Social Psychology*, 39, 333–51.

39. Imada, A.S., & Hakel, M.D. (1977). "Influence of Nonverbal Communication and Rater Proximity on Impressions and Decisions in Simulated Employment Interviews." *Journal of Applied Psychology*, 62, 295–300.

40. Baron, R.A. (1986). "Self-Presentation in Job Interviews: When There Can Be 'Too Much of a Good Thing.' " *Journal of Applied Social Psychology*, 16, 16–28.

41. See Note 38.

42. Rowe, M.P., & Baker, M. (1984). "Are You Hearing Enough Employee Concerns?" *Harvard Business Review* (May–June): 127–35.

ADDITIONAL CASES AND EXERCISES:
APPLYING WHAT YOU'VE LEARNED

The Fired (?) Coach

Bob Kemper
Associate Professor of Management
Northern Arizona University

Stuart Monroe
Monroe Consulting
Flagstaff, Arizona

Bobby Burns is placing the last few items from his desk drawers into a box. He is vacating his office so that it may be occupied by his successor. Bobby has just completed his first losing season in four years as football coach at Prairie State University (PSU). He resigned just three days ago. The resignation came two games prior to the end of the football season. PSU had lost to Akron 52 to 7 on Saturday. The loss to Akron was the sixth straight and left PSU's record at two wins and seven losses.

Three days ago Bobby was head football coach. Today he is unemployed and his six assistants will be unemployed at the end of the academic semester.

Bobby remembers going to Athletic Director Charlie Beix's office for a regular Monday morning meeting. He knew Charlie would want to talk about the loss to Akron, the 2–7 season, and next year. When he entered Charlie's office he had no plans to resign. He was looking ahead to next year. He had planned to retire as a winner. His current PSU record was 26 wins and 28 losses. The only way he would consider resigning would be if he found out that PSU's officials were dissatisfied with the direction of the football program.

When Bobby entered Charlie's office, Charlie was busy at his desk writing some notes on a piece of paper. Charlie continued his writing without making eye contact with Bobby. It was about two minutes before Charlie finished the paperwork. Charlie then moved his chair away from the desk, leaned back in the chair, and then held the pencil in both hands in front of his forehead as if he were doing a chin-up on the pencil.

Bobby started the conversation by asking Charlie if he was disappointed. Beix answered, "Yes, I am." Bobby then asked, "Are the officials (PSU's) disappointed?" To this question Beix answered, "Yes, they are." Bobby replied, "Hey, that's good, I'm outta here."

Early Monday afternoon Athletic Director Beix met with the local press and announced Coach Burns's retirement effective immediately. The name of the interim coach was announced. Beix told the press that the resignation was Coach Burns's idea. "He came into my office this morning and volunteered to resign."

Bobby was very upset later that Monday afternoon when he found out that his six assistant football coaches immediately received separation notices effective at the end of the calendar year. Although this action was standard university procedure, it did not sit well with Bobby. He might not have resigned if he had realized what a burden his resignation would be for his assistant coaches.

It was this anger that prompted Bobby to tell local reporters Tuesday morning that he had not wanted to resign when he had met with Charlie Beix on Monday

101
ADDITIONAL
CASES AND
EXERCISES:
APPLYING WHAT
YOU'VE LEARNED

morning. Bobby recollects that he knew he was fueling a controversy when he insinuated that he had been fired while Athletic Director Beix was telling the same reporters Beix had voluntarily resigned. Some players became bitter about the "resignation." Others felt Coach Burns stepped down because, at age sixty-five, he was tired and drained from a frustrating season of close losses.

On Wednesday morning a *Metropolis Republic* columnist described the Burns resignation as a mess. "Fergus Falls, an unlikely setting for a major league flap, sounds a lot like East Lansing (Michigan State University) or Ann Arbor (University of Michigan) today. Nasty allegations are all over town. . . . the mess over the impending departure of football Coach Bobby Burns is silly. PSU's quiet campus is not a football factory. It never has been. The school plays the game, but not amid all the pressures and temptations that scar the big-time campuses. . . . The mudslinging began minutes after Tuesday's announcement that Burns would leave PSU before the season's final two games. Burns's offensive coordinator, Harry Pringle, condemned Athletic Director Charlie Beix. 'To me this place reeks of cronyism. Beix has his little fiefdom and all his buddies.' " The same reporter quoted Beix as saying, "Pringle is a hothead."

Then another columnist quoted Beix as stating, "He came in Monday and talked to me. It was his idea to come in. He knew that (his) time was up. Look at his age (sixty-five), the poor guy." Charlie Beix later stated that he was misquoted.

The box is filled. Bobby is ready to leave his successor's office for the last time. He regrets that he interpreted Beix's "disappointed in the season" as "dissatisfied with the direction of the football program." He now knows that the university officials were not dissatisfied with the direction of the football program at PSU and that he could have coached a fifth year at PSU. On the other hand, he reminds himself as he closes the door, perhaps it is time to retire when you are disappointed in the 2–7 season, disappointed in the 52 to 7 loss to Akron, and disappointed that the team did not live up to your expectation—a conference championship.

Questions

1. What messages were poorly encoded by Bobby and Charlie? How could these messages be improved?

2. What messages were poorly decoded by Bobby and Charlie? How could the decoding be improved?

3. What feedback messages were given by Bobby and Charlie? How could these feedback messages be improved?

4. What transmission channels were used by Bobby and Charlie?

5. What role did PSU's "organizational structure" play in Bobby's resignation?

6. What are the formal and informal communication channels at PSU? What was their effect before and after Bobby's resignation?

7. What was the problem with the verbal communications between Bobby

102

CHAPTER 3
COMMUNICATION:
THE FINE ART OF
GETTING YOUR
MESSAGE ACROSS

and Charlie? What form could be used to improve the verbal communications?

8. What was the message from the nonverbal communications between Bobby and Charlie? What could be done to improve the nonverbal communication?

9. What role did timing and listening play in Bobby's resignation? What could Bobby and Charlie have done to prevent the misunderstanding?

Communication Patterns at Work: A Personal Analysis

Most likely you are or have been employed by some organization. Consequently, you have had some experience with communication structure and patterns in work environments. Analyze the communication patterns in your present work environment according to the criteria listed below. For each of these items simply indicate your feeling about your present or most recent place of employment. Then rate your overall impression about the effectiveness of communication in your work environment.

1. The degree of upward flow of communication:

1	2	3	4	5
Very little	Some	Average	Quite a bit	A lot

2. The use of an open door policy:

1	2	3	4	5
Very little	Some	Average	Quite a bit	A lot

3. Communication by rumors:

1	2	3	4	5
Very little	Some	Average	Quite a bit	A lot

4. Reluctance to transmit negative information (MUM effect):

1	2	3	4	5
Very little	Some	Average	Quite a bit	A lot

5. How satisfied are the employees at this work environment with the system of communication?

1	2	3	4	5
Very satisfied	Satisfied	In-between	Dissatisfied	Very dissatisfied

6. To what extent do problems occur because of lack of communication between management and employees?

1	2	3	4	5
Hardly ever	Sometimes	In-between	Often	Very often

Now obtain a total score for items 1 through 4. If you obtain a high score for the first four items (e.g., 16 or higher), you probably indicated dissatisfaction and the existence of problems on items 5 and 6. You might ask your instructor to write the results for all students in your class on the board so that you can see whether there is a consistent pattern of this type.

Producing a Rumor Mill

103

ADDITIONAL
CASES AND
EXERCISES:
APPLYING WHAT
YOU'VE LEARNED

Rumors are everpresent in groups and organizations. Once they get started, they may become very distorted and end up very different from the original version because of the leveling, sharpening, and assimilation (changing the story into more familiar terms) that may occur. To demonstrate this, use a simple story, preferably taken from another culture so as to be a little unusual.

Ten people in the class should play the role of rumor transmitters. They should stay outside the classroom until called into the class for the rumor exercise. One of the students should begin by reading this story to one of the students. This student in turn will repeat the story from memory to another student, and so on until all of the ten students have heard the rumor. Then the last student gives his or her final version to the class. This one should differ radically from the original. The class should take notes during this process of instances of leveling, sharpening, and assimilation.

4

Motivation: The Force Behind Behavior

Study

Learning Objectives

After reading this chapter,
you should be able to:

1. Describe Maslow's need theory and its implications for work motivation.

2. Describe Herzberg's motivation-maintenance theory and its major predictions concerning work motivation.

3. Explain why certain expectancies held by employees can strongly affect their work motivation.

4. Explain how feelings of being treated fairly or unfairly can influence work motivation.

5. Describe several techniques for enhancing motivation at work, including management by objectives, goal setting, job enrichment, and organizational behavior modification.

hat an exciting day it was for Jennifer and Valerie. They had been friends since third grade and had shared many of their high school experiences. Now they were driving together to their final high school event. Today was graduation day at Lamar High School. Although they were close friends, they were different in many ways. Jennifer was a fairly serious student while Valerie did just enough to get by and was mainly interested in a good social life.

"Isn't it great that we're all finished" said Valerie. "I'm really looking forward to having a good time this summer."

"Must be nice," Jennifer replied. "I'm afraid I'm going to have to work most of the summer to help pay for my college expenses. Lone Star U isn't cheap, but it has an excellent program in accounting."

Jennifer's parents had only a modest income and she was determined to have a profession in which she could afford all the things her parents could not—a nice house, nice furniture, vacations in Europe.

Valerie, on the other hand, came from a fairly well-to-do family. She had little desire to work hard for those things she had always taken for granted.

"I really don't want to go to college for a while," she confessed. "My uncle runs a resort in the Bahamas and he has invited me to spend a year there as a waitress. That should give me plenty of time for the beach."

"It looks like we'll really be going in different directions now," mused Jennifer. "Oh, well, to each her own."

What makes Jennifer and Valerie so different? We might say they differ in their **motivation.** Jennifer is motivated by eventual career success, while Valerie appears to be motivated mainly by having a good time. This led to them making quite different choices during their high school careers and again as they make plans for the future. It is hard to say what will happen to Valerie, but we can be pretty confident that Jennifer will work hard to achieve her goals.

All of us differ, as do Jennifer and Valerie, in our motivation. Some people are more motivated than others. Some may be strongly motivated by material success, while others may be more concerned with the welfare of others. These differences in motivation may account in large part for the differences we observe in people's choices of careers and lifestyles and how hard they work in school or at work. Many contrasting views of motivation exist.[1] However, most agree on the following basic point: *Motivation is an internal force or process that both energizes and guides behavior.* The energizing aspect of motivation is obvious. Unless we are activated in some manner, we are likely to do little (or even nothing) in a given situation. Thus motivation refers in part to the force or energy that gets the "motor of behavior" running (see Figure 4.1). The guiding component of motivation, too, is straightforward. As you know from your own experience, human beings do not usually flail about, performing one aimless action after another. Instead, most of their behaviors are directed toward *specific goals*. And this, too, is where motivation enters the picture. It does not simply activate us and get us moving; it gets us moving toward specific goals. It is also important in maintaining the behavior directed at a particular goal. Most goals will take time to achieve, and only individuals who are motivated to persist will attain them.

There are, of course, many physiological, psychological, and social sources of motivation for our behavior. In fact, any particular behavior might be motivated by several sources of motivation. For example, going to college can be motivated by the desire to learn, to obtain a degree that will lead to a good job, and to have a good time socially. The extent to which students are motivated will determine the choice of a particular school or major and how much time is spent studying and socializing. Motivation plays a key role in all aspects of human behavior—everything from satisfying basic biological urges through the appreciation of art and music or the mastery of complex skills. Human relations is most interested in the impact of motivation on work and work settings. The major question we will address in this chapter, then, is this: What factors affect individuals' motivation to work—to perform their jobs in the most efficient and effective manner possible?

In order to answer this question, we first examine several major theories of motivation—perspectives that attempt to explain its nature and impact on work. Then we will turn to a number of techniques designed to enhance work motivation—concrete steps that can be taken to increase an employee's effort on the job.

FIGURE 4.1 Motivation: The Energy behind Actions
As shown here, an important part of motivation is the energy that activates behavior. (Reprinted with special permission of King Features Syndicate.)

MOTIVATION AND WORK: SOME BASIC VIEWS

It has often been said that the key task performed by managers is motivating their employees—somehow building a fire underneath them so they accomplish their work efficiently. But how can this task best be carried out? In order to know, we must understand the nature of motivation generally, and of work motivation in particular. The theories we will now consider all seek to shed light on these issues.

Maslow's Need Theory: From Deficiency to Growth

Mahatma Gandhi, the famous Indian leader, once remarked: "Even God cannot talk to a hungry man except in terms of bread." What he meant by this remark was this: When people's basic biological needs are unsatisfied, their attention will be riveted on these, and efforts to communicate with them about other matters will probably fail. This basic truth lies at the heart of one highly influential theory of human motivation, Abraham Maslow's **need hierarchy theory.**[2]

This theory begins with two reasonable assumptions: (1) human beings have many different needs, ranging from lower-level biological ones through higher-level psychological ones; (2) these needs exist in a hierarchy, so that before higher-level needs can become motivators and affect behavior, lower-level needs must be at least partly satisfied. But what are these lower-level and higher-level needs? Maslow offers some intriguing answers.

Briefly, he suggests that all human beings possess five distinct types of needs. At the lowest or most basic level are the **physiological needs.** These include our needs for food, water, and oxygen, to mention just a few. Obviously, satisfaction of these needs is essential if life is to continue. Next are what Maslow terms the **safety needs.** These involve our desire to be safe from physical or psychological harm—from such threats as accident, injury, and illness. Interestingly, although modern life in Western nations is free from some threats that sent chills up and down the spines of our ancestors, such as famine and plague, many other dangers still exist. For example, at present many persons fear economic depression and being assaulted by criminals in their homes or on the streets of major cities. Thus concluding that our safety needs are usually fulfilled is not entirely justified. A third level of needs involves our desire to form friendships with others, to belong, and to be loved and accepted. These are the **social or belonging needs,** and they are visible in our willingness to join various organizations and form close relationships with others. Together, the three types of needs we have just described are labeled by Maslow as the **deficiency needs.** This term reflects his belief that unless such needs are met, an individual cannot hope to develop a healthy personality.

But deficiency needs are only part of the total picture. In addition, we possess two other types of needs. The first of these are the **esteem or ego needs.** These center around our desire to maintain self-respect and to gain the admiration or respect of others. Such needs are shown in our strivings for prestige, achievement, and status. Finally, at the very top of the need hierarchy are needs for **self-actualization or self-realization.** These center around our desire to find out who we really are, and to develop ourselves to our fullest possible potential. Together, these strivings for esteem and self-actualization are termed **growth needs** by Maslow. Unless they are satisfied, personal growth cannot continue.

Maslow's Theory and Motivation at Work: The Crucial Links   By now you are probably convinced that human beings possess many different needs. Moreover, you may agree that these can be arranged in order from lower-level ones through higher-level ones. But what, you may wonder, does all this have to do with motivation at work? What does knowing about all these needs and their arrangement really buy us? Maslow's theory has direct application to work and work settings in several ways. First, it calls attention to the fact that unless individuals satisfy their basic needs, they will not be able to concentrate on higher-level ones. This contains a practical message for managers and organizations. In essence, it indicates that unless employees earn enough to satisfy their physiological needs, feel safe and secure in their jobs, and enjoy good social relations with others, they will not be able to turn their attention to such matters as getting ahead, achievements, and development of their full potential. In short, they will not be able to work in a highly efficient and productive manner. This general principle holds for all employees, at all levels. But, as you can probably see, it is especially applicable to persons performing creative, demanding jobs. If such individuals are concerned with satisfying lower-level, deficiency needs, they will be unable to develop their skills and talents to the fullest—and this may prove very costly to them and to their companies. Fortunately, most organizations are aware of this fact. Thus top-level people, whether managers, engineers, scientists, or artists, are generally provided with generous salaries, a high level of job security, and many desirable benefits. The result: They can indeed focus on the satisfactions of achievement in their fields, and on full application of their expertise, training, and talent. Maslow's theory underscores the importance of placing such persons in precisely these circumstances, and it helps explain why treating them with respect and generosity may pay off.

Maslow's theory also underscores the fact that companies need to be concerned with the multiple needs of employees so that they will be satisfied and effective workers. To provide for physiological needs, companies need to provide adequate salaries, rest breaks, and, if possible, exercise and physical fitness programs.[3] Safety needs can be met by providing a safe and secure work environment, and life and health insurance plans. Company social events and athletic activities may serve to satisfy *social needs*. Award banquets and status symbols such as private offices and private parking spots may be designed to meet esteem needs. By allowing for individual creativity and input, companies may enable employees to find self-fulfillment in their work and satisfy self-actualization needs.

Research testing Maslow's theory has supported the distinction between deficiency needs and growth needs. Unfortunately, the research has shown that not all workers are able to satisfy their higher-order needs on the job. For example, Porter found that whereas lower-level managers were only able to satisfy their deficiency needs on the job, managers from the higher echelons of organizations were able to satisfy these as well as their growth needs.[4] Also it appears that full-time homemakers had higher levels of deficiency needs than married women employed outside the home.[5] Presumably, this is because they do not have a job through which these needs can be fulfilled. The growth needs of working women are also higher than those of full-time homemakers, presumably because their deficiency needs are already satisfied on the job. This evidence is clearly consistent with Maslow's ideas about the satisfaction of deficiency needs prior to growth needs.

Despite this general evidence, Maslow's theory has not received a great deal of support with respect to the specific things it proposes—namely, the exact needs that exist and the order in which they are activated.[6] Many researchers have failed to confirm that there are only five basic categories of needs. Also, these needs have not been found to be activated in the exact order specified by Maslow.

Alderfer's ERG Theory In response to these criticisms, an alternative formulation has been proposed by Clayton Alderfer.[7] This approach, known as **ERG theory,** is much simpler. Not only does Alderfer specify that there are only three types of needs instead of five, but that these are not necessarily activated in any specific order. In fact, Alderfer postulates that any need may be activated at any time.

The three needs specified by *ERG theory* are the needs for existence, relatedness, and growth. *Existence* needs correspond to Maslow's physiological needs and safety needs. *Relatedness* needs correspond to Maslow's social needs—the need for meaningful social relationships. Finally, *growth* needs correspond to the esteem needs and self-actualization needs in Maslow's theory—the need for developing one's potential. A summary of Maslow's need hierarchy theory and the corresponding needs identified by Alderfer's ERG theory is shown in Table 4.1.

Clearly, ERG theory is much less restrictive than Maslow's need hierarchy theory. Its advantage is that it fits better with research evidence suggesting that although basic categories of needs do exist, they are not exactly as specified by Maslow.[8] Despite the fact that need theorists are not in complete agreement about the exact number of needs that exist and the relationships between them, they do agree that satisfying human needs is an important part of motivating behavior on the job.

Motivation-Maintenance Theory: From Satisfaction to Motivation

It seems only reasonable to suggest that people who are generally satisfied with their jobs show higher levels of motivation to perform them than people who are dissatisfied in this respect. If this is indeed the case, then it is important to know just what conditions produce satisfaction or dissatisfaction on the job. We will return to this topic in detail in Chapter 11. Here, we simply wish to call

TABLE 4.1
Need Theories: A Comparison

The five needs identified by Maslow's *need hierarchy theory* correspond to the three needs of Alderfer's *ERG theory*. Maslow's theory specifies that needs are activated in order from the lowest to the highest level, while Alderfer's theory specifies that needs may be activated in any order.

Maslow's Need Hierarchy Theory	Alderfer's ERG Theory
Growth Needs:	
5. Self-actualization	Growth
4. Esteem	
Deficiency Needs:	
3. Social	Relatedness
2. Safety	
1. Physiological	Existence

attention to the key role of job satisfaction or dissatisfaction in motivation to work.

At first glance, it is tempting to assume that a single set of factors accounts for both satisfaction and dissatisfaction. That is, we might assume that certain conditions either increase or decrease job satisfaction, depending on the extent to which they are present in work settings. According to a theory offered by Herzberg,[9] though, this is not actually so. Rather, it appears that job satisfaction (plus high levels of work motivation) and job dissatisfaction (along with low levels of such motivation) spring from somewhat different sources. Since this is a surprising conclusion, you may find it interesting to learn how Herzberg reached it.

Herzberg began by conducting a study in which more than 200 engineers and accountants were asked to describe times when they felt especially satisfied or dissatisfied with their jobs. (This is sometimes known as the *critical incident* technique.) Careful analysis of their answers pointed to an intriguing pattern of results. When describing incidents in which they felt dissatisfied, most persons mentioned conditions surrounding their jobs, rather than the work itself. For instance, they commented on such factors as physical working conditions, pay, security, and interpersonal relations. To the extent these conditions were positive, feelings of dissatisfaction were prevented. Given their role in preventing such negative reactions, Herzberg termed these factors **hygienes** and **maintenance factors.** In contrast, when describing incidents in which they felt especially satisfied or happy with their jobs, subjects usually mentioned factors relating more directly to the work they performed. For example, they spoke about the nature of their jobs and daily tasks, achievement in these, promotion opportunities, recognition from management, increased responsibility, and the chance for personal growth.

Because such factors contributed to job satisfaction, Herzberg termed them **motivators.** (See Figure 4.2 for a summary of both motivators and hygienes.)

As we have already noted, motivators seem related to the jobs individuals perform, while hygienes relate to conditions surrounding their work. But there is another way of viewing these two groups of factors as well. Hygienes seem to involve the satisfaction of lower-level deficiency needs, while motivators involve

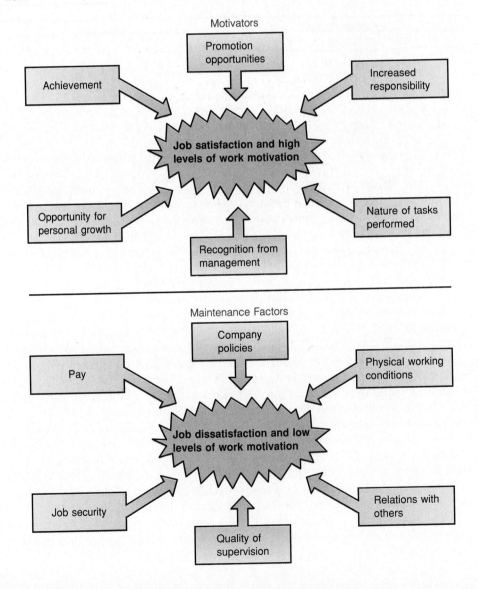

FIGURE 4.2 Herzberg's Motivation-Maintenance Theory
According to a theory proposed by Herzberg, job satisfaction, and high levels of work motivation stem from one set of factors relating to the work itself. In contrast, job dissatisfaction and low levels of work motivation stem from another set of factors relating to the conditions surrounding work.

Motivators

Promotion opportunities

Achievement

Increased responsibility

Job satisfaction and high levels of work motivation

Opportunity for personal growth

Nature of tasks performed

Recognition from management

Maintenance Factors

Company policies

Pay

Physical working conditions

Job dissatisfaction and low levels of work motivation

Job security

Relations with others

Quality of supervision

the satisfaction of higher-level growth needs. For example, recall that hygienes (or maintenance factors) involve such conditions as the pay one receives, social relations with others, and physical working conditions. Obviously, these factors are related to physiological, safety, and social needs. In contrast, motivators involve such conditions as opportunities for growth, increased responsibility, and promotion. Here, self-esteem and self-actualization needs seem more central. Thus, taking Herzberg's theory and related research findings into account, the bottom line seems to go something like this: To the extent individuals satisfy their basic deficiency needs at work, feelings of dissatisfaction will be prevented. However, the fulfillment of such needs is, by itself, not enough to produce high levels of satisfaction or motivation. To attain these positive results, opportunities for the fulfillment of higher-level needs, too, must be provided. In sum, the key to high morale and high productivity at work seems to lie not simply in offering employees good pay, job security, and pleasant working conditions, but also in ensuring that they have ample opportunities to grow. (See **Human Relations in Action:** How Satisfied Are You with Your Job?)

Expectancy Theory: Motivation and Belief

Imagine two people facing very different situations. One believes it really makes little difference how hard she works. Extra effort will not necessarily improve her job performance, and even if it does, no one will notice or care. The other is certain that if he puts out more effort, his performance will improve. He also believes that better performance, in turn, will yield many valued rewards (e.g., raises, promotions, and the like). Which of these two persons will be more motivated to work hard? The answer is so obvious that it hardly requires stating: the second.

* Miracle Food Mart.

While this example is extremely simple (perhaps unrealistically so), it calls attention to the key assumptions of a third major view of motivation: **expectancy theory** (or **expectancy/valence theory,** as it is sometimes known).[10,11] This approach assumes that motivation to work is strongly determined by certain beliefs or expectancies held by individuals. We have already hinted at each of these, but it is probably useful to make them explicit.

First, work motivation hinges on individuals' *expectancy* that increased effort will result in enhanced performance. Usually, of course, this is the case: Most persons *do* believe that the harder they work, the more productive they will be. But this is not always so. For example, a salesperson may believe that if she really bears down, she'll come across as using a "hard sell," and so actually hurt her chances for success. Similarly, production workers may conclude that they can keep up with their jobs through moderate effort, and that working harder will do no good; after all, the flow of parts past their stations will not increase. Expectancy theory suggests that individuals will be motivated to work only to the extent that they expect high levels of effort to result in improved performance. If they do not believe this is the case, they may well slack off and take it easy on their jobs.

Second, expectancy theory indicates that work motivation is closely linked to the view that good performance will yield *rewards* or is instrumental in doing so.

Only if individuals believe that good performance will be recognized and rewarded will they be motivated to work hard (see Figure 4.3). In contrast, if they feel that excellence will be ignored or overlooked, their work motivation may drop sharply, or virtually disappear!

A third aspect of the theory centers around the concept of *valence*—the personal value attached by individuals to various rewards they believe they can gain through their jobs. To the extent these rewards are highly valued, work motivation will be high. However, to the extent they are lacking in such value, motivation will be low. This makes good sense; after all, why should individuals work hard to attain outcomes they do not really want?

Expectancy theory claims that motivation is a multiplicative function of all three components. This means that higher levels of motivation will result when valence, instrumentality, and expectancy are all high than when they are all low. The multiplicative assumption of the theory also implies that if any one of the components is zero, then the overall level of motivation will be zero. So, even if a worker believes that her effort will result in performance, which will result in reward, motivation may be zero if the valence of the reward received is zero.

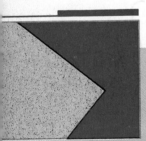

HUMAN RELATIONS IN ACTION

How Satisfied Are You with Your Job? Testing Motivation-Maintenance Theory

Many students work while they go to college or during vacation periods. Some of the features of these jobs may be quite positive, while others may be somewhat negative. For the items listed below, indicate whether you are dissatisfied or satisfied with these in your present job. (If you do not have a job now, you can rate your last job.)

		Satisfied	Dissatisfied
1.	Pay	✓ Satisfied	____ Dissatisfied
2.	Job security	✓ Satisfied	____ Dissatisfied
3.	Promotion opportunities	____ Satisfied	✓ Dissatisfied
4.	Recognition for good work	____ Satisfied	✓ Dissatisfied
5.	Physical working conditions	____ Satisfied	✓ Dissatisfied
6.	Relations with other workers	✓ Satisfied	____ Dissatisfied
7.	Opportunity for growth or learning	____ Satisfied	✓ Dissatisfied
8.	Degree of responsibility	____ Satisfied	✓ Dissatisfied
9.	Company policies	✓ Satisfied	____ Dissatisfied
10.	Quality of supervisors	____ Satisfied	✓ Dissatisfied
11.	Nature of work	____ Satisfied	✓ Dissatisfied
12.	Opportunities for achievement	____ Satisfied	✓ Dissatisfied

Figure 4.4 summarizes the definitions of the components of expectancy theory and shows the interrelationships between them.

Figure 4.4 also shows that expectancy theory assumes that motivation is not equivalent to job performance, but that it is just one of several determinants of job performance. In particular, the theory assumes that *skills and abilities* also contribute to a person's job performance. It is no secret that some people are better suited to perform their jobs than others by virtue of the unique characteristics and special skills or abilities they bring to their jobs. For example, a tall, strong, well-coordinated person is likely to make a better professional basketball player than a short, weak, klutz, even if the shorter person is highly motivated to succeed.

Expectancy theory also recognizes that job performance will be influenced by a worker's *role perceptions*. How well workers perform their jobs will depend, in part, on what they believe is expected of them. An assistant manager, for example, may believe his or her primary job responsibility is to train employees. But if the manager believes the assistant manager should be doing paperwork instead, he or she may be seen as a poor performer. Of course, such poor performance results

Now indicate on the following scale how satisfied you are with your job.

_____ Very   _____ Satisfied   _____ Neutral   _____ Dissatisfied   _✓_ Very
satisfied   dissatisfied

Motivation score   Maintenance score
_____ Satisfied   _6_ Dissatisfied   _4_ Satisfied   _2_ Dissatisfied

Scoring

Add up the number of times you checked satisfied and the number of times you checked dissatisfied on items 3, 4, 7, 8, 11, and 12. Write these numbers under "motivation score." Do the same for items 1, 2, 5, 6, 9, and 10 and write the scores under "maintenance score". Do these scores relate to your job satisfaction as suggested by Herzberg's motivation-maintenance theory? If you are very satisfied or satisfied with your job, you probably have a high motivation score for motivators. If you are very dissatisfied, you probably have a high dissatisfaction score for maintenance. You can ask your instructor to collect this information from all the students in the class to see what percentage of the time the predictions fit with motivation-maintenance theory.

FIGURE 4.3 Expectancy Theory: The Rewards of Rewards
Expectancy theory emphasizes the use of rewards to increase work motivation. As shown here, giving such rewards may be rewarding in themselves. (Reprinted with special permission of King Features Syndicate.)

not necessarily from poor motivation but from misunderstanding concerning the role one is expected to play in the organization.

Finally, expectancy theory also recognizes the role of *opportunities to perform* one's job. It is possible that even the best workers will perform at low levels if their opportunities are limited. A good example may be seen in the work of salespersons. Even the most highly motivated salesperson will perform poorly if opportunities are restricted—if the available inventory is very low (as is sometimes the case among certain popular cars), or if the customers are unable to afford

FIGURE 4.4 Expectancy Theory: An Overview
According to *expectancy theory*, motivation is the product of three types of beliefs: expectancy (effort will result in performance), multiplied by instrumentality (performance will result in rewards), multiplied by valence of rewards (the perceived value of the rewards). It also recognizes that motivation is only one of several factors responsible for job performance.

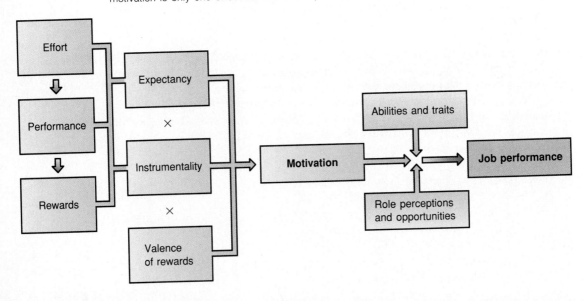

TABLE 4.2
How to Motivate Employees: Some Suggestions from Expectancy Theory

Expectancy theory makes some specific recommendations about how to enhance motivation. Various organizational practices can help implement these recommendations. A few of these are summarized here.

Recommendation	Practice
Clarify the expectation that working hard will improve job performance	Design jobs in a way that makes the desired performance more attainable
Clearly link valued rewards to the job performance needed to attain them	Institute pay-for-performance plan, paying for meritorious work
Administer rewards that have a high positive valence to workers	Use a cafeteria-style benefit plan, allowing workers to select the fringe benefits they most value

the product (as is sometimes the case among salespersons whose territories are heavily populated by unemployed persons).

It is important to recognize that expectancy theory views motivation as just one of several determinants of job performance. Motivation, together with a person's skills and abilities, role perceptions, and opportunities, will combine to influence job performance. Expectancy theory generated a great deal of research and has been successfully applied to understanding behavior in a wide range of organizational settings.[12] However, although some specific aspects of the theory have been supported (particularly the impact of expectancy and instrumentality on motivation),[13] others have not (such as the contribution of valence to motivation, and the multiplicative assumption).[14] However, it does suggest a number of ways in which one can motivate workers. These are summarized in Table 4.2.

One important suggestion would be to *clarify workers' expectancies that their efforts will lead to performance.* It is important to make it clear to people what is expected of them *and* to make it possible for them to attain that level of performance. A second practical suggestion from expectancy theory is to *clearly link valued rewards and performance.* Managers should attempt to enhance workers' beliefs about instrumentality—that is, to make it clear to them exactly what job behaviors will lead to what rewards. To the extent that it is possible for employees to be paid in ways that are directly linked to their performance—such as through piece-rate incentive systems, or sales commission plans—expectancy theory specifies that it would be effective to do so because this would enhance beliefs about instrumentality. Indeed, a great deal of research has shown that performance increases can result from carefully implemented merit systems—what is frequently referred to as *pay-for-performance* systems.[15]

Finally, one of the most obvious practical suggestions from expectancy theory is to *administer rewards that are positively valent to employees.* The carrot at the end of the stick must be a tasty one, according to the theory, for it to have potential as a motivator. These days, when the composition of the work force is changing, with increasing numbers of unmarried parents and single people working, it would be a mistake to assume that all employees care about having the same rewards made available to them by their companies. Some might recognize the incentive value of a pay raise, while others might prefer additional vacation days, improved insurance benefits, or day care facilities for children. With this in mind, more and more companies are instituting *cafeteria-style benefit plans*— incentive systems through which the employees get to select their fringe benefits from a menu of available alternatives (see Figure 4.5). Given that fringe benefits represent an average of 37 percent of payroll costs, more and more companies are recognizing the value of administering them flexibly.[16]

Equity Theory: Fairness and Motivation at Work

Imagine that at some point in the future, you hold a job with a large company. In general, you are quite satisfied with it and view it in positive terms. Then one day you discover a disturbing fact: Another member of your department, who does work similar to your own and has just about the same amount of training and experience, earns $5,000 a year more than you do! How would this knowledge affect your motivation? In all likelihood, it would decrease it sharply. *After all, you might reason to yourself, why should I work as hard as he does for less pay?*

Your reaction in this respect would be quite understandable, for in our dealings with others, we all prefer to feel that we are being treated fairly. This central fact lies at the core of the final theory of motivation we will consider: **equity theory.**[17] Actually, equity theory is more than just a theory of work motivation. It applies to a wide range of human relationships, from romantic ones at one extreme to purely economic ones at the other. But it has important implications for motivation in work settings, and it is on these that we will focus here.

Basically, equity theory suggests that people will be most satisfied with their jobs, and most strongly motivated to work at them, when they believe they are being treated fairly. But how, precisely, do individuals decide whether this is the case or not? The answer seems to involve a special type of relative judgment in which we compare ourselves with others. In this judgment we first examine our own **inputs** (everything we contribute to our jobs) and our own **outcomes** (all the benefits we derive from them). Then, we compare these with the equivalent values for others. If our ratio of outcomes-to-inputs seems roughly equivalent to theirs, **equity** exists; we conclude that we are in fact being treated fairly relative to others. If, instead, our ratio of outcomes-to-inputs is *not* similar to theirs, **inequity** may exist; in this case, we conclude that something is "out of whack" and that fairness does not prevail. For example, we may discover that another person enjoys a more favorable outcome-to-input ratio than we do: He receives higher pay for the same work. Alternatively, we may find that another person has a less favorable outcome-to-input ratio: He receives fewer or smaller benefits for the same amount of work. The conditions leading to the feelings of equity and inequity are summarized in Figure 4.6.

It is important to note that for equity to exist, it is *not* necessary that everyone in an organization provide the same inputs or receive the same rewards—far from it. All that is essential is that the *ratio* of outcomes to inputs remain fairly constant. Thus it is perfectly reasonable for persons who make large contributions (by virtue

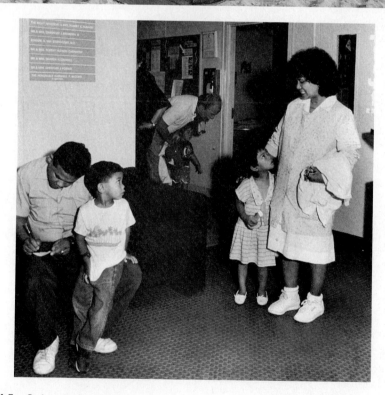

FIGURE 4.5 Cafeteria-Style Benefit Plans: One Way to Enhance Motivation
Many companies now use cafeteria-style benefit plans that allow employees to choose among a
variety of benefits like those shown here.

of their training, experience, talent, or effort) to receive larger rewards than persons who make small contributions. In fact, it is this matching of outcomes to contributions that is central to perceived fairness in work settings.

Unfortunately, of course, equity does not always prevail. For various reasons, some persons tend to reap larger benefits than they deserve, while others get the short end of the stick and receive less than is fair. What happens in such cases? As you might anticipate those who are *overrewarded* tend to feel guilty, while those who are underrewarded may feel angry (see Figure 4.7).

According to equity theory, people are motivated to escape those negative emotional states of anger and guilt. Equity theory recognizes several ways of resolving inequitable states (refer to the summary in Table 4.3). For example, underpaid persons may respond by lowering their inputs. They may not work as

FIGURE 4.6 Equity Theory: An Overview
To judge equity or inequity, employees can compare the ratios of their own outcomes/inputs to the corresponding ratios of others. The resulting states—either overpayment inequity, underpayment inequity, or equitable payment—and their associated emotional responses, are summarized here.

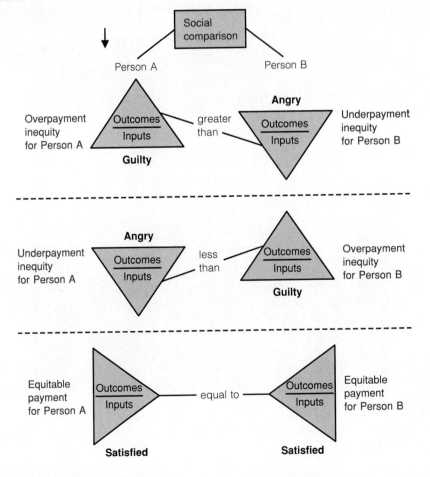

FIGURE 4.7 Anger: A Likely Reaction to Inequity
When employees feel they have been treated unfairly or inequitably, they may feel angry and become involved in protests.

hard—for example, by arriving at work later, leaving early, taking longer breaks, doing less work, or performing lower quality work. In an extreme case, they may even quit their jobs. They may also attempt to raise their outcomes—for example, by asking the boss for a raise (see Figure 4.8), or even taking home company property (such as tools, or office supplies). All these examples may be considered *behavioral* reactions to inequity because they represent things people can do to change their existing inputs or outcomes.

In addition to these behavioral reactions to *underpayment inequity,* there are also some likely *psychological* reactions. Assuming that many workers may feel uncomfortable stealing from their employers (as they should) or would be unwilling to restrict their productivity or to ask for a raise, they may resort to resolving the perceived inequity by changing the way they think about the situation. For example, an underpaid worker may attempt to rationalize that another's inputs are really higher than his own, thereby convincing himself that the other's higher outcomes are justified. One recent study even found that workers who received a 6 percent pay cut rationalized that their pay was still equitable by coming to think of their work environments in more favorable terms.[18] In this manner, by coming to perceive the situation as equitable, people can effectively reduce their inequity distress.

TABLE 4.3
Possible Reactions to Inequity: A Summary

People can respond to overpayment and underpayment inequities in behavioral and/or psychological ways. A few of these are summarized here. These reactions help change the perceived inequities into a state of perceived equity.

	Type of Reaction	
Type of Inequity	**Behavioral** (What you can *do* is . . .)	**Psychological** (What you can *think* is . . .)
Overpayment inequity	Raise own inputs (e.g., work harder), or lower own outcomes (e.g., work through a paid vacation)	Convince yourself that your own outcomes are deserved based on your own inputs (e.g., rationalize that you work harder than others and so you deserve more pay)
Underpayment inequity	Lower own inputs (e.g., reduce effort), or raise own outcomes (e.g., get a raise in pay)	Convince yourself that others' inputs are really higher than your own (e.g., rationalize that the comparison worker is really more qualified, and so deserves higher outcomes)

FIGURE 4.8 Inequity: One Behavioral Reaction
One behavioral reaction to perceived wage inequity is to ask for a pay raise. Unfortunately, this may not always be a successful tactic. (Herman © 1989 Universal Press Syndicate. Reprinted with permission. All rights reserved.)

"Have you given any thought to my pay raise?"

A similar set of behavioral and psychological reactions can be identified for *overpayment inequity.* A salaried worker who feels overpaid may raise his or her inputs by working harder or for longer hours. Similarly, workers who lower their own outcomes—for example, by not taking advantage of company-provided fringe benefits—may be seen as redressing an overpayment inequity. In addition, overpaid persons may readily convince themselves psychologically that they are really worth their higher outcomes by virtue of their superior inputs. Workers who receive substantial pay raises may not feel too distressed about it for the same reason. Research has generally supported the theory's claim that people will respond to overpayment and underpayment inequities as we have just described.[19,20]

Adjustments in the inputs to a job or outcomes from it are steps individuals can take to deal with feelings of inequity. It is important to note that organizations, too, can play a role in this regard. For example, they can attempt to establish the fairest pay and promotion policies possible. Inequity in these procedures, either real or imagined, is a major source of unhappiness among employees in many companies. Thus making certain that they are as fair as possible is a good way to head off possible trouble. Similarly, organizations can attempt to distribute work assignments in a balanced and reasonable manner. By doing so, instances in which some persons are overworked while others are on a permanent semi-vacation can be reduced. Finally, organizations can attempt to disperse various "perks" (perquisites) such as fancy titles or desirable offices in a rational rather than a seemingly random fashion. This can help keep feelings of resentment, as well as undesirable forms of organizational politics, to a minimum.

In these and other ways, feelings of fairness or equity can be encouraged in various work settings. To the extent that such reactions prevail, and feelings of unfairness (inequity) are minimized, and motivation, job satisfaction, and efficiency may be enhanced. Given the value of such gains, it is clear that there are many practical as well as ethical grounds for adhering as closely as possible to basic principles of fair play. (For a concrete example of how the principles of motivation discussed so far may play a role at work, see the **Case in Point** on page 124.)

ENHANCING MOTIVATION AT WORK: SOME USEFUL TECHNIQUES

Each of the theories we have examined so far offers, or at least implies, specific steps that can be taken to increase motivation at work. These have often been put to practical use, and in many instances have yielded valuable benefits.[21] But they are not the only techniques available. Several others, not as closely tied to broad or sweeping theories of work motivation, have also been developed. Because these, too, have proven quite effective, we will describe several here. The most important of these are *Management by Objectives (MBO), goal setting, job enrichment,* and *behavior modification.*

Management by Objectives: The Benefits of Having Clear-cut Goals

According to an old saying, "It is usually easier to get somewhere if you know where you are going." What this statement implies, of course, is that in general, it is easier to reach various goals if they are clearly defined. This is far from a surprising conclusion. Yet, it is often ignored by large organizations. Goals are stated in very general terms such as "high efficiency," "a good public image," or "excellent standards of quality," and no indication of precisely what they mean is provided. As a result, employees—from management on down—may be uncertain as to just what they are trying to accomplish, and the entire company can seem to be very much adrift.

The potential costs of such uncertainty are given full attention in a popular technique for enhancing motivation at work—**Management by objectives** (or *MBO* for short).[22] In essence, this approach is designed to enhance progress toward key organizational goals by making these highly specific and by outlining concrete steps for their attainment. Often, it proceeds through four distinct stages. First, supervisors and their subordinates meet and agree on specific goals for their company or department. These should be measurable so that progress toward them can be assessed, and time-bounded—linked to a specific timetable. Second,

CASE IN POINT

A Problem of Motivation

It was a typically busy lunch hour at Manny's Sandwich Shop. Manny's specializes in custom sandwiches with all the trimmings and is a popular stop for the high school students during their lunch break.

"Where is Brian?" yelled Manny to the counter crew from the back room. "He was supposed to be here at 11:30 and it is already 11:45. I'm getting fed up with him."

Brian Williams had been working at Manny's for four months and had begun as a highly motivated employee. He was always punctual, courteous with the customers, and hard-working. Yet lately he had developed a somewhat negative attitude about working at Manny's and was starting to be erratic about showing up on time for work. Manny wandered up to the counter to help out with the customers. He was lucky to have two really good workers in Joe and Sally. They were hired about the same time as Brian and had never been any problem. As they were working the counter, Manny questioned them about Brian.

"What do you guys think the problem is?"

Joe replied first. "I think the problem started when both of us got raises this past month. Brian thought he should have had a raise too since he has been here as long as we have."

concrete steps for reaching these goals within the time frame established are outlined, and then put into practice. A third and crucial step involves procedures for monitoring progress toward key goals in a consistent and regular manner. Finally, total progress is reviewed, and if objectives have been met, new goals are established. If initial goals have not yet been achieved, additional steps for doing so are developed, and a new timetable is established. (See Figure 4.9 for a summary of the major phases of MBO.)

At present, MBO is one of the most widely used techniques for enhancing work motivation.[23] One reason for this popularity may lie in the fact that in a sense, MBO is *self-correcting*. Because it states objective, quantifiable goals and insists on periodic measurement of progress toward them, it is a continuing process, open to adjustment and feedback. This is a highly attractive feature. Second, through its emphasis on agreement between supervisors and subordinates, MBO may contribute to *close cooperation* across levels of an organization. This, too, probably contributes to its widespread acceptance. Finally—and perhaps most important—MBO *seems to work,* and it does help many organizations reach their goals. In fact, one review of more than 185 studies concerned with MBO reported that a large majority offered support for its success.[24] Why is this the case? Why precisely does MBO seem to work so well in so many situations? Probably, there is no simple answer, for MBO is a complex process. But growing evidence points

"Oh come on," Manny replied shaking his head, "you two have worked longer hours and are always willing to help out when I need you. Brian only wants to work a limited schedule and he has not yet helped out in the pinch."

Sally nodded in agreement and added that Brian had complained that he didn't know what was expected of him. He had taken the job because he wanted to work during the lunch hour and keep his evenings free to play on his softball team. He did not realize that he would be expected to work some evenings as well. At this point Sally noticed Brian driving into the parking lot.

"He's here now, Manny. I guess you'll get your chance to find out for yourself now."

"I sure am going to settle this problem once and for all!" said Manny as he walked back to his office. "Tell him to come directly to see me."

Questions

1. What motivational factors appear to lie behind Brian's behavior? Can you relate the concepts of equity and expectancy theory to this scenario?

2. How would you evaluate working at a sandwich shop in terms of the motivators and maintenance factors of Herzberg's theory?

3. How do you think Manny should deal with Brian? Are there any particular techniques suggested in this chapter that might be helpful?

to the importance of setting concrete goals. Specifically, many investigations indicate that the establishment of concrete goals often produces beneficial effects on both motivation and performance.[25]

Motivating by Goal Setting

Research has suggested that certain techniques of **goal setting** are most effective. The first requirement of an effective goal setting procedure is to make the goals very *clear* or specific. This gives employees something to "shoot for" and has been shown to increase productivity in a variety of companies.[26,27] Yet, just any goal will not work. It is best if the goals are *difficult* but attainable.[28] Such goals may be seen as a realistic challenge. If the goals are seen as too difficult or unrealistic, employees may simply ignore them (see Figure 4.10). It also helps if workers are involved in setting the goals and if the reason behind the goals are explained. Under these conditions, workers are more likely to accept the goals as reasonable. Finally, providing *feedback* about the level in quality of performance seems to be important in motivating people to strive for the goals. Combining feedback with goal setting seems to be most effective in facilitating the performance of individuals or groups.[29,30]

FIGURE 4.9 MBO: An Overview
As shown here, management by objectives (MBO) often proceeds through several distinct stages.

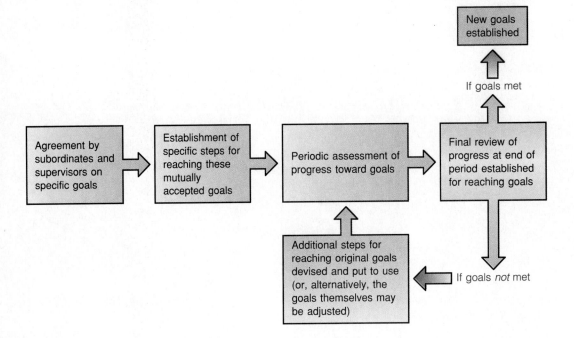

Job Enrichment: Making Jobs More Meaningful

Suppose that you do precisely the same dull things at work each day. Further, imagine that you have no say over what tasks you perform, and your supervisor checks up on you regularly to make sure you are not goofing off. Yet, despite this, she provides little feedback on how well you are doing. What do you think your motivation would be under these conditions? The answer is pretty clear: low, very low, or nonexistent. Unfortunately, the conditions just described are ones associated with many production or office jobs even today.

Can anything be done about this situation? Can jobs be changed so that they enhance rather than destroy employee motivation to perform them? Many human relations experts believe that they can. In fact, efforts to change jobs in these ways have been going on for several decades.[31] In general, such changes are known as **job enrichment,** and to quote one expert on this process, they involve efforts to "help individuals gain the chance to experience the kick that comes from doing a job well, and . . . once again care about their work."[32] A wide range of procedures have been found useful in this regard. Among the most important, though, are these.

First, efforts should be undertaken to make jobs more meaningful to the people who perform them—to make them seem important, valuable, and worthwhile. This can be accomplished in several ways, such as increasing the variety of tasks performed, or enlarging the scope of a job so that it involves completing a whole piece of work rather than only a part.

(handwritten margin note: very important again miracle.)

FIGURE 4.10 Job Performance: It Depends on the Acceptance of Difficult Goals
Research and theory on goal setting suggests that people will work hard to attain difficult goals that they accept, until they reach the limits of their capabilities. However, as goals get too difficult, they may be rejected, and performance will suffer. (*Source:* Adapted from Locke & Latham (1984); see Note 28.)

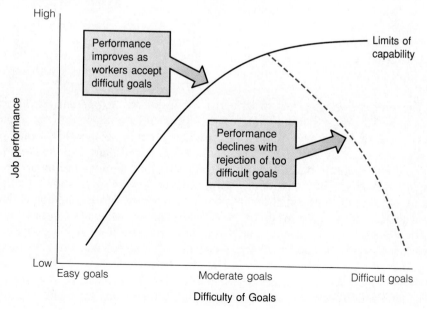

Second, individuals should be provided with increased *autonomy*—more freedom to perform their jobs in the manner they wish, without undue control from supervisors. This helps employees feel more directly responsible for the work they perform, and can increase their motivation.

Third, individuals should receive regular and informative *feedback*—information on how well they are doing their jobs. Such information often assists them in improving their performance, and also contributes to a sense of personal control over outcomes. These reactions, in turn, can sharply enhance work motivation.

When jobs are altered so as to maximize the features just described, positive results often follow. For example, when Volvo, the largest Swedish automobile manufacturer, instituted changes based on principles of job enrichment, absenteeism dropped by more than 35 percent, and the quality of the cars produced rose sharply[33] (see Figure 4.11). Similarly, when clerical workers in South Africa were provided with the opportunity to set their own schedules and inspect their own work (increased autonomy), given daily feedback, and offered a greater variety, their reported motivation and job satisfaction increased. Similarly, absenteeism and turnover among these employees dropped considerably.[34] In sum, it appears that steps designed to make work more interesting and meaningful to employees may yield handsome dividends in terms of enhanced motivation—and everything that this implies.

Behavior Modification: Learning to Be Productive

Let's begin with a basic fact of life: Behavior often produces effects. Winking at someone in a bar is likely to produce one kind of outcome; giving them an icy stare is likely to produce another. Similarly, telling your boss what a great job he is doing and how much you admire him may yield one result; telling him that he is an incompetent boob and that you know more about the business than he does will probably yield another. Now for another basic fact: The nature of the effects produced by any action determine whether it will be repeated or abandoned. In general, actions we perform that yield positive results are strengthened—our tendency to perform them again is increased. Actions that yield negative effects, in contrast, tend to be avoided—in fact, we may learn not to perform them.

The process we have just described is often known as *operant conditioning* and is one of the most general—and basic—forms of learning we can accomplish. Indeed, scientists who have studied this process in detail believe that it may play a key role in virtually all forms of human behavior, everything from making love or learning to speak to figuring out how to program a computer or how to design complex machinery. But what does all this have to do with motivation? Actually, it turns out, quite a bit. Since our tendency to perform various actions is determined at least in part, by whether they yield positive or negative results, some human relations experts have reasoned as follows. Perhaps if we arrange conditions in work settings so that positive behavior by employees (behavior that contributes to productivity or efficiency) is rewarded, the tendency to perform these actions will be strengthened. In other words, perhaps if employees are rewarded for engaging in actions considered desirable by their supervisors, they will soon reach

FIGURE 4.11 Job Enrichment: Changing Jobs for the Better
After Volvo instituted job enrichment, job performance improved sharply.

the point at which they *want* to perform these behaviors rather than other, less desirable ones. If such effects occur, of course, we might suggest that in one sense, their motivation to work has been increased.

Many attempts have been made to apply this reasoning—and the process of operant conditioning—to the task of improving output or productivity in work settings.[35] Since the goal of such efforts is that of modifying the behavior of employees, these procedures are often termed **OB Mod** (short for **organizational behavior modification**). The basic principle on which they rest is straightforward: Arrange conditions so that employees receive various rewards for behaving in ways that contribute to the progress and well-being of their organizations. While this principle is fairly easy to grasp, the problems involved in actually applying it to changing human behavior often turn out to be immense. Thus a great deal of expertise is required in order to design effective programs of this type. Obviously, we can't provide you with such detailed training here. What we can do, though, is briefly describe some of the key steps involved in the process of OB Mod.

OB Mod: The Basic Steps Such procedures begin with the identification of what are termed the critical behaviors—those actions that exert a strong impact on key aspects of job performance. Only after these are identified can the process continue. Next, the rate at which these behaviors are being performed must be observed. This is essential, for without it, there is no way of knowing whether efforts at OB Mod have actually produced any change—any increase in desired actions on the part of employees. The third step is perhaps the most complex. It involves a detailed analysis of just what conditions lead to the occurrence of various actions by employees, and what consequences (positive or negative) follow these actions. For example, it might be observed that "looking busy," even when there is no work to do, is rewarded: It provides employees with the chance to write personal letters, balance their checkbooks, and so on. However, finishing one's work promptly and efficiently may yield negative outcomes: It leads to even more work being piled on the diligent person's desk! In a fourth step, specific tactics for modifying the behavior in question are devised. Usually this involves arranging conditions so that employees gain positive reinforcers (rewards) only by performing the desired behaviors. In short, conditions must be such that they gain raises, promotions, praise, or other outcomes they desire only by working in an efficient and productive manner. (Individuals differ greatly in the goals they seek and, thus, in precisely what they find reinforcing. It is crucial to take such differences into account in formulating any effective program of OB Mod.) A final step involves the systematic evaluation of outcomes. Behavior prior to the start of the OB Mod program is compared with that at its conclusion to see whether the goals sought have actually been attained.

O.B. Mod: Does It Really Work? As we noted earlier, OB Mod is derived largely from basic principles of operant conditioning. This form of learning appears to play a major role in a wide range of human behavior. For this reason, it can be expected that, when carried out with skill and care, OB Mod will really work—it will produce major changes in employee behavior and motivation. In fact, a growing body of evidence suggests that this is the case. For example, in one recent study efforts were made to improve the job performance of retail clerks working in a large department store.[36] A careful analysis revealed that such performance would be enhanced if the clerks remained near the merchandise on display, greeted customers within five seconds of their arrival, and kept the display shelves filled to at least 70 percent of their capacity. In order to encourage such actions, clerks in one group (the *experimental condition*) were offered time off with pay and a chance to win a free vacation for reaching improved levels of performance with respect to these behaviors (e.g., for keeping their shelves fully stocked). In contrast, clerks in a second (*control*) group were never offered these incentives. The behavior of persons in both groups was observed for twenty days while these rewards were available (only to those in the experimental condition, of course), and for twenty additional days after they were removed. As you can see from Figure 4.12, results were impressive: On-the-job performance improved greatly among persons in the experimental group, but did not change among those in the control condition.

The fact that similar results have been attained in other studies conducted in different settings (e.g., hospitals, freight companies, factories) points to the following general conclusion: Arranging conditions at work so that employees can attain valued rewards only by behaving in certain desired ways may be an effective means of enhancing both performance and motivation.

SUMMARY

Motivation is generally defined as the internal force that energizes and guides behavior. Many different theories of work motivation have been proposed. Ac-

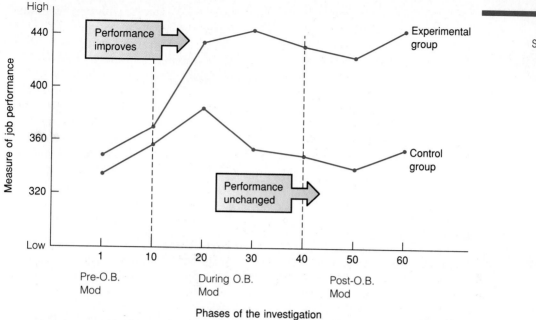

FIGURE 4.12 O.B. Mod: A Successful Example

When clerks in a large department store were offered valued rewards for engaging in key behaviors related to their jobs (the *experimental group*), their performance of these actions increased. In contrast, clerks never offered rewards for performing these behaviors (the *control* group) showed little change in performance during the same period of time. (*Source:* Based on data from Luthans et al. (1981); see Note 36.)

cording to one, **Maslow's need hierarchy theory,** human beings have many different needs, arranged in a hierarchy. Lower-level, deficiency needs must be at least partly satisfied before higher-level, growth needs can be activated. In contrast, Alderfer's **ERG theory** proposes that we are motivated by basic physiological or safety needs (**existence**), social needs (**relatedness**), and esteem needs (**growth**). A second approach, Herzberg's **motivation-maintenance theory,** suggests that certain factors (especially relating to the conditions surrounding work) affect the satisfaction of lower-level needs; thus they primarily influence job dissatisfaction. In contrast, other factors (relating to work itself) affect the satisfaction of higher-level needs and are more closely related to job satisfaction. **Expectancy theory,** a third approach to work motivation, suggests that individuals' willingness to expend effort on their jobs is strongly affected by certain expectancies. Among the most important of these are the expectancy that effort will improve performance, and the expectancy that good performance will yield valued rewards. A fourth perspective, **equity theory,** indicates that work motivation will be higher under conditions where individuals believe they are being treated fairly than under conditions where they believe they are being treated unfairly.

Many tactics for enhancing work motivation have been developed. Perhaps the most popular of these is **Management by Objectives (MBO).** This procedure involves agreement between supervisors and subordinates on concrete goals to be sought and steps for attaining them. A related strategy involves **goal setting.** By providing clear and challenging goals, one can often enhance worker motivation and performance. **Job enrichment,** a second strategy for enhancing work motivation, centers around efforts to make jobs more meaningful to the persons who perform them. Useful steps in this regard include making jobs more varied in content, giving employees greater autonomy and providing them with informative feedback. A third tactic effective in increasing work motivation is **organizational behavior modification (OB Mod).** This procedure, which derives from basic principles of operant conditioning, seeks to arrange conditions at work so that employees can attain valued rewards only by performing desired organizational behaviors. Existing evidence suggests that if used with skill and care, OB Mod can be highly successful in altering work-related behavior.

KEY TERMS

deficiency needs: According to Maslow's need theory, the lower-level needs that must be at least partly satisfied before higher-level growth needs can be activated.

equity: The state in which one worker's outcome/input ratio is equivalent to that of another worker with whom this person compares him or herself.

equity theory: The theory stating that workers strive to maintain ratios of their own outcomes (rewards) to their own inputs (contributions) that are equal to the outcome/input ratios of other workers with whom they compare themselves.

ERG theory: An alternative to Maslow's need hierarchy theory; proposed by Alderfer, it asserts that there are three basic human needs: existence, relatedness, and growth.

esteem needs: According to Maslow's need theory, the need to attain self-respect and the respect of others.

expectancy theory: A theory asserting that workers' motivation is based on their beliefs about the probability that effort will lead to performance (expectancy), multiplied by the probability that performance will lead to reward (instrumentality), multiplied by the perceived value (valence) of the reward.

goal setting: The process of determining specific levels of performance for workers to attain.

inequity: The undesirable condition in which a worker's outcome/input ratio is not equal to that of another person who is used for comparison. If this inequity favors a person, the result is *overpayment inequity,* which leads to feelings of guilt. If this inequity is to a person's disadvantage, the result is *underpayment inequity,* which leads to feelings of anger.

inputs: Workers' contributions to their jobs, such as their experience, qualifications, or the amount of time worked.

job enrichment: The practice of giving workers a high degree of control over their work, from planning and organization, through implementing the job and evaluating the results.

maintenance factors (hygienes): In Herzberg's motivation-maintenance theory, factors that prevent job dissatisfaction or reduction in work motivation.

Management by Objectives (MBO): A technique for enhancing work motivation; it is based largely on the establishment of jointly agreed-upon goals by management and employees, concrete steps for reaching the goals, and periodic assessment of progress toward them.

motivation: The set of processes that arouse, direct, and maintain human behavior toward the attainment of some goal.

motivation-maintenance theory: Herzberg's theory suggesting that different factors contribute to job satisfaction and/or high levels of work motivation and job dissatisfaction and/or low levels of work motivation.

motivators: In Herzberg's theory, factors that contribute to job satisfaction and/or high levels of work motivation.

need hierarchy theory: Maslow's theory that there are five human needs (physiological, safety, social, esteem, and self-actualization) and that these are arranged in such a way that lower, more basic needs must be satisfied before higher-level needs become activated.

organizational behavior modification (OB Mod): A technique for changing the behavior of employees in ways viewed as desirable by their organization. It is based largely upon the following principle: Determine what outcomes employees find rewarding, and then arrange conditions so that these can be obtained only by working in an efficient and productive manner.

outcomes: The rewards a worker receives from his or her job, such as salary and recognition.

physiological needs: Basic biological needs, such as the need for food, water, and oxygen.

safety needs: Our need to feel safe from threats to our physical or psychological well being.

self-actualization needs: The need to find out who we really are and to develop to our fullest potential.

social needs: Our need to form friendships with others, to belong, and to love and be loved.

NOTES

1. Steers, R.M., & Porter, L.W., eds. (1989). *Motivation and Work Behavior*, 5th ed. New York: McGraw-Hill.

2. Maslow, A.H. (1970). *Motivation and Personality*, 2d ed. New York: Harper & Row.

3. Falkenberg, L.E. (1987). "Employee Fitness Programs: Their Impact on the Employee and the Organization." *Academy of Management Review, 12,* 511–22.

4. Porter, L.W. (1961). "A Study of Perceived Need Satisfaction in Bottom and Middle Management Jobs." *Journal of Applied Psychology, 45,* 1–10.

5. Betz, E.L. (1982). "Need Fulfillment in the Career Development of Women." *Journal of Vocational Behavior, 20,* 53–66.

6. Wahba, M.A., & Bridwell, L.G. (1976). "Maslow Reconsidered: A Review of Research on the Need Hierarchy Theory." *Organizational Behavior and Human Performance, 15,* 212–40.

7. Alderfer, C.P. (1972). *Existence, Relatedness, and Growth.* New York: Free Press.

8. Salancik, G.R., & Pfeffer, J. (1977), "An Examination of Need-Satisfaction Models of Job Satisfaction." *Administrative Science Quarterly, 22,* 427–56.

9. Herzberg, F.H. (1966). "Work and the nature of man." Cleveland, OH: World.

10. Vroom, V.H. (1964). *Work and Motivation.* New York: Wiley.

11. Porter, L.W., & Lawler, E.G., (1968). *Managerial Attitudes and Performance.* Homewood, Ill.: Irwin.

12. Mitchell, T.R. (1983). "Expectancy-Value Models in Organizational Psychology." In N. Feather, ed., *Expectancy, Incentive, and Action,* pp. 293–314. Hillsdale, N.J.: Lawrence Erlbaum Associates.

13. Heneman, R.L. (1984). *Pay for Performance: Exploring the Merit System.* New York: Pergamon Press.

14. Miller, L.E., & Grush, J.E. (1988). "Improving Predictions in Expectancy Theory Research: Effects of Personality, Expectancies, and Norms." *Academy of Management Journal, 31*, 107–22.

15. Harrell, A., & Stahl, M. (1986). "Additive Information Processing and the Relationship Between Expectancy of Success and Motivational Force." *Academy of Management Journal, 29*, 424–33.

16. Foegen, J.H. (1982). "Fringe benefits are being diversified too." *Industry Week* (October 18): 56–58.

17. Adams, J.S. (1965). "Inequity in social exchange." In L. Berkowitz, ed., *Advances in Experimental Social Psychology*, p. 2. New York: Academic Press.

18. Greenberg, J. (1989). "Cognitive Re-evaluation of Outcomes in Response to Underpayment Inequity." *Academy of Management Journal, 32*, 174–184.

19. Greenberg, J. (1987). "A Taxonomy of Organizational Justice Theories." *Academy of Management Review, 12*, 9–22.

20. Pritchard, R.D., Dunnette, M.D., & Jorgenson, D.O. (1972). "Effects of Perceptions of Equity and Inequity on Worker Performance and Satisfaction." *Journal of Applied Psychology, 57*, 75–94.

21. Campbell, J.P., & Pritchard, R.D. (1976). "Motivation Theory in Industrial and Organizational Psychology." In M.D. Dunnette, ed., *Handbook of Industrial and Organizational Psychology*. Chicago: Rand McNally.

22. Greenwood, R.G. (1981). "Management by Objectives: As Developed by Peter Drucker, Assisted by Harold Smiddy." *Academy of Management Review, 6*, 225–30.

23. Jun, J.S. (1976). "A Symposium: Management by Objectives in the Public Sector." *Public Administration Review, 36*, 1–5.

24. Kondrasuk, J.N. (1981). "Studies in MBO Effectiveness." *Academy of Management Review, 6*, 419–30.

25. Locke, E.A. (1968). "Toward a Theory of Task Motivation and Incentives." *Organizational Behavior and Human Performance, 3*, 157–89.

26. Latham, G.P., & Lee, T.W. (1986). "Goal Setting." In E.A. Locke, ed., *Generalizing from Laboratory to Field Settings*, pp. 100–17. Lexington, Mass.: Lexington Books.

27. Latham, G.P., & Locke, E. (1979). "Goal Setting—A Motivational Technique that Works." *Organizational Dynamics, 8*(2), 68–80.

28. Locke, E.A., & Latham, G.P. (1984). *Goal Setting for Individuals, Groups, and Organizations*. Chicago: Science Research Associates.

29. Chhokar, J.S., & Wallin, J.A. (1984). "A field study of the effects of feedback frequency on performance." *Journal of Applied Psychology, 69*, 524–30.

30. Pritchard, R.D., Jones, S.D., Roth, P.L., Stuebing, K.K., & Ekeberg, S.E. (1988). "Effects of Group Feedback, Goal Setting, and Incentives on Organizational Productivity." *Journal of Applied Psychology, 73*, 337–58.

31. Herzberg, F. (1976). *The Managerial Choice*. Homewood, Ill.: Dow Jones–Irwin.

32. Hackman, J.R. (1976). "Work design." In J.R. Hackman and J.L. Suttle, eds., *Improving Life at Work*. Santa Monica, Calif.: Goodyear.

33. Gyllenhammar, P.G. (1977). *People at Work*. Reading, Mass.: Addison-Wesley.

34. Orpen, C. (1979). "The Effects of Job Enrichment on Employee Satisfaction, Motivation, Involvement, and Performance: A Field Experiment." *Human Relations, 32*, 189–217.

35. Luthans, F., & Kreitner, R. (1975). *Organizational Behavior Modification*. Glenview, Ill.: Scott, Foresman.

36. Luthans, F., Paul, R., & Baker, D. (1981). "An Experimental Analysis of the Impact of a Contingent Reinforcement Intervention on Salespersons' Performance Behaviors." *Journal of Applied Psychology*, 1981, 66, 314–323.

ADDITIONAL CASES AND EXERCISES: APPLYING WHAT YOU'VE LEARNED

The Withdrawn Professor

Bob Kemper
Associate Professor of Management
Northern Arizona University

Stuart Monroe
Monroe Consulting
Flagstaff, Arizona

Clyde Howard reaches across his desk and grabs a file folder. He makes sure it is the official personnel file of Dr. Edward Norvell. It is. He looks at the clock on the wall. It is 10:50 A.M. In ten minutes Clyde will be meeting with Dr. Norvell, assistant professor of engineering, and Bill Bradford, president of the Associated Students of Engineering. Clyde has mixed feelings about the scheduled meeting. He is especially worried about his colleague, Ed Norvell.

As dean of the engineering department at Prairie State University, Clyde knows Ed Norvell to be an outstanding instructor. Only six months ago, a department of engineering faculty teaching evaluation committee, as part of the annual faculty evaluation process, rated Dr. Norvell as "outstanding." As Clyde scans through Dr. Norvell's file he is reminded that Ed has been cited as "outstanding" twice in three years by the committee. On page four of the file, he is reminded that Dr. Norvell was awarded the department's "Professor of the Year" award.

Clyde recalls the standing ovation Ed was given at the engineering college's annual award banquet just two years ago. He remembers Ed and his wife, Linda, as they jointly accepted Ed's award. Ed and Linda—young, motivated, bright-eyed, and dedicated. This is how Clyde prefers to remember Ed and Linda.

Today Clyde is worried about Ed. Five months ago Linda died while giving birth to Ed's second son. Now, some faculty and most students insist that Ed should be forced out of the classroom—at least temporarily. They cite the "no office hours policy," disorganized lectures, unwillingness to go over examination questions, and frequent tardiness as reasons for replacing Ed.

The once sympathetic students are now demanding that university officials appoint other faculty members to cover Dr. Norvell's classes. Students see Dr. Norvell's classes as stepping stones to other engineering courses and they fear that Dr. Norvell's current teaching activity will leave them unprepared for more advanced courses. They feel that although Dr. Norvell gives passing grades to everyone, they may not be gaining the basic knowledge that is necessary for engineers faced with new technological advances.

Clyde has been sympathetic to the student demands. However, he believes his hands are tied—Dr. Norvell will not accept help, will not allow anyone else to teach "his courses," will not allow anyone to finish an important research contract for the University, and will not take an offered paid leave of absence. In fact, when university officials previously attempted to counsel Dr. Norvell, he stopped talking. He simply "does not want to talk about this situation." Ed's last meeting with officials ended when he stated, "If you don't like the way I do research and the way I teach, fire me!"

Dr. Howard believes that Dr. Norvell just needs time to adjust to his wife's death and to his new situation; he continues to prefer that Dr. Norvell be allowed to work out his problems on his own, even though it may take another semester for this to happen.

It is now 11 A.M.—time for Ed and Bill to enter the office. Bill will be asking Clyde and Ed what can be done to salvage Dr. Norvell's courses and research. Clyde will be forced to negotiate a satisfactory solution on behalf of the university and its students. Clyde has alerted the president of Prairie State University to the situation and has been instructed to take any action necessary to get the situation settled.

Questions

1. What changed? Was it Ed's performance and motivation after his wife's death? (Use Maslow's theory, EGR theory, Herzberg's theory, expectancy theory, and equity theory to explain your answers.)

2. Why is Ed unwilling to talk about the situation? Why is he willing to challenge Clyde to fire him when confronted about his behavior?

3. What steps could Ed take to improve his academic performance? (Use the chapter's theories and motivation methods to explain your answer.)

4. What steps could Clyde take to enhance Ed's academic performance? (Use MBO, job enrichment, and behavior modification methods to determine the steps.)

5. What do you recommend Clyde do with (a) student complaints and (b) Ed? Why do you recommend these courses of action?

The Power of Positive Reinforcement: A First-hand Look

Why do people say the things they do? Your initial answer is probably something like "because they want to communicate with others," or perhaps "because they want to influence the people around them." Both of these answers are true, and people do often make verbal statements for these reasons. But there is another factor that strongly affects what they (and we) say: the reactions of persons around them. For example, imagine that you make some statement and everyone nearby reacts with shock and disapproval. Clearly, you may be less likely to make the same or a similar statement again. Or, imagine that you utter some words and everyone nearby voices approval and pleasure. In this case, your tendency to repeat such phrases may be strengthened. In short, operant conditioning, too, may play a key role in determining what thoughts we choose to state out loud, and what thoughts we choose to keep to ourselves.

You can readily demonstrate this basic fact, and so gain first-hand experience with the power of positive reinforcement. All you need is the cooperation of a friend who has not taken a course in human relations or psychology, and a piece of paper with the numbers 1 to 100 written on it. Tell your friend that you are conducting a simple study of language, and that you want her to construct 100

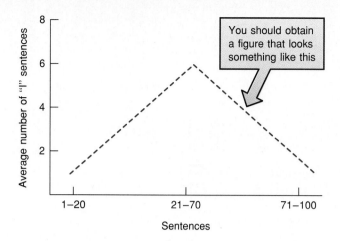

You should obtain a figure that looks something like this

different sentences, one at a time. Seat your subject in a comfortable chair, and let her begin. (Be sure to place yourself outside her field of view, so that you cannot provide any clues through smiles, nods, and so on.) For the first twenty sentences, simply sit quietly. Then beginning with sentence twenty-one, and continuing for the next fifty, say "mm-hmm" in as natural a voice as possible each time your subject starts with the word "I." Each time she does, place a check next to the corresponding number on your sheet of paper. Because that sound "mm-hmm" signifies approval to most people, your subject will probably show an increasing use of "I" sentences during this period. Then, for the last thirty sentences, stop providing this verbal reinforcement. Once the "mm-hmm" is removed, your subject will probably show a gradual drop in the use of sentences beginning with "I."

To see if these effects have occurred, simply go back and count the number of "I" sentences during the first twenty. Now, divide by two to get the average number in each ten sentences. Next, count the number of "I" sentences between sentence twenty-one and sentence seventy. Then divide by five. Finally count the number of "I" sentences for trials seventy-one through one hundred; divide by three. If you plot the numbers you find in the graph above, you should attain a pattern resembling an upside-down letter V.

Now stop and think for a moment: If merely uttering the sound "mm-hmm" can affect what another person says, imagine how much stronger the impact of praise, approval, and other forms of verbal reinforcement can be. This is truly what we mean by the phrase "the power of positive reinforcement!"

Personality: Understanding How and Why Individuals Differ

Study

Learning Objectives

After reading this chapter,
you should be able to:

1. Define personality and indicate why it is relevant to human relations.

2. Describe Freud's psychoanalytic theory and the learning-oriented approach to personality.

3. Summarize the major characteristics of Type A and Type B individuals, and indicate how these affect their work and personal lives.

4. Mention some key traits and beliefs of Machiavellian persons, and list several tactics for defending yourself against them.

5. Explain how achievement, power, and affiliation motivation influence organizational behavior.

6. Discuss the characteristics of people with social skills.

7. Explain what the self-concept is, how it develops, and why it often operates in a self-fulfilling manner.

ohn and Sue Alexander were relaxing over their Friday night dinner. This was a treat they looked forward to after surviving another week at work. Sue managed the sports department at a large department store and John was an engineer for a computer manufacturer.

"I sure had some strange people in today," mused Sue.

"Why, did you have some engineers stopping by," joked John.

"No," laughed Sue, "I seem to get a lot of these high level executives. They're always in a hurry on their lunch hour looking for the latest sports equipment. It seems like their favorite sport is racquetball. Maybe they can vent their frustrations that way. One of them put up a big fuss because we didn't carry her favorite line of equipment. I'd be surprised if these people don't drop dead from a heart attack one of these days."

"I don't think I could take being around these types of people," John said. "I work with some strange characters too, but at least they're a little less easily frustrated. I guess in my line of work, you have to be pretty patient, since it usually takes a while to figure things out. What bothers me about the people in my group is that they are mostly concerned with pleasing the boss. It seems that only Larry Rupp and I stand up to the bosses every once in a while."

"Well, maybe we should trade people," said Sue. "I could use a few more agreeable people at work."

"That's a deal," laughed John.

It takes all types to make the world go round but sometimes we may run into too many of one type. This apparently happened to Sue and John. You yourself may have had similar experiences. Some jobs or places seem to attract certain types of people. Yet even at a particular job, there is likely to be a variety of types of people. In this chapter we will focus on some of the major dimensions of **personality** along which people differ.[1] As we will see, personality may have strong impact on human relations.

But making this statement is one thing; following through on it is another. As you probably realize, human beings differ from one another in what seems to be a limitless number of ways—everything from purely physical traits such as height or eye color, through complex attitudes and values. Because of this, a logical question arises: Which of these many kinds of differences are most important—most worthy of our attention? All are certainly of *some* interest, but many experts currently feel that from the perspective of human relations, differences in personality are among the most crucial. In short, they believe that understanding how individuals differ with respect to lasting traits, characteristics, and behaviors can yield important practical benefits.

In keeping with this view, this chapter focuses on several aspects of personality.

First, it considers a few contrasting *theories of personality*—grand and sweeping efforts to account for a wide range of differences between individuals. Second, it examines key *work-related traits*—traits that seem to exert an important effect on human behavior and human relations in work settings. Third, it discusses the role of various motives and social skills on behavior in work settings. Finally, it addresses both the nature and impact of the *self-concept*—each individual's private picture of his or her own unique pattern of traits.

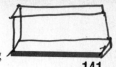

141
THEORIES OF
PERSONALITY: WIDE-
ANGLE VIEWS OF
THE NATURE
OF INDIVIDUAL
DIFFERENCES

THEORIES OF PERSONALITY: WIDE-ANGLE VIEWS OF THE NATURE OF INDIVIDUAL DIFFERENCES

Why do human beings behave as they do? What accounts for their individuality and uniqueness? How does personality develop and grow over time? It is to answer questions such as these that broad and sweeping theories of personality are constructed. And building such frameworks has been a popular task. Indeed, at present dozens (perhaps even hundreds) of such theories exist. For this reason, describing even a small sample of these views is totally out of the question. While we cannot undertake this task, we can at least acquaint you with three approaches that have gained widespread acceptance and remain influential today. These are Sigmund Freud's **psychoanalytic theory, learning-oriented theories** of personality, and the **humanistic perspective.**

Freud's View of Personality: In Search of Hidden Forces

At this point, you may be thinking, *Ah Freud, you old devil, I knew you'd turn up somewhere in this book; you always do. But why do I have to read about you once again, even in a text on human relations?* This is a reasonable question and you have every right to ask it. But the answer, too, is quite straightforward: Freud's views about personality and human behavior have been tremendously influential. In fact, they have been absorbed into the basic fiber of Western culture. As a result, ideas first stated by Freud are now often voiced (and accepted) by persons who do not recognize their source. Thus you are almost as likely to meet assumptions about human nature derived from Freud's thought in corporate board-rooms as in a psychiatrist's office. For these reasons, it is probably useful for you to have a clear idea of some of his basic proposals. Freud's theory, of course, is complex and is not easy to summarize in a few short pages. However, he felt that full understanding of human behavior must involve attention to three basic topics: *levels of consciousness, major structures of personality,* and the *role of early experiences.* Thus we will focus on these key aspects of his thought.

Levels of Consciousness   As the captain of the ill-fated Titanic discovered, most of an iceberg lies hidden beneath the surface of the sea; only a small portion is visible. According to Freud, the human mind has a similar structure. Above the surface, and readily open to our mental inspection, is the *conscious.* This includes

142
CHAPTER 5
PERSONALITY:
UNDERSTANDING
HOW AND WHY
INDIVIDUALS DIFFER

our current thoughts—whatever we are thinking about at a given moment. Beneath the conscious is the *preconscious*. This portion of the mind includes memories that are not currently in our thoughts but that can be brought to mind if the need arises. Finally, under the preconscious, and forming the bulk of the mind, is the *unconscious*—thoughts, desires, and urges of which we remain largely unaware. According to Freud, some material here was always unconscious. But a large portion of it was *repressed*—thrust out of consciousness because it was anxiety-provoking (e.g., unacceptable sexual desires, shameful experiences). The key point to remember about all of this is: Because many thoughts, fears, motives, and impulses are unconscious, it is often difficult for us to identify the actual causes behind our own or others' behavior. Thus, in this respect at least, there is often much more to personality than at first meets the eye.

The Building Blocks of Personality: Id, Ego, and Superego   Have you ever seen a cartoon in which one of the characters is urged by his "good self" to take one course of action and by his "bad self" to take another? If so, you already have a rough idea of some of the major structures of personality described by Freud. Briefly, Freud proposed that personality consists of three major parts: **id, ego, and superego.** As we will now see, he could actually have used the words "desire," "reason," and "conscience" instead, for these are the aspects of behavior to which his colorful terms refer.

To begin at the beginning, the *id* (desire) can be viewed as the motor or energy of human personality. It consists of our primitive, innate urges for gratification of various needs. According to Freud, the id is totally unconscious and operates in accordance with the *pleasure principle*—the demand for immediate gratification. Unfortunately, of course, such outcomes are usually available only in our dreams or fantasies; frustration is a far more common experience than instant, total fulfillment of all our desires.

It is out of this sad fact that the *ego* develops. Basically, the task of this structure is that of mediating between the wild desires of the id and the demands of reality. The ego operates in accordance with what Freud termed the *reality principle,* holding the impulses of the id in check until conditions are appropriate for their satisfaction. Only then is gratification permitted. As you can readily guess, the ego is partly conscious. But please note that it is not entirely so. In fact, according to Freud, none of the structures of personality operate solely at the level of consciousness.

The final structure described by Freud is the *superego*. This, too, controls satisfaction of id impulses, permitting their fulfillment only under certain circumstances. In contrast to the ego, though, the superego is concerned with *morality*. That is, it can tell "right" from "wrong." Thus the superego permits gratification of id impulses only when this is morally correct—not simply when it is safe or convenient, as required by the ego. For example, the superego might prevent an ambitious young man from spreading a malicious (and false) rumor about a rival, even though doing so will help him gain the promotion he is seeking. Similarly, it might prevent a saleswoman from providing false information to a potential customer, even though this may cost her a large commission. In short, even when conditions are such that we *could* get what we want, the superego may intervene and prevent us from doing so because such actions would be "wrong." If you have ever struggled with your own conscience—and lost—you know how unbending, persuasive, and harsh a superego can be.

The three basic structures of personality outlined by Freud, as well as the major functions they perform and the rules by which they operate, are summarized in Figure 5.1. Please examine it carefully before proceeding.

143
THEORIES OF
PERSONALITY: WIDE-
ANGLE VIEWS OF
THE NATURE
OF INDIVIDUAL
DIFFERENCES

The Importance of Early Experience   Freud believed that during our development as children, we are constantly confronted with a variety of conflicts among the id, ego, and superego. How these conflicts are handled by our parents and ourselves have important implications for our personality development. Thus Freud believed that early experiences are important in shaping our adult personalities (see Figure 5.2). For example, people whose desires for food and drink were constantly attended to by their parents (possibly to the point of overfeeding) when they were children may come to expect others to be similarly attentive to their needs as adults. These people may prefer jobs in which they are told what to do and do not need to show much initiative. Although many of the specific aspects of Freud's theory remain subject to criticism and lack research support, the role of early experiences has received strong support from learning-oriented theories of personality.

FIGURE 5.1 Personality: Freud's View of Its Basic Nature
Freud believed that in order to comprehend human personality, we must understand its three major components: id, ego, superego. The nature and functions of each of these structures are illustrated here.

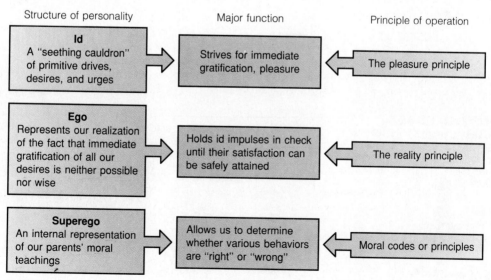

144

CHAPTER 5
PERSONALITY:
UNDERSTANDING
HOW AND WHY
INDIVIDUALS DIFFER

Learning-Oriented Theories of Personality: Experience as a Basis for Uniqueness

According to Freud, the key to understanding human personality lies in comprehending hidden, inner struggles between the id, ego, and superego. As we noted earlier, this view has gained widespread acceptance. But it has certainly *not* gone unchallenged. Other theories have adopted a radically different approach to understanding the nature and development of personality. In brief, they suggest that the key to understanding both the uniqueness of human beings and their possession of lasting, stable traits lies in a basic behavioral process: learning.[2]

In order to explain this approach adequately, we must first indicate what is meant by **learning.** Generally, it refers to any fairly permanent change in behavior induced through experience. Thus any time your behavior is altered in a relatively lasting way by some experience you have had—some interaction with the social or physical world around you—learning has occurred. But how can this basic process account for the development of each of the hundreds of specific traits human beings possess? The answer is slightly complicated, because several types of learning exist, and each of these can play a more or less important role with respect to any given trait. Perhaps it will be useful to consider two of these, to see how they might contribute to the uniqueness of each individual's personality.

The first type of learning, generally known as *operant conditioning,* occurs when individuals learn to perform behaviors that yield desirable outcomes (e.g., praise, money, success) or when they learn to perform actions that help them avoid undesirable results (e.g., failure, cold, hunger).[3] Operant conditioning is common, and it plays an important role in the formation of many traits. To see how this is so, consider two children. One is consistently praised by her parents for showing ambition and initiative. The other is consistently criticized for competing with others or trying to "show them up." How will they differ as adults?

FIGURE 5.2 Childhood Experiences: Important but Not Always Remembered
According to Freud's psychoanalytic theory, to understand ourselves as adults, we must understand our childhood experiences. Of course this may be easier said than done, as demonstrated by Calvin and Hobbes. (Calvin and Hobbes © 1989 Universal Press Syndicate. Reprinted with permission. All rights reserved.)

Many factors contribute to the answer, but the chances are good the first child will be competitive and high in achievement motivation, while the second will be passive and unambitious (see Figure 5.3).

A second type of learning that may also contribute to the formation of personality is known as *modeling* (or *observational learning*). Here, the behavior of one individual is changed in a lasting manner through exposure to the actions of one or more other persons. Such learning seems to play an important role in the development of a wide range of traits—everything from aggressiveness and bigotry on the one hand to altruism and generosity on the other.[4] Moreover, it can operate even when the persons being observed have no intention of influencing the individuals who watch them (e.g., young children). For example, bigoted adults who demonstrate negative feelings toward the members of certain minority groups may encourage similar reactions on the part of children even if the adults state that they "disapprove" of prejudice. In such cases, actions do indeed seem to speak louder than words!

In these and other ways, various forms of learning may underlie even complex human traits. People, it now appears, are strongly shaped or molded by their experiences. Thus it may be the sum total of these effects that constitutes the underlying foundations of personality.

Humanistic Theories of Personality: Accent on Growth

At first glance, Freud's theory and the learning-oriented approach probably strike you as completely different. In fact, they *do* contrast sharply in language and specific content. Yet, if we dig just beneath the surface, a surprising fact emerges: Both share a common theme. According to each of these perspectives,

FIGURE 5.3 Learning: Its Impact on One Important Trait
One child (top panel) is praised by her parents for showing ambition. Another (bottom panel) is criticized for showing such behavior. Because of *operant conditioning,* the first becomes ambitious and achievement-oriented, while the other shows opposite behavior.

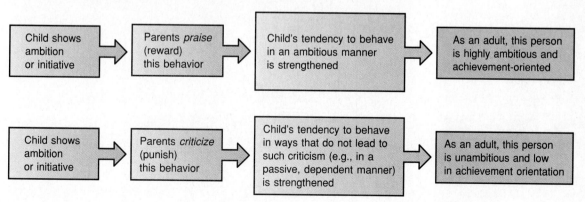

146

CHAPTER 5
PERSONALITY:
UNDERSTANDING
HOW AND WHY
INDIVIDUALS DIFFER

human behavior is strongly shaped by specific internal and external factors. Freud suggests that the most important of these involve inner conflicts, primitive instincts, and hidden motives. Learning theory, in contrast, emphasizes the importance of past experience and basic processes of learning. Yet, both theories view behavior as largely *determined* by specific, identifiable factors. In this regard, they both go a long way toward abolishing the concept of free will. Why do people act as they do? The answer offered by Freud and learning theorists alike is this: Because they are pushed or directed to do so by a wide range of causal factors. Notions of choice, rational thought, or personal freedom do not enter into the picture.

Disturbed by what they viewed as an overly mechanistic approach to human behavior, a third group of theorists adopted a sharply different view of personality known as the **humanistic perspective.**[5] Two points are central to this approach. First, humanistic theorists propose that, contrary to what Freud and learning-oriented theories contend, human behavior is *not* totally determined by internal and external factors. Instead, it is shaped, in part, by personal choice and each individual's subjective view of the world and his or her own experience in it. Second, humanistic theories place great emphasis on positive aspects of personality. They suggest that human beings possess strong tendencies toward growth, and are actively motivated to maximize their personal freedom and potential (see Figure 5.4). Only when environmental conditions block these growth tendencies do personal difficulties arise.

These ideas have been quite influential and have exerted a strong effect on

FIGURE 5.4 Humanistic Perspective: There Are Many Reasons for Living
Humanistic theories emphasize that human beings possess strong tendencies toward personal choice, freedom, and growth. Do you think Ziggy is a humanist? (Ziggy © Ziggy & Friends. Distributed by Universal Press Syndicate. Reprinted with permission. All rights reserved.)

the field of human relations. Thus we will return to them—and to specific humanistic theories—at several points in this book. (We have already considered one such theory, Maslow's need hierarchy, in Chapter 4.) At the moment, we will simply call attention to some major implications of this viewpoint. First, according to the humanistic approach, we cannot hope to understand specific persons or predict their behavior from knowledge of the objective conditions around them. This is helpful, but is not enough. We must also understand their subjective point of view—how *they* interpret and understand their experiences. Second, and perhaps more important, the humanistic perspective is very optimistic with respect to the capacity of human beings to accept responsibility, acquire new skills, and behave in constructive ways. Since individuals are strongly motivated to attain maximum growth and freedom, they will, if given half a chance, continue to improve in many different ways. In short, the humanistic approach is highly consistent with Theory Y or the human resources model described in Chapter 1. Little wonder, then, that it is accepted (at least in part) by many members of our field.

PERSONALITY: ITS IMPACT IN WORK SETTINGS

During your career, you will encounter hundreds of people. These individuals will differ from one another on countless dimensions—all the ones you can think of now, plus many others that are sure to take you by surprise. Obviously, though, not all of these differences are related to behavior or human relations in work settings. Only some are of major importance in this regard. But which ones? Actually, this is a tricky question, for the specific traits or characteristics that are of greatest importance can vary widely with the type of work being performed. For example, having an outgoing, friendly personality may be closely linked to success in the field of sales, but probably has far less impact on performance as an accountant. Similarly, a good ability to estimate length or weight may contribute to success among carpenters, but has little bearing on the productivity of librarians. Some traits, though, do seem to exert important effects on work-related behavior in a wide range of contexts. It is on these that we will focus here. Specifically, we will examine the nature and impact of two intriguing traits: the **Type A–Type B** dimension and **Machiavellianism.** Then we will discuss differences in **work-related motives** and **social skills.** An additional characteristic—**self-esteem**—will be considered in our discussion of the **self-concept.**

The Type A–Type B Dimension: Who Succeeds—and Who Survives

Think back over all the persons you have known. Can you recall someone who always seemed to work under great pressure, was hard-driving and com-

148

CHAPTER 5
PERSONALITY:
UNDERSTANDING
HOW AND WHY
INDIVIDUALS DIFFER

petitive, and who was both impatient and aggressive? Now, in contrast, try to think of someone who showed the opposite pattern—an individual who was generally relaxed and easy-going, sociable, and not very competitive. The two persons you now have in mind represent contrasting patterns of behavior labeled, respectively, **Type A** and **Type B**[6] (see Figure 5.5). While these are clearly extremes on a continuous dimension, it appears that most people actually fall into one category or the other.[7] Specifically, about 40 percent of the population is Type A and 60 percent is Type B.

FIGURE 5.5   Type A and Type B: Drastic Differences in Style
Which of these men is likely to be a Type A and which a Type B? What personal characteristics are evident from these pictures?

Obviously, the differences between Type A and Type B persons have important implications for behavior in work settings. For example, hard-driving, competitive individuals would be expected to act differently than relaxed, easy-going individuals while performing many jobs. As we shall see, this is in fact the case. But Type A and Type B persons also differ in other key respects that are perhaps less apparent. The most important of these involve personal health and social relations.

The Type A Pattern and Health   Actually, initial research interest in the Type A–Type B dimension was begun by an unsettling finding: Persons showing the Type A cluster of traits are more than twice as likely as those showing the Type B cluster to experience serious heart disease.[8] Further, they are also more likely to suffer a second heart attack if the first one is not fatal. In short, Type A individuals appear to pay a high price for their hard-driving, high-pressure lifestyle.

Additional findings help explain why Type A individuals are more likely to experience serious heart disease than Type B's. Quite simply, they seem to respond to stress with more pronounced physiological reactions than Type B's.[9] This fact is illustrated clearly in an investigation by Hill and her colleagues.[10] These researchers studied the behavior of first-year medical students at three times: during a vacation period, during a stressful examination period, and again during a second vacation period. They found that several of the typical components of Type A behavior described above (e.g., loud, explosive speech, short response latency) increased among Type A's during the high-stress exam period (see Figure 5.6). Type A's also showed larger increases than Type B's in resting heart rate during the examination period. It appears that during periods of stress, Type A's subject their cardiovascular systems to greater "wear-and-tear." Since the competitive, hard-driving style of Type A's often leads them to *seek* stress-induced challenge, it is not surprising that their health then suffers.

The Type A Pattern and Interpersonal Relations   In addition to differences in personal health and task performance, Type A and Type B persons also demonstrate contrasting styles of interpersonal behavior. First, because they are always in a hurry, Type As tend to become impatient with other persons, and frequently grow angry if others delay them in any way. Second, when given a choice, Type As prefer to work by themselves rather than with others. They are definitely loners, not team players. Third, Type As are more irritable and aggressive than Type Bs. They lose their tempers frequently, and are more likely to lash out at others for even slight provocations.[11] As a result of these tendencies, Type As report becoming involved in more conflicts at work than Type Bs. In one recent study on this issue, Baron asked managers at a large food-processing company to indicate the frequency with which they experience conflict with subordinates, peers, and supervisors.[12] As you can see from Table 5.1, those classified as Type A reported a significantly higher frequency of conflict than those classified as

150
CHAPTER 5
PERSONALITY:
UNDERSTANDING
HOW AND WHY
INDIVIDUALS DIFFER

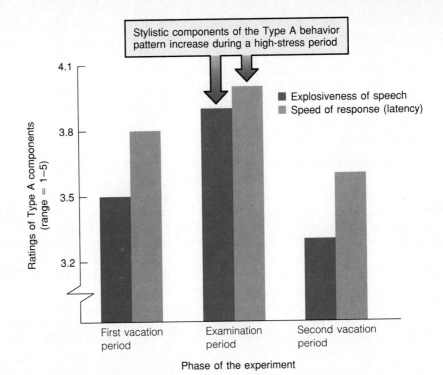

FIGURE 5.6 Type A Behavior Under Stress Increased in Intensity
First-year medical students classified as Type A showed more components of the Type A behavior patterns during a high-stress examination period than during vacation periods that preceded and followed such stress. (*Source:* Based on data from Hill et al. (1987); see Note 10.)

TABLE 5.1
Conflict and the Type A Behavior Pattern: A Difference in Style

Type A managers report a higher incidence of conflict (on a 7-point scale) than other managers with subordinates and peers. Type A managers also report a slightly higher incidence of conflict with supervisors. (*Source:* Based on data from Baron (1989); see Note 12.)

	Type B	Indeterminate	Type A
Subordinates	2.45	3.21	3.49
Peers	2.45	3.19	3.00
Supervisors	2.77	2.41	2.75

Type B, or managers who did not fall clearly into either category. Clearly, several characteristics of Type As seem to get them into more than their share of interpersonal difficulties at work.

The Type A Pattern and Performance   It was noted earlier that Type A and Type B persons differ with respect to performance. Here, we return to this important point. At first, you might expect such differences to be quite simple. Specifically, you might guess that Type As, with their hard-driving, competitive style will always (or at least usually) surpass Type Bs.[13] In fact, the situation is much more complex. On the one hand, it is true that Type As work faster on many tasks than Type Bs, even when no pressure or deadline is involved. And Type As often seek more challenge in their work and daily lives than Type Bs. For example, when given a choice, they select more difficult tasks than Type Bs.[14] On the other hand, there appear to be situations in which Type Bs—not Type As—have the edge. For example, Type As frequently do worse on tasks requiring patience or careful, considered judgment.[15] In such cases, they are in too much of a hurry for their own good!

More importantly, surveys reveal that most members of top management are Type Bs, not Type As.[16] Several factors probably contribute to this somewhat surprising finding. First, it is possible that Type As simply do not last long enough to rise to the very highest management levels—the health risks described above tend to remove them from contention at an early age! Second, it is also possible that the impatient, always-in-a-hurry tendencies of Type As are incompatible with the skills needed by top-level executives. As you know, one of the key functions performed by such persons is decision-making; and the decisions involved are far from simple. In order to make them effectively, executives must weigh and consider a huge amount of information. Type As, because of their tendency to "rush, rush, rush!" do not appear well-suited for such tasks. Finally, the impatient, aggressive style of Type As may lead them to make many enemies, a factor that can count heavily against them when the possibility of promotion to top-level jobs arises.

In sum, available evidence suggests that Type As tend to do better than Type Bs on some tasks, especially those involving time pressure or solitary work. However, they may actually do worse than Type Bs on tasks involving complex judgment, accuracy rather than speed, and working as part of a team. Thus neither pattern appears to have an overall advantage over the other. Rather, the nature of the tasks to be performed may be crucial in determining whether Type As or Type Bs will excel. (To find out whether you are a Type A or a Type B, consult the **Human Relations in Action** on page 152.)

Machiavellianism: Manipulating Others as a Way of Life

In 1513 an Italian philosopher named Niccolo Machiavelli (see Figure 5.7) write a book entitled, *The Prince*. In it he outlined a general strategy for seizing

HUMAN RELATIONS IN ACTION

Are You a Type A or a Type B? A Quick Self-Assessment

Now that we have considered the Type A–Type B dimension and pointed out some of its consequences, you may find it interesting to discover where you stand on this dimension. You can do this by responding to the questions below. For each, simply circle the choice that seems most appropriate for you.

1. Is your everyday life filled mostly by:
   a. Problems needing solution
   b. Challenges needing to be met
   c. A rather predictable routine of events
   d. Not enough things to keep you interested or busy
2. When you are under pressure or stress, do you usually:
   a. Do something about it immediately
   b. Plan carefully before taking any action
3. Ordinarily, how rapidly do you eat?
   a. I'm usually the first one finished
   b. I eat a little faster than average
   c. I eat at about the same speed as most people
   d. I eat more slowly than most people
4. When you listen to someone talking, and this person takes too long to come to the point, do you feel like hurrying him or her along?
   a. Frequently
   b. Occasionally
   c. Almost never
5. Do most people consider you to be:
   a. Definitely hard-driving and competitive
   b. Probably hard-driving and competitive
   c. Probably more relaxed and easy going
   d. Definitely more relaxed and easy going
6. Would people who know you well agree that you have less energy than most people?
   a. Definitely yes
   b. Probably yes
   c. Probably no
   d. Definitely no
7. Do you ever set deadlines or quotas for yourself in courses or other things?
   a. No
   b. Yes, but only occasionally
   c. Yes, at least once a week
8. Do you maintain a regular study schedule during vacations such as Thanksgiving, Christmas, and Easter?
   a. Yes
   b. No
   c. Sometimes

9. When you are in a group, do the other people tend to look to you to provide leadership?
   a. Rarely
   b. About as often as they look to others
   c. More often than they look to others
10. Compared with the average student at this school, I am:
    a. Much more responsible
    b. A little more responsible
    c. A little less responsible
    d. Much less responsible

To obtain your score, follow the key shown in Table 5.2. Add one point each time your answer to a given item agrees with the answer(s) shown in the key.

If you scored 7 or higher, you can consider yourself Type A. In contrast, if you scored 3 or below, you are probably Type B. (If you scored between 4 and 6, you are average on this dimension, and not clearly Type A or Type B.) In interpreting your score on this dimension, please keep two facts in mind. First, there are both advantages and disadvantages associated with being either Type A or Type B. Thus, which you prefer is largely a matter of individual taste and personal goals. Second, as is true of most aspects of personality, some degree of change is possible. If you are currently Type A but wish to shift toward the Type B end of the dimension, you can do so. In fact practical techniques for accomplishing this goal have already been developed. So, if you believe you may profit from this kind of change, please see your instructor; she or he can probably put you in touch with individuals trained to help you in this respect.

TABLE 5.2

For each item, give yourself one point if you chose the answer shown here. Please note: In some cases, more than one answer should receive a point. Compute your total score adding all your points.

Item	Choice
1	a, b
2	a
3	a, b
4	a
5	a, b
6	d
7	c
8	a
9	c
10	a

154

CHAPTER 5
PERSONALITY:
UNDERSTANDING
HOW AND WHY
INDIVIDUALS DIFFER

FIGURE 5.7   Machiavelli: The Great Manipulator
Niccolo Machiavelli became famous for his strategies on how to manipulate people.

and holding political power. The basic idea behind this approach was simple: Other people can readily be manipulated, or used for our own purposes, if we stick to a few basic rules. Among the guiding principles he recommended were: (1) Break your word to others whenever it suits you or helps you reach your goals; (2) Never show humility—only great confidence (or even arrogance) is helpful; (3) It is much better to be feared than loved. In more general terms, Machiavelli urged those who desired power to adopt a totally cold and pragmatic approach to life. Let other people be moved by friendship, loyalty, or morality, he suggested. A truly successful leader should always be above such influences. Primarily, he or she should be willing to *do whatever is needed to get his or her way*.

Machiavelli and the rulers he advised are long departed. But the basic ideas he proposed are still very much alive. In fact, they are readily visible in several books that have recently made their way onto the bestseller lists—volumes such as Korda's *Power: How to Use It*, and Ringer's *Winning through Intimidation*. The existence of these and related books suggests that people are as fascinated by Machiavelli's approach today as they were in the early 1500s.

But it is one thing to be intrigued by such tactics, and quite another to put them to practical use. *Surely*, you may now be thinking, *very few people could ever live by the ruthless, self-centered creed proposed by Machiavelli*. While this is a comforting thought, it is not supported by modern research.[17,18] When large numbers of persons complete a test designed to measure acceptance of a Machiavellian approach to life (the *Mach Scale*), many receive high scores. That is, many indicate strong acceptance of the ruthless code of behavior Machiavelli recommended. Such persons are often described as *High Machs* (short for High Machiavellians) and, unfortunately, they are not rare. In fact, High Machs have been identified among children as young as ten years of age![19] Given the relatively high frequency of High Mach persons, you are almost certain to encounter one or more in your own career. For this reason, it is important for you to understand how such individuals operate—how they attempt to manipulate others for their own gain—and how you can protect yourself against them. It is on these points that we will now focus.

High Machs: How They Operate   How do High Machs "do their thing"? How do they succeed in manipulating others and using them for their own ends? Several factors seem to play a role in this regard. First, High Machs follow Machiavelli's advice about being *pragmatic*. As far as they are concerned, any means is justified so long as it helps them toward their goals. Thus they are perfectly willing to lie, cheat, play "dirty tricks," or engage in virtually any actions that succeed (refer to our discussion of organizational politics in Chapter 7). Second, High Machs often possess characteristics associated with success in persuading others. They are confident, eloquent, and competent. When these traits are combined with their pure pragmatism, the result can be quite devastating. Third, High Machs are often very adept at choosing situations in which their preferred tactics are most likely to work. Such situations are ones in which they can interact face-to-face with the persons they intend to manipulate, in which there are few clear rules, and in which others' emotions are running high. Since High Machs themselves never let their hearts rule their heads, they can take full advantage of the fact that others' emotions make them especially vulnerable to manipulation. Finally, High Machs are skilled at various political maneuvers, such as forming coalitions with others. And as you might expect, in these coalitions, most of the advantages are theirs.

At this point, you may find it interesting to consider a brief description of High Machs in operation. In a well-known study, ten one-dollar bills were placed on a table in front of a group of three subjects.[20] These persons were told the money would belong to any two of them who agreed on how to divide it; the third individual would be totally "cut out." One of the three persons in each group was a High Mach, one was a Low Mach, and the other was in between. Who do you think did best? As you see from Figure 5.8, the High Machs won hands down. In fact, they obtained several times as much as the Low Mach players. They did this in ways you might expect: by lying to the other players (e.g., promising each more than they intended to deliver), by playing one off against the other, and by pretending to care about their partner's winnings when, in fact, this was of no interest to them at all.

High Machs: Defending Yourself against Them   By now, you may be discouraged. We've noted that High Machs exist and are far from rare. We've described their

156

CHAPTER 5

PERSONALITY:
UNDERSTANDING
HOW AND WHY
INDIVIDUALS DIFFER

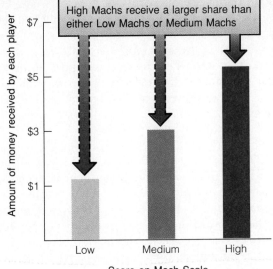

FIGURE 5.8 High Machs: One Demonstration of Their Skill

In a clever demonstration of the persuasive skills of High Mach persons, ten one-dollar bills were placed in front of groups of three subjects (a High Mach, Medium Mach, and Low Mach). The money would belong to any two of the individuals who could agree on how to divide it. As shown here, High Machs did much better in this situation than either Medium or Low Machs—they walked away with a larger share of the money. (*Source:* Based on data from Christie and Geis, (1970); see Note 20.)

ruthless, cold-blooded approach to human relations. And we've observed that they are usually quite effective in manipulating or persuading others. Does this mean that we must either surrender to them or sink to their level? Fortunately, it does not. There are several techniques that we can use to defend ourselves against even super-High Machs. And most of these, it turns out, are based on the old phrase, "To be forewarned is to be forearmed." In a nutshell, understanding the nature of High Machs, and recognizing their presence, can go a long way toward helping us resist their actions. A few concrete suggestions for putting this general principle to use are outlined below. Please consider them carefully; the career you save may be your own!

1. *Expose them for what they are:* One reason High Machs can get away with breaking promises, lying to others, and so on is that, often their victims choose to remain silent. After all, when one has been "had," one doesn't want to tell the world about it! Don't cooperate in this way—don't be a "good victim." If someone has treated you unfairly, tell others about it. You may ultimately save yourself and your friends a lot of future trouble.

157
WORK-RELATED
MOTIVES:
ACHIEVEMENT,
POWER, AND
AFFILIATION

2. *Pay attention to what others do, not what they say:* High Machs are often masters at deception. They frequently succeed in convincing others that they have their best interests at heart, just when they are busy cutting the ground out from beneath them. While it is often difficult to see through such maneuvers, progress in this direction can often be made by focusing on what others *do* rather than on what they *say.* If their actions suggest that they are cold-bloodedly manipulating the persons around them, even while loudly proclaiming commitment to such principles as loyalty and fair play, the chances are good that they are Machiavellian in orientation and should be carefully avoided.

3. *Avoid situations that give High Machs an edge:* In order to ensure their success, High Machs prefer to operate in certain types of situations—ones in which others' emotions run high and they are uncertain about how to proceed. The reason for this preference is simple: High Machs realize that under such conditions many persons will be distracted and less likely to recognize the fact that they are being manipulated for someone else's gain. It is usually wise, therefore, to avoid such situations. And if this is not possible, at least refrain from making important decisions or commitments in them. Such restraint may make it harder for High Mach persons to use you for their own benefit.

4. *Learn to resist influence:* As we will see in Chapter 7, there are many techniques for resisting influences from others. The better you are at using these, the less likely you are to be manipulated by High Machs.

5. *Learn to exert influence:* This is the other side of the coin. If you become skilled at persuading or influencing others, you can "fight fire with fire"—you can prevent High Machs from influencing you. Of course, the goals behind your efforts at persuasion will almost certainly be more altruistic or humane than those of the High Machs you confront.

WORK-RELATED MOTIVES: ACHIEVEMENT, POWER, AND AFFILIATION

The main theme of this chapter is that people differ greatly and that some of these differences have important effects on behavior in work settings. So far, we have focused on differences in specific traits or characteristics (Type A behavior, Machiavellianism). Here, we will turn to yet another way in which people differ: with respect to certain *motives.* We are confident that you are already well aware of such differences. For example, some people seem to yearn for success. Others concentrate on status; they want to be admired and respected by others. And some individuals seem to be primarily concerned with friendship or love;

158

CHAPTER 5
PERSONALITY:
UNDERSTANDING
HOW AND WHY
INDIVIDUALS DIFFER

pleasant, satisfying relations with others are what they crave most. Do such differences in motivation play a role in work settings? The answer is obvious: They do. Differences with respect to several basic motives can affect performance on many tasks, success in leadership roles, and a wide range of other outcomes. We will now examine the impact of three such motives—**need for achievement, need for power,** and **need for affiliation.**

Achievement Motivation: The Quest for Excellence

As its name suggests, the achievement motivation (sometimes termed the *need for achievement*) relates to the strength of individuals' desire to excel—to succeed at difficult tasks and do them better than others. Persons high in such motivation have several characteristics.[21] First, they are task-oriented in outlook. Their major concern is getting things done and accomplishing concrete goals. Good relations with others are of secondary importance. Second, they tend to prefer situations involving moderate levels of risk or difficulty. In contrast, persons low in achievement motivation tend to prefer situations involving either very low or very high levels of risk. Why this preference for moderate risk among persons high in the achievement motive? Because situations involving moderate risk are ones in which the odds of success are good but are still sufficiently challenging to make the effort worthwhile. Persons low in achievement motivation prefer either very low or high levels of risk because with low risk, they are almost certain to succeed, while with high risk they can attribute failure to external factors. Third, persons high in achievement motivation strongly desire feedback on their performance. This allows them to adjust their goals in terms of current conditions and to know just when, and to what degree, they have succeeded.

Given their strong desire to excel, one would expect that persons high in achievement motivation will attain greater success in their careers than others. To some extent, this is true. Persons high in achievement motivation gain promotions more rapidly than persons low in such motivation, at least early in their careers.[22] However, persons high in achievement motivation may not always be good managers for several reasons. First, persons high in achievement motivation want to do everything themselves—they are reluctant to delegate. This gets them into serious trouble in many organizations. Second, they desire immediate feedback on their work. Often, this is unavailable, and its absence can interfere with their efficiency.

Affiliation and Power Motivation: Two Sides of the Same Coin?

At first glance, the desire to be in charge (power motivation) and the desire to have close, friendly relations with others (*affiliation motivation*) would appear to be unrelated. Yet it seems that the two are often linked. First, consider the question of managerial success. What kind of individuals are most successful in this role? One possibility, suggested by McClelland and Boyatzis is as follows: Persons *high* in power motivation but *low* in affiliation motivation.[23] Such persons will focus on gaining influence over others while at the same time being able to make difficult decisions without worrying unduly about being disliked by their subordinates. Individuals who possess this combination of traits—known as the **leadership motivation pattern** (or LMP) appear to be more effective managers than persons who do not (see Figure 5.9).

It is quite evident that individual differences with respect to several motives are closely linked to important aspects of behavior. The nature of this relationship, however, is far from simple. To understand how individuals' motives influence their job performance or careers, we must take account not only of the motives themselves but also of the combinations or patterns in which they occur, the specific jobs being performed, and the organizational context in which these motives operate. Only when the complex interplay of such factors is given full consideration can knowledge about individuals' motives yield valuable insights into their behavior at work.

SOCIAL SKILLS: INDIVIDUAL DIFFERENCES IN THE ABILITY TO GET ALONG WITH OTHERS

Imagine that you are working with two different people. One is viewed as brilliant and hard-working by most other members of her organization. However, she is also widely disliked and perceived as hard to get along with. The other is viewed as merely competent in job skills and average in effort but is extremely popular with peers, subordinates, and supervisors. Which individual is likely to get the next promotion? The odds are quite good that the second individual will get the nod. It seems that often being liked by others is a much better predictor of success than intellectual brilliance, high motivation, or other desirable qualities. While this may strike you as somewhat unfair, it appears to be a fact of life in most work settings.

Given the above state of affairs, it is important to know what factors determine whether or not a certain person is liked or disliked by others. As indicated in Chapter 6, many factors play a role. One important characteristic is the possession of various *social skills*.[24] These skills involve the ability to communicate effectively with others. People possessing a high level of such skills communicate well and clearly, are perceived as honest and credible, and make very good first impressions.[25] Persons lacking in such skills are relatively poor at interpersonal communication and are perceived negatively by the people around them. In recent years, efforts have been made to identify the basic or most important components of social skills. The results of such research suggest that six are most important: (1) *emotional expressivity*—the ability to express emotions nonverbally (e.g., through facial expressions, gestures); (2) *emotional sensitivity*—the ability to

160
CHAPTER 5
PERSONALITY:
UNDERSTANDING
HOW AND WHY
INDIVIDUALS DIFFER

FIGURE 5.9 Executives: What Are Their Motives?
Donald Trump (Atlantic City, Trump Shuttle) and Lee Iacocca (Chrysler) have been successful as heads of major corporations. How do you think these men measure up on the motives of achievement, power, and affiliation?

"read" the emotional and nonverbal communication of others; (3) *emotional control*—skill in stifling spontaneous expressions when necessary, and skill at feigning emotions that are not really experienced; (4) *social expressivity*—the ability to speak fluently and engage others in social interaction; (5) *social sensitivity*—the ability to understand others' verbal statements, plus general knowledge of social norms (knowing what is considered appropriate in various situations); and (6) *social control*—skill at self-presentation (presenting oneself to others in a positive light) and at playing various social roles (e.g., the respectful subordinate, the caring supervisor). A questionnaire (known as the *Social Skills Inventory*) has been devised by Riggio to measure individual differences in such skills; sample items from it are presented in Table 5.3.[26]

People who are high in these types of social skills are not only liked more than low social skill individuals, but also viewed as more honest and believable, both when telling the truth and when lying, than persons low in social skills.[27] These results suggest that one reason socially skilled individuals are often successful in their careers is that they are trusted more by others, and so are more effective at persuasion. Whatever the precise mechanisms involved, though, one fact is clear: Expressive, articulate, tactful persons have a definite edge in many situations. Fortunately, training programs designed to enhance various social skills exist, and some, at least, appear to be quite effective.[28] Several of these programs are highly popular, and are completed by thousands of persons each year. Participation in them may well prove worthwhile for individuals who suspect that their careers, and personal adjustment, are being hampered by deficits in this important dimension.

SELF-CONCEPT AND SELF-ESTEEM: UNDERSTANDING YOUR OWN PERSONALITY

Suppose that at this moment, you were asked to describe your most important traits—the ones that make you a unique individual and set you apart from all

---

TABLE 5.3
Social Skills: Some Sample Items

Items similar to the ones presented here are used to measure individual differences in social skills. (*Source:* Based on items by Riggio (1986); see Note 24.)

Aspect of Social Skills	Sample Item
Emotional expressivity	I have been told that I have an expressive face.
Emotional sensitivity	I can always tell how people feel about me.
Emotional control	I can hide my real feelings from just about anyone.
Social expressivity	I usually take the first step and introduce myself to strangers.
Social sensitivity	I often worry about making a good impression on others.
Social control	I find it easy to play different roles in different situations.

162

CHAPTER 5
PERSONALITY:
UNDERSTANDING
HOW AND WHY
INDIVIDUALS DIFFEF

the others. Would you find this task difficult? Probably not. The reason for this is simple: By the time we are adults, most of us possess a clearly developed self-concept. That is, we have a stable and (we believe) a fairly accurate picture of our own personalities. We know—or think we know—that we are bright or dull, attractive or unattractive, ambitious or complacent, and so on. Obviously, these images we hold of ourselves are important and can exert major effects on our lives. But where do they come from? Are they generally accurate? And what are their effects? Research on the self-concept has provided intriguing answers to each of these questions.[29]

Self-Concept: How Does It Develop?

How do we come to know ourselves—to understand our own traits and characteristics? Your first answer might be: "Directly, by looking inward." This is an appealing solution, and one most people accept. After all, we have access to all of our own thoughts, feelings, and behaviors, so combining these into a unified picture of ourselves should be a fairly simple task, right? Wrong! Actually, it turns out that there are very few instances in which we can come to know ourselves in this direct fashion. To see why this is so, consider the following question: How do you know whether you are charming or boring? Can you tell by looking into a mirror, or by sitting in some corner and thinking quietly about yourself? Probably not. Rather, the best way to answer this question would be through direct experience. Your interactions with the persons around you would provide clues as to whether you are a charmer or a crashing bore. If others constantly seek your company, hang on your every word, and tell you that you are fascinating, you will probably conclude that you are indeed charming. If, in contrast, they cross the street to avoid conversations with you, yawn constantly as you speak to them, and tell you that you are dull, you will decide that you are not as charming as you hoped.

In sum, contrary to what common sense suggests, we cannot really look into a mirror—or simply inward—and form an accurate self-concept. Rather, we must usually base such images of our own personality on information provided by others. In answer to the question at the start of this discussion, then, we can state that the self-concept derives primarily from four sources: (1) our social interactions with others, (2) comparing ourselves with them, (3) their comments or statements about us, and (4) careful observation of our own feelings, thoughts, and behavior (see Figures 5.10 and 5.11).

Self-Concept: Is It Accurate?

Given that the self-concept derives from several sources and that these can act as checks on each other, it is only reasonable to expect that in most cases, it will be fairly accurate. And in fact, this is true. The experiences of daily life simply do not permit our self-concept to depart too radically from reality. Thus

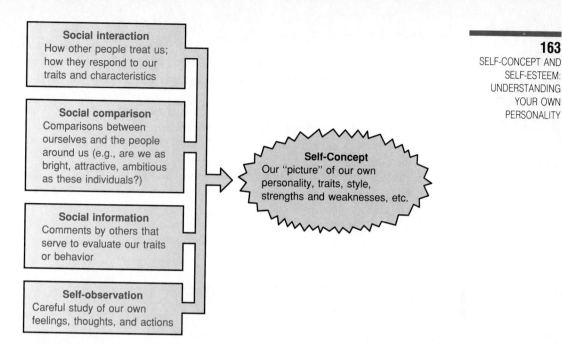

Social interaction
How other people treat us; how they respond to our traits and characteristics

Social comparison
Comparisons between ourselves and the people around us (e.g., are we as bright, attractive, ambitious as these individuals?)

Social information
Comments by others that serve to evaluate our traits or behavior

Self-observation
Careful study of our own feelings, thoughts, and actions

Self-Concept
Our "picture" of our own personality, traits, style, strengths and weaknesses, etc.

163
SELF-CONCEPT AND
SELF-ESTEEM:
UNDERSTANDING
YOUR OWN
PERSONALITY

FIGURE 5.10 Self-Concept: Its Basic Foundations
As shown here, our self-concept is based largely on information from four distinct sources: (1) our social interactions with others, (2) comparisons between ourselves and other persons, (3) information about us others provide, and (4) careful study of our own feelings and actions.

the views most of us hold about our major traits tend to be fairly, if not perfectly, correct. However, there are many cases in which the gap between an individual's self-concept and the way in which he or she is perceived by others can become quite large. Several factors contribute to such errors. For example, many persons

FIGURE 5.11 Self-Concept: One Important Source
Our self-concept derives from a variety of sources, including comments or statements from others. (Reprinted by permission of UFS, Inc.)

164

CHAPTER 5
PERSONALITY:
UNDERSTANDING
HOW AND WHY
INDIVIDUALS DIFFER

are reluctant to transmit negative feedback to others. As a result, individuals who possess undesirable traits often fail to receive input pointing to this fact. Similarly, some persons seem to reject information that is inconsistent with their current self-concept. As a result, it becomes very much a closed system, no longer open to change.

Regardless of how such gaps between self-concept and reality develop, they can have serious consequences. If individuals believe they possess more of desirable traits than is actually the case, they may form overly optimistic expectations—ones that may later be crushed. Similarly, if they do not recognize traits they *do* possess, they may miss important opportunities. And they will often be puzzled by their treatment at the hands of others who *do* notice these traits and act accordingly. For these and other reasons, a self-concept that accurately reflects your real traits is almost always preferable to one that does not, even if the latter is more flattering to your "image."

Self-Concept: Some Major Effects

Imagine two people who work for the same company. They actually possess similar personalities and similar job-related skills. However, one has a positive self-concept—he believes he is a talented employee and a desirable human being. In short, he possesses high self-esteem: he evaluates himself positively. In contrast, the other has a negative self-concept—he assumes he is barely adequate in both departments. In other words, he possesses low self-esteem. Which one will do better work? A good guess is the one with high self-esteem will. Many studies indicate that when individuals feel good about themselves (i.e., have a positive self-concept), their morale, motivation, and productivity are all enhanced. When they hold a negative view of their own self-worth, the opposite may be true.[30,31]

Unfortunately, though, this is only part of the total picture. Low self-esteem (i.e., a negative self-concept) also seems to have other costs as well. One of the most important of these involves the ability of individuals to conduct an adequate job search. Recent evidence suggests that persons suffering from low self-esteem are far less effective in this crucial task than those possessing high self-esteem. Such effects are shown clearly in a study conducted by Ellis and Taylor.[32] These researchers measured the self-esteem of a large number of business-school seniors. They then examined the relationship between such self-esteem and the success of these persons in the actual job-search process. Results indicate that subjects low in self-esteem did more poorly than those high in this trait. Persons low in self-esteem were less likely than those high in self-esteem to make use of informal job sources (e.g., friends and relatives) or ones requiring a high level of initiative (e.g., direct application). Since such sources are often very helpful, this was a major drawback. Similarly, low self-esteem individuals actually received lower ratings from interviewers, both in interviews conducted on campus and ones conducted at various companies. Finally, low self-esteem individuals received fewer job offers than those high in self-esteem. As you can see, then, possession of a negative self-concept proved costly in this important area of life.

Looking back over our comments so far, we are sure you will agree that the effects of low self-esteem are unfortunate to say the least. Possessing a negative self-concept seems to interfere with job satisfaction, motivation, performance, and even with finding a good position. Thus it is a serious problem for many persons. This fact leads to an important question: Can anything be done to help individuals suffering from low self-esteem? Fortunately, the answer seems to be "yes." Moreover, assisting such persons does not seem to require years of therapy or counseling. Instead, growing evidence suggests that this problem can often be alleviated merely by inducing low self-esteem persons to change their attributions about the causes of their own outcomes. Often, it appears, low self-esteem persons attribute successes to *external causes*—good luck ("I got lucky") or an easy task. In contrast, they attribute failures to *internal causes* ("I knew I really didn't have it in me"). If, instead, they can be induced to view their failures as stemming from external causes and their successes as deriving from internal ones, their self-esteem can be greatly improved (see Figure 5.12).

That such shifts can be readily produced is indicated by the results of a study conducted by Brockner and Guare.[33] In this investigation, college students previously found to be either low or high in self-esteem first worked on an insoluble concept formation task. (They were told that some stimuli they examined all shared a characteristic in common and were asked to identify it. In fact, the stimuli did *not* share a common characteristic.) After this failure experience, they worked on a solvable anagrams task. At this time, some individuals were led to attribute their previous poor performance to *external* causes (the task was very hard). Others were led to attribute their failure on the first task to *internal* causes (they were unable to cope with it), and still others were not given any information designed to affect their attributions. It was predicted that among low self-esteem subjects, those who attributed past failure to external causes would now do better on the anagrams tasks than those who attributed it to internal causes or those who were given no attribution-shaping information. Since high self-esteem subjects would tend to attribute failure to external causes, no such effects were expected among this group. As you can see from Figure 5.13, results supported both predictions.

165
SELF-CONCEPT AND
SELF-ESTEEM:
UNDERSTANDING
YOUR OWN
PERSONALITY

FIGURE 5.12 Self-Esteem and Attributions for Successes and Failures
Persons low in self-esteem often demonstrate a pattern of attributions for successes and failures opposite to that of persons high in self-esteem. They blame themselves for negative outcomes and refuse to take credit for positive ones.

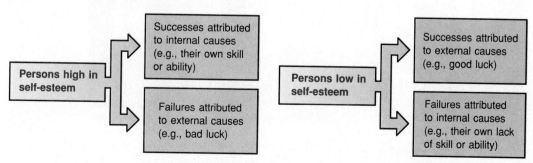

166

CHAPTER 5

PERSONALITY:
UNDERSTANDING
HOW AND WHY
INDIVIDUALS DIFFER

These findings suggest that both performance and underlying self-esteem can be enhanced by inducing individuals to interpret failures as stemming from external causes. Of course, in order for such shifts to be of practical value, they must be general in nature, rather than restricted to one specific task. Also, it would not be wise to induce low self-esteem persons to attribute *all* failures to external causes; some do stem from internal factors. In many cases, though, it appears that getting such persons to change their attributions about their task-related outcomes may be a valuable strategy—one that can quickly help them escape from the many harmful effects produced by their own negative self-concept. For an example of someone who appears to have a problem with self-esteem, see the **Case in Point** on page 167.

FIGURE 5.13 Overcoming Low Self-Esteem: An Attributional Approach
When low self-esteem individuals were induced to attribute failure on one task to external causes, they did much better on a second task. In contrast, information on the causes of failure had little impact on the performance of high self-esteem subjects. (*Source:* Based on data from Brockner and Guare (1983); see Note 33.)

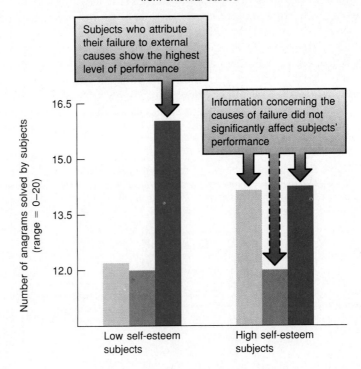

Esteem Is In the Eye of the Beholder

Ann and Kim were sitting in the employee cafeteria of Karma Plastics Corporation. They had been working in the accounting department together for about six months but had not gotten to know each other very well. Kim was rather shy and introverted and usually ate alone. Today Ann had gone out of her way to suggest that they have lunch together. They were both twenty-six-year-old single parents and Ann thought they should get to know each other a little better. As they were talking, Ann began to realize that there were some fundamental differences between them. While Ann considered herself an optimist who had a generally positive attitude toward the world and herself, Kim seemed to be really down on herself.

"It sure is nice of you to ask me to go to lunch with you, Ann, but I'm sorry I'm not a great conversationalist. I've never been very good with small talk."

"Come on!" Ann replied. "You certainly have had no trouble keeping us talking."

Kim smiled and looked away for a moment. "Maybe that's because I haven't had much chance to talk to people here. Of course, after I screwed up the invoices for that big order last week, I just wanted to hide. That was really stupid of me. Mr. Nall really got mad at me for that screwup!"

Ann shook her head in disagreement. "But that really wasn't your fault. He shouldn't have let you work on the new billing system until you had finished the training program. It's the fault of management for rushing us to do tasks for which we are not fully trained."

Kim did not seem to agree. "Maybe so, but I should have picked it up a bit faster. Nancy always seems to learn the new procedures faster than I do. I'm surprised I'm still here."

At this point, both of them noticed that their lunch break was about over and began to pick up their trays.

"Well, maybe we can do this again sometime," Ann remarked as they were leaving. However, there was a notable lack of enthusiasm in her voice as they walked back to work.

Questions

1. How would you characterize Kim's self-concept?

2. Do you get any clues from the conversation about characteristics that Kim shares with other low self-esteem people and how low self-esteem is maintained?

3. How do you think she came to have her low self-esteem in the first place? Do you think being a single parent makes her situation even more difficult?

4. Are there some ways Kim's fellow employees can help her build up her self-esteem?

168

CHAPTER 5

PERSONALITY:
UNDERSTANDING
HOW AND WHY
INDIVIDUALS DIFFER

SUMMARY

Personality refers to the unique pattern of traits and behaviors that sets each individual apart from others and is relatively stable over time. Many theories have been advanced to account for such individual differences. One of the most famous is Freud's **psychoanalytic theory,** which focuses on the interplay among three major structures of personality **(id, ego,** and **superego).** Another theory is the **learning-oriented approach.** According to this view, individuals' unique experiences with the world around them account for the large differences in their lasting traits.

Several specific traits or characteristics appear to be closely linked to behavior and relations to work settings. One of these is the **Type A–Type B** personality dimension. Type A individuals are impatient, hard-driving, and aggressive. In contrast, Type Bs are easy-going, calm, and relaxed. Type As are more than twice as likely to suffer serious heart attacks as Type B's. Type A's outperform Type B's on tasks involving time pressure or multiple demands. However, they do more poorly than Type B's on tasks involving delaying responses or complex judgments.

Individuals who adopt a manipulative approach to life are known as **High Machiavellian** (or **High Machs** for short). Such persons believe it is appropriate to lie to others if this helps them attain their goals. They also assume that most persons are vicious, immoral, and untrustworthy. Because they quickly master techniques for manipulating and deceiving others, High Machs often succeed in getting their way in many situations.

Three work-related motives—**achievement, power,** and **affiliation**—play an important role in work situations. People high in achievement motivation have a strong desire to excel but do not necessarily make good managers. People who are high in power motivation and low in affiliation motivation—the **leadership motivation pattern**—appear to be quite effective as managers.

Another important factor in success at work is one's social skill. This is the ability to communicate effectively with others. This ability actually consists of multiple components of emotional and social **expressivity,** emotional and social **sensitivity,** and emotional and social **control.** Individuals high in social skills are typically liked and tend to be more successful in their careers.

Each of us has a **self-concept**—a picture of our own traits and personality. It is acquired largely from our interactions with other persons and the information about us they provide. In most cases, the self-concept is fairly accurate. However, in some, it is inaccurate, and individuals are badly mistaken about the traits they do or do not possess. A positive self-concept is important for success in both work and social contexts.

KEY TERMS

achievement motivation: The desire to meet standards of excellence and accomplish tasks more successfully than others.

affiliation motive: The desire to establish and maintain positive relations with others.

ego: According to Freud, one of the three basic structures of personality. It is the function of the ego to hold basic drives or impulses in check until they can be satisfied under safe conditions.

humanistic perspective: Theories of personality that emphasize tendencies toward growth and the role of personal choice or free will in human behavior.

id: According to Freud, one of the three basic structures of personality. The id is the source of all basic drives, urges, and impulses.

leadership motivation pattern: A pattern consisting of a high need for power and a low need for affiliation. This pattern of motives appears to be related to managerial success.

learning: The process through which lasting changes in behavior are induced through experience.

learning-oriented approach: A group of theories that view personality as stemming mainly from learning. According to these theories, each individual acquires a unique pattern of traits from having unique experiences with the world.

Machiavellianism: A personality trait involving a willingness to manipulate others in order to attain one's goals. Individuals high on this dimension (High Machs) believe it is appropriate to lie to others, and view them as basically dishonest and immoral.

personality: Refers to the unique pattern of traits and behaviors that sets each individual apart from others and is relatively stable over time.

power motive: The desire to exert influence over others.

psychoanalytic theory: Freud's famous theory of the nature of personality and its role in the development of various behavior disorders.

self-concept: The picture of one's own personality, reflecting everything believed to be true about one's traits, behaviors, and abilities.

self-esteem: The extent to which individuals perceive their traits and characteristics in a positive or negative manner.

social skills: The ability to communicate effectively with others.

superego: According to Freud, one of the basic structures of personality. The superego evaluates behavior and impulses on the basis of codes or principles of morality. Thus it serves as the conscience.

Type A–Type B personality dimension: A personality dimension with important implications for health, social relations, and job performance. At one end is Type A—hard-driving, competitive, impatient. At the other end is Type B—relaxed, easygoing, unambitious. Not surprisingly, Type As are more than twice as likely as Type Bs to have serious heart attacks.

NOTES

1. Carver, C.S., & Scheier, M.F. (1988). *Perspectives in Personality*. Boston: Allyn and Bacon.
2. Mischel, W. (1982). *Personality*. New York: Holt, Rinehart and Winston.
3. Hulse, S.H., Deese, J., & Egeth, H. (1980). *The Psychology of Learning*, 5th ed. New York: McGraw-Hill.
4. Bandura, A. (1977). *Social Learning Theory*. Englewood Cliffs, N.J.: Prentice-Hall.
5. Rogers, C.R. (1977). *Carl Rogers on Personal Power: Inner Strength and Its Revolutionary Impact*. New York: Delacorte.
6. Glass, D.C. (1977). *Behavior Patterns, Stress, and Coronary Disease*. Hillsdale, N.J.: Erlbaum.
7. James, S.P., Campbell, I.M., & Lovegrove, S.A. (1984). "Personality Differentiation in a Police-Selection Interview." *Journal of Applied Psychology, 69,* 129–34.

170

CHAPTER 5
PERSONALITY:
UNDERSTANDING
HOW AND WHY
INDIVIDUALS DIFFER

8. Friedman, M., & Rosenman, R.H. (1974). *Type A Behavior and Your Heart*. New York: Knopf.

9. Holmes, D.S., McGilley, B.M., & Houston, B.K. (1984). "Task-Related Arousal of Type A and Type B Persons: Levels of Challenge and Response Specificity." *Journal of Personality and Social Psychology, 46*, 1322–27.

10. Hill, D.R., Krantz, D.S., Contrada, R.J., Hedges, S.M., & Ratliff-Crain, J.A. (1987). "Stability and Change in Type A Components and Cardiovascular Reactivity in Medical Students During Periods of Academic Stress." *Journal of Applied Social Psychology, 17*, 679–98.

11. Holmes, D.S., & Will, M.J. (1985). "Expression of Interpersonal Aggression by Angered and Nonangered Persons with the Type A and Type B Behavior Patterns." *Journal of Personality and Social Psychology, 48*, 723–27.

12. Baron, R.A. (1989). "Personality and Organizational Conflict: Effects of the Type A Behavior Pattern and Self-Monitoring." *Organizational Behavior and Human Decision Processes, 44*, 291–296.

13. Carver, C.S., Coleman, A.E., & Glass, D.C. (1976). "The Coronary-Prone Behavior Pattern and the Suppression of Fatigue on a Treadmill Test." *Journal of Personality and Social Psychology, 33*, 460–66.

14. Ortega, D.F., & Pipal, J.E. (1984). "Challenge Seeking and the Type A-Coronary Prone Behavior Pattern." *Journal of Personality and Social Psychology, 46*, 1328–34.

15. Glass, D.C., Snyder, M.L., & Hollis, J. (1974). "Time Urgency and the Type A Coronary-Prone Behavior Pattern." *Journal of Applied Social Psychology, 4*, 125–40.

16. Friedman, M., & Rosenham, R.H. (1974). *Type A Behavior and Your Heart*. New York: Knopf.

17. Christie, R., & Geis, F.L., eds. (1970). *Studies in Machiavellianism*, New York: Academic Press.

18. Hunter, J.E., Gerbing, D.W., & Boster, F.J. (1982). "Machiavellian Beliefs and Personality: Construct Invalidity of the Machiavellianism Dimension." *Journal of Personality and Social Psychology, 43*, 1293–305.

19. Kraut, R.E., & Paice, J.D. (1976). "Machiavellianism in Parents and Their Children." *Journal of Personality and Social Psychology, 33*, 782–86.

20. Christie, R., & Geis, F.L. (1970). "The Ten Dollar Game." In R. Christie and F.L. Geis, eds., *Studies in Machiavellianism*. New York: Academic Press.

21. McClelland, D.C. (1961). *The Achieving Society*. Princeton, N.J.: Van Nostrand.

22. McClelland, D.C. (1977). "Entrepreneurship and Management in the Years Ahead." In C.A. Bramlette, Jr., ed., *The Individual and the Future of Organizations*. Atlanta: Georgia State University, College of Business Administration.

23. McClelland, D.C., & Boyatzis, R.E. (1982). "Leadership Motive Pattern and Long-Term Success in Management." *Journal of Applied Psychology, 67*, 737–43.

24. Riggio, R.E. (1986). "Assessment of Basic Social Skills." *Journal of Personality and Social Psychology, 51*, 649–60.

25. Friedman, H.S., Riggio, R.E., & Casella, D.F. (1988). "Nonverbal Skill, Personal Charisma, and Initial Attraction." *Personality and Social Psychology Bulletin, 14*, 203–11.

26. See Note 24.

27. Riggio, R.E., Tucker, J., & Throckmorton, B. (1987). "Social Skills and Deception Ability." *Personality and Social Psychology Bulletin, 13*, 568–77.

28. Friedman, H.S. (1979). "The Concept of Skill in Nonverbal Communication: Implications for Understanding Social Interactions." In R. Rosenthal, ed., *Skill in Nonverbal Communication*. Cambridge: Oelgeschlager, Gunn and Hain.

29. Tharenou, P. (1979). "Employee Self-Esteem: A Review of the Literature." *Journal of Vocational Behavior, 15,* 316–46.

30. Mossholder, K.W., Bedeian, A.G., & Armenakis, A. (1982). "Group Process-Work Outcome Relationships: A Note of the Moderating Impact of Self-Esteem." *Academy of Management Journal, 25,* 575–85.

31. See Note 22.

32. Ellis, R.A., & Taylor, M.S. (1983). "Role of Self-Esteem Within the Job-Search Process." *Journal of Applied Psychology, 68,* 632–40.

33. Brockner, J., & Guare, J. (1983). "Improving the Performance of Low Self-Esteem Individuals: An Attributional Approach." *Academy of Management Journal, 26,* 642–56.

ADDITIONAL CASES AND EXERCISES: APPLYING WHAT YOU'VE LEARNED

Social Skills Are Job Skills Too

William Ickes
Professor of Psychology
University of Texas at Arlington

Allen Rodriguez has just been passed over for a promotion to chief of production, and he is busy venting his frustration on one of his co-workers, Gordon Carlisle.

"It's just not *fair*!" Allen insists for the fourteenth time. "The group I supervise had the highest production levels in the entire plant for the third year in a row. Frank Soza's group was only second-highest during each of those years. Why should *he* get the promotion instead of me?"

"I've been trying to tell you, Allen. We've *all* been trying to tell you."

"Tell me what? That I don't play the 'social game' as well as Frank? That I don't stand around listening to people as much; that I'm in too big a hurry to get things done? I've heard all that stuff before, and it just isn't relevant. My job is to get the highest level of productivity from my people, not to waste time standing around talking to them or to indulge them in bringing up problems."

"What you don't understand, Allen, is that *social skills are job skills too*. It's true that you are very effective in getting the most work out of your people, but think about the cost to *them*. You're always on someone's case, pressuring them to do better. If you spot a problem, you're there in a flash to jump on it, doling out big doses of criticism but hardly ever any praise. And it's true that you don't listen to people; Jessie Phillips got so frustrated trying to explain to you that she needed some leave time to visit her daughter in the hospital that she finally had to go over your head to arrange it."

"So what's the bottom line here? Am I supposed to be a manager, or am I supposed to be a psychiatrist or some kind of glorified babysitter?"

"You're supposed to be the kind of manager that other people can talk to. It's no surprise to most of us that Frank Soza got the promotion instead of you. He listens to people, and he takes their perspective into account before answering. He lets them know that he understands their concerns and respects their position even if he has to adopt a different one. Most importantly, he does his best to *resolve* the problems people bring to him; he doesn't just bulldoze right over them."

"Well, Soza's the way he is and I'm the way I am. I've been this way for thirty-six years and I can't change now."

"How do you know, Allen, unless you try? The senior management keeps recommending that you participate in the company's seminars on social skills training. They seem to think that you could benefit from learning a different way of relating to others. Who are you really hurting by *not* participating—yourself or them?"

Questions

173

ADDITIONAL
CASES AND
EXERCISES:
APPLYING WHAT
YOU'VE LEARNED

1. What social skills do you think Allen needs to develop in his relationships with co-workers?

2. How important are social skills in most work settings? Why should they count as much or more than other job-relevant skills when people are selected for positions of responsibility within an organization?

3. People often seem to be more willing to learn new technical skills than they are to learn new social skills. Why?

4. Why are the efforts of senior management to improve their employees' social skills sometimes resented? How could they present opportunities for social skills training in a way that would create less resentment and reluctance on the part of employees?

Assessing Your Own Self-Concept: Accurate? Or Out of Line?

Everyone has a self-concept; of this there can be no doubt. But, as noted earlier in this chapter, not everyone's self-concept is equally accurate. Some persons have a good grasp of their own major traits and characteristics: They see themselves much as others do. In contrast, other persons possess a self-concept that is out of phase with their true traits or characteristics. As we noted earlier, this can have serious consequences. Where do you stand on this dimension? Is your self-concept largely accurate? Or does it depart from reality in important ways? In order to get some preliminary insights into this crucial question, follow the procedures outlined below.

(1) List on a piece of paper what you feel are your five most important traits. (2) Ask at least ten people that you know to make a list of what *they* feel are your five most important characteristics. Try to get the help of friends, family, co-workers, and others—people who know you and see you regularly in various roles and contexts. (3) Compare the lists you obtained from these other people with your own list. Score one point each time a trait on your own list was also included by one of the people you approached. (Be sure to give yourself credit for synonyms. For example, if you described yourself as friendly, and one of the people you approached described you as sociable, score a point. Similarly, if you described yourself as ambitious and one of the people who helped you listed the trait achievement-oriented, score a point.)

If you attain a score of at least 20 (assuming you had ten people list your major traits), your self-concept is probably fairly accurate: other people do see you in the way you see yourself. If your score is five or less, though, there is a good chance your current self-concept is not accurate. If this is the case, you may want to give some careful thought to adjusting it at least to a degree.

Interpersonal Relations: From Getting Along to Loving

Learning Objectives

After reading this chapter,
you should be able to:

1. Discuss the different reasons that people have for joining groups.

2. Describe the major factors that lead to liking and friendship.

3. Understand the different theories of love.

4. Explain how relationships develop.

5. Discuss the major findings on romance in the workplace.

read & study
this chapter

I t was Joe Garcia's first day at his new job. He had just graduated from college with a degree in computer programming and was excited about his new job with Software Analysts. Elaine Solomon was in charge of introducing him to his new co-workers.

"Welcome to the company, Joe," said Elaine with smile.

Elaine was quite an attractive young lady and about the same age as Joe. So it was probably not surprising that Joe grinned as he responded, "Thanks I'm really looking forward to getting to know everyone."

"Well, I think you'll like your co-workers. We're all about the same age and we get along really well. We often socialize as a group after work. Most Friday evenings we go to some local club or restaurant to blow off steam."

"That's good to hear," said Joe. "I'm new in town and haven't met too many people yet. I could use a little boost to my social life."

As they went to the different offices, Elaine continued to fill Joe in on the various do's and don't's of the company.

"They're really sticklers for timeliness here," she said. "If you're late for work, you better have a good reason. And dating among employees is definitely out!"

"Why is that?" asked Joe, looking a bit surprised. He had seen some rather attractive female employees, and the thought of getting to know them had already crept into his mind. He was particularly attracted to Elaine because of her good looks and pleasant interpersonal style.

Elaine acted as if she didn't notice Joe's surprise, and matter of factly explained that this was a policy instituted by the boss.

"He simply feels that romantic relationships at work will lower productivity and cause conflicts. That doesn't mean that people here can't be good friends though," she said with a twinkle in her eye. *Now what did she mean by that,* Joe thought to himself. Oh well, it will take a while to learn the ropes here and to *really* get to know everybody. I guess there's no reason to rush.

Joe's dilemma is similar to that experienced by people every day. Companies are constantly hiring new employees. These newcomers have to become integrated into the social life of the organization. Co-workers may be an important source of personal and interpersonal rewards. They may help us feel important, provide for a social life, and be a source of friendship. Sometimes fellow employees may become quite attracted to each other and begin dating. They may even fall in love and decide to get married. This could present problems at work, especially if one of the partners has management responsibility. Other employees may be concerned about favoritism and may be jealous. So the whole issue of interpersonal relations in the workplace is important since effective work environments require compatible interpersonal relations. In this chapter we will analyze interpersonal relations in general and try to understand the implications of this knowledge for relations in work environments. First, we will deal with the factors that motivate people to seek out *interpersonal contact* and *relationships*. Then we will examine those factors that lead us to become *attracted* to other individuals and to fall in *love* with them. Finally, we will examine *how relationships develop* and the role of *romantic relationships* in the workplace.

AFFILIATION: GETTING TOGETHER WITH OTHERS

Most of us are involved in a lot of different relationships. We have our families, different groups of friends, social clubs, and acquaintances from work. Some people are much more involved in social activities with these groups than others, and some people may avoid involvement in groups as much as possible. What motivates us to be involved in groups and why do we differ so much in our social inclinations? First, some have argued that our tendency to **affiliate** with others is an *inborn need*. People simply need people to survive and they may have an instinctual tendency to seek out the company of others. Certainly there are times when there is safety in numbers, and it is important for infants and parents to maintain close ties. However, there seem to be other factors involved. We may learn to develop *positive associations* with the presence of others. As infants, many of our needs were met by our parents or others, and this may have led to development of strong affiliative tendencies because of these generally positive associations. Of course, if our early experiences were mostly negative, we would not be so inclined to affiliate. We may become loners or hostile to others. The fact that child abuse tends to be passed on from one generation to another is evidence for this.[1]

A third possible basis for affiliation is our *need for social stimulation.* It is often presumed that we seek an optimum level of stimulation. If we get too little stimulation from our various activities, we may become bored and restless and seek out more stimulation. Social activities may serve as an important source of stimulation. However, if we get too much stimulation, we may be overwhelmed and stressed and attempt to reduce the level of stimulation. Studies with animals have provided some evidence for the importance of social stimulation in affiliation,[2] and studies with humans found that people with high needs for stimulation are more likely to be involved in a lot of social activities.[3]

Although each of the above factors is probably responsible to some extent for our affiliative activities,[4] current thinking about affiliation focuses primarily on two factors—*exchange of rewards* and *social comparison*. It is obvious that we obtain many benefits or rewards from affiliating with others. Our families may provide protection and emotional and financial support. Social interest groups provide stimulation and church groups may provide stimulation as well as social support. Some rewards such as financial success and sports championships can only be obtained by the efficient combination of efforts of work groups or teams. Some groups may provide important social contacts or prestige (e.g., civic clubs

178

CHAPTER 6

INTERPERSONAL
RELATIONS: FROM
GETTING ALONG TO
LOVING

and college fraternities and sororities). People can also bask in the reflected glory of their groups. This can be seen in the pride that fans take when their teams win or their organization is successful.

Two Types of Social Rewards: Intimacy and Involvement

It appears that we are motivated to be involved in groups because of the various rewards they may provide for us. Shaver and Burhmester have argued that there are basically two types of rewards or social provisions that individuals seek in groups: *psychological intimacy* and *integrated involvement.*[5] **Psychological intimacy** represents the direct benefits derived from social contact such as affection, opportunity for emotional expression, and security. **Integrated involvement** consists of those benefits that come from involvement in various group activities. These activities can provide enjoyment, a sense of social identity, a feeling of being needed, and approval for successful performance. Figure 6.1 provides a more detailed list of the types of provisions involved in each of the two categories. Shaver and Burhmester propose that unless both of these provisions are satisfied by groups in our lives, there will be a sense of emptiness or loneliness. In other words, we need to feel that others care and to have the opportunity to care for others as well as the opportunity to feel important or needed by others. If these needs are not satisfied, then feelings of loneliness may come about. Lack of intimacy is associated with anxiety, insecurity, depression, and the reporting of a variety of physical and mental problems. Lack of integrated involvement can result in feelings of boredom, alienation, and anger. (See Figure 6.1.)

You can see that it is important to people to find fulfillment of their various needs in groups. For a group to be successful, it is also important that the group satisfies the diverse needs of its members. Church, work, and social groups that satisfy both the needs for intimacy and integrated involvement are probably going to be most successful. Part of the success of Japanese companies lies in their attempts to satisfy these diverse needs. These companies encourage employee input and involvement in management and production and provide a lot of social activities for their employees. As you will learn in our discussion of leadership in Chapter 8, leaders who are concerned both with the maintenance of good relations among group members and the achievement of goals or productivity are the most effective. Of course, it is not necessary to satisfy both sets of needs in the same group. But it is easy to see why people would feel a strong sense of commitment to groups that are able to do this.

Fear and Affiliation: Is There Safety in Numbers?

You have probably had occasions when you were really afraid to be alone. You may have been home alone at night and heard strange noises outside. You may have been walking alone down a dark alley or mistakenly driven into a dangerous area of a city. At these times you may have strongly wished that you were in the company of some friends. You could have discussed your plight with them and they could have aided you in dealing with the situation. Although it may seem obvious that there is a greater feeling of safety in potentially dangerous situations when we are with a group of individuals, it may surprise you to learn that just being in a group may *reduce* our fear even if the group members can't

	Provisions	Consequences of Insufficient Provisions
Psychological intimacy	Affection and warmth Unconditional positive regard Self-disclosure Lack of defensiveness Security and emotional support Giving and receiving nurturance	Loneliness Low self-esteem Anxiety Insecurity Pent-up feelings Mental and physical symptoms
Integrated involvement	Enjoyable, involving activities Social identity Being needed for skills Social comparison Power and influence Conditional positive regard Support for beliefs and values	Boredom Feeling of not being needed Feeling unimportant

FIGURE 6.1 Social Provisions: Rewards from Groups
According to Shaver and Burhmester, there are two basic types of provisions or rewards that individuals need from groups—psychological intimacy and integrated involvement. If these needs are not met, then individuals may experience different aspects of loneliness. (*Source:* Adapted from Shaver and Burhmester (1983); see Note 5.)

do anything to help us avoid a threatening event. This was found in studies by Schachter where subjects were expecting to experience painful shocks as part of an experiment. They were then allowed to either wait alone or with others who also were part of the experiment. Most preferred to wait with others rather than alone. In contrast, when the shock expected was very mild, most preferred to wait alone.[6]

Two explanations for this phenomenon were *direct anxiety reduction* and *social comparison*. In a fearful situation, students may have sought out the company of others for their potential calming influence. They may also have desired to take advantage of an opportunity to compare their feelings or anxieties with those of others. Both of these ideas gained some support (see Figure 6.2). Just waiting with others does lead to a reduced level of anxiety, but people seem to prefer waiting with others only when these people are confronted with the same experience. Only then can there be a reasonable basis of comparison.[7]

Social Comparison: The Drive to Check Our Opinions and Abilities

The research by Schachter has shown that people can be motivated to be with others in order to compare their feelings with those of others. This tendency of **social comparison** appears to be very general. You probably remember times when you wondered how others felt about some issue because you weren't sure whether your opinions were correct. In his social comparison theory, Festinger proposed that we have a strong *drive* to compare our opinions and abilities with those of others.[8] Our opinions about many issues are rather subjective since there

180

CHAPTER 6

INTERPERSONAL
RELATIONS: FROM
GETTING ALONG TO
LOVING

is no objective way of determining who is right or wrong. For example, is free enterprise the best economic system? Is an attempt to land people on Mars a worthwhile way for our country to allot its resources?

How can we increase our certainty that our opinions are correct? One of the best ways is to seek confirmation from those with whom we agree on many other issues. So it is only natural that we seek out people who are *similar* to us in age, background, and life perspective to discuss these issues and to validate our opinions. These people may *not* always agree with us, but they are more likely to agree than those who are radically different in many ways. If we have no particular opinion on an issue, we may in fact acquire the opinions held by such reference groups.

Although we may seek out similar others for comparison of opinions, in the case of abilities we may seek out people who appear to be slightly better than us. This is probably motivated by a desire to maintain or increase our self-esteem. The worst that can happen is that the experience will confirm that this individual *is* in fact better. If by chance we perform about as well or even better, that would be a boost to our self-esteem. Comparison with someone who is less capable could actually backfire if we happen to do worse than this person.

It is interesting that these two types of social comparison mesh quite nicely with the different types of social needs we discussed earlier—intimacy and integrated involvement. Social comparison of opinions with similar others is motivated by a desire for confirmation or social support (intimacy) while comparison of abilities with superior others is motivated by the desire to feel important or competent (integrated involvement). Both types of social comparison are likely to play an important role in relations at work. Most of us gravitate to people at work who have relatively similar opinions or values. However, we may try to match our work skills or abilities with someone at a slightly higher level or status.

INTERPERSONAL ATTRACTION: LIKING AND FRIENDSHIP

Who are your best friends? What are they like? Do you have a lot in common with them? Do you think they are intelligent, honest, and good-looking? How

FIGURE 6.2 Affiliation in Groups: Two Bases for Reduced Fear
When people are fearful, they tend to seek the company of others to engage in social comparison and direct anxiety reduction.

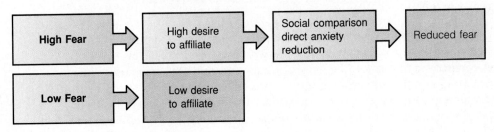

did you meet and become friends? These kinds of issues are the concern of studies of interpersonal attraction. Most of us have certain people of the same and opposite sex that we consider our friends. What determines whether we become friends with someone?

Propinquity and Familiarity: The Benefits of Closeness

One obvious factor in friendships is the need at some point in time to be in close *proximity* to each other. Either because of residential location, seating position, location of work sites, or involvement in various groups, we tend to come into contact with certain people. We may not particularly like some of them, but we may be attracted to others. Not surprisingly, it has been found that most friendships and romantic relationships start with people who work or live close to each other. A casual reading of the marriage or engagement section of your newspaper will show that many of the couples went to the same university or high school or worked at the same company.

One factor that aids our attraction to people in close proximity is that we are attracted more to *familiar* people than to strangers. Studies have shown that the more frequently we encounter a stranger, the more favorably we feel about them. This was first shown in carefully controlled laboratory studies where it was impossible to interact. Otherwise, the tone of the interaction might overwhelm any effects of mere exposure. In other words, familiarity appears to breed attraction and not contempt. This is particularly true if the stimulus objects to which we are exposed are fairly complex and our initial reactions are neutral, as is presumably the case with most strangers.[9] It appears that the same familiarity effect is used effectively by politicians and advertisers. We certainly encounter a lot of advertising and political campaigns that focus primarily on brand or name familiarity.

Attractive Features: Can We Make a Deal?

Of course, just because someone is nearby and familiar does not mean that he or she will be liked or become our friend. One important factor determining our choice of friends is their characteristics. We tend to like people who have attractive features—intelligence, good personality, good looks, talents, and attractive possessions (see Figure 6.3). In the case of romantic friendships, it appears that looks are particularly important. We are strongly attracted to individuals of the opposite sex who are physically attractive and may be more affected by this factor than others such as intelligence and personality in initial encounters. Unfortunately, we tend to assume that individuals who are above average in physical attractiveness are also above average in intelligence, mental health, and happiness. There is in fact no support for such ideas.[10]

Although we are often attracted to physically attractive people, we may not actually seek out a particularly attractive person as a friend or date. Here, our choices seem to be governed by reality in that we tend to select people who are similar in physical attractiveness.[11] In fact people seem to follow a rather economic perspective in selecting prospective romantic partners. We may determine roughly

182

CHAPTER 6
INTERPERSONAL
RELATIONS: FROM
GETTING ALONG TO
LOVING

our value on the dating market by taking into account looks, education, income, job, and other personal assets. In this way wealthy old men may end up marrying beautiful young women. This may be seen as a fair trade. Of course, we might take a little risk and try for someone who may be slightly above our own estimated value. Who knows, we might get lucky. This approach would be consistent with the comparison of abilities idea discussed earlier.

Similarity: The Glue of Relationships

Not only do people strive for similarity in terms of overall "value," they also seem to be attracted to people who are *similar* in important dimensions such as values, opinions, race, socioeconomic level, and personality. Laboratory studies have shown that liking for others is increased to the extent that their opinions are in agreement with ours.[12] Studies with friends and marital partners have similarly found evidence for the important role of similarity. Friends in high school may select among themselves on the basis of their activities and involvement in drugs or alcohol.[13] Marriage partners tend to be similar in a variety of personality traits such as extraversion and dominance.[14] Even more important, similarity is important in satisfaction with relationships. When college students were asked to indicate the reasons for the breakup of romantic relationships, they frequently cited boredom and differences in interests, sexual attitudes, background, and marriage ideas. In the case of marriage, success rates also tend to be higher with couples who have more in common (e.g., education, age).[15]

Do opposites attract? Contrary to all of the evidence cited so far, it has often been suggested that opposites attract and might actually make better marriage partners. One basis for this idea is that individuals with different characteristics can *complement* each other's weaknesses.[16] So the shy accountant wife can keep the financial aspect of the family in order, while the sociable salesperson husband can deal with social conflicts and arrange the social activities. While this kind of complementarity may have some merits, the basic differences in social inclinations

FIGURE 6.3 Interpersonal Attraction: The Role of Attractive Features
Interpersonal attraction is often influenced by positive features of individuals, including valued possessions or income. (Cathy © 1989 Universal Press Syndicate. Reprinted with permission. All rights reserved.)

are likely to cause problems in the relationship. How can they ever agree on how to spend their spare time? So it is not surprising that similarity rather than complementarity is the main determinant of marital success.[17] That does not mean that complementarity along some dimensions may not be useful (e.g., one person prefers outside housework and the other inside housework), but such differences should not reflect basic differences in personality or values that are likely to lead to continual conflict in the relationship.

LOVE: WHAT ABOUT THAT SPECIAL THING?

They say that **love** makes the world go 'round. Certainly if you listen to the songs on the radio, you would begin to believe this. It is the focal point of many contemporary songs, books, plays, and television fare. Why all the fuss? Is it such a special phenomenon? Well, if it is, it took psychologists a while to decide to look at it scientifically, but now there is an increasingly sophisticated body of research.

Theoretical Perspectives: The Different Faces of Love

Although we use the word "love" to describe special feelings associated with a variety of relationships (romantic, family), you no doubt realize that the nature of "love" varies among relationships and within the same relationship. We will briefly examine some of the perspectives that have been developed about love and its variations.

Reinforcement Affect You have probably seen the bumper sticker on cars that says, "If it feels good, do it!" This sentiment is the basis of a hedonistic approach to life, which is concerned primarily with satisfaction of one's needs. Events that satisfy such needs are often called rewards or reinforcements and presumably produce positive emotional reactions. To the extent that a relationship is associated with a lot of rewards, strong positive feelings could develop. These rewards can come directly from the relationship—affection, attention, and praise—or from pleasant events that accompany the relationship—parties, movies, or a romantic evening. This principle underlies the Byrne-Clore *reinforcement-affect model* of attraction.[18] This model focuses on similarity of opinions and values. Since agreement from others serves to validate our view of the world, agreements may serve as a powerful reward and produce positive feelings or affect. From this perspective, love is simply a strong degree of liking produced by rewards associated with a relationship (see Figure 6.4).

Exchange Versus Communal Relationships So far, our discussion may make fairly good sense to you. Certainly, you wouldn't fall in love with someone unless you had a lot of positive feelings about this person. But just receiving rewards

184
CHAPTER 6
INTERPERSONAL
RELATIONS: FROM
GETTING ALONG TO
LOVING

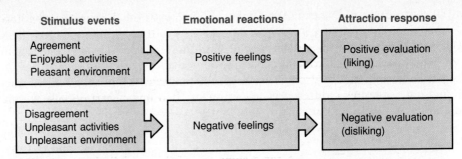

FIGURE 6.4 Reinforcement-Affect Model: The Role of Rewards in Liking
One influential model of attraction is the Byrne-Clore reinforcement-affect model, which suggests that liking or disliking is derived from positive or negative feelings associated with rewarding or punishing events that are part of a relationship.

may not be sufficient to produce a compatible love relationship. One important factor is *equity* (see Chapter 4) of rewards. That is, individuals supposedly seek a fair balance or exchange of rewards in a relationship. If one partner is providing most of the rewards or benefits (such as providing most of the affection or doing most of the work), this partner is likely to become dissatisfied and the relationship may break up.[19] However, moderate differences among the partners in how much they bring to the relationship may not be a serious problem in relationships that involve strong caring and affection. These are sometimes called *communal relationships* and in these relationships the partners may be concerned primarily with satisfying each other's needs than with a fair balancing of rewards.[20]

Liking Versus Loving   But, you say, is that all there is? Recent developments suggest that there is much more. First, it appears that *loving* and *liking* are actually somewhat *distinct* states.[21] Friendship or liking seems to involve a primarily positive evaluation of another person. Love, on the other hand, may involve a number of other factors. Rubin developed a love scale indicating that being in love consisted of three components: (1) a strong need for *affiliation* or *dependency*—"I just can't do without him/her;" (2) a desire to be *helpful*—"I would do almost anything for her;" (3) a sense of *exclusiveness* about the other person—"I feel very possessive about him." This scale is a fairly good predictor of desire to get married and how much couples will gaze into each other's eyes. So it seems to give a fairly good glimpse of this state called love.

Passionate Love   One feature that often characterizes falling in love is a high level of *emotionality* or excitement. You have just found this wonderful and attractive new person and can't get this person out of your mind. This level of excitement and arousal may be both positive and negative. The attention, sexual excitement, and getting to know someone new may all contribute to a generally positive feeling. Yet there is also some sense of uncertainty about the future of the romance. Will it last? Does the other person love me as much as I love him or her? You may be frustrated by separation or you may experience feelings of jealousy.

This arousal and excitement aspect of love is the central focus of Walster and Berscheid's *three-factor theory of love*.[22] According to this model, passionate love requires (1) an appropriate and desirable love object, (2) culturally based beliefs and expectations about love, and (3) a heightened level of emotional arousal. Supposedly, when we are strongly aroused in the presence of an attractive person, we may interpret this emotional state as love. We do this in part because in our culture we have learned that emotional states called love occur under such circumstances. The high level of arousal or excitement can be the result of sexual attraction as well as some of the other elements of the relationship such as anxiety and uncertainty (see Figure 6.5 for a summary of this model). It can also come from sources outside of the relationship. Any factor that causes us to be aroused in the presence of an attractive individual, even the threat of shock, may lead to the inference of love.[23] For example, one study compared the reactions of men to an attractive interviewer after they had either crossed an unstable bridge over a deep gorge or a stable bridge close to the ground. Those who crossed the scary bridge responded with sexual answers to ambiguous pictures when the interviewer was female and were most likely to try to contact her at a later time.[24] So it appears that they misinterpreted the arousal produced by the bridge as sexual attraction to the female interviewer.

The transfer of excitement from one source to feelings about another may explain why love and hate may sometimes go together.[25] The sexual arousal and excitement of a love relationship may *transfer* to the anger produced in relationships by conflicts or jealousies. Some of the violent outbreaks that accompany attempts by one person to break off a relationship while the other is still passionately in love may be related to this factor. So it is probably best to go slowly in winding down or cooling relationships.

It appears that the passionate phase of love lasts only a few months for most couples. It is difficult to maintain the level of excitement about the relationship as the couple becomes more familiar with each other. Some of the initial uncertainty is gone and there is no longer the thrill of discovery inherent in any new relationship. There may still be strong sexual attraction, but there is likely to be

FIGURE 6.5 Passionate Love: A Three-Factor Model
Three-factor theory of passionate love proposes that this type of love requires an attractive person of the opposite sex, cultural beliefs about love, and interpretation of emotional arousal as love.

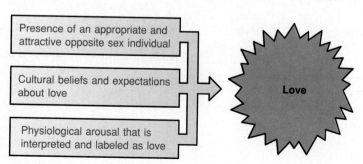

186

CHAPTER 6

INTERPERSONAL
RELATIONS: FROM
GETTING ALONG TO
LOVING

less of the idealization that was part of the early phase of the love affair. However, there may still be strong feelings of affection and caring as the couple goes into what is called a *companionate love phase.*[26]

An Integrative Perspective: Putting It All Together

The story of love appears to be pretty complex. There are different types of love and different factors involved in the love experience. Sternberg has recently proposed that the different types of love relationships can be understood as varying on three basic dimensions—*passion, intimacy,* and *decision/commitment.*[27] *Passion* represents the emotional and arousal factors involved in love. *Intimacy* is the feeling of closeness and attachment. *Decision/commitment* is the decision that one is in love and that one is going to try maintain the relationship for a long period of time. Table 6.1 shows how different types of love relationships can be understood as varying on these three dimensions. For example, if only intimacy is present, one is experiencing liking, while passionate love (infatuation) would involve passion but little intimacy or commitment. A combination of passion and intimacy is romantic love. Companionate love involves intimacy and commitment but little passion. The ultimate or complete love that many strive for in romantic relationships comes from a combination of all three components—passion, intimacy, and commitment. How many of the different types of love listed in Table 6.1 have you experienced?

Keeping Love Alive: How to Keep the Flames Going

Although love can be one of the most beautiful experiences in a person's life, it may also lead to a lot of misery. Many relationships end in painful ways for

TABLE 6.1
Love: An Integrative Approach

Sternberg proposed that different types of love are based on different degrees of passion, intimacy, and decision/commitment. How these contribute to different types of love is shown in this table. (*Source:* Based on suggestions by Sternberg (1987); see Note 27.)

Type of Love	Love Components		
	Passion	Intimacy	Decision/Commitment
Liking	No	Yes	No
Infatuation	Yes	No	No
Romantic	Yes	Yes	No
Companionate	No	Yes	Yes
Consummate	Yes	Yes	Yes

one or both members. About half of the marriages in the United States end in divorce, and children suffer greatly from the resultant "broken homes." Is there anything that can be done to avoid these breakups of long-term relationships? One obvious way is to educate people about the *importance of similarity* in relationships. If a couple differs greatly in personality, values, and interests, they should think twice about getting involved in a long-term relationship. Once a couple is committed to a long-term relationship, they can do their best to keep the passion, intimacy, and commitment levels in their relationship strong. Admittedly, that may take some active effort, but it is exactly these efforts that were associated with falling in love. First, we can keep passion in a long-term relationship by maintaining some degree of novelty, unpredictability, mystery, and excitement. We could give unexpected presents, get involved in some novel activities, and try to get away for pleasant and romantic trips. It is also important to make attempts to remain attractive to the other person by our dress, hygiene, and actions. Intimacy can be maintained by sharing concerns and experiences, getting involved in mutually rewarding activities, and demonstrating concern for our partner's welfare. Feelings of commitment would tend to increase naturally over time as we come to share many possessions, experiences, and possibly children. However, such feelings can be enhanced by investing time and energy in a relationship. It is important for couples to give their relationship priority and to try to engage in activities that help strengthen it. If people become totally absorbed in their work or school, this commitment may begin to diminish. What we are suggesting is thus quite simple. We should continue to do those things that made us fall in love in the first place. We may fall out of love not because the feelings of love automatically diminish with time, but because we stop acting out those behaviors that were involved in falling in love and are required to nourish its maintenance.

THE DEVELOPMENT OF RELATIONSHIPS: HOW DO THEY GET STARTED?

How do you go about making friends? Do you just walk up to somebody and start talking? How do you progress from casual conversation to the level of friendship? How do you become better acquainted with your fellow worker? These are the types of issues that concern researchers who study the development of interpersonal relations. Although there are many different ways that we can go about making friends, there appears to be some general consistency in this process. First of all, it appears to happen in a rather gradual manner as we progress from *awareness* of each other, to *superficial contact,* and then to a degree of *mutuality.*[28] Mutuality includes three dimensions of relationships—*involvement, commitment,* and *symmetry.* Involvement is the degree to which the friends share their time, interests, and activities with one another. Commitment is the degree of obligation they feel to one another. Symmetry is the extent to which they contribute equally to the relationship.

188

CHAPTER 6

INTERPERSONAL
RELATIONS: FROM
GETTING ALONG TO
LOVING

Self-Disclosure: The Process of Getting Close

Yet how do we develop some sense of mutuality? One of the main factors appears to be the process of **self-disclosure**.[29] Self-disclosures are personal statements that we make about ourselves in relationships. These statements reveal information that would not otherwise be known to this person. They can be fairly superficial or quite intimate. In the early stages of a relationship we tend to restrict ourselves mostly to superficial self-disclosures such as statements about work, sports, and the weather. As we get to know the other person better, we may begin to divulge more and more personal information such as religious and sexual views. This process takes place rather gradually, typically by means of reciprocity. That is, we tend to determine the amount and intimacy of self-disclosure by that of the other person. The more he or she discloses, the more we do also. Of course, there are limits. If someone begins to disclose intimate information almost immediately, we may think this person is abnormal and pull back in our relationship. There also has to be one person who sets the pace for the relationship, otherwise there would be no movement. People who tend to be more comfortable in making self-disclosures may be the pace setters. Of course, if someone is shy, very little reciprocity may occur no matter what the other person does.

An interesting aspect of the self-disclosure process is that the *degree of reciprocity* varies with the stage of the relationship. During the early phases, there is a lot of reciprocity of nonintimate information but very little reciprocity of intimate information.[30] The reciprocity of nonintimate information declines as the relationship develops since it appears to be more important for formation of relationships than for their maintenance. In contrast, the reciprocity of intimate information goes up during the middle phases of a relationship. There is now some element of trust and reciprocity of personal information may be important for demonstrating this feature to one another. However, as the relationship continues to develop, this type of reciprocity may also no longer be necessary. This doesn't mean that self-disclosure is not occurring. There is simply no concern about responding to a partner's self-disclosures with similar self-disclosures. Just listening and commenting may be sufficient to satisfy the needs of the relationship at that point in its development (see Figure 6.6 for a summary of this discussion).

Exchange Theory of Relationships: The Give and Take of Life

We have already discussed *exchange theory* as it relates to liking and loving. It is actually a broad theory of relationships that helps us understand the process of developing and maintaining relationships.[31] The major elements of this theory are *rewards* and *costs*. People are motivated to maximize rewards and minimize their costs. Therefore any acts by members in a relationship that are rewarding should strengthen the desire to maintain the relationship, while acts that are punishing or unpleasant should lessen the desire for a relationship. Development of a relationship can be seen as an exchange of rewards and costs. When primarily positive behaviors or rewards are being exchanged, there is a tendency to reciprocate these (see Figure 6.7). The relationship is seen as quite rewarding by both partners. If there are a lot of negative behaviors exchanged or there is a lack of

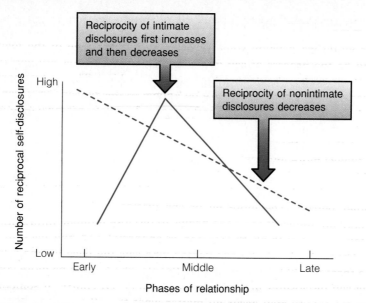

FIGURE 6.6 Reciprocity of Self-Disclosure: Changes Over Time
Reciprocity of self-disclosure varies over the course of a relationship. The exact patterns also depend on whether the information being disclosed is intimate or nonintimate. (*Source:* Adapted from Won-Doornink (1979); see Note 30.)

positive behaviors, the relationship will not be seen as very rewarding. There is a lot of evidence for the importance of rewards in relationships. For example, someone saying he or she likes you can serve as a very strong reward and in turn strongly influence your attraction to that individual.

Comparison Levels However, just because we are experiencing a lot of rewards in a relationship does not mean that we will be happy with it. Our happiness in a relationship also depends on our **comparison level (CL).**[32] This is the reward

FIGURE 6.7 Exchange of Rewards: One Basis for Relationship Development
In developing relationships, exchange or reciprocity of positive behaviors is an important part of the process. Yet as in this case, such exchanges may sometimes be misinterpreted. (Reprinted by permission of UFS, Inc.)

190

CHAPTER 6

INTERPERSONAL
RELATIONS: FROM
GETTING ALONG TO
LOVING

level we expect in a relationship based on our past experiences and expectations derived from other sources such as friends or the media. If the outcomes we obtain in a relationship are *below* this comparison level, we will be dissatisfied. If they are *above* the comparison level, we will be satisfied (see Figure 6.8). So as they say, happiness is relative. If you expect a lot, you will be happy only when you receive a high level of rewards. If you expect very little, you may be satisfied with only a modestly rewarding relationship. Of course, if the relationship is very rewarding, it eventually will raise your comparison level to a point where the satisfaction will be reduced. Support for the comparison level idea comes from a study in which people who won a million dollars in a lottery were compared with those who had an accident that paralyzed them for life.[33] The accident victims took more pleasure in everyday events than did the lottery winners. Apparently, the high comparison level of the lottery winners made the little everyday rewards seem insignificant, but the low comparison level of the accident victims enabled them to appreciate their value.

While comparison level influences our satisfaction in a relationship, whether we stay in a relationship will depend on the rewards we can gain in other alternative relationships—**comparison level for alternatives (CL alt).**[34] If we feel that we can gain more rewards in some other relationship, we may leave the present one for this new one. This helps explain the frequent changes in relationships that can occur both before and after marriage. Yet sometimes people will stay in an

FIGURE 6.8 Comparison Level: A Basis for Satisfaction or Dissatisfaction
According to the concept of *comparison level,* our level of satisfaction with a relationship at any point in time is determined by whether our outcomes are above or below our present comparison level. After a period of rather positive experiences or outcomes, the CL may shift to a higher level as in Phase 2. However, if there is a series of negative outcomes, the CL could shift again to a lower level (Phase 3). (*Source:* Based on suggestions by Thibaut and Kelley (1959); see Note 31.)

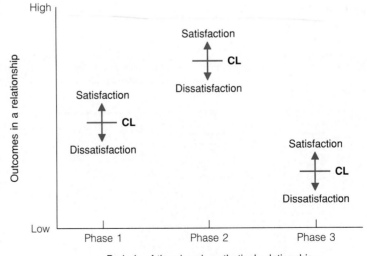

unhappy relationship because they feel that they have no alternative. Battered wives are an example. A third factor that may keep people in relationship is their **investments** in it. Some may feel they have contributed too much to a relationship (financially and emotionally) to leave it for another attractive relationship.[35]

Exchange theory provides a rather straightforward explanation of why relationships form and break up. There are, however, many other factors that play a role in relationships. We have discussed several of these in other chapters (e.g., attributions, social influence, communication). These factors of course influence relationships in work settings as well. The **Case in Point** on page 192 exemplifies how relationship problems in workplaces can often be traced to some of the principles we have discussed.

ROMANCE IN THE WORKPLACE: DO WORK AND LOVE MIX?

There have been drastic changes in the proportion of men and women in the workplace over the past few decades. Although women still dominate some of their traditional job categories such as secretaries and nurses, increasing numbers are involved in a wide variety of professional and corporate positions. As a result, men and women now find themselves working as colleagues in such areas as sales, research, and management (see Figure 6.9). While these changes are certainly positive ones from the standpoint of advancing the equality of women in the workplace, it has also provided increased opportunities for the development of heterosexual romance. Is this a positive or negative development? Certainly those

FIGURE 6.9 Workplace Romance: An Increasingly Common Phenomenon
Today men and women find themselves colleagues in a wide variety of work settings. This has increased the frequency of workplace romance.

192
CHAPTER 6
INTERPERSONAL
RELATIONS: FROM
GETTING ALONG TO
LOVING

who have found a romantic partner may view it positively. But what about their fellow workers and bosses? What happens to the effectiveness at work? Does the romance interfere with job performance and produce conflicts among employees? Or does romance provide an added reason to be highly motivated at work? These questions have received increased attention from researchers in the past few years.

Some Basic Features: Who and Why

Romantic involvement seems to be a rather common occurrence, with about 70 percent of workplaces having at least one reported romance.[36] The likelihood of romance may be partly facilitated by the proximity factor. Simply working in close proximity provides opportunities for communication and interaction. This gives people a chance to discover similarities in values and opinions. Many jobs or organizations would tend to attract employees who are fairly similar in these areas. For example, those working for an American automobile manufacturer are likely to be positively disposed to having strong restrictions on the importation of foreign-made automobiles.

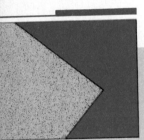

CASE IN POINT

Some Bad Relations!

"Can I come in for a minute, Mr. Glidson?"

"Sure, Jane, what can I do for you?"

"Well, frankly I've had it with Don Callan. I really can't work with him any more."

Mr. Glidson, director of personnel at Aero Shipping, sat back and looked sympathetically at Jane Myers. She had worked at the company for about two years and had been a dependable and congenial employee. Don Callan had only been with the company for two months, but he was also a good worker. He had not yet missed a workday, he was always on time, and he was willing to work overtime if necessary. Mr. Glidson did not want to lose either one of these employees. He decided that he had better get to the bottom of the problem.

"What has Don done to get you so upset?"

Jane sat up straight, took a deep breath, and then started to detail her various complaints. "Basically, Don has no social skills. He is always cutting me down and will disagree with me on an issue just to get me mad. Sometimes I try to get things started on the right foot by giving a compliment, but he just ignores it. Actually, it's pretty hard to compliment him since he does very little about his looks. I think he wears the same clothes most of the week."

Mr. Glidson nodded in agreement at the last comment.

"He sure could improve his appearance a bit, but when you're handling

While shared similarities may aid the attraction process, the romantic couples often differ in a number of ways. The men in such relationships tend to be older, better educated, and of higher status.[37] This could be viewed as an exchange process in that higher status of the male is exchanged for the youthfulness of the female. The exchange does not appear to be based solely on the attractiveness of the female, since the partners tend to be viewed as similar in physical attractiveness.[38] So it seems that attraction in the workplace develops in about the same way as it does in most other situations.

People may get involved in a romance at work for a variety of reasons. Most of these can be understood in terms of three types of motivation—love, ego, and job.[39] Love motivation involves a sincere desire for romance and a long-term companion. Those motivated by ego are interested in the excitement, adventure, and sexual experiences provided by the relationship. Job-motivated people are interested in the work-related benefits provided by the relationship, such as security, power, improved job conditions, and advancement. Of course, the partners in the work romance may either be similar or different in their motives for the relationship. As a result, there are many different types of romance relationships.[40] In some, both partners may be motivated by love and ego, resulting in a passionate

packages all day, wearing nice clothes probably isn't as important as it would be in an office."

"Yes, but that doesn't mean that you don't have to try to be a reasonable human being," Jane replied, becoming more emotional by the minute. "I think he has some basic personality problem because he never opens up about himself. I don't really know much more about him as a person now than I did the first week he worked for us. I sure miss working with Jim Bone. We really got along well."

"Yes that Jim is a fine person," Mr. Glidson mused as he began shuffling some papers on his desk. "He certainly deserved his promotion and is really doing well in his new department. But that doesn't help us now, does it? Well, maybe I should begin by having a talk with Don. I'd hate to lose either one of you."

Questions

1. What principles of good relations or interpersonal attraction does Don appear to be violating?

2. Do you think Jane's prior experience with Jim had something to do with the strength of her reactions to Don? What principle from exchange theory may have come into play here?

3. What do you think Mr. Glidson should do? Should he just get rid of Don or should he try to improve Don's interpersonal style? What specific suggestions do you have for such an improvement program?

194

CHAPTER 6
INTERPERSONAL
RELATIONS: FROM
GETTING ALONG TO
LOVING

love relationship. This is the most common relationship found in the workplace. When both partners are motivated primarily by love, a companionate relationship is likely to develop. A fling is the result of two people motivated exclusively by ego. Sometimes the male in the relationship is motivated primarily by a desire for job power and control. He may seek out a female who has greater influence or power than he does to further these goals. The form of this relationship that involves a male with ego and job motives and a female with love and job motives is called male-dominated utilitarian. When the female is motivated by ego and job but the male only by ego, a female-dominated utilitarian relationship exists. This typically involves low status or power females forming relationships with older, high-power males. We have summarized the types of workplace romances and their reported frequency in Table 6.2. How many of these have you observed or experienced?

Romance and Job Performance: Pluses and Minuses

While work romances may fulfill a variety of needs in the participants, they are not without controversy. Some researchers have suggested that such relationships interfere with the effective functioning of organizations.[41] The participants may be less effective at work because of their increased preoccupation with one another. Gossip, suspicion, and jealousy may negatively affect the work atmosphere. If the romance is between managers or between people of different rank, their ability to be effective managers may be hurt. Their credibility and objectivity in the eyes of the other employees may be lowered. Certainly, they will be unable to appraise the performance of the romantic partner objectively. Once romances end, bad feelings between the participants may persist.

Most popular discussions in newspapers of workplace romance focus on the

---

TABLE 6.2
Job Romance: Three Basic Motives

On the basis of the three basic motives for work romance (love, ego, and job), five different types of relationships can develop. (*Source:* Adapted from Dillard and Segrin, (1987); see Note 40.)

Partners	Motives	Relationship	Frequency
Male	Love, Ego	Passionate love	36%
Female	Love, Ego		
Male	Love	Companionate love	23%
Female	Love		
Male	Ego	Fling	19%
Female	Ego		
Male	Ego, Job	Male-dominated utilitarian	8%
Female	Love, Job		
Male	Ego	Female-dominated utilitarian	14%
Female	Ego, Job		

negative elements of such relationships, but until recently, solid evidence on the impact of romance on job effectiveness was not available. There are no studies providing objective evidence of the effects of workplace romance on productivity and organizational functioning. However, several studies have obtained subjective impressions from people in the workplace about the effects of romances in which they were involved or which they observed. The results so far are rather mixed. In many cases there are no observed changes in productivity attributed to the romance.[42] In other cases, both positive and negative effects on work performance have been observed. For example, in one study it was found that there was a slight tendency for people involved in organizational romance to begin arriving late or leaving early, to complain more, or have increased absence from work. However, there was also a strong increase in enthusiasm for work.[43] (See Figure 6.10 for a summary of these findings.) The group most likely to show an improvement in job performance are females who are love-motivated.[44] Possibly, the positive feelings about the love relationship "spill over" into positive feelings about the job. So while there may be drawbacks to office romance, these may be counteracted by the increased enthusiasm such romances produce, especially among female workers. Before you read the next section, complete the questions about workplace romance in the **Human Relations in Action** on page 196.

FIGURE 6.10 Effects of Workplace Romance: Not Always Negative
Individuals involved in organizational romance may show a variety of changes in the workplace. While there is some tendency for more complaints, absenteeism, and tardiness, there is also an increased enthusiasm. (*Source:* From Dillard and Broetzmann (1989); Note 43.)

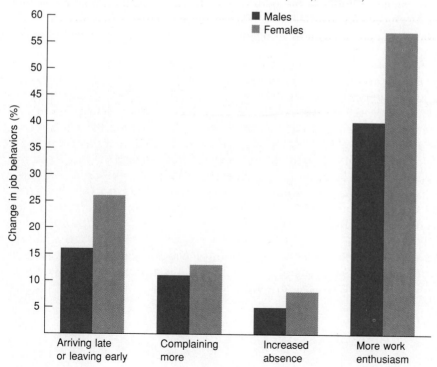

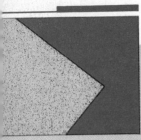

HUMAN RELATIONS IN ACTION

Workplace Romance: An Assessment

As we have been discussing, romance between co-workers is becoming a fairly frequent occurrence. Have you ever been involved in such a relationship? If not, have you worked in places where you had the opportunity to observe such a relationship develop? If so, what happened to the work habits of those involved? Answer the following questions in terms of your experience. If you have been involved in a work romance, answer the questions on the basis of this romance. If you have only observed romance at work, answer the questions on the basis of this experience. If you have not experienced or observed workplace romance, answer the questions on the basis of what you expect. Answer these questions about both the male and female partner in the relationship.

1. Was there increased tardiness or early departure from work?

   Male: Yes _____ No _____   Female: Yes _____ No _____

2. Was there more complaining about work?

   Male: Yes _____ No _____   Female: Yes _____ No _____

3. Was there increased absenteeism?

   Male: Yes _____ No _____   Female: Yes _____ No _____

4. Was there more enthusiasm for work?

   Male: Yes _____ No _____   Female: Yes _____ No _____

You can compare your answers with the results presented in Figure 6.10. You can see that the most likely changes in job-related behaviors are in changes in arrival and departure times and increased enthusiasm for work, especially among females. Does this fit with your pattern of answers? Of course, more reliable information can be obtained by combining the answers from the whole class. Ask your teacher to collect this information, either by a show of hands or by using the form in the Student Study Guide. Separate sets of scores should be computed for people who were involved in relationships, those who observed relationships, and those who are just giving their expectations. What do you find? Are the results comparable to those in Figure 6.10 for the different groups? The study by Dillard and Broetzmann suggests that the impressions of those involved in relationships and those of observers should not differ much.[45] However, those who are giving their expectations may give the most negative picture, since it is generally presumed that office romance is harmful.[46] If the results of the class do not fit with these expected patterns of results, you might want to discuss possible reasons for this discrepancy.

Handling Work Romance: Some Guidelines

It is quite apparent that the effects of work romance can be rather varied. Sometimes romance can be quite disruptive and interfere with job performance. At other times, it may help create increased enthusiasm for the job. So it is difficult to develop a single policy that encompasses every situation, and it probably does not surprise you that the most common technique of dealing with work romance is to do nothing.[47] This may not always be the best policy. Management needs to be sensitive to the broad variety of motives that lie behind such romance and the varied effects it can have. Prohibiting the development of romantic relationships may not be feasible and may cut off the potential for the development of relationships that are positive both for the participants and the corporation. In particular, relationships that are seen as motivated by love may be least problematic.[48] However, relationships that appear to be exploitative or disruptive should not be ignored. The participants should be counseled about the impact of their relationship on the workplace and steps should be taken to minimize the negative effects. They may have to limit their interaction at work or they may need to be moved to different departments. If the relationship continues to be a problem, one or both of the partners may have to leave.

SUMMARY

We **affiliate** with others for a wide variety of reasons. Two major factors appear to be the opportunity for social comparison and the opportunity for the exchange of social rewards. Two types of rewards that others provide are psychological intimacy and integrated involvement. When we are in a state of fear, we may have an increased desire to affiliate with others to obtain direct anxiety reduction or the opportunity for social comparison.

We tend to like people who are familiar or have attractive features. Contrary to common expectations, we appear to be attracted most to those who are similar to us along such dimensions as opinions and personality.

Love appears to be partly based on positive emotions related to the exchange of rewards. There are many types of love—ranging from passionate to companionate. It has been proposed that the different types of love relationships that exist vary on the three basic dimensions of passion, intimacy, and decision/commitment.

Self-disclosures play an important role in relationships since they enable the development of intimacy. The rewards and costs associated with a relationship are also important. Satisfaction with a relationship may depend on the extent to which our outcomes exceed our **comparison level.** Our commitment to a relationship depends on our **comparison level for alternatives** and our **investment** in a relationship.

Workplace romance is an increasingly frequent phenomenon. People become involved in such romances due to a wide variety of motives. While such romances may have some negative effects on job performance, these may be counteracted in part by an increase in enthusiasm for the job.

198

CHAPTER 6

INTERPERSONAL
RELATIONS: FROM
GETTING ALONG TO
LOVING

KEY TERMS

affiliation: The tendency to associate with other people.

comparison level (CL): The reward level we expect in a relationship is based on our past experiences and expectations derived from other sources such as friends or the media. The comparison level becomes the standard by which satisfaction in a relationship is measured.

comparison level for alternatives (CL alt): The level of rewards that we feel we can obtain in relationships other than the one in which we are presently involved. This comparison level determines the extent to which we are inclined to stay in a relationship.

integrated involvement: Rewards or benefits that come from being involved in group activities. Among these are a feeling of being needed and approval for successful performance.

investment: One's contribution to a relationship. The greater one's investment, the greater one's commitment to the relationship.

love: A strong affectional relationship between people. There appear to be many variations of this type of relationship in terms of degree of passion, intimacy, and commitment.

psychological intimacy: Direct rewards or benefits derived from social contact such as affection and the opportunity for emotional expression. This is one of the major reasons individuals may join groups.

self-disclosure: Personal statements about oneself revealing information that would not otherwise be known. These types of statements are important in the development of intimacy in relationships.

social comparison: The process of comparing our abilities and opinions with those of others. In the case of opinions, we tend to compare ourselves to those who are similar, whereas in the case of abilities we tend to compare ourselves with those who appear to be slightly superior.

NOTES

1. Park, R.D., & Slaby, R.G. (1983). "The Development of Aggression." In E.M. Hetherington, ed., *Handbook of Child Psychology,* vol. 4, pp. 547–641. New York: John Wiley.

2. Latane, B., & Glass, D.C. (1968). "Social and Nonsocial Attraction in Rats." *Journal of Personality and Social Psychology, 9,* 142–46.

3. Zuckerman, M. (1979). *Sensation Seeking: Beyond Optimal Level of Arousal.* Hillsdale, N.J.: Lawrence Erlbaum Associates.

4. Hill, C.A. (1987). "Affiliation Motivation: People Who Need People But in Different Ways." *Journal of Personality and Social Psychology, 52,* 1008–18.

5. Shaver, P., & Burhmester, D. (1983). "Loneliness, Sex-Role Orientation, and Group Life: A Social Needs Perspective." In P.B. Paulus, ed., *Basic Group Processes,* pp. 259–88. New York: Springer-Verlag.

6. Schachter, S. (1959). *The Psychology of Affiliation.* Stanford, Calif.: Stanford University Press.

7. Wrightsman, L.S. (1960). "Effects of Waiting with Others on Changes in Level of Felt Anxiety." *Journal of Abnormal and Social Psychology, 61,* 216–22.

8. Festinger, L. (1954). "A theory of Social Comparison Processes." *Human Relations, 7,* 117–40.

9. Bornstein, R.F. (1989). "Exposure and affect: Overview and Meta-analysis of research, 1968–1987." *Psychological Bulletin, 106,* 265–89.

10. Berscheid, E., Dion, K., Walster, E., & Walster, G.W. (1971). Physical Attractiveness and Dating Choice: A Test of the Matching Hypothesis." *Journal of Experimental Social Psychology, 7,* 173–89.

11. Berscheid, E. (1985). "Interpersonal Attraction." In G. Lindzey and E. Aronson, eds., *Handbook of Social Psychology,* 3d ed., vol. 2, pp. 413–84, New York: Random House.

12. Byrne, D., Clore, G.L., & Smeaton, G. (1986). "The Attraction Hypothesis: Do Similar Attitudes Affect Anything?" *Journal of Personality and Social Psychology, 51,* 1167–70.

13. Kandell, D.B. (1978). "Similarity in Real-Life Adolescent Friendship Pairs." *Journal of Personality and Social Psychology, 36,* 306–12.

14. Buss, D.M., & Barnes, M. (1986). "Preferences in Human Mate Selection." *Journal of Personality and Social Psychology, 50,* 559–70.

15. Cate, R.D., & Lloyd, S.A. (1988). "Courtship." In S.W. Duck, ed., *Handbook of Personal Relationships,* pp. 409–27. New York: John Wiley.

16. Winch, R.F. (1958). *Mate Selection: A Study in Complementary Needs.* New York: Harper & Row.

17. Meyer, J.P., & Pepper, S. (1977). "Need Compatibility and Marital Adjustment in Young Married Couples." *Journal of Personality and Social Psychology, 35,* 331–42.

18. Byrne, D., & Clore, G.L. (1970). "A Reinforcement-Affect Model of Evaluative Responses." *Personality: An International Journal, 1,* 103–28.

19. See Note 15.

20. Clark, M.S., & Mills, J. (1979). "Interpersonal Attraction in Exchange and Communal Relationships." *Journal of Personality and Social Psychology, 37,* 12–24.

21. Rubin, Z. (1970). "Measurement of Romantic Love." *Journal of Personality and Social Psychology, 16,* 1243–46.

22. Walster, E., & Berscheid, E. (1974). "A Little Bit About Love: A Minor Essay on a Major Topic. In T.L. Huston, ed. *Foundations of Interpersonal Attraction.* New York: Academic Press.

23. Kenrick, D.T., & Cialdini, R.B. (1977). "Romantic Attraction: Misattribution Versus Reinforcement Explanations." *Journal of Personality and Social Psychology, 35,* 381–91.

24. Dutton, D.G., & Aron, A.P. (1974). "Some Evidence for Heightened Sexual Attraction Under Conditions of High Anxiety." *Journal of Personality and Social Psychology, 30,* 510–17.

25. Zillmann, D. (1984). *Connections Between Sex and Aggression.* Hillsdale, N.J.: Erlbaum.

26. Hatfield, E. (1982). "Passionate Love, Companionate Love, and Intimacy." In M. Fisher and G. Stricker, eds. *Intimacy,* pp. 267–92. New York: Plenum.

27. Sternberg, R.J. (1987). "Liking Versus Loving: A Comparative Evaluation of Theories." *Psychological Bulletin, 102,* 331–45.

28. Levinger, G., & Snoek, J.D. (1972). *Attraction in Relationships: A New Look at Interpersonal Attraction.* Morristown, N.J.: General Learning Press.

29. Archer, R.L., & Earle, W.B. (1983). "The Interpersonal Orientations of Disclosure." In P.B. Paulus, ed. *Basic Group Processes,* pp. 289–314. New York: Springer-Verlag.

30. Won-Doornink, M.J. (1979). "On Getting to Know You: The Association Between the Stage of a Relationship and Reciprocity of Self-Disclosure." *Journal of Experimental Social Psychology, 15,* 229–41.

31. Thibaut, J.W., & Kelley, H.H. (1959). *The Social Psychology of Groups.* New York: John Wiley.

32. See Note 31.

200

CHAPTER 6

INTERPERSONAL
RELATIONS: FROM
GETTING ALONG TO
LOVING

33. Brickman, P., Coates, D., & Janoff-Bulman, R. (1978). "Lottery Winners and Accident Victims: Is Happiness Relative?" *Journal of Personality and Social Psychology, 36*, 917–27.

34. See Note 31.

35. Rusbult, C.E. (1983). "A Longitudinal Test of the Investment Model: The Development (and Deterioration) of Satisfaction and Commitment in Heterosexual Involvements." *Journal of Personality and Social Psychology, 45*, 101–17.

36. Dillard, J.P., & Miller, K.I. (1988). "Intimate Relationships in Task Environments." In S.W. Duck, ed. *Handbook of Personal Relationships*. New York: John Wiley.

37. Miller, K.I., & Ellis, B.H. (1987). "Stereotypical Views of Intimate Relationships in Organizations." Paper presented at the annual meeting of the International Communication Association, Montreal (May).

38. Dillard, J.P., & Witteman, H. (1985). "Romantic Relationships at Work: Organizational and Personal Influences." *Human Communication Research, 12*, 99–116.

39. Quinn, R.E. (1977). "Coping with Cupid: The Formation, Impact, and Management of Romantic Relationships in Organizations." *Administrative Science Quarterly, 22*, 30–45.

40. Dillard, J.P., & Segrin, C. (1987). "Intimate Relationships in Organizations: Relational Types, Illicitness, and Power." Paper presented at the annual meeting of International Communication Association, Montreal (May).

41. Collins, E.G.C. (1983). "Managers and Lovers." *Harvard Business Review, 83*, 142–53.

42. See Note 36.

43. Dillard, J.P., & Broetzmann, S.M. (1989). "Romantic Relationships at Work: Perceived Changes in Job-Related Behaviors as a Function of Participant's Motive, Partner's Motive, and Gender." *Journal of Applied Social Psychology, 19*, 93–110.

44. Dillard, J.P. (1987). "Close Relationships at Work: Perceptions of the Motives and Performance of Relational Participants." *Journal of Social and Personal Relationships, 4*, 179–93.

45. See Note 43.

46. See Note 41.

47. See Note 39.

48. See Note 43.

49. Lee, J.A. (1973). *The Colors of Love: An Exploration of the Ways of Loving*. Don Mills, Ontario: New Press.

50. Hendrick, C., & Hendrick, S.S. (1989). "Research on Love: Does It Measure Up?" *Journal of Personality and Social Psychology, 56*, 784–94.

51. Hendrick, S.S., Hendrick, C., & Adler, N.L. (1988). "Romantic Relationships: Love Satisfaction and Staying Together." *Journal of Personality and Social Psychology, 54*, 980–88.

52. Ainsworth, M.D.S., Blehar, M.C., Waters, E., & Wall, S. (1978). *Patterns of Attachment: A Psychological Study of a Strange Situation*. Hillsdale, N.J.: Lawrence Erlbaum Associates.

53. Hazan, C., & Shaver, P. (1987). "Romantic Love Conceptualized as an Attachment Process." *Journal of Personality and Social Psychology, 52*, 511–24.

ADDITIONAL CASES AND EXERCISES: APPLYING WHAT YOU'VE LEARNED

What Is Your Love Style?

The items below indicate different approaches to or feelings about love. Some of the items describe a specific relationship while others refer to general feelings about love. Answer these questions in light of your present or most current love relationship. If you have not yet been in love, give your answers on the basis of how you think you would react. Simply complete the scale by filling in the spaces with *Y* if the item accurately describes your general approach or feelings or *N* if the item does not describe your general approach or feelings.

_____ **1.** My lover and I were meant for each other.

_____ **2.** My lover and I have the right chemistry.

_____ **3.** My lover and I really understand each other.

_____ **4.** What my lover doesn't know about me won't hurt him/her.

_____ **5.** I don't like it when my lover gets too dependent on me.

_____ **6.** I like to keep my lover a little unsure about my commitment to him/her.

_____ **7.** Love that grows out of a long friendship is best.

_____ **8.** I have to care for someone before I can fall in love with that person.

_____ **9.** Love is basically a deep friendship.

_____ **10.** It is important to know about a person's background before making a commitment.

_____ **11.** In choosing a partner, it is important to know whether or not this person will be a good parent.

_____ **12.** It is best to fall in love with someone with a similar background.

_____ **13.** When my lover doesn't pay attention to me, I get very upset.

_____ **14.** When I am in love, I find it hard to concentrate on other things.

_____ **15.** When I am in love, I am often too excited to sleep.

_____ **16.** I place my lover's happiness before my own.

_____ **17.** I am happy to give up my own wishes and desires so that my lover can achieve his/hers.

_____ **18.** I would rather have bad things happen to myself than to my lover.

Instructions for scoring. On the basis of detailed interviews, Lee proposed that there are six love styles—romantic love (*eros*), game-playing love (*ludus*), friendship love (*storge*), possessive/dependent (*mania*), pragmatic or logical (*pragma*), and unselfish and all giving (*agape*).[49] The items above are similar to those used by Hendrick and Hendrick.[50] The six love styles are represented by the following items: eros (items 1–3); ludus (items 4–6); storge (items 7–9); pragma (items 10–12); mania (items 13–15); agape (items 16–18). If you answered two or more of

202

CHAPTER 6
INTERPERSONAL
RELATIONS: FROM
GETTING ALONG TO
LOVING

the items for a love style with Y, you probably are inclined toward that type of love style. You may, of course, be high in two or more of the love styles. For example, if you are high on mania, you could also be high on eros. Or you could be high on both storge and agape. You might ask your instructor to obtain the scores (anonymously, of course) from each student in your class. This would enable the instructor to report on the frequency of occurrence of the various love styles or love style combinations. If you also provide information about gender, age, and whether you are currently in love, the influence of these factors could also be examined.

There is some evidence for sex differences in love styles. Males tend to be higher in ludic love and females in erotic, storgic, pragmatic, and manic love. It is likely that we will become more storgic and agapic and less erotic and manic in our love styles as we get older or over time in a relationship with a particular person. One question that probably has come to your mind is whether certain styles are related to more successful relationships. Not surprisingly, it has been found that relationships that were more erotic and less ludic seem to last longer.[51]

Attachment Style: One Basis for Love

All of us have somewhat different styles of love. Listed below are three alternative styles that characterize love relationships. Which one of these best describes you? Please make a checkmark by the one that is most appropriate for you.

_____ 1. I find it relatively easy to get close to others and am comfortable depending on them and having them depend on me. I don't often worry about being abandoned or about someone getting too close to me.

_____ 2. I am somewhat uncomfortable being close to others. I find it difficult to trust them completely and difficult to allow myself to depend on them. I am nervous when anyone gets too close, and often, love partners want me to be more intimate than I feel comfortable being.

_____ 3. I find that others are reluctant to get as close as I would like. I often worry that my partner doesn't really love me or won't want to stay with me. I want to merge completely with another person, and this desire sometimes scares people away.

Young infants may show three different types of attachment to their parents—secure, avoidant, and ambivalent.[52] The secure type are able to relate in a fairly normal manner with their parents. They play normally in their presence, may cry if they leave, and are easily comforted when they return. The avoidant type may act as if the parent is not present during play situations and when a parent returns after a brief absence. The anxious-ambivalent mix typical attachment behavior with anger, anxiety, and rejection of the parents' attempts at physical contact. These styles may derive in part from the way the child is handled by the parents and according to Hazan and Shaver may in turn be reflected in our love styles.[53] The first one describes the secure style and is endorsed by about 55 percent. The second style is avoidant and chosen by about 25 percent. The third is anxious ambivalent and chosen by about 20 percent. You might ask your instructor to collect this information from the entire class to see how similar these results are to those of the Hazan and Shaver study.

Interpersonal Relations at Work: Keys to Success

Those of you who have had experience in the workplace know that many of the problems one encounters there have their basis in the relationships among the workers and between the workers and management. Managers may have poor interpersonal skills and be unable to motivate their employees. They may not be sensitive to the emotional and social needs of their employees. There may be conflicts among employees about raises, favoritism, job schedules, and assignments. New employees may have a hard time being accepted by the older ones. Sometimes love affairs develop between employees or between a manager and an employee. These can lead to further conflicts on the job. As you can see, unless interpersonal relations are effectively managed in the work environment, it will be difficult to achieve both efficiency and interpersonal harmony.

On the basis of the material from this chapter, list what you think would be the key rules people should follow to ensure effective human relations in the workplace. Try to come up with ten of these and compare them with those of other students. Your instructor might want to collect this information from the class to determine the most frequently suggested rules.

CHAPTER

Persuasion, Influence, and Power: Getting Your Way from Others

PERSUASION: THE FINE ART OF CHANGING
OTHERS' MINDS

Persuasion: Why, Sometimes, It Succeeds
Persuasion: Why It Often Fails
Changing Our Own Attitudes: A Bit of Dissonance

COMPLIANCE: TO ASK—SOMETIMES—IS
TO RECEIVE

Ingratiation: Liking as a First Step toward Influence
Multiple Requests: The Old "One-Two" Punch Strikes Again

POWER: BEYOND INFLUENCE AND PERSUASION

Individual Power: Its Basic Sources

ORGANIZATIONAL POLITICS: TECHNIQUES FOR
GAINING AND USING POWER IN WORK SETTINGS

SPECIAL SECTIONS

CASE IN POINT
A Little Compliance for a Big Sale
HUMAN RELATIONS IN ACTION
Measuring Your Own Power: A Quick Self-Assessment
ADDITIONAL CASES AND EXERCISES: APPLYING WHAT
   YOU'VE LEARNED

important

Learning Objectives

After reading this chapter,
you should be able to:

1. List several factors that determine
   whether attempts at persuasion will
   succeed or fail.

2. Describe at least two reasons why human
   beings are so good at resisting persuasion.

3. Explain how dissonance affects
   persuasion.

4. Explain the nature of ingratiation, and
   why it often succeeds.

5. Describe the "foot-in-the-door" and the
   "door-in-the-face" tactics for gaining
   compliance, and explain why each
   succeeds.

6. Define power, and list some of the major
   sources from which it derives.

7. Describe several steps that may prove
   useful in gaining and using power in
   organizational settings.

Study theory X & Y

iles Wills is the sales manager of one of the top new car dealers in the country. Today, he's breaking in a newly hired sales person, Nels Gustafson. Nels has had some experience in used car sales, but this is his first opportunity to get involved in new car sales.

"Selling is a real art, Nels. It takes some special skills and sensitivities," says Miles as they walk around the new car lot. "First you have to establish a favorable impression with the customers. They have to see you as someone who knows what he's talking about and who's trustworthy. So it's important to know your product well so you answer their questions in a confident and straightforward way. It's also important to develop a good rapport with the customer. Engage in small talk, find some areas of agreement and give some compliments about the behavior of the children."

"That part about the kids may not be easy," counters Nels.

Miles smiles and nods in agreement. "True, and whatever you do, make sure they don't see your actions as phony. You must persuade them that you have their self-interest at heart."

"But so far all you've talked about is selling myself instead of cars," Nels protests.

"Well, that's the important first step, but you're right, there is more than that," Miles responds as they stop at one of their top-selling cars. "You've got to persuade them that this car is better suited for them than competitors' cars. But you don't want to pressure them too hard or you'll turn them off. The key is to get them on your side step by step."

"I suppose you mean I should get them to take test drives?" asks Nels.

"Exactly," nods Miles, "and make sure you get them to sit down in your office afterward. Then we have a great chance to make that sale."

Just then Nels sees a young family walking on the lot. "I think I've just spotted my first sale," says Nels excitedly.

"Go for it," Miles says, nodding his approval.

Most of us have at one time or another been exposed to the various "tricks" of expert sales people. Their task of course is to do their best to make a sale. Since it is often difficult to choose between similar products, the influence of sales people may be critical. Although they may spend some time educating customers about a product, the most effective sales people are also likely to use a variety of techniques like those employed by Miles Wills, sales manager, to persuade potential buyers about the merits of his automobiles to make a sale.

Have you ever had the following daydream: Somehow, you acquire a special power that permits you to control all the people around you. Through this power, you can get them to behave in any way you wish and to do anything you want.

This is a provocative fantasy, and for good reason. Other people play a crucial role in our lives, both on and off the job. Thus the ability to totally control their behavior would be useful to say the least!

Unfortunately, of course, no magic formula for attaining such control exists. People have minds of their own and usually do what we want only part of the time. While total control over others seems to be an impossible dream, there are many tactics we can use to maximize our impact on them. Like Miles in our example, we can engage in many actions designed to "load the dice in our favor" and increase our success at influencing others. During the years ahead, you will both use and be the recipient of such tactics on countless occasions. Indeed, it is probably safe to say that attempts at influence are one of the common forms of behavior you will encounter in the world of work. For this reason, it is important that you understand their basic nature and know how to guard against them. Both of these topics, plus several others, will be examined in this chapter. Specifically, we will begin with a discussion of **persuasion**—the attempt by one person to change the behavior of others through convincing appeals and arguments. We will then examine a mixed bag of tactics useful in attaining **compliance**—a technique helpful in getting others to agree to your requests. Finally, we will turn to **power**—the strongest and most impressive form of influence.

PERSUASION: THE FINE ART OF CHANGING OTHERS' MINDS

You attend a meeting in your department and hear two people argue for different policies. You watch TV and are numbed by a seemingly endless string of commercials. Your spouse tries to talk you into taking your vacation at the seaside rather than in the mountains. What do all of these incidents have in common? One answer, of course, is that they all involve *communication*—the process of transmitting information to another person or group (see Chapter 3). But going beyond this basic fact, these incidents also share another feature: All involve *attempts at persuasion*. In each, one or more persons tried to change your behavior by getting you to see the world the way they do—by getting you to share their views. Thus persuasion involves communication for a specific purpose: changing someone's mind. More precisely, it can be defined as efforts by one or more persons to alter the beliefs or behavior of one or more others through what seem to be logical arguments and convincing facts. Of course, the arguments presented are often far from logical and the facts anything *but* accurate. Generally, though, these flaws are concealed, and persuasion maintains at least an outward appearance of reason and authority.

Persuasion is a very common form of influence—perhaps *the* most common one in use.[1] Thus each day you are sure to be subjected to efforts along these lines as everyone from your boss through politicians and advertisers attempts to change your behavior in various ways. Fortunately, of course, most of these efforts fail. Only a small fraction of the persuasive appeals we receive manage to alter our views or our actions. And this fact, in turn, raises two intriguing questions:

208

CHAPTER 7

PERSUASION,
INFLUENCE, AND
POWER: GETTING
YOUR WAY FROM
OTHERS

Why is this the case? Why are some attempts at persuasion effective while others fail? And, second, why are we so successful in resisting such appeals? We will now consider both of these issues.

Persuasion: Why, Sometimes, It Succeeds

As we noted in our discussion of communication (see Chapter 3), many factors seem to play a role in determining the success of persuasive appeals. The most important of these, though, tend to fall under two major headings: (1) characteristics of the persons doing the persuading (often termed *communicators*), and (2) various aspects of what they actually say—features of the persuasive appeal themselves.

Characteristics of Would-be Persuaders: Attractiveness, Style, and Credibility

2 major chatagories are Character & Appeal.

Suppose that at some time in the future, your job involves ordering supplies for your company. In this role, you are visited by two sales persons representing competing firms. The first is well-groomed and attractive. When describing her company's products, she speaks in an eloquent, forceful, and enthusiastic manner. Finally, she tries to help you choose the products your company needs most— *not* the ones that will yield her the largest commission. In contrast, the second sales person is sloppy, poorly groomed, and unattractive. He speaks in a halting and unconvincing manner. And he has consistently tried to get you to order the most expensive products on his list, just to increase his own gains. Which of these two persons will be more successful in affecting your decisions? The answer is obvious: the first. Of course, this is a simple and extreme case. Still, it serves to call attention to three of the factors most important in determining the success of attempts at persuasion: a communicator's *attractiveness, style* of presentation, and *credibility.*

attractiveness

With respect to attractiveness, it is clear that communicators we like (either because of their appearance or personality) are much more effective in changing our views and our behavior than ones we do not like[2] (see Figure 7.1). This occurs for the following reason. When we like certain individuals, we tend to lower our "defenses" and interpret much of what they say in a positive, favorable light. Little wonder, then, that they are effective in exerting influence on us.

Turning to personal style, a number of different factors affect persuasion. One of the most important of these, however, is a communicator's *speed of speech.* Many research studies indicate that would-be persuaders who talk rapidly are more successful in changing listeners' views or behavior than ones who speak at a more leisurely pace.[3] The reason for this is as follows: When another person speaks quickly and smoothly, we interpret such eloquence as a sign of underlying knowledge. That is, we conclude that they really know what they are talking about! In contrast, if they speak at a slow rate, we conclude that they really don't know much about the subject of their presentation. In any case, regardless of the mechanism involved, it is clear that where persuasion is concerned, "fast talkers" definitely have an edge.

FIGURE 7.1 Communicator Attractiveness: Influential in Politics
Vice President Dan Quayle looks somewhat like actor Robert Redford. His youth and good looks may have influenced his selection as a vice-presidential candidate.

Finally, a communicator's *credibility,* too, is important (see Figure 7.2). Credibility refers to the perception that a communicator can be believed or trusted. As you might guess, persons viewed as high in credibility are much more effective at persuasion than ones who are viewed as low in credibility. Two factors seem to play a key role in shaping such judgments. First, communicators who are high in *expertise* are viewed as more credible than those who are low in expertise. Second, communicators who do not seem to have much to gain from influencing others or who at least appear to take others' interest into account are seen as higher in credibility than those appearing to operate entirely out of self-interest. Thus, as in the example above, a sales person who seems concerned about customers' well-being will be higher in credibility—and thus more successful at persuasion—than one who seems to focus only on maximizing her or his own commissions.

In sum, it appears that several factors contribute to effectiveness at persuasion. If you want to maximize your own success at this important task, therefore, you should take steps to (1) enhance your attractiveness, (2) improve the smoothness, speed, and eloquence of your delivery, and (3) increase your image of credibility. To the extent you do, you may well enhance your ability to change the views and actions of the persons around you (see Figure 7.3). And this, of course, can be an important "plus" both for your career and your personal life.

The Contents of Persuasive Appeals: What You Say Matters, Too Suppose one day you go to hear a lecture on success by a famous expert. As the author of several best-selling books and the winner of many awards, this person's expertise and honesty are beyond question. Further, as she is introduced, you notice that

210

CHAPTER 7

PERSUASION,
INFLUENCE, AND
POWER: GETTING
YOUR WAY FROM
OTHERS

FIGURE 7.2   Communicator Credibility: A Valuable Commodity
Communicator credibility is very important for someone to be persuasive. When communicators such as evangelists and politicians are seen as being motivated by self-interest, they may lose credibility. (Ziggy © 1989 Ziggy & Friends./Distributed by Universal Press Syndicate. Reprinted with permission. All rights reserved.)

she is impeccably groomed and highly attractive. The room becomes hushed when she begins. At her first words—"Do you want to know the secret of success?"—hundreds of people lean forward to catch the pearls of wisdom about to follow. "Well, my friends," she continues, "I will tell you. After twenty years of experience and study, I am convinced that the secret of success is—shredded bean curd. Yes, only by eating several pounds a day of this wonderful food can you hope to get ahead in today's competitive world . . ." For a moment, there is stunned silence. Then, howls of laughter erupt all over the room, and soon it is obvious that the speech cannot continue. The speaker has totally blown her credibility!

FIGURE 7.3   Effective Persuasion: Some Key Factors
As shown here, several personal characteristics contribute to success at persuasion.

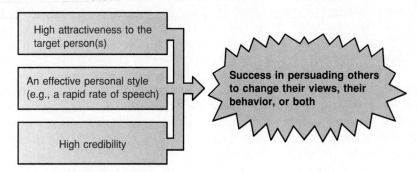

Admittedly, this is a bizarre exaggeration. Yet, it serves to call attention to a key point: The success of a persuasive appeal depends on its content as well as its source. In short, *what* is said, as well as *who* says it, is important. But what, precisely, should go into attempts at persuasion in order to maximize effectiveness? Since each persuasive appeal deals with a unique set of issues, it is obviously not possible to specify the exact words each should contain—this will depend very much on the specific situation. But research findings do point to several general guidelines that are helpful in constructing almost *any* persuasive message. By paying close attention to these, you can probably enhance the impact of your own attempts at persuasion, whether they are delivered directly to one other person, or indirectly to a larger audience. For this reason, they are worth noting carefully.

First, it is often useful to present *two-sided* rather than *one-sided* arguments.[4] Specifically, you should not simply offer support for your own view: In addition, you should mention—and then refute—opposing positions or suggestions. By following this course of action, you not only build up enthusiasm for your own position but also weaken that of others. As a result, your success at persuasion may be increased.

Second, it may help to build an emotional element (e.g., mild anxiety) into your appeals. Specifically, you should suggest that failure to adopt your suggestions will lead to negative outcomes, and then offer individuals concrete ways of avoiding these unpleasant results. If you succeed in getting your audience worried, they may quickly adopt the actions you recommend. And, of course, these should be the ones you wanted them to perform all along. Such *fear appeals,* as they are often termed, seem to be effective in many contexts.[5] But they should not be overdone. If you paint *too* frightening a picture of what will happen if people reject your suggestions, the process may backfire and actually reduce your persuasiveness.

Third, be sure to tailor your appeals to the people you are addressing. This should be done in at least two ways. The first is to be sure that your comments do not "go over their heads." One of the major reasons why even carefully planned persuasive messages fail is that the persons who hear them do not have the background or technical knowledge to understand them. And, of course, if they do not comprehend what is being said, the chances of influencing them drop close to zero. The second is to be sure to avoid stating views that are radically different from those held by the audience. A large amount of research on persuasion indicates that when individuals receive messages presenting views sharply different from their own, they tend to reject these out of hand. This is because they find them to be extreme or outlandish, and feel that they are not worthy of their attention. In contrast, if they receive appeals containing views only moderately different from their own, they may consider these carefully, and be influenced.[6] So, where persuasion is concerned, moderation—not extremity—is usually more effective (see Figure 7.4).

We could readily continue with this discussion, for many factors seem to play a role in the process of persuasion. Instead, though, we'd like to note that research on this process has recently taken a somewhat different path. Rather than asking "What kinds of messages produce the most attitude change?" recent studies have

212

CHAPTER 7
PERSUASION,
INFLUENCE, AND
POWER: GETTING
YOUR WAY FROM
OTHERS

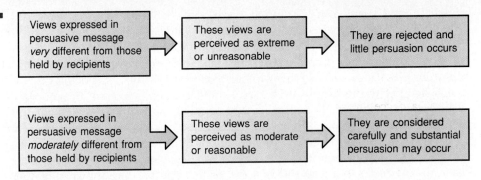

FIGURE 7.4 Moderation: Why It Often Helps in Persuasion
When the views contained in persuasive messages are very different from the ones held by recipients, they may perceive them as extreme and reject them out of hand. If, in contrast, the views contained in the messages are only moderately different from those held by the recipients, they may consider them carefully and be influenced.

focused on another question: "What cognitive processes determine whether someone will or will not be persuaded?" In other words, efforts have been made to tie the process of persuasion more closely to current knowledge about human cognition generally, and **social cognition**—the manner in which we process, store, and remember social information. It has been found that there are two distinct ways in which persuasion and attitude change occur.[7] In the first, we think about the arguments presented in a careful, rational manner. They remain at the center of our attention, and we are persuaded because, logically, they make sense. This is known as the *central route* to persuasion. In the second—the *peripheral route*—we do not give the arguments presented our full attention. Rather, we are distracted by other events, or perhaps by our thoughts about the style or appearance of the would-be persuader. Here, persuasion occurs in a kind of automatic manner. Both kinds of persuasion occur in organizational settings. An example of the first is provided by a situation in which, because of a convincing and fact-filled presentation by an individual from marketing, a group of executives decides to change their product-mix for the coming year. An example of the second would occur when a buyer for a large company is swayed to place an order with one potential supplier because the sales person from that supplier is witty and charming. (See Figure 7.5 for an overview of these two distinct routes to persuasion.)

Persuasion: Why It Often Fails

From our discussion of persuasion so far, you might well conclude that it is a fairly easy task. Strong appeals from attractive and credible communicators, you may have decided, always (or at least usually) work. They succeed in changing the behavior of the persons who receive them. Is this really the case? Even a moment's reflection suggests that it is not. Each day we are subject to many attempts at persuasion. Commercials, political speeches, suggestions from friends and co-workers—all are designed to alter our views in some way. If we yielded to all of these appeals, or even a small fraction of them, we would soon be in a pathetic state. Our views and our behavior would show a strange pattern of shifts, reversals, and re-reversals. In short, we would be mere leaves in the persuasive breeze. Obviously, this is not the case. Our views and our behavior do *not* change on a momentary basis. In fact, they generally show a great deal of stability. For this reason, it is probably fair to conclude that most attempts at persuasion fail. Why? What forces permit us to resist even impressive efforts to change our views and behavior? Actually, several factors play a role in this respect. Among the most important, though, are two: **reactance** and **forewarning.**

Reactance: "Oh, Yeah?" "Says Who?" "Watch Who You're Pushing!" Here is a basic fact of human behavior: *People don't like to be pushed around.* In fact, when they feel that someone is trying to tell them what to do or is threatening their personal freedom, they often react in a surprising way: They lean over backwards to do the *opposite* of what is demanded of them (see Figure 7.6). This tendency—usually known as *reactance*—is quite strong.[8] It occurs in many situations and can be observed among children as well as adults. Reactance is one major reason why we are so effective at resisting persuasion. After all, when individuals are exposed to persuasive appeals, they can usually tell that someone is trying to influence them. Under some conditions (for example, if they perceive that this person has a right to guide their behavior), they may accept such persuasion, or at least listen to it. But in many other cases, they view such efforts as unjustified. Then reactance occurs, and any hope of persuasion goes right out the window.

FIGURE 7.5 Persuasion: Two Basic Mechanisms
Research findings indicate that persuasion can occur through two distinct processes. In the first (the central route), persuasion takes place because target persons direct careful attention to arguments that are convincing and logical. In the second (the peripheral route), it occurs because target persons are distracted by other stimuli or events, and do not notice that the arguments presented are weak and unconvincing.

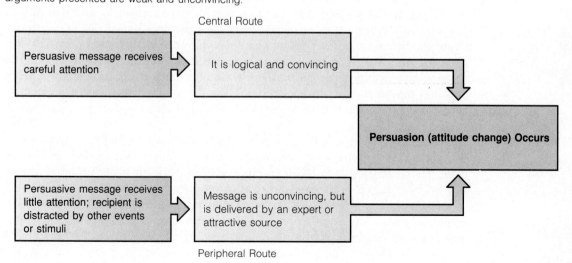

214

CHAPTER 7

PERSUASION,
INFLUENCE, AND
POWER: GETTING
YOUR WAY FROM
OTHERS

FIGURE 7.6 Reactance: Resistance to Influence
When we are told what to do, we may experience *reactance* and do exactly the opposite.
(Reprinted by permission Tribune Media Services.)

Reactance has important implications for managers or anyone else who wishes to exert influence on others. Primarily, the message is this: If you want to be an effective persuader, beware of reactance. Don't be too pushy and don't threaten others' personal freedom. Instead, always leave the persons you want to influence some room for maneuver, and at least the illusion of free choice. If you do (and if you follow the other guidelines offered above), you stand a good chance of altering their views and behavior. If you don't, reactance may set in, and your chance of producing lasting, beneficial change may totally vanish.

Knowing that Persuasion Is on the Way: Why (Sometimes) to be Forewarned Is Indeed to be Forearmed A second reason why we are often so effective at resisting persuasion is this: In most cases, we know full well when efforts at persuasion are coming. For example, we know that a political speech is designed to affect our vote, that memos from various persons in our company are aimed at changing our views, and that ads have the goal of selling us some product. Thus it is probably quite rare for any would-be persuader to catch us totally unprepared. Growing evidence suggests that such advance knowledge of persuasive intent can help us resist it. That is, we are less likely to be affected by a persuasive appeal if we know in advance that it is designed to alter our views than if we do not possess this knowledge.[9] Moreover, this is especially true with respect to views or behaviors we hold to be important. These beneficial efforts, in turn, seem to stem from a simple fact. If we know in advance that someone is trying to persuade us, we can formulate counterarguments against his or her views. As a result, we are better able to refute this person's appeal when it is actually presented. For this and other reasons, to be forewarned is indeed to be forearmed, at least in cases where we care enough about the issues in question to make active use of this knowledge (i.e., to create our own counterarguments).

The practical implications of forewarning, too, are clear. First, if you are a would-be persuader, avoid tipping your hand as long as possible. The less time you give your audience to prepare defenses against your messages, the better you will do. Second, if you are the target of persuasion and wish to defend against it, try to see it coming from as far off as possible. And then, make as much use of this advance knowledge as possible. If you do, your ability to resist may be greatly enhanced.

To conclude: because of the operation of reactance, forewarning, and other factors, resistance to persuasion is often great. Of course, persuasive appeals *do* produce change in some cases. To deny this would be to suggest that advertising, propaganda, and sales efforts always fail. But the opposite conclusion—that human beings are helpless pawns in the hands of powerful persuaders—is equally false. Resisting persuasion is an ancient human art, and there is every reason to believe that it is as successful today as it was in the past. Because of this, exerting such influence on others is often much easier to plan or imagine than it is to actually achieve.

Changing Our Own Attitudes: A Bit of Dissonance

Suppose that as graduation approaches, a college student receives two job offers. After much agonizing, she selects one. Will her attitudes toward the two companies now change? If she is like most people, they may. After the student accepts one of the two jobs, she may find that her evaluation of this position, and the company that offered it, has improved: It now seems better than it did initially, before the decision was reached. Conversely, she may find that her attitude toward the rejected firm has become less favorable. The same process occurs after other kinds of decisions, too. Whether individuals choose among cars, schools, lovers, or courses of action, they often experience a positive shift in attitudes toward the chosen alternative, and a negative shift in attitudes toward the others. Why? The answer seems to lie in a process known as **cognitive dissonance.**[10]

In simplest terms, dissonance refers to the fact that human beings dislike inconsistency. When we say one thing but do another, or discover that one attitude we hold is inconsistent with another that we also accept, an unpleasant state of *dissonance* arises. We notice the inconsistency between our words and deeds, or between our various attitudes, and react negatively to it. As the above example suggests, dissonance is also generated by many decisions. When we choose one alternative, we must necessarily forgo the benefits of the others. As a result, post-decision dissonance arises.

Many factors determine the magnitude of dissonance and the precise ways in which we seek to reduce it. Since it is usually easier to change our attitudes than our overt behavior, cognitive dissonance often leads to attitude change. We've already noted how this occurs following decisions: Chosen alternatives are enhanced while rejected onces are derogated. In other cases, we may change our attitudes to bring them into line with our overt actions, or alter our attitude to make it more consistent with others. For example, suppose that you believe quite strongly in affirmative action (special efforts to hire and promote members of minority groups who have previously been the victims of discrimination). At the

216

CHAPTER 7

PERSUASION,
INFLUENCE, AND
POWER: GETTING
YOUR WAY FROM
OTHERS

same time, you also believe in promotion on the basis of merit. No problems arise until one day a person from a minority group is promoted over one of your close friends at work, despite the fact that your friend has more experience and is better qualified in several ways. Confronted with this situation, you experience dissonance: Your two attitudes are inconsistent. What happens next? The chances are good that one or the other of these views will change. You may become less favorable toward affirmative action or less supportive of promotion-by-merit (see Figure 7.7).

Because it is an unpleasant state most persons wish to reduce, dissonance can be used as an important wedge for persuasion.[11] If would-be persuaders can place individuals in a situation where they will experience dissonance unless they alter their attitudes in desired directions, considerable success can be obtained. In organizations, tactics based on dissonance are applied in a number of contexts. One of the most important of these is their use by persons favoring the adoption of some plan or course of action. Such individuals often concentrate their efforts on getting decision-makers in their organization to make an initial, tentative commitment to the plan. They realize that once this is done, the would-be targets may become quite reluctant to pull out and reverse their decision, even if initial results are negative. Several factors play a role in such reluctance to cut one's losses, but dissonance appears to be one of them. In situations where an initial investment in some course of action has been made, but outcomes are negative, the persons involved face the following situation: They realize that they chose this plan voluntarily, and hold at least mildly positive attitudes about it. Yet, such views are inconsistent with the knowledge that the plan is not succeeding. This

FIGURE 7.7 Cognitive Dissonance as a Source of Attitude Change
When individuals notice that two attitudes they hold are inconsistent, an unpleasant state of dissonance occurs. This generates pressures to change one, or perhaps both, of the attitudes.

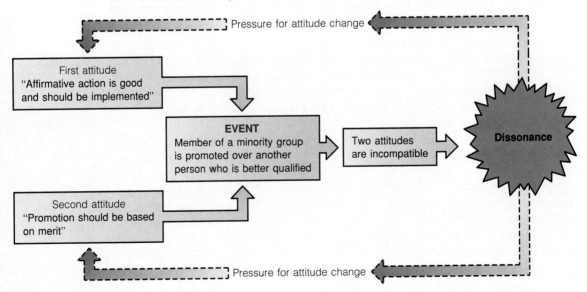

results in dissonance, which can be reduced in either of two ways: pulling out and cutting one's losses, or concluding that the plan *will* work, if given enough time, or if more resources are invested in it. Since it is easier to change one's beliefs than one's behavior, the latter tendency often prevails, with the result that what started out as a very tentative commitment grows stronger and stronger over time—just as the persuaders originally intended.

In sum, the induction of dissonance can be a powerful tactic of persuasion. In fact, as expressed in the heading of this section, under the right conditions, persons experiencing this unpleasant cognitive state become virtual allies of those who wish to persuade them: They generate internal pressures to change their own attitudes!

COMPLIANCE: TO ASK—SOMETIMES—IS TO RECEIVE

Suppose that you want another person to do something for you—anything from helping you with your work to scratching your back (figuratively or literally). How would you go about getting this individual to comply—to do what you want? The most direct approach, of course, is that of simply asking for the favor you desire. This type of influence is called **compliance.** As you know from your own experience, this is a common tactic. Individuals *do* frequently make direct requests to others. As you probably also know, however, efforts to win compliance in this manner often fail. The recipients of such requests delay responding, pretend not to understand, or simply refuse. Because of this, individuals seeking to exert such influence on others usually refrain from presenting their requests "cold." Rather, they engage in preliminary steps designed to tip the balance in their favor, and to enhance their chances of success. In short, they try to "soften up" the target of their requests before making them. Many different tactics can be used for this purpose, and several of these are highly effective. Here, we focus on two that seem to work very well in a wide range of situations: *ingratiation* and *multiple requests.*

Ingratiation: Liking as a First Step toward Influence

Most of us are aware of the following basic fact: If other persons like us, they are usually more willing to grant our requests than if they do not like us. This fact, in turn, points to a useful technique for gaining compliance from others: **ingratiation.** Briefly, ingratiation involves efforts on our part to increase others' liking for us. Once this has been attained, we reason, their willingness to agree to various requests will be enhanced. Actually, several different procedures seem effective in this regard. First, we can seek to convince other persons that we share their opinions, or are similar to them in other respects. A large body of research findings indicates that similarity often generates a high degree of liking.[12] Second,

218

CHAPTER 7

PERSUASION,
INFLUENCE, AND
POWER: GETTING
YOUR WAY FROM
OTHERS

we can concentrate on demonstrating outstanding task performance. In general, persons who perform at high levels are evaluated more favorably than those who perform less adequately. And such positive reactions seem to generalize, spreading from task performance to a wide range of personal characteristics.[13] By far the most common tactic of ingratiation, though, involves the communication of high personal regard to the target persons. This tactic, usually known as *other-enhancement*, may take the form of flattery (exaggerated praise) showing *interest* (eye contact), and giving positive nonverbal cues such as smiling.[14] Other tactics involve *impression management* or *self-presentation*—efforts by the ingratiator to create a favorable impression on the target person. This can involve efforts to enhance one's personal appearance through dress and grooming,[15] presenting information which suggests that one possesses desirable characteristics (e.g., sincerity, competence, intelligence, friendliness), or merely associating oneself with positive events or people they already like. In this latter category, ingratiators can "name drop," thus linking themselves to important or respected persons, and can casually introduce evidence of their past accomplishments into the conversation. Additional tactics include *self-deprecation*—providing negative information about oneself as a means of promoting the image of modesty, and *self-disclosure*, offering personal information about oneself even if it is not requested. This latter tactic fosters the *impression* that the ingratiator is honest and likes the target person.

Do such tactics work? A growing body of evidence suggests that if used with skill and care, they do. It is now well established that job applicants who dress and groom appropriately, and who emit positive nonverbal cues (e.g., they smile frequently, maintain eye-contact with the interviewer), receive higher ratings than applicants who do not engage in such actions.[16] However, additional evidence suggests that as is true in other contexts involving ingratiation, these tactics can be overdone. For example, when applicants with poor credentials emit many *nonverbal cues*, they are down-rated relative to ones who do not engage in such behavior.[17] Similarly, Baron found that job applicants who both wore perfume and emitted many positive nonverbal cues were rated less favorably than ones who employed only one of these tactics.[18] The use of too many ingratiatory tactics seemed to backfire and reduce rather than enhance reactions to the applicants. Possibly when ingratiation techniques become too direct or numerous, it may become obvious that an attempt is being made to manipulate our feelings. This may result in anger or irritation rather than liking. So the best approach is probably to be as subtle or natural as possible in showing positive feelings for others. In any case, regardless of the precise methods used, if ingratiation is carried out with skill, it can serve as an effective strategy for increasing compliance.

Multiple Requests: The Old "One-Two" Punch Strikes Again

Often, when people want others to do something for them, they do not begin with their basic request. Instead, they use a kind of "one-two" punch designed to enhance their chances of success. The idea behind this approach is simple: One request can serve a kind of set-up for another. That is, an initial request can help "soften up" the target person so that he or she is more likely to comply with a second—and perhaps more important—one. Two strategies that are used quite frequently in this manner are the *foot-in-the-door* and the *door-in-the-face* (see Figure 7.8).

The Foot-in-the-Door: Small Request First, Large Request Second   As the saying goes, "Give them an inch and they'll take a mile." What it refers to is the fact that often, individuals seeking compliance with their wishes begin with a small or trivial request. Then, once this has been granted, they escalate to a larger or more important one. This technique—often known as the **foot-in-the-door technique**—is common and can be observed in many different settings. For example, sales persons often begin by asking potential customers to accept a free sample or even merely a brochure describing their products. Only later, after these requests have been granted, do they try to close an order. Similarly, individuals seeking help with their work often start with requests for trivial amounts of aid (e.g., lend them a pencil, answer a simple question). After they are granted, they gradually move to more and more effortful tasks. Finally, use of the foot-in-the-door technique in romance (and seduction!) is well known ("Oh come on, just one little drink . . ."). In these and many other instances, the basic strategy is much the same: Somehow, get another person to agree to a small initial request and thereby increase the chances that he or she will later agree to other (and larger) ones.

But does this strategy really work? Does beginning with a small request and then shifting to a larger one actually increase the chances that this second favor will be granted? A large body of research findings indicates that this is so.[19] For example, consider a famous study conducted by Freedman and Fraser.[20] In this investigation, hundreds of homemakers were called on the phone by a male experimenter who identified himself as a member of a consumers' group. Some were called twice, and so were exposed to the foot-in-the-door tactic: First they

FIGURE 7.8   Compliance Techniques: Important in Sales
Although many door-to-door salesmen may use the foot-in-the-door and door-in-the-face technique, this salesman is able to have Dagwood fall for a somewhat different technique. (Reprinted with special permission of King Features Syndicate.)

220

CHAPTER 7
PERSUASION,
INFLUENCE, AND
POWER: GETTING
YOUR WAY FROM
OTHERS

were presented with a trivial request, and then later, they were confronted with a much larger one. Other subjects, in contrast, were called only once and were hit with the large request "cold." The small request was a simple one: Would the subjects answer a few simple questions about the soaps they used at home? The second request, made several days later, was much larger. In this case, the experimenter asked if his organization could send a five-or-six-person crew to the subject's home to conduct a thorough inventory of all products on hand. It was explained that this survey would take about two hours and that the crew would require complete freedom to search through the house—including all closets, cabinets, and drawers. As you can see, this was truly a gigantic request. Yet, among subjects exposed to the foot-in-the-door approach (i.e., those called twice), fully 52.8 percent agreed! In contrast, only 22.2 percent of the individuals called only once and exposed to the large request "cold" (without any previous small request) consented. These results suggest that the technique of starting with a small request and then moving to a large one can be highly effective.

Additional research offers an explanation for why the foot-in-the-door tactic works. Apparently, once individuals agree to a small initial request, they undergo subtle shifts in their self-perceptions. Specifically, they come to see themselves as the kind of person "who does that sort of thing"—the kind of person who agrees to help others when they request it. Thus, when contacted again and asked for a second favor, they agree in order to be consistent with their changed (and enhanced) self-image.[21]

Of course, the foot-in-the-door technique does not succeed under all conditions. For example, as you might well guess, it often fails when the second request involves behaviors that are costly or very unpleasant. (Would you loan $50 to a friend just because you loaned her $1 a few days ago?) But in many settings, and with respect to many target actions, the tactic of beginning with a small request and then shifting to a larger one can indeed be effective. For this reason, you are sure to encounter it in your own life—both on and off the job—on many occasions (see Figure 7.9).

The Door-in-the-Face: Large Request First, Small Request Second While the technique of beginning with a small request and then moving to a larger one is quite successful, an opposite strategy, too, may succeed. Here, we start by asking for a large favor—one which other persons are almost certain to refuse. And then, when they do, we shift to a smaller request—the one we really wanted all along. This approach is known as the **door-in-the-face technique** (referring to the "door" that is, at first, slammed in our face!) and is also very common.[22]

For example, consider the following scene, one that actually occurs in many companies on a regular basis. An individual in the sales department has closed a big order and wants to make sure that it is shipped on time. His customer wants it about two weeks, so he calls shipping and indicates he wants it out of the warehouse by the end of the week. The shipping manager reacts with an agonizing shriek, shouting that it can't possibly be done in less than a month. At this point, the caller counters with a request that it be shipped in ten days to two weeks.

FIGURE 7.9 Foot-in-the-Door Technique: Used in Door-to-Door Sales
A number of companies have been quite successful by relying only on door-to-door sales. These companies often have their sales people use foot-in-the-door techniques by having customers accept a small gift prior to attempting to sell products.

The shipping manager, somewhat relieved, indicates that he will do what he can to meet this deadline. Thus by beginning with a large request—one he really did not want—the sales person has managed to get the outcome he *did* desire. He has, in short, used the door-in-the-face tactic to good advantage.

Research evidence also lends support to the effectiveness of this general strategy.[23] That is, following this "start big–shift small" approach does often yield more compliance than simply beginning with the small request itself. Moreover, the reason for this success, too, is clear. Apparently, when an individual starts with a large request and then backs down to a smaller one, this puts pressure on the person with whom he is dealing to make a similar concession. "After all," the targets of persuasion seem to reason, "the requester has retreated in order to meet me halfway; how can I refuse to do likewise?" Another possibility involves concern over *self-presentation*—presenting ourselves in a favorable light to others. If we refuse a large and unreasonable request, this appears justifiable and our image doesn't suffer. If we then also refuse a much smaller request from the same source, however, we may appear unreasonable. Thus we may yield to the door-in-the-face tactic because of our concern that failing to do so will cause us to look rigid to others.[24]

The moral, then, is clear: Beware of persons who begin with unreasonable demands and then back down to smaller ones. They may be setting you up for the kill with a carefully developed strategy for gaining compliance. For an example of someone using many of the techniques we have discussed, see the **Case in Point** on page 222.

222

CHAPTER 7

PERSUASION,
INFLUENCE, AND
POWER: GETTING
YOUR WAY FROM
OTHERS

POWER: BEYOND INFLUENCE AND PERSUASION

Imagine the following scene: An office supervisor is trying to persuade a keypuncher to come to work on Saturday in order to finish a big job. The keypuncher refuses, stating that he has better things to do with his weekends. The supervisor tries every persuasive trick at her disposal. She appeals to the

CASE IN POINT

A Little Compliance for a Big Sale

Stan Kirby is sitting at his desk at Hansen's Chevrolet reading the morning paper. It is the usual slow beginning for a Saturday. Not too many customers show up until late in the morning, but the sales people have to be there just in case. Of course, Saturday is always a big day for sales, but lately business has been slow. Stan really needs to sell a few cars today to get his commissions back up to par. It's a good thing they had that special sales seminar last week. That really helped him sharpen his technique a bit. He is looking forward to really letting out all the stops today. As he puts down his paper, he notices a young family has just arrived and is looking over the latest minivan. He quickly jumps up and walks over to the potential customers, the Waterman family.

"Hi folks, welcome to Hansen's, I'm Stan Kirby. Isn't that a beautiful automobile?" After the usual exchange of introductions, Stan proceeds to strike up a broad-ranging conversation while they walk across the lot.

"So you're also a big fisherman, John. I tell you, I don't think I've ever met a fisherman I didn't like. Oh, by the way, this wagon would be great for your fishing trips with or without the family. Do the kids like to fish too?" John Waterman nods affirmatively as he and his family continue to look over the car lot. "You know I have kids about the age of yours. We really do enjoy getting out to do some fishing on Sundays." They have come to the end of the lot and the Watermans have still not expressed any strong interest in one of the cars on the lot.

At this point John stops and begins to turn back. "Stan, I'm not sure I see exactly what we are looking for. We want a minivan but we wanted one with a sunroof, and I don't see one on the lot. We're also not sure whether we like the way the passenger seats are arranged."

Stan pulls the list of cars in stock out of his jacket and scans it for a few minutes. "You're right, we don't have any sunroofs right now, but we're due to get a few in next week. But you can't really appreciate these cars unless you take a test drive. Why don't all of you take this one for a spin to see how you like it."

employee's loyalty, describes the serious problems that will arise if the job is not finished on time, and praises his excellent past work. All is to no avail; the keypuncher still refuses. Just then, the head of the division strolls by and asks what's happening. The supervisor explains the situation and the division head turns to the reluctant employee: "Jones," he says in a deep voice, "I want you to come in on Saturday."

"Well, if you really need me . . ." the target of this firm command murmurs weakly. The matter is closed; the keypuncher will report for duty bright and early Saturday morning.

"Oh, I really don't think we have the time because we still have several other places we want to check out," John responds.

Now Stan is getting worried. He's spent quite a bit of time with this family and they are about to slip out without even trying out one of his cars. Well he's not about to give up yet. He still has one more technique up his sleeve.

"John, have you heard about our new try it for a week program?"

John looks up with a little air of surprise that Stan is still going at it. "No," he says, in a rather uninterested tone.

"Well this program lets you take the car for a week to see if it suits you and your family," Stan continues. "Of course, there is no obligation for you to keep the car if you do not want it after one week."

John still does not appear very interested. "No, I don't think we're ready to try that yet."

"Well, in that case, John, you should at least invest about ten minutes in a test drive so that you can compare our wagon to the competition," responds Stan with continued determination.

John looks at his wife and the kids who are getting a little restless. "Well, all right. Maybe we'll take it for a short drive around the block, but then we'll have to be on our way."

"Great! Just wait here while I get the keys to this one!" Stan says enthusiastically as he walks over to the office to get the keys. Maybe this would be his lucky day after all!

Questions

1. Do you think Stan will make the sale? Why or why not?
2. What specific techniques of compliance did Stan use?
3. Do you think he used them effectively? In what ways could he have improved his approach? What additional techniques could he have used?
4. How do you deal with sales people who try to use these techniques on you?

224

CHAPTER 7

PERSUASION,
INFLUENCE, AND
POWER: GETTING
YOUR WAY FROM
OTHERS

This incident illustrates the basic difference between influence and power. Actually, as you can readily see, the difference is largely one of degree. While influence refers to the capacity to change others' behavior in some desired manner, power refers to the ability to do so *regularly* and *strongly*. In fact, according to some experts on this topic, power refers mainly to the ability to control others' actions to promote one's own goals even without their consent, against their will, and without their knowledge or understanding.[25] In short, power is influence carried to its ultimate extreme.

As you already know from your own experience, power is a desirable commodity. In fact, it is something many people seek and enjoy. In a key sense, this is far from surprising. First, power comes closer than any other form of influence to the daydream of total control over others described at the start of this chapter. Second, the other side of its coin is **status**—and a lot of it. Powerful people, as a rule, acquire a great deal of status. They enjoy high levels of respect and prestige. Moreover, they usually hold many desirable privileges not shared by others. Little wonder, then, that power is sought by many. (But it should be noted that although many successful managers and executives have a strong drive for power, possession of this motive does not seem essential for good job performance. In fact, findings suggest that high need for power may interfere with administrative efficiency and can also produce low morale among subordinates.[26] Thus the link between power motivation and effectiveness as a manager seems to be complex.)

But where precisely does power come from? For example, why was the division head able to command obedience from the keypuncher while the office supervisor was not? And how can individuals attain such influence? How, in short, can they grab their slice of the power pie? It is on these major questions that we now focus.

Individual Power: Its Basic Sources

Power can stem from many different sources—everything from inherited royalty on the one hand to sheer brute strength on the other. Careful analysis suggests, however, that in most cases, it derives from five distinct sources.[27]

Reward Power: Control Over Valued Resources A major source of personal power involves control of valued rewards or resources. Individuals able to determine who gets raises, promotions, or various "perks" are usually able to exert tremendous influence over others. In fact, with a little practice, they can usually get these persons to jump through hoops! The reason for this is simple: Only by doing what the power-holder wants can these individuals hope to attain valued rewards. **Reward power** offers a good explanation for the reactions of the keypuncher in the example described above. This person probably realized that the head of the department could determine the size of his next raise, and whether he would be promoted. Thus it is not surprising that he quickly yielded to the request (or demand) from this person that he work on Saturday.

Coercive Power: Control Over Punishments   The other side of the coin from reward power involves the ability to inflict punishments of various kinds on others, a capacity known as **coercive power.** Basically, this form of power rests mainly on fear. Individuals realize that if they do not behave as the power-holder wishes, they will suffer unpleasant outcomes or events. For example, persons holding coercive power can fire employees, lower their pay, criticize them publicly, or give them poor references. The open use of coercive power is generally frowned on in most work settings, and for good reason. Exposing employees to strong punishment or censure can often lead them to nurse a grudge against their manager or the company. Needless to say, this can be devastating to morale. For this and other reasons, coercive power is generally used as sparingly as possible. And when it is enforced, it is often concealed behind a velvet glove. Even then, however, it is readily recognized by most persons and can exert important effects on their behavior.

Legitimate Power: Control Based on Rank   Have you ever seen thousands of people bow down before a queen, king, or religious leader? If so, you are already familiar with a third major basis for power. Such persons and also top executives, elected government officials, and even sports coaches, all exercise authority over others by virtue of the jobs or titles that they hold. In short, people obey their directives because it is considered appropriate and legitimate for CEOs (chief executive officers), presidents, and head coaches to be in charge. Because power stemming from this source (known as **legitimate power**) is viewed as justified, it is often less likely to stir resentment (or reactance) among those who must obey.

Referent Power: Control Based on Attraction   We noted earlier that individuals are more willing to accept influence from someone they like than from someone they dislike. This fact points to a fourth major source of power: that based on attraction. When individuals are greatly admired by others, they can often exert a tremendous amount of influence on them. In fact, exercising such **referent power** may be a trivially easy task, for many persons are both willing and eager to obey directives from those they admire. Dramatic examples of referent power in action are provided by charismatic political leaders, athletes, and movie stars. But this type of power can also be observed in work settings, where popular executives often inspire great respect—and willingness to obey—among their staffs. In short, where power is concerned, being liked is often a major step toward being able to exert considerable control over others.

Expert Power: Control Based on Expertise   A final source of power—that deriving from expertise—is easily illustrated. Suppose one day you visit your accountant. After examining your records, he recommends you send a huge payment to the government at once. Will you comply? Probably, you will. Painful as this action is, you realize that your accountant knows best where tax matters are concerned. The fact that you follow his directions, though, demonstrates the impact of **expert power**—the ability of persons possessing special knowledge to

226

CHAPTER 7
PERSUASION,
INFLUENCE, AND
POWER: GETTING
YOUR WAY FROM
OTHERS

exert strong influence over others. In most cases, expert power is restricted to issues or behaviors related to the expert's knowledge. In some instances, though, it seems to spill over into additional areas as well, perhaps because a high degree of expertise often confers high status. Advertisers make use of this fact when they have their products endorsed by celebrities or athletes who actually know little about them (see Figure 7.10 for an example). In any case, there is little doubt that technical skill or expertise, too, can serve as a major source of power.

Various Bases of Power: Independent or Linked?   Before concluding this discussion of the various types of power, we should touch on one final question: Are they independent or closely linked? The answer is clear: In many instances, they are highly interdependent. First, different types of power tend to occur in combination, so that, for example, individuals high in reward power are often high in coercive power, as well. Second, the presence and use of one type of power often affects other types. For example, use of coercive power can often reduce referent power because people usually dislike those who punish them. Similarly, because legitimate power is often associated with high status, its presence can often enhance attraction toward its holders, and so increase their referent power. We could go on to consider other examples but by now the main point should be clear: While power can stem from many different sources, in actual use the different types tend to be intricately linked.[28] (How much power do you possess? For a quick overall estimate, see **Human Relations in Action** on page 228.)

FIGURE 7.10   Expert Power: Used in Advertising
Well-known actors and athletes are often used in advertising because their high status gives them *expert power.*

ORGANIZATIONAL POLITICS: TECHNIQUES FOR GAINING AND USING POWER IN WORK SETTINGS

In the best of all possible worlds, organizations would be totally fair places in which to work. Promotions, raises, and other rewards would be distributed solely on the basis of merit or past performance. And major decisions related to policy and other matters would always be based on careful examination of all available data. Unfortunately, of course, reality departs greatly from this picture of perfection. Work settings are not always governed by principles of fair play and rationality. In fact, they often appear to be highly political in nature, with individuals and groups constantly jockeying for position and power. The rules of this game, which is generally known as **organizational politics,** are complex and everchanging.[29] But the stakes are so high that sooner or later nearly everyone must play. And though the cast of characters shifts over time, the major focus remains the same: gaining and using power.

Unfortunately, organizational politics play a major role in most work settings. Thus, who you know, who you can count on as allies, and who owes you favors are often more important in determining the fate of your career than your actual performance. Further, winners of this game tend to be the ones who control an organization, regardless of what the formal organizational chart seems to say. Given the obvious importance of this political process, we wish we could now arm you with a firm set of guidelines for winning—steps for getting your share of power and using it effectively. But—alas!—this goal is far easier to state than to attain. The situations involved are complex, and each work setting is, in a sense, unique. Also, little firm evidence about the relative success of various political strategies currently exists. For these reasons, it is impossible to offer a short list of "no-fail" techniques. What we can do, though, is provide you with a summary of several general tactics—ones that fit with what we know about power and influence, and so seem quite promising. If you use them well and with care, they may contribute to your success in the political maneuvering you are sure to encounter. But please note: The tactics listed below are only general suggestions and guidelines. There is no guarantee that they will always, or even usually, work. Since you are likely to meet most of them in the years ahead even if you don't use them yourself, being familiar with them may be helpful.

1. *Cultivate the right allies.* Having allies who will support your views and positions is almost a "must." Thus it is important to make such arrangements of mutual support as quickly as possible. But be sure to choose your partners carefully. Forming alliances with persons who are clearly rising stars is likely to prove more advantageous than associating with co-workers whose careers are on the skids.

2. *Count on reciprocity.* As a general rule, it is helpful to do favors for others. Once you do, you can remind them of this at times when calling in these IOUs will do you the most good. But again, don't do favors

228

CHAPTER 7

PERSUASION,
INFLUENCE, AND
POWER: GETTING
YOUR WAY FROM
OTHERS

for just anyone: Try to concentrate on helping those who will be able to return your kindness in the future.

3. *Always project an image of competence and confidence.* It has long been said that "nothing succeeds like success." And in organizational politics, this seems to be true with a vengeance. If you always appear to be on top of your job, and to know just what you are doing, you may soon pick up a positive "halo." Even better, you may be invited to join various

political authority →

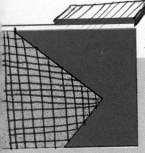

HUMAN RELATIONS IN ACTION

Measuring Your Own Power: A Quick Self-Assessment

Now that we have examined the major sources and types of power, you may find yourself wondering: "How much power do I have myself?" Actually, answering this question is no simple task. Power, to a large extent, is in the eye of the beholder. Thus it is not simply what you can do to—or for—other people that counts; what they believe you can do is important, too. But leaving this issue aside for the moment, you can gain at least a degree of insight into your own power (either at home or at work) by answering the questions below (check one space for each question):

1. *Reward power:* To what extent can you influence the rewards of other persons—their promotions, raises, job assignments, emotional well-being?

_____ Not at all

_____ Somewhat

_____ Very much

2. *Coercive power:* To what extent can you influence the negative outcomes received by others—dock their pay, fire them, give them poor references, and the like?

_____ Not at all

_____ Somewhat

_____ Very much

3. *Legitimate power:* To what extent does your position or title give you the authority to tell others what to do?

_____ Not at all

_____ Somewhat

_____ Very much

groups or cliques whose fortunes are on the rise. So, keep your image as bright and shiny as possible.

4. *Remember that being liked is a plus.* While some kinds of power are hard to attain on your own (e.g., reward or legitimate power), referent power can be cultivated. Through careful use of ingratiation and related techniques, you can increase your appeal to others—especially to key persons in your organization. Being liked by such individuals may give a big boost to your career.

New Knowledge is power / - nuclear bomb / - computer.

4. *Referent power:* To what extent do other people like or admire you, and so show willingness to do what you want?

    _____ Not at all

    _____ Somewhat

    _____ Very much

5. *Expert power:* To what extent do other people seek your advice or suggestions concerning technical matters or special skills that you possess?

    _____ Not at all

    _____ Somewhat

    _____ Very much

Scoring

Give yourself 1 point for each "Not at all" answer, 5 points for each "Somewhat" answer, and 10 points for each "Very much" answer. Then add all your scores together.

Interpretation

If you scored 40 or higher, welcome to the power elite; you seem to exert considerable power or influence over others. If you scored between 20 and 35, you are currently exerting a moderate degree of power over others. If you scored between 5 and 15, your power quotient is quite low. If this is the case, though, don't despair. Instead, read the section on organizational politics, where specific hints for increasing your personal power are presented.

230

CHAPTER 7

PERSUASION,
INFLUENCE, AND
POWER: GETTING
YOUR WAY FROM
OTHERS

5. *Learn to be persuasive.* Forceful arguments eloquently stated are often highly effective in swaying others. So take great pains to develop your persuasive skills to the highest degree possible. The payoffs may be substantial.

6. *First impressions count.* As note in Chapter 2, first impressions do count. Thus it is important for you to look good on any project or assignment right from the start. If you do, important people in your organization will tend to remember this positive impression, and your position in the political arena may improve greatly.

If the tactics just outlined strike you as Machiavellian in nature (refer to Chapter 5), we can say this in their defense: They are mild and benevolent in comparison to another group of strategies known as "dirty tricks."[30] These include such practices as (1) spreading false rumors about opponents, (2) channeling communication so that opponents fail to receive vital information, and (3) conducting meetings according to a *hidden agenda* so that you, but not your opponents, are prepared to discuss certain topics. These procedures are clearly unethical and violate basic principles of fair play and justice. Thus we certainly do not wish to recommend them here. But the world of work, unfortunately, has its full share of unprincipled persons. Thus, for your own protection, you should be familiar with such tactics, and be prepared to defend against them. Only if you are will you have a good chance of surviving in the complex, and often harsh, arena of organizational politics.

SUMMARY

We often wish to change the behavior of others in various ways. Many techniques for accomplishing this goal exist. One of the most effective of these is **persuasion**—the attempt to change others' minds (and hence their actions) through persuasive appeals. The effectiveness of such efforts is strongly affected by characteristics of the persons doing the persuading (e.g., their attractiveness, style, credibility). It is also influenced by the contents of the persuasive message. Some attitude change is the result of attempts to reduce **dissonance.** Because of **reactance** and **fore-warning,** individuals are often successful in resisting even powerful efforts at persuasion.

Additional techniques for exerting influence over others focus on **compliance**—getting them to agree to various requests. **Ingratiation,** efforts to enhance our appeal to other persons, is often successful in this regard. Another tactic for attaining compliance involves **multiple requests** (e.g., the foot-in-the-door and the door-in-the-face techniques). Here, we begin with one request and then shift to another, the one we really desire.

Power is the ability to change the behavior of others regularly, strongly, and even against their will. Power stems from several sources, including control over rewards or punishments, expertise, legitimacy, and personal attractiveness. These sources combine and interact so that possession of one type of power often affects the possession or use of others. Organizations are highly political in nature, with various individuals and groups constantly jockeying for power. Among the tactics for obtaining power are courting the right allies, projecting an image of competence, being persuasive, and creating a positive first impression.

KEY TERMS

coercive power: Power stemming from control over punishments and negative outcomes. The use of coercive power is generally discouraged in most work settings.

cognitive dissonance: A state of discomfort that exists whenever attitudes are inconsistent with one another.

compliance: A form of influence based on direct requests.

door-in-the-face technique: A tactic for enhancing compliance based on the strategy of beginning with a large request and then, when this is rejected, backing down to a smaller one.

expert power: Power based on the possession of special knowledge or skill.

foot-in-the-door technique: A tactic for gaining increased compliance based on the strategy of beginning with a small request and then, when this is granted, moving to a much larger request.

forewarning: Advance knowledge of the persuasive intent of a spoken, written, or televised message. When individuals know that attempts at persuasion are about to be made, their ability to resist such appeals is often increased.

ingratiation: A technique for gaining compliance in which a requester first attempts to increase his or her appeal to the target person. Once this is attained, various requests or other forms of influence follow.

legitimate power: Power based on an individual's position or rank.

organizational politics: Tactics for gaining, holding, and using power within organizations.

persuasion: A technique for changing others' behavior by what appear to be logical arguments contained in persuasive appeals.

power: The ability to affect the behavior of others regularly and strongly, even against their will.

reactance: The negative state experienced by individuals when they feel that others are trying to "push them around" or threaten their personal freedom.

referent power: Power based on personal attractiveness.

reward power: Power stemming from the ability to control various rewards sought by other persons.

social cognition: The manner in which we process, store, and remember social information.

status: The level of respect, prestige, and special privilege assigned to a specific individual by other members of his or her group or organization.

NOTES

1. Rajecki, D.W. (1990). *Attitudes: Themes and Advances.* Sunderland, Mass.: Sinauer Associates.
2. Kiesler, C.A., & Kiesler, S. (1969). *Conformity.* Reading, Mass.: Addison-Wesley.
3. Miller, N., Maruyama, G., Beaber, R.J., & Valone, K. (1976). "Speed of Speech and Persuasion." *Journal of Personality and Social Psychology, 34,* 615–24.

232

CHAPTER 7

PERSUASION,
INFLUENCE, AND
POWER: GETTING
YOUR WAY FROM
OTHERS

4. See Note 1.

5. Mewborn, C.R., & Rogers, R.W. (1979). "Effects of Threatening and Reassuring Components of Fear Appeals on Physiological and Verbal Measures of Emotion and Attitudes." *Journal of Experimental Social Psychology, 15,* 242–53.

6. See Note 1.

7. Petty, R.E., & Cacioppo, J.T. (1986). *Attitude Change: Central and Peripheral Routes to Persuasion.* New York: Springer-Verlag.

8. Petty, R.E., & Cacioppo (1981). *Attitudes and Persuasion: Classical and Contemporary Approaches.* Dubuque, Iowa: William C. Brown.

9. See Note 8.

10. Festinger, L. (1957). *A Theory of Cognitive Dissonance.* Evanston, Ill.: Row, Peterson.

11. See Note 7.

12. Byrne, D. (1971). *The Attraction Paradigm.* New York: Academic Press.

13. Wall, J.A., & Adams, J.S. (1974). "Some Variables Affecting a Constituent's Evaluations of and Behavior Toward a Boundary Role Occupant." *Organizational Behavior and Human Performance, 11,* 290–308.

14. Liden, R.C., & Mitchell, T.R. (1988). "Ingratiatory Behaviors in Organizational Settings." *Academy of Management Review, 13,* 572–87.

15. Baron, R.A. (1986). "Self-Presentation in Job Interviews: When There Can Be 'Too Much of a Good Thing.' "*Journal of Applied Social Psychology, 16,* 16–28.

16. Avery, R.D., & Campion, J.E. (1982). "The Employment Interview: A Summary and Review of Recent Research." *Personnel Psychology, 35,* 281–322.

17. Rasmussen, K.G., Jr. (1984). "Nonverbal Behavior, Verbal Behavior, Resume Credentials, and Selection Interview Outcomes." *Journal of Applied Psychology, 69,* 551–56.

18. See Note 15.

19. Beamon, A.L., Cole, M., Preston, M., Klentz, B., & Steblay, N.M. (1983). "Fifteen Years of the Foot-in-the-Door Research: A Meta-Analysis." *Personality and Social Psychology Bulletin, 9,* 181–86.

20. Freedman, J.L., & Fraser, S.C. (1966). "Compliance Without Pressure: The Foot-in-the-Door Technique." *Journal of Personality and Social Psychology, 4,* 195–202.

21. DeJong, W., & Musili, L. (1982). "External Pressure to Comply: Handicapped Versus Nonhandicapped Requesters and the Foot-in-the-Door Phenomenon." *Personality and Social Psychology Bulletin, 8,* 522–27.

22. Cialdini, R.B. (1988). *Influence: Science and Practice,* 2nd ed. Glenview, Ill.: Scott, Foresman.

23. Cialdini, R.B., Vincent, J.E., Lewis, Catalan, J., Wheeler, D., & Darby, B.L. (1975). "Reciprocal Concessions Procedure for Inducing Compliance: The door-in-the-face technique." *Journal of Personality and Social Psychology, 31,* 206–15.

24. Pendleton, M.G., & Batson, C.D. (1979). "Self-Presentation and the Door-in-the-Face Technique for Inducing Compliance." *Personality and Social Psychology Bulletin, 5,* 77–81.

25. Grimes, A.J. (1978). "Authority, Power, Influence, and Social Control: A Theoretical Synthesis." *Academy of Management Review, 3,* 724–35.

26. Cornelius, E.T. III, & Lane, F.B. (1984). "The Power Motive and Managerial Success in a Professionally Oriented Service Industry Organization." *Journal of Applied Psychology, 69,* 32–39.

27. French, J.R.P., & Raven, B. (1959). "The Bases of Social Power." In D. Cartwright, ed. *Studies in Social Power.* Ann Arbor: University of Michigan Press.

28. Green, C.N., & Podsakoff, P.M. (1981). "Effects of Withdrawal of a Performance Contingent Reward on Supervisory Influence and Power." *Academy of Management Journal,* 24, 527–42.
29. Mayes, B.T., & Allen, R.W. (1977). "Toward a Definition of Organizational Politics." *Academy of Management Review,* 2, 672–78.
30. Cavanagh, G.F., Moberg, D.J., & Velasquez, M. (1981). "The Ethics of Organizational Politics." *Academy of Management Review, 6,* 363–74.

ADDITIONAL CASES AND EXERCISES: APPLYING WHAT YOU'VE LEARNED

The Schedule Change

Don H. Hockenbury
Psychology Instructor
Tulsa Junior College

Sandra E. Hockenbury
Adjunct Instructor
Tulsa Junior College

Mark's boss, Ed Bagley, was adamantly against changing the work schedule once it was posted. "If you want different hours," he said repeatedly to all his employees, "tell me in advance, otherwise I don't want to hear about it." But Mark wanted to take an introductory accounting course at the local college on Monday and Wednesday afternoons for eight weeks during October and November. That meant Mark would have to ask Mr. Bagley to modify the October and November schedules to accommodate his request. In Mark's mind, the chances of getting his boss to agree seemed destined to fail until he mentioned the problem to his co-worker, Laura, during lunch.

"Of course you should ask him for a schedule modification to take the class!" Laura said encouragingly.

"But didn't Bagley turn down Susan's request for a schedule change just two weeks ago?"

"He sure did," Laura nodded, then smiled. "But he approved my schedule change last month so I could take a four-day weekend to visit my sister," she said.

"I don't get it. Why would he say yes to you and no to Susan?"

"Because how you ask for the request is just as important as what you ask for!" Laura responded.

"I thought we were supposed to put our requests in writing, not talk to him," Mark pointed out.

"And that's part of the reason so many people get their requests turned down," Laura said confidently.

"So I should try to talk with him face-to-face rather than write a note. What else should I do?" Mark asked, now genuinely curious.

"There are several things you can do to improve your chances of persuading him to give you the schedule change," Laura began explaining.

That afternoon Mark set up an appointment to talk with Mr. Bagley the following morning at 10:30. That night at home he wrote down the various reasons why he thought Mr. Bagley should be willing to work with him on modifying his schedule. He practiced explaining his reasons in front of the mirror in his bedroom until he felt confident and relaxed with what he was going to say. He assembled everything he needed for the meeting, including a copy of the college's class schedule to show Mr. Bagley that the course was not available at any other time.

The next day Mark arrived about five minutes early for the appointment with Mr. Bagley. Although Mark always dressed neatly for work, he took extra care on this particular day to look nicer than usual. While he waited for Mr. Bagley, Mark rehearsed his various reasons and arguments in his mind. Finally, Mr. Bagley's secretary told Mark that Mr. Bagley was ready to see him.

As Mark walked into the office, Mr. Bagley was jotting down notes on a pad of paper on his desk. He failed to acknowledge Mark as he walked in, so Mark spoke first.

"Hi, Mr. Bagley," Mark said confidently. "I appreciate your taking the time to talk to me this morning."

Mr. Bagley finally quit writing on the note pad. "What did you need to see me about?" he asked dryly, sitting back in his chair.

"Do you mind if I sit down?" Mark asked directly, but politely.

Mr. Bagley nodded approval.

"Well, Mr. Bagley, I don't want you to think that I'm unhappy with my job, but I've been thinking about going back to college on a part-time basis. In fact, because of some of the different projects I've worked on here at your company, I'm thinking about possibly getting a degree in accounting. That's why I wanted to take an introduction to accounting class at the state college. Do you think that would be a good idea, sir?"

Mr. Bagley seemed mildly startled by the question. "Well, Mark, I'm not sure what to say here. If you're interested in that kind of work, I'm certain it would probably be a good place to start."

"That's what I thought, too, but I wanted to make sure you felt the same way because I've always valued your opinion, Mr. Bagley," Mark said sincerely. "I should also mention that Mrs. Caraway, in accounting, said that if I did well in the class that she would consider me for an accounting clerk position."

"Well, I certainly think that's a reasonable course of action to follow, Mark," Mr. Bagley smiled slightly, his tone softening a little.

"There are just two things that I hope you can help me with, Mr. Bagley," Mark continued, speaking more quickly. "The only time the accounting course if offered is on Monday and Wednesday afternoons from noon to 1:30 P.M. That would mean taking additional time for my lunch hour that I'd like to make up by coming in early or staying late, or switching hours with someone else, whichever you think would work better. The second thing I'd like to talk to you about is the possibility of the company paying for the class because I think the company will directly benefit from it."

Mr. Bagley sat forward, clearing his throat. "Mark, the company has never paid for our employees to attend college classes."

"Even if the class would directly benefit the company?" Mark asked, looking surprised.

"No, we sure don't," Mr. Bagley said flatly.

Gosh, I'm sorry, Mr. Bagley. I wouldn't have suggested that except that I know several people whose companies do that type of thing."

"Well, we don't do that here," Mr. Bagley repeated.

Mark paused for a second, frowning slightly. "Well, then, if I pay for the class myself, do you think we could at least work with my schedule so I could attend this class during October and November?"

236

CHAPTER 7
PERSUASION,
INFLUENCE, AND
POWER: GETTING
YOUR WAY FROM
OTHERS

Mr. Bagley was drumming his fingers on the edge of his desk. "Let me look at the schedule this morning and you can check with my secretary this afternoon. I'm sure we can work something out."

Questions

1. Assess Mark's persuader characteristics in terms of interpersonal style, attractiveness, and credibility.

2. Mark knew full well before the meeting that the company did not pay for employees to attend classes. Which strategy was he using?

3. Was Mark's mild use of ingratiation appropriate or inappropriate?

4. What do you think would have happened if Mark had tried the same persuasive appeal in a written memo rather than face-to-face? Why?

5. Analyze the situation for the different types of power being displayed.

Persuasion and Influence: A Daily Dose

At several points in this chapter, it was noted that attempts at persuasion and influence are common. You can demonstrate the accuracy of this suggestion quite readily by following these simple directions. Choose one day when you will be in contact with many different people in several different contexts. (A day when you plan to stay home alone, or go somewhere far away from other people is *not* a good choice.) During this day, keep a record of each time another person asks you to do something, tries to change your attitude, gives you a direct order, or seeks to influence you in any manner. For each of these incidents, record (1) who attempted to influence you, (2) how (what specific tactics they used), (3) the context in which this attempt occurred, and (4) whether and to what extent it succeeded. (Use Form A on page 237 for your records.)

As another part of this demonstration, turn the matter around, and also keep a record of every instance in which *you* try to influence or persuade others. Here, record (1) whom you tried to influence, (2) how you tried to do this, (3) the context in which your effort at persuasion took place, and (4) the extent to which it succeeded. (Use Form B for your records.)

By the end of the day, we think you will be convinced of three basic facts: (1) Persuasion and influence *are* very common; you will observe many instances in which others tried to influence you and in which you attempted to persuade them; (2) different tactics are used in different situations, and (3) while not all efforts at persuasion succeed, many do produce at least some movement in the direction desired by their users. Putting all these together, you can also reach a more general conclusion: Persuasion and influence are indeed a basic fact of human relations!

Persons Attempting Influence	Situation/context in Which This Occurred	Specific Tactics Used	Extent to Which They Succeeded

FORM A
Occasions when someone tried to influence you

FORM B
Occasions when you tried to influence others

Persons You Tried to Influence	Situation/context in Which This Occurred	Specific Tactics Used	Extent to Which You Succeeded

CHAPTER

8

Leadership: Who Does It, How, and with What Effect?

Study

Learning Objectives

After reading this chapter,
you should be able to:

1. Define *leadership*.

2. Discuss the trait, situational, and
   interactionist approaches to leadership.

3. Describe several key dimensions of leader
   behavior.

4. Summarize the main points of the major
   theories of leadership (*contingency theory,
   path-goal theory*).

5. Indicate how leaders' relations with their
   subordinates can affect subordinates'
   performance and careers.

6. Explain why leaders are not always
   essential for high levels of performance.

7. Explain why different styles of leadership
   may be required at different points in the
   development of work groups.

ike Brooks and Dan Newton are two veteran players on the Houston Driller minor league team. Both are exhausted after a tough workout, and are lounging in the dugout before going to the showers.

"It's sure a lot tougher around here with Mitch," moans Dan. Mitch Wilson is the new manager. The team had not done well the last few years under their previous manager, Larry Salazar.

"Larry sure was more easygoing and personable than Mitch," sighs Mike. "I sure miss him. He was like a father to me."

"Maybe that was the problem," mused Dan. "We weren't afraid of him, so we probably didn't work as hard as we should have. With these long seasons, it's easy to backslide."

"That's for sure," agreed Mike. "Mitch certainly has a different style. He's all business. No small talk, and he keeps his distance. All he seems to care about is performance."

"Maybe that's what we need to turn this team around," says Dan as he starts to go to the showers.

"Yeh, but I still miss good ol' Larry," sighs Mike as he slowly gets up to follow Dan.

At different times during your life, you have belonged to many groups—from informal play gangs to work teams in a large company. Think back over some of these now. For each, can you recall one member who was more influential than the others? Probably you can, for in almost every group one individual wields more control than all the rest. Such persons are usually described as **leaders,** and their impact on other members can be profound. When we use the term *leadership,* then, we refer to the exercise of a special type of influence—that exerted by one member of an organization (or group) over one or several other members.

In work settings formal leaders are generally appointed to their positions. Thus specific persons are named office manager, director of sales, or vice president for human resources. In other contexts, though, leaders may be chosen by members of their groups, or may emerge in an informal manner. Regardless of how they gain their authority, leaders usually play a key role in the groups they head (see Figure 8.1). Indeed, if they are suddenly removed through illness or transfer to another job, both productivity and morale may suffer greatly. In extreme cases, groups or work units may become incapable of carrying out their major functions until a new leader is obtained. Because leadership plays a key role in many organizational settings, it is important for you to gain a basic understanding of this process. In short, it is essential for you to know something about leaders— who they are, how they operate, and the effects they produce. To provide you with such knowledge, we will focus on three major topics. First, we will consider

w Miller

Attila The Horizontally Mobile

FIGURE 8.1 Leaders: Influential in Groups
Leaders have played key roles in their groups throughout the ages. (Drawing by W. Miller; ©
1989 The New Yorker Magazine, Inc.)

the question of *who becomes a leader*—why certain persons rise to positions of power and influence. Second, we will describe several *leadership styles*—contrasting approaches adopted by leaders in their efforts to influence other persons. (Two such styles were briefly mentioned in the introduction to this chapter.) Finally, we will turn to *leader effectiveness,* and consider several factors that determine the degree to which leaders are successful in directing their groups or subordinates.

WHO BECOMES A LEADER? THREE CONTRASTING ANSWERS

Few people become leaders. In fact, the vast majority of human beings spend their lives following rather than issuing directives. Relatively few attain even modest authority over others. And only a tiny number rise to positions from which they can exert influence over thousands or even millions of persons. These facts lead to an intriguing question: What factors set such persons apart from the rest of us? In other words, why do they and not others become leaders? Many answers to this puzzle have been offered. Most, though, attribute leadership to (1) something about the *persons* in question (i.e., their possession of special traits), (2) something about the *situations* in which they find themselves, and (3) a *combination* of these factors.

The Trait Approach: In Search of "Born Leaders"

Are some people born to lead? Common sense seems to suggest that this is so. Great leaders such as Joan of Arc, George Washington, Winston Churchill, Mikhail Gorbachev, and Martin Luther King, Jr., do seem to differ from "ordinary" human beings in several ways (see Figure 8.2). They also appear to share

no such thing as a born leader.

certain traits, such as iron wills, boundless energy, and driving ambition. To a lesser degree, even leaders lacking such worldwide fame seem different from their followers. Top executives, many politicians, and even sports celebrities often seem "larger than life," and possess an "aura" that sets them apart from other persons. On the basis of such observations, early researchers interested in leadership formulated a view known as the **great person theory.** According to this approach, all leaders possess key traits that set them apart from most other persons. Further, these traits remain the same across time and across different groups. Thus all leaders have similar traits regardless of the time period in which they live and the type of group they lead. Consistent with this view, the central task of leadership research was seen as that of identifying these traits, and many researchers launched energetic efforts to accomplish this task.

Sad to relate, this work generally failed. Try as they might, supporters of the great person theory were unable to develop a short list of traits that produce

FIGURE 8.2 Some Great Leaders: Evidence for the Great Person Theory
Great leaders, such as those shown here, differ from their followers in traits such as energy, ambition, and strength of will. This is consistent with the *great person theory* of leadership.

leadership ability. In fact, after several decades of work on this topic, there seemed to be almost as many different lists of "key" leadership traits as there were individual investigators! More recent efforts to determine whether leaders and followers differ in measurable ways have been a bit more successful. For example, it has been found that persons who possess certain patterns of motives (e.g., a high need for power coupled with a high self-control) tend to be more successful in leadership roles than persons who do not show these patterns.[1] Similarly, it has been observed that political leaders tend to be higher in such traits as self-confidence, need for achievement, and dominance than nonleaders.[2] Third, some leaders are viewed as being **charismatic** because they are willing to go against the status quo, have a strong vision or goal, and are willing to take risks.[3]

It is important not to misunderstand this concept: None of these findings suggest that all leaders share the same traits, or that possession of these characteristics is required for leadership for all times and in all places. However, they do suggest that personal factors *can* play a role in leadership in some cases, and that in this respect, at least, there may be a small grain of truth in the *great person* perspective.

The Situational Approach: Technical Skill Versus Charisma

Imagine the following scene: The top executives of a giant corporation are on their way to an important meeting. It is being held far out in the desert, at an estate owned by the president of another company with which they plan to merge. On the way, their limousine breaks down, many miles from any town. Who takes charge? Surprisingly, it is the driver—the only person who knows enough about motors to get the car started again. As he oversees repairs, he gives direct orders to vice presidents, members of the board, and other top officials. They willingly obey his commands without a murmur. Later, when they arrive at the meeting, the driver surrenders his authority and becomes an obedient subordinate once again.

While it may seem a bit farfetched, this incident actually illustrates an important point about leadership—one totally overlooked by the trait approach just described. Briefly, it is this: In many cases, the person most likely to act as a leader is not necessarily the awe-inspiring "great woman or man," whose charisma, charm, or power hypnotizes others into blind submission. Rather, it is the individual whose skills and competence happen to be most useful to the group in a given context. According to this view, often known as the **situational approach,** different persons may well rise to positions of authority under different conditions. What is crucial in determining who will take charge is the contribution each can make to the group and its current needs. Thus under appropriate circumstances even normally meek, shy, and retiring persons may come forward to direct the actions of others if they are best able to meet the group's requirements.

different persons may arise to positions of authority under different conditions.

In addition, the situational approach suggests that when one individual remains in a position of leadership over time, this person *must* adjust his or her behavior to shifts in situational factors. In short, leaders must be flexible, and take account of changes in important variables such as their subordinates' motivation, confi-

244

CHAPTER 8
LEADERSHIP: WHO
DOES IT? HOW AND
WITH WHAT EFFECT?

dence, and ability to perform their jobs.[4,5] Only if leaders show such flexibility will their effectiveness remain high.

In sum, the situational view argues that external pressures and factors, *not* personal characteristics or traits, are of central importance in determining who will become a leader, and how successful such persons will be in performing this role. According to this view, the key question we should ask about leadership is not "What kind of person becomes a leader?" Rather, it should be "What skills, knowledge, or abilities are needed by a group in a given situation, and who can best provide them?" If we can answer this question, the situational view contends, we can accurately predict who will lead at a given time, and with what degree of success.

The Interactionist Approach: Leadership as a Two-Way Street

The trait and situational approaches described above offer sharply contrasting views of leadership. Yet they are similar in one key respect: Each presents a relatively simple answer to the question "Who becomes a leader?" The trait approach replies: "Those persons possessing special characteristics." The situational approach answers: "Those individuals whose skills are most useful to a group in a given context." Simple answers are always appealing, and these are no exception. At present, though, most experts on leadership have concluded that neither, by itself, is sufficient. Instead, they believe that both personal and situational factors must be taken into account. In other words, they believe that it is the *interaction* between the traits possessed by individuals and situational conditions that determine who will rise to positions of power or influence (see Figure 8.3). Perhaps some concrete examples will help illustrate the nature of this key point.

FIGURE 8.3 Leadership: The Interactionist Approach
According to the *interactionist approach,* determining which member of a group becomes its leader is affected both by personal characteristics and by situational factors. Thus an individual with one set of traits or skills may rise to leadership under one set of conditions, while another person, with very different traits, may attain this position under other circumstances.

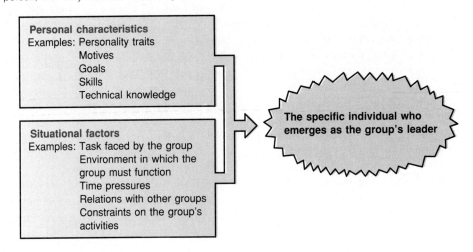

First, consider a team of experts assembled by a large consulting firm and assigned the task of solving a problem posed by one of the firm's clients. Which member will assume leadership in this context? Probably, the one who is most creative—most successful in proposing new avenues of attack on the problems or most effective in pulling the diverse skills of various team members together. In this context, then, creativity and an ability to combine diverse points of view may be the most important factors determining leadership. This occurs because in this particular situation these skills are the most desirable ones. Now, in contrast, consider a group of assembly-line workers in a large furniture factory. Who will emerge as the leader here? Perhaps in this case it will be the person who is most vocal in presenting complaints to the foreman. Or it may be the worker with the greatest seniority. It might even be the one who can consume the most beer at a local tavern! In any case, the characteristics related to leadership in this group would almost certainly be different from those in the first.

245
LEADERSHIP STYLES:
CONTRASTING
APPROACHES TO THE
TASK OF DIRECTING
OTHERS

By now, the major point should be clear. According to the **interactionist view,** there is no simple answer to the question "Who becomes a leader?" Rather, this approach realizes that different kinds of persons possessing different patterns of traits will rise to positions of authority in different situations. Clearly, this view is more complex than the trait or situational theories outlined earlier. However, it offers two major advantages over these older approaches. First, it is almost certainly more accurate than either. Thus, while it is not as simple or easy to grasp, it is closer to the truth. Second, it is optimistic in its implications about who can become a leader. Briefly, the interactionist approach suggests that almost anyone, possessing practically any combination of traits, can become a leader in *some* context. Thus, if any individual is not viewed as "leadership material" in a particular job or career, this person can move to another position in which the traits he or she possesses are highly valued. Of course, certain traits seem to contribute to leadership in almost any situation. These include intelligence, ambition, decisiveness, and self-assurance. But aside from these basics, a wide range of personal skills and characteristics can contribute to success and influence in different careers. As we will note in Chapter 14, effective career planning or development should involve two crucial steps: (1) Try to identify your own major traits; (2) Select a career in which these will be valued and used to the fullest. Together, these steps will help ensure that you reach the highest level of success and leadership you are capable of attaining. (See Chapter 14 for further discussion of career development and planning.)

LEADERSHIP STYLES: CONTRASTING APPROACHES TO THE TASK OF DIRECTING OTHERS

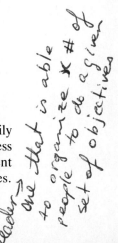

While leaders do not seem to differ from followers in a small number of easily stated ways, they *do* differ markedly from one another. Different leaders possess different motives and seek sharply contrasting goals. In addition, they use different techniques for exerting influence over other persons and directing their activities.

leader→ one that is able to organize x # of people to do a given set of objectives

Since such differences in leadership style strongly affect the atmosphere and functioning of groups, they are important and worth considering with care. It is on such differences that we focus in this section.

In one sense, there are probably as many unique styles of leadership as there are individual leaders. Each determines what works best for him or her and then uses this approach in a fairly consistent manner. But most differences between leaders seem to relate to two key dimensions. The first ranges from a **democratic** or **participative** style of leadership at one end to an **autocratic** or **directive** one at the other. The second covers the ground from primary concern with *output* or *productivity,* through primary concern with *people* and positive human relations. We will now examine differences in leadership style relating to each of these dimensions.

autocratic – does things alone/plans.

(Democratic) ~~Participative~~ versus Autocratic Leaders: Contrasting Styles, Contrasting Effects

Think back to your days in elementary school. Did you ever have a teacher who wanted to control virtually everything—someone who made all the decisions, insisted on performing tasks in certain ways, and who generally ruled the room with an "iron fist"? In contrast, did you ever have a teacher who allowed the class much more freedom—someone who encouraged students to vote on activities and projects, to do things in their own way, and who generally created a warm, friendly atmosphere? If so, you have already had direct experience with two contrasting styles of leadership: *autocratic* and *participative.*

In the past, these styles were viewed as end-points along a single dimension. However, as noted by Muczyk and Reimann, they actually seem to involve two separate dimensions.[6] The first is the extent to which leaders permit subordinates to take part in decisions: This is the *autocratic-democratic* dimension. The second involves the extent to which leaders direct the activities of subordinates and tell them how they are to carry out their jobs; this is the *permissive-directive* dimension. Combining these two dimensions yields four possible patterns, which Muczyk and Reimann label (1) directive autocrat, (2) permissive autocrat, (3) directive democrat, and (4) permissive democrat. (These patterns are described in Table 8.1.) While any attempt to divide human beings into discrete categories has its limitations, these patterns do seem to make good sense; many managers adopt a style of leadership that fits roughly into one of these categories.

One question that may have come to mind is whether one pattern is superior to the others in many, if not most, situations. Evidence so far suggests this is not the case. All four styles seem to involve a mixed pattern of advantages and disadvantages. The relative success of each depends quite heavily on conditions existing within a given organization and its specific stage of development. For example, consider managers who might be described as *directive autocrats.* They make decisions without consulting subordinates and supervise their work activities very closely (see Figure 8.4). This pattern may not be desirable with capable and highly motivated employees. However, it may be highly successful when employees are inexperienced or underqualified for their jobs or when subordinates adopt an adversarial stance toward management and must be closely supervised.

247

LEADERSHIP STYLES:
CONTRASTING
APPROACHES TO THE
TASK OF DIRECTING
OTHERS

TABLE 8.1
Leadership: Some Contrasting Styles

According to one recent study, leaders often adopt one of the four distinct styles described here. *Source:* Based on suggestions by Muczyk and Reimann (1987); see Note 6.

Leadership Style or Type	Description
Directive autocrat	Makes decisions unilaterally; closely supervises activities of subordinates
Permissive autocrat	Makes decisions unilaterally; allows subordinates considerable latitude in carrying out assigned tasks
Directive democrat	Makes decisions participatively; closely supervises activities of subordinates
Permissive democrat	Makes decisions participatively; allows subordinates considerable latitude in carrying out assigned tasks

In contrast, consider the case of *permissive autocrats* (leaders who combine permissive supervision with an autocratic style of making decisions). This pattern may be useful in dealing with employees who have a high level of technical skill and want to be left alone to manage their own jobs (e.g., scientists, engineers, computer programmers) but who have little desire to participate in routine decision-making. The remaining two patterns (directive democrat and permissive democrat) are also most suited to specific working conditions. The key task for leaders, then, is to match their own style to the needs of their organization, and to change as these shift and evolve. What happens when leaders in organizations do not demonstrate such flexibility? Their organization is likely to suffer and they are likely to be replaced (see Figure 8.5).

To conclude, no single style of leadership is best under all conditions and in all situations. However, recognizing the importance of differences in this respect can be a constructive first step toward ensuring that the style most suited to a given set of conditions is in fact adopted.

FIGURE 8.4 Autocratic Decision Style: Ignoring Subordinate Views
Although Hagar has consulted his subordinates about a raise, he ignores their views. This reflects an *autocratic* style. (Reprinted with special permission of King Features Syndicate.)

But given that many managers adopt either a relatively autocratic or relatively participative style of leadership, another question arises: Where precisely, do such preferences come from? One answer involves the personalities of individual managers. Some persons, because of their own attitudes or traits, are simply more comfortable with one of these styles. For example, some people have a strong need for power—they like telling others what to do and exercising authority.[7] Obviously, such persons tend to prefer an autocratic leadership style, since it is consistent with their own motives and tendencies. In contrast, other persons are deeply concerned with being liked by others—they have a strong need for approval. Because of this goal, they are inclined to adopt a participative leadership style—one that often leads to positive reactions among subordinates. One basis for managers' choices between these contrasting approaches to leadership, then, involves their own personalities.

A second factor that plays a key role in this respect centers on managers' views of human nature and behavior in work settings—the famous *Theory X* and *Theory Y* we examined in Chapter 1. As you may recall from our earlier discussion, Theory X managers assume that people are lazy and lacking in ambition and that they resist change and wish to avoid responsibility. Consistent with this view, they conclude that it is their task to direct, motivate, and control employees. Of course, these managers strongly prefer an autocratic style of leadership. Indeed, they view it as necessary and see little choice in the matter. In contrast, Theory Y managers adopt a more positive view of human nature. They believe that people are capable of self-direction and self-control, and will work hard to attain valued

FIGURE 8.5 Leader Flexibility: An Important Factor for Long-Term Success
Major league managers are often changed when owners want a different style of leadership. Billy Martin's style appeared to be very effective at certain times, not so effective at others. Therefore he experienced a lot of job changes. Tommy Lasorda's style seems to have been flexible enough so that he has maintained his position over many years.

goals. Managers who accept this view tend to prefer a participative or democratic style. And this, too, makes sense. After all, since they believe that people will tend to "do right" if given half a chance, efforts to control them at every step are unnecessary and may even be counterproductive. In sum, managers' acceptance of the contrasting views of human nature summarized by Theory X and Theory Y can also play a key role in their preference for an autocratic or democratic leadership style.

Before concluding, we should mention one additional factor that seems to affect managers' leadership style. In a word, this factor is gender. Research findings indicate that, in general, female managers are more participative or democratic than males. For example, in one study on this topic (conducted by Jago and Vroom) male and female managers and also male and female students (both undergraduates and graduates) completed a questionnaire designed to measure the amount of participation they would permit their subordinates to have in reaching various decisions.[8] As you can see from Figure 8.6, results indicated that in all three groups, females reported a more participative style than males. Additional findings indicate this difference stems from the fact that both men and women view an autocratic leadership style as less appropriate for female managers. Thus they evaluate females who adopt this approach more negatively than males

249

LEADERSHIP STYLES:
CONTRASTING
APPROACHES TO THE
TASK OF DIRECTING
OTHERS

FIGURE 8.6 Leadership Style: An Intriguing Sex Difference
Females report being more participative in leadership style than males. Moreover, this is true among undergraduate students, MBA students, and practicing managers. *Source:* Based on data from Jago and Vroom (1982); see Note 8.

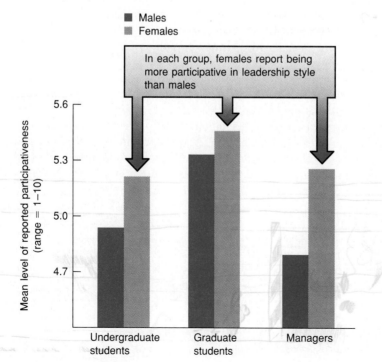

250

CHAPTER 8
LEADERSHIP: WHO
DOES IT? HOW AND
WITH WHAT EFFECT?

who choose the same pattern. Being aware of these reactions, female managers tend to prefer a participative style. Of course, other factors, too, may play a role in generating this difference between male and female managers. Regardless of the precise nature of the causes, though, it is clear that females do tend to be more participative in their approach to leadership than males.

Person-Oriented versus Production-Oriented Leaders: Showing Consideration or Initiating Structure

Have you ever seen a film version of Dickens's *A Christmas Carol*? If so, you are already familiar with the extremes along another key dimension (or really two dimensions) of leader behavior. Prior to his night with the spirits, Scrooge was interested in only one thing: carrying out his business in the most efficient and profitable manner possible. He had little interest in establishing friendly relations with his subordinates. After visits from the ghosts of Christmas Past, Present, and Future, though, all this changed. Scrooge's major concern became that of furthering the welfare of his long-suffering clerk, Bob Cratchit. Efficiency and profit were less important, and took a back seat to friendly human relations.

While few people ever experience such radical shifts in style as Dickens's character, a great deal of evidence suggests that leaders differ greatly along both of these dimensions.[9] Some are *production-oriented* and focus mainly on getting the job done. Others are lower on this dimension and show less concern with attaining high levels of output or efficiency. Similarly, some leaders are *people-oriented,* and show deep concern with establishing good relations with their subordinates. In contrast, others are low on this dimension, and do not really care much about the quality of their relations with subordinates.

At first glance, you might assume that these two dimensions (often termed **initiating structure** and **showing consideration**) are closely linked. That is, you might well guess that persons high on one must necessarily be low on the other. However, this is not the case. The two dimensions actually seem to be independent, so that a given manager can be high on both, high on one and low on the other, and so on. This basic fact was emphasized some years ago by Blake and Mouton, in well-known research on management style.[10] They developed a special questionnaire designed to measure managers' positions along both dimensions. On the basis of answers to this questionnaire, individuals are assigned two numbers: one representing their position on concern with production, and the other representing their position on concern with people. In both cases, scores can range from low (1) to high (9). For example, a manager who shows little concern with either production or people would receive a score of 1,1. Blake and Mouton describe this as an *impoverished style* of management and this term seems appropriate; indeed it is difficult to see how a person with this style could serve as an effective leader. In contrast, a manager who shows high concern with production but little concern with people would receive a score of 9,1. This is termed *task management* and is obviously a common approach in work settings. The opposite pattern is one in which a manager shows high concern with people but low concern with production (1,9). This is described as the *country-club* style of management. As a final example, consider a manager who shows moderate concern with both people and production. Such a person would receive a score of 5,5—a pattern Blake and Mouton term *middle-of-the-road* management. Of course, other scores, too, are possible (e.g., 3,9; 7,4; 9,5; 2,8). In fact, since concern with people and concern with production are measured on nine-point scales, eighty-one combinations exist. All these patterns can be represented on a grid such as the one shown in Figure 8.7. Be sure to note the positions of the styles discussed above (e.g., the country-club and task management styles).

Now let us turn to a very practical question. Assuming that leaders vary greatly in their concern for production and their concern for people, what combination of these styles is best? This turns out to be a difficult question to answer for two reasons. First, as you might guess, concern for people mainly affects morale or job satisfaction, while concern for productivity mainly affects output or efficiency. Thus there tends to be a degree of trade-off between them: High concern with people raises morale but may lower output, while high concern with productivity may enhance output but lower job satisfaction. Second, there are complex interactions between these factors. For example, a high level of people-

FIGURE 8.7 The Managerial Grid: A Useful Technique for Representing Leadership Style Grids such as this one are often used to represent a manager's position on two key dimensions: concern for people and concern for production. *Source:* Based on a figure developed by Blake and Mouton (1985); see Note 12.

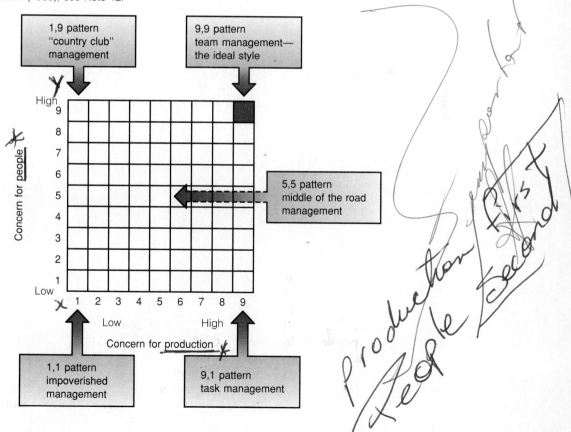

concern on the part of a manager can yield a favorable work atmosphere and so enhance productivity as well as morale. Similarly, a high level of concern for productivity can sometimes enhance morale, especially when a work group faces stressful conditions and needs strong direction from its leader.[11] Because of such effects, there can be no simple answer to the question "Which pattern is best?" This depends on the specific situation faced by a group. Having pointed out the complexities, we can now add that in many situations, leaders who are high on *both* dimensions (those showing the 9,9 pattern) seem to be the most effective.[12] Blake and Mouton term this *team management*. Apparently, the high concern for subordinates shown by such leaders encourages commitment and positive feelings among these persons, while their high concern with productivity converts this positive morale into good, efficient performance. In many cases, then, interest in people and interest in productivity are not incompatible approaches. On the contrary, they may combine to yield highly desirable results. However, not all of us may react the same way to different leadership styles. To check on how your own preferences may play a role, see the **Human Relations in Action** section below.

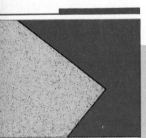

HUMAN RELATIONS IN ACTION

What Leadership Style Do You Prefer?

We have been discussing different styles of leadership. The major styles are (1) directive and production-oriented or (2) participative and people-oriented. These styles may be differentially effective in various work situations. One factor that may influence the effectiveness of a particular leadership style is the attitude of the potential followers. Some may strongly prefer a participative or people-oriented approach, others a directive and task-oriented style. Which of these contrasting styles do you think you prefer? To gain some insight into this issue, respond to the statements below. If you agree with a statement write *Y*. If you disagree, write *N*.

_____ **1.** I like to know exactly what is expected of me at work.

_____ **2.** I like a leader who monitors workers closely.

_____ **3.** Leaders should primarily be concerned with promoting worker morale.

_____ **4.** One of the most important characteristics of a leader is willingness to listen to subordinates.

_____ **5.** The most important quality for a leader is the ability to get the job done.

LEADER EFFECTIVENESS: WHO SUCCEEDS AND WHO FAILS?

Most groups have a leader. Yet not all groups perform effectively or attain their major goals. One reason for this basic fact centers on differences in leader effectiveness. All leaders, it appears, are *not* created equal. Good ones assist their groups in many ways and help ensure their success. But poor ones, like the proverbial "lead weight," drag the groups they head down to failure and despair. Differences in leader competence, then, are important and have a wide range of practical implications. But what factors cause a leader to be effective—or ineffective? Why, in short, are some persons so successful in this role and others so disappointing? Our discussion of leadership would be sadly incomplete without some attention to these matters. Thus in this final section we will focus on two frameworks offering valuable insights into the nature and causes of leader competence: Fiedler's *contingency theory* of leader effectiveness, and House's *path-goal theory* of leadership.

---

      6. It is more important for a leader to have good relations with workers than constantly focusing on productivity.

      7. Leaders should keep their distance socially from their employees.

      8. People will take advantage of leaders who are friendly and oriented toward having good relations with employees.

      9. Employees should play an important role in management decisions.

      10. It is important for leaders to show a personal interest in employees.

If you answered *Y* to three or more of items 1, 2, 5, 7, and 8 and *N* to three or more of items 3, 4, 6, 9, and 10, you are probably direction-oriented. That is, you are probably best-suited for work situations oriented to productivity and formal leader/follower relations. If you answered *Y* to three or more of the items 3, 4, 6, 9, and 10 and *N* to three or more of the items 1, 2, 5, 7, and 8, you are participation-oriented and probably would work best in situations where there is likely to be a focus on developing positive and informal leader/follower relations. Those of you who do not show a definite pattern in one direction or the other may do well under either type of leadership situation.

Fiedler's Contingency Model: Matching Leaders and Tasks

Leadership, we have repeatedly noted, does not occur in a vacuum. Rather, leaders attempt to exert their influence on group members within the context of specific situations. Given that these can vary greatly along many dimensions, it seems reasonable to expect that no single style or approach to leadership will always be best. Rather, the most effective strategy will vary from one situation to another.

This basic fact lies at the heart of a theory of leader effectiveness developed by Fiedler.[13] Fiedler describes his model as a **contingency approach,** and this term seems apt, for the basic assumption of the theory is this: The contribution of a leader to successful performance by his or her group is determined both by the leader's traits and by various features of the situation in which the group operates. To fully understand leader effectiveness, the theory contends, both factors must be taken into account.

With respect to characteristics possessed by leaders, Fiedler has focused most attention on what he terms *esteem for least preferred co-worker* (or *LPC* for short). This refers to leaders' tendency to evaluate the person with whom they find it most difficult to work in a favorable or unfavorable manner. Leaders who perceive this person in negative terms (*low LPC leaders*) seem primarily motivated to attain successful task performance. In short, they are primarily *production-oriented*. In contrast, leaders who perceive their least preferred co-worker in a positive light (*high LPC leaders*) seem concerned mainly with establishing good relations with their subordinates; they are primarily *people-oriented*.

But which of these two types of leaders is more effective? Fiedler's answer: it depends. And what it depends on is several situational factors. Specifically, Fiedler suggests that whether low LPC or high LPC leaders prove more effective depends on the degree to which the situation provides the leader with *control* or *influence* over group members. This, in turn, is determined largely by three factors: the nature of the leader's *relations with group members* (the extent to which he or she enjoys their support and loyalty), the *structure of the task* faced by the group (ranging from unstructured to highly structured), and the leader's *position power* (ability to enforce the compliance of subordinates). Combining these three factors, the leader's situational control can range from very high (positive relations with members, a highly structured task, high position power) to very low (negative relations with members, an unstructured task, low position power.)

Now that we have examined both the leader characteristics and situational factors Fiedler views as most important, we can return to the central question: When are different types of leaders most effective? Fiedler suggests that low LPC leaders (those who are task-oriented) will be superior when situational control is either low or high. However, high LPC leaders (those who are people-oriented) will "shine" when situational control is moderate (see Figure 8.8). The reasoning behind these predictions can be summarized as follows.

Under conditions of low situational control, groups need considerable direction and structure to accomplish their tasks. Since low LPC leaders, with their focus on task performance, are more likely to provide this than high LPC leaders, they will usually be superior in such cases. Similarly, low LPC leaders will also

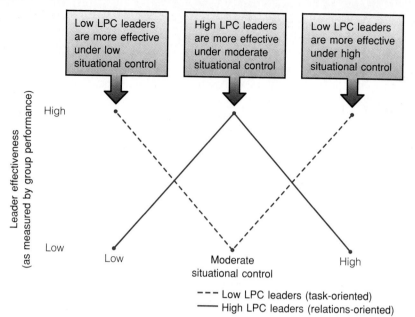

FIGURE 8.8 Contingency Theory: Some Major Predictions

Fiedler's *contingency theory* predicts that low LPC leaders (those who are primarily task-oriented) will be superior to high LPC leaders (those who are primarily people-oriented) when situational control is either very low or high. The opposite will be true when situational control is moderate. (Source: Adapted from suggestions by Fiedler: See note 13)

have an edge in situations that offer the leader a *high* degree of situational control. Here, low LPC leaders realize that their goal of task accomplishment is likely to be met. As a result, they may relax and adopt a "hands-off" style—one that aids their groups in this context. In contrast, high LPC leaders, realizing that they already enjoy good relations with their followers, may shift their attention to task performance. As a result, they may begin behaving in ways their subordinates perceive as needless meddling!

Turning to situations offering the leader *moderate* control, a different set of circumstances prevails. Here, conditions are mixed, and attention to positive human relations is often needed to "smooth ruffled feathers" and ensure good performance. High LPC leaders, with their people-orientation, often have an important edge in such situations—especially since low LPC leaders may be worried about attaining good performance and tend to act in directive, autocratic ways.

To summarize: Fiedler predicts that low LPC leaders, with their focus on task performance, will prove more effective under conditions of either low or high situational control. In contrast, high LPC leaders, with their focus on personal relations, will have a major edge under conditions where such control is moderate.

As you can probably see, Fiedler's theory is fully consistent with the interactionist view of leadership discussed earlier in this chapter. That is, it takes full account of the fact that leader effectiveness depends both on characteristics of leaders themselves, and on a number of situational factors. But now for the $64,000 question: How has the theory fared when put to actual test? In general, quite well. A recent review of more than 170 studies undertaken to test various aspects of Fiedler's view indicates that a large majority obtained positive results.[14] Further, the contingency theory has recently been put to practical use in a training program known as *leader match*.[15] Here, actual leaders (from business, education, the military) are trained to modify various aspects of the situations they face so as to make these more consistent with their preferred leadership style. In this way, of course, they help maximize their own effectiveness as leaders.

While the above results are encouraging and lend support to the theory, not all findings have been consistent with it. While laboratory studies have tended to support Fiedler's view, field investigations (those carried out with existing groups operating in a wide range of contexts) have not been as favorable.[16] Such investigations have sometimes yielded results contrary to what contingency theory would

CASE IN POINT

A Bad Match?

Shana Moore has an important position with Electronics Incorporated. She supervises the computer development and manufacturing branch. The company specializes in small portable computers and its products have been well received. They are well-designed and have a lot of built-in software. However, lately there have been increasing complaints about minor problems with the computers. Most of these are related to quality control in the manufacturing process. John Van Zinderen, vice president of the company, is concerned about this problem and has called Shana in for a discussion of the situation.

"Shana, you know we're having some problems of quality control with our computers. I'd like to know why you think this is going on."

Shana nodded in agreement. "Yes, I'm aware of the problem. It really surprises me. I have really good relations with the workers in manufacturing. I show a lot of interest in them as individuals, listen to their suggestions, and try to involve them in decisions. Morale seems to be really high. The same is true for the people in the engineering and software develpment department."

Van Zinderen leaned back in his chair and tapped his pencil on his desk for a few minutes. All of a sudden he sat up with a gleam in his eye.

"You know what strikes me? We're not having any problems with our engineering and software development. Our major problems are in the manufacturing process. Part of the problem may be the people involved. It could also be that your management style is better suited for the engineering and software section. These people are already highly motivated and primarily need continued encouragement and feelings of freedom. The people in manufacturing are primarily predict. The theory has been criticized on several bases. For example, a degree of ambiguity exists with respect to classifying specific situations along the dimension of situational control. Unless situations can be accurately classified as very low, low, moderate, and so on in this regard, predictions concerning leader effectiveness are difficult to make. Similarly, some critics have questioned the adequacy of the questionnaire used to assess leaders' standings on the LPC dimension. In particular, the reliability of this measure does not seem to be as high as that of other widely used tests.[17] Despite these problems. Fiedler's theory is widely recognized as one that has added much to our understanding of the factors influencing leader effectiveness. For an example of a potential mismatch between leadership style and the situation, see the **Case in Point** section, which starts on page 256.

Path-Goal Theory: Leaders as Guides to Valued Outcomes

Individuals rarely work for nothing. Rather, as we have seen before, they usually seek—and expect to attain—specific goals through their job-related be-

involved in straightforward tasks that can get pretty boring. They may need a little more directive supervision and monitoring to keep them working at high levels."

Now it was Shana's turn to sit up straight, and look directly at Van Zinderen. "So you think I'm the problem?" she asked. "Maybe you should find someone else for my job."

To her surprise Mr. Van Zinderen broke out in a smile. "No, I'm afraid you are mistaken if you think I want to get rid of you. We need good people like you in our company. What I'm suggesting is that you may want to adjust your management style in manufacturing somewhat. That doesn't mean that you have to become unfriendly to your employees. You probably should make it clear to these people that you are also very interested in their productivity by monitoring it more carefully."

Questions

1. How would you characterize Shana's leadership style in terms of the different models of leadership discussed?

2. Analyze the dilemma of Shana's leadership style from the perspective of the different leadership models. To what extent does Mr. Van Zinderen's analysis and suggestion for change fit or conflict with these different models?

3. Do you think Shana will be able to adjust her style or should Van Zinderen assign a different supervisor to manufacturing? Why or why not?

258

CHAPTER 8
LEADERSHIP: WHO
DOES IT? HOW AND
WITH WHAT EFFECT?

havior. This basic fact about human motivation serves as the basis for another major approach to understanding leader effectiveness: the **path-goal theory** of leadership.[18] This theory contends that subordinates will react favorably to a leader only to the extent that they perceive this person as helping them progress toward various goals by clarifying actual paths to such rewards. More precisely, the theory proposes that actions by a leader that clarify the nature of the task and reduce or eliminate obstacles will increase perceptions on the part of subordinates that working hard will lead to good performance and that good performance, in turn, will be recognized and rewarded. Under such conditions, House suggests, job satisfaction, motivation, and actual performance will all be enhanced. (As you can see, this *path-goal theory* of leadership is closely related to expectancy theory; refer to our discussion of this theory in Chapter 4.)

How can leaders best accomplish these tasks? Well, it depends on the style of leader behavior and certain contingency factors. Path-goal theory suggests that leaders can adopt four basic styles:

1. *Instrumental* (directive): A style that provides specific guidance, establishing work schedules, and setting rules.

2. *Supportive:* A style that seeks to establish good relations with subordinates, permitting them to participate in decisions.

3. *Participative:* A style focused on consulting with subordinates, permitting them to participate in decisions.

4. *Achievement-oriented:* A style that sets challenging goals and seeks improvements in performance.

It should be noted that these styles are not mutually exclusive; in fact, the same leader can adopt them at different times and in different situations.

Which of these contrasting styles is best from the point of view of maximizing subordinate satisfaction and motivation? This depends on the *contingency factors.* One of these is the characteristics of subordinates. For example, if followers are high in ability, an instrumental style of leadership may be unnecessary; instead, a less structured, supportive one may be preferable. On the other hand, if subordinates are low in ability, the opposite may be true; such persons need considerable guidance to help them attain their goals. Similarly, persons high in need for affiliation (close, friendly ties with others) may strongly prefer a supportive or participative style of leadership. Those who are high in the need for achievement may strongly prefer an achievement-oriented leader.

Second, the most effective leadership style depends on several aspects of *work environments.* For example, path-goal theory predicts that when tasks are unstructured and nonroutine, an instrumental approach by the leader may be best; much clarification and guidance is needed. However, when tasks are structured and highly routine, such leadership may actually get in the way of good performance and may be resented by subordinates. (See Figure 8.9 for an overview of all these aspects of path-goal theory.)

Although path-goal theory is relatively new, it has been subjected to empirical tests in several studies.[19] In general, results have been consistent with major predictions derived from the theory, although not uniformly so. In sum, path-

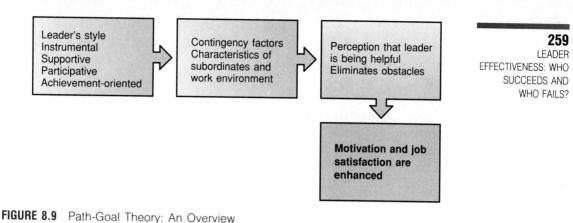

FIGURE 8.9 Path-Goal Theory: An Overview
According to path-goal theory, perceptions among employees that leaders are helping them to reach valued goals enhance both motivation and job satisfaction. Such perceptions, in turn, are fostered when a leader's style is consistent with the needs and characteristics of subordinates (e.g., their level of experience, achievement motivation) and aspects of the work environment (e.g., requirements of the tasks being performed). *Source:* Based on suggestions by House and Baetz (1979); see Note 18.

goal theory indicates that a high degree of leader effectiveness can most readily be attained through a careful matching of leader behavior to the specific work situation and the needs or values of employees. When a close match of this type is achieved, subordinates will perceive the leader as helpful and essential and will be ready to follow his or her directives. When leader behavior is instead "out of phase" with work requirements and employees' values, this person will be viewed in a less favorable light, and his or her effectiveness will be sharply reduced. To a surprising degree, then, leader effectiveness appears to rest as much in the eyes (and needs) of subordinates as in the actual behavior or style of leaders.

Substitutes for Leadership

In this chapter, we have emphasized that the style, actions, and degree of effectiveness of leaders all exert major effects on subordinates. Yet, you have probably been part of groups in which the designated leaders actually had little influence—groups in which these people were mere figureheads with little impact on subordinates. The leaders may simply have been weak and unsuited for their jobs. Another intriguing possibility is that in some contexts, other factors may actually **substitute** for a leader's influence and make it superfluous. According to a framework developed by Kerr and Jermier, many different variables can produce such effects.[20] First, a high level of knowledge, commitment, or experience on the part of subordinates may make it unnecessary for anyone to tell them what to do or how to proceed. Second, jobs themselves may be structured in ways that make direction and influence from a leader redundant. Third, work norms and strong feelings of cohesion among employees may directly affect job performance and render the presence of a leader unnecessary. Fourth, the technology associated with certain jobs may strongly determine the decisions and actions of persons performing them, leaving little room for input from a leader.

Situational Leadership Theory: Follower Maturity and Leadership Style

In an organization with a stable work force, many persons—including leaders and their subordinates—will work together for years or even decades. Since change is indeed the only constant where human beings are concerned, these individuals, and their relationships, will alter over time. One such change involves increasing maturity on the part of subordinates. As these persons grow older and obtain more job-related experience, they will become more mature in many respects. Will such shifts be reflected in their needs for various types of leadership? A theory proposed by Hersey and Blanchard suggests that they will.[21] In a view known as **situational leadership theory,** they propose the following sequence. Initially, when subordinate maturity is relatively low, the need for directive actions by the leader (initiating structure) will be high. Later, as they master their jobs, the need for emotional support (showing consideration) will increase. Finally, as they attain full maturity, the need for this, too, will decrease. Then, supervisory actions by their leaders will become superfluous in many respects. (See Figure 8.10 for a summary of this theory.)

Are these assertions about the changing course of leadership requirements over time accurate? Situational leadership theory is quite new, so little evidence about it currently exists.[22] However, findings do suggest that situational leadership theory may be most applicable to newly hired employees—ones who require a high degree of structuring from their supervisors.[23] However, it may be less applicable to more experienced, and more mature, individuals. Whatever its ultimate fate, the theory does emphasize an important fact: A style of leadership that is adaptive and successful at one point in time may not necessarily be so at others. Thus, once more, we are left with the same basic message for leaders or would-be leaders: *Flexibility* is, perhaps, the most important route to success.

SUMMARY

In most groups, one individual exerts more influence than any of the others. Such persons are generally termed **leaders,** and play a crucial role in the groups or organizations they head. At one time, it was assumed that all leaders share certain traits, and that they rise to positions of authority because of these special characteristics. Now, however, it is realized that **situational factors** (e.g., the tasks faced by a group, the environment in which it must operate) are also important. Thus according to the modern **interactionist perspective,** different individuals possessing different patterns of traits will tend to become leaders in different kinds of situations.

Leaders differ greatly in their approach or style. Some are **autocratic** and wish to be totally in control of groups they direct. Others are more **participative** and share authority and decision-making with their subordinates. The choice between these styles is affected by several factors, including a leader's acceptance of Theory X or Theory Y, and his or her own personality. Leaders also differ greatly in terms of their **concern with production** and their **concern with people.** Some evidence suggests that leaders who are high on both of these dimensions may be the most effective in a wide range of situations.

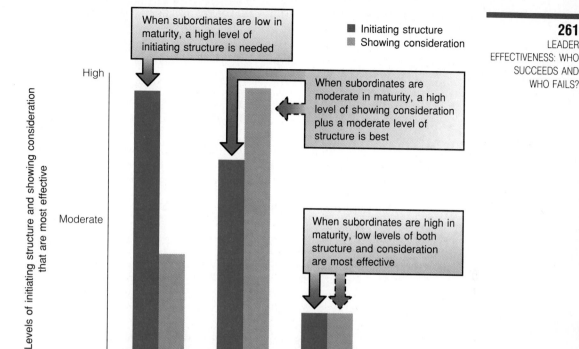

■ Initiating structure
■ Showing consideration

When subordinates are low in maturity, a high level of initiating structure is needed

When subordinates are moderate in maturity, a high level of showing consideration plus a moderate level of structure is best

When subordinates are high in maturity, low levels of both structure and consideration are most effective

Levels of initiating structure and showing consideration that are most effective

High

Moderate

Low

Low   Moderate   High

Maturity of subordinates

FIGURE 8.10 Situational Leadership Theory: A Summary

According to *situational leadership theory,* the most effective style of leadership changes as subordinates increase in maturity. At first, an approach high in initiating structure but low in showing consideration is best. Later, as subordinates become more mature, a style high in showing consideration but moderate in initiating structure is preferable. Finally, when subordinates attain a high degree of maturity, a leadership style low in both factors is best.
Source: Based on suggestions by Hersey and Blanchard (1982); see Note 21.

Many factors determine a leader's effectiveness. According to Fiedler's *contingency theory,* both the leader's characteristics and several aspects of the situation are crucial in this respect. Specifically, this theory contends that production-oriented leaders are more effective than people-oriented ones under conditions where the leader has either high or low control over the group. In contrast, people-oriented leaders are more effective under conditions where the leader has moderate control over the group. An alternative view of leader effectiveness—House's *path-goal theory*—suggests that a leader's effectiveness depends on the perception, among subordinates, that he or she is helping them toward valued goals. To the extent subordinates view the leader as helping in this regard, they will accept directives and influence from this person, and leader effectiveness will be high. To the extent they view the leader as unnecessary or as interfering with movement toward valued goals, however, they will refuse to accept such influence and leader effectiveness will be low.

262

CHAPTER 8
LEADERSHIP: WHO
DOES IT? HOW AND
WITH WHAT EFFECT?

In some situations other factors may *substitute* for leadership, making a leader's role somewhat superfluous. Highly experienced workers, highly structured jobs, and strong work norms may serve as such substitutes. In a similar vein, as work groups mature, they may require different types of leadership. This is the basic idea behind *situational leadership theory*.

KEY TERMS

autocratic leadership style: A style in which the leader attempts to control virtually every aspect of group functioning (e.g., all work activities, decision-making).

charismatic leaders: Leaders who exert powerful effects on their followers and to whom several special traits are attributed (e.g., possession of an idealized vision or goal, willingness to engage in unconventional behaviors to reach it, etc.).

contingency theory of leader effectiveness: A theory suggesting that leader effectiveness is determined both by characteristics of the leader and the degree of situational control this person can exert over subordinates.

democratic leadership style: A form of participative leadership in which the leader allows subordinates to make decisions through a "majority rules" approach.

great person theory: The view that leaders possess special traits that set them apart from others, and that these traits are responsible for their assuming positions of power and authority.

initiating structure: A style of leadership focused mainly on productivity or successful task accomplishment. Leaders high on this dimension often engage in such actions as organizing work activities, setting deadlines, and assigning individuals to specific tasks; also called task-orientation.

interactionist view of leadership: A view contending that the particular member of a group who becomes its leader depends both on personal characteristics of such an individual and on many situational factors.

leaders: Those individuals within work or social groups who exert the most influence on other members.

participative leadership style: A style in which the leader permits subordinates to have input in decisions and affords them a considerable degree of freedom with respect to routine job activities.

path-goal theory: A theory of leadership suggesting that subordinates will accept influence from the leader and work effectively under this person's direction only to the extent that they perceive the leader as helping them attain valued goals.

showing consideration: A style of leadership focused mainly on the establishment of positive relations between the leader and other group members; also called people-orientation.

situational approach: A view suggesting that the person who becomes the leader of a specific group is determined largely by situational factors (e.g., the technical skill or knowledge needed for a particular task).

situational leadership theory: A theory suggesting that the most effective style of leadership varies with the maturity or experience of subordinates.

substitutes for leadership: The view that high levels of skill among workers or certain features of technology and organizational structure can sometimes serve as substitutes for leaders, rendering their guidance or influence superfluous.

trait approach to leadership: A view suggesting that leaders differ from other persons with respect to certain key traits, and that all leaders—regardless of the time period in which they live or the kind of groups they lead—share these traits.

NOTES

1. McClelland, D.C., & Boyatzis, R.E. (1982). "Leadership Motive Pattern and Long-Term Success in Management." *Journal of Applied Psychology, 67,* 737–43.

2. Costantini, E., & Craik, K.H. (1980). "Personality and Politicians: California Party Leaders, 1960–1976." *Journal of Personality and Social Psychology, 38,* 641–66.

3. Conger, J.A., & Kanungo, R.N. (1987). Toward a behavioral theory of charismatic leadership in organizational settings. *Academy of Management Review, 12,* 637–647.

4. Hersey, P., & Blanchard, K.H. (1982). *Management of Organization Behavior*, 4th ed. Englewood Cliff, N.J.: Prentice-Hall.

5. Graeff, C.L. (1983). "The Situational Leadership Theory: A Critical Review." *Academy of Management Review, 8,* 285–91.

6. Muczyk, J.P., & Reimann, B.C. (1987). "The Case of Directive Leadership." *Academy of Management Executive, 1,* 301–11.

7. McClelland, D.C., & Burnham, D.H. (1976). "Power Is the Great Motivator." *Harvard Business Review*, March-April.

8. Jago, A.G., & Vroom, V.C. (1982). "Sex Differences in the Incidence and Evaluation of Participative Leader Behavior." *Journal of Applied Psychology, 67,* 776–83.

9. Halpin, A.W., & Winer, B.J. (1957). "A Factorial Study of the Leader Behavior Descriptions." In R.M. Stogdill and A.E. Coons, eds. *Leader Behavior: Its Description and Measurement.* Columbus: Ohio State University, Bureau of Business Research.

10. Blake, R., & Mouton, J. (1978). *The New Managerial Grid.* Houston: Gulf.

11. Fleishman, E.A. (1973). "Twenty Years of Consideration and Structure." In E.A. Fleishman and J.G. Hunt, eds. *Current developments in the Study of Leadership.* Carbondale: Southern Illinois University Press.

12. Blake, R.R., & Mouton, J.S. (1985). *The Managerial Grid III.* Houston: Gulf.

13. Fiedler, F.E. (1978). "Contingency and the Leadership Process. In L. Berkowitz, ed. *Advances in Experimental Social Psychology*, vol. 11, New York: Academic Press.

14. Strube, M.J., & Garcia, J.E. (1981). "A Meta-Analytic Investigation of Fiedler's Contingency Model of Leadership Effectiveness." *Psychological Bulletin, 90,* 307–21.

15. Fiedler, F.E., Mahar, L., & Schmidt, S. "Four Validation Studies of Contingency Model Training." Seattle: University of Washington, Organizational Research Tech. Rep., 75–70.

16. Peters, L.H., Hartke, D.D., & Pohlman, J.T. (1985). "Fiedler's Contingency Theory of Leadership: An Application of the Meta-analysis Procedures of Schmidt and Hunter." *Psychological Bulletin, 97,* 274–85.

17. Ashour, A.S. (1973). "The Contingency Model of Leadership Effectiveness: An Evaluation." *Organizational Behavior and Human Performance, 9,* 339–55.

18. House, R.J., & Baetz, M.L. (1979). "Leadership: Some Generalizations and New Research Directions." In B.M. Staw, ed. *Research in Organizational Behavior.* Greenwich, Conn.: JAI Press.

19. Schriesheim, C.A., & Denisi, A.S. (1981). "Task Dimensions as Moderators of the Effects of Instrumental Leadership: A Two-Sample Replicated Test of Path-Goal Leadership Theory." *Journal of Applied Psychology, 66,* 589–97.

20. Kerr, S., & Jermier, J.M. (1978). "Substitutes for Leadership: Their Meaning and Measurement." *Organizational Behavior and Human Performance, 22,* 375–403.

21. See Note 4.

22. Hambleton, R.K., & Gumpert, R. (1982). "The Validity of Hersey and Blanchard's Theory of Leader Effectiveness." *Group and Organization Studies, 7,* 225–42.

23. Vecchio, R.P. (1987). "Situational Leadership Theory: An Examination of a Perspective Theory." *Journal of Applied Psychology, 72,* 444–51.

The Oz Ice Cream Parlor

Don H. Hockenbury
Psychology Instructor
Tulsa Junior College

Sandra E. Hockenbury
Adjunct Instructor
Tulsa Junior College

Eight years ago, shortly after graduating from college, Jerry and Lauree opened the Oz Ice Cream Parlor with the help of a small business loan. Their idea was deceptively simple: Provide a party atmosphere and entice customers with low-cost giveaways. For example, anyone who had a double-dip cone or sundae got a free small soft drink or coffee. Children would always get a balloon, a little toy, or a paper hat. If you came in on your birthday, you got a free double-dip cone. Customers never knew what to expect; once or twice a month a clown, mime, or juggler might perform. There was something for everyone who simply walked through the door. The Oz Ice Cream Parlor became known as a fun, inexpensive place for the entire family to enjoy.

It took almost two years before the business finally began operating in the black, but soon Oz started melting the competition. Lauree and Jerry involved their employees in virtually every decision that was made. The atmosphere at the original Oz was one of genuine group effort and commitment. Jerry and Lauree kept their employees loyal by offering flexible scheduling, monthly cash recognition awards for customer service, cash awards for ideas and suggestions, and regular raises. They fostered camaraderie among the workers by hosting frequent parties and barbecues for the Oz staff and by sponsoring a volleyball and softball team for the employees.

By the fourth year of operation, Oz had expanded to a second location at one of the busiest malls in the area. Either Lauree or Jerry was at each location every day. In the sixth year, two more ice cream parlors were added and discussions began about branching throughout the state and, possibly, the region. With four stores now to oversee, Jerry and Lauree cut back on the number of hours they spent each day at the ice cream parlors. They moved the Oz Ice Cream office from their spare bedroom at home to a downtown office building. In time, Jerry and Lauree realized that the business had simply gotten too big for them to personally supervise every parlor. With a great deal of reluctance, they decided that they needed at least two on-site managers to be responsible for the day-to-day operations of the ice cream parlors. Lauree and Jerry would, of course, still make all the major decisions, but they would let the professional managers handle the routine operations.

Six months after they hired Bob to manage the two northside stores, and Frank to manage the two southside parlors. Lauree and Jerry sat down with their accountant to go over the financial statements for each store. Profits were up at all four stores, but for different reasons. The northside stores showed increased expenditures but also increased sales that more than compensated for the additional costs. Bob was asking them to approve three new positions and thought that they should seriously consider expanding the floor space of the original parlors or move to a larger location. Frank's southside stores also showed increased profits, but for an entirely different reason: Although sales were actually down by almost 15 percent, costs had been cut by 25 percent, so the result was a hefty increase in profits. In addition, two employees had quit over the past six months and another four employees were working fewer hours. Frank didn't think that the two employees who quit needed to be replaced. In fact, he was talking about laying off one or two more workers.

"I don't understand, Lauree," Jerry frowned as they looked at the operating figures. "Frank thinks we should cut back on the hours at the southside stores, but just last year those ice cream parlors were booming. In fact, didn't you say last year that you thought we needed more room at the parlor in the mall?"

"That's what I thought," Lauree nodded, equally puzzled. "And there's another thing I don't understand. Marty Hodges has submitted his two-week notice to quit. Why would Marty quit? He's one of our oldest employees—in fact, the free balloons and toys were his original idea."

"He's got a dynamite volleyball serve, too!" Jerry said. "The Oz Ice Creamers will certainly miss him this summer."

"Maybe we need to talk to Marty before he quits," Lauree suggested. "I think I'll call him and see if he can stop by today."

Marty reluctantly agreed to stop by Lauree and Jerry's house after the parlor closed that night. Hesitant at first, Marty finally opened up and expressed his concerns.

"Well, to be quite honest with you, Lauree, when I first started working for you and Jerry there was this wonderful feeling of togetherness among the employees. We were like one big family, all working to try to give the customer the best service possible. You know how much I've loved working at Oz these past few years. In many ways, I really did consider it my home away from home.

"But things are different now," Marty continued. "Frank has a whole different approach to running the business, and I can't really argue with him. I guess there was a lot of waste in the old days, but I just don't like his system of doing things."

"What kind of system, Marty?" Jerry asked.

"Well, Frank keeps track of things, like how long it takes each of us to wait on a customer. He says that we should spend less time talking to the customers and to each other and more time taking orders and keeping the store clean and the freezers stocked. And he notices little things like whether we give the customer a little extra on their sundaes or cones, you know. He showed us all the difference between a level scoop and a heaping scoop, and let us know that he wanted us to use the level measure, not the heaping measure! And you know, he's right; we really did give away a lot of free ice cream and chocolate sprinkles that way. But you know, lots of people would drive right past three other ice cream stores to come to Oz, just because they knew they'd get a little extra for their money. You know, when you've been at a place for as long as I have, you get to know your regulars. And to tell the truth, a lot of them just don't come by that often anymore."

Marty paused and shrugged his shoulders. "Plus, you know how we always encouraged people to try new and different flavors? Frank told us to stop suggesting to people that they sample a few flavors before they placed their orders. He said, 'If they ask for a sample, of course, we have to give it to them, but just don't put the idea in their head.' Well, I kinda feel sorry for the little kids that don't have much money to spend, so I used to tell them to go ahead and sample away. I know that was giving away the ice cream for free, but the sample spoons are awfully little, and the kids really appreciated it, I could tell, and so did their parents. Well, Frank caught me telling one of the little ones to go ahead and try a few flavors, and he really let me have it, right in front of all the other workers. He said that if I didn't agree with his decisions, that was my problem, not his, and that I could either do as he said or leave."

"I see," said Jerry quietly. "In other words, he said, do as I tell you, whether you agree with it or not."

"Basically," Marty nodded. "And I guess that he has the right to say that, since he *is* the boss. But on the other hand, I really didn't want to work there anymore if that was going to be his attitude toward me. And not just toward me, but toward the customers and the other workers. Heck, Frank wouldn't even let the mime who performs at Oz every month have free ice cream anymore."

"That's amazing," said Lauree, shaking her head. "I think we're getting the picture. Thanks, Marty, for being honest with us. But before you turn in your resignation, maybe you'd like to stop over at the northside stores. Maybe you'd be interested in a transfer, rather than a new job."

Questions

1. From the information provided, which of the four leadership types shown in Table 8.1 seem to depict Jerry, Lauree, Bob, and Frank?

2. Analyze the different leaders in this situation on the dimensions of consideration and initiating structure.

3. Use the path-goal model of leadership effectiveness to explain employees' responses to the different managers.

4. Evaluate the pros and cons of Frank's leadership style for the Oz Ice Cream Parlor business.

5. If you were the owner of this ice cream chain, what would you do with the information Marty shared with you?

Leaders: Alike or Different?

A major theme of this chapter has been this: All leaders are not alike. Depending on the type of group they lead and the type of situation they confront, they can show sharply contrasting traits. In short, different kinds of people rise to positions of leadership in different kinds of settings. You can demonstrate this fact for yourself, and gain some insight into the major characteristics of leaders, by following these procedures.

First, identify persons who are widely recognized as leaders in several areas of life: business, religion, the military, politics, and sports. For each one, list the three traits that you feel were most directly responsible for this person's rise to "the top." Now, expand your survey by asking several of your friends to do the same.

After you have collected this information, examine the traits you and your friends have listed for the leaders in each field. In all probability, you'll find that these lists are only partially overlapping. For example, with respect to leaders in business, you and your friends may well have mentioned such traits as ambition, self-confidence, and dominance. In contrast, with respect to leaders of religion, you and your friends may have listed such characteristics as kindness, compassion, and sympathy. Compare the various lists of traits and note the differences between them. Finally, try to understand why different traits are needed for successful leadership in different fields or occupations.

Group Behavior and Influence: How Do Groups Affect Us?

Learning Objectives

After reading this chapter,
you should be able to:

1. Define some of the goals that groups can help us satisfy.

2. Describe the way in which people become socialized as group members.

3. Describe the stages of group development.

4. Discuss the ways in which diffusion of responsibility can affect bystander intervention, deindividuation, and social loafing.

5. Describe the phenomenon of social facilitation and explain why it occurs.

6. Identify the major factors that influence the performance of brainstorming groups.

7. Discuss the factors that underly the group polarization effect.

8. Describe the basic characteristics of groupthink.

he employees of Mayland Department Store were having their monthly meeting to share their various concerns and ideas with the manager, Ms. Cole. The store was about to enter its Christmas merchandising phase, and Ms. Cole was interested in getting some new ideas from the employees. Most of the employees had worked for the store more than a year, but Joe Sloan had only worked there for a month and this was his first meeting. He wasn't sure how it would go. Being new to the store, he had some ideas about how to improve some of the procedures, but he wasn't sure that the input of a new employee would be valued. Ms. Cole began the meeting thanking the employees for their good work the past month and encouraging them to continue their efforts during the Christmas season. One of her main concerns for this meeting was whether to stay open on Sundays during this period. Ms. Cole asked the group what they thought about this.

One of the more senior employees, Jack Myers, thought it was a good idea. "We'll probably get a lot more business this way. Many families are so busy during the week that Sunday is one of the few times they can do their shopping."

"I agree," Susan Altman said. "It will probably be one of our busiest days."

Quickly there seemed to be general agreement that it was a good idea. However, a few of the employees had not expressed their opinions yet. Joe had some qualms and wondered about the extra costs of paying higher wages on Sundays and the possibility that people would simply spread their shopping out to seven days instead of doing the same amount of shopping in six days. Since most of the other department stores were closed on Sundays, would they also open an extra day?

Yet most of the people in the group seemed to feel positive about it, and Joe did not know how the input from a new employee would be accepted. They would probably not pay much attention to it since he was new. Or maybe they would object to his disagreeing with the view of more experienced employees. All of a sudden, Ms. Cole looked him straight in the eyes. "Well Joe, what do you think? You're the new person on the block, so to speak. Do you think it's a good idea for us to open on Sundays?"

Now he was on the spot. What should he say? After a short pause, he blurted out, "Eh, well, it seems to be a pretty good idea, but . . ."

"But what?" Ms. Cole prompted. "Do you have some reservations about it?"

"Well, I'm not sure I'll be able to work on both Saturdays and Sundays because of my studies."

"Oh, I think we can work around that," said Ms. Cole. "Are there any other comments? If not, then we will adjourn the meeting. Thanks for your input, and let's do our best to have a successful Christmas season."

As Joe left the meeting, he was a little angry with himself. Why had he not spoken up frankly? Maybe the others were right anyway. Well, there was no use fussing about it now. It was time to get back to work.

Joe's experience is probably typical of many group meetings. Most people feel a need to get along in a group and may not fully express opinions that may conflict with those of the group. In this chapter we will deal with the various factors that influence our behavior in groups. Many studies have suggested that groups have a strong impact on our behavior. Some of these effects may be quite counterproductive. We will look carefully at the variety of factors that play a role in group behavior and how these factors can either lead to positive or negative results for groups. But first we will briefly discuss some basic characteristics of groups.

GROUPS: WHAT ARE THEY AND WHAT DO THEY DO?

What are **groups?** We usually think of groups as consisting of two or more individuals having some common bond, goal, or task. Sometimes they are simply temporary collections of people such as groups at spectator events. Some groups such as clubs, churches, and families may have strong bonds and maintain long-term relationships. Although there are obviously many types of groups, we can formally define *groups* as *a collection of two or more interacting individuals who share common goals, have a stable relationship, and see themselves as a group*[1] (see Figure 9.1). Most groups exist because they share common goals or interests. Unless some degree of verbal or nonverbal interaction takes place among group members, there is not likely to be a sense of group identity. A group typically has some degree of stability in that it is not constantly changing and it has a core group of members. Fraternities and sororities reflect these features quite nicely. There is likely to be much social interaction among members. Although there is always some turnover, the change in membership is gradual and provides for some degree of stability. The members share common goals about the importance of social life on campus and have strong perceptions of their group identity.

FIGURE 9.1 A Group: Its Basic Characteristics
The four major defining characteristics of a group are summarized here. As shown, to be a group, there must be two or more people in social interaction who share common goals, have a stable group structure, and who perceive themselves as being a group.

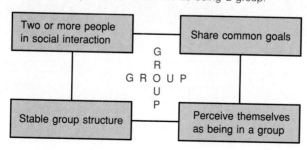

272

CHAPTER 9
GROUP BEHAVIOR
AND INFLUENCE:
HOW DO GROUPS
AFFECT US?

Joining Groups: Why People Need People

People join groups for a wide variety of reasons. Groups may satisfy a number of *psychological* or *social needs*. For example, groups may allow people to fulfill their needs for belonging, control, and attention or affection. They may also be a source of approval and social support and can help reduce fear in stressful settings.[2] However, our social and personal needs are not the only consideration in joining groups. Groups also help us achieve tasks and *goals* that are not possible as individuals. This is obvious in the case of many competitive sports and in business ventures, but it is also true for most other groups. There are three basic goals that groups can help us attain—*utilitarian, knowledge,* and *identity.*[3] Utilitarian goals are those related to satisfying personal and social needs such as those for money, achievement, and influence. Knowledge goals involve obtaining information and developing a consensus about issues with others. Groups can also aid us in establishing a positive social identity. This, of course, comes about rather naturally when we are part of a successful group (see Table 9.1 for a summary). Yet even those who belong to relatively unsuccessful or underprivileged groups may feel positive about their group membership.[4] Why is this so? Possibly, group members compare themselves primarily with others in their own group in establishing their identity. Even though the group may not be very successful, as individuals they may find that they measure up quite well within their own group and thus have a fairly positive self-concept.

Group Socialization: Becoming a Group Member

Although you may belong to a number of groups, you are probably not at the same level of involvement in all of them. You may be a key leader in one, a newcomer in another, and about to quit a third. Our membership in groups is usually not static, but subject to change over a period of time. According to Moreland and Levine, membership seems to go through a series of phases that vary in how committed one is to the group.[5] At first the member and the group *investigate* each other to see whether group membership should be considered. Once group membership is decided on, a person may enter the group and begin

---

TABLE 9.1
Group Goals: Reasons for Joining Groups

Groups help us satisfy a variety of goals. Three primary types of goals are utilitarian, knowledge, and identity.

Utilitarian	Knowledge	Identity
Money	Information	Social comparison
Achievement	Consensus	Positive self-concept
Influence		

a period of *socialization* in which the group attempts to help the individual become a full-fledged member. If all goes well and both the newcomer and the group are satisfied with each other, full *acceptance* of group membership may occur. The person is now a full member and has a strong commitment to the group. However, for a variety of reasons, some people may lose interest in being group members. They may become bored or get involved in conflicts with other group members. They may become marginal members, and unless efforts are made to *resocialize* such individuals and increase their commitment, they may eventually quit or *exit* from the group and enter a phase of *remembrance*. During the remembrance phase, the individual and the group may actively think about or evaluate the past relationship. The various phases of group membership are shown in Figure 9.2. Can you place your membership in different groups into the categories shown? Can you apply this model to your experiences in social groups (e.g., fraternities or sororities), teams, or work groups? (See Figure 9.3.)

Group Development: Changes in the Life of the Group

Just as our relationship to a group may vary over time, so may the characteristics of the group itself. A group may go through at least five stages of **group development** as shown in Table 9.2.[6] The first stage is *forming* and involves the

FIGURE 9.2 Group Socialization: Phases of Group Membership
According to the Moreland and Levine model of socialization in small groups, group membership goes through different phases that involve different degrees of commitment and a variety of role transitions. Adapted from Moreland and Levine (1989); see Note 5.

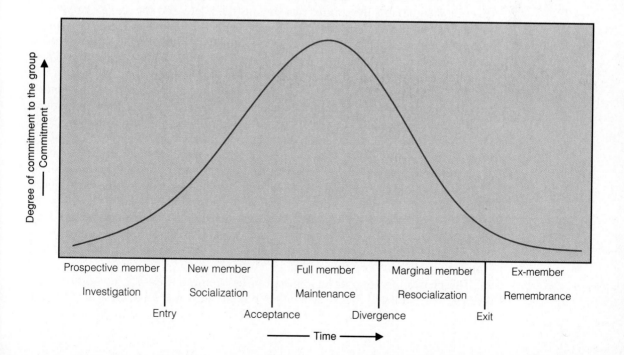

274
CHAPTER 9
GROUP BEHAVIOR
AND INFLUENCE:
HOW DO GROUPS
AFFECT US?

FIGURE 9.3 Initiation Activities: One Part of Group Socialization
In many fraternities or sororities, elaborate initiation rites are part of the socialization experience.

process of getting to know other group members and learning the ground rules. The members may be unsure as to how to act and who is going to be the leader. Once these uncertainties are cleared up and individuals come to think of themselves as members of the group, this stage is complete and the stage of *storming* begins. At this point, there may be a lot of conflict as members resist the control of their leaders and compete for attractive positions or roles. If these conflicts are not resolved, the group may not survive. However, if the conflicts are resolved in a reasonable fashion and there is acceptance of the leadership, the group goes into the *norming* stage. At this point the group members become closer emotionally and develop a common perspective about how the group will operate. They share feelings and try to develop mutually satisfactory solutions to problems. There is a sense of camaraderie and feelings of shared responsibility for the group's activities. Once this phase is complete, the group is ready to begin *performing*. They can now focus their energies on the tasks at hand. As long as groups are successful or have goals to achieve, they are motivated to maintain their existence. However, once its goals have been achieved, a group may begin *adjourning*, as in the case of fund-raising groups or special task forces. However, groups may also start to disband as key members leave, conflicts arise, and the common goals or beliefs no longer bind the group members. This may be especially true for groups that are not very successful.

The phases of group development can be seen quite clearly in sports teams. At first the members check each other out to see who is the best at different

TABLE 9.2
The Five Stages of Group Development

As outlined in this model, groups go through several stages of development. *Source:* Based on information in Tuckman and Jensen (1977); see Note 6.

Stage	Primary Characteristic
1. Forming	Members get to know each other and seek to establish ground rules.
2. Storming	Members come to resist control of group leaders and show hostility.
3. Norming	Members work together and develop close relationships and feelings of camaraderie.
4. Performing	Group members work toward getting their job done.
5. Adjourning	Groups may disband either after meeting their goals, or because members leave.

positions and who is likely to be a team leader (forming). Then there is competition for starting positions and the positions of team captains (storming). Once this is resolved, the group begins to work together to become an effective team and may begin socializing together and wearing their team jackets or shirts (norming). They are now ready to devote their energies to doing their best to help the team win (performing). Of course, once the season is over, the team disbands (adjourning) until another team is formed the following season.

Although this model of group development is descriptive of the life of many groups, each group's development process is rather unique and may not follow this pattern precisely. Research indicates that some of the stages may be combined and that they may not always occur in the same order. The time a group spends in each phase is also likely to vary. However, the model does suggest a natural progression of stages through which many groups move and helps us understand why some work groups are effective and others are not.

DIFFUSION OF RESPONSIBILITY: HIDING IN GROUPS

Have you ever felt like you had too many responsibilities and decisions to make? Sometimes we get overwhelmed with all we have to do at work, at home, and in school, and it is difficult to find time to relax. Although we may relax alone, we often seek out groups for leisure activities. We may go to happy hour or parties after work or get involved in group activities such as camping or theater. Groups do seem to be effective in reducing our levels of stress by providing social support (Chapter 13). However, there is also a more subtle way in which groups can affect us. It appears that when we are involved in group situations, we tend

276

CHAPTER 9
GROUP BEHAVIOR
AND INFLUENCE:
HOW DO GROUPS
AFFECT US?

to relax in a number of ways. This relaxation seems to stem from a lessened feeling of responsibility.

Bystander Intervention

This phenomenon was first demonstrated vividly by studies on *bystander intervention* by Latane and Darley.[7] They were trying to understand the fact that in many emergencies, groups of bystanders may not intervene to help. One dramatic case involved Kitty Genovese who was stabbed repeatedly in New York City while thirty-seven neighbors looked on. Not one onlooker intervened by helping directly or calling the police. Latane and Darley theorized that one reason for this lack of helping was that individuals in a group of bystanders felt a reduced responsibility to help because others in the group were also capable of helping (see Figure 9.4). This **diffusion of responsibility** in groups was studied by having students exposed to another student (actually an experimental assistant) who appeared to be having an epileptic seizure. The students were placed in individual rooms and were taking turns talking over a microphone when the apparent epileptic seizure occurred. The groups had two, three, and six members, including the experimental assistant. As suggested by the diffusion of responsibility hypothesis, the larger the group of bystanders, the less likely it was that the epileptic student would be helped. When the subject was the only bystander, the victim was always helped. With two bystanders, the victim was helped only 85 percent of the time. With five bystanders, helping was reduced to 62 percent. Similar results have been obtained in many other studies.[8]

The bystander intervention studies have shown that merely being part of a group can lessen one's feelings of responsibility for action in a time of need. This may account partly for the failure of employees to report work-related problems such as dishonesty or poor work performance by fellow employees. However, such lowered feelings of responsibility can also occur in other group settings. You have probably participated in some exciting group activities in which you got so involved that you lost some degree of self-control. You might have said or done things you would not ordinarily have done. Sometimes individuals in groups such as youth gangs or mobs act out in fairly aggressive or violent ways. The phe-

FIGURE 9.4 Diffusion of Responsibility: One Cause of Reduced Helping
When there is an emergency and someone needs help, the degree of responsibility is divided by the number of others present. Therefore we feel less responsibility with larger groups and are less likely to help. *Source:* Adapted from Latane and Darley (1970); see Note 7.

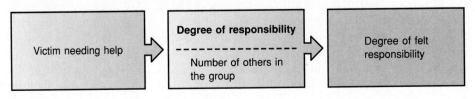

nomenon of lost self-control in groups has been the concern of studies on deindividuation.

Deindividuation: Loss of Self-Control in Groups

The behavior of crowds has intrigued scholars for some time. Le Bon observed the wild behavior of the crowds during the French Revolution and proposed that some sort of "group mind" had taken control of the crowd. As a result, individuals were behaving in very extreme ways, as exemplified by condemning many people to death by guillotine. The extreme behaviors exhibited by crowds may be understood in part through the concept of deindividuation. **Deindividuation** is a state of lessened self-awareness that occurs because of involvement in group situations and is related to a lowering of self control over behavior.[9] As a result, individuals may exhibit antisocial or aggressive behaviors. They are also more susceptible to the influence of other people. Your experience in large crowd events or at parties probably fits with some of these proposals. People may get somewhat disinhibited at these events and act in ways that they would not ordinarily. The use of alcohol adds fuel to the fire since this increases loss of self-awareness and control.

Of course, not all group situations lead to deindividuation or antisocial behavior. A variety of studies have shown that group size, anonymity, and active group involvement all can increase uninhibited behavior.[10] Deindividuation will occur primarily in situations where there is a degree of anonymity and people are actively engrossed in group activities such as dancing or shouting. The Mardi Gras celebration in New Orleans exemplifies this clearly. Many of the participants wear masks and are strangers to one another, and they are actively involved in a variety of group activities (see Figure 9.5).

The research on deindividuation has thus complemented the perspective gained from the research on bystander intervention. It has shown that a lowering of feelings of responsibility and self-awareness in groups may not only lead to lack of helping but may actually be associated with destructive or antisocial behaviors. Therefore it is important for us to be aware of the consequences of our involvement in groups, whether it be a gang, work group, or party. As long as there is some degree of accountability, problems are not likely to occur. However, when accountability is reduced, and arousal and cohesiveness are increased by group activities, and there is some use of alcohol, problems are most likely to occur.

Social Loafing: How to Get Less Out of More

So far we have discussed the ways in which individuals may behave somewhat irresponsibly in groups. When groups make people feel less accountable or responsible, individuals seem to be less motivated to behave in accord with normative standards of behavior. Interestingly, this type of phenomenon can also be observed in work situations. One of the first such observations was made by Ringlemann, who noted that as the number of individuals in a group pulling on a rope increased,

278
CHAPTER 9
GROUP BEHAVIOR
AND INFLUENCE:
HOW DO GROUPS
AFFECT US?

FIGURE 9.5 Mardi Gras: One Deindividuation Experience
Mardi Gras celebrations in New Orleans provide an opportunity for many people to experience deindividuation with the use of masks and active group participation.

the amount of force each individual was exerting was reduced. Doesn't this contradict what you might have expected? It would seem natural for people in the group to be motivated to work harder for the group goal. Yet research has demonstrated that motivation losses in groups, called **social loafing** do occur whenever efforts of individuals are combined into a group product.[11]

Research has shown that social loafing can occur on a variety of tasks. The basic characteristics of these tasks is that they are **additive.** This means that individuals in the group do their own individual task and the sum of all of the individual efforts is the group product. This is typical of many work situations such as telemarketing, car sales, and painting in which individuals may work independently with a group of individuals. Social loafing has been found in studies where individuals were asked to clap, shout loudly, or generate uses for a simple object.

Yet why do people loaf on such tasks? One major reason seems to be the fact that in many such situations people may not be individually identifiable in that their performances are combined into a group score. Under such conditions people may feel little concern about the quality of their performance. Identifiability is important mainly because it allows the individual's performance to be evaluated.[12] When individual performance can be evaluated by others, people seem to be motivated to exert more effort on a task. This probably makes sense to you since you may tend to work harder when the boss or the manager is around to observe your work than when he or she is not.

Counteracting Social Loafing   There appear to be three major ways to counteract people's tendency to loaf in large work groups. One is to increase *accountability* by making sure that each person's performance can be assessed or evaluated.[13] This can be done in a variety of ways that depend to a large extent on the type of work situation. For example, procedures could be designed to keep track of the work each person accomplishes. This can be seen in factories that pay on the basis of amount of work done by each individual (piece rate) and stores that pay on a commission basis.

It may also be useful to complement the accountability strategy with one focusing on the intrinsic merits of the task. Studies have shown that when people feel that the task on which they are working is unique or challenging, they may not loaf even if their performance is pooled with that of the group. Under such conditions people may be motivated by the opportunity to make a unique contribution or to test their skills.[14]

The final way of overcoming social loafing might be called *group pride*. If people feel that the performance of their group can be compared with that of other groups, they may be motivated to work hard so that their group will do well relative to the other groups. This can be seen most clearly when one team competes with another. In the same way, stores or companies may have competitions with one another. This effect has been shown in several studies where groups in which performance was pooled were provided with either an objective standard of ideal performance or the average performance of previous participants. In both cases, the social loafing effect was eliminated.[15] (Table 9.3 provides a summary of those factors that influence the degree of social loafing in groups.)

Applicability of Social Loafing   Although there is much evidence for social loafing in laboratory studies, there is little evidence thus far for the role of this factor in

TABLE 9.3
Social Loafing: Some Influential Factors

The extent to which social loafing will occur or will be reduced or prevented depends on the factors outlined below.

Factors that Increase Loafing	Factors that Reduce Loafing
Lack of identifiability	Individual identifiability
No individual evaluation	Individual or group evaluation
Task is easy, boring, or same as that of others	Individual or group standards of evaluation
	Task is difficult, interesting, or different from others

280

CHAPTER 9
GROUP BEHAVIOR
AND INFLUENCE:
HOW DO GROUPS
AFFECT US?

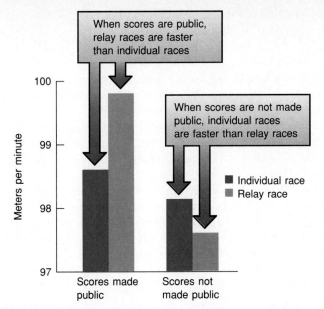

FIGURE 9.6   Loafing and Athletes: Accountability in Swimming Relay Races
When scores are publicly announced, swimmers have better times (in meters per minute) in relay races than in individual ones. When they are not announced or made public, swimmers have slower times in relay races. *Source:* Adapted from Williams et al. (1989); see Note 16.

real-life working situations. Your own experience probably suggests that it does play a role in such situations. The fact that economies based on the socialistic system of pooling individual contributions (e.g., communes or collective farms or industries) have not been very productive is consistent with a social loafing perspective. In any case, anyone concerned with achieving a high level of productivity out of a group should be aware of the potential problems caused by social loafing and the ways in which it can be avoided.

Although studies of social loafing in workplaces have yet to be done, there is some research demonstrating its role in athletics. In one study swimmers were asked to swim laps either individually or as part of a relay team.[16] When these scores were not made public, they swam slower in relays than individually (see Figure 9.6). While this is evidence for social loafing, the study also found that groups can serve to motivate better performance as well. When swimmer's scores were publicly identifiable, they swam faster in relays than individually. What accounts for this facilitative effect of groups? We will help solve this puzzle in the next section.

SOCIAL FACILITATION: MOTIVATION AND INTERFERENCE IN GROUPS

Even though much evidence exists for the loss of motivation in groups, you probably are aware of situations in which you have been strongly motivated in group situations. If you have participated in team sports, taken part in recitals, or competed in games, you know that in these types of situations your adrenaline may really start going. This type of phenomenon has been studied for a long time with both animals and humans. These studies have generally led to a consistent pattern of results. Whenever we are in the presence of another person who is either observing our performance or doing the same task, the performance of simple or well-learned behaviors or tasks is facilitated and the performance of complex or poorly learned tasks is hindered. For example, when people are jogging, they jog faster when others are watching, but when people are trying to solve arithmetic problems they do poorly when others are watching.[17] These findings have important implications for work situations. Menial or fairly simple work may be done best in groups or while being monitored. Complicated jobs that involve learning and creativity might be done best in isolation. Why is this the case? Many ideas have been proposed and examined. We will briefly discuss a number of them.

Theories of Social Facilitation: Arousal and Evaluation

Some researchers have argued that the presence of other members of the same species increases one's level of excitation or **arousal**.[18] This enhanced state of excitation in turn enhances the occurrence of *dominant* or strong responses and hinders the occurrence of *subordinate* or weak ones. On simple or well-learned tasks, the correct responses are presumably dominant—that is, they have become strongly trained or automatic. On complex or poorly learned tasks, the correct responses are fairly weak or subordinate (see Figure 9.7). Many studies support this arousal model. For example, in one study subjects were asked to do a complex motor task over a period of trials either alone or in front of an audience. On the initial learning trials, the incorrect responses are presumably dominant and audience presence should interfere with performance. As the trials progress, the correct responses should gain in strength and eventually become dominant. At that point, they should be facilitated by audience presence. This is exactly what was found[19] (see Figure 9.8).

Although the arousal model accounts fairly well for many of the findings obtained in this area of study, a number of other proposals have been generated

FIGURE 9.7 Social Facilitation: Arousal Theory Interpretation
The arousal theory of social facilitation. *Source:* Based on Zajonc (1980); see Note 18.

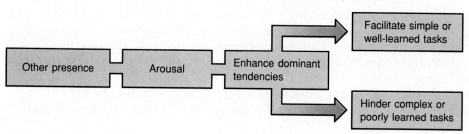

282

CHAPTER 9
GROUP BEHAVIOR
AND INFLUENCE:
HOW DO GROUPS
AFFECT US?

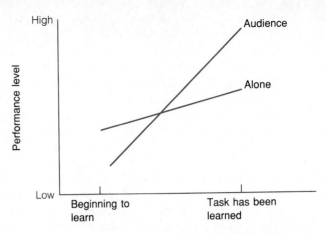

FIGURE 9.8 The Effects of Audiences: Depend On the Stage of Learning
When we are learning a task, we learn better alone than in front of an audience. Once we have
learned the task quite well, we may do better in front of an audience than alone. *Source:*
Adapted from Martens (1969); see Note 19.

about the factors that underlie the observed effects. It is rather obvious that many
of the group situations we have discussed involve an element of evaluation or
competition. When we are being observed by others while doing some task, we
may be concerned about what the observers think of our performance. When
doing a task in groups, we may be concerned about how well we are doing relative
to the other group members. This **evaluation apprehension** may be an important
factor in the occurrence of excitation or arousal. Research has generally supported
the importance of evaluation as a factor in task performance.[20] However, it also
appears that in situations where there is little opportunity for evaluation, the
effects of the presence of others can still be observed. For example, in one study
students were asked to type their name into a computer (simple task) and then
to type their name backwards while inserting numbers between each letter (difficult
task).[21] They did this either alone, while the experimenter peered over their
shoulder (evaluation condition), or while a subject from another experiment sat
in the room facing away from the subjects and wearing a blindfold and headphones
(mere presence). Both of the presence conditions facilitated the performance of
the simple task and hindered that of the complex one (see Figure 9.9). So while
concern of evaluation by others has a strong effect on how well we do on tasks,
the mere presence of another person can also be influential.

Why does the presence of others have an effect even when no evaluation is
possible? Possibly whenever people are around us, we have a need to monitor
them since we never know for sure what is going to happen. This state of enhanced
preparedness or monitoring may be the basis for enhanced arousal in the presence
of others.[22] So at work, our performance of various tasks may be influenced both
by the mere presence of co-workers and by their potential evaluation of us. Of
course, whether this is beneficial for productivity depends on the complexity of
the task.

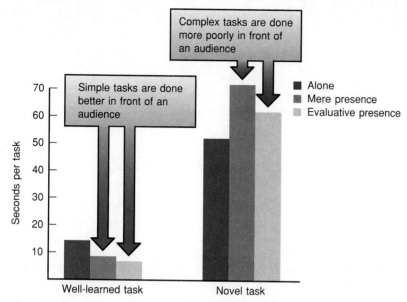

FIGURE 9.9 Mere Presence and Evaluation: Both Important in Social Facilitation
When subjects do the simple task of typing in their name, they do this in less time when others are present. When they have to type their name backwards interspersed with ascending numbers, they do this more slowly in the presence of others. *Source:* From Schmitt et al. (1986); see Note 21.

BRAINSTORMING: CREATIVITY IN GROUPS?

When groups or organizations are trying to decide on some new courses of action or solutions to problems, they often resort to some version of a technique called **brainstorming.**[23] This typically involves the free exchange of ideas in a group to come up with novel ideas. It is presumed that group brainstorming will stimulate its members to come up with a lot of novel ideas. You have probably participated in groups of that sort. How successful were they? Very likely it may have appeared that you generated quite a few good ideas and that the group was a success. The problem with such observations is that they do not take into account what you might have been able to do if the group members brainstormed by themselves. This issue has been carefully examined in research on brainstorming.

Studies on brainstorming emphasize a number of rules for the group to follow in generating ideas. Group members should feel free to express any or all ideas, no matter how unusual. There is an emphasis on number of ideas—the more

284

CHAPTER 9
GROUP BEHAVIOR
AND INFLUENCE:
HOW DO GROUPS
AFFECT US?

ideas the better. There should be no criticism or evaluation of ideas while they are being generated, and group members are encouraged to build on each other's ideas.

Contrary to early enthusiasm for the effectiveness of brainstorming, it now appears that brainstorming in groups is *not* particularly effective. When such brainstorming is compared with the efforts of the same number of individuals brainstorming alone, the groups of individuals (called *nominal groups*) almost always outperform the real groups both in terms of number and quality of ideas.[24]

Factors That Inhibit Effective Brainstorming

Why do brainstorming groups fare so poorly? A number of factors appear to be responsible. Even though there is an emphasis on being noncritical, there is still likely to be a concern with what others are thinking of one's ideas. As we have seen with the social facilitation phenomenon, such *evaluative concerns* will inhibit the performance of creativity tasks. People in brainstorming groups may also be prone to free ride or *loaf* since they may feel that their efforts are dispensable and no clear accountability for performance exists. While both of these factors do seem to be involved to some extent, recent research suggests that the most important factor is the interference or *blocking* that occurs when one person is trying to think up ideas while listening to those of others.[25] Finally, since a fairly large number of ideas are generated in any group in a short period of time, the group may quickly feel that they have generated a sufficient number of good ideas. Groups typically stop generating ideas before the time period allotted is over. An individual brainstorming alone may keep on going for the entire period of time since they may be concerned about generating as many ideas as other individuals. When a group is given information about how much a group of individuals can generate, they greatly increase their output of ideas.[26] However, they still do not outperform a group of individuals who are given a similarly high standard of comparison. (See Figure 9.10 for a summary of factors that inhibit group brainstorming.)

Improving Group Brainstorming

A number of procedures have been suggested to improve the performance of brainstorming groups. Prior practice with brainstorming seems to help.[27] This can aid the group in becoming better coordinated in the generation of ideas in a group. To optimize the fact that individuals may more efficiently generate ideas in isolation than in a group, a procedure in which individuals first generate ideas alone, then share these ideas in a group, and then brainstorm again as individuals may be optimal. This type of procedure is employed in the *nominal group technique*.[28] This technique involves presentation of the topic to the group, individual generation of ideas, and subsequent sharing of them in the group in sequence, allowing for clarification but not critiquing of the ideas presented. The ideas are then discussed and subsequently ranked individually.

Another structured approach that appears to be fairly effective is called *synectics*.[29] The main concern of this approach is to increase divergent thinking and

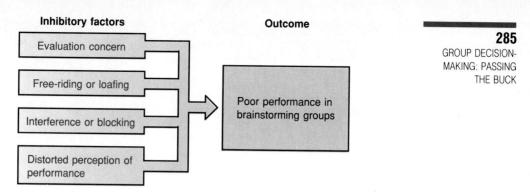

Inhibitory factors

Evaluation concern

Free-riding or loafing

Interference or blocking

Distorted perception of performance

Outcome

Poor performance in brainstorming groups

FIGURE 9.10 Brainstorming: Some Inhibitory Factors
Research has shown that group brainstorming is not very effective when compared to individual brainstorming. This appears to be related to the factors outlined here.

to come up with unusual ideas. Groups have a tendency to convergent thinking—coming up with fairly expected or uncontroversial ideas. To promote divergent thinking, synectics emphasizes a spectrum policy, which holds that few ideas are all good or all bad and that it is important to look at all sides of an issue. During dry spells where few ideas are being generated, the group is asked to use metaphors, analogies, or fantasy to generate further ideas.

Although the above techniques appear to be effective, no group brainstorming technique yet has been shown to surpass an individual brainstorming procedure. This does not mean that group brainstorming should be completely avoided. Group brainstorming may increase positive group feelings or cohesiveness and a feeling of commitment to the ideas finally decided on by the group. However, to optimize the generation of the largest number of the most creative ideas, groups should supplement their group brainstorming with some sort of individual brainstorming activity. It also appears best to use small groups such as pairs. Working with only one other person would limit many of the negative effects of groups but still offer the benefit of being stimulated by another person's ideas. Table 9.4 provides a summary of the various ways brainstorming can be made more effective.

There are also some personal characteristics that influence how effectively we function in groups. The **Human Relations in Action** section on page 286 may help you assess your general suitability for working in groups.

GROUP DECISION-MAKING: PASSING THE BUCK

It seems that in our democratic society, practically every major decision is made by a group of individuals. Judges, juries, legislatures, committees, and task forces are just some of the groups that dominate decisions in our society. Most

286

CHAPTER 9

GROUP BEHAVIOR
AND INFLUENCE:
HOW DO GROUPS
AFFECT US?

TABLE 9.4
Better Brainstorming: Some Techniques

Although group brainstorming may not be as effective as individual brainstorming, there are some ways to optimize the effectiveness of brainstorming groups.

Techniques for Facilitating Group Brainstorming Effectiveness

Seek group members having prior practice with group brainstorming.

Generate ideas alone first, then in the group.

Use spectrum policy—look at all sides of an issue.

Organize small groups or pairs.

Establish groups with a variety of perspectives, talents, and knowledge bases.

Give the groups some goals for which to aim.

universities have various committees that are responsible for major decisions, and corporations are run largely on the basis of staff and board meetings. Of course, there are cases where strong and fairly independent leaders make crucial decisions by themselves. But these seem to be the exceptions rather than the rule.

Even though the idea of group decision-making fits with the democratic aspirations of many nations, how effective is this process? Do groups generate high

HUMAN RELATIONS IN ACTION

Group Seekers and Avoiders: How Well-Suited Are You for Working in Groups?

While some of us enjoy group activities and working in groups, others prefer solitary activities or working alone. There may be many factors that underlie this difference in orientation. The items below represent some of these and are designed to determine how you feel about groups in general. Simply write Y (yes) or N (no) for each of the following questions.

_____ 1. I usually feel uncomfortable with a group of people that I don't know.

_____ 2. I enjoy parties.

_____ 3. I do not have much confidence in social situations.

_____ 4. I am basically a shy person.

_____ 5. I like going on job interviews.

_____ 6. I usually feel anxious when I speak in front of a group.

quality solutions? How effective are groups in making decisions? As with brainstorming, the basis of comparison used for judging group decision-making is the performance of a group of individuals.

A major problem with group decision-making is that the group tends to be disorganized in its approach to the problem. Unless a formalized structure is imposed by some outside force or by a group leader, most groups do not attempt to develop a system for approaching the problem or the decision. Basically, groups seem to go with the flow, which is usually the first plausible idea presented. As soon as this idea is accepted by a majority of the group, the group rarely reverses itself. This has been called the *strength in numbers effect,* in that decisions tend to go in the direction of the largest subgroup that agrees on a particular course of action.[32] This same type of phenomenon underlies two other interesting group decision phenomena—group polarization and groupthink.

Group Polarization

Think about the groups to which you belong. Why do you belong to them? What are the people in them like? Most likely you belong to groups whose members are much like you in many ways. People tend to join groups composed of members that have values and opinions similar to their own. This is obvious in the case of political and church groups, but it is also characteristic of more informal social and work groups. When group members get together, they often

---

_____ **7.** Large groups make me nervous.

_____ **8.** I would rather work on a group project than an individual project.

_____ **9.** I am basically a loner.

_____ **10.** I find that groups bring out the best in me.

To score your questionnaire, count the number of times your answers coincided with the following answer pattern: 1 = Y, 2 = N, 3 = Y, 4 = Y, 5 = N, 6 = Y, 7 = Y, 8 = N, 9 = Y, 10 = N. If you come up with a score of 8 or higher, you would probably prefer to avoid most group situations—that is, you may be a group avoider. However, if you have a score of 2 or lower, you probably seek out group situations and activities—that is, you are a group seeker. Unfortunately it is not always possible to choose your preferred situation. When people do get into situations that conflict with their preferences, they may not function as well as they would otherwise. For example, group avoiders may not do as well as group seekers on group tasks like brainstorming or group decision making.[30,31] If you find this is true for you, you might try to match your activities and work with your group preference style.

288

CHAPTER 9

GROUP BEHAVIOR
AND INFLUENCE:
HOW DO GROUPS
AFFECT US?

discuss their opinions on various issues. Given the degree of similarity among group members, they are likely to be in general agreement on many issues. Interestingly, such discussions may lead them to become even more strongly convinced of their general point of view about an issue.

Early studies of this type of situation noticed that groups tended to become more *risky* after group discussion in comparison to the feelings expressed by the individuals before the discussion. This intrigued scholars because it had been expected that group decision-making would be more cautious than individual decisions. Yet soon it was found that groups could shift toward caution as well as toward risk. Later studies demonstrated that shifts toward more extreme positions could be obtained for a wide variety of issues and the phenomenon came to be known as **group polarization.**[33,34] (See Figure 9.11 for a demonstration of this phenomenon.) What was going on to produce this type of polarization in groups?

One critical factor appears to be that the group was already leaning in one direction or another from some neutral position. When these group members who are already of the same mind on some issue come together to discuss it, the comparison of views (*social comparison*) and exchange of ideas (*information*) seems to generate more momentum in an already favored direction.[35] When views are compared in such a group, individuals may discover that others hold the position either as strongly or more strongly than they do. Since they supposedly value being extreme on this issue (e.g., being conservative or liberal), they may change their opinions somewhat to more strongly reflect the valued direction. There is an additional effect of the information exchanged. Group members hear new arguments that provide additional support for their favored position. In fact, the number of arguments in support of the generally favored direction greatly outnumber those in support of the opposition direction. So you can see that under such circumstances people would begin to feel even more strongly about an issue (see Figure 9.12).

This group polarization phenomenon has been demonstrated with laboratory groups using many types of issues. It obviously has important implications for any group situation where like-minded individuals (e.g., judges, corporations, political parties, and gangs) gather to discuss issues. In fact, individuals in extremist groups appear to show increased polarization as they become more involved with such groups. One clear example of this type is a study by Myers and Bishop that examined polarization on racial issues.[36] Groups of white students were assessed

FIGURE 9.11 Group Polarization: The Basic Phenomenon
The group polarization effect involves people becoming more extreme in their opinions after group discussion. The basis of this effect seems to be social comparison of views and exchange of information.

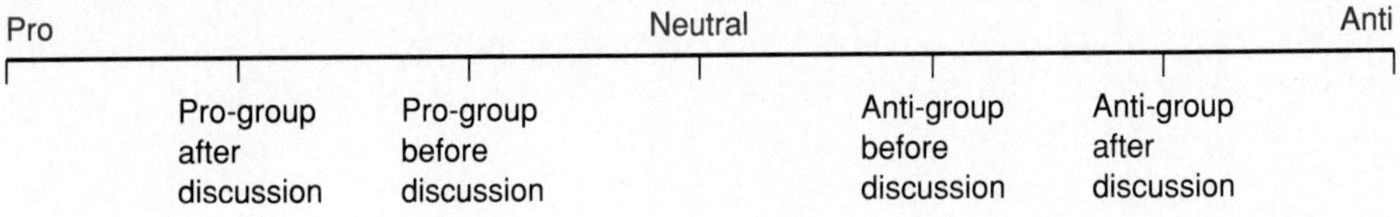

Pro			Neutral			Anti
	Pro-group after discussion	Pro-group before discussion		Anti-group before discussion	Anti-group after discussion	

FIGURE 9.12 Social Comparison: An Important Source of Influence
In group discussions we are often influenced by the views of others through the social comparison process. (Reprinted with special permission of King Features Syndicate.)

for their attitudes about a number of issues related to the integration movement (e.g., forced busing, black power). On the basis of this questionnaire, they were assigned to groups that were either all pro-integration or all anti-integration. They were given an opportunity to discuss one particular topic related to the race issue and then the attitudes of group members were reassessed. As expected, the members of the two groups became more extreme in their favored direction. The anti-black group members became more anti-black, while the pro-black groups became more pro-black. Groups that discussed issues unrelated to race showed little change in racial attitudes (see Figure 9.13).

Since we choose most groups to which we belong on the basis of similarity of interests, opinions, or values, it seems likely that group polarization is a common experience in many groups. It is therefore important for us to be aware of the group polarization effect and to avoid blind acceptance of extremist positions. The world has suffered much from leaders or groups who have championed extremist positions. This is often associated with intergroup discrimination and violence. Hopefully, we will never forget the lessons of Nazi Germany! Yet polarization is also important for understanding the workings of informal and work groups. We can assume that there is usually little harm in groups feeling strongly about a particular position or cause. However, as individuals we should always make sure that we are not being driven to make decisions or to take actions that we will later regret. It appears that such bad decisions are unfortunately not uncommon, as we will see in our discussion of groupthink.

Groupthink: Defective Decision-Making in Groups

Many of you probably have vivid memories of the tragic explosion of the Challenger shuttle seventy-four seconds after launch on January 28, 1986. Seven astronauts, including teacher Christa McAuliffe, lost their lives (see Figure 9.14). This terrible tragedy was a real shock to the United States. We have always taken great pride in our space program and it seemed to be a constant source of successes. This program apparently could do no wrong. The last Challenger mission was highly publicized because it was the first flight in which a civilian would participate. So the leaders of the program felt a lot of pressure to put their best foot forward.

290
CHAPTER 9
GROUP BEHAVIOR
AND INFLUENCE:
HOW DO GROUPS
AFFECT US?

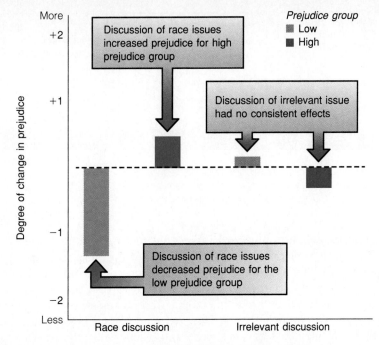

FIGURE 9.13 Group Polarization of Prejudice: One Important Example
Group discussion of race issues can increase feelings of prejudice for highly prejudiced groups but reduce it for unprejudiced ones. *Source:* Adapted from Myers and Bishop (1970); see Note 36.

FIGURE 9.14 Groupthink: Sometimes a Recipe for Disaster
Groupthink may have been responsible for a number of bad group decisions, including the decision to launch the Challenger despite unusually cold weather.

Not only was the whole nation watching, but this was an important opportunity to generate more enthusiasm for additional funding for the program. Unfortunately, the weather would not cooperate. The temperature dropped to freezing and the launch had to be delayed. Conditions soon improved, but they were still below those recommended by engineers. The O rings that connected the different sections of the shuttle tended to become brittle in cold weather and not function appropriately. Some problems with these rings had already been encountered in prior launches. The engineers from the company that designed the O rings objected to the impending launch. However, they were overruled by higher-level officials in their company and in the space program who felt that they were being overly cautious. After all, there had not been any serious problems, and minor variations from the standards probably would not be a problem. Besides, continual delays in the launch would not look good from a public relations point of view. The high-level officials did not think the concerns were serious enough to pass on to the top official in the project. Unfortunately, they were wrong.

The above scenario highlights the serious consequences that can result when groups do not carefully evaluate alternative courses of action. Janis has analyzed a number of well-known examples of this type and has labeled the overall process **groupthink.**[37] Some historic examples are the Bay of Pigs fiasco, which was an unsuccessful attempt to invade Cuba after Castro's revolution, the failure of the generals to prepare for possible Japanese attacks on Pearl Harbor, and the escalation of the Vietnam War. Of course, it is always easy to Monday-morning quarterback any wrong decision. Wrong group decisions are not necessarily a result of groupthink, and most decisions groups make are fairly straightforward and reasonable. Groupthink is involved primarily when a group is more concerned about agreement than about a careful assessment of alternative courses of action, and it is a potentially serious problem in cases of complex decisions that will have significant consequences.

Concurrence Seeking   The driving force of groupthink is called the **concurrence-seeking** tendency. Members of many groups like to get along with one another and come to some concurrence or agreement on important issues. Otherwise there would be conflict and possible hostilities among group members. Concurrence seeking is especially important for groups that are already highly cohesive. Such groups have strong interpersonal bonds and probably have similar opinions and values on many issues (remember our discussion of group polarization). So it would seem only natural that they would want to minimize conflict. In addition to group cohesiveness, Janis and Mann have proposed that a number of factors lead to a strengthening of the *concurrence-seeking* tendency (Figure 9.15). If the group is insulated from other groups, it is unlikely to have the benefit of alternative views. If it does not have systematic procedures to search out and appraise information and alternative positions, it is likely to go with the first reasonable idea. If the leader of the group pressures the group to come to a decision or to support a particular course of action, there is an increased tendency for premature agree-

292

CHAPTER 9
GROUP BEHAVIOR
AND INFLUENCE:
HOW DO GROUPS
AFFECT US?

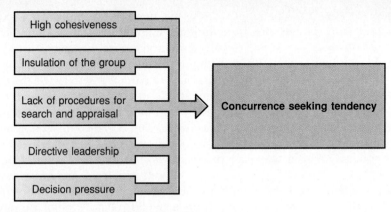

FIGURE 9.15 Groupthink: Facilitating Conditions
A variety of conditions can increase groupthink.

ment (see Figure 9.16). Finally, if there is a lot of pressure to come up with a decision and little sense that a better solution than the one being proposed by a leader or influential group member will be found, there will be a strong tendency to seek a quick concurrence among the group. These types of features unfortunately characterize many decision-making groups in government and industry. As a result, many decisions primarily reflect a premature group consensus rather than a careful consideration of alternatives.

Symptoms of Groupthink In his study of cases of groupthink, Janis found that groups prone to groupthink were characterized by certain features or symptoms. First, such groups evidence a lot of *pressure to uniformity*. There is *direct pressure* by group members on dissenters to go along with the group consensus. Because of concerns about reaction to dissension, group members practice *self-censorship* by not expressing reservations they have about an impending decision. Certain members of the group may act as *mindguards* to keep people in line with the group consensus or to keep dissenting information from reaching the group. As a result of the lack of public dissension, the group may develop an *illusion of*

FIGURE 9.16 Leader Pressure: One Factor in Groupthink
When leaders pressure groups to support a particular position, they tend to be more prone to groupthink. (Reprinted with special permission of King Features Syndicate.)

unanimity. A second major feature associated with groupthink is considerable *misperception* or distortion of the actual state of affairs. The group may feel that it is invulnerable to failure and that it is morally superior to other groups. Groups that are in conflict with one's own group may be viewed in a very biased fashion as being low in capability. Once the consensus has been developed, the group may *rationalize* away any information that does not fit with the decision. The last four factors can often be found at the basis of decisions by countries to go to war or to engage in certain battles. They can also be important factors in the underestimation of competitors in business, as in the case of the U.S. automakers lack of regard for the capability of the Japanese to develop a competitive automobile industry.

Defective Decision-Making   Groups that are engaging in groupthink tend to use a number of decision-making procedures that help lead them to defective decisions. They do a generally poor search of information relevant to the decision. They do not engage in a complete survey of alternatives and objectives and fail to examine sufficiently the risks involved in the preferred choice. The information that is available is processed in a biased fashion by emphasizing information supporting the decision and ignoring or deemphasizing inconsistent information. The group also fails to reappraise or evaluate the alternatives once a preliminary consensus has been reached or work out contingency plans to be used in case the proposed course of action fails (see Figure 9.17). As you can see, this type of approach to group decision-making is a recipe for disaster. Of course, not all groups do such a poor job at decision-making, but careful examination of poor decisions in business and government often reveals the existence of many of the factors emphasized in the groupthink model.

Avoiding Groupthink   Fortunately, there are some simple steps that groups can take to avoid falling into the groupthink trap. First, it is important that the group make a commitment to coming up with the best decision possible rather than simply reaching consensus with a minimum of conflict. The group leader can play an important role in promoting such an approach to group decision-making and not pressuring the group toward a particular point of view.

Second, to make the best possible decision, the group should use a number

FIGURE 9.17 Groupthink: Some Major Symptoms
A summary of the groupthink model. *Source:* Adapted from Janis (1982); see Note 37.

Symptoms of groupthink	Symptoms of defective decision making
Illusion of invulnerability Collective rationalization Belief in morality of the group Stereotyping of outgroups Direct pressure on dissenters Self-censorship Illusion of unanimity Mindguards	Incomplete survey of alternatives Incomplete survey of objectives Failure to examine risks of favorite choice Poor information search Selective bias in processing available information Failure to reassess alternatives Failure to work out contingency plans

294

CHAPTER 9

GROUP BEHAVIOR
AND INFLUENCE:
HOW DO GROUPS
AFFECT US?

of procedures. There should be a broad-ranging and nonevaluative search of information relevant to the decision. The effective use of brainstorming may be beneficial at this stage. If feasible, several independent groups should be composed with different leaders. These groups might in turn subdivide periodically into smaller subgroups representing a reasonable cross-section of the group in terms of skills and perspectives. This procedure would increase the opportunity for diverse views to be aired and evaluated in the different groups. If all of the subgroups come to a similar consensus, the larger group could have a reasonable degree of confidence in the decision. If not, it would stimulate the subgroups to do a careful assessment of the basis for their differences and hopefully lead to a carefully considered final decision.

CASE IN POINT

Marketing Strategy: Another Case of Groupthink?

It was the day of the weekly managers' meeting of Charmante Cosmetics. This was an opportunity for the managers of the different departments to share ideas and suggest possible new marketing strategies. Mr. Kinder, the vice-president of the company called the meeting to order.

"Hello everyone; good to see all of you are in town for a change. This should be a great opportunity to do some serious brainstorming. Joe, don't we have an exciting new product that may need some special marketing efforts?"

Mr. Kinder was looking at Joe Pascale, the head of the marketing division who was always anxious to come up with some new strategies to outdo the competition. Joe was one of the more dynamic managers in the company and well-liked by almost everyone. Joe perked up in his chair and nodded his head.

"We sure do, Mr. Kinder. We have just finished testing a new skin moistener that can also serve as a sunblocking agent. So we should have a real winner here."

There was a buzz of excitement around the room. This type of product could really help put them into a profitable position. Thoughts of raises and profit sharing were undoubtedly going through the managers' minds.

"This certainly comes at a good time," noted Lori Miller, the accounting manager. "We've had a tough year so far. We lost a few big accounts and some of our new fragrances are not doing as well as we expected. I think we should go with an all out media blitz—radio, TV, and magazines."

Marsha Ewell was not quite as excited as the rest of the group about the new product. She was rather new to the company, having been recently hired as distribution manager from a competitor. "This could be a really great product for us, but aren't we rushing it a bit? After all, we've done very little test marketing

Third, some input from knowledgeable outsiders who are not subject to the pressures of an existing group may also be helpful. These people may either provide further support for the decision or challenge some of the assumptions on which it is based. Finally, for important decisions, second chance meetings should be scheduled. At these meetings, the members of the group could air any second thoughts or doubts that have arisen since the decision was made. Although these steps will not ensure that good decisions will always be made, they will prevent bad decisions resulting from groupthink. In any case, always be alert for elements of groupthink in groups in which you are involved and be ready to make suggestions for countering such problems. See the **Case in Point** on page 294 for an example.

with this product. It would be good to find out what segment of the population would be most interested in this type of product. I am afraid that if we are not successful in our initial marketing efforts, this product may get a bad image with our clients. They may not be willing to allot the promotional space necessary during the first year."

Joe looked a little annoyed. "Look, we need a winner, and if we don't move fast on this product, some other company may beat us out with a similar product."

Mr. Kinder looked around the room with a questioning expression on his face. "What do the rest of you think? Should we go all out right away or go with a step-by-step approach?"

There was an eerie quiet for a minute or so. Then one by one there seemed to be more and more people going along with the idea of a broad-based marketing effort.

"Well, Joe, it looks like we've got a winner here. Go for it! Now that we have resolved this item, what else do we need to take up?"

Questions

1. What do you think about the decision-making process that occurred in this group? Can you find some elements of group polarization and groupthink?

2. Why do you think Joe seemed to be more influential than Marsha?

3. If you had been in charge of the meeting, how would you have run it? What could have been done to bring out a broader range of views and opinions?

4. What procedures from brainstorming could have been applied to make this a more effective decision-making group?

296

CHAPTER 9
GROUP BEHAVIOR
AND INFLUENCE:
HOW DO GROUPS
AFFECT US?

SUMMARY

Groups are defined as a collection of two or more interacting individuals with a stable pattern of relationships between them who share common goals and who perceive themselves as being a group. Many interesting processes can take place in groups. When people join groups, they typically go through a *socialization phase* in which a person can be transferred from a newcomer to a full-fledged member. Groups also go through various phases. The five stages appear to be *forming, storming, norming, performing,* and *adjourning.*

In some group situations, individuals may feel a lowered sense of individual responsibility. In emergency situations, **diffusion of responsibility** may occur, which leads to reduced helping in the presence of other bystanders. *In some cases, group activity may lead people to lose their sense of self-awareness and become deindividuated.* When people perform tasks in groups, lessened feelings of responsibility may be reflected in lowering of performance or in social loafing.

Individual productivity is influenced by the presence of other group members. Sometimes, a person's performance improves in the presence of others (when the job they are doing is well-learned), and sometimes performance declines in the presence of others (when the job is novel). This phenomenon is known as **social facilitation.** These effects have been attributed to the *mere presence* of others, and to the *evaluation apprehension* caused by others.

Groups are often asked to **brainstorm** by exchanging ideas freely about some problem or issue. Research indicates that these groups actually produce fewer ideas than a comparable number of individuals brainstorming alone. However, there are a number of techniques that can be used to enhance the generation of ideas in groups, such as synectics or the nominal group technique.

When groups discuss problems or issues, they may demonstrate a tendency toward **polarization.** Groups that are already inclined in a particular direction may move even more strongly in that same direction after group discussion. This effect seems to be the result of the exchange of information and the social comparison of views that occur during the discussion.

The failure of groups to carefully evaluate alternative courses of action when they make decisions has been termed **groupthink.** Groupthink results from the desire of group members to get along with each other and to come to an agreement or concurrence on important issues. Fortunately, there are a number of procedures that can be employed to eliminate or limit the occurrence of groupthink.

KEY TERMS

additive tasks: Group tasks in which the individual efforts of several persons are added together to form the group's product.

arousal theory of social facilitation: A theory stating that the presence of others increases arousal, which increases people's tendencies to perform the dominant response. If that response is well-learned, performance will improve, but if it is novel, performance will be impaired.

brainstorming: A technique designed to enhance creativity in problem-solving groups by emphasizing the free exchange of novel ideas. These groups are not as effective as commonly thought.

concurrence seeking: The tendency of group members to strive for agreement on important issues.

deindividuation: A state of lessened self-awareness that occurs because of involvement in group situations; it is related to a lowering of self-control over behavior.

diffusion of responsibility: The reduced feelings of responsibility that members of groups may have in emergency situations because others are available to help.

evaluation apprehension: The fear of being evaluated or judged by another person.

group: A collection of two or more interacting individuals with a stable pattern of relationships between them who share common goals and who perceive themselves as a group.

group development: The five stages—forming, storming, norming, performing, and adjourning—that groups appear to go through as they develop.

group polarization: A process that occurs when groups of like-minded individuals discussing issues become more extreme in the direction of their initial attitudes of beliefs.

group socialization: The process of socialization that occurs in groups, as members pass from investigation to remembrance.

groupthink: The tendency of groups to make decisions without carefully evaluating alternative courses of action.

social loafing: The tendency for group members to exert less individual effort on an additive task as the size of the group increases.

NOTES

1. Forsythe, D.L. (1983). *An Introduction to Group Dynamics.* Monterey, Calif.: Brooks/Cole.

2. Hill, C.A. (1987). "Affiliation Motivation: People Who Need People . . . but in Different Ways." *Journal of Personality and Social Psychology, 52,* 1008–18.

3. Mackie, D.M., & Goethals, G.R. (1987). "Individual and Group Goals." In C. Hendrick, ed., *Group Processes: Review of Personality and Social Psychology,* vol. 8, pp. 144–66. Newbury Park, Calif.: Sage Publications.

4. Abrams, D., & Hogg, M.A. (1988). "Comments on the Motivational Status of Self-Esteem in Social Identity and Intergroup Discrimination." *European Journal of Social Psychology, 18,* 317–34.

5. Moreland, R.L., & Levine, J.M. (1989). "Newcomers and Oldtimers in Small Groups." In P.B. Paulus, ed. *Psychology of Group Influence,* pp. 143–86. Hillsdale, N.J.: Lawrence Erlbaum Associates.

6. Tuckman, B.W., & Jensen, M.A. (1977). "Stages of Small Group Development Revisited." *Group and Organization Studies, 2,* 419–27.

7. Latane, B., & Darley, J.M. (1970). *The Unresponsive Bystander: Why Doesn't He Help?* New York: Appleton-Century-Crofts.

8. Latane, B., & Nida, S. (1981). "Ten Years of Research on Group Size and Helping." *Psychological Bulletin, 89,* 308–24.

9. Diener, E. (1980). "Deindividuation: The Absence of Self-Awareness and Self-Regulation in Group Members." In P.B. Paulus, ed. *The Psychology of Group Influence,* pp. 209–242. Hillsdale, N.J.: Lawrence Erlbaum Associates.

10. Prentice-Dunn, S., & Rogers, R.W. (1989). "Deindividuation and the Self-Regulation of Behavior." In P.B. Paulus, ed. *Psychology of Group Influence,* pp. 87–109. Hillsdale, N.J.: Lawrence Erlbaum Associates.

11. Latane, B., Williams, K., & Harkins, S. (1979). "Many Hands Make Light of Work: The Causes and Consequences of Social Loafing." *Journal of Personality and Social Psychology, 37,* 822–32.

298

CHAPTER 9
GROUP BEHAVIOR
AND INFLUENCE:
HOW DO GROUPS
AFFECT US?

12. Harkins, S. (1987). "Social Loafing and Social Facilitation." *Journal of Experimental Social Psychology, 23,* 1–18.

13. Weldon, E., & Mustari, E.L. (1988). "Feel Dispensability in Groups of Coactors: The Effects of Shared Responsibility and Explicit Anonymity on Cognitive Effort." *Organizational Behavior and Human Decision Processes, 41,* 330–51.

14. Harkins, S.G., & Petty, R.E. (1982). "Effects of Task Difficulty and Task Uniqueness on Social Loafing." *Journal of Personality and Social Psychology, 43,* 1214–29.

15. Harkins, S.G., & Szymanski, K. (1989). "Social Loafing and Group Evaluation." *Journal of Personality and Social Psychology, 56,* 934–41.

16. Williams, K.D., Nida, S.A., Baca, L.D., & Latane, B. (1989). "Social Loafing and Swimming: Effects of Identifiability on Individual and Relay Performance on Intercollegiate Swimmers." *Basic and Applied Social Psychology, 10,* 73–82.

17. Geen, R.G. (1989). "Alternative Conceptions of Social Facilitation." In P.B. Paulus, ed. *Psychology of Group Influence*, 2d ed. pp. 15–51. Hillsdale, N.J.: Lawrence Erlbaum Associates.

18. Zajonc, R.B. (1980). "Compresence." In P.B. Paulus, ed. *Psychology of Group Influence*, pp. 35–60. Hillsdale, N.J.: Lawrence Erlbaum Associates.

19. Martens, R. (1969). "Effect of an Audience on Learning and Performance of a Complex Motor Skill." *Journal of Personality and Social Psychology, 12,* 252–60.

20. See Note 17.

21. Schmitt, B.H., Gilovich, T., Goore, N., & Joseph L. (1986). "Mere Presence and Social Facilitation: One More Time." *Journal of Experimental Social Psychology, 22,* 242–48.

22. Guerin, B. (1986). "Mere Presence Effects in Humans: A Review." *Journal of Experimental Social Psychology, 22,* 38–77.

23. Osborn, A.F. (1957). *Applied Imagination.* New York: Scribner.

24. Diehl, M., & Stroebe, W. (1987). "Productivity Loss in Brainstorming Groups: Toward the Solution of a Riddle." *Journal of Personality and Social Psychology, 53,* 497–509.

25. See Note 24.

26. Dzindolet, M.T., & Paulus, P.B. (1990). *The Role of Performance Perceptions and Standards in Brainstorming.* Paper presented at Southwestern Psychological Association Convention.

27. Bouchard, T.J. (1972). "Training, Motivation, and Personality as Determinants of the Effectiveness of Brainstorming Groups and Individuals." *Journal of Applied Psychology, 56,* 324–31.

28. Delbecq, A.L., Van de Ven, A.H., & Gustafson, D.H. (1975). *Group Techniques for Program Planning: A Guide to Nominal Group and Delphi Processes.* Glenview, Ill.: Scott, Foresman.

29. Prince, G. (1970). *The Practice of Creativity.* New York: Harper and Row.

30. Baum, A., & Valins, S. (1979). "Architectural Mediation of Residential Density and Control: Crowding and the Regulation of Social Contact." In L. Berkowitz, ed. *Advances in Experimental Social Psychology*, vol. 12, pp. 132–72. New York: Academic Press.

31. Paulus, P.B., Camacho, L.M., & Dzindolet, M.T. (1990). *Cognitive Factors in Group Brainstorming.* Paper presented at a symposium of Cognition and Affect in Social Processes at the International Congress of Applied Psychology in Kyoto, Japan.

32. Stasser, G., Kerr, N.L., & Davis, J.H. (1989). "Influence Processes and Consensus Models in Decision-Making Groups." In P.B. Paulus, ed. *Psychology of Group Influence*, 2d ed., pp. 279–326. Hillsdale, N.J.: Lawrence Erlbaum Associates.

33. Moscovici, S., & Zavalloni, M. (1969). "The Group as a Polarizer of Attitudes." *Journal of Personality and Social Psychology, 12,* 125–35.

34. Myers, D.G. (1982). "Polarizing Effects of Social Interaction." In H. Brandstatter, J.H. Davis, & G. Stocker-Kreichgauer, eds. *Group Decision Making*, pp. 125–61. London: Academic Press.

35. Kaplan, M.F., & Miller, C.E. (1983). "Group Discussion and Judgement." In P.B. Paulus, ed. *Basic Group Processes*, pp. 65–94. New York: Springer-Verlag.

36. Myers, D.G., & Bishop, G.D. (1970). "Discussion Effects of Racial Attitudes." *Science, 169,* 778–79.

37. Janis, I.L. (1982). *Groupthink.* (2nd edition) Boston: Houghton-Mifflin.

ADDITIONAL CASES AND EXERCISES: APPLYING WHAT YOU'VE LEARNED

Company Socialization Practices

On page 272 we discussed the phases that group members go through as they become members of a group. One major phase is the socialization of newcomers by the older members. This involves telling them about the rules, norms, and traditions of the group. This is an important phase for new employees in corporations. If they are appropriately socialized, they may develop a sense of commitment to the company and cohesiveness with the rest of the employees. Companies vary in the extent to which they have procedures in place to facilitate the socialization process of new employees. You may want to investigate this issue with a number of major companies in your area. If they have a personnel office, this may be the best place to start your interview process. You should ask the following questions:

1. What sort of programs do you have for new employees to become acquainted with the other employees?

2. Do you have any training programs that familiarize them with company policies, traditions, and history?

3. Do you have a mentorship program in which one of the older employees serves as a guide and resource for the new employee during the first few months?

4. Do you have any organized social events or activities for new employees to become acquainted with one another?

5. Is there an opportunity for new employees to provide feedback to their superiors about adjustment problems they may be experiencing?

6. How much turnover do you have among new employees in the first year?

Groupthink and Life

We have discussed a number of examples of groupthink in this chapter. However, you have probably experienced some examples of this phenomenon as part of your involvement in a variety of groups. You may want to share these experiences with other students in the class. For each of these examples, how many symptoms of groupthink did you notice? How many symptoms of defective decision-making were evident? Which symptoms seem to be the most common? Do you think some of the suggestions provided about avoiding groupthink would have been helpful in these situations?

Social Loafing at the Post Office

The mail-sorting facility at Worthside was having a problem keeping up with the increasing volume of mail. Worthside had been growing at a rapid rate ever since the new office park opened near the edge of town. The volume of mail had doubled just in the past year. Fortunately, the postmaster had been able to double the number of employees to help with the job of sorting the mail. There are now thirty employees involved in this task compared to only fifteen a year ago. Yet productivity has not doubled. It seems to take more than twice the time to sort the present volume of mail. The postmaster is at a loss to figure out the cause of this dilemma. Do you think social loafing could be the culprit here? Why do you think it is a possibility? Are there some characteristics of mail sorting that make it relatively susceptible to loafing? What could the postmaster do to eliminate the social loafing?

Coordination in Work Settings: Cooperation, Competition, or Conflict

Learning Objectives

After reading this chapter,
you should be able to:

1. Explain why coordination is often
   essential in organizations.

2. Identify key individual and organizational
   factors that determine the occurrence of
   cooperation in work settings.

3. Describe major causes of conflict within
   organizations.

4. Discuss the positive as well as negative
   effects of conflict.

5. Indicate several techniques through which
   conflict can be *managed* or *resolved*.

usan Kearney was furious. "That @#@##$% Laura English. She's always causing trouble for us."

"Why are you so upset," asked Jane Oliver, a friend of Susan's. "I've never seen you like this."

Susan was the president of the Psychology Club and had been working hard on her new program all year. To get things off to a good start, she had planned a "kick-off" weekend. Laura English was president of Psi Chi, the psychological honor society, which was limited to only the top students. Susan had been trying to get these students involved in the psychology club as well. Unfortunately, Laura had scheduled a party for Psi Chi on the same night.

"I bet she did it on purpose," Susan yelled as she pounded her fist on the desk. "She thinks they're too good for us. Well, I'll show her. The next time they set up a donut sale in the lobby to raise money, we'll do one at the same time. We'll beat her at her own game."

Jane noticed that Susan had calmed down considerably and was now smiling.

"I'm not sure that's going to solve the problem though," said Jane as they walked together to their next class.

"Maybe not," agreed Susan, "but . . ."

Most of us belong to a variety of groups and have had experiences where one of our groups got into conflict with another one. It may have started over a rather minor incident but quickly escalated into a full-scale conflict. Conflicts can happen not only between groups, but also among members of the same group and can be very destructive to the overall harmony and functioning of the group. In this chapter, we will discuss the problem of maintaining coordination and cooperation among individuals and groups and how we can manage conflicts when they do arise.

All the persons and units within an organization are interdependent: What happens to one affects what happens to the others. If the organization prospers, there are rewards for everyone; if it does poorly, however, no one is likely to benefit (except, perhaps, competitors!). Given these basic facts, it seems only reasonable to assume that *coordination* should be the byword in all work settings. All units and individuals within an organization should work together as closely and smoothly as possible.

As incidents such as the one outlined above suggest, though, this ideal is not always attained. Sometimes different units or persons in a business ignore one another, or fail to coordinate their actions in basic ways (see Figure 10.1). In other cases, they may actually compete, seeking to attain certain goals at the expense of other people or groups. And in even more extreme cases, open confrontation or conflict may develop. Obviously, all of these departures from max-

FIGURE 10.1 Coordination: Why It's Often Essential
When individuals or groups fail to coordinate their actions, the results can be disastrous!
(Reprinted with special permission of King Features Syndicate.)

imum coordination can be costly. In fact, they can greatly reduce an organization's efficiency, productivity, and morale.[1]

Coordination, then, is a key process in almost all work settings—one fully deserving of our careful attention. For this reason, it will be the central focus of this chapter. Specifically, our discussion of coordination in the world of work will proceed as follows. First, we will consider **cooperation** and **competition,** paying special attention to factors that seem to tip the balance in favor of one or the other of these contrasting patterns of behavior. Second, we will turn to conflict— an unsettlingly common event in many work settings. Here, we will focus on the causes of conflict (various factors that seem to lead to its occurrence), the effects it produces (which, as we will see, can be beneficial as well as harmful), and various tactics for its effective management or resolution.

COOPERATION AND COMPETITION: WORKING WITH—OR AGAINST—OTHERS

Have you ever heard the phrase "the milk of human kindness?" If so, you probably know that individuals sometimes engage in one-way assistance. That is, they offer help to others without receiving anything obvious in return. (Note the word *obvious,* though, for even in such cases, they may receive *some* benefit for their help—praises, enhancement of their own self-image, and so on). While such one-way assistance certainly occurs, another pattern of interpersonal behavior is far more common. Here, two or more persons work together in order to enhance the outcomes each receives. Such mutual, two-way assistance is generally termed *cooperation* and represents a common form of coordination in work settings. For example, it occurs when several workers pool their efforts to lift a heavy load, when engineers work together to design new equipment, and when executives pool their expertise in order to reach an important decision. In all such cases, the basic strategy is much the same: The persons involved work together and coordinate their actions in order to reach goals or levels of performance they

306

CHAPTER 10

COORDINATION IN
WORK SETTINGS:
COOPERATION,
COMPETITION, OR
CONFLICT

could not attain alone, and then, once the mutual goal is reached, it is shared among all the participants in some fair manner. In sum, cooperation often pays—and pays quite handsomely at that!

The obvious benefits yielded by cooperation raise an intriguing question: Why does it sometimes fail to occur? Why don't people seeking the same goal always join forces to reach it? Several factors help account for this puzzling lack of coordination. First, a clash of personalities or values may be involved. Some people simply find it unpleasant or distasteful to work closely with certain individuals and so refuse to do so. Second, while individuals or departments may be seeking the same overall goals (the success of their company), their sub-goals may differ sharply (e.g., each unit may wish to outshine the others, or to increase its own power and status). Finally, and by far most important, cooperation cannot develop in many situations because the goals sought by several persons or units simply cannot be shared. To the extent this is true, of course, it makes little sense for them to work together. For example, if two persons are seeking the same promotion, they cannot join forces to attain it—this prize can go to only one. In this and many other instances cooperation is literally impossible. Thus an alternative form of behavior known as *competition* may arise. Here, persons or departments strive to maximize their own outcomes, often at the expense of others. Because many valued goals (e.g., status, promotions, bonuses, certain types of power) are sought by more persons or departments than can hope to attain them, competition, too, is common in work settings. In fact, it is a basic aspect of life in most organizations.

In many instances, the choice between cooperation and competition is an obvious one. Indeed, there may really be no choice at all. But in others the individuals or groups involved may find that they do have some room to maneuver. They can choose to work with others or against them. This was true in the example at the beginning of this chapter. There, the two clubs might well have attempted to coordinate their activities and cooperate. Instead, people in the honor society chose to ignore the needs of those in the Psychology Club. The result: a destructive conflict quickly took shape.

The fact that individuals often have to make a choice between competition or cooperation raises a basic question: What factors tip the balance toward one or the other of these contrasting patterns? That is, what conditions lead individuals or groups to opt for cooperation, or for competition? Much research has focused on this practical question, and as a result, many factors have been identified. Among the most important, though, seem to be these: (1) the principle of reciprocity, (2) group size, and (3) certain traits possessed by individuals.

Reciprocity and Cooperation: Reacting to the Behavior of Others

Throughout our lives we are urged to "do unto others as we would have others do unto us." Despite such recommendations, we usually seem to act in another manner. Briefly, we treat others as they have treated us. In short we follow the rule of **reciprocity**—a principle perhaps best expressed as "an eye for an eye and a tooth for a tooth." This tendency to adhere to reciprocity is both general and strong. Thus it can be observed among forms of behavior as diverse as helping, on one hand, and aggression, on the other. And growing research evidence suggests that our choice between cooperation and competition poses no exception to this powerful rule. When others act competitively, we usually respond with mistrust and confrontation. If they behave in a moderately cooperative fashion, we tend to return such actions. And if they behave in a highly cooperative way, we sometimes return high levels of coordination. The word "sometimes" should be stressed, however, for this appears to be true only under certain conditions. If one individual or group offers a high level of cooperation to another but makes it clear that such behavior will continue only if it is returned, cooperation may well be enhanced. In contrast, if a high level of cooperation is offered with "no strings attached"—without any requirement that it be returned—a different pattern may emerge. Here, many persons may be strongly tempted to take unfair advantage of their opponent and may respond to this person or group's trust with attempts at exploitation.[2] Fortunately, such conditions are fairly rare in work settings. Most people realize that they must reciprocate when cooperation is received from others, or it will be withdrawn. Even then the tendency to reciprocate cooperation is not perfect, however.

In judging the level of cooperation of others and adjusting our response to it, we tend to fall prey to the same type of *self-serving bias* described in Chapter 2. We often perceive others' level of cooperation as lower than it really is, and our own level of cooperation as somewhat higher than reality would dictate. The result: In our dealings with others, we tend to *undermatch* the level of cooperation they demonstrate.[3] The fact that cooperation is usually reciprocal in nature points to the following practical conclusion: The key task with respect to such coordination may simply be getting it started. Once employees or organizational units have begun to cooperate with one another, the process may be self-perpetuating. Clearly, managers should thus do everything in their power to set the stage for such developments.

Communication: Potential Benefits, Potential Costs

In many situations where cooperation could potentially develop but does not, its absence is blamed on a "failure to communicate." It is suggested that better or more frequent contact between the persons or groups involved might have facilitated such coordination. Is this suggestion accurate? In one sense, it is. Some forms of communication do indeed seem to increase interpersonal trust and do, therefore, enhance actual cooperation. For example, an open exchange of views may convince all parties that working together is the best strategy, and that a fair division of responsibilities and rewards is possible. Similarly, unless some minimal level of communication exists, close coordination of work activities may be impossible; after all, each individual or group will have little idea about what the others are doing.

It is also clear, however, that not all types of communication yield such beneficial outcomes. In fact, research findings indicate that at least one type of contact between persons or groups—communication involving the use of *threat*—can reduce rather than encourage cooperation (see Figure 10.2).

308

CHAPTER 10

COORDINATION IN
WORK SETTINGS:
COOPERATION,
COMPETITION, OR
CONFLICT

FIGURE 10.2 Threats: Usually a Poor Technique

Sometimes individuals, such as the manager, worker, and union organizer shown here, use threats in trying to achieve their goals. Research has shown that this can actually backfire and lead to less cooperation.

Threats take many different forms, but they typically involve statements suggesting that negative consequences will be delivered if the recipient does not behave or refrain from behaving in some manner. For example, a manager may warn her subordinate that if he continues to tie up the phones with personal calls, his phone privileges will be revoked. Similarly, during negotiations, representatives from one company may inform those from another that they will end the current discussions unless one of their requests is met. While the use of such tactics is tempting, they often produce mixed effects at best. In many cases, they anger recipients, and so stiffen their resolve to resist. Even in cases where threats appear to succeed, and produce immediate yielding or surrender, they may leave behind a residue of resentment that can return to haunt those who have issued threats. And of course, threats often stimulate *counterthreats,* creating a damaging spiral that can lead, ultimately, to open and costly conflict.[4] While threats may succeed in obtaining concessions and compliance in the short-run, they tend to interfere with establishment of long-term lasting patterns of coordination. For this reason, threats appear to be one type of communication managers should avoid on most occasions.

Group Size and Cooperation: Another Reason Why "Bigger" Is Not Always "Better"

One complaint often heard in organizations—especially in those experiencing rapid growth—is this: "My department (or work group) is getting so big it's hard to coordinate." In short, many managers (and employees, too) seem to feel that as their organizations or departments grow, coordination within them becomes harder and harder to achieve. Are these beliefs justified? Is cooperation harder to attain as group size increases? Unfortunately, research findings confirm that it is. As the number of individuals participating in almost any task-performing group rises, the level of cooperation and coordination within that group seems to drop.[5] Several factors contribute to this disturbing pattern.

First, the greater the number of persons present, the greater the likelihood that at least one will act in an exploitative, selfish manner. Such behavior may then permeate the group through the principle of reciprocity described above. Second, as groups increase in size, communication among members—and communication with other groups—may become more difficult (refer to Chapter 3). Third, as the number of individuals in a work group increases, **diffusion of responsibility** may develop. That is, each participant comes to feel less responsible for the group's performance, and this, too, may hinder efforts at coordination.

On the face of it, these facts seem to indicate that as organizations grow in size, they must necessarily become less efficient and less pleasant places in which to work. Too often, this seems to be true. However, the high levels of efficiency attained by some giant corporations suggest that increasing size does not necessarily go hand-in-hand with reduced productivity or with employee dissatisfaction. Why? What is the secret of avoiding these negative outcomes? The answer seems to lie in a relatively simple principle: *division*. Specifically, as groups become larger and more unwieldy, they may be divided into several smaller subunits. That this general strategy can succeed is supported both by the results of systematic research and by the outcome of practical programs along these lines adopted by several major companies. With respect to laboratory research, it has been found that cooperation is in fact enhanced by dividing large groups into smaller ones. For example, one recent study reported that reducing the size of work groups by one-third increased the level of cooperation among group members by as much as 40 to 50 percent.[6] Turning to programs adopted by large corporations, similar positive results have been reported. For example, when Volvo assigned production-line employees to relatively small work groups (about fifteen to twenty-five members), both absenteeism and turnover dropped substantially.[7] Moreover, product quality (although not output) also rose. Of course, several other changes were instituted at the same time (e.g., alterations in the way cars were assembled), so these may have contributed to the positive results as well. At the least, though, these findings agree with those uncovered in systematic research studies. Thus, considered together, these two sources of evidence suggest that reducing the size of work groups may be a useful tactic for enhancing cooperation and overcoming the potentially disruptive effects of bigness.

The Role of Individual Factors: Personality and Cooperation

In Chapter 5, we called attention to the fact that human beings differ in almost a limitless number of ways. It thus seems reasonable to ask whether the tendency to cooperate with others is included among these differences. The answer is a definite "yes." Individuals do differ greatly in the tendency to cooperate, and

310

CHAPTER 10

COORDINATION IN
WORK SETTINGS:
COOPERATION,
COMPETITION, OR
CONFLICT

several personality traits seem to be closely linked to such differences. We will consider some of them here.

Cooperators, Competitors, and Individualists: Contrasting Orientations toward Coordination   Think of the many persons you have known. Can you remember several who were highly competitive—persons who viewed every situation as one in which they must defeat others? Similarly, can you recall individuals who were almost always cooperative—persons who tried to avoid competition whenever they could? You probably have little difficulty bringing examples of both types to mind, for our experience indicates there are large differences in the tendencies to cooperate and to compete. Not surprisingly, the existence of such differences has also been confirmed by careful research.[8] Specifically, it appears that most individuals fall into one of four major categories with respect to their overall orientation toward cooperation.

First, there are **competitors.** These are persons whose primary motive is that of doing better than the persons around them. For this reason, they will often settle for negative results, as long as these exceed those of their opponents. Second, there are **cooperators.** Such persons are primarily concerned with maximizing both their own gains and those of others. They want all the co-workers in their department or group to obtain positive outcomes and are unhappy unless this is the case. Next, there are **individualists.** These are persons whose major motive is that of maximizing their own gains. Generally, they have little interest in the outcomes of others and do not care whether others do better or worse than themselves. All that really interests them is the size of their own payoffs. Finally, a few persons can be described as **equalizers.** Their major goal is minimizing differences between their own performance or outcomes and those of others. In short, they wish to ensure that everyone with whom they work receives the same basic results.

While many individuals seem to fall into one of these categories, others demonstrate a mixture of these perspectives. Substantial numbers seem to combine an individualistic orientation with a competitive one: They want to do as well as they can but are also interested in surpassing others when this is possible. Similarly, some persons combine an individualistic orientation with a desire for equality. They want to do as well as they can but do not want their outcomes to get too far out of line with those of others. Interestingly, men and women show a somewhat different pattern of these orientations. Among males, the single largest group was competitors; fully one-third showed this orientation, while another 18 percent showed an individualistic pattern. In contrast, among females, the single largest group was cooperators (about 20 percent), followed closely by competitors (about 15 percent).[9]

As you might suspect, persons showing different perspectives toward working with others tend to behave quite differently.[10] Competitors frequently attempt to exploit the people around them, and cooperate only when they see no other choice. In contrast, cooperators prefer friendly ties with co-workers, and would rather work with them than against them. Individualists are flexible—they choose whatever strategy will succeed in a given situation. In addition, they often prefer to work alone, concentrating solely on their own outcomes rather than those of others. Persons with a mixed orientation are harder to predict: they often oscillate or adopt intermediate approaches in working with others.

Managers should be aware of such differences, for they are relevant to several key personnel decisions (e.g., hiring, promotion, work assignments). Persons with a competitive orientation may be highly effective in situations where representatives of several organizations must compete against one another. However, they may wreak havoc in contexts requiring prolonged team work. In contrast, cooperators may shine as team players but do poorly in some types of negotiations. Equalizers may excel in positions requiring the fair distribution of resources among various groups (e.g., scheduling of space or equipment). But they may run into problems if, as managers, they must evaluate the performance of subordinates and recommend differential raises or promotions for them. In sum, individual differences with respect to such preferences or orientations are important and can affect performance in a wide range of positions. (What is your own orientation toward cooperation and competition? To find out, see the **Human Relations in Action** section on page 312.)

CONFLICT: ITS CAUSES, EFFECTS, AND MANAGEMENT

Imagine a dimension stretching from positive actions at one end to negative actions at the opposite end. On the positive side would lie helping or altruism. Toward the middle (but still on the positive side) would be cooperation. Farther out, and now past the midpoint, would be competition. And beyond this, even closer to the negative end, would be conflict (see Figure 10.3). In short, conflict can be viewed as a more extreme—and therefore potentially more disruptive—pattern than even intense competition.

But what, precisely, is conflict? One useful definition is as follows: **Conflict** involves direct confrontations between groups or individuals, usually arising in situations where each side perceives that the other is about to frustrate (or has

FIGURE 10.3 Coordination: The Range Is Great
Coordination within an organization can range from very high levels at one extreme (e.g., helping, cooperation) through very low levels at the other (e.g., conflict).

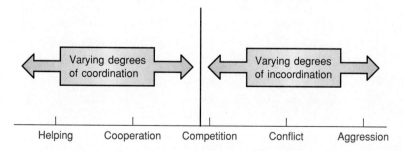

312

CHAPTER 10

COORDINATION IN
WORK SETTINGS:
COOPERATION,
COMPETITION, OR
CONFLICT

already frustrated) some of its major interests.[11] In short, conflict involves opposing interests, the recognition of such opposition, and the belief that one's opponent is out to thwart these essential concerns (Figure 10.4).

Unfortunately, conflict is an all-too-common occurrence in work settings. For this reason, it has long been of major interest to human relations experts. In this discussion, therefore, we will examine conflict from several perspectives. First, we will consider some of the factors that lead to its emergence. Second, we will examine some of its major effects. These, you may be surprised to learn, can be beneficial as well as disruptive. And finally, we will turn to several tactics for resolving or managing conflict—procedures for directing it into constructive rather than destructive pathways.

Conflict: Its Major Causes

As we noted earlier, conflict centers around opposing interests (Figure 10.5). It usually occurs in situations where groups or individuals realize that their interests are opposed to those of others, and in which they expect these persons or groups to thwart their concerns. But what conditions, specifically, lead to open conflict? As we shall now see, several play a role.

Interdependence? "Why Can't They Do Their Job Right, Anyway?"   In most organizations, various units and individuals are highly interdependent. In fact, in

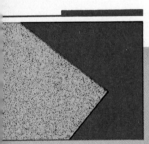

HUMAN RELATIONS IN ACTION

Are You a Cooperator, Competitor, Individualist, or Equalizer?

What is your own orientation toward coordination? To gain some insight into this important matter, indicate whether you think each of the statements below is true (T) or false (F).

_____   1.   In dealing with others, my major concern is getting what I want; what happens to them is not very important to me.

_____   2.   If I had to choose between doing well on some task and doing poorly but still better than other persons, I would prefer the latter.

_____   3.   I am not satisfied with a relationship or business arrangement unless the other people in it are satisfied too.

_____   4.   I like it best if my fellow workers and I are about equally successful.

_____   5.   In doing my work, I tend to set my own standards; I'm not very concerned with how others do theirs.

_____   6.   It is exciting to pit my abilities, skills, and intelligence against those of others.

many cases they cannot complete their own work unless they receive appropriate input or assistance from others. For example, in a factory all parts must be available for proper assembly, and the entire unit must be put together before it can be painted or tested. Such *interdependence* can often serve as a major cause of conflict. The reason for this is simple: Each group or department requires input from others. When this is delayed or not provided, a group's work is disrupted. The result: The affected persons or departments blame others for this thwarting, and conflict is initiated. As you probably know, such reactions are quite common. Gripes often take the form of blaming "those people in production," or those "fellows in the main office." In short, each unit's problems are attributed, fairly or unfairly, to the shortcomings of other departments. Unfortunately, such blame-fixing usually becomes reciprocal, with each side holding the other responsible for most of its difficulties. Thus a great deal of careful planning is needed if this basic cause of organizational conflict is to be avoided.

The Problem of Limited Resources: "We've Got to Get Our Share." Unfortunately no organization, no matter how successful, has unlimited resources. Space, money, materials, labor—all must be conserved and used to the greatest advantage. But what division of these resources among various departments or individuals is best? Not surprisingly, bitter disputes about this issue often erupt. Each unit tends to ask for more than the others feel is fair, and each strives to ensure that it doesn't receive the "short end of the stick." Indeed, from the

_____ **7.** If I were to receive a larger reward than another person, even though we both did the same work, I would be quite unhappy.

_____ **8.** If I were to get a bigger raise than my co-workers, I would feel uncomfortable.

If you marked "true" for items 1 and 5, you are probably an individualist—you are mainly concerned with your own outcomes and have little interest in those of others. If you marked "true" for items 2 and 6, you are probably a competitor—your main concern is being better than others, overcoming them in competitive situations. If you marked "true" for items 3 and 7, you are a co-operator—you prefer to maximize the other person's outcomes as well as your own. Finally, if you marked "true" for items 4 and 8, you are an equalizer—you prefer to minimize differences between yourself and others. Of course, you may well show a mixed pattern (e.g., an individualist orientation coupled with some elements of competitiveness). In any case, examine your answers to these questions carefully: they may reveal much about your own orientation toward working with—or against—others.

314
CHAPTER 10
COORDINATION IN
WORK SETTINGS:
COOPERATION,
COMPETITION, OR
CONFLICT

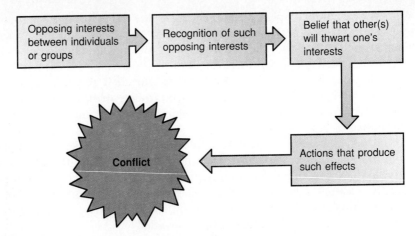

FIGURE 10.4 Organizational Conflict: Its Basic Nature
Conflict involves opposing or incompatible interests between groups or individuals, the
recognition of such opposing interests, and the belief that others will act on such opposing
interests. *Source:* Based on suggestions by Thomas (1989); see Note 1.

perspective of organizational politics, supervisors who succeed in such disputes
are perceived as effective, and often gain in power and status. Those who bring
home less than their subordinates believe is fair are viewed in a much more
negative light. Whatever the final outcome, though, this continuous struggle within
organizations for a share of available resources is clearly a major cause of confrontation and conflict.

FIGURE 10.5 Conflict: A Result of Opposing Interests
Because management and labor often have opposing interests, conflicts often arise, as in the
case of major league baseball player strikes.

Reward Structures: Building Conflict into the System Suppose that at a particular company, bonuses and raises are distributed to production-line staff on the basis of total output: the higher the overall production, the more reward they receive. Similarly, imagine that among service personnel—people who must deal with customer complaints—a somewhat different reward system operates. Here, the lower the total costs of service during a given period, the greater the raises and bonuses. Is there a potential basis for conflict in this set-up? You bet there is! From the point of view of production workers, faster is better—the more they produce, the higher their pay. In a sense, conflict between these two groups is practically assured. The reward system adopted by their company pits the interests of one group directly against those of the other (see Figure 10.6). The moral in this example is simple: When planning reward systems, such problems should be carefully avoided. If they are not, serious conflict may be fostered in situations where, with a little care, it might have been avoided.

Interpersonal Relations and Conflict: From Grudges to Criticism The causes of conflict we have considered so far all relate to aspects of organizations themselves. But conflict actually occurs between individuals. In fact, it is specific persons who decide to threaten or thwart others' interests—not departments or other organizational units. This basic fact calls attention to another cause of conflict in work settings: faulty interpersonal relations between key individuals.

There are many sources of conflict in interpersonal relations. First, consider the impact of lasting *grudges*. When individuals are angered by others, and es-

FIGURE 10.6 Organizational Reward Systems: A Potential Source of Conflict
In this hypothetical setting, production workers are rewarded for high output, while service employees are rewarded for holding costs to a minimum. The result: conflict between these two groups.

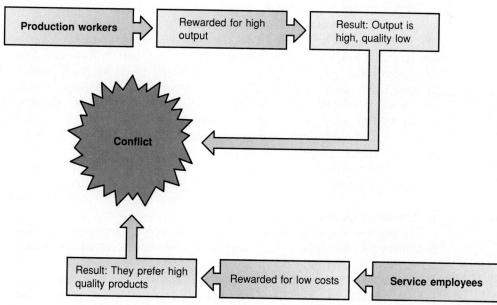

316

CHAPTER 10
COORDINATION IN
WORK SETTINGS:
COOPERATION,
COMPETITION, OR
CONFLICT

pecially when they are made to "lose face" (to look foolish publicly), they may develop strong, negative attitudes toward the persons responsible for these outcomes. As a result, they spend considerable time and effort planning or actually seeking revenge for these wrongs. Unfortunately, such grudges can persist for years, with obvious negative effects for the organizations or work groups in question.

Second, conflict often stems from or is intensified by faulty *attributions*—errors concerning the causes behind others' behavior. When individuals find their interests have been hindered by another person, they generally try to determine *why* this person acted this way. Was it a desire to harm them or give them a hard time? Or did the provoker's actions stem from factors beyond his or her control? When people infer some negative motive, anger and subsequent conflict are more likely and more intense than when they assume this is not the case.[12] For example, in one study on this issue, students engaged in simulated negotiations with another person (actually an accomplice).[13] Both persons played the role of executives representing different departments within a large organization; they bargained over the division of $1 million in surplus funds between their respective departments. The accomplice adopted a very confrontational stance, demanding $800,000 out of $1 million in available funds for his or her own department, and offered only two small concessions during the negotiations. As the bargaining proceeded, the accomplice made several statements indicating that he or she had been ordered to behave in this "tough" manner by his or her constituents. In other words, the accomplice adopted a bargaining tactic often described as the "my hands are tied" strategy. In one condition, subjects received information suggesting these claims were true, while in another, they learned that they were false. As predicted, participants reported more negative reactions to the accomplice, and stronger tendencies to avoid and compete with this person on future occasions, when they learned that he or she had misrepresented the causes behind his or her behavior (see Figure 10.7).

A third interpersonal factor of considerable importance in generating instances of organizational conflict might be termed *faulty communication*. This refers to the fact that individuals often communicate with others in a manner that angers or annoys them, even though they do not intend to do so. Such faulty communication often involves a lack of clarity—for example, a manager is certain that she communicated her wishes clearly to a subordinate when in fact, the subordinate is confused about exactly what he is supposed to do. When the manager later finds that the task has not been completed, she is annoyed. And the subordinate, in turn, is angered by what he considers to be unfair treatment. In other cases, faulty communication centers around inappropriate *criticism*—negative feedback delivered in a manner that angers the recipient instead of helping this person to do a better job. The negative effects of such *destructive criticism* have been demonstrated clearly in a study by Baron.[14]

In this investigation, subjects were asked to prepare an ad campaign for an imaginary product (a new shampoo), and they then received feedback on their work from another person (an accomplice of the researcher). In one condition (*constructive criticism*), this feedback was negative but was consistent with established principles for providing such feedback in an effective manner. Thus it was

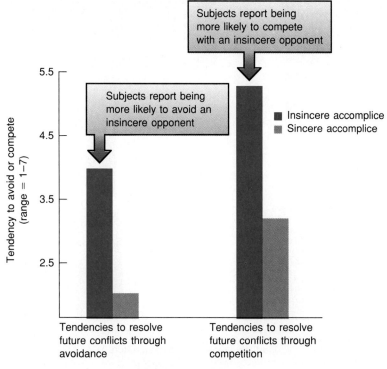

FIGURE 10.7 Insincerity as a Cause of Future Conflict
Subjects reacted more negatively to an opponent whose claims about the causes behind his or
her "tough" bargaining stance seemed false than to one whose claims in this regard seemed
true. These findings indicate that attributions often play an important role in organizational
conflict. *Source:* Based on data from Baron (1988); see Note 13.

considerate in tone, specific in content, contained no threats, and made no internal
attributions for the supposedly poor performance. In a second condition (*destructive criticism*), feedback was negative but, in addition, violated basic principles of
effective feedback. It was harsh in tone, general rather than specific in content,
was threatening, and placed the blame for poor performance squarely on the
subject. After receiving one of these types of criticism, subjects rated their current
feelings (anger, tension), and their likelihood of resolving future conflicts with
the accomplice in each of five ways (through competition, compromise, collaboration, accommodation, or avoidance). Results indicated that subjects who received destructive criticism reported being angrier and more upset than those who
received constructive criticism. In addition, those who received destructive criticism, as compared to those who received constructive criticism, reported being
more likely to resolve future conflicts through avoidance or competition, and less
likely to resolve them through collaboration (see Figure 10.8). In a follow-up
study, it was found that destructive criticism also reduced subjects' self-set goals
and feelings of self-efficacy (i.e., perceived ability to perform various tasks). These

318

CHAPTER 10

COORDINATION IN
WORK SETTINGS:
COOPERATION,
COMPETITION, OR
CONFLICT

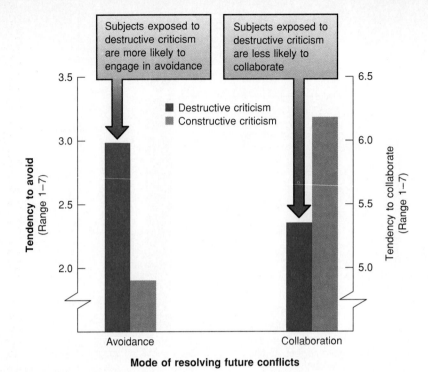

FIGURE 10.8 Some Negative Effects of Destructive Criticism
Individuals exposed to destructive criticism reported being more likely to resolve future conflicts with the criticizer through competition and less likely to resolve them through collaboration than individuals exposed to constructive criticism. *Source:* Based on data from Baron (1988); see Note 14.

findings suggest that harsh, destructive criticism is one type of communication managers (and others) would do well to avoid. Such criticism induces feelings of anger, may contribute to the occurrence of costly conflicts, and may also exert negative effects on motivation and self-efficacy. Truly, this seems to be a devastating combination!

In sum, considerable evidence suggests that conflict in work settings often stems from the relations between individuals as well as from underlying structural (organization-based) factors (see Figure 10.9). At first glance, this finding might appear to be quite pessimistic in its implications for the reduction or management of such conflict; after all, it adds several potential causes to the ones that have traditionally been viewed as important in this respect. In fact, it can actually be interpreted as being quite optimistic in this regard. Interpersonal behavior can readily be modified. Indeed in many cases it may be easier to change than organizational structure, and easier to modify than built-in underlying conflicts of interest. For this reason, understanding the interpersonal causes of organizational conflict may offer important and practical benefits.

Organizational factors

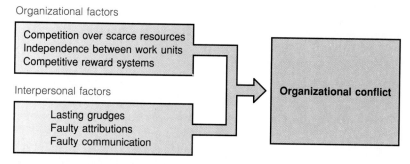

Interpersonal factors

FIGURE 10.9 Organizational Causes of Conflict
Organizational and interpersonal factors contribute to the occurrence of conflict in work settings.

Conflict: A Look at Its Major Effects

Many processes affecting human behavior seem to operate like the proverbial "double-edged sword." Depending on who wields them, they can produce mainly harmful or mainly beneficial effects. To mention one example, persuasion can be used to enhance personal health by convincing people to quit smoking, or to induce consumers to buy products they do not really need. Surprising as it may seem, this same general principle applies to conflict. Depending on what and how it occurs, it can yield either harmful or beneficial outcomes. Because the effects of both types are quite varied in scope, we will now consider them separately.

Conflict: The Negative Side of the Coin Some of the negative effects of conflict are obvious. For example, conflict often generates strong negative feelings among the parties concerned, interferes with communication between them, and all but eliminates any coordination with their activities. In these ways, of course, it can seriously impair effective organizational functioning.

Other effects of conflict, though, are a bit more subtle. First, it has been found that when groups experience conflict, their leaders often shift from democratic to autocratic practices (see Chapter 8).[15] The reason for this seems to be straightforward: Groups experiencing stress require firm direction from their leaders. Thus when conflict develops, these persons shift to more authoritarian tactics—tactics that are accepted without protest by their subordinates. Groups experiencing conflict thus tend to be far less pleasant to work in than groups not encountering such stress.

Conflict also increases the tendency of both sides to engage in *negative stereotyping*. The members of each group emphasize the differences between themselves and their opponents and come to perceive others in an increasingly negative

320

CHAPTER 10

COORDINATION IN
WORK SETTINGS:
COOPERATION,
COMPETITION, OR
CONFLICT

light. "You know what marketing people are like" and "All those staff people are the same" are just two statements that capture the essence of such thinking. In short, conflict tends to heighten our tendency to divide the world into two opposing camps—"us" and "them"—with all the unfortunate outcomes this implies.

Finally, conflict leads each side to close ranks and emphasize loyalty to their own department or group. This effectively prevents opponents from taking each other's perspective and tends to lessen the chances for an effective, satisfactory compromise. As you can readily see, conflict has a number of negative, costly effects.

The Positive Side of the Coin   Nevertheless, the total picture is not entirely bleak. While conflict often exerts a disruptive effect on organizations and work settings, there are certain conditions under which it can actually be helpful.[16] First, conflict can serve to bring problems that have previously been ignored out into the open. In this way, it can facilitate their solutions. All too often, issues that are unpleasant or "sticky" are swept under the corporate rug. As a result, they tend to persist. Once open conflict breaks out, however, this approach is no longer possible, and problems that require attention may finally receive it.

Second, conflict can sometimes lead to the consideration of new ideas and approaches. This occurs because once conflict erupts, an organization cannot go on conducting business as usual. Instead, new solutions or policies may be needed. To the extent conflict facilitates the emergence of these, it can indeed be useful.

Finally, it may encourage the opposing sides to carefully monitor each other's performance—a process that increases effort and productivity on both sides. In these ways, conflict can actually contribute to effective organizational functioning. Of course, it is important to note that this will be the case only when it is carefully managed or controlled. If conflicts are allowed to become extreme and intense, strong negative feelings may be generated on both sides. Then, rationality and the potential benefits just described may fly quickly out of the window! If such pitfalls can be avoided, however, conflict can play a useful role. Indeed, it can turn out to be an effective tool for inducing positive organizational change. (See Figure 10.10 for a summary of both the potential costs and benefits of conflict.)

Conflict: Its Effective Management

While conflict seems capable of producing positive as well as negative effects, one fact about it is clear: If allowed to continue, it will ultimately exert a disruptive influence on an organization. After all, while a conflict persists, valuable resources better used elsewhere will be committed to it. Even worse, growing evidence suggests that the more each side has invested in a conflict—the more losses they have experienced as a result of their disagreement—the harder it is for them to bring it to an end. Thus there are strong reasons for attempting to resolve existing conflicts as quickly as possible. How can this be accomplished? Fortunately, a number of tactics for attaining this goal exist and seem effective. We will consider several of these briefly.

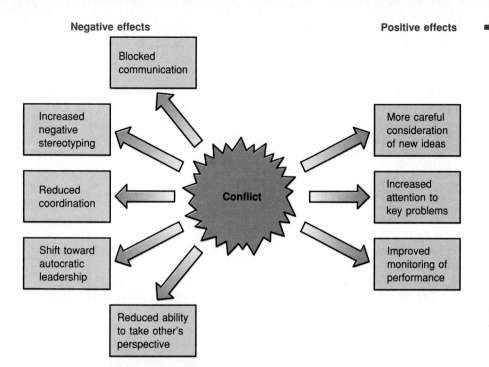

Negative effects   Positive effects

- Blocked communication
- Increased negative stereotyping
- Reduced coordination
- Shift toward autocratic leadership
- Reduced ability to take other's perspective

- More careful consideration of new ideas
- Increased attention to key problems
- Improved monitoring of performance

Conflict

FIGURE 10.10 Conflict: Mixed Effects
As shown here, conflict can produce beneficial as well as harmful effects.

Bargaining: The Give-and-Take Road to Resolution By far, the most common tactic used for resolving organizational conflicts is **bargaining** or **negotiation.**[17] (See Figure 10.11.) As you probably already know, this process consists of a mutual trading of offers, counteroffers, and (hopefully) concessions between the parties involved or their representatives. If the process is successful, a solution acceptable to both sides is attained, and the conflict is brought to a close. The catch, of course, is that often, the process is *not* successful. Negotiations frequently dead-

FIGURE 10.11 Negotiation: A Common Tactic
Negotiation is a common tactic to resolve a variety of disputes. (Reprinted with special permission of King Features Syndicate.)

322

CHAPTER 10

COORDINATION IN
WORK SETTINGS:
COOPERATION,
COMPETITION, OR
CONFLICT

lock, with the result that conflict is intensified rather than reduced. A major question concerning bargaining, then, is this: What factors either increase or reduce the likelihood of its success? Research findings point to some intriguing answers.

First, open and direct communication between the opposing sides is beneficial, especially if this continues throughout the entire process.[18] Only one type of contact between opponents should be avoided: implicit or explicit *threats*. When these are used, tempers tend to flare, and the chances of an agreement can be sharply reduced. Second, willingness to make concessions, even small ones, is extremely helpful. When one side to a conflict makes such a move, the rule of reciprocity (which, we noted earlier, is quite general in its effects) dictates the other should do likewise. This fact points to another interesting conclusion about bargaining: In general, it is best to begin with a position you do not really expect to attain. By doing so, you leave yourself room for maneuvering and for a number of small concessions. But beware of starting with too extreme an offer: This can anger your opponent and stiffen his or her resistance.

On the other side of the coin, several additional factors seem to reduce the chances of success in bargaining. For example, if one or both sides believe that they have an "out"—some other option aside from reaching an agreement with their opponent—they may refuse to grant concessions and so block a solution.[19] And the more attractive this option (e.g., the more attractive a deal offered them by someone else), the tougher and less flexible they tend to be. Similarly, when negotiators represent others and are accountable to them for their actions, they often adopt a tougher stance and make it more unlikely that agreement will be reached.[20] Third, if bargainers perceive their task as "beating" their opponents rather than finding a solution acceptable to both sides, the chances of success decrease. After all, if they perceive the situation as a kind of contest, both sides cannot win, and neither wishes to lose.[21]

Another group of factors that determine the nature and outcomes of bargaining involve the cognitive set or focus adopted by negotiators. Several carefully conducted studies suggest that when bargainers adopt a *positive frame*—when they focus on the potential benefits of negotiations and on the settlements that may result—bargaining is facilitated. In contrast, when they adopt a *negative frame,* and focus on potential losses or costs, bargaining is impaired.[22] In short, expectations or cognitive sets shape reality, determining the nature and course of actual bargaining.

Perhaps the single most important factor determining the success of negotiations in producing settlements satisfactory to both sides, however, involves participants' overall orientation toward this process. Persons taking part in negotiations can approach such discussions from either of two distinct perspectives.[23] On the one hand, they can view them as "win-lose" (*distributive*) situations in which gains by one side are necessarily linked with losses for the other. On the other hand, such persons can approach negotiations as potential "win-win" situations—ones in which the interests of the two sides are not necessarily incompatible, and in which the potential gains of both can be maximized. Not all situations offer the potential for such agreements, of course, but many that at first glance seem to involve simple head-on clashes between the two sides do, in fact, provide such possibilities. If participants are willing to explore all options carefully and exert the effort required to identify creative potential solutions, they can attain **integrative agreements**—ones that offer greater joint benefits than simple compromise (splitting all differences down the middle).

How can such integrative agreements be attained? Pruitt and his colleagues suggest the possibilities summarized in Table 10.1. As you can see, these involve several distinct tactics. In *nonspecific compensation,* each side receives different benefits, and the question of whether outcomes are precisely equal in magnitude is ignored. In *logrolling,* each side makes concessions on relatively unimportant issues in order to attain concessions on issues it views as more central to its needs.

Research findings suggest that when parties to a dispute strive for integrative agreements, joint outcomes do indeed increase. Moreover, the nature of their discussion also changes. *Contentious tactics* such as threats or taking strong firm, unyielding positions decrease, and the open exchange of accurate information between the two sides increases. Thus not only does integrative bargaining increase the outcomes of both sides, it may enhance their relationships too. Given such benefits, it seems clear that encouraging such an approach to negotiations is one highly effective strategy for managing real or potential conflicts.

Third-Party Intervention: Help from the Outside   Despite the best efforts of both sides, negotiations sometimes deadlock. When they do, the aid of a third party, someone not directly involved in the dispute, is often sought. Such *third party intervention* can take many different forms, but the most common are **mediation**

TABLE 10.1
Techniques for Attaining Integrative Agreements

Several strategies can be used to attain integrative agreements through bargaining. *Source:* Based on suggestions by Pruitt et al. (1983); see Note 23.

Type of Agreement	Description
Broadening the Pie	Available resources are broadened so that both sides can obtain their major goals
Nonspecific compensation	One side gets what it wants; the other is compensated on an unrelated issue
Logrolling	Each party makes concessions on low priority issues in exchange for concessions on issues that are of higher value to it
Cost cutting	One party gets what it desires and the costs to the other party are reduced or eliminated
Bridging	Neither party gets its initial demands, but a new option that satisfies the major interests of both sides is developed

324

CHAPTER 10

COORDINATION IN
WORK SETTINGS:
COOPERATION,
COMPETITION, OR
CONFLICT

and **arbitration.**[24] In mediation, the third party attempts, through various tactics, to facilitate voluntary agreements between the disputants. Mediators have no formal power and cannot impose an agreement on the two sides. Instead, they seek to clarify the issues involved and enhance communication between the opponents. Mediators sometimes offer specific recommendations for compromise or integrative solutions; in other cases, they merely guide disputants toward developing such solutions themselves. In sum, their role is primarily that of *facilitator*—helping the two sides toward agreements they both find acceptable.

In contrast, *arbitrators* do have the power to impose (or at least strongly recommend) the terms of an agreement. In *binding arbitration,* the two sides agree in advance to accept these terms. In *voluntary arbitration,* the two sides retain the freedom to reject the recommended agreement (although the personal stature and expertise of the arbitrator may make it difficult for them to do so). In *conventional* arbitration, the arbitrator can offer any package of terms he or she wishes. However, in *final offer arbitration,* the arbitrator merely chooses between final offers made by the disputants.

Both mediation and arbitration can be helpful in resolving organizational conflicts. However, both suffer from certain drawbacks. Because it requires voluntary compliance by the parties to a dispute, mediation often proves ineffective. Indeed, it may simply serve to underscore the depth of the differences between the two sides. Arbitration suffers from several potential problems. First, it may exert a *chilling effect* on negotiations, bringing voluntary progress to a halt. Since both sides know the arbitrator will resolve the dispute for them, they see little point in engaging in serious bargaining which, after all, is hard work. Second, one or both sides may come to suspect that the arbitrator is biased. The result: Disputants become increasingly reluctant to agree to arbitration. Finally, there is some indication that commitment to arbitrated settlements is weaker than that to directly negotiated ones.

In most instances, mediation and arbitration are relatively formal procedures involving the services of persons from outside an organization. Are they also used by practicing managers to resolve disputes between persons under their authority? Research suggests this is not the case. Apparently, managers often seek to resolve conflicts between their subordinates in ways other than standard mediation or arbitration.[25]

By taking these factors into account, groups or individuals participating in bargaining can increase the likelihood of an agreement and avoid some key pitfalls (see Figure 10.12). Thus, under appropriate conditions, bargaining can be a highly effective technique for resolving even bitter and prolonged conflicts.

The Induction of Superordinate Goals: Converting "Them" into "Us"   Another useful strategy for resolving conflicts stems from a basic aspect of social perception we have already met. Briefly, most individuals possess a strong tendency to divide the social world into two distinct categories: *them* and *us*. Persons falling into the former category are viewed as different from ourselves, and usually evoke negative feelings and attitudes. In contrast, those included in the "us" category are seen as being similar to ourselves, and generally elicit positive reactions. In short, we

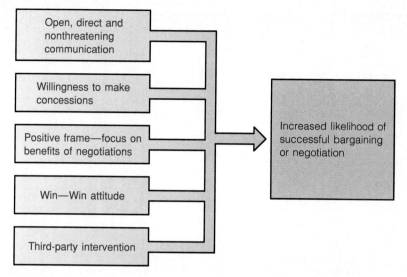

FIGURE 10.12 Bargaining and Negotiation: One Way of Managing Conflicts
Bargaining and negotiation can be a useful way of managing or resolving conflicts. Some of the techniques that have been useful in increasing the chances of agreement are shown here.

divide the social world into "in-group" members and "out-group" members, and demonstrate sharply different reactions to persons falling into each category.

This tendency has important implications for resolving many conflicts. Often, each side in a conflict views the other as belonging to the out-group. As a result, each tends to hold negative attitudes toward their opponents. One effective technique for resolving such conflicts, then, might involve a shift in perceptions, so that each side comes to view the other as basically similar rather than dissimilar to itself—as part of the "us" category, rather than as part of the "them" category. How can this step be accomplished? Research findings suggest that one approach lies in the establishment of some **superordinate goal.** That is, conditions can be arranged so that the two sides no longer compete; rather, they must work together to attain a goal of interest to both. Recent events in the American automobile industry suggest that this strategy can often be effective in reducing even intense conflict. Faced with growing competition from foreign companies, labor and management—traditional opponents—agreed to bury the hatchet at least temporarily and to work together to fend off this threat to their common livelihood. Thus workers agreed to reductions in pay and other benefits, and management agreed to pass on the savings so obtained to consumers in the form of lower prices. The result: positive outcomes for both sides. The benefits of superordinate goals have also been demonstrated in classic research by Sherif and his associates. These investigators found that when opposing groups had to work together to achieve common goals, their perceptions of each other improved, while conflict decreased.[26] In sum, it appears that either reminding the parties to a conflict of their shared goal (e.g., the overall success of their organization), or actually establishing such objectives can be a highly effective means for resolving confrontations (see

326

CHAPTER 10

COORDINATION IN
WORK SETTINGS:
COOPERATION,
COMPETITION, OR
CONFLICT

FIGURE 10.13 Superordinate Goals: One Way to Reduce Conflicts
When groups are involved in common activities or have common goals (e.g. protest movements),
they tend to overlook their differences.

HUMAN RELATIONS IN ACTION

How Do You Deal with Conflict?

All of us deal with conflict in different ways. Some of us try to avoid or minimize
conflict at all costs; others may thrive on conflict and may be very difficult people
with which to negotiate. A third group may see conflict as a necessary evil and
try to make the best of such situations. The following questionnaire is designed
to determine your conflict style. Simply place a *T* next to the items with which
you agree and an *F* next to those with which you disagree.

Conflict Style Scale

_____ 1. When there is a conflict among groups, I like to be right in the middle
of it.

_____ 2. I find conflicts among people or groups very uncomfortable.

_____ 3. When I'm involved in a conflict, I don't let it linger but get to work
to try to resolve it.

_____ 4. Sometimes I try to produce a conflict in a group on purpose just for
the excitement of it.

_____ 5. I enjoy helping people or groups resolve their conflict.

_____ 6. Whenever I have a conflict with someone, I tend to withdraw into
my own shell and ignore that person.

Figure 10.13). All of us have different ways of dealing with conflict. To see what your style is, see the **Human Relations in Action** section on page 326.

SUMMARY

Coordination is a key process in most work settings. Yet it is not always attained. Sometimes individuals or departments cooperate, but on other occasions they fail to coordinate their actions, or may even engage in open competition. Several factors seem to determine which of these patterns emerges. In general, cooperation is reciprocated, so that a cooperative approach by one person or group is matched by others. However, if an individual or department offers total cooperation with no requirement that it be returned, exploitation may follow. Open and nonthreatening communication can facilitate cooperation. Cooperation tends to drop as group size increases, but this trend can be halted or reversed by dividing large groups into smaller units. Personal factors, too, play a role in cooperation. Some individuals prefer to cooperate, while other prefer to compete.

    Conflict occurs when groups or individuals perceive that others are about to frustrate or have already frustrated their major interests. It stems from many causes, including the interdependence of work units, certain types of organizational reward systems, and the continuous struggle over organizational resources. In

----

   ——   **7.** I usually try to get my own way in most situations.

   ——   **8.** I hold grudges for long periods of time.

   ——   **9.** I avoid criticizing people for their mistakes and try to help them avoid these in the future.

   ——   **10.** I tend to let others have their way just to minimize conflicts.

   ——   **11.** I often find myself involved in resolving conflicts between friends.

   ——   **12.** I tend to keep my feelings to myself if I think they might produce some conflict.

If you have marked "true" for items 2, 6, 10, and 12, you have an *avoidant style* of dealing with conflict—you try to avoid it if at all possible. If you answered "true" for questions 1, 4, 7, and 8, you are a *conflict seeker*. You tend to enjoy conflicts and may even try to generate them. If you answered "true" for items 3, 5, 9, and 11, you take a *problem-solving* approach to conflict. You try to find ways to help people and groups deal with conflicts. Although from the perspective of this chapter the problem-solving approach may be most helpful for groups, sometimes the other styles may also be beneficial. Groups that have become lethargic may need some conflict to energize them. When important issues are not on the line, avoidance of conflict is certainly desirable.

328
CHAPTER 10
COORDINATION IN
WORK SETTINGS:
COOPERATION,
COMPETITION, OR
CONFLICT

addition, it may be fostered by grudges or other forms of faulty interpersonal relations. Many of the effects produced by competition are negative. These include interference with effective communication, and negative stereotyping. Under some conditions, however, conflict can yield beneficial effects. It can lead to the consideration of new ideas or procedures, and it can bring important organizational problems out into the open. Several techniques for managing conflict exist. These include *bargaining* and *negotiation, third-party intervention,* and the induction of *superordinate goals* (ones shared by all parties to a conflict).

KEY TERMS

arbitration: A form of third-party intervention in disputes in which the intervening person has the power to determine the terms of an agreement.

bargaining: A process in which two or more sides exchange offers, counteroffers, and concessions in an attempt to resolve their disagreement; also called negotiation.

competition: A situation in which individuals or groups attempt to maximize their own outcomes, often at the expense of others.

competitors: Individuals who are mainly concerned with doing better than others. Such persons prefer competition to cooperation in most cases.

conflict: Confrontations between individuals or groups in situations where each side perceives the other as thwarting or about to thwart its major interests.

conflict management: Procedures designed to hold conflict in check, to minimize its destructive impact, and to maximize its beneficial efforts.

cooperation: A situation in which two or more persons or groups coordinate their behavior to reach a common goal.

cooperators: Individuals who are concerned with maximizing their own gains as well as those of others.

diffusion of responsibility: The tendency of individuals to assume that others will take responsibility for needed actions.

equalizers: Individuals primarily concerned with ensuring equality of outcomes among all persons who work together on joint projects.

individualists: Persons who are concerned only with their own gains. In general, they pay little attention to the gains of others.

integrative agreements: Agreements between negotiators that maximize the joint outcomes of all parties.

mediation: A form of third-party intervention in disputes in which the intervener does not have the authority to dictate an agreement. Mediators simply attempt to enhance communication between opposing sides and to provide conditions that will facilitate acceptable agreements.

reciprocity: A basic human relations principle stating that we act toward others as they have behaved toward us.

superordinate goals: Goals shared by all members of an organization. When the parties to a conflict are made aware of these goals, the conflict may be resolved or lessened.

NOTES

1. Thomas, K.W. (1989). "Conflict and Negotiation Processes in Organizations." In M.D. Dunnette, ed. *Handbook of Industrial and Organizational Psychology*, 2d ed. Chicago: Rand McNally.
2. Shure, G.H., Meeker, R.J., & Hansford, E.A. (1965). "The Effectiveness of Pacifist Strategies in Bargaining Games." *Journal of Conflict Resolution, 9,* 106–17.

3. Youngs, G.A. Jr., (1986). "Patterns of Threat and Punishment Reciprocity in a Conflict Setting." *Journal of Personality and Social Psychology, 51,* 541–46.

4. See Note 3.

5. Fox, J., & Guyer, M. (1978). "Public Choice and Cooperation in N-person Prisoner's Dilemma." *Journal of Conflict Resolution, 22,* 468–81.

6. Komorita, S.S., & Lapworth, C.W. (1982). "Cooperative Choice Among Individuals Versus Groups in an N-person Dilemma Situation." *Journal of Personality and Social Psychology, 42,* 487–96.

7. Gyllenhammar, P.G. (1977). *People at Work.* Reading, Mass.: Addison-Wesley.

8. Knight, G.P., & Dubro, A.F. (1984). "Cooperative, Competitive, and Individualistic Social Values: An Individualized Regression and Clustering Approach." *Journal of Personality and Social Psychology, 46,* 98–105.

9. See Note 8.

10. Kuhlman, D.M., & Marshello, A.F.J. (1975). "Individual Differences in Game Motivation as Moderators of Pre-programmed Strategy Effects in Prisoner's Dilemma." *Journal of Personality and Social Psychology, 32,* 922–32.

11. See Note 1.

12. Johnson, T.E., & Rule, B.G. (1986). "Mitigating Circumstance Information, Censure, and Aggression." *Journal of Personality and Social Psychology, 50,* 537–42.

13. Baron, R.A. (1988). "Attributions and Organizational Conflict: The Mediating Role of Apparent Sincerity." *Organizational Behavior and Human Decision Processes, 41,* 111–27.

14. Baron, R.A. (1988). "Negative Effects of Destructive Criticism: Impact on Conflict, Self-Efficacy, and Task Performance." *Journal of Applied Psychology, 73,* 199–207.

15. Fodor, E.M. (1976). "Group Stress, Authoritarian Style of Control, and Use of Power." *Journal of Applied Psychology, 61,* 313–18.

16. Robbins, S.P. (1974). *Managing Organizational Conflict.* Englewood Cliffs, N.J.: Prentice-Hall.

17. Lewicki, R.J., & Litterer, J.A. (1985). *Negotiation.* Homewood, Ill.: Irwin.

18. Stech, F., & McClintock, C.G. (1981). "Effects of Communication Timing on Duopoly Bargaining Outcomes." *Journal of Personality and Social Psychology, 40,* 664–74.

19. Komorita, S.S., Lapworth, C.W., & Tuomonis, T.M. (1981). "The Effects of Certain Versus Risky Alternatives in Bargaining." *Journal of Experimental Social Psychology, 17,* 525–44.

20. Breaugh, J.A., & Klimoski, R.J. (1981). "Social Forces in Negotiation Simulations." *Personality and Social Psychology Bulletin, 7,* 290–95.

21. Brown, B.R. (1970). "Face-saving Following Experimentally Induced Embarrassment." *Journal of Experimental Social Psychology, 6,* 255–71.

22. Huber, V.L., Neale, M.A., & Northcraft, G.B. (1987). "Decision bias and Personnel Selection Strategies." *Organizational Behavior and Human Decision Processes, 40,* 136–47.

23. Pruitt, D.G., Carnevale, J.D., Ben-Yoav, O., Nochajski, T.H., & Van Slyck, M.R. (1983). "Incentives for Cooperation in Integrative Bargaining." In R. Tietz, *Aspiration Levels in Bargaining and Economic Decision-Making.* Berlin: Springer-Verlag.

24. Carnevale, J.D., & Conlon, D.E. (1988). "Time Pressure and Strategic Choice in Mediation." *Organizational Behavior and Human Decision Processes, 42,* 111–33.

25. Sheppard, B.H. (1984). "Third-party Conflict Intervention: A Procedural Framework." In B. Staw and L. Cummings, eds. *Research in Organizational Behavior, 6,* 141–90. Greenwich, Conn.: JAI Press.

26. Sherif, M., Harvey, O.J., White, B.J., Hood, W.R., & Sherif, C.W. (1961). *Intergroup Conflict and Cooperation: The Robbers' Cave Experiment.* Norman: University of Oklahoma Press.

ADDITIONAL CASES AND EXERCISES: APPLYING WHAT YOU'VE LEARNED

Problems in the Library

Don H. Hockenbury
Psychology Instructor
Tulsa Junior College

Sandra E. Hockenbury
Adjunct Instructor
Tulsa Junior College

The notice had been slipped into last week's pay envelope. Its message was to the point: MEETING FOR ALL PART-TIME STUDENT STAFF, 3:30 P.M. THURSDAY. ATTENDANCE COMPULSORY. Mrs. Griffler, the new assistant librarian, sat at the head of a long table in the library conference room, around which sat twelve college students. All of them were work-study students who needed their jobs to help pay their college tuition. In any case, as in most years, the students were a mixed group: some were extremely conscientious, while others . . .

Mrs. Griffler cleared her throat and spoke. "I called this meeting because I've received a number of complaints from both our library users and our full-time staff. Basically, you folks just aren't pulling your weight this semester, and I felt that a meeting was necessary before things got much worse."

Mrs. Griffler paused, and looked around the table for response. Silence.

"What kinds of problems?" asked Karen, one of the more conscientious students.

"Well, to be more specific, one problem is that the check-out desks often aren't fully staffed," Mrs. Griffler responded. "Library users get rather irritable when they have to wait to check out a book, especially at this time of year when students are writing term papers. Plus, it makes it much easier for people to walk out with books, even with our electronic detection system.

"Also, I've noticed that library books frequently aren't shelved properly, or even shelved at all!" she continued. "I've gone into the stacks sometimes and found piles of books sitting on tables or even on the floor. You know that each of you is responsible for shelving the books returned during your work period."

Janeen, a new student, interrupted. "Yes, but some periods are much busier than others! Lots of people drop off books in the morning on their way to class, and there simply isn't any way that I can reshelve them all before I leave at noon," she complained.

Fern, who had worked in the library longer than anyone else at the table, spoke up. "Well, maybe if you came in on time you'd have the time to do your job properly!"

"You know I've had trouble with my ride in the morning. And the bus doesn't run in my neighborhood," Janeen countered defensively.

Mrs. Griffler intervened. "Well, is it true that most of the books are returned during Janeen's shift?"

Terry broke in. "I really don't think that's accurate. Just as many people drop their books off in the evening on their way home, and I don't have any trouble getting my books reshelved. There are a lot of people who study at the library at night, too, and that means lots of questions and reference books left out. But somehow I manage to get all my work done. Frankly, I'm a little offended at this whole meeting. *Some* of us are doing our jobs, and doing them pretty well for the measly minimum wage the college pays us."

"Terry, I know that you're an excellent worker," Mrs. Griffler replied, "and that we can always count on you to make sure things are done properly. I know you even stay late sometimes to make sure that everything's been taken care of. But the only way these problems will get resolved is if we all work together.

"And Janeen, I know that you have had problems getting here in the morning. But I've also heard reports that you make a lot of personal phone calls from the circulation desk. Is that true?"

"No more than anyone else!" Janeen said. "Fern talks on the phone all the time, and you can't believe the number of times people have come to me with their questions because the so-called information desk was tied up because she was talking to her boyfriend, Erv!"

"That's not true!" Fern said. "I remember the day she's talking about. It only happened once! My boyfriend's grandfather died, and he was really upset. Besides, more than once I've worked overtime without pay putting away the books that Janeen didn't reshelve or waiting for Dean to get here so I could go home. Otherwise there would be no one at the circulation desk at all!"

"Hey, wait a minute!" Dean sat up. "Why should I break my neck to get here on time when Janeen comes strolling in half an hour late?"

Mrs. Griffler sighed. "All of you, calm down!" she said firmly. "Look, the only way for this library to run smoothly is if we all cooperate. But first we have to be responsible for doing our own job well. It's great that some of you are willing to help out by staying late, but it's not fair to expect any of you to cover someone else's responsibilities as well as your own."

Beck interrupted. "Why can't we all just do our own jobs and mind our own business? I don't think it's up to me to worry about everybody else. If they're not getting their work done, hey, that's their problem, not mine! Talk to them about it, but don't breathe down my neck!"

Mrs. Griffler frowned slightly. "The only problem with that attitude is that sometimes we *do* need each other's help. There are rush periods at the library, and sometimes personal factors will interfere with our job performance, even if we try hard to avoid it."

"Now, I think we all agree that books need to be reshelved properly and promptly, and that the circulation desks should *always* be staffed. And I think that we also agree that it is important that each of us be at work on time. So, Janeen and Dean, I'd like you to put forth a little extra effort to get to the library on time. If we continue to have the tardiness problems, we'll have to put in a time clock for work-study students. I think that's only fair.

"The problem of reshelving books seems a little more complicated. Perhaps the rule that everyone reshelve all the books that are returned on his or her shift is a little rigid. I have noticed that some shifts are definitely busier than others. The early morning seems to have fewer people asking questions, but a lot of books in the overnight book drops that need to be reshelved. Does anyone have any suggestions for handling this problem?"

332

CHAPTER 10
COORDINATION IN
WORK SETTINGS:
COOPERATION,
COMPETITION, OR
CONFLICT

Paul spoke up. "Nobody really seems to know how many books are returned during the different shifts, how many people are checking out books, or how many people are calling the information desk. Maybe if we tracked all this stuff for a couple of weeks, we'd have a better idea of what's fair."

"That's fair!" Asha agreed from across the table. "If we knew when most of the books were returned, we could plan to have more staff time devoted to the shelving rather than the circulation desk. Or maybe the next shift would know that they would be expected to reshelve some of the books from the earlier shift."

Mrs. Griffler smiled. "That's an excellent idea! Paul, I want you, Fern, Janeen, and Asha to work on putting together a tracking system for library use. We'll circulate it to the entire staff. Now, you're an intelligent group of students—that's why you have scholarships. What other great ideas are you hiding?"

Questions

1. What were some of the causes of the problems in the library? What principles of cooperation and conflict were operating?

2. Were different orientations toward coordination displayed at the meeting? Which students seemed to be cooperators? Competitors? Individualists?

3. Evaluate Mrs. Griffler's method of conflict management. What principles did she follow? Was she successful or unsuccessful?

4. What additional steps would you recommend to handle the problems in the library? What would you do to make sure that they don't recur?

Conflict and the Question "Why?"

Suppose that another person thwarts your interests or goals—how will you react? Your first answer might be "with anger" or "with attempts to pay him or her back." But think again: The answer is actually "it depends." And what it depends on, quite strongly, is your interpretation of the reasons behind the other's action. In short, it is not simply what others do that matters; our explanations for why they have acted in these ways is important too. To see why this is so, consider the following situation.

You and another person represent different departments in a single company. You face the task of dividing some money between your two units. Your opponent acts in a confrontational manner, demanding the lion's share of the funds. How will you react? As noted above, the answer depends on your understanding of the causes of the confrontational behavior. For each of the potential causes below, indicate how likely you would be to become angry with your opponent. Write a number from 1 (not likely) to 7 (very likely) in the blank space next to each cause.

_____ 1. The behavior stemmed mainly from external causes (e.g., orders from the department to behave this way).

—— **2.** The behavior stemmed mainly from sincere beliefs that his (her) department is really more deserving of the funds.

—— **3.** The behavior stemmed mainly from a competitive personality.

—— **4.** The behavior stemmed mainly from the fact that he (she) is temporarily in a bad mood.

If you are like most people, you probably wrote the highest number next to the third term, and somewhat lower numbers next to the others. The reason behind this is clear: We are not more likely to blame others for negative behavior, and to become angry with them, when it seems to stem from their own traits or motives than when it seems to derive from other causes. Such attributions play an important role in many aspects of human relations, and conflict is certainly no exception to this general rule.

CHAPTER 11

Work-Related Attitudes: Job Satisfaction

Learning Objectives

After reading this chapter,
you should be able to:

1. Indicate how job satisfaction can be
   measured.

2. List a number of different factors that
   influence job satisfaction.

3. Describe the prevalence of job
   satisfaction.

4. Outline the major effects of job
   satisfaction in work settings and
   elsewhere.

im Byrne has really been looking forward to his ten-year high school class reunion, and now he can hardly believe it is really happening. He's having a great time seeing all his old friends, and even some of his old enemies. A lot of talk is centering on jobs. Most of his friends went to college and have spent a few years developing their careers. Although they seem generally happy with their jobs, some of them openly admit they're not very happy with their present situation. One of these is his best friend, Jeff Hyland. He's an accountant with a hospital supply company.

"I can't complain about the benefits," he says, "but there just isn't enough work to keep me busy. It's the same old stuff every week and there is no chance for advancement since there's only one accountant position."

"That's too bad," said Tim sympathetically. "I really like my job as toy buyer for Sanger Harris."

Sanger Harris is a large chain of up-scale department stores. Tim gets to travel to various toy shows as far away as Hong Kong.

"What I like best about my job is that my bosses are really supportive. They know it takes a few years to learn the ropes. It's also nice to know that if you're successful you can move up the corporate ladder pretty quickly. Hey, Jeff, let's get off this job talk and talk about what's really important, old times. Remember when . . ."

As you can readily see, **job satisfaction** is of great practical importance. It is only reasonable to assume that individuals who hold mainly positive *attitudes* toward their jobs or their companies will often behave very differently from those who hold negative views in these respects (see Figure 11.1). There is a large body of research findings suggesting that this is in fact the case,[1] but it is important to note that job satisfaction does not always influence on-the-job behavior in ways you might predict. Similarly, it is not always enhanced by factors or techniques that might seem, at first, to be useful in this respect. Job satisfaction also seems to exert far-ranging and often unexpected effects on behavior outside work settings as well.[2]

The present chapter summarizes existing knowledge about several key aspects of job satisfaction. First, it will indicate how such reactions are measured and made visible. Second, it will examine some of the major causes of job satisfaction—factors that tend to enhance or reduce its presence. Third, it will focus on the prevalence of job satisfaction—the extent to which employees are generally satisfied or dissatisfied with their work. And finally, it will address the effects of job satisfaction—the impact of such attitudes on a wide range of work-related behaviors.

FIGURE 11.1 Employee Attitudes: How They Affect Job Behavior
The attitudes of employees toward their jobs may have an important influence on on-the-job behavior. (Cathy © 1989 Universal Press Syndicate. Reprinted with permission. All rights reserved.)

MEASUREMENT OF JOB SATISFACTION: ASSESSING REACTIONS TO WORK

As you probably already know, individuals do not go about proclaiming their attitudes to everyone they meet. On the contrary, they generally keep their views on politics, religion, sex, and other matters important to them. Attitudes about work are no exception to this general rule. In fact, most persons express these views in an open and frank manner only to a select group of friends or relatives— and certainly not to their managers or supervisors. For this reason, measuring job satisfaction is often a tougher task than you might at first assume. Fortunately, however, several techniques for assessing this important aspect of the work environment exist. Among the most useful of these are (1) indirect methods, based on *employee behavior;* (2) *confrontation meetings* or gripe sessions; and (3) systematic *job satisfaction surveys.*

Indirect Methods: Gauging Job Satisfaction from Employee Behavior

Suppose that a company adopts a new pay plan. Within three months, the number of employees quitting rises sharply. Does this change tell us anything about reactions to the plan, and workers' satisfaction with their jobs? Probably, it does. And in this case, the message is negative: For some reason, the pay plan has sharply reduced employee morale. Now consider another example. A manager learns that 5 percent of the employees in this company are absent each day. In contrast, fully 10 percent of the employees at the competing firm are absent. Does this tell him anything about the relative levels of satisfaction in the two businesses? It does. And here, the manager has reason to be pleased: It appears that workers in his company are more satisfied than the competitor's. Of course, factors other than job satisfaction may contribute to this difference. (For example, the competitor's plant may be located in a less convenient spot.) But assuming that such variables do not play a role, the lower rate of absenteeism at the manager's own plant suggests higher employee morale.

We could consider other examples, but the main point is clear: We can often learn much about employee satisfaction (or dissatisfaction) through indirect means. Specifically, we can gain such knowledge by examining changes in certain aspects of employees' behavior, or by comparing their actions with those of other groups of workers. Changes or differences in turnover, absenteeism, lateness, grievances, output, thefts, and even accidents may all point to shifts in job satisfaction, or to contrasting levels of satisfaction among various groups of employees. In some cases, then, we can learn much about such critical, work-related attitudes without asking anyone about them.

Confrontation Meetings: Getting Gripes Out into the Open

Another useful technique for measuring job satisfaction involves special meetings in which individuals are encouraged to "lay it on the line," and discuss their pet peeves and complaints. If such sessions are conducted with care, problems that might otherwise remain hidden may be brought out into the open (see Figure 11.2). Then steps can be taken to correct or eliminate them. One danger in such meetings, of course, is that emotions tend to rise, so that even fairly minor problems may be blown up into seemingly large ones. However, this can usually be avoided by urging participants to emphasize the positive—not only calling attention to problems but also suggesting ways of dealing with them. When this is done, **confrontation meetings** can be a useful technique for learning about—

FIGURE 11.2 Confrontation Sessions: One Way of Measuring Job Satisfaction
Confrontation meetings or gripe sessions can often provide useful information on current job satisfaction among employees.

and coming to grips with—factors or situations that tend to reduce employee morale.

Questionnaires and Surveys: Measuring Job Satisfaction through Self-Report

While job satisfaction is often measured through the behavioral means outlined above, the most common approach involves the use of special *surveys* or *questionnaires*. Briefly, employees are asked to complete special forms on which they report or rate their current reactions to their jobs. A number of scales have been developed for this purpose, and they vary greatly in scope. For example, in the popular **Job Descriptive Index,** or JDI, individuals are presented with lists of adjectives and asked to indicate whether each one does or does not describe a particular aspect of their work.[3] An interesting feature of this scale is that it measures reactions to five distinct aspects of jobs: the work itself, pay, promotion opportunities, supervision, and people (co-workers).

In another widely used measure of job satisfaction (the *Minnesota Satisfaction Questionnaire*), individuals rate the extent to which they are satisfied with various aspects of their present job (e.g., their degree of responsibility, opportunities for advancement, and pay[4]). Such ratings range from "not at all satisfied" on the one hand to "extremely satisfied" on the other. Obviously, the higher the ratings individuals report, the greater their degree of satisfaction with various aspects of their job.

Other scales relating to job satisfaction focus, in more detail, on specific facets of such attitudes. For example, the **Pay Satisfaction Questionnaire,** as its name suggests, is primarily concerned with attitudes about various aspects of pay. This scale measures individuals' reactions to *pay level* (how much they actually receive), *raises, pay structure, and administration* (how pay is allocated by rank, and how it is actually distributed to employees—weekly, monthly, and so on), and *benefits* (sick leave, vacations, insurance, etc.)[5] Items similar to those included on this scale and the other scales discussed are presented in Table 11.1.

By means of these and other surveys, a fairly clear picture of employee satisfaction and dissatisfaction can generally be acquired. As we will soon see, this information is often quite useful in predicting turnover, absenteeism, and other aspects of work-related behavior. Thus information on employees' attitudes toward their jobs can often be of great practical value.

JOB SATISFACTION: SOME MAJOR CAUSES

Job satisfaction varies greatly from individual to individual and also from organization to organization. While some persons report mainly positive reactions

TABLE 11.1
A Sample of Items Measuring Job Satisfaction

The items shown here are similar to those used on three popular measures of job satisfaction. (Note that the items shown are *not* identical to those on the actual scales.) *Source:* Based on items from the JDI, MSQ, and PSQ; see Notes 3, 4, and 5.

Job Descriptive Index (JDI)

Enter "Yes," "No," or "?" for each description or word below.

Work itself:	_____	Routine
	_____	Satisfactory
	_____	Good
Promotions:	_____	Dead-end job
	_____	Few promotions
	_____	Good opportunity for promotion

Minnesota Satisfaction Questionnaire (MSQ)

Indicate the extent to which you are satisfied with each aspect of your present job. Enter one number next to each aspect.

1 = Not at all satisfied
2 = Not satisfied
3 = Neither satisfied nor dissatisfied
4 = Satisfied
5 = Extremely satisfied

_____ Utilization of your abilities

_____ Authority

_____ Company policies and practices

_____ Independence

_____ Supervision-human relations

Pay Satisfaction Questionnaire

Item	Aspect of pay
My current pay	Pay level
Size of my salary	Pay level
Typical raises	Raises
How raises are determined	Raises
Number of benefits	Benefits

to their work, others offer nonstop gripes about real or imagined problems. Further, while morale and satisfaction are high in some companies, they are low or almost nonexistent in others. Why is this so?

What factors contribute to job satisfaction or dissatisfaction? The answer to this question has obvious practical value, for if we understand the causes of job satisfaction (or dissatisfaction), we can take appropriate steps to increase positive attitudes among employees. You will not be surprised to learn, therefore, that efforts to solve this particular puzzle have continued without pause for several decades. The results of this ongoing work have been revealing. But taken as a whole, they point to the following general conclusion: *Understanding job satisfaction is a complex task.* Many different factors seem to contribute to satisfaction or dissatisfaction among employees. In fact, so many of these exist that it would be impossible to examine all of them here. Instead, we will focus on those that seem to be among the most important. While these are highly diverse, they generally fall into two major groups: Factors relating to work settings and factors relating to individuals.

Focus on Work Settings: External Causes of Job Satisfaction

Most research on the causes of job satisfaction has focused on various aspects of work settings themselves—on conditions faced by employees that either increase or reduce their satisfaction with their jobs. Here, everything from the nature of the work being performed to reward systems and relations with co-workers or supervisors appear to play a role.

First, with respect to work itself, job satisfaction is enhanced by tasks that are mentally challenging and interesting but not too tiring. In short, people like to be challenged but not overwhelmed.

A second group of factors affecting employees' attitudes toward their jobs centers around the *reward system* used by an organization—the procedures followed in distributing such benefits as raises, bonuses, and promotions. Growing evidence indicates that job satisfaction is enhanced by systems that are fair (e.g., ones that distribute rewards in accordance with each person's contributions), and ones that afford individuals a feeling of control—the belief that they can influence the rewards they receive. In contrast, systems that omit either of these conditions tend to produce lower levels of reported satisfaction among employees.

General working conditions, too, can strongly affect positive or negative attitudes toward one's job. In most cases, a work environment that is comfortable, and relatively low in physical and psychological stress, and one that facilitates the attainment of work goals will tend to produce high levels of satisfaction among employees.[6] In contrast, environments that are uncomfortable, high in stress, or prevent achievement of work goals tend to lead to low levels of reported job satisfaction (see Figure 11.3).

Still another set of factors affecting employee attitudes centers around interpersonal relations.[7] Friendly, positive relations with co-workers and supervisors contribute to high levels of job satisfaction. Negative relations, in contrast, tend to be associated with lower levels of satisfaction. Similarly, participation in work-related decisions can contribute to positive attitudes among employees; exclusion from this process may have the opposite effect. Finally, employees tend to report higher levels of job satisfaction when they are surrounded by others who share their major values. When, in contrast, they find themselves in contact with persons

FIGURE 11.3 Working Conditions: One Factor in Job Satisfaction
Our satisfaction with our job may be influenced by working conditions. Do you think the two different environments shown above will yield very different job-satisfaction levels?

holding different views or beliefs (either about work or other matters), they may react negatively.

Of course, many other aspects of work settings, too, can affect the attitudes of employees toward their jobs. But the ones mentioned here seem to be among the most important and the most general in their effects.

Focus on Individuals: Internal Causes of Job Satisfaction

Have you ever known someone who was easy to please—someone who was satisfied under almost any conditions? Similarly, have you ever known someone who was just the opposite—an individual who was almost never happy, no matter how many benefits he or she enjoyed? (See Figure 11.4.) Probably, you have known people of both types, which points to another major set of factors affecting job satisfaction: personal characteristics of individuals. In short, there are certain traits or perspectives that people carry with them from situation to situation that may strongly affect their degree of satisfaction with any given job. So far, researchers have directed less attention to such factors than to ones directly involved with work settings. But we can at least mention a few that have already been identified.

First, individuals who are high in self-esteem or who have a positive self-image appear to be more satisfied with their jobs than persons who are low in self-esteem or who have a negative self-image.[8] Perhaps this is because high self-esteem persons tend to perceive everything they do in a favorable light. Or perhaps it is because they are actually more competent and successful than others. Whatever the reason, the higher an individual's self-image, the more likely he or she is to report being happy and satisfied on the job.

Similarly, persons who are high in the ability to withstand stress tend to report higher job satisfaction than persons low in this ability.[9] Third, individuals who believe that they can influence or control their own outcomes tend to report higher job satisfaction than those who feel that such outcomes are outside their personal influence.[10] Finally, persons who are high in status and seniority often report higher levels of satisfaction than ones who are low in status or seniority.[11] Such findings probably stem, at least in part, from the fact that persons in the former group actually enjoy better working conditions than those in the latter. However, they may also reflect the fact that persons happy in a given job or organization tend to remain in it, and thus are higher in status and seniority as a result of their positive attitudes.

Furthermore, individuals with positive expectations about their jobs—especially about the job's ability to satisfy basic needs—appear to be higher in satisfaction than those lacking in such expectations. Evidence for this intriguing conclusion is provided by a study carried out by Pulakos and Schmitt.[12] These

FIGURE 11.4 The Constant Complainer: One Internal Cause of Job Dissatisfaction
Some employees always seem to be dissatisfied, no matter what benefits are provided. This demonstrates the important role of internal causes of job satisfaction. (Reprinted with special permission of King Features Syndicate.)

researchers asked graduating high school seniors to rate the importance of various outcomes they hoped to attain from their future jobs (e.g., good pay, security, new skills, and knowledge), and also to rate the likelihood that their jobs would provide these outcomes. Then, at nine and again at twenty months after graduation, the same individuals completed a measure of job satisfaction. Results were clear: the more positive participants' initial expectations about their future jobs, the higher their reported satisfaction with them after they had gained employment. These findings, and those of other studies, suggest that positive expectations may often be fulfilled, at least with respect to job satisfaction. However, note that there are definite limits to this relationship. Positive expectations may foster high levels of job satisfaction as long as such expectations are *realistic* and have some chance of being met. If they are unreasonably high, bitter disappointment may result, and satisfaction may, in the long run, be reduced.[13] For this reason, it is important for organizations to avoid building up false hopes among prospective employees. If they do, they may well be setting the stage for disillusionment and other negative reactions. (See the **Case in Point** section below for a concrete example of such efforts.) As long as these pitfalls are avoided and expectations

CASE IN POINT

On the Costs of Shattered Dreams

As the door swings shut behind him, Todd Defollett turns and gives it an ironic salute: "So long, Standard," he mutters. "Am I ever glad to be leaving you!"

Todd has just come from his exit interview with Pam Tilset, the director of personnel. It had been pleasant enough, but he was glad it is over and that he is now officially "out." As he walks down the path toward the parking garage, Todd remembers his interview with Hector Polenti eighteen months earlier. That meeting, too, had been very pleasant. In fact, it had led directly to his being offered, and his accepting, a job at Standard Industries. When he left the building on *that* day, his mind had been filled with images of a challenging and rewarding career. The type of work he'd be doing, the opportunities for advancement, general working conditions—all had sounded great. In fact, for several days after the interview he had been on pins and needles, just hoping the phone would ring. When it did and he learned that he had the job, he literally jumped into the air for joy.

And then came reality, with all its disappointments and disillusionment. He had been promised a great deal of freedom and autonomy; none was delivered. He had been told he would participate in the decision-making process; this was not the case. He had been given a glowing description of the daily work he would do; it turned out to be painfully dull and repetitive. And no one had bothered to inform him about the required hours of overtime on Saturdays, the tedious about one's job remain realistic, however, a positive, hopeful approach may be a major "plus."

Finally, and not surprisingly, it appears that people who enjoy good personal adjustment away from work tend to report greater satisfaction with their jobs than those whose personal lives are marked by stress and unhappiness. This may be the case because the same skills that help well-adjusted persons succeed in their personal lives are also useful to them in work settings (e.g., the ability to get along with others, a high degree of self-confidence). Whatever the reason, individuals who are happy and well-adjusted off the job also tend to be satisfied on the job as well.

345

THE PREVALENCE OF JOB SATISFACTION: HOW MUCH DO PEOPLE LIKE THEIR WORK?

THE PREVALENCE OF JOB SATISFACTION: HOW MUCH DO PEOPLE LIKE THEIR WORK?

Suppose that you approached a large sample of individuals doing many different jobs in many locations and asked them to rate their satisfaction with their

---

travel he had to do, or the pointless forms required by the company for almost everything. Yes, he had been misled all right, and he was still angry about it. In fact, his feeling of having been "had" was one of his major reasons for quitting.

If only they had told me the truth, Todd muses to himself. Maybe then I wouldn't have been so disappointed. I mean, really, conditions at Standard aren't all that bad. Plus, the job market is pretty tight right now. But they led me to expect far too much, so it was a big letdown when I found out what was really going on. I don't like being told a pack of lies, and I doubt that many other people do either. Misleading new people like that is a big mistake—it makes them mistrustful of the whole company. Yeah, I've had enough. Let them find someone else to play the sucker game. I'd rather work someplace where I know what I'm getting into.

Questions

1. Do you think Todd's major reason for leaving is really the gap between what he was promised and what his job was really like? Or are other factors involved?

2. If you were running Standard Industries, would you change this policy of promising new employees more than the company can actually deliver?

3. Why do you think Standard Industries adopted this tactic to begin with?

4. What else could Todd have done, aside from quitting, to change the situation?

work. What would you find? Would you report a reasonable degree of satisfaction? Would you be deluged with complaints and strong statements of dissatisfaction? Judging from images of the world of work contained in recent movies and magazine articles, you might predict the latter outcome—that is, you might expect to uncover huge pools of anger and discontent. Few characters in films are shown enjoying their work, and many articles in newspapers and periodicals focus on the boredom and despair experienced by industrial and even white-collar workers. Surprisingly, though, large-scale surveys of job satisfaction do not support this gloomy picture. On the contrary, most point to the conclusion that a large majority of persons are relatively satisfied with their jobs. For example, one survey that has continued for more than twenty years indicates that between 81 and 92 percent of employees are reasonably happy with their jobs (see Figure 11.5).[14]

Such findings paint a comforting picture of conditions in work settings. But how do they square with such facts as rising **absenteeism** and **turnover** in many businesses, major declines in productivity (which have only recently begun to be reversed), and the growing incidence of industrial theft and sabotage? If workers are so happy with their jobs, why do such conditions exist? The answer, it appears, is this: The overall situation is far more complex than first meets the eye.

First, while job satisfaction is generally high, these positive reactions are not

FIGURE 11.5 Reported Job Satisfaction: Higher than You Might Guess
Contrary to popular belief, most persons report being quite satisfied with their jobs. Further, job satisfaction has neither increased nor decreased greatly in recent decades. *Source:* Based on data from Quinn and Staines (1979); see Note 14.

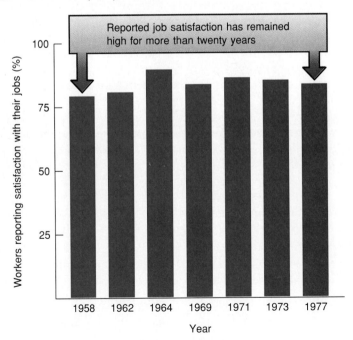

uniform across all aspects of work and work settings. For example, satisfaction with pay is generally lower than satisfaction with quality of supervision or with such factors as having enough time, help, and equipment to get one's job done properly. Thus when we ask "how satisfied are employees generally?" we may overlook important aspects of this issue.

347

THE PREVALENCE OF JOB SATISFACTION: HOW MUCH DO PEOPLE LIKE THEIR WORK?

Second, in some respects, the high levels of satisfaction noted above may be more apparent than real. In fact, they may stem as much from the way in which job satisfaction is measured as from high levels of positive reactions among employees. That this is the case is suggested by the findings of several studies in which employees were asked to indicate whether they would choose the same work again if they could start all over. The results of such investigations have been less encouraging than those reported earlier. For example, only 41 percent of all white-collar workers surveyed reported that they would choose the same line of work again. Among blue-collar employees, the figure was only 24 percent.[15] In short, many persons seem to feel that they would be happier in some other career.

But if this is so, why do so many report that they are satisfied with their present jobs? Many factors probably play a role in producing this puzzling pattern (e.g., strong feelings about the necessity of holding a job, the desire to avoid looking like a constant complainer). One of the most important of these may involve the operation of a process known as **cognitive dissonance.** Briefly, this refers to the fact that human beings strongly dislike inconsistency. They dislike inconsistency between various attitudes they hold (for example, if one attitude contradicts the other). Also, they dislike inconsistency between their attitudes and their overt behavior.[16] In fact, when either type of inconsistency occurs, they experience an unpleasant state known as *dissonance,* and they often attempt to reduce or eliminate its presence.

Now consider how cognitive dissonance may contribute to the strong tendency of most persons to report liking their current jobs. In general, individuals realize they will probably have to stay in the job they now hold or one quite similar to it—economic conditions rarely permit the luxury of great job-to-job mobility. Thus, if they report being dissatisfied with their job, dissonance may result. After all, stating that one dislikes one's job is inconsistent with the knowledge that holding it is a fairly permanent (and necessary) fact of life. In order to avoid such inconsistency, therefore, many persons may choose to both describe and view their jobs in a relatively favorable light. By doing so, they can avoid unpleasant feelings of inconsistency or dissonance; and as you well know, holding all forms of discomfort to a minimum is a basic principle of human life! At the moment, no direct evidence exists for the contribution of dissonance to the high levels of job satisfaction uncovered in many surveys. However, an extensive body of research does support the impact of dissonance on many other types of attitudes. Thus the possibility that it also affects reported job satisfaction seems feasible.

A third important factor to keep in mind concerning the prevalence of job satisfaction is this: It varies greatly across different groups of employees. As you might expect, managers, technical and professional workers, and the self-employed generally report higher satisfaction than blue-collar personnel.[17] Similarly, older workers often report greater satisfaction with their jobs than younger ones. Members of minority groups tend to indicate lower overall levels of satisfaction than do others. Finally, there appear to be some differences between males and females in this respect, although the pattern here seems to be changing. In the past, it was often found that men reported higher job satisfaction than women. Recent investigations indicate, however, that such differences may be declining, perhaps because of the removal of many barriers to female employment and advancement.[18] Yet some differences continue to exist.

In one investigation on this topic, Varca, Shaffer and McCauley measured job satisfaction among 400 college graduates (half male, half female).[19] Important differences between the sexes were uncovered, at least with respect to satisfaction with pay and opportunities for promotion. Among persons holding relatively high-level jobs (e.g., marketing manager), males reported greater satisfaction than females. Among those holding low-level jobs (e.g., waitress), in contrast, the pattern was reversed. Here, females reported greater satisfaction with their current jobs than did males (see Figure 11.6). One possible explanation for these results may involve the specific *reference groups* chosen by males and females—the groups

FIGURE 11.6   Job Satisfaction: Some Intriguing Sex Differences
Among persons holding high-level jobs, males report greater satisfaction with pay and promotion opportunities than females. Among persons holding low-level jobs, the opposite seems to be true—females report greater satisfaction. *Source:* Varca, Shaffer, and McCauley (1983); see Note 19.

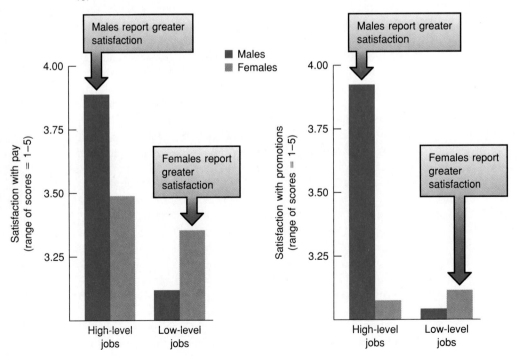

with whom they choose to compare themselves, in order to determine how well they are doing in their jobs. Females holding low-level jobs may compare their pay and promotion opportunities only with those of other women holding the same kind of position. As a result, they tend to be relatively satisfied with the outcome. In contrast, males holding such jobs may compare themselves with persons holding higher level positions, and so become dissatisfied. Similarly, females in higher level occupations may compare their pay and promotion opportunities with those of males holding similar jobs. If, as was often true in the past, they observe a disparity in favor of the men, their job satisfaction may be sharply reduced. At the moment, it is difficult to determine whether these or other factors contributed to the results observed by Varca, Shaffer, and McCauley. Whatever the causes, however, one point is clear: Important differences in job satisfaction continue to exist between the sexes and should not be overlooked.

JOB SATISFACTION: WHAT ARE ITS EFFECTS?

Throughout this discussion we have made an important implicit assumption: that job satisfaction exerts strong effects on behavior in work settings. On the face of it, this is an eminently reasonable suggestion. After all, the way people feel and think about their jobs should in fact influence the way in which they perform them. But is this really the case? Actually, we gave the game away earlier when we noted that many research findings point to an important job satisfaction–work behavior link. You may also recall that we noted that the impact of job satisfaction on work behavior is not always straightforward. In fact, as we shall soon see, it is sometimes downright puzzling!

Why is this the case? Part of the answer lies in the fact that job satisfaction is an attitude (or, perhaps, a cluster of related attitudes). And attitudes, in turn, do not always affect behavior in a simple or clear-cut way. Sometimes attitudes direct our words and deeds, and sometimes they do not. Many factors (e.g., the strength of our views, their degree of specificity) seem to determine which of these outcomes prevails. For example, many people continue to smoke despite knowing this is harmful to their health. Most of us have occasionally said things we don't really believe because good manners or plain common sense require us to do so. Given that the link between attitudes and behavior is quite complex, it is not surprising that the impact of job satisfaction on many work settings is also far from simple. Keep this fact in mind as we examine some of its major effects.

Job Satisfaction, Absenteeism, and Turnover

Imagine two employees, both of whom hate to get up in the morning and dislike fighting their way through the morning rush hour to work. One likes her job very much while the other dislikes it. Which is more likely to call in sick or miss work for other reasons? The answer is obvious: The one who dislikes her job. That job satisfaction does affect absence from work in this manner is indicated by the findings of many investigations. In general, these studies report that the lower an individual's satisfaction with his or her job, the more likely that person is to be absent from work.[20] The strength of this relationship, though, is quite modest. That is, while job satisfaction exerts some effect on absenteeism, its impact is far from overpowering.

Similar findings have been obtained with respect to turnover. Once more, the lower an individual's level of satisfaction with his or her job, the more likely this person is to resign and seek other opportunities. Again, the strength of this relationship is modest.[21] This fact, in turn, raises an interesting question: Why aren't the links between job satisfaction and both absenteeism and turnover even stronger? The answer is simple: These behaviors—as well as others relating to work—are affected by many factors. Job satisfaction is only one of these. To mention just two illustrations of this point, absence from work is probably affected by weather, traffic conditions, and the distance employees must travel to work, as well as by their attitudes toward their jobs. Similarly, turnover is probably affected by general economic conditions and alternative employment opportunities, as well as by job satisfaction.[22] In view of the impact of these and many other factors, it is not surprising that the relationship between job satisfaction and turnover or absenteeism is so modest. Indeed, it would be far more surprising if these links were extremely powerful. (The link between job satisfaction and absenteeism can be demonstrated by following the instructions in the **Human Relations in Action** section on pages 352–53.)

Job Satisfaction and Productivity: The Missing Link?

It has often been assumed that happy workers are productive workers, and at first glance this assertion makes good sense. Won't persons who are pleased with their jobs put out more effort than those who are unhappy and dissatisfied? Such arguments seem persuasive, and even today most managers seem to accept them as valid. Actually, though, there is little support for their validity. Most studies designed to examine the possibility of a link between job satisfaction and productivity have yielded negative results. Contrary to what "common sense" suggests, productivity does *not* seem to rise with increased satisfaction or to fall with growing dissatisfaction.[23] While this finding may strike you as puzzling, there are several reasons for its existence. We will touch on three of these here.

First, in many work settings, there is little room for large changes in performance. Jobs are structured so that the persons holding them must perform at a minimal level. If they do not, they cannot retain the position. But there is also little room for *exceeding* this standard. Even if an employee speeds up his or her own output, this may be useless if co-workers continue to work at the same pace. Given the interdependence of employees in most businesses, the individual putting out maximum effort may find that co-workers may simply not be ready to benefit from what this person produces. In short, in many cases, even high levels of job satisfaction can do little to raise productivity. As a result, the potential link between these variables is weakened.

Second, certain values held by individuals may sometimes be more important in determining their job-related behavior than positive or negative attitudes toward their work. For example, individuals who believe firmly in the value and necessity of work will probably demonstrate a high level of effort even if they detest their jobs. Similarly, persons who desire the approval of others may voluntarily restrict their own output to avoid "showing up" their co-workers, even if they greatly enjoy their work. In these and many related instances, job satisfaction may fail to exert strong or direct effects on performance.

Finally, it may actually be the case that job satisfaction and productivity are not directly linked. Rather, any apparent relationship between them may stem from the fact that both are related to a third factor—the receipt of various rewards. As suggested by Porter and Lawler, the situation may go something like this.[24] Job performance leads to various rewards (e.g., pay, promotion, feelings of accomplishment). If these are judged to be fair, the individuals involved may come to perceive a contingency between their performance and these rewards. This, in turn, may have two effects. First, it may encourage high levels of effort and so good performance. Second, it may lead to a high level of job satisfaction. In short, high productivity and high satisfaction may both stem from the same conditions. The two factors themselves, however, are not directly linked. (See Figure 11.7 for a summary of these suggestions.)

For these and other reasons, job satisfaction may fail to exert direct effects

FIGURE 11.7 Job Satisfaction and Performance: One Explanation for the Absence of a Strong Link
According to Porter and Lawler, job satisfaction and performance are not directly linked. Instead, both stem from employees' perceptions that there is a contingency between their output and the rewards they receive. *Source:* Based on suggestions by Porter and Lawler (1968); see Note 24.

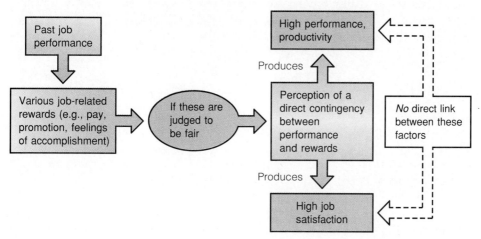

on productivity. As already noted, though, it does appear to influence both absenteeism and turnover. Further, it may also affect additional aspects of job performance, such as the rate at which new skills are mastered, or the frequency of what have been termed "citizenship behaviors"—actions by employees that serve to "lubricate the social machinery" of their organization. These include helping co-workers with their jobs, promoting a positive work climate, cheerfully putting up with temporary inconveniences, and similar helpful actions. While such behaviors are not directly reported in weekly summaries of output or sales, they

HUMAN RELATIONS IN ACTION

Job Satisfaction and Absenteeism: Seeing for Yourself

While job satisfaction exerts only a modest impact upon absence from work, you can readily demonstrate this effect for yourself. In order to do so, you must first obtain the cooperation of about ten to twenty currently employed people. Once you do, proceed as follows:

1. Have them complete the self-checklist below. (This is a brief measure of job satisfaction.)

2. Have them indicate the total number of times they have been absent from work during the past year.

3. Enter a point corresponding to each person's job satisfaction and absences on the graph. Then, draw a line around all of these points. The

A Self-Checklist

For each item, circle one number to indicate how you feel.

On My Current Job This Is How I Feel About:	Not at All Satisfied	Slightly Satisfied	Satisfied	Very Satisfied	Extremely Satisfied
1. My pay	1	2	3	4	5
2. My work itself	1	2	3	4	5
3. My working conditions	1	2	3	4	5
4. My co-workers	1	2	3	4	5
5. My level of responsibility	1	2	3	4	5
6. My supervision	1	2	3	4	5

can greatly enhance the smooth functioning of an organization. Thus they represent an important contribution of high levels of job satisfaction to organizational effectiveness.[25]

Job Satisfaction and Life Satisfaction: Is There a "Spillover"?

Work is an important part of our daily lives. In fact, for most of us, it forms a central aspect of our self-concept. We define ourselves, at least in part, by our careers or professions. Further, while fantasies of a life of total leisure are in-

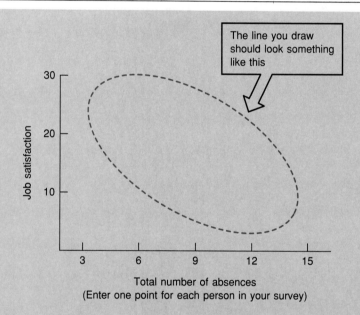

figure you see will probably be an ellipse (something shaped like a fat sausage or the Goodyear blimp). And it will probably point downward toward the right. The thinner it is, the stronger the relationship (correlation) between job satisfaction and absenteeism you have uncovered. The fact that the ellipse points down and to the right indicates that the higher the job satisfaction, the less likely individuals are to be absent from work.

To score the checklist, simply add the numbers circled by each participant. Scores range from 6, indicating very low job satisfaction, through 30, indicating very high job satisfaction.

triguing to say the least, few people can really imagine a full or satisfying life that does not involve some type of productive work. Given these facts, it makes sense to ask the following question: Does satisfaction with one's career or job spill over into one's personal life? The answer suggested by research findings appears to be yes. A number of studies indicate that satisfaction on the job is indeed related to satisfaction with one's life in general.[26] Moreover, at least one investigation suggests that this link is a causal one.[27] That is, changes in job satisfaction do in fact appear to cause changes in general **life satisfaction.** (In contrast, evidence for an impact of general life satisfaction on job satisfaction is somewhat weaker.) It has also been found that when men come home from work, stressed and fatigued, they have a reduced involvement in housework and an increase in negative marital interactions.[28] The findings on "spillover" suggest that efforts to enhance employees' satisfaction with their jobs and reduce their stress may yield handsome rewards indeed. Not only will they improve the quality of life at work; they may also enhance the quality of life in general. Certainly these are benefits worth pursuing.

Job Satisfaction and Personal Health

Before concluding, we can add one final bit of icing to the cake: Additional evidence suggests that job satisfaction can even contribute to personal health. First, it has been found that such satisfaction is linked to longevity: Persons satisfied with their jobs actually tend to live longer than those who are dissatisfied with their jobs![29] Second, high levels of job satisfaction are associated with several aspects of mental well-being, such as reduced anxiety, high self-esteem, and good social adjustment.[30] If managers or organizations needed any further inducement for paying close attention to the satisfaction of their employees (as well as their own), these intriguing results provide it. As was stated at the start of this chapter, employees' attitudes toward their jobs definitely seem to exert important and far-reaching effects on many aspects of their behavior.

SUMMARY

Attitudes held by individuals about their work are often termed **job satisfaction.** Such reactions can be measured by indirect means (e.g., by observing changes in absenteeism or turnover), through confrontation meetings, or by means of systematic questionnaires and surveys.

Job satisfaction is influenced by a wide range of factors. Many of these involve various aspects of work settings, such as the work itself, the reward systems employed by an organization, and general work conditions. In addition, interpersonal relations between employees or between employees and supervisors are important. Other factors affecting job satisfaction involve certain characteristics of individual employees, such as their self-esteem or expectations about their jobs.

Contrary to popular belief, most individuals report a fairly high level of satisfaction with their jobs. However, such satisfaction may be more apparent than real. For example, it may stem from individuals' realization that they have little choice but to work. Job satisfaction also differs across various groups of employees. It is higher among professional and technical workers than among blue-collar workers, and higher among older than younger employees. Women tend to report lower levels of job satisfaction than men, especially when they occupy high-status jobs.

Job satisfaction is related both to employee *turnover* and *absence from work*. However, it does not exert clear or consistent effects upon performance. High levels of job satisfaction appear to spill over into general life satisfaction and may even enhance personal health.

KEY TERMS

absenteeism: Occasions on which employees are absent from work. Absenteeism is one aspect of work-related behavior affected by job satisfaction.

cognitive dissonance: An unpleasant state that occurs when individuals become aware of inconsistency between their attitudes, or between their attitudes and their behavior.

confrontation meetings: Special sessions in which employees are given an opportunity to voice their complaints and call attention to specific organizational problems. Comments made during such meetings can provide a useful index of current job satisfaction.

job descriptive index (JDI): A widely used measure of job satisfaction in which individuals indicate whether various adjectives describe particular aspects of their jobs.

job satisfaction: The degree of positive attitudes felt toward a job.

life satisfaction: The level of satisfaction felt about life away from work.

pay satisfaction questionnaire: A measure of job satisfaction that measures attitudes about various aspects of one's pay.

turnover: The rate at which employees quit or otherwise voluntarily leave their jobs.

NOTES

1. Locke, E.A. (1976). "The Nature and Causes of Job Satisfaction." In M. Dunnette, ed. *Handbook of Industrial and Organizational Psychology.* Chicago: Rand McNally.

2. Orpen, R.P. (1978). "Work and Nonwork Satisfaction: A Causal-Correlational Analysis." *Journal of Applied Psychology, 63,* 530–32.

3. Smith, P.C., Kendall, L.M., & Hulin, C.L. (1969). *The Measurement of Satisfaction in Work and Retirement.* Chicago: Rand McNally.

4. Weiss, D.J., Dawis, R.W., England, G.W., & Lofquist, L.H. (1967). *Manual for the Minnesota Satisfaction Questionnaire* (Minnesota Studies on Vocational Rehabilitation, vol. 22). Minneapolis: Industrial Relations Center, Work Adjustment Project.

5. Scarpello, V., Huber, V., & Vandenberg, R.J. (1988). "Compensation Satisfaction: Its Measurement and Dimensionality." *Journal of Applied Psychology, 73,* 163–71.

6. Sundstrom, E. (1986). *Workplace.* Cambridge, England: Cambridge University Press.

7. Bateman, T.S., & Strasser, S. (1984). "A Longitudinal Analysis of the Antecedents of Organizational Commitment." *Academy of Management Journal, 27,* 95–112.

8. Locke, E.A. (1976). "The Nature and Causes of Job Satisfaction." In M. Dunnette, ed., *Handbook of Industrial and Organizational Psychology.* Chicago: Rand McNally.

9. Scheier, M.F., Weintraub, J.K., & Carver, C.S. (1986). "Coping with Stress: Divergent strategies of optimists and pessimists." *Journal of Personality and Social Psychology, 51,* 1257–64.

10. Andrisani, P.J., & Nesetl, C. (1976). "Internal-External Control as a Contributor to and Outcome of Work Experience." *Journal of Applied Psychology, 61,* 156–65.

11. See Note 8.

12. Pulakos, E.D., & Schmitt, N. (1983). "A Longitudinal Study of a Valence Model Approach for the Prediction of Job Satisfaction of New Employees." *Journal of Applied Psychology, 68,* 307–12.

13. Wanous, J.P. (1980). *Organizational Entry: Recruitment, Selection, and Socialization of Newcomers.* Reading, Mass.: Addison-Wesley.

14. Quinn, R.P., & Staines, G.L. (1979). *The 1977 Quality of Employment Survey.* Ann Arbor: Institute for Social Research.

15. Kahn, R.L. (1972). "The Meaning of Work: Interpretations and Proposals for Measurement." In A.A. Campbell and P.E. Converse, eds. *The Human Meaning of Social Change.* New York: Basic Books.

16. Festinger, L. (1957). *A Theory of Cognitive Dissonance.* Evanston, Ill.: Row, Peterson.

17. Weaver, C.N. (1980). "Job Satisfaction in the United States in the 1970s." *Journal of Applied Psychology, 65,* 364–67.

18. Sauser, W.I. Jr., & York, C.M. (1978). "Sex Differences in Job Satisfaction: A Reexamination." *Personnel Psychology, 31,* 537–47.

19. Varca, P.E., Shaffer, G.S., & McCauley, C.D. (1983). "Sex Differences in Job Satisfaction Revisited." *Academy of Management Journal, 26,* 348–53.

20. Porter, L.W., & Steers, R.M. (1973). "Causes of Employee Turnover: A Test of the Mobley, Griffeth, Hand, and Meglino Model." *Journal of Applied Psychology, 67,* 53–59.

21. Mowday, R.T., Koberg, C.S., & McArthur, A.W. (1984). "The Psychology of the Withdrawal Process: A Cross-Validational Test of Mobley's Intermediate Linkages Model of Turnover in Two Samples." *Academy of Management Journal, 27,* 79–94.

22. Carsten, J.M., & Spector, P.E. (1987). "Unemployment, Job Satisfaction, and Employee Turnover: A Meta-analytic Test of the Muchinsky Model." *Journal of Applied Psychology, 72,* 374–81.

23. Iaffaldano, M.T., & Muchinsky, P.M. (1985). "Job Satisfaction and Job Performance: A Meta-analysis." *Psychological Bulletin, 97,* 251–73.

24. Porter, L.W., & Lawler, E.E. (1968). *Managerial Attitudes and Performance.* Homewood, Ill.: Dorsey Press.

25. Bateman, T.S., & Organ, B.W. (1983). "Job Satisfaction and the Good Soldier: The Relationship Between Affect and Employee 'Citizenship.'" *Academy of Management Journal, 26,* 587–95.

26. Rice, R.W., Near, J.P., & Hunt, R.G. (1980). "The Job Satisfaction/Life-Satisfaction" relationship: A review of empirical research. *Basic and Applied Social Psychology,* 1980, 1, 37–64.

27. Chacko, T.I. (1983). "Job and Life Satisfactions: A Causal Analysis of their Relationships." *Academy of Management Journal, 26,* 163–69.

28. Crouter, A.C., Perry-Jenkins, M., Huston, T.L., & Crawford, D.W. (1989). "The

Influence of Work Induced Psychological States on Behavior at Home." *Basic and Applied Social Psychology, 10,* 273–92.

29. Palmore, E. (1969). "Predicting Longevity: A Follow-up Controlling for Age." *The Gerontologist, 9,* 247–50.

30. Kornhauser, A.W. (1965). *Mental Health of the Industrial Worker: A Detroit Study.* New York: Wiley.

ADDITIONAL CASES AND EXERCISES: APPLYING WHAT YOU'VE LEARNED

"I Can't Git No Satisfaction!"

Don H. Hockenbury
Psychology Instructor
Tulsa Junior College

Sandra E. Hockenbury
Adjunct Instructor
Tulsa Junior College

Bryan Gaines never expected anything to come of the application he had mailed six weeks earlier to Turnbow Corporation. But, much to his surprise, he was offered a job on Friday of the same week he interviewed for it. The personnel director at Turnbow Corporation told Bryan he could have the weekend to decide whether or not he was going to take the position. That Friday night Bryan had dinner with two good friends as he tried to sort out what he was going to do.

"I don't know why you're going back and forth on this, Bryan. It seems pretty clear cut to me," Kathy observed as she studied the menu. "You've done nothing but gripe about your job at Wedgewood since you began four years ago."

"Yeah, but I've made some friends here," Bryan replied, nervously drumming his fingers on the tabletop.

"Friends? What friends? You have friends at Wedgewood?" Martin quipped, glancing up from his menu.

"Well, I've been getting along better with Walker for the last couple of weeks," Bryan replied lamely.

"Walker is the one who's been driving you bonkers since day one," Martin observed. "As I recall, you've said repeatedly that tile mold has a higher IQ than Walker."

"Why are you suddenly getting so wishy-washy? I thought this was what you wanted!" Kathy threw one hand up in exasperation.

"So did I, but now I'm not so sure. That's why I wanted the two of you to help me sort this out," Bryan replied as he fiddled with his menu.

"So talk!" Martin sat forward, pushing his menu aside.

"We're all ears!" Kathy scooted up her chair.

For the next couple of hours, the three of them talked about Bryan's dilemma. Bryan began working at Wedgewood almost four years ago, less than a month after he graduated from college. He began as a low-level manager with the understanding that he was being groomed for more advanced positions. In his mind, Bryan created his own timetable of when these events should happen. However, his movement up the management ladder was much slower than he expected.

Bryan was worried that the position at Turnbow would suffer from the same problem as his current job—little responsibility or autonomy, across the board raises with no consideration of performance, little opportunity to affect policy, and a snail's pace of advancement. However, Turnbow Corporation had a reputation as being very progressive in its treatment of its employees. When Kathy and Martin both pressed Bryan to give reasons for staying at Wedgewood, his explanation seemed weak.

"It sounds like you're afraid to change," Kathy observed.

Bryan shrugged his shoulders. "I don't know, maybe Wedgewood isn't as bad as it seems. At least I have a safe niche there and someday I'll be an upper level manager, if I don't die of old age first."

"Maybe you just like to complain," Martin suggested.

Bryan frowned immediately. "What's that supposed to mean?"

"Exactly what I said," Martin replied straightforwardly. "Some people seem to thrive on bitching about their jobs and their lives. Maybe you don't really want things to get better because then you wouldn't have as much to complain about. Everything you've said about Wedgewood makes it sound like you're wasting your time there. On the other hand, the job at Turnbow sounds like it has potential for you to get some recognition for your work and even move up the corporate ladder. Granted, both jobs pay virtually the same amount of money but the opportunities at Turnbow seem enormous compared to Wedgewood. There's not one reason why you shouldn't give your two week notice on Monday morning at Wedgewood. Unless, of course, you get more satisfaction out of complaining than gaining."

"Gee, you can always count on your friends," Bryan said sarcastically.

"Hey, Bryan, do you want me to be honest or just pamper your ego?" Martin countered.

"Is that what you think, too?" he asked Kathy.

"Well, Bryan," Kathy began slowly, "I don't know if complaining is just a habit for you or if you're actually dissatisfied with life itself. Either way, Bryan, I think you need to look at your attitudes. Don't get me wrong, Bryan, I find my share of things to complain about with my job, not the least of which is the fact that I've been passed over twice for promotions for someone less qualified than me. But I don't just complain. I've got resumes in at two different companies. I'm going to try to make things different."

"You know, Bryan, it could be that you just expect too much from people and situations," Martin suggested. "I remember when you began your job at Wedgewood, you had this whole strategy mapped out for how you were going to be a division manager within five years. Remember that?"

Bryan smiled with slight embarrassment as he remembered the plan.

"Hey, Bryan, I'm still planning to be the director of marketing at my company by the time I'm 30! I've still got four years left to get that done!" Martin laughed, reminding the other two of his own boastful dreams. "I guess what I'm trying to say is that it's okay to have dreams, Bryan. We all have dreams and goals. But I think sometimes your expectations are too high for situations and the people in those situations. You seem to set yourself up to be disappointed because you expect too much from people and situations. I think you should try to be more positive *and* more realistic."

Questions

1. Identify the areas where cognitive dissonance is playing a role in this situation. Describe the different conflicts operating and the attempts to remove the dissonance.

2. Identify the internal and external causes of job dissatisfaction that seem to be operating with Bryan.

3. Do you agree or disagree with Martin's assertion that some people seem to thrive on complaining about their jobs and other aspects of their lives? If so, how much impact could an individual like that have on other employees in a job situation? In everyday life? What suggestions would you have to help a co-worker or friend who's chronically dissatisfied change?

4. Does Bryan seem to have realistic expectations for himself and the job situation? Or are his ideas just fanciful daydreams? Either way, what could Bryan do to be more realistic in this expectations of his job, himself, and other people?

5. Finally, should Bryan: (a) take the new job with Turnbow Corporation, (b) stay with his old job at Wedgewood, or (c) burn his three-piece suits and become a stage manager for the Rolling Stones?

Job Satisfaction—High or Low? It Depends (in Part) on How You Ask

Earlier in this chapter, it was noted that most people report being fairly satisfied with their work. Yet, many also indicate they would choose a different career or job if they felt they could start over. These findings suggest that whether job satisfaction appears to be high or low depends, quite strongly, on just how such reactions are measured. If you approach people and ask them: "Is your present job or career Okay?" most will answer, "Sure." If, instead, you ask: "Could you do better if you started over?" most will again answer in the affirmative. So, in measuring job satisfaction and reaching conclusions about its prevalence, it is important to be aware of just how the basic questions are asked. You can readily demonstrate the importance of this factor for yourself.

First, approach ten people in various jobs or careers and ask them to answer the question, "How satisfied are you with your current job or career?" (Indicate their response by circling one number on the scale below.)

Not at all satisfied						Very satisfied
1	2	3	4	5	6	7

Now ask the same people to respond to the following question: "If you could start over, would you choose the same job or career?" (Again, circle one number below.)

Definitely would not						Definitely would
1	2	3	4	5	6	7

Now compute an average for responses to the first question and for responses to the second. At first glance, you might guess that these two numbers would be quite similar. After all, if people report being satisfied with their jobs or careers, they should also indicate that they would choose them again. In fact, though, you will probably find the second number is somewhat lower than the first. In short, people will tell you: "Yes, I like my present job," but "No, I wouldn't necessarily choose it again."

If you want to go further with this demonstration, divide your subjects into groups according to the status of their jobs: low, moderate, high. If you compute averages for each of these groups, you may find that the numbers for the two questions above are most similar in the high-status group, and least similar in the low-status group.

Prejudice and Discrimination: Negative Attitudes and Relations in the Workplace

Learning Objectives

After reading this chapter,
you should be able to:

1. Define prejudice and discrimination, and distinguish between them.

2. Describe several factors that contribute to the development of prejudice.

3. List several factors that currently operate against success by females in work settings.

4. Indicate how, and to what extent, male and female managers differ.

5. Describe several techniques for reducing or eliminating prejudice.

It has been six weeks since Debra Seiter graduated from Midwestern Community College, where she concentrated on taking secretarial courses. Debra is highly motivated and can do basic bookkeeping and most clerical tasks. Yet so far she has had no luck finding a job. She has filled out over ten applications, but always hears the same refrain—"We've found someone with somewhat better qualifications, but we wish you the best of luck in finding a suitable position." She has started to get a bit frustrated.

It may take a little more than luck. Debra has cerebral palsy, which affects her speech and motor movements. Yet she can still carry out many of the clerical tasks required in these jobs. *What is it?* she wonders. *Are the others really more qualified, or are they just uncomfortable with having someone with my disability around the office? You'd think some company would be willing to take a chance on me. How else am I going to be able to prove myself?*

Debra's dilemma may seem unusual to you in some ways. After all, how many people with cerebral palsy are in the job market? Yet this same type of dilemma is faced by many people who have some obvious disability as well as those who may be treated unfairly on the basis of appearance, background, race, or gender. In an ideal world, only ability would be considered in hiring and promotion. Yet we know that many people are the victims of prejudice. That is, they are denied employment because of personal characteristics—factors that probably have little or no bearing on their ability to perform various tasks relating to work.

Certainly, it would be more comforting to assume that Debra's troubles stem mainly from job-related factors, such as her lack of experience and training. Unfortunately, it is impossible to rule out the potential role of prejudice, as well. Even today, after several decades of rapid social change, such negative reactions persist, and exert a major impact in work settings. Prejudice thus remains a serious problem for employers and employees alike and it is worthy of our careful attention. In this chapter we will consider several aspects of prejudice and discrimination in the world of work. Specifically, our discussion will proceed as follows. First, we will define prejudice more precisely and distinguish it from *discrimination*. Second, we will consider the bases from which it springs—possible origins of hatred and intolerance. Third, we will turn to an especially timely and important form of prejudice—that based on sex. Finally, we will review several steps that can be taken, both by individuals and by businesses, to overcome the negative effects of prejudice.

PREJUDICE AND DISCRIMINATION: WHAT THEY ARE AND HOW THEY DIFFER

In newscasts and magazine articles, the terms *prejudice* and *discrimination* are often used as synonyms. But human relations experts who study these topics usually distinguish between them. They use the term prejudice to refer to a special type of attitude—generally, a negative one toward the members of one distinct social group. In contrast, they use the term *discrimination* to refer to specific negative actions directed against these individuals. The same distinction will be adopted throughout this chapter.

Prejudice: Social Identity as a Basis for Rejection

As we have just seen, human relations experts generally view prejudice as a special type of attitude.[1] More precisely, they often define it in the following manner: ***Prejudice** is a negative attitude toward the members of some specific group, held simply because those individuals belong to that group.* When we say that a given person is prejudiced against members of some social group, then, we mean that he or she tends to reject these members or evaluate them negatively merely because they belong to that group. Their individual behaviors, skills, or characteristics are not taken into account.

Since it is a special type of attitude, prejudice possesses the three basic components shared by all attitudes: *cognitive, affective,* and *behavioral* aspects. The *cognitive* component of prejudice refers to beliefs and expectations about the members of particular groups. Often, such beliefs form clusters of preconceived notions known as **stereotypes.** These are of major importance, for once formed, they exert several powerful effects. First, they lead individuals who accept them to assume that all members of a given group possess the same traits or behave in the same manner. Second, stereotypes often distort social perception, so that no matter how other persons act, their behavior is interpreted as lending support to these preconceived beliefs. And third, stereotypes often demonstrate an unsettling, self-fulfilling nature.[2] Once we believe members of a given social group possess certain traits, we tend to treat them as if these beliefs were true. This may then cause them to act in ways that confirm our stereotype. For example, consider a manager who believes that workers over age fifty-five simply can't cut it—they are far less productive than younger workers. Because of this belief, she tends to assign them relatively easy tasks and sets very low goals for them. These individuals, recognizing the manager's low expectations, experience a drop in self-confidence. This, in turn, impairs their ability to perform competently. The result: The manager's initial, false beliefs bring about their own confirmation! (See Figure 12.1 for an illustration of this process.)

The *affective* component refers to the negative feelings or emotions prejudiced persons experience when in the presence of members of specific groups or when they merely think about them. Direct evidence for such reactions has been ob-

366
CHAPTER 12
PREJUDICE AND
DISCRIMINATION:
NEGATIVE ATTITUDES
AND RELATIONS IN
THE WORKPLACE

tained in several studies designed to assess emotional reactions to members of one's own and a different racial group. Results indicate that many persons do indeed experience greater anxiety and emotional arousal when interacting with persons belonging to another racial group than when interacting with members of their own.[3] Finally, the *behavioral* aspect of prejudice involves tendencies to act in negative ways toward the persons or groups who are the object of such attitudes. When these tendencies spill over into overt actions, they constitute **discrimination.**

Discrimination: Prejudice in Action

As we noted in Chapter 11, attitudes are not always reflected in overt actions. In fact, there is often a large gap between the views individuals hold and their actual behavior. Prejudice is no exception to this general rule. In many situations, persons holding even strong negative views about the members of various racial or ethnic groups cannot express these hatreds directly. Laws, fear of retaliation, and social pressure all prevent them from engaging in openly negative actions against the targets of their hatred. In other cases, though, such restraining forces are absent. Then, the negative beliefs, feelings, and behavior tendencies that constitute prejudice may find expression in overt actions. Such behaviors are usually known as *discrimination* and can take many different forms. At relatively mild levels, they may involve simple avoidance: Prejudiced persons have as little contact as possible with the groups they dislike—at work and in their personal lives. At stronger levels, they can involve exclusion: Members of disliked groups

FIGURE 12.1 Stereotypes: Their Self-Fulfilling Nature
Because a manager expects older workers to be inefficient and incompetent, she assigns them easy tasks and sets low goals for them. The employees recognize her low expectations and so suffer reductions in self-confidence. This impairs their ability to perform well and so tends to confirm the manager's initial false beliefs (i.e., her stereotype of older workers).

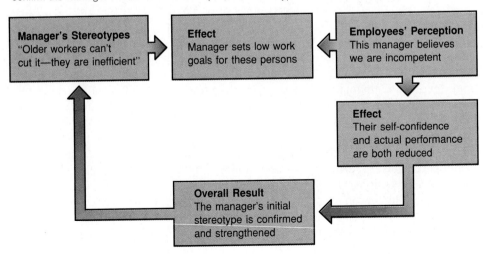

are prevented from living in certain neighborhoods, from sending their children to certain schools, and from joining certain social organizations (clubs, churches). Finally, in extreme cases, discrimination can involve direct physical assaults, or even the mass murder of one group by members of another.

Needless to say, all of these forms of discrimination are important and can exert harmful effects on the targets of prejudice. Of greatest concern to many human relations experts, however, are several practices, known together as job discrimination. Such discrimination includes reluctance to hire persons belonging to certain groups, failure to promote them, and attempts to pay them less than other employees are paid for their job or specialty. In the past, practices of this type were quite widespread, and the victims included racial and ethnic minorities, women, older workers, and sometimes even young workers. Fortunately, this situation has altered greatly in recent decades, largely because of legislation making such actions illegal. Thus, in its more blatant forms at least, such discrimination definitely seems to be on the wane (see Figure 12.2). But it has far from totally vanished, and the struggle to eliminate it from all work settings is a continuous process. In addition, several subtler forms of job discrimination persist. These include withholding aid or assistance from persons belonging to certain groups so that their job performance suffers, and *tokenism*—hiring or promoting a few "token" women, blacks, or Hispanics in order to comply with the letter if not the spirit of the law. Such subtler forms of discrimination are often harder to spot than the obvious practices of the past. Yet they still exert negative effects on the persons toward whom they are directed.

FIGURE 12.2 Minorities in High Places: The New Look
Although subtle forms of discrimination still exist, many members of minority groups have reached high positions in government and industry.

368

CHAPTER 12
PREJUDICE AND
DISCRIMINATION:
NEGATIVE ATTITUDES
AND RELATIONS IN
THE WORKPLACE

Tokenism: A Subtle Form of Discrimination   Imagine that you were hired for a job you really wanted, and at a higher starting salary than you expected. At first, you would be happy about your good fortune. Now, assume that one day, you learn that you got the job mainly because you belong to a specific group—one underrepresented at the company. How would you react? Most likely you would be upset. After all, few persons would enjoy discovering that they were hired as a *token* member of a specific racial, ethnic, or religious group, rather than on the basis of their qualifications. For example, in one study on this topic, young women holding management-level jobs were asked to rate the extent to which several factors (their ability, experience, education, or sex) played a role in their being hired. They also rated their attitudes toward their companies and satisfaction with their supervisors and work. When women who rated their ability as the most important factor in being hired were compared with those who rated their sex as most important, unsettling differences emerged. Those who felt they were mere tokens reported significantly lower commitment and satisfaction than those who felt they had been hired on the basis of their ability.[4]

Wherever it occurs, tokenism seems to have at least two negative effects. On the one hand, it lets bigoted people off the hook; they can point to tokenistic actions as proof that they are not really prejudiced or that they have followed the letter if not the spirit of antidiscrimination laws. On the other hand, it can be damaging to the self-esteem and confidence of the targets of prejudice, including those few persons who are selected as tokens. Clearly, then, it is one subtle form of discrimination worth preventing.

EXPLANATIONS OF PREJUDICE: THE ORIGINS OF HATE

Where does prejudice come from? Why do individuals so often hold strong negative attitudes toward members of groups other than their own? These are important questions, for understanding the origins of prejudice may help us to develop effective strategies for overcoming its impact in work settings. Unfortunately, prejudice is far too complex in scope to permit us the luxury of simple answers. Instead, it appears to stem from several different sources, none of which should be ignored. Among the most important of these are (1) *intergroup conflict,* (2) *social categorization,* and (3) *early learning experiences.*

Intergroup Conflict: Competition as a Basis for Bigotry

In recent years, a growing number of Cubans have moved to the United States. Most have settled in southern Florida, with the result that Miami is today virtually a bilingual city. Indeed, in many locations Spanish, not English, is the language in daily use. Since the Cubans came seeking political freedom, and since Cuba and Florida have long enjoyed a great deal of trade and commerce, it might be expected that this immigration would go smoothly. In fact, it has not. Many long-time residents of Miami have objected strongly to this sudden influx of "foreigners." And many people—blacks and whites alike—have voiced negative attitudes about Cubans in general. In short, prejudice has reared its ugly head in an area previously more famous for its palm trees and tropical climate. Why has this been the case? According to one explanation for the occurrence of prejudice, the answer is competition. As Cubans arrived in growing numbers, they came into competition with previous residents for jobs, housing, and schools. This competition, in turn, stimulated the development of anti-Cuban attitudes. In short, one major explanation for the occurrence of prejudice suggests that it often stems from direct economic competition between distinct social groups. This is known as *realistic conflict theory*.

Unfortunately, this view has been confirmed both by systematic research and careful observation of events occurring in many societies. With respect to research, it has been found that when groups are placed in direct competition for valued rewards, they do come to dislike and disparage one another.[5] They label one another as "enemies," view their own groups as morally superior, and draw the boundaries between themselves and their opponents even more firmly. The result, of course, is that what starts out as simple competition, relatively free from animosity and hatred, gradually develops into full-scale, emotion-laden prejudice (see Figure 12.3). Turning to observation of societal events, it appears that prejudice and job discrimination do tend to increase at times when economic conditions are poor and jobs are scarce.[6] In view of these two kinds of evidence, it seems reasonable to conclude that one important basis for the emergence of strong intergroup prejudice is direct economic competition.

FIGURE 12.3 Competition: One Source of Prejudice
According to *realistic conflict theory*, prejudice sometimes develops out of competition for scarce resources.

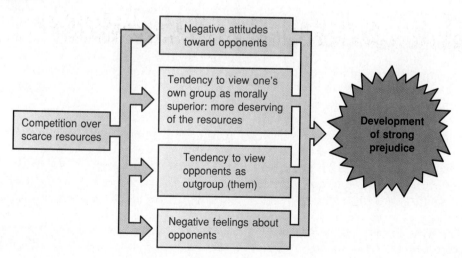

370

CHAPTER 12

PREJUDICE AND
DISCRIMINATION:
NEGATIVE ATTITUDES
AND RELATIONS IN
THE WORKPLACE

"Us" versus "Them": Social Categorization as a Basis for Prejudice

A second factor contributing to prejudice is, in some respects, even more disturbing because it seems to be built directly into our perceptions of the social world. Briefly, growing evidence indicates that human beings have a strong tendency to divide all the people around them into two distinct groups.[7] Either these individuals are similar to themselves in key respects and are seen as part of their own "in-group," or they are viewed as different and are assigned to the "out-group." If this tendency to divide the social world into these two distinct categories (**social categorization**) stopped there, it would be of little significance. Unfortunately, this is not the case. Instead, sharply contrasting feelings and beliefs are usually attached to members of the in-group and members of the out-group. While persons in the "us" category are viewed in highly favorable terms, those in the "them" category are seen in a more negative light. They are assumed to possess undesirable characteristics and are often strongly disliked, or at least mistrusted. And they are seen as much more similar to one another than persons in our in-group.[8] In short, while individuals belonging to our own group are known to

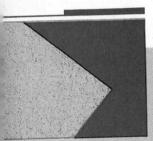

HUMAN RELATIONS IN ACTION

"Ah, They're All Alike": Demonstrating the Illusion of Out-group Homogeneity

Earlier, we noted that one basis for prejudice seems to lie in our tendency to perceive all members of any group other than our own as similar. This is sometimes known as the **illusion of out-group homogeneity** and it is, in fact, an illusion: There is no reason to believe that people in other groups are any more alike than people in our own group. Yet, despite this fact, our tendency to jump to such conclusions is quite strong. You can demonstrate its impact for yourself by obtaining the help of several friends and following the directions below. (Be sure to choose friends who have not read this book or taken a course in human relations.) Work with one person at a time.

First, tell each person that you are going to ask him or her to estimate how much the people in various groups differ from one another by writing a number from 1 to 7 on a piece of paper. If your friend feels that the people in the group you name vary only a little (they are all pretty much the same), he or she should enter the number 1. If, in contrast, your friend thinks that these people vary a great deal, he or she should enter the number 7. Numbers in between, of course, reflect different degrees of perceived variability.

Now present your first example. Read this statement: *To what extent do people in (name a foreign country; e.g., Britain if you live in the United States) vary in their political views?*

differ in many respects, those in the out-group are viewed as being very much alike. "You know what *they're* like" is a phrase that captures the essence of this view. (You can demonstrate this unsettling tendency for yourself by performing the exercise in the **Human Relations in Action** on page 370.)

Unfortunately, this inclination to divide the world into "us" and "them" is very powerful. Indeed, it seems to occur even in situations where the basis for such distinctions is flimsy, to say the least. Similarly, our tendency to hold more positive attitudes toward members of our in-group than toward members of various out-groups is also very strong. Why is this so? One possibility is that individuals seek to enhance their self-esteem by becoming identified with specific social groups. This tactic can succeed, however, only to the extent that the persons involved perceive these groups as somehow superior to other, competing groups.[9] Since all individuals are subject to the same forces, the final result is inevitable: Each group seeks to view itself as somehow better than its rivals, and prejudice arises out of this clash of social perceptions (see Figure 12.4). This type of process is termed *social competition,*[10] and it may set the stage for strong discriminatory actions in work settings and elsewhere.

Next, read the following statement: *To what extent do people in (name your own country) vary in their political views?*

In each case, remind your friend to enter a number from 1 to 7.

Now present your second example. Read this statement: *To what extent do (name your friend's own age group—for example, people in their twenties) vary in physical fitness?*

Then read this statement: *To what extent do middle-aged people vary in physical fitness?*

At this point, you are ready to examine your results. First, obtain an average score for each item. (Simply add together the numbers selected by each of your friends and then divide by the number of persons you had participate.) Now, compare these numbers. You will probably find that for both items your friends assigned a higher number to their own groups than to other groups. That is, they perceive more variability among persons in their own country or age group than among persons in some other country or age group. This tendency to view people in other groups as more alike than people belonging to our own group is, in a sense, the entering wedge of prejudice. If the members of some group are perceived as all being pretty much alike, there is no reason to bother with them as individuals, or to take into account their personal needs and traits. By encouraging such false beliefs, the illusion of outgroup homogeneity, which might seem neutral in itself, can play a destructive role in human relations.

372

CHAPTER 12
PREJUDICE AND
DISCRIMINATION:
NEGATIVE ATTITUDES
AND RELATIONS IN
THE WORKPLACE

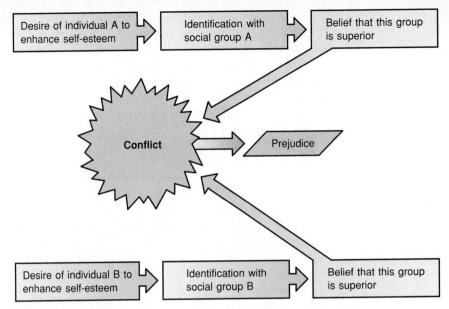

FIGURE 12.4 Ingroup Identification: One Potential Source of Prejudice
Prejudice sometimes arises out of social competition. Individuals may attempt to enhance their self-esteem by identifying with groups they view as superior to others. Since the members of many groups have the same desire, conflict between them occurs. Prejudice then follows this clash of social perception. *Source:* Based on suggestions by Tajfel (1982); see Note 10.

The Role of Social Learning: Early Experience as a Basis for Prejudice

Heroines and heroes may be born, but bigots are clearly made. Few persons would suggest that children enter the world with racial hatreds, sexist attitudes, or techniques of job discrimination firmly in place. Rather, it is clear that such reactions must be acquired (see Figure 12.5). The social learning view of prejudice takes full account of this basic fact. According to this view, individuals acquire prejudice toward various groups because they hear such views expressed by parents, friends, teachers, and others, and because they are directly rewarded (with praise and approval) for adopting them. The mass media also seems to play a major role in "training for prejudice." For example, until recently, the members of racial and ethnic minorities, as well as women, were presented in a negative light on television and in movies (see Figure 12.6). Specifically, they were depicted as being low in intelligence, lacking in ambition, and suited only to simple or low-level jobs. Fortunately, this situation has changed somewhat in recent years in the United States, Canada, and other nations. Members of various minorities and females are now shown in a wider range of roles, and in higher status jobs, than was true in the past. Even today, though, there is still room for improvement. Until such changes occur, and all traces of racism, sexism, and other forms of bigotry are removed from the mass media, their potential for contributing to such reactions will remain.

THE FAMILY CIRCUS®   By Bil Keane

"Does Mommy know you're playing
with her toys?"

FIGURE 12.5   Sex-Role Attitudes Develop Early
Sexist attitudes can be acquired very early in a child's development. If these attitudes are not learned at home, they may be derived from exposure to the mass media. (Reprinted with special permission of King Features Syndicate, Inc.)

FIGURE 12.6   The Mass Media: A Source of Bigotry
Television programs in the past often cast members of minority groups in roles consistent with negative stereotypes, such as Eddie "Rochester" Anderson in the Jack Benny show. This has changed dramatically in recent years.

374

CHAPTER 12

PREJUDICE AND
DISCRIMINATION:
NEGATIVE ATTITUDES
AND RELATIONS IN
THE WORKPLACE

The Roots of Prejudice: Summing Up

As even this brief discussion suggests, prejudice stems from many different causes. Direct economic competition, parental influence, media influence, and basic ways of perceiving the social world around us all play a role in its occurrence. At first glance, knowledge of all these different factors may strike you as confusing, and perhaps even unnecessary. Actually, though, it is of great practical value. Only by understanding the roots of prejudice can we hope to devise effective techniques for reducing its impact and occurrence. Thus we will soon have reason to draw on the information presented in this section. Before doing so, though, we will examine one specific form of prejudice—a type that plays a key role in many work settings and that has recently been the focus of a great deal of political, legislative, and research interest: prejudice based on sex.

PREJUDICE BASED ON SEX: A SPECIAL, TIMELY CASE

Females constitute a majority of the world's population. Yet, despite this fact, they have been treated very much like a "minority group" in most cultures throughout history. They have been largely excluded from economic and political power. They have been the object of pronounced negative stereotyping. And they have often suffered overt discrimination; for example, they have been barred from many jobs, certain types of training, and from various social organizations. Fortunately, overt practices such as these appear to be decreasing, at least in many places and to some degree. Further, the past decade has witnessed major shifts in beliefs about the traits of men and women, and the supposed differences between them. As you probably know, such shifts have generally been in the direction of realizing that males and females are not nearly as different in many respects as society once assumed.[11] Despite such changes, discrimination based on sex (or **sexism,** as it is often termed) still persists in many settings, including businesses and other organizations. Given the negative effects produced by such prejudice, and the major social changes that have stemmed from efforts to overcome it, there can be little doubt that it is a timely topic, with important implications for human relations. Thus we will consider it here in some detail.

Discrimination against Females: Subtle but Significant

In the past thirty years women have made significant advances. At the beginning of the 1990s, they make up about 54 percent of the college undergraduates in the United States. About 60 percent of women are in the work force. The number of female lawyers, judges, doctors, and engineers have increased greatly (see Figure 12.7). Yet there are a number of indications that serious problems remain. Women who work full-time earn only two-thirds as much as men. Only a small percentage of the top executives of major companies are female. The majority of women are still stuck in low-paying "pink collar" jobs, such as clerk, receptionist, secretary, and service worker.[12]

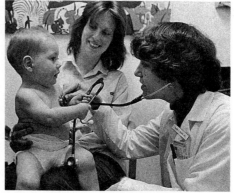

FIGURE 12.7 Female Careers: Increasingly Popular Choices
Women are increasingly entering professions once dominated by men—as in the case of the design engineer and medical doctor shown here.

Why do females still lag behind males economically in many ways? One major reason is that females in the United States are primarily responsible for child-rearing and household tasks. This limits their ability to pursue demanding educational and occupational goals. Although laws and court rulings have significantly reduced direct discrimination against women, there still exist a number of subtle factors that help maintain a second-class status for females in the world of work.

The Role of Sex-Role Stereotypes   One such force involves the persistence of traditional views about the characteristics supposedly possessed by men and women (as in the case of the boss in Figure 12.8). Such views (often known as *sex-role stereotypes*) suggest that males tend to be aggressive, forceful, persistent, and decisive, while females tend to be passive, submissive, dependent, and emotional. Growing evidence indicates that such differences are largely false: Males and females do not differ as consistently or to as large a degree in these ways as sex-role stereotypes suggest. Yet, such beliefs persist and continue to play a role in

FIGURE 12.8 Sex Role Stereotypes: Often Incorrect
We are increasingly learning that traditional views of men and women (sex-role stereotypes) are not very accurate. (Reprinted with special permission of King Features Syndicate, Inc.)

376

CHAPTER 12
PREJUDICE AND
DISCRIMINATION:
NEGATIVE ATTITUDES
AND RELATIONS IN
THE WORKPLACE

organizational settings. One reason this occurs is that the traits attributed to males by these stereotypes are ones that seem consistent with managerial success, while the traits attributed to females are ones that seem inconsistent with such success. The result: Females are perceived as less suited for managerial positions, even when they possess appropriate credentials.

Evidence for the operation of such sex-role stereotypes has been obtained by Heilman and her colleagues in a series of studies.[13] In these experiments, it has been repeatedly found that females are perceived as less suited for jobs traditionally filled by males, and that any characteristics that serve to emphasize or activate female sex-role stereotypes tend to intensify such negative effects. For example, females who are physically attractive are perceived as being more feminine and therefore as less suited for managerial roles than females who are less physically attractive. Interestingly, the impact of sex-role stereotypes can be countered if clear evidence for a woman's ability or competence is provided. In such cases, females applying for traditionally male-dominated jobs (e.g., sports photographer) actually receive *higher* ratings than males.[14] Apparently, this occurs because they are perceived as a special subgroup—one that is even more competent than males for such jobs. In general, though, traditional sex-role stereotypes tend to operate against success and advancement by women in work settings.

The Role of Expectations Another factor impeding advancement by females in at least some work settings involves their expectations. In general, women seem to hold lower expectations about their careers than do men. For example, among recent business graduates, females expect to receive lower starting and peak salaries than males.[15] Several factors probably contribute to such differences (e.g., the fact that females specialize in lower-paying areas than do males; their observation that on an average, females do, in fact, tend to earn less than males in most organizations). Whatever the basis, it is a general rule in life that people tend to get what they expect. Thus the lower expectations held by females may be one factor operating against them in many instances.

The Role of Self-Confidence Confidence, it is often said, is the single best predictor of success. People who expect to succeed often do; those who expect to fail find that these predictions, too, are confirmed. Unfortunately, women tend to express lower self-confidence than men do in many achievement situations. Thus the fact that they have not as yet attained full equality with men in many work settings may stem, at least in part, from this factor. Evidence suggesting that this is indeed the case has been reported by McCarty.[16]

In a laboratory study on this issue, she asked male and female students to work on tasks involving creativity. Subjects performed three such tasks (devising unique uses for ordinary objects such as a pencil or wire hanger), and received feedback about their performance on each one. Some learned that they had done very well (positive feedback), others that they had done quite poorly (negative feedback), while still others received no feedback whatsoever. Subjects were asked to rate their self-confidence both before working on the tasks and again after receiving feedback. As you can see from Figure 12.9, women reported lower levels of self-confidence before working on the tasks. More importantly, while positive

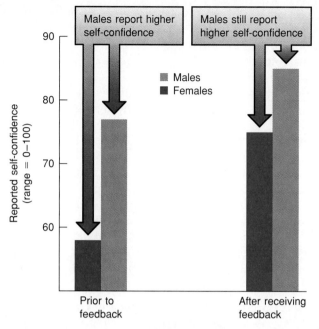

FIGURE 12.9 Feedback and Self-Confidence Among Males and Females
Females reported lower self-confidence than males before receiving feedback about their performance. After receiving positive feedback, their self-confidence increased but it was still lower than that of males. (Only data for the positive feedback condition are shown.) *Source:* Based on data from McCarty (1986); see Note 16.

feedback did increase their self-confidence, it did not eliminate the difference in favor of men; women continued to report lower self-confidence throughout the study. Finally, men who received no feedback duing the study reported self-confidence as high as that of women who had received positive feedback.

Together, these findings suggest that positive feedback about task performance may be especially important for women. Even in its absence, men express relatively high degrees of self-confidence. However, women report similar levels of confidence only in the context of encouraging feedback. This is a point managers who wish to foster advancement among women would do well to consider.

Devaluing Female Achievement: Luck, Skill, or Effort? When individuals perform some task, the success or failure they achieve can be attributed to several potential causes. Specifically, a given level of performance can be viewed as stemming mainly from internal factors such as ability and effort, or external factors such as luck or low task difficulty. As you might well guess, in most cases, good performance stemming from ability or effort is viewed as more deserving of recognition than similar performance deriving from luck or an easy task.[17] For this reason, raises, promotions, and other corporate rewards are frequently dispensed to persons viewed as having succeeded because of high ability or out-

378

CHAPTER 12
PREJUDICE AND
DISCRIMINATION:
NEGATIVE ATTITUDES
AND RELATIONS IN
THE WORKPLACE

standing effort. In contrast, such rewards are given far less frequently to persons seen as having succeeded because of luck or an easy job.

All this probably strikes you as quite reasonable, and to a degree it is. But now consider the following fact: Growing evidence suggests that many persons attribute successful performance by males and females to different factors. Briefly, success by males is often attributed to their ability or effort. In contrast, similar levels of performance by females are often viewed as stemming mainly from luck or from the difficulty of the task.[18] In short, if a man succeeds, it is assumed he worked very hard or that he possesses a high level of ability. If a woman attains the same level of performance, however, it is often assumed that she "lucked out," or that the task she faced really was not very difficult (see Figure 12.10).

Needless to say, these tendencies operate against the advancement of women in business settings. After all, even when women attain the same level of performance as their male colleagues, this success is discounted or devalued. Fortunately, evidence indicates that such bias may be decreasing, at least in some business settings.[19] However, to the extent it persists, it can be damaging, to say the least (see the **Case in Point** on page 380).

Women as Managers: Do They Really Differ?

According to widely accepted cultural stereotypes, males and females differ greatly. Females supposedly show such traits as submissiveness, gentleness, emotionality, and lack of ambition. In contrast, males are assumed to demonstrate such traits as decisiveness, ambition, dominance, and self-confidence.[20] If these stereotypes are correct—even to a small degree—we may expect men and women to differ greatly as managers. That is, once they attain managerial rank, females

FIGURE 12.10 Successful Performance: Different Explanations for Males and Females
Growing evidence suggests that successful performance by females and by males is often attributed to different causes. While successful performance by males is usually seen as deriving from high ability or effort, similar performance by females is often perceived as stemming mainly from good luck or an easy task.

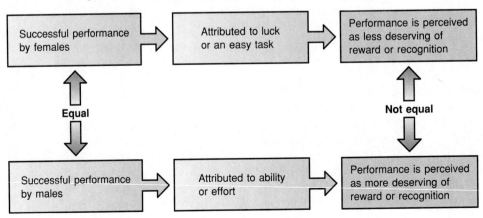

might well adopt different styles or practices than men. Is this actually the case? Do male and female managers really differ in the ways that cultural expectations predict? Many research studies have sought to answer these questions, and in general results have been quite consistent. They point to the following conclusion: Potential differences between male and female managers have been greatly overemphasized. Men and women do not seem to differ greatly either in the traits they bring with them to management jobs, or in the practices and styles they adopt in them.

First, consider the traits of male and female managers. As noted above, cultural stereotypes suggest that men and women differ sharply in this respect. Further, these differences seem to favor males. Presumably, they possess the traits necessary for management roles to a greater extent than do females; supposedly, men are more assertive, dominant, and decisive. Actual research, though, has failed to offer support for such predictions. For example, in one investigation, large numbers of male and female business students completed several measures of personality—tests designed to assess their relative standing on a wide range of traits.[21] When the scores of male and female students were compared, males were *not* more assertive, practical, venturesome, or self-assured than females. In fact, in several cases, the opposite was true (see Figure 12.11). In short, males and females do not seem to differ with respect to the traits that they bring with them to their management jobs.

Turning to actual performance on the job, results have been similar. Again, few differences between male and female managers emerge. Perhaps the most convincing evidence in this regard has been gathered by Donnell and Hall in a large scale study.[22] These researchers actually conducted five separate but related investigations designed to uncover any differences in the behavior of male and female managers. Almost 2,000 persons participated in the study, and in each case comparisons betwen male and female managers were based on carefully matched samples. That is, only individuals who were quite similar in terms of age, rank, and type of organization in which they worked were compared.

Once matched samples were obtained, the behavior of male and female managers was compared along five key dimensions previously found to be closely linked to managerial success. These included (1) managerial philosophy—beliefs that shape an individual's approach to management process; (2) motivational dynamics—the manager's own motives and their effects on his or her subordinates; (3) participative practices—the degree to which a manager is sensitive to the needs of subordinates; (4) interpersonal competence—a manager's ability to deal effectively with others; and (5) managerial style—whether a manager is primarily concerned with people, production, or both. The results of the entire project were clear and pointed to a firm conclusion: Contrary to popular belief, women do *not* differ from men in terms of key aspects of their behavior as managers. Indeed, of forty-three separate comparisons relating to the five factors listed above, only two showed significant differences between males and females. And, even here, one of the differences favored females (they were more achieving in their motivation profiles than were men), while the other favored males (they were more open and candid with colleagues than were women). In short, the findings of the

380

CHAPTER 12

PREJUDICE AND
DISCRIMINATION:
NEGATIVE ATTITUDES
AND RELATIONS IN
THE WORKPLACE

study indicated that females and males behave in much the same fashion when serving as managers.

Needless to say, these findings make any traces of prejudice against women in work settings even more ridiculous than would be true if important differences between the sexes actually existed. After all, if female and male managers show virtually identical patterns of behavior, why should the question of sex enter into the picture at all? The answer, you will probably agree, is simple: It shouldn't!

Sexism in Work Settings: Some Positive News

It is quite clear from our discussion that females have suffered significantly from various forms of prejudice based on gender. Yet females have also made significant strides in a wide variety of areas in terms of educational and career

CASE IN POINT

Not Bad, for a Woman

Carla Parker is up for evaluation and possible promotion. Eighteen months ago she joined UBX Systems, Inc., as its first female engineer. Now, three people—Jack Feldman, her supervisor; Bob Rollins, head of Employee Relations; and Steve Johnson, Chief Engineer—are reviewing her record. Putting aside her folder and leaning back in his chair, Jack begins: "She looks pretty good on paper," he remarks. "In fact, I think she's doing a fine job for us. I have to admit that at first I was a bit surprised. We've never had a woman in that job before, and I had some doubts. But I don't anymore. I think she's a good, solid performer. Let's give her a merit raise."

Steve Johnson looks doubtful. "Well, I agree that her record looks pretty strong, Jack, but there's one thing that bothers me. Since she's been with us, she's never really had any tough jobs or emergencies. Everything's been pretty easy and pretty routine. How do we know what she'll do when the going gets rough? It's one thing to do well when everything's going smoothly, and another to deliver in the crunch. I have some concerns about that."

"I don't agree," replied Jack. "That AMPAD job was pretty sticky, but she handled it really well. And after all, we don't get that many special problems or emergencies these days anyway."

"Maybe so, maybe so," Steve admits with some reluctance. "But there's another thing, too. One of the people who work for her came to me the other day to complain. Seems he didn't like her style. I haven't been able to pinpoint the problem yet, but there does seem to be something going on that the old-timers don't like."

"Ha! I know who that was," exclaims Bob. "It must have been Mike Haggerty. And I know what's eating him, too. He just doesn't like having a woman boss.

achievements. Even more encouraging, there are indications that sexist attitudes also seem to be weakening. Recent studies indicate lack of bias in on-the-job evaluations, job interviews, and evaluation as leaders.[23,24] Thus there seem to be major shifts toward reduced sex discrimination in the world of work. Females, it seems, are receiving more equitable treatment now than in the past. Of course, this does not imply that sexism is no longer of major importance in work settings. On the contrary, women and other disadvantaged groups continue to face serious problems in this regard. It does appear, however, that at least some types of prejudice are on the wane and are less influential—and harmful—than they were in the past. It is our hope, of course, that such trends will continue and that at some point in the future, the impact of sexism and other forms of prejudice will vanish in work settings and in all other contexts as well.

He can't adjust—too old, I guess. You know, I've watched Carla in action a lot of times and I think she's doing just fine. In fact, I don't see that she really does anything different from Tom Bellasco, the person she replaced."

"Well," Steve answers, "I wouldn't like taking orders from a woman, myself." Then, smiling in an unpleasant way, he continues: "But I guess it wouldn't be so hard to take from Carla. Yeah, she's a real cutie, all right. And nice legs, too—I think I could get along with her just fine . . ."

At these comments, Bob grows angry. "Hey, come off it, Steve! That stuff is way out of line. We're here to talk about her work, not her sex appeal. It's a good thing some of our female employees can't hear you; you'd be in big trouble—and you'd deserve it, too."

Steve is taken aback, and looks slightly embarrassed. But he recovers quickly. In fact he, too, grows angry: "OK, let's stick to the point. And my feeling is that taking everything into account, she's not ready for promotion or a bonus raise. She's doing okay, for a woman, but I'm not going to approve any special rewards for her yet. Let's give her another six months or a year and see what happens. I'll bet she folds in the end."

Questions

1. Which of the three people present at this evaluation qualifies for the booby prize "head chauvinist?"

2. What forms of bias against women can you spot in this meeting?

3. How might these be reduced or eliminated?

4. If Carla is not promoted and fails to receive a merit raise, should she lodge a formal complaint or grievance?

382

CHAPTER 12

PREJUDICE AND
DISCRIMINATION:
NEGATIVE ATTITUDES
AND RELATIONS IN
THE WORKPLACE

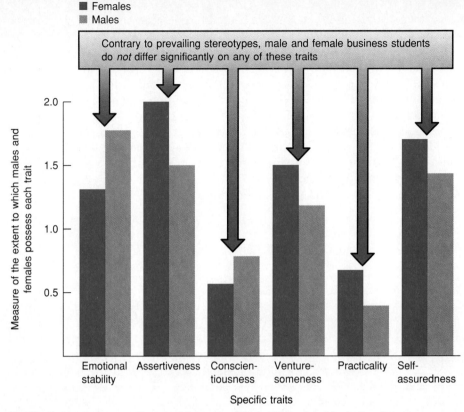

FIGURE 12.11 Male and Female Managers: Their Traits Are Much the Same
In a study which compared the personality traits of male and female business students (future
managers), few differences emerged. In cases where the sexes did seem to differ females often
had the edge—they scored higher on traits linked to future success as a manager. *Source:*
Based on data from Steinberg and Shapiro (1982); see Note 21.

Sexual Harassment: A Serious Problem in the Workplace

While there have been some positive changes in the area of sexism, another
problem seems to be occurring with increasing frequency: *sexual harassment.*[25]
This term refers to unwanted contact or communication of a sexual nature, and
it can range from forced physical contact and sexual propositions linked to threats
or promises of change in job status, through offensive remarks or unwanted
nonverbal attention (e.g., stares, gestures, whistles), and repeated requests for
dates (refer to Figure 12.12). Women are the overwhelming victims of such actions,
but men, too, are subject to sexual harassment on some occasions.

Unfortunately, the incidence of sexual harassment appears to have increased
in recent decades. Surveys reveal that more than 25 percent of female employees
of the federal government in the United States have experienced sexual harassment
at least once during their careers. Similarly, the number of complaints filed with
the Equal Employment Opportunity Commission rose from 4,272 in 1981 to 7,273
in 1985. Of course, it is difficult to know whether this is due to harassment or

FIGURE 12.12 Sexual Harassment: An Increasing Problem
With increasing numbers of women in the workplace, incidents of sexual harassment are becoming more frequent.

merely a greater willingness of employees to report its occurrence. Whichever interpretation is more accurate, however, it is clear that being subjected to sexual harassment is a highly unpleasant and stressful experience for the persons involved.

Can organizations, and individual managers, do anything to reduce the frequency of such objectionable behavior? Growing evidence suggests that they can. In fact, taking a number of recent studies on this topic into account, the following recommendations seem useful:

1. Develop formal policies concerning sexual harassment—ones that clearly specify the type of behavior that will constitute such harassment. These policies, and potential penalties, should then be communicated in a clear manner to all employees.

2. Establish an in-house mechanism for complaints about sexual harassment. In other words, employees should have some means of voicing such complaints without turning at once to legal action.

3. Inform employees that it is their duty to serve as witnesses to instances of sexual harassment, if they are in a position to observe their occurrence. In short, efforts should be made to overcome the natural reluctance of many persons to become involved in such proceedings by explaining that eliminating sexual harassment is in the best interests of all employees and the entire organization.

Findings indicate that courts are most likely to rule in favor of employees complaining of sexual harassment when they have been subjected to serious forms of harassment (e.g., forced physical contact, sexual propositions linked to job outcomes), when they have witnesses to such harassment, and when they informed

384

CHAPTER 12

PREJUDICE AND
DISCRIMINATION:
NEGATIVE ATTITUDES
AND RELATIONS IN
THE WORKPLACE

management of the problem prior to taking legal action, but no steps were then taken to correct the situation.[26] In view of these results, it certainly seems wise for all organizations to implement the recommendations contained in points (1) and (2) above. Doing so will help reduce the incidence and severity of sexual harassment. And this, in turn, will contribute to the welfare of both individual employees and the entire organization.

REDUCING PREJUDICE AND DISCRIMINATION: COMPLEX PROBLEMS DEMAND COMPLEX SOLUTIONS

Prejudice and discrimination create tremendous problems both for individuals and for entire societies. Because of their presence, basic rights are often violated, injustice is fostered, and valuable pools of talent are wasted. Given these major costs, efforts to overcome the negative impact of prejudice and discrimination seem well justified. But do techniques for accomplishing this valuable goal exist? Can prejudice and discrimination actually be overcome? Fortunately, the answer appears to be "yes." When used with skill and care, several strategies appear to be successful in reducing prejudice and in eliminating the discriminatory practices it often breeds. Several of these are described below. Note that none, by itself, offers a perfect solution to the problem of prejudice. Rather, since prejudice stems from several different sources, a combination of tactics is probably needed to make serious dents in its armor.

Breaking the Chain of Bigotry: On Learning Not to Hate

We noted earlier that prejudice, like other attitudes, is learned. Children acquire their hatred of various groups largely through training provided by their parents, teachers, friends, or the mass media. Given this fact, it is apparent that one means for countering the impact of prejudice is that of somehow breaking this chain of bigotry—somehow preventing youngsters from acquiring such negative views early in life. This can be accomplished in several different ways. First, educational campaigns can call parents' attention to the important future costs attached to these attitudes. Second, teachers and schools can make special efforts to counter the training in prejudice many children receive at home. Third, changes can be made in the contents of television shows and other forms of the mass media, so that they expose audiences to positive, rather than negative, views toward minorities, women, the aged, the handicapped, and other groups that have often been the subject of discrimination. Of course, none of these steps is easy, and all require careful planning. However, growing evidence suggests that such procedures can help. For example, when children are exposed to television programs showing females in a positive light, their acceptance of negative sexual stereotypes is reduced.[27] Findings such as this indicate that systematic efforts to "nip prejudice in the bud" may well yield impressive, beneficial results.

Increased Intergroup Contact: The Positive Effects of Acquaintance

385
REDUCING PREJUDICE
AND DISCRIMINATION:
COMPLEX PROBLEMS
DEMAND COMPLEX
SOLUTIONS

One major source of prejudice seems to lie in our tendency to divide the social world into two opposing camps: "them" and "us." And closely associated with this process is our belief that people belonging to various out-groups (groups other than our own) are markedly different from ourselves. To the extent prejudice stems from these factors (and considerable evidence indicates that it does), another tactic for reducing its occurrence is suggested: increased contact with members of out-groups. If we actually meet such persons and interact with them on a regular basis, several beneficial changes may occur.[28] First, we may soon come to realize that they are much more similar to ourselves than we initially assumed. This growing recognition of similarity, in turn, may lead to increased liking for them. Second, as we get to know individual members of other groups, stereotypes about them—especially negative ones—are likely to be shattered. After all, it is hard to assume that all members of some group are alike when we learn through direct experience that they are not. And third, increased contact with members of other groups may lead to more positive views toward them simply because repeated exposure to almost any person or stimulus tends to produce such results—something known as the *mere exposure effect.* In sum, there are several reasons why increased contact with members of other groups may enhance our attitudes toward them, and so overcome prejudice. (See Figure 12.13, for a summary of these suggestions.)

In order for such effects to occur, however, certain conditions must prevail.[29] First, intergroup contact must take place in a context where the two groups

FIGURE 12.13 Intergroup Contact: The Basis for Its Beneficial Effects
As shown here, increased contact between different social groups can reduce prejudice in several ways.

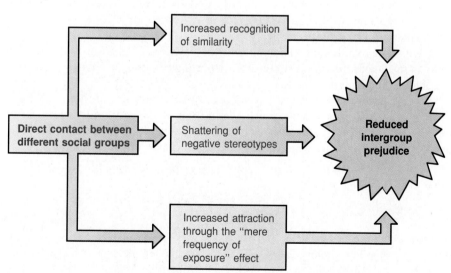

386
CHAPTER 12
PREJUDICE AND
DISCRIMINATION:
NEGATIVE ATTITUDES
AND RELATIONS IN
THE WORKPLACE

involved are approximately equal in social, economic, and task-related status. If, instead, they differ in these respects, communication between them may be difficult, and prejudice can actually be increased. Second, it is crucial that the two groups engage in relatively informal contacts. Formal or restricted ones do not seem helpful in countering stereotyping beliefs. Finally, the groups must meet under cooperative conditions, where they can work with rather than against one another. When such conditions are met, direct contact between members of different racial or ethnic groups can lead to sharp reductions in prejudice. In short, at such times, getting to know others better can serve as a useful step toward viewing them in more positive ways.

SUMMARY

Prejudice may be defined as a negative attitude toward the members of some group held by the members of another group. In contrast, **discrimination** refers to negative actions against the objects of prejudice. These can range from simple avoidance to exclusion of, or even direct assaults against, persons belonging to a disliked group. *Job discrimination* involves actions such as reluctance to hire persons from certain groups, failure to promote them, and attempts to pay them less than they deserve.

Prejudice seems to stem from several different sources. Sometimes it derives from direct economic competition between different groups. It is also encouraged by a strong tendency to divide the social world into two basic categories: "us" (in-group) and "them" (out-group). Finally, children often acquire prejudiced attitudes from their parents, friends, teachers, and the mass media.

Although females constitute a majority of the world's population, they have often been treated as a minority group. They have been excluded from economic and political power, have suffered overt discrimination, and have been the object of stereotyping. At present, blatant forms of discrimination against women in work settings seem to be decreasing. However, more subtle forms of bias against them persist, such as the tendency to devalue their achievements and to discount the competence of female leaders. Growing evidence suggests that when they serve as managers, females do not differ from males either in their personal traits or in their job-related behavior.

Several different strategies may be effective in reducing prejudice. First, educational campaigns may help prevent the formation of prejudiced views early in life. Second, increased contact between the members of groups holding prejudiced views may help eliminate negative stereotypes and may improve relations between them.

KEY TERMS

discrimination: Negative actions directed toward persons who are the object of prejudice.

illusion of out-group homogeneity: The tendency to view persons belonging to other groups as varying less than persons in our own group. Out-group members are all perceived as being very much alike.

intergroup conflict: A major cause of prejudice involving direct competition between various social groups for jobs, housing, educational opportunities, and so on.

intergroup contact: A technique for reducing prejudice based on increased contact between the members of different social groups.

prejudice: A negative attitude toward members of some specific group, held simply because those individuals belong to that group.

sexism: Prejudice toward other persons on the basis of their sex.

social categorization: Our basic tendency to divide the social world into two categories: the group to which we belong ("us") and groups to which we do not belong ("them").

stereotypes: Beliefs and expectations about the members of some social group. Stereotypes lead the persons holding them to assume that all members of a group possess the same traits and behave in the same manner.

NOTES

1. Katz, P.A., ed. (1976). *Toward the Elimination of Racism.* Elmsford, N.Y.: Pergamon Press.

2. Skrypnek, B.J., & Snyder, M. (1982). "On the Self-Perpetuating Nature of Stereotypes About Women and Men." *Journal of Experimental Social Psychology, 18,* 277–91.

3. Stephan, W.G., & Stephan, C.W. (1988). "Emotional Reactions to Interracial Achievement Outcomes." *Journal of Applied Social Psychology, 19,* 608–21.

4. Chacko, T.I. (1982). "Women and Equal Employment Opportunity: Some Unintended Effects." *Journal of Applied Psychology, 67,* 119–23.

5. Sherif, M., Harvey, O.J., White, B.J., Hood, W.R., & Sherif, C.W. (1961). *Intergroup Conflict and Cooperation: The Robbers' Cave Experiment.* Norman: University of Oklahoma Press.

6. Hepworth, J.T., & West, S.G. (1988). "Lynchings and the Economy: A Time-Series Reanalysis of Hovland and Sears (1940)." *Journal of Personality and Social Psychology, 55,* 239–47.

7. Locksley, A., Ortiz, V., & Hepburn, C. (1980). "Social Categorization and Discriminatory Behavior: Extinguishing the Minimal Intergroup Discrimination Effect." *Journal of Personality and Social Psychology, 39,* 773–83.

8. Schaller, M., & Maass, A. (1989). "Illusory Correlation and Social Categorization: Toward an Integration of Motivational and Cognitive Factors in Stereotype Formation." *Journal of Personality and Social Psychology, 56,* 709–21.

9. Turner, J.C., & Oakes, P.J. (1989). "Self-categorization Theory and Social Influence." In P.B. Paulus, ed. *Psychology of Group Influence.* Hillsdale, N.J.: Lawrence Erlbaum Associates.

10. Tajfel, H. (1982). *Social Identity and Intergroup Relations.* Cambridge: Cambridge University Press.

11. Helmreich, R.L., Spence, J.T., & Gibson, R.H. (1980). "Sex-Role Attitudes: 1972–1980." *Personality and Social Psychology Bulletin, 8,* 656–63.

12. Wallis, C. (Dec. 4, 1989). "Onward, Women!" *Time.*

13. Heilman, M.E., & Martell, R.F. (1986). "Exposure to Successful Women: Antidote to Sex Discrimination in Applicant Screening Decisions?" *Organizational Behavior and Human Decision Processes, 37,* 376–90.

14. Heilman, M.E., Martell, R.F., & Simon, M.C. (1988). "The Vagaries of Sex Bias: Conditions Regulating the Undervaluation, Equivaluation, and Overvaluation of Female Job Applicants." *Organizational Behavior and Human Decision Processes, 41,* 98–110.

388

CHAPTER 12
PREJUDICE AND
DISCRIMINATION:
NEGATIVE ATTITUDES
AND RELATIONS IN
THE WORKPLACE

15. Major, B., & Konar, E. (1984). "An Investigation of Sex Differences in Pay Expectations and Their Possible Causes." *Academy of Management Journal, 27,* 777–92.

16. McCarty, P.A. (1986). "Effects of Feedback on the Self-Confidence of Men and Women." *Academy of Management Journal, 29,* 840–47.

17. Mitchell, T.R., & Kalb, L.S. (1982). "Effects of Job Experience on Supervisor Attributions for a Subordinate's Poor Performance." *Journal of Applied Psychology, 67,* 181–88.

18. Stevens, G.E., & DeNisi, A.S. (1980). "Women as Managers: Attitudes and Attributions for Performance by Men and Women." *Academy of Management Journal, 23,* 355–61.

19. Peters, L.H., O'Connor, E.J., Weekely, J., Pooyan, A., Frank, B., & Erekrantz, B. (1984). "Sex Bias and Managerial Evaluations: A Replication and Extension." *Journal of Applied Psychology, 69,* 349–52.

20. Basow, S.A. (1981). *Sex-role Stereotypes: Traditions and Alternatives.* Monterey, Calif.: Brooks/Cole.

21. Steinberg, R., & Shapiro, S. (1982). "Sex Differences in Personality Traits of Female and Male Master of Business Administration Students." *Journal of Applied Psychology, 67,* 306–10.

22. Donnell, S.M., & Hall, J. (1980). "Men and Women as Managers: A Significant Case of No Significant Difference." *Organizational Dynamics,* 60–77.

23. Goktepe, J.R., & Schneier, C.E. (1989). "Role of Sex, Gender Roles, and Attraction in Predicting Emergent Leaders." *Journal of Applied Psychology, 74,* 165–67.

24. Graves, L.M., & Powell, L.M. (1988). "An Investigation of Sex Discrimination in Recruiters' Evaluations of Actual Applicants." *Journal of Applied Psychology, 73,* 20–29.

25. Terpstra, D.E., & Baker, D.D. (1988). "Outcomes of Sexual Harassment Charges." *Academy of Management Journal, 31,* 185–94.

26. See Note 25.

27. Liebert, R.M., Neale, J.M., & Sprafkin, J. (1982). *The Early Window: Effects of Television on Children and Youth,* 2d ed. New York: Pergamon.

28. Pettigrew, T.F. (1981). "Extending the Stereotype Concept." In D.L. Hamilton, ed. *Cognitive processes in Stereotyping and Intergroup Behavior,* pp. 303–31. Hillsdale, N.J.: Lawrence Erlbaum Associates.

29. Cook, S.W. (1985). "Experimenting on Social Issues: The Case of School Desegregation." *American Psychologist, 40,* 452–60.

ADDITIONAL CASES AND EXERCISES: APPLYING WHAT YOU'VE LEARNED

Real Men Don't Type

Don H. Hockenbury
Psychology Instructor
Tulsa Junior College

Sandra E. Hockenbury
Adjunct Instructor
Tulsa Junior College

Last week the four secretaries at the Cox & Devine Law Firm received a memo indicating that a fifth secretary was being hired for the summer. The new secretary, the memo said, was being hired to cover the vacation time of the four full-time secretaries so that work loads would remain pretty much constant throughout the summer months. All four secretaries were relieved when they got the memo, because several problems had occurred the previous summer when staff members had gone on vacation. The memo indicated that the new secretary, Meredith Lewis, would begin on Wednesday. The only other information the memo gave about the new secretary was that Meredith was a pre-law student at the local university and was home for summer break.

On the Tuesday before Meredith was to begin work, the four regular secretaries decided they would take Meredith to lunch on Wednesday as a welcoming gesture. Everyone was looking forward to meeting her and they speculated openly about what she would be like.

"At least we probably won't have to teach her about legal terminology," Sue speculated. "I mean, after all, she's a pre-law student so she must know something about how to type contracts and briefs."

"We may have to teach her about our new word processing system though, now that we've got access to the computerized case searches," Marsha suggested.

The other two women, Kelsy and Judy, were more worried that she might be a know-it-all because she was a pre-law major.

On Wednesday morning, as the secretaries were getting their morning coffee and surveying the stacks of work on their desks, the senior law partner, Roger Cox, walked into the office with a tall, lanky young man at his side.

"Ladies, could I have your attention for a moment," Mr. Cox began. "I'd like you to meet Meredith Lewis, the summer secretary."

The four secretaries stared at the young man in silence.

"Hi, it's a pleasure to meet you," Meredith smiled at them.

"Sue, I'd appreciate it if you'd show Meredith around the office today and orient him to the way we do things," Mr. Cox said, oblivious to the reaction of the four secretaries. "You're going to have to pick things up quickly, Meredith, because one of the secretaries is starting on vacation next week, right? I don't remember which one of you is going on vacation."

"I am," Kelsy reminded him.

"Ah! Okay, good. Well, Kelsy, maybe you should show Meredith around today and explain to him which projects you're working on so that he can take over your position next week. Does that sound okay?"

390

CHAPTER 12

PREJUDICE AND
DISCRIMINATION:
NEGATIVE ATTITUDES
AND RELATIONS IN
THE WORKPLACE

Kelsy nodded agreement, still looking at the lanky young man with suspicion.

For the remainder of the morning Kelsy described procedures in the law office to Meredith and, in particular, she showed him the projects she was currently working on. Meredith took numerous notes, asked questions occasionally, and seemed intensely interested in learning all that he could.

At 10:30 that morning the four secretaries took their coffee break and went down to the lobby of the office building. Meredith wasn't invited to go along. Instead, they had him answer the phones while they were away from their desks. During the coffee break, it was decided to cancel the idea of taking the "new girl" to lunch.

"Can you believe this?" Sue complained to the other women on their coffee break. "They hired some guy to do our jobs? I'll bet he doesn't even know how to type!"

"No, he's a great typist!" Kelsy pointed out. "He types right around seventy words per minute."

"Why'd they hire this guy anyway? Why couldn't they hire a female secretary? Guys aren't secretaries unless they're weird or something is wrong with them," Judy said accusingly.

"Well, I don't want that guy sitting at my desk and going through my drawers," Sue said. "In fact, I think I'm going to complain about this because it's not right to have some guy doing our jobs."

"This is going to be a long summer," Marsha said with annoyance. "If this guy thinks he's going to have some kind of buddy-buddy relationship with us then he's got another thing coming. If he's like most men, he'll probably start telling us how we should be doing our jobs instead of us telling him what he should be doing. Besides, I hate talking about football."

"Well, I don't think we should help make him look good," Judy added. "If he's going to survive this summer he'll have to make it on his own."

Kelsy quietly listened to others make their comments. Finally, when there was a lull in the conversation, she spoke up. "I don't think you're being fair," she said firmly, the other three women glancing at her. "He told me he's been working in his dad's law office since he was fourteen years old. He already knows how to type contracts, depositions, and briefs. He's even had some experience typing courtroom transcripts. He seems really familiar with legal terminology, court procedures, and even billing methods. When I was explaining things to him this morning, he asked really good questions and took notes. I don't know about you, but I think he's going to be a great help to us this summer, even if he is a guy."

"You just like him because he's got a cute little fanny," Sue chided her.

"Is that why they hired you?" Kelsy shot back at her.

"Not Sue, but maybe Judy!" Marsha laughed, trying to get the group to lighten up.

"Well, I don't know about the three of you, but when I was hired I appreciated the help that I got from the other secretaries in learning my way around this law firm. I don't think we need to hold it against this guy because he'd rather be a secretary for the summer instead ot working for the highway department filling in potholes on Interstate 90," Kelsy said with conviction.

"Well, I still think they should have hired a woman," Judy said again. "But I agree with Sue, he does have a cute little tush."

"You're hopeless!" Kelsy threw her hands up in exasperation.

"I agree with Kelsy," Marsha said firmly. "I don't think we should isolate him because, after all, they did hire him to help us. I mean, if it was a choice between him or no help at all for the summer, which would you rather have?"

"I'd rather have Paul Newman," Sue quipped.

"Skip Paul Newman, Kevin Costner is my first choice!" Judy chimed in.

"You're hopeless! You're all hopeless!" Kelsy said, shaking her head.

"Well, all I can say is that Mr. Football has to take his turn making the coffee," Sue said flatly.

When the four secretaries returned from their break they found a freshly brewed pot of coffee, compliments of Meredith.

"By the way," Meredith said when they got back. "Do you think we could have lunch together today so we can get to know each other?"

The four secretaries paused, glancing at each other.

"That sounds like a great idea!" Kelsy spoke up. "In fact, we were planning to buy you lunch today."

"As long as we don't talk about football," Marsha groaned.

Meredith looked puzzled. "Why would I talk about football? I never watch football."

Questions

1. Identify the cognitive, affective, and behavioral components of the stereotype the full-time secretaries initially had of their new co-worker.

2. Speculate on how social learning theory contributed to the initial reactions of the four full-time secretaries to their new office mate.

3. What kinds of things can Meredith do to avoid an atmosphere of "females versus male" over the course of the summer?

4. Other than simply telling the regular secretaries that Meredith was a male, how could this situation have been handled differently to avoid the initial negative reaction that the regular secretaries had?

5. If the four regular secretaries had decided to discriminate against Meredith by isolating and excluding him, how should he have handled it in order to potentially produce a more positive atmosphere?

Prejudice and the Mass Media: Television Then and Now

Earlier in this chapter, it was noted that one means for reducing prejudice and discrimination might involve changes in the mass media. Specifically, if women, members of various minorities, the handicapped, and others were portrayed in a positive manner, perhaps negative beliefs about them could be changed, and prejudice itself reduced. While the total picture is still far from perfect, major shifts of this type have occurred in many television programs. In contrast to the situation prevailing in past decades, women and minorities are now often presented

392

CHAPTER 12
PREJUDICE AND
DISCRIMINATION:
NEGATIVE ATTITUDES
AND RELATIONS IN
THE WORKPLACE

FORM A New Programs

Name of Program	Age, Sex, Background of Character Observed	Role or Job Held By This Person	Major Traits Shown By This Person

FORM B Old Programs

Name of Program	Age, Sex, Background of Character Observed	Role or Job Held By This Person	Major Traits Shown By This Person

as holding high-status jobs and as possessing many positive traits. You can demonstrate the magnitude of this shift yourself by following these simple procedures.

First, select about five popular television shows—shows that you and many people you know regularly watch. For each, keep a record of the manner in which women, minorities, handicapped people, and the aged are depicted. (Use Form A for this task.) Now, for comparison, select five shows first produced in past decades (shows from the 1950s and 1960s are best.) Use Form B to keep track of how women, minorities, and other disadvantaged groups were portrayed in these shows.

Finally, examine your results. You will probably find that as compared to the older shows, new ones depict minorities, women, and other disadvantaged groups in a much more favorable light. The impact of such shifts is difficult to assess, and probably won't be visible for many years. But at least some steps in the right direction appear to have been taken.

Occupations and Sex-Role Stereotypes

Robert D. Goddard III
Associate Professor, Department of Management
Appalachian State University

In order to better understand sex-role stereotyping and occupations, try to find at least one man in a traditionally female-dominated occupation (secretary, telephone operator, nurse, elementary teacher, or the like), and one woman in a male-dominated occupation (military officer, police officer, fire fighter, construction worker) and interview them. Ask them the following questions:

1. Did you become a (nurse/fire fighter/operator) as a result of a conscious desire to break new ground, so to speak, in your field?

2. Have you suffered from discrimination or prejudice as a result of your occupational decision? If so, what form has it taken? If not, why were you accepted so readily?

3. Do you believe that successful performance on the job is related to ability, or to luck?

4. What advice would you give to people going into occupations traditionally dominated by members of the opposite sex to help them avoid the effects of discrimination or prejudice?

CHAPTER

13

Stress and Burnout: Key Problems at Work

Learning Objectives

After reading this chapter,
you should be able to:

1. Discuss the basic characteristics of stress.

2. Describe several major work-related causes of stress.

3. Discuss how life events and daily hassles are related to stress.

4. Explain how reactions to stress are affected by several personal characteristics (e.g., optimism, hardiness).

5. Describe the impact of stress on personal health, task performance, and the use of alcohol and drugs.

6. Define burnout and indicate why it occurs.

7. Describe several personal and organizational techniques for managing stress.

t looks like it is going to be another one of those days for Laurie Elwell. She is frantically trying to get her kids out of the house in time to meet the school bus.

"Come on Chris and Leigh, you're going to be late again! I have to get out of here you know."

Laurie works as an accountant for a large firm. The end of the month reports are due in a couple of days, so she can't afford to be late.

I wish I could just take a day off to relax, she thinks. *I've been working under one deadline after another. It never seems to let up.* To add to Laurie's problems, she's been having conflicts with her boss, Shirley Canalas. Shirley often wants her to work late on weekends, but Laurie wants to be home with the kids. She's afraid she might lose her job over this. Lately, she's been having a lot of headaches and feels exhausted most of the time. *Maybe I should go see a doctor,* she thinks. *Better yet, maybe I should find a new job.*

You have probably faced situations similar to Laurie's. All of us periodically *have* to deal with pressures at home, at work, and at school. At times we may feel like we can't handle any more. We may feel tense or depressed, have trouble sleeping, and reach a stage of physical and emotional exhaustion. If you've even had this type of experience, you've encountered one of the most common problems of the twentieth century—**stress.**

Unfortunately, such conditions are far from rare in the world of work, or in modern life generally. Even worse, when they occur, they often exert far-ranging negative effects on the persons exposed to them. For these reasons, stress is a timely topic, fully deserving of our close attention. This chapter, therefore, focuses on stress and on the closely related topic of **burnout.** Our examination of these topics will proceed as follows. First, we will examine the basic nature of stress. Then we will consider several causes of stress—factors that lead to its occurrence. Third, we will discuss personal factors that influence the way we react to stress. Next, we will examine the effects of stress. Since burnout is one of the most serious of these, it will be discussed later. Finally, we will turn to several techniques for managing stress—tactics for reducing or countering its negative impact.

STRESS: ITS BASIC NATURE

How would you describe the experience of stress? Most people think of stress as an unpleasant emotional state accompanied by high levels of arousal. To a degree, such descriptions are accurate; Stress does indeed involve a subjective, emotional component. However, experts on this subject now agree that this is only part of the total picture. To fully understand stress and its many effects, we must understand three related issues.[1]

First, we must consider *physiological aspects* of stress. According to Selye, a leading expert on this topic, these can be divided into several distinct stages.[2] When first confronted with any threat to our safety or well-being, we experience an immediate and vigorous *alarm reaction*. Arousal rises quickly to high levels, and many physiological changes that prepare our bodies for strenuous activity (as in flight or combat) take place. This initial reaction is soon replaced by a second stage known as *resistance*. Here, activation remains relatively high but drops to levels that are more sustainable over relatively long periods of time. Finally, if stress persists, the body's resources may become depleted and a final stage known as *exhaustion* occurs. At this point, the ability to cope (at least physically) decreases sharply, and severe biological damage may result if stress persists. (See Figure 13.1 for a summary of these physiological reactions.)

Second, in order to fully understand stress it is necessary to consider the external events or stimuli that induce it—the nature of various **stressors.** What is it about these stimuli that produces stress? What do they have in common? It appears that many events we find stressful share the following properties: (1) they are so intense, in some respect, that they produce a state of *overload*—we can no longer adapt to them; (2) they evoke simultaneous incompatible tendencies (e.g., tendencies to both approach and avoid some object or activity); and (3) they are uncontrollable—outside our ability to change or influence.

FIGURE 13.1 Physiological Reactions to Stress: Three Stages

When we are exposed to stress, several physiological changes occur. First, we experience a vigorous *alarm reaction*. This is followed by a stage of *resistance* in which we actively seek to cope with the source of stress. If stress persists, a final stage of *exhaustion* may occur, in which our ability to cope with stress drops to low levels. *Source:* Based on research by Selye (1976); see Note 2.

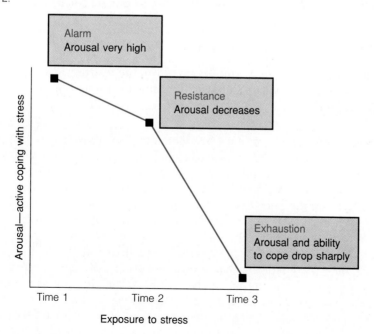

Perhaps most important of all, stress involves the operation of several cognitive factors. Perhaps the most central of these is individuals' *cognitive appraisals* of a given situation or potential stressor. In simple terms, stress occurs only to the extent that the persons involved perceive (1) that the situation is somehow threatening to their important goals, and (2) they will be unable to cope with these potential dangers or demands.[3] In short, stress does not simply shape our thoughts; in many cases, it derives from and is strongly affected by them.

To understand the nature of stress, therefore, it is necessary to consider the emotional and physiological reactions it involves, the external conditions that produce it, and the cognitive processes that play a role in its occurrence.[4] Taking all these factors into account, we can define stress as follows: *It is a pattern of negative emotional and physiological reactions occurring in situations where individuals perceive threats to their important goals that they may be unable to meet.*[5] In short, stress occurs where individuals feel, rightly or wrongly, that they may soon be overwhelmed by events or circumstances that exceed their personal resources.[6]

STRESS: ITS MAJOR CAUSES

Stress and work—somehow, the two words seem to go together. And the reason for this is obvious: Most of us experience at least some degree of stress in our jobs. In fact, like Laurie in our opening example, we are exposed to many events and conditions that cause us to feel pressured or in danger of being pushed to our personal limits. Factors contributing to stress at work vary greatly in their nature and scope. Most, however, fall into two major categories: ones relating to our jobs or organization, and ones relating to our personal characteristics.

Work-Related Causes of Stress

What aspects of jobs or organizations contribute to stress? Unfortunately, the list is long. Here, we will consider several of the most important of these sources of strain and discomfort.

Occupational Demands: Some Jobs Are More Stressful Than Others   Think about the following jobs: production manager, librarian, emergency room physician, janitor, firefighter, college professor, airline pilot. Do they differ in degree of stressfulness? Obviously, they do. Some, such as emergency room physician, firefighter, and airline pilot expose the persons who hold them to high levels of stress. Others, such as college professor, janitor, and librarian do not. This basic fact—that some jobs are much more stressful than others—has been confirmed by the results of a careful survey involving more than 130 different occupations.[7] Results of this survey indicate that several jobs (e.g., physician, office manager, foreman, waitress or waiter) are quite high in stress. In contrast, others (e.g., maid, craft workers, farm laborer) are much lower in this regard (see Figure 13.2). Occasionally, jobs change in the amount of stress involved. For example, working for the post office used to be considered a fairly easy-going job. However, with changes in technology and increased pressures for productivity, the job of postal worker has become much more stressful.[8]

Why are some jobs more stressful than others? It appears that several features of jobs are indeed related to the levels of stress they generate.[9] For example, the greater the extent to which a given job requires (1) decisions, (2) the constant monitoring of devices or materials, (3) repeated exchange of information with others, (4) unpleasant physical conditions, and (5) performing unstructured rather than structured tasks, the more stressful it tends to be (see Figure 13.3). Moreover—and this is the most important point—such relationships were found to be quite general in nature. Thus the greater the extent to which virtually *any* job possesses these characteristics, the higher the level of stress it produces among persons holding it, regardless of the specific tasks being performed.

These findings and related evidence in other studies indicate that one major source of stress at work involves the nature and demands of various jobs.[10] For this reason, it is probably wise to take two key factors into account whenever you consider a career in some field, or a job in a specific company: the level of stress it will involve, and your own ability to handle such pressures. Given the powerful impact of stress on our physical and mental well-being (effects we will soon review), this may be one case where it really pays to "look before you leap!" (For specific suggestions on how to assess various aspects of different careers, please see Chapter 14.) How much stress do you encounter on the job you now hold? For some revealing insights into this important question, see the **Human Relations in Action** on page 402.

Role Conflict: Stress from Conflicting Demands Consider the following situation. Because she has done such excellent work, a young engineer is promoted and becomes one of her company's key troubleshooters. Her new job requires her to

FIGURE 13.2 Job Stress: Varies with Jobs
Some jobs are typically more stressful (such as firefighting) than others (e.g., artist).

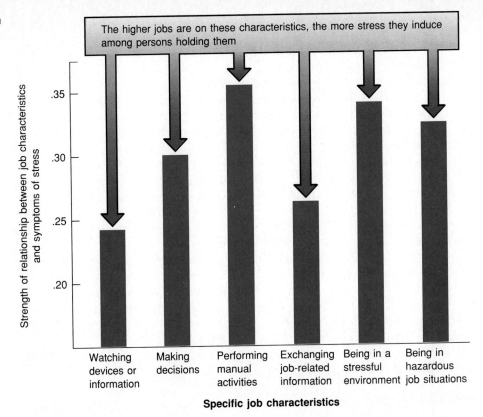

FIGURE 13.3 Job Characteristics: Contributing to Stress
Certain characteristics of jobs tend to make them stressful. The ones shown here all seem to contribute to the "stress quotient" of various jobs. Note that the higher the values shown, the greater the contribution of each job characteristic to stress. *Source:* Based on data from Shaw and Riskind (1983); see Note 9.

visit various plants to help the local people at these locations solve various problems. Because her company's factories are located hundreds of miles apart, she must travel often, and she is away from home at least two weekends every month. Her supervisor is very pleased with her work and gives her more and more assignments. Her husband and two children, though, miss her very much and put increasing pressure on her to give up the new job and stay home with them. Is this a stressful situation for the young woman concerned? You bet it is! She finds herself pulled in two directions at once by the needs and expectations of two groups of persons: her family and people at work. Moreover, there seems to be no easy or simple way to reconcile these conflicting demands. The result: she experiences a considerable degree of role conflict. Unfortunately, since most people play several different roles in their lives and must deal with groups of persons holding contrasting expectations about their behavior, **role conflict** is quite common.[11] In fact, it is often an important source of stress both on and off the job.

Interestingly, recent evidence gathered by Newton and Keenan indicates that the adverse effects of role conflict are less pronounced in work settings characterized by warmth and support than in those where such factors are lacking.[12] These findings suggest that while a degree of role conflict is probably unavoidable in many contexts, its contribution to overall levels of stress can be reduced by other, positive conditions.

Role Ambiguity: Stress from Uncertainty   Even if an individual avoids the stress associated with role conflict, she or he may still encounter an even more common source of job-related stress: **role ambiguity.** This occurs when individuals are uncertain about several matters relating to their jobs: the scope of their responsibilities, exactly what's expected of them, how to divide their time between various duties. Most persons dislike such uncertainty and find it quite stressful. Since we seldom possess complete or totally satisfactory knowledge about such matters, role ambiguity is quite common. In fact, 35 to 60 percent of employees surveyed report experiencing it to some degree.[13] Clearly, then, it is a major cause of stress in many work settings.

Overload and Underload: Doing Too Much or Too Little   When the phrase "job stress" is mentioned, most people envision scenes like the ones shown in Figure 13.4. That is, they imagine either a harried executive attempting to dictate a letter, talk on three phones, and conduct an interview all at once, or a post office employee frantically trying to zip through letters, one per second. In short, they conjure up an image of someone caught in the trap of trying to do too much in too little time. In this case, common belief is not far off the mark, for overload is in fact a major cause of stress at work. Actually, a distinction is often made between **quantitative overload**—a situation in which an individual is confronted with more work than can be completed in a given period of time, and **qualitative overload**—the belief by an employee that he or she lacks the skills or abilities required to perform a given job. Both types of overload are unpleasant, and research findings suggest that both can lead to high levels of stress.[14]

But overload is only part of the total picture. While being asked to do too much on one's job can be stressful, so, too, is the opposite—being asked to do too little. In fact, there seems to be considerable truth to the following saying: "The hardest job in the world is doing nothing—you can't stop and take a break." Such *underload* (or underutilization) leads to boredom and monotony. In this respect, it can be quite stressful. Again, a distinction between **quantitative underload** and **qualitative underload** is often drawn. Quantitative underload refers to the boredom that results when employees have so little to do that they find themselves sitting around much of the time. In contrast, qualitative underload refers to the lack of mental stimulation that accompanies many routine, repetitive jobs. Thus an individual experiencing qualitative underload can be doing quite a bit but still be bored to tears.

Most persons find either type of underload stressful, and for good reason. First, everyone wishes to feel useful and needed. Thus discovering that we are accomplishing next to nothing on our job may be damaging to our self-esteem. Second, human beings seem to possess a basic need for stimulation. Contrary to what common sense suggests, their preferred state is definitely *not* that of staring blankly into space. On the contrary, most people prefer to be active and to be doing interesting things at least part of the time. For these reasons, jobs that demand too little can be as stressful as those that demand too much. In sum, it appears that, with respect to the amount of work or effort demanded from individuals by their jobs, the middle course is best. The most desirable, and least stressful, jobs seem to be those that keep their holders busy but do not overtax their abilities, or lead them to feel unable to cope. Figure 13.5 summarizes the stressful impact of underload and overload.

Responsibility for Others: Often, a Heavy Burden   In any organization, there is a division of responsibility. Some persons deal primarily with financial matters such as budgets, others handle the flow of supplies or maintenance equipment, and still others deal primarily with people. Are there any differences in the level of stress associated with these contrasting types of responsibility? Research suggests that there are. In general, people responsible for other people—those who must deal with, motivate, and make decisions about others—experience higher levels of stress than persons who handle other aspects of a business.[15] Such persons are more likely to report feelings of tension and anxiety and to demonstrate physical symptoms of stress, such as ulcers and hypertension, than their counterparts in finance, supply, and so on. The basis for this difference is obvious. Supervisors and managers must witness the pain of persons who are fired or passed

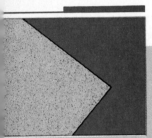

HUMAN RELATIONS IN ACTION

Stress: Too Much or Too Little?

Our comments so far seem to suggest that *any* exposure to stress is harmful. In fact, however, this is not the case. While stress often exerts negative effects on individuals and organizations, it has a positive side, too.[16] Many persons seem to do their best work when facing deadlines or other types of pressure. And many report enjoying the feelings of arousal or activation that accompany moderate levels of stress. Conversely, most persons become bored or apathetic if their jobs present them with no challenge whatsoever. In sum, it appears that extremely low levels of stress (or its total absence), as well as very high levels of such pressure, can be damaging to performance and morale. We will return to the relationship between stress and job performance later. At this point, though, you can determine how much stress you are currently facing on your own job by answering the questions below. Simply place a check next to each item in column 1 and column 2 that describes your current job.

Column 1	*Column 2*
_____ I don't have enough responsibility.	_____ I have too much responsibility.
_____ I have too much training for my job.	_____ I wish I had more training so I could do my job better.

over for promotion. As you can imagine, such experiences are often very stressful. So, being responsible for other persons *is* often a heavy burden, and one that exacts a toll in terms of job-related stress.

Lack of Social Support: The Costs of Isolation   You have probably noticed that often when people are under stress, they seek *support* and comfort from others. While this support and comfort may make them feel better, does it actually reduce the effects of stress? In general, the answer seems to be "yes." When individuals believe that they have the friendship and support of others at work, their ability to resist the adverse effects of stress seems to increase. For example, in one investigation on this topic, Oullette-Kobasa and Pucetti studied managers at a large public utility who were experiencing high levels of stress. They found that among such persons, those who felt they had the support of their immediate supervisors reported fewer physical symptoms associated with stress than managers who did not feel that they enjoyed such support.[17]

How does social support assist individuals in dealing with stress? Several mechanisms may play a role. First, having friends to whom they can turn in time of difficulty may help individuals to perceive stressful events as less threatening and more under their control than would otherwise be the case. Second, such persons can suggest useful strategies for dealing with sources of stress. Third, they

_____ My job lacks variety.

_____ I often have too much time on my hands.

_____ My job is not challenging.

_____ I don't have enough work to do much of the time.

_____ I am bored by the routine nature of my job.

_____ I have to force myself to stay alert.

_____ Sometimes, I have to search for things to do.

_____ I have to do too many different things.

_____ I don't have enough time to complete my work.

_____ I find my job too challenging.

_____ I don't have time to visit with friends because of my workload.

_____ I often find the pace of my job overwhelming.

_____ My work continues at such a fast pace that I don't have time to recover.

_____ I find that I often have to take work home with me.

If you checked five or more items in column 1, you probably experience very little or no stress on your current job; in fact, you may well find it boring or routine. If you checked five or more items in Column 2, in contrast, you currently face very high levels of stress. In that case, you will probably find our discussion of techniques for managing stress (presented later in this chapter) very helpful.

FIGURE 13.4 Overload: Two Examples

Overload, or being required to do too much, is one major cause of stress at work.

can help reduce the negative feelings that often accompany exposure to stressful events.[18]

Lack of Participation in Decisions: Helplessness Strikes Again   As we have noted on several occasions, most of us want to feel we have at least some control over our own fate. The opposite belief—that we are helpless pawns tossed about by forces beyond our control—is quite disturbing (see Figure 13.6). Unfortunately, one factor contributing to such feelings is common in work settings: lack of participation by employees in decisions affecting their jobs. Most persons feel that they know a lot about their work. Thus, when they are prevented from offering input into decisions relating to them, they experience feelings of being "left out" and reactions of helplessness, and so they encounter considerable stress.[19]

Other Organizational Sources of Stress: Evaluation, Working Conditions, and Change   The factors described above appear to be among the most important sources of stress within organizations. However, several others exist, too, and should briefly be mentioned here. First, there is the process of *performance appraisal* or *evaluation*. Being evaluated by others is a stressful experience, especially when the results of such appraisal have important effects on one's career. For this reason, as well as others, it is important that such appraisals be conducted in as fair and impartial a manner as possible. Second, *working conditions* are often an important source of stress. Extreme heat or cold, loud noise, crowding, repeated interruptions—all these, plus several other aspects of work settings can act as stressors and strongly affect the persons who must endure them.[20] Finally, stress often derives from *change* within an organization. Alterations in company policy, reorganizations in corporate structure, and major shifts in personnel or leadership can all produce high levels of stress among employees. We will return

FIGURE 13.5   Overload and Underload: Contrasting Patterns
Both overload and underload can serve as sources of stress at work. Two distinct patterns (quantitative and qualitative) exist for each.

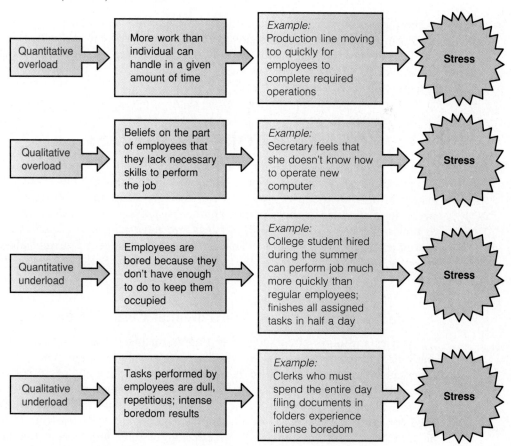

FIGURE 13.6 Lack of Control: A Disturbing State of Affairs
Most people desire some feeling of control over their lives, and like Ziggy, they may become
disturbed when things seem out of control. (Ziggy © 1989 Ziggy & Friends./Distributed by
Universal Press Syndicate. Reprinted with permission. All rights reserved.)

to the topic of change in work settings in Chapter 15. A summary of all of the
organizational sources of stress considered so far is provided in Figure 13.7. As
this figure—and our comments so far—suggest, sources of stress abound in the
modern world of work. Little wonder, then, that coping with such conditions is
a major task faced by most of us in the 1990s.

PERSONAL FACTORS AND STRESS

Let's begin this section with two basic facts: (1) what happens to people off
the job often affects the way they behave at work, and (2) the characteristics
people bring with them to their jobs can strongly affect the ways they react to
stress. In the context of these points, another basic fact becomes clear: If we wish
to fully understand stress in work settings, we must take into account personal
as well as organizational factors. That is, we must consider the current lifestyles,
attitudes, and characteristics of the persons in question. Some of these personal
factors will now be considered.

Life Events and Stress: The Potential Costs of Change

Movies and plays often suggest an important link between certain events in
one's life and personal health. Specifically, they often show individuals who have
experienced traumatic events (e.g., the death of a loved one, divorce) pining
away until they become seriously ill, or even die. This suggestion of a link between
stressful life events and health is intriguing and has important implications for
behavior in work settings. After all, employees who are suffering from ill health
or deep depression are unlikely to be effective at their jobs. But is this picture
accurate? The answer appears to be "yes." Many studies indicate that when

individuals undergo stressful changes in their lives, their personal health does indeed suffer.[21] Some of the events related to such changes are listed in Table 13.1. As you can see, events near the top of the table are very upsetting and stressful, while ones farther down are only mildly stress-inducing. (Note that death of a spouse is assigned 100 points while other life events receive smaller values reflecting their degree of stressfulness relative to this shattering event.) Research suggests that the greater the number and intensity of stressful life events individuals experienced, the greater their likelihood of developing serious illness. For example, persons who report life events totaling 150 to 300 points have about a 50 percent chance of becoming seriously ill during the next year. Those who experience events totaling more than 300 points have a 70 percent chance of such outcomes.

For example, in one study on this topic, Holmes and Masuda asked patients at a university medical center to report all significant life changes (events) during the past eighteen months.[22] Persons who experienced events totalling 300 points or more showed a much higher incidence of illness during the next nine months than those with 200 points or less (49 percent versus 9 percent).

The Hassles of Our Lives

Traumatic life events are relatively rare. Many persons live for years, or even decades, without experiencing any of them. Unfortunately, the daily life of most

FIGURE 13.7 Work-Related Causes of Stress: A Summary
Stress stems from many factors relating to work. Some of the most important of these are shown here.

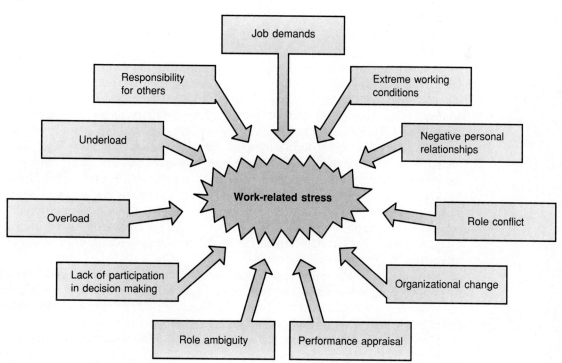

TABLE 13.1
Life Events: Some Are More Stressful Than Others

When asked to assign arbitrary points (1 to 100) to various life events according to the degree of readjustment they required, a large group of individuals provided these values. The higher the numbers shown, the more stressful the events listed. *Source:* Based on data from Holmes & Masuda (1974); see Note 22.

Event	Relative Stressfulness
Death of a spouse	100
Divorce	73
Marital separation	65
Jail term	63
Death of a close family member	63
Personal injury or illness	53
Marriage	50
Fired from job	47
Retirement	45
Pregnancy	40
Death of a close friend	37
Son or daughter leaving home	29
Trouble with in-laws	28
Trouble with boss	23
Change in residence	20
Vacation	13
Christmas	12

of us is filled with countless minor sources of stress that seem to make up for their relatively low intensity by their high frequency of occurrence. That such *daily hassles* are an important cause of stress is suggested by the findings of several studies by Lazarus and his colleagues.[23] These researchers have developed a *Hassles Scale* on which individuals indicate the extent to which they have been "hassled" by common events during the past month. As shown in Table 13.2, items included in this scale deal with a wide range of everyday events (e.g., having too many things to do at once, shopping, concerns over money). Scores on the Hassles Scale are related to both reports of psychological symptoms and physical health. The more stress people report as a result of such daily hassles, the poorer their psychological and physical health. Indeed, some findings suggest that stress induced by daily hassles has stronger effects on health than that resulting from traumatic life events.[24]

In sum, while traumatic life events such as the death of loved ones or the loss of one's job are stressful and exert adverse effects on health, the minor hassles of daily life—perhaps because of their frequent, repetitive nature—may sometimes prove even more crucial in this respect. Whatever their relative importance, both traumatic life events and daily hassles are important sources of stress for

TABLE 13.2
Daily Hassles: A Common Source of Stress

The everyday events and concerns shown here are ones that many persons describe as common sources of stress. *Source:* Based on information in Lazarus et al. (1985); see Note 23.

Household hassles	Preparing meals
	Shopping
Time pressure hassles	Too many things to do
	Too many responsibilities
Inner concern hassles	Being lonely
	Fear of confrontation
Environmental hassles	Neighborhood deterioration
	Noise
	Crime
Financial responsibility	Concerns about owing money
	Financial responsibility for someone who doesn't live with you

many persons. And since this stress is often carried into the workplace by the persons involved, it is certainly worth noting in this discussion of stress and its impact in work settings.

Individual Differences in Resistance to Stress: Optimism, Pessimism, and Hardiness

You have probably observed that individuals differ greatly in their resistance to stress. Some suffer ill effects after exposure to brief periods of relatively mild stress, while others are able to function effectively even after prolonged exposure to much stronger levels of stress. How do such persons differ? There appear to be a number of key characteristics that play an important role.

Optimism: A Buffer against Stress One personal factor that seems to play an important role in determining resistance to stress is the familiar dimension of *optimism-pessimism*. Optimists, of course, are people who see the glass as half full; they are hopeful in their outlook on life, interpret a wide range of situations in a positive light, and tend to expect favorable outcomes and results. Pessimists, in contrast, are individuals who see the glass as half empty; they interpret many situations negatively, and expect unfavorable outcomes and results. Recent studies indicate that, as you might well guess, optimists are much more stress-resistant than pessimists. For example, optimists are much less likely than pessimists to report physical illness and symptoms during highly stressful periods such as final exams.[25] Optimists and pessimists seem to adopt sharply contrasting tactics for coping with stress. Optimists engage in *problem-focused coping*—making and enacting specific plans for dealing with sources of stress (see Figure 13.8 for a humorous example). In addition, they seek *social support*—the advice and help of friends and others, and refrain from engaging in other activities until current

FIGURE 13.8 Problem-Focused Coping: Getting a Handle on Stress
Cathy appears to be engaging in *problem-focused* coping, although the specific goal attained does not effectively deal with the source of stress. (Cathy © 1989 Universal Press Syndicate. Reprinted with permission. All rights reserved.)

problems are solved and stress is reduced. On the other hand, pessimists tend to adopt different strategies, such as giving up in their efforts to reach goals with which stress is interfering, and denying that the stressful events have even occurred.[26] (See Figure 13.9). Needless to say, the former strategies are often more effective than the latter.

Hardiness: Viewing Stress as a Challenge Another characteristic that seems to distinguish stress-resistant people from those who are more susceptible to its harmful effects is known as **hardiness.**[27] Actually, this term refers to a cluster of characteristics rather than just one. Hardy persons seem to differ from others in three respects: (1) *commitment*—they have deeper involvement in their jobs and other life activities; (2) *control*—they believe that they can, in fact, influence important events in their lives and the outcomes they experience; and (3) *challenge*—they perceive change as a challenge and an opportunity to grow rather than as a threat to their security.

Together, these characteristics tend to arm hardy persons with high resistance to stress. Several studies with persons of different occupations have found that persons classified as high in hardiness indeed report better health than those low in hardiness, even when they had recently encountered major stressful life changes. Together, such findings suggest that hardiness is a useful concept in understanding the impact of stress.

STRESS: SOME IMPORTANT EFFECTS

By now, you are probably convinced that stress derives from many sources and is quite common at work. What you may still not fully realize, though, is just how powerful and far-reaching its effects can be. Systematic research on this topic indicates that stress influences our physical well-being, our psychological states, our personal adjustment, and many aspects of our behavior. In fact, there is hardly any aspect of our lives that it does not affect. Information about the specific nature of these effects follows. But be prepared for some intriguing—and unsettling—surprises.

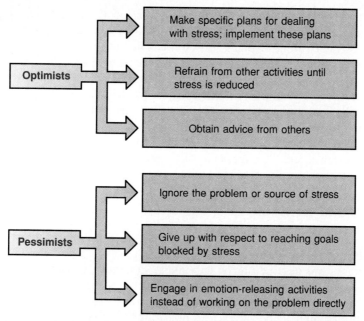

FIGURE 13.9 Optimists and Pessimists: Different Ways of Coping with Stress
Optimists and pessimists adopt different strategies for coping with stress. In general, those chosen by optimists are more effective. *Source:* Based on suggestions by Scheier, Weintraub, & Carver (1986); see Note 26.

Stress and Health: The Silent Killer

Here comes the first of the surprises we promised: At the present time, most medical experts believe that from *50 percent to 70 percent of physical illnesses are related to stress.*[28] Moreover, included among these stress-related diseases are some of the most serious and fatal ones known to medical science. We have already touched on evidence linking stress to heart disease (see our discussion on the Type A personality pattern in Chapter 5). Here, we will simply add that high levels of stress are also linked to the following major health problems: high blood pressure, arteriosclerosis (hardening of the arteries), ulcers, and diabetes. In short, stress is implicated in the occurrence of some of the leading causes of death among human beings. If you needed any further basis for giving it careful consideration in your own life, this fact should provide it!

Stress: Its Effects on Our Mental States

At present, most behavioral scientists believe that mind and body are closely connected. Events and conditions affecting one often affect the other. Given this view, it is not surprising to learn that as stress affects our basic bodily processes, it also influences our psychological states. Several such effects have been uncovered. First, as you might well expect, exposure to stress often induces negative changes in mood or emotions. Persons experiencing stress frequently report such feelings as anxiety, depression, irritation, and fatigue. Second, exposure to stress—especially stress relating to one's job—may result in lowered self-esteem.[29] This seems to stem from the fact that persons experiencing stress often feel unable to cope with their job. This, in turn, affects feelings of competence and self-worth, and reduces self-esteem. Third, and perhaps most important, stress is often associated with reductions in job satisfaction.[30] Considering the negative and unpleasant nature of intense, continued stress, this is far from surprising. In any case, given the important links between job satisfaction and key forms of behavior at work (reviewed in Chapter 11), the effect of stress on such attitudes has important practical implications.

Stress and Behavior at Work

At one time, it was generally believed that stress improved performance on a wide range of tasks. Specifically, the relationship between stress and performance on many tasks was assumed to be curvilinear in nature, so that at first, increases in stress (from none to low or moderate levels), were energizing, and led to improved performance. Beyond some point, however, additional increments in stress were assumed to be distracting or to interfere with performance in other ways. Thus, at high or very high levels of stress, performance would actually fall (Figure 13.10).

While this relationship may hold true under some conditions, growing evidence suggests that stress exerts mainly negative effects on task performance. In other words, performance can be disrupted even by relatively low levels of stress. Evidence for this is provided by a study conducted by Motowidlo, Packard, and Manning.[31] These researchers asked a large group of nurses to describe their own levels of work-related stress. Ratings of their actual job performance were then obtained from supervisors or co-workers. Results indicated that the higher the nurses' feelings of stress, the lower their job performance. In other words, there was no evidence for initial increments in performance, as the curvilinear hypothesis would suggest.

These findings, and those of several other studies indicate that in many real-life settings, performance may be reduced even by low or moderate levels of stress. Why is this the case? Shouldn't the activation produced by moderate levels of stress facilitate performance in many situations? Although this possibility remains and may apply in some situations, there are several reasons why even moderate levels of stress might be expected to interfere with task performance. First, even relatively mild stress can be distracting. Individuals experiencing it may focus on the unpleasant feelings and emotions stress involves rather than on the task at hand. As a result their performance suffers. Second, prolonged or repeated exposure to even mild levels of stress may exert harmful effects on health, and this may interfere with effective performance. Finally, as shown in Figure 13.10, as arousal increases, task performance may at first rise, but at some point, begins to fall.[32] The precise point where the fall occurs seems to depend, to a large extent, on the complexity of the task being performed. The greater the complexity, the lower the levels of arousal at which a downturn in performance occurs. Are the tasks performed by today's employees more complex than those

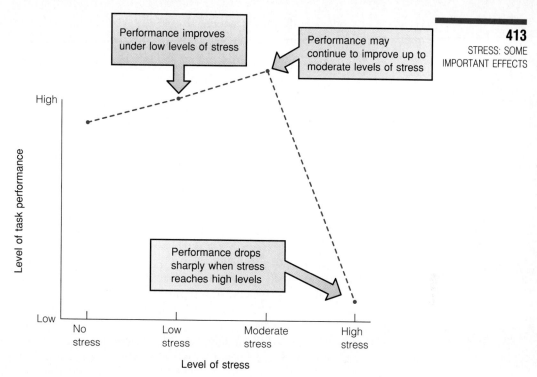

FIGURE 13.10 Stress and Task Performance: One Possibility
At one time, it was widely believed that as stress rises from very low to moderate levels, performance improves, but that beyond this point, performance drops as stress continues to rise. However, recent evidence suggests that the relationship between stress and performance is probably more complex than this.

in the past? Many observers contend that they are. For this reason, too, even relatively mild levels of stress may interfere with performance in today's complex world of work.

There are exceptions to the general rule that stress interferes with task performance. First, some individuals, at least, do seem to "rise to the occasion" and turn in exceptional performances at times of high stress. This may result from the fact that they are truly expert in the tasks being performed, so that the inflection point in the arousal-performance function described previously is very high (refer again to Figure 13.10). Alternatively, it may be the case that for persons who are exceptionally skilled at a given task, even very high levels of stress are cognitively appraised as a *challenge* rather than a *threat*.

Second, large individual differences seem to exist with respect to the impact of stress on task performance. As your own experience may suggest, some individuals do indeed seem to thrive on stress: They actively seek arousal and high levels of sensation or stimulation. For such persons, stress is exhilarating and may enhance their performance. In contrast, other persons react in an opposite manner. They seek to avoid arousal and high levels of sensation. Such individuals find stress upsetting, and it may interfere with their performance on many tasks.[33]

In summary, in many situations stress can indeed interfere with performance.

However, its precise effects depend on several different factors (e.g., complexity of the task being performed, personal characteristics of the individuals involved, their previous experience with this task). In view of such complexity, generalizations about the impact of stress on task performance should be made with considerable caution.

Task performance is not the only aspect of work behavior influenced by stress. In addition, stress is modestly related to absenteeism and turnover.[34] This is hardly surprising, for when individuals find their jobs highly stressful, they may well seek to avoid them. High levels of job stress are also linked to two other very important problems, alcoholism and drug abuse.

Alcohol, Drugs, and Stress: Flight from Reality

Stress, as we have repeatedly noted, is unpleasant. For this reason, most persons attempt to eliminate or reduce it whenever possible. For an overwhelming majority of individuals, this involves efforts to actively cope with the causes of stress, whether these involve problems at home or on the job. Some, however, adopt a different strategy. Instead of attempting to deal directly with stress, they seek to withdraw from it. One of the major tactics such persons use for accomplishing this goal is that of retreating into an alcohol or drug-induced haze.

Unfortunately abuse of these substances is all too common. In fact, shocking as it may seem, the National Institute on Alcohol Abuse and Alcoholism estimates that nearly ten million persons in the United States can be classified as alcoholic: They drink to the point at which their health, economic, or social functioning is impaired. In other words, more than 5 percent of the entire United States labor force suffers from alcohol-related problems. Drug abuse, too, is disturbingly common. Marijuana, cocaine, tranquilizers, amphetamines, and even heroin are all in widespread use and can be encountered everywhere from the loading dock to the corporate boardroom.

We should hasten to note, of course, that individuals use—and abuse—these substances for many reasons; escaping from stress is only one of them. Yet, when asked why they turned to alcohol or drugs in the first place, many individuals mention intense boredom, role conflicts, anxiety over careers, and other factors closely related to stress.

Whatever the specific reasons behind alcoholism and drug abuse, though, there is little doubt that these problems have serious costs for individuals and organizations alike. From the point of view of individuals, the costs are all too obvious. Abuse of alcohol and drugs can adversely affect personal health, destroy careers, wreck marriages, break up families, and lead to crime. The costs for organizations, too, are staggering. For example, alcoholic employees are absent from work and experience accidents from two or four times as often as other employees. The toll exacted by drug abusers may be even higher. Such persons show drastically reduced productivity (after all, how can you do your job when in a drug-induced fog?), and may account for a large share of company thefts.[35] In short, alcoholism and drug abuse are extremely costly problems—ones worthy of careful attention.

In the past, these attempts to escape from reality were viewed largely as criminal actions and were seen as cause for immediate dismissal. More recently, though, public attitudes have shifted, and they have come to be seen largely as serious but treatable illnesses. As this new perspective has gained acceptance, and as businesses have recognized the tremendous costs associated with alcoholism and drug abuse, many companies have established special programs designed to help affected employees. These *employee assistance programs,* as they are often known, seek to help either by directly providing employees with counseling and treatment, or by directing them to various agencies that can offer such assistance. Since recognizing a problem is usually the first step toward its solution, these developments, preliminary as they are, provide some basis for optimism. Nevertheless, alcoholism and drug abuse remain serious problems in the world of work, and ones for which there are no obvious or simple remedies. For this reason, they must be included on any list of the damaging effects of stress.

Burnout: When Stress Consumes

When most people begin their careers, they are full of hope, enthusiasm, and energy. They have many exciting plans and look forward to a bright if not dazzling future. All too often, though, these early dreams of success, contributions, and achievement rapidly fade. Individuals find that they cannot change things very much, that many of the activities they must perform are boring, and that each day they must cope with a number of unpleasant and stressful events. For most persons, the result of this collision between youthful dreams and reality is a period of adjustment. After it is complete, they continue with their careers in an orderly and usually satisfying manner. For others, though, the outcome is much less positive. Such persons become greatly dissatisfied with their work. They experience mental and physical fatigue. They develop negative feelings about their jobs and about life in general. They become **burnout** victims.[36] People who suffer from burnout demonstrate several distinct characteristics.[37]

First, victims of burnout suffer from *physical exhaustion.* They have low energy and feel tired most of the time. In addition, they report many symptoms of physical strain such as frequent headaches, nausea, poor sleep, and changes in eating habits (e.g., loss of appetite). Second, they experience *emotional exhaustion.* Depression, feelings of helplessness and feelings of being trapped in one's job are all part of the picture. Third, persons suffering from burnout often demonstrate *mental or attitudinal exhaustion.* They become cynical about others, hold negative attitudes toward them, and tend to derogate themselves, their jobs, their organizations, and even life in general. To put it simply, they come to view the world around them through dark gray rather than rose-colored glasses. Finally, they often report feelings of *low personal accomplishment.* Persons suffering from burnout conclude that they haven't been able to accomplish much in the past, and assume that they probably won't succeed in this respect in the future. In sum, burnout can be defined as a *syndrome of emotional, physical, and mental exhaustion coupled with feelings of low self-esteem or low self-efficacy, resulting from prolonged exposure to intense stress.* (See Figure 13.11 for a summary of the major components of the burnout syndrome.)

Burnout: Some Major Causes What are the causes of burnout? As we have already noted, the primary factor appears to be prolonged exposure to stress.

However, a number of conditions within an organization plus several personal characteristics seem to determine whether, and to what degree, specific individuals experience burnout. For example, job conditions implying that one's efforts are useless, ineffective, or unappreciated seem to contribute to burnout.[38] Under such conditions, individuals develop the feelings of low personal accomplishment that are an important part of burnout. Similarly, poor opportunities for promotion and the presence of inflexible rules and procedures lead employees to feel trapped in an unfair system, and contribute to the development of negative views about their jobs.[39] Another important factor contributing to burnout is the *leadership style* adopted by employees' supervisors. Apparently, the lower the amount of consideration demonstrated by their supervisors (i.e., the lower their concern with employees' welfare or with maintaining friendly relations with them), the higher employees' reported levels of burnout.[40]

Now that you understand the major characteristics and causes of burnout, you might want to see if you are a candidate for burnout. To do so, complete the **Human Relations in Action** on page 418.

Burnout: Some Major Effects   Whatever the precise causes of burnout, once it develops, it has important consequences. First, it may lead individuals to seek new jobs or careers. In one study concerned with the impact of burnout, Jackson, Schwab, and Schuler asked several hundred teachers to complete a questionnaire

FIGURE 13.11   Burnout: Its Major Components

When individuals are exposed to high levels of stress over prolonged periods of time, they may experience burnout. This is a syndrome involving physical, mental, and attitudinal exhaustion, plus feelings of low personal accomplishment.

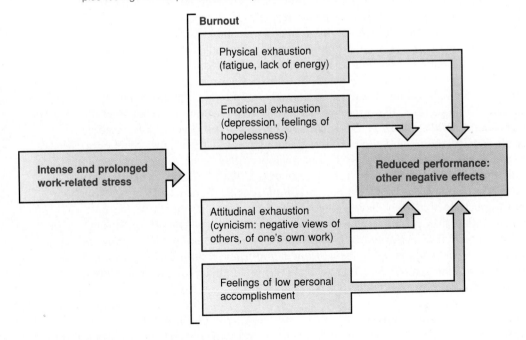

designed to measure burnout and to report on the extent to which they would prefer to be in another job or career.[41] As expected, the greater the teachers' degree of burnout, the more likely they were to prefer another job and to be actively considering a change of occupation.

Second, persons suffering from burnout may seek administrative roles where they can hide from jobs they have grown to hate behind huge piles of forms. While this pattern certainly occurs, it appears to be relatively rare. Most victims of burnout seem either to change jobs or to withdraw psychologically and mark time until retirement.

Burnout: Countering Its Effects If our discussion so far has left you slightly depressed, don't give up hope. Growing evidence suggests that burnout can be reversed. With appropriate help, victims of burnout can recover from their physical and psychological exhaustion. If ongoing stress is reduced, if individuals gain added support from friends and co-workers, and if they cultivate hobbies and other outside interests, at least some persons, it appears, can return to positive attitudes and renewed productivity. Such results can only be attained, however, through active efforts designed to overcome burnout and to change the conditions from which it develops. Below are some key steps that often prove helpful in this respect.

1. Realizing that there is a problem: This is the essential first step. Only if individuals recognize that they face a problem can they engage in active efforts to overcome it. So, admitting that they have experienced burnout, or are in the process of experiencing it, is a must.

2. Reordering priorities and goals: A major factor leading to burnout is the attempt to do too much for too long a time. In a sense, people do burn themselves out. In order to reverse this process, such persons must reorder their priorities and adjust their goals. They must recognize that they can't do everything, and that they have limits. Once they do, they may begin to eliminate some of the self-imposed sources of stress from their lives. Recovery from burnout then becomes possible.

3. Building in opportunities for positive experiences: Burnout often occurs because the persons involved have experienced too many demands, conflicts, and pressures but too few rewards or successes. If such individuals wish to reverse the devastating effects of burnout, they must restructure their lives so that they get their share of positive outcomes. This can be done by learning to relax (e.g., taking short vacations), seeking new skills, (e.g., through job-related training), or simply by learning to take pride in their own accomplishments. The positive feelings generated by such experiences can help counter the mental and emotional exhaustion induced by burnout, and so set victims back on the road to recovery.

4. Establishing a network of social support: Persons suffering from burnout often feel isolated from others. They lack a group of friends who can appreciate their work, listen to their problems, and provide them with emotional support. Thus one effective means of countering burnout is that of developing a network of social support. The effort involved in

acquiring a group of close friends may be high, but the rewards make it well worth the effort.

5. Compartmentalizing life: Persons seeking to avoid or counter burnout should also learn to divide their lives into separate compartments: life at work and life away from work. While on the job, they should in fact work hard and seek to reach their goals. When the day is through, though, they must try to leave the stresses of their career behind them. By doing so, they can gain the time needed to recover from such strain and can avoid the intense emotional pressure responsible for burnout.

Through these and related steps, individuals can turn the tables on burnout. Instead of being its helpless victims, they can avoid its development or even convert it into the basis for important personal growth. In short, when tedium and burnout are handled effectively, they can actually leave individuals stronger, wiser, and more in touch with their own basic values than was true initially. (It should be noted that personal efforts to counter or overcome burnout are often effective. If they fail to produce positive results, though, don't give up. Instead, seek the help of counselors or other professionals specially trained to assist individuals in overcoming such problems.)

HUMAN RELATIONS IN ACTION

Measuring Your Burnout Potential: A Self-Diagnosis

What are the chances that you will experience burnout? To gain some insight into this important question, complete the following questionnaire.

How often do you have any of the following experiences? Please use the following scale: 1 (never); 2 (once or twice); 3 (rarely); 4 (sometimes); 5 (often); 6 (usually); 7 (always).

_____ 1. Being tired

_____ 2. Feeling depressed

_____ 3. Having a good day

_____ 4. Being physically exhausted

_____ 5. Being emotionally exhausted

_____ 6. Being happy

_____ 7. Being "wiped out"

_____ 8. Feeling weak and helpless

_____ 9. Feeling hopeless

_____ 10. Feeling rejected

_____ 11. Feeling "burned out"

_____ 12. Being unhappy

_____ 13. Feeling rundown

_____ 14. Feeling trapped

_____ 15. Feeling worthless

MANAGING STRESS: SOME USEFUL TECHNIQUES

Stress derives from many sources. For this reason, it is probably impossible to completely eliminate it from work settings. While it cannot be totally removed, it can be managed. We will now describe several techniques for accomplishing this task.

Personal Tactics for Coping with Stress

What can individuals do to help themselves cope with stress? Fortunately, there are several things they can do. First, and perhaps foremost, they can concentrate on increasing their physical fitness. A large body of evidence suggests that individuals who exercise, and so strengthen their cardiovascular system and endurance, are much less likely to suffer from several types of stress-related illness (e.g., heart disease, hypertension) than those who are less physically fit.[42] Moreover, it doesn't seem to matter how such fitness is attained—through jogging, swimming, sports, aerobic dancing, or any other means. As this link between physical fitness and health has become increasingly clear, many companies have

---

_____ **16.** Being weary

_____ **17.** Being troubled

_____ **18.** Feeling disillusioned and resentful about people

_____ **19.** Feeling optimistic

_____ **20.** Feeling energetic

_____ **21.** Feeling anxious

Now, compute your score as follows:

1. Add the values you wrote next to items 1, 2, 4, 5, 7, 8, 9, 10, 11, 12, 13, 14, 15, 16, 17, 18, 21.

2. Add the values you wrote next to items 3, 6, 19, 20.

3. Subtract the second total from 32.

4. Now add your total in (1) to your total in (3). Divide this by 21. The result is your _burnout potential_ score.

If this score is between 2 and 3, you are doing quite well; it is unlikely that you will soon experience burnout. If it is between 3 and 4, you may be on the road to this pattern, and should consider taking steps to change your priorities or lifestyle. If your score is over 4, watch out! You are already experiencing symptoms of burnout, and should take immediate actions to counter its effects. (See our discussion of such steps on pages 417–18.) (Scale adapted from one used by Pines et al., 1981; Note 38.)

added **employee fitness programs.** These are programs, run and funded by organizations, to improve the physical fitness of their employees. Such programs are based, in part, on the assumption that improved physical fitness increases individuals' resistance to the adverse effects of stress. However, their growing popularity also derives from findings suggesting that physical fitness reduces absenteeism and enhances productivity, that employee fitness programs contribute to commitment and other positive attitudes among employees.[43,44] Given these important benefits, it is not surprising that such programs have grown in popularity and are now widespread throughout many industries.

But improving our physical fitness is not the only thing we can do to help increase our resistance to stress. Several other techniques exist as well. For example, employees can undergo *coping skills training*—a procedure in which they learn to recognize situations that cause them to feel helpless (i.e., unable to cope), plus specific tactics for dealing with such events. Many techniques of stress management, however, center around a common theme: teaching individuals special procedures for replacing strain and tension with relaxation. One of the most popular of these is **relaxation training** (see Figure 13.12). Here, individuals learn how to relax their muscles in a systematic manner (e.g., from the feet upward to the head). Such relaxation feels good and does seem helpful in reducing emotional tension. A related tactic involves learning to breathe in a deep and regular manner. Such breathing, too, can lower tension. A third and somewhat different technique is known as **meditation.** Individuals practicing meditation assume a comfortable position, close their eyes, and attempt to clear all disturbing thoughts from their minds. Then, they silently repeat a single syllable, or *mantra,* over and over again. When performed correctly, meditation seems to produce feelings of relaxation and well-being. It also affects basic bodily functions in a way suggestive of relaxation (e.g.; it lowers oxygen consumption and produces brain-wave patterns indicative of a calm mental state).[45]

FIGURE 13.12 Relaxation Training: Managing Stress
Relaxation training is a popular technique of stress management.

A final tactic for replacing strain with relaxation is known as *biofeedback*. In this approach, individuals are connected to sensitive equipment that can detect small changes in their bodily functions (e.g., increases or decreases in blood pressure). Whenever these functions exceed target levels (e.g., whenever blood pressure is too high), a tone sounds or a light flashes. Individuals then attempt to stop the tone or light by lowering their blood pressure, slowing their pulse, and so on. Surprising as it may seem, most persons are able to master this technique, although they cannot report precisely *how* they manage to produce these effects.

Through relaxation training, meditation, biofeedback, and related techniques, individuals can learn to manage stress. In this way, they can stop acting as their own worst enemies and can take an active role in enhancing both their health and their careers.

Organizational Strategies for Managing Stress

While individuals can increase their own resistance to stress and can master techniques for reducing its impact when it occurs, they cannot, by themselves, eliminate many causes of stress from their work environment. For this reason organizations, too, can play a key role in stress management. Specifically, they can adopt changes in their own structure or alter jobs so as to reduce stress among their employees.

Changes in Organizational Structure and Function Several steps involving shifts in organizational policy or function appear to be useful in reducing on-the-job stress. First, such beneficial effects can sometimes be produced by *decentralization*—a process in which authority is spread more widely through an organization. This seems to reduce feelings of helplessness among employees, and so reduces overall stress. Second, stress can be reduced through adjustments in *reward systems*. When performance appraisals are viewed as reasonable and the distribution of rewards is seen as fair, the stress stemming from legitimate concerns over such matters is minimized. (Recall our discussion of equity theory in Chapter 4.) Third, stress can be reduced by permitting employees to *participate* in the decision-making process. As we noted earlier, lack of such participation often serves as a major source of tension. Finally, stress can be reduced by improving and broadening lines of *communication*.

Changes in the Nature of Specific Jobs In addition to the changes just outlined, stress can often be reduced by alterations in the scope of specific jobs. For example, the stress resulting from boring, repetitious tasks can be reduced through job enlargement. Here, efforts are made to broaden the scope of such jobs so that they include more varied activities. Second, stress stemming from feelings of helplessness or lack of control can be reduced by job enrichment—procedures in which employees are provided with more responsibility for planning and directing their own work. Finally, stress can be reduced through the elimination of hazardous and unpleasant working conditions.

When organizations adopt the changes mentioned above, they can help to make life at work far less stressful and thus far more satisfying and rewarding. By doing so, they not only enhance the health and well-being of their employees but guarantee their own success and survival as well.

SUMMARY

When individuals perceive that their ability to cope may soon be overwhelmed, they often experience **stress.** Stress stems from many causes. Several of these relate to work itself (e.g., demands of a given job, role conflict, overload, lack of participation in decision making). Others involve personal characteristics of individuals, such as major events in their lives, daily hassles, or individual differences.

Stress exerts harmful effects on health. In addition, it can produce depression, lowered self-esteem, and reductions in job satisfaction. The relationship between stress and performance appears to be complex and may depend on such factors as the complexity of the tasks performed and the specific stressors involved. Prolonged exposure to intense emotional stress can lead to **burnout.** Persons suffering from this reaction experience physical, emotional, and mental exhaustion, and may be unable to cope with their jobs or personal lives. Some victims of burnout leave their fields, while others seek refuge in administrative positions. Still others mark time until retirement and so become "deadwood." Fortunately, several techniques for preventing or reversing burnout exist.

Individuals can manage stress by enhancing their own physical fitness, or by engaging in several tactics designed to substitute relaxation for tension. Organizations can help reduce stress among their employees by altering their internal structure or function (e.g., by decentralizing, by improving communication). In addition, they can restructure jobs so as to lessen tension.

KEY TERMS

burnout: A syndrome resulting from prolonged exposure to stress, consisting of physical, emotional, and mental exhaustion plus feelings of low personal accomplishment.

employee fitness programs: Organization-sponsored programs to enhance the physical fitness of employees.

hardiness: A combination of traits (commitment to work, a sense of personal control, viewing change as a challenge rather than as a threat) that enables individuals to resist the harmful effects of stress.

meditation: A technique for inducing relaxation in which individuals clear disturbing thoughts from their minds and then repeat a single syllable (mantra) over and over again.

qualitative overload: The belief of an employee that he or she lacks the skills or abilities required to perform a specific job.

qualitative underload: The lack of mental stimulation that accompanies many routine, repetitive jobs.

quantitative overload: A situation in which individuals are confronted with more work than can be completed in a given period of time.

quantitative underload: A situation in which individuals have so little to do that they find themselves sitting around much of the time.

relaxation training: Special training in which individuals learn to relax one group of muscles at a time. This, in turn, often causes them to experience reduction in tension.

role ambiguity: Uncertainty among employees about the key requirements of their jobs and how they should divide their time among various tasks.

role conflict: A situation that occurs when different groups of persons with whom an individual must deal hold conflicting expectations about his or her behavior. Such role conflict often contributes to stress.

stress: The physical, psychological, and behavioral reactions experienced by individuals in situations where they feel that they are in danger of being overwhelmed—pushed beyond their abilities or limits.

stressors: Various aspects of the world around us that contribute to stress.

NOTES

1. Kahn, R. (1989). "Stress and Behavior in Work Settings." In M.D. Dunnette, ed. *Handbook of Industrial and Organizational Psychology*, 2d ed. Chicago: Rand McNally.

2. Selye, H. (1976). *Stress in Health and Disease.* Boston: Butterworth.

3. Lazarus, R.S., & Folkman, S. (1984). *Stress, Appraisal, and Coping.* New York: Springer.

4. Lazarus, R.S., Delongis, A., Folkman, S., & Gruen, R. (1985). "Stress and Adaptational Outcomes: The Problem of Confounded Measures." *American Psychologist, 40,* 770–79.

5. See Note 1.

6. McGrath, J.E. (1976). "Stress and Behavior in Organizations." In M.D. Dunnette, ed. *Handbook of Industrial and Organizational Psychology.* Chicago: Rand McNally.

7. National Institute for Occupational Safety and Health, Department of Health, Education, and Welfare (1978). Washington, D.C.: Government Printing Office.

8. Carlson, M. (Dec. 25, 1989). "Mailroom Mayhem." *Time,* 30–31.

9. Shaw, J.B., & Riskind, J.H. (1983). "Predicting job stress using data from the position analysis questionnaire." *Journal of Applied Psychology, 68,* 253–61.

10. Prasuraman, S., & Alutto, J.A. (1981). "An examination of the organizational antecedents of stressors at work." *Academy of Management Journal, 24,* 48–67.

11. Cooke, R.A., & Rousseau, D.M. (1984). "Stress and Strain from Family Roles and Work-Role Expectations." *Journal of Applied Psychology, 69,* 252–60.

12. Newton, T.J., & Keenan, A. (1987). "Role Stress Reexamined: An Investigation of Role Stress Predictors." *Organizational Behavior and Human Decision Processes, 40,* 346–68.

13. See Note 6.

14. French, J.R.P., & Caplan, R.D. (1972). "Organizational Stress and Individual Strain." In A.J. Morrow, ed. *The Failure of Success.* New York: Amacom.

15. McLean, A.A. (1980). *Work Stress.* Reading, Mass.: Addison-Wesley.

16. Matteson, M.T., & Ivancevich, J. (1982). *Managing Job Stress and Health: The Intelligent Person's Guide.* New York: Free Press.

17. Oullette-Kobasa, S.C., & Pucetti, M.C. (1983). "Personality and Social Resources in Stress Resistance." *Journal of Personality and Social Psychology*, 45, 839–50.

18. Costanza, R.S., Derlega, V.J., & Winstead, B.A. (1988). "Positive and Negative Forms of Social Support: Effects of Conversational Topics on Coping with Stress Among Same-Sex Friends." *Journal of Experimental Social Psychology, 24,* 182–93.

19. Jackson, S.E. (1983) Participation in decision-making as a strategy for reducing job-related strain. *Journal of Applied Psychology*, 68, 3–19.

20. Oldham, G.R., & Fried, Y. (1987). "Employee Reactions to Workspace Characteristics." *Journal of Applied Psychology, 72,* 75–80.

21. Gunderson, E., & Rahe, R. (1974). *Life Stress and Illness.* Springfield, Ill.: Charles C. Thomas.

22. Holmes, T.H., & Masuda, M. (1974). "Life Change and Illness Susceptibility." In B.S. Dohrenwend & B.P. Dohrenwend, eds. *Stressful Life Events: Their Nature and Effects,* pp. 45–72. New York: Wiley.

23. Lazarus, R.S., Delongis, A., Folkman, S., & Gruen, R. (1985). "Stress and Adaptational Outcomes: The Problem of Confounded Measures." *American Psychologist, 40,* 770–79.

24. Weinberger, M., Hiner, S.L., & Tierney, W.M. (1987). "In Support of Hassles as a Measure of Stress in Predicting Health Outcomes." *Journal of Biological Medicine, 10,* 19–31.

25. Scheier, M.F., & Carver, C.S. (1985). "Optimism, Coping, and Health: Assessment and Implications of Generalized Outcome Expectancies." *Health Psychology, 4,* 219–47.

26. Scheier, M.F., Weinbtraub, J.K., & Carver, C.S. (1986). "Coping with Stress: Divergent Strategies of Optimists and Pessimists." *Journal of Personality and Social Psychology, 51,* 1257–64.

27. Kobasa, S.C. (1979). "Stressful Life Events, Personality and Health: An Inquiry into Hardiness." *Journal of Personality and Social Psychology, 37,* 1–11.

28. Frese, M. (1985). "Stress at Work and Psychosomatic Complaints: A Causal Interpretation." *Journal of Applied Psychology, 70,* 314–28.

29. See Note 6.

30. See Note 16.

31. Motowidlo, S.J., Packard, J.S., & Manning, M.R. (1986). "Occupational Stress: Its Causes and Consequences for Job Performance." *Journal of Applied Psychology,* 71, 618–29.

32. Berlyne, D.E. (1967). "Arousal and Reinforcement." In D. Levine, ed. *Nebraska Symposium on Motivation*, vol. 15, 279–86. Lincoln: University of Nebraska Press.

33. Martin, R.A., Kuiper, N.A., Olinger, L.J., & Dobbin, J. (1988). "Is Stress Always Bad? Telic Versus Paratelic Dominance as a Stress-Mediating Variable." *Journal of Personality and Social Psychology*, 53, 970–82.

34. Beehr, T.A., & Newman, J.E. (1978). "Job Stress, Employee Health, and Organizational Effectiveness: A Facet Analysis, Model and Literature Review." *Personnel Psychology*, 31, 665–99.

35. Hollinger, R.C., & Clark, J.P. (1983). *Theft by employees.* Lexington, Mass.: Lexington Books.

36. Maslach, C., & Jackson, S.E. (1984). "Burnout in Organizational Settings." In S. Oskamp, ed. *Applied Social Psychology Annual*, vol. 5, pp. 135–54. Beverly Hills: Sage.

37. Maslach, C. (1982). "Understanding Burnout: Definitional Issues in Analyzing a Complex Phenomenon." In W.S. Paine, ed. *Job Stress and Burnout: Research Theory, and Intervention Perspectives.* Beverly Hills: Sage.

38. Pines, A.M., Aronson, E., & Kafry, D. (1981). *Burnout: From Tedium to Personal Growth.* New York: Freeman.

39. Gaines, J., & Jermier, J.M. (1983). "Emotional Exhaustion in High Stress Organizations." *Academy of Management Journal, 26,* 567–86.

40. Seltzer, J., & Numerof, R.E. (1988). "Supervisory Leadership and Subordinate Burnout." *Academy of Management Journal, 31,* 439–46.

41. Jackson, S.E., Schwab, R.L., & Schuler, R.S. (1986). "Toward an Understanding of the Burnout Phenomenon." *Journal of Applied Psychology, 71,* 630–40.

42. See Note 11.

43. Shepherd, R.J., Cox, M., & Corey, P. (1981). "Fitness Program Participation: Its Effect on Workers' Performance." *Journal of Occupational Medicine, 23,* 359–63.

44. Cox, M., Shephard, R., & Corey, R. (1981). "Influence of an Employee Fitness Programme upon Fitness, Productivity and Absenteeism." *Ergonomics, 24,* 795–806.

45. Wallace, B., & Fisher, L.E. (1987). *Consciousness and Behavior*, 2d ed. Boston: Allyn & Bacon.

ADDITIONAL CASES AND EXERCISES: APPLYING WHAT YOU'VE LEARNED

Stressed-Out Sally

Don H. Hockenbury
Psychology Instructor
Tulsa Junior College

Sandra E. Hockenbury
Adjunct Instructor
Tulsa Junior College

Sorting through her boss's morning mail, Sally opened an envelope from the Human Resources Department. A two-day management seminar on "Executive Burnout: Dealing with Stress on the Job" had been scheduled for the following week. Of course, hourly workers like Sally were not invited. "Burnout" seemed to be the latest buzz word around the offices of CREON, Inc., where Sally had worked as a secretary for the last three years. In a relatively short period of time, CREON had become very successful in the highly competitive and volatile field of computer network systems. The management was proud of the company's high profile, rapid growth, and its "lean and mean" mentality. The young executives and managers were highly competitive and seemed to pride themselves on the number of evenings and weekends spent in the office. Sally had heard a few of them privately sneer at those who allowed family and friends to interfere with work. Lately, she had overheard several of the managers comparing their symptoms of "burnout" and as they competed in everything else, they seemed to vie with each other as to who exhibited the most symptoms. The seminar was being held at a nice hotel downtown and featured catered lunches and a wine and cheese reception for the participants at the end of the seminar.

Mr. Vance, Sally's boss, passed her desk on his way to a meeting outside the office. "Nice job on that report, Sally—as usual," he said. "I can always count on you. By the way, this has to go out in overnight mail today."

He tossed a lengthy handwritten memo on her desk. Once again, it was a rush job. Mr. Vance's handwriting was atrocious, but his spelling and grammar were worse. Sally knew he counted on her to "clean up" his careless writing and turn his memo into a polished final product. At first he had been surprised at her suggestions, then grateful, but now he considered it just part of her job. Sally knew that none of the other secretaries did the same. Betty said, "Her name is on it, not mine!" and typed her boss's letters and memos exactly as Ms. Wilson handed them to her, but Sally just couldn't allow the reports to go out without looking perfect, even though she often had to work through her lunch hour or stay late to finish them. Just the other day she had overheard the vice president complimenting Mr. Vance on his well-written, well-prepared reports.

Wearily, Sally turned to her computer terminal. It was only 9 A.M., but her in-basket was already overflowing. There was a fifty-page report that needed twenty collated copies for this afternoon's meeting. She walked down the hall to the office copier. Unfortunately, the copy machine was broken again, and four other secretaries were waiting in line, each claiming that her copy job needed priority. She waited for several minutes, but then gave up and went back to her desk.

Three phone messages were waiting for her. The first one was from the day care center, saying that her daughter, Jenny, was sick. Sally could only hope that she would be able to reach her mother to see if she could pick Jenny up and take care of her until Sally could get home from work. The second one was from Sara's third-grade teacher, requesting a conference for next Thursday at 3 P.M.

Mr. Vance was fond of saying that he understood the problems of working mothers because, after all, he had four children of his own. However, he had frowned the last time she had asked him for permission to leave early to attend a parent-teacher meeting. And he hadn't been exactly pleased when Sally had missed a day of work last week because Sara had been too sick to go to school. Although Mr. Vance claimed to have empathy for mothers employed outside the home, he enjoyed the luxury of a salary that easily allowed his wife to care for their children at home. On the other hand, Sally's ex-husband was four months behind on child support. She couldn't afford a lawyer to do anything about it, and the state would not intervene until he was six months overdue.

Finally, there was a phone message from Barbara, the office manager, to meet in Barbara's office this afternoon. Sally sighed; she thought she knew what the meeting would be about. Sally had been fifteen minutes late three times in the past two weeks. Sally's neighbor Bonnie drove Sara to school each morning along with her own children, but she had been late picking Sara up.

Longingly, Sally eyed her college textbooks, stacked on the corner of her filing cabinet. She had hoped to get in a good hour's study time today during her lunch hour, but if she was to get the report copied and the memo out in today's mail, she was going to have to work through lunch hour again. Sally was taking two night courses at the local community college, trying to finish the college degree that she had started several years before. She had always gotten high evaluations on her performance reviews at work, but last month Mr. Vance had told her quite frankly that she could progress no further at CREON without a four-year degree. If she could continue taking two courses a semester, she would earn an associate's degree in a year and a half. A four-year degree seemed to be an impossible goal, although she was pulling a B-plus average and had been encouraged to continue her schooling by her instructors. Her English teacher had told Sally that she was one of the brightest students she had ever had and was encouraging her to look into the fields of journalism or teaching for a new career. Today Sally needed to study for her upcoming biology midterm; she'd been only three points shy of an A on her first test, and she was determined to do better on this one. But lately it all seemed so overwhelming. She loved her college course, but was it worth it? Maybe she should quit school and wait until Sara and Jenny were a little bit older to try again. Suddenly Sally felt an almost irresistible urge to put her head on her desk and cry.

Questions

1. Who is more likely to suffer from burnout: Sally or Mr. Vance? Why?
2. Identify the key sources of stress and burnout in Sally's life.
3. What conflicting roles is Sally juggling?
4. What concrete steps could Sally take to improve her work environment?

5. What steps could Sally take to reduce her level of stress?
6. What steps could Sally take to improve her network of social support at work and in her personal life?

What Is Your Hassles Score?

It appears that everyday hassles are an important source of stress in our lives. The scale below is designed to help you assess the extent to which you are experiencing a high level of hassles.

Instructions: Please indicate the extent to which you have been "hassled" (irritated, annoyed, bothered) by each of the factors listed below. Circle one number for each item.

		Somewhat hassled	Moderately hassled	Extremely hassled
1.	Preparing meals	1	2	3
2.	Shopping	1	2	3
3.	Home repairs/maintenance	1	2	3
4.	Too many things to do/not enough time	1	2	3
5.	Too many responsibilities	1	2	3
6.	Being lonely	1	2	3
7.	Inner conflicts	1	2	3
8.	Concern about crime	1	2	3
9.	Financial responsibility	1	2	3
10.	Concerns about owing money	1	2	3
11.	Problems getting along with co-workers	1	2	3
12.	Concerns about job security	1	2	3
13.	Concerns about investments or taxes	1	2	3

To obtain your score, simply add the numbers you circled for each item. A score of 15 or lower indicates a low level, 16 to 21 a moderate level, and 22 and above a high level. If you are at a high level, you may want to use some of the strategies discussed in this chapter to reduce this level.

CHAPTER

14

Career Choice and Development: Planning for Success

Learning Objectives

After reading this chapter,
you should be able to:

1. List some of the major factors that play a role in career choice.

2. Describe a more systematic approach to this process than most people seem to follow.

3. Explain how programs based on human resource planning can be of help to you in career development.

4. Outline the major steps in a systematic approach to personal career development.

5. Define the term *career* and explain how changes in individuals' jobs and work-related experiences reflect different stages in their lives.

6. Describe important issues individuals must confront in the early, middle, and later stages of their careers.

7. Define the term *organizational socialization* and indicate how this process takes place.

ood's Department Stores were having a new employee seminar. They were hiring a large number of new employees for a newly opened store. John Samuels, vice president in charge of sales, was addressing the group.

"We are really excited about the prospect of all of you being part of our company. I think you will find Good's to be an exciting place to work. There's a lot of opportunity for advancement. A good number of the people in our various stores have been with us for twenty years. So you can see that you have a good future with us."

As John Samuels looked over the group of new employees he noticed that they seemed to be reacting positively to his message. There certainly seemed to be some capable and highly motivated people in the group. Yet he also knew that only a small percentage of these people would stay with the company. They would leave for many reasons beyond the company's control, such as changes in family situation. However, a large percentage would leave because they would discover they were not well-suited for a career in sales. So as part of his speeches to new employees, Samuels always included a few warnings about the drawbacks of working in sales.

He continued his speech by pointing out some of these problems. "You realize, of course, that the career of a salesperson can be demanding. You have to deal with a lot of unpleasant customers without bruising your good humor. Some days or months, sales will be slow and your income will suffer. A large percentage of your customers will not buy even when you put forth your best efforts to make a sale. So you have to be willing to face these types of challenges if you are going to be a success in sales. If you think you can keep a positive attitude toward people and selling even when times are tough, you're the kind of person we want and who will be successful in our company."

A long time ago in a simpler world that now seems far, far away, people entered a job and stayed in it for the rest of their working lives. Today, of course, the situation is radically different. Most people realize that their first job is unlikely to be their last one. In fact, many would be quite upset if they suspected that this was the case. They expect change and look forward to progress. They anticipate promotions, rising status, growing income, and increasing autonomy. In short, they expect their careers to develop and to do so along mainly positive lines. But—and here comes the paradox—while they expect such progress, they often do nothing to ensure it. They fail to engage in the careful planning that is essential to continued progress, and ignore long-term trends that may affect the future of various careers. As a result, they miss out on golden opportunities, they experience crushed hopes, and they often end up in occupational blind alleys (see Figure 14.1).

FIGURE 14.1 Cul-de-Sacs: One Result of Lack of Career Planning
Lack of career planning can lead one into occupational blind alleys or "cul-de-sacs." (Duffy ©
1985 Universal Press Syndicate. Reprinted with permission. All rights reserved.)

Can you personally avoid such difficulties? Our answer is "yes," but only if
you adopt the right strategies. Good things sometimes happen in life without any
effort on our part—we just sort of "luck out." But usually they don't occur unless
we take active steps to *make* them happen. This seems to be the rule with respect
to successful careers. They don't appear out of thin air and drop softly into our
laps. Rather, they are usually the result of careful planning plus a lot of hard
work. How, then, can you plan for your own success? How can you make your
own career rewarding and enjoyable? Unfortunately, we can't provide you with
a simple, no-fail answer. The world of work is far too complex a place for this
kind of luxury. But we don't have to leave you out in the cold wondering either.

In recent years, human relations experts have devoted growing attention to
the topic of careers—how they develop, how they are pursued, and why, sometimes, they go on the rocks.[1] More formally, **careers** can be defined as the sequence
of attitudes and behaviors associated with work-related activities experienced by
individuals over the span of their working lives.[2] In this chapter, we will focus
on the rapidly growing body of knowledge such experts have acquired. Specifically,
we examine four distinct but related issues. First, we will delve into the question
of how individuals *choose* their careers—why they select one field over others.
Second, we will turn to the ways careers develop over time, both with and without
careful long-range planning. Third, we analyze how career issues change over the
course of our working career. Finally, we will examine organizational socialization—how people become part of an organization. Our hope, of course, is that
armed with the information presented here, you will be better able to plan and
pursue a challenging and rewarding future.

GETTING STARTED: CHOOSING THE RIGHT CAREER

How many different jobs can you bring to mind? Probably you can think of
dozens with little or no effort. Even if you listed hundreds, though, you would
still only be scratching the surface. In the 1990s, there are literally thousands of

432

CHAPTER 14

CAREER CHOICE AND
DEVELOPMENT:
PLANNING FOR
SUCCESS

careers we can pursue. The existence of this tremendous range of choices, in turn, raises an intriguing question: How do individuals ever zero in on a specific job? Why do some choose to become accountants, others carpenters, and still others doctors, farmers, or computer programmers? Further, by what mysterious process do people ever end up in jobs such as the ones shown in Figure 14.2? As you can readily guess, there are no simple answers to these questions. Rather, careful study of the way individuals choose their careers indicates that many factors play a role in this process.[3] In this discussion, we will first examine some of the more important of these factors. We will then suggest a useful technique for selecting an appropriate career—a technique based largely on detailed self-appraisal, careful study of the requirements of various jobs, and a search for a close match between the two.

Career Choice: Some Key Factors

If you stopped ten different people on the street and asked them how they ended up in their present job or career, you would probably receive ten different

FIGURE 14.2 Choosing the Right Career: Some Unconventional Outcomes
Can you guess why these people chose their unusual occupations?

answers. This is hardly surprising, for people are unique and their working lives reflect this basic fact. Taking a step back from their replies, however, you might begin to notice several common themes in their comments. Each of these—described below—calls attention to an important factor in individual career choice.

The Intrinsic Appeal of a Job or Field   Have you ever fantasized about becoming a surgeon, a movie star, or a great detective? If so, you are already familiar with one reason why individuals choose certain careers: They offer a high degree of excitement, challenge, and reward. Needless to say, not all fields are as attractive as the ones named above. But human beings, as you know, differ tremendously in their preferences. Thus almost any career you can imagine—no matter how dull it may seem to you—will appear wildly desirable to others. Clearly, one major factor in individual career choice, then, is personal interest. Because of their unique pattern of traits, abilities, and past experiences, specific persons are drawn to certain fields. And when they follow these preferences, they may embark on careers that occupy the rest of their working lives.

The Role of Social Influence   As we noted in Chapter 7, people spend a lot of time and effort attempting to influence others. They often seek to change their attitudes, alter their behavior, or both. And they seek to accomplish these goals through persuasion and other tactics of social influence. Not surprisingly, these same processes often play a role in career choice. First, parents, teachers, and other adults may attempt to steer members of the younger generation into certain jobs or careers. In order to do so, they may dangle various rewards in front of them for "correct" choices (e.g., for deciding to pursue careers in law, medicine, engineering, or business). And they may withhold support (both social and financial) when a "difficult" daughter or son insists, instead, on selecting a field they do not favor. As you may already know, such pressure tactics often work—they do nudge many persons into careers that are perceived as safe, conventional, and financially rewarding by their families.

But direct persuasion is not the only way social influence affects career choice. Another and more subtle aspect of this process involves the impact of **social models.** At one time or another, almost all of us have had heroes or heroines—people we admire greatly and would like to emulate. Such individuals may not even be aware of our existence, let alone our admiration for them; they may be famous celebrities we never met, or even figures from history who lived centuries in the past. Yet, their impact on us can be powerful indeed. How many scientists were inspired to choose their careers by accounts of the life of Albert Einstein or Marie Curie? How many musicians decided to take up their instruments after hearing the music of Beethoven or Mozart? It is impossible to tell, but research on the impact of social models suggests that the number is probably large.[4] It should be noted that such modeling effects are not in any way restricted to high-level or high-status careers. Many carpenters, electricians, miners, and salespeople report having entered their field because of early exposure to members of these occupations—members they liked or admired.

In sum, in choosing a career, as in making virtually every other decision, we are often strongly influenced by the words, deeds, or examples of the people

434
CHAPTER 14
CAREER CHOICE AND
DEVELOPMENT:
PLANNING FOR
SUCCESS

around us. In this sense, then, career choice is not nearly as random or unpredictable as some would believe.

Accident and Inertia: Life without a Game Plan To illustrate a third major influence on career choice, let's go back to those imaginary ten people mentioned earlier—the ones you stopped and asked, "How did you choose your present job?" If they were feeling especially honest, several would probably answer something like "Well, I kind of drifted into it." And others might state "Hm—it was really sort of by accident." Through such remarks, they would reveal that they ended up in their present career without any initial plan to do so. At first glance this probably seems surprising. After all, how can people leave anything as important as this to chance? The answer, however, is simple: There are many (countless?) ways in which unforeseen events can shape our ultimate career choice. In fact, such influence often occurs without our awareness.

For example, consider the following fact: Many persons end up in a given occupation because at some point they held a temporary job in it, such as summer employment. When they first accepted this job, they had no plans to pursue it on a permanent basis—they simply needed extra income and took whatever position was available. As they became familiar with their work, learned the ropes of their organization, and formed friendships with other employees, though, they found it increasingly tempting to stay put, or at least to return after completing their education. In such cases, a combination of accident (finding a specific job in the first place) and inertia (staying in it because they already know how to perform it) can shape the course of individuals' future careers. Similarly, consider this: Many persons enter college with the intention of majoring in one field. Then, quite by accident, they take a course outside their chosen area and find it especially interesting. As a result, they take more courses in this field. Soon they may discover that they are actually ready to shift majors—and career plans. In these and many other ways, accidental events—even events that seem quite trivial when they first occur—can exert powerful effects on our lifelong careers.

Career Choice: A Better Approach

Choosing a career is an important matter—one of the most crucial decisions we ever face. Ideally then it should be a rational systematic process; as noted earlier, though, it is not. Most persons seem to select a career largely on the basis of personal interests, social influence from others, or mere accident. This would pose no special problems if most were ultimately satisfied with their choices. But—alas!—they are not. Surveys suggest that, given the opportunity to choose again, many individuals would select a different career.[5] This proportion varies greatly across different occupations, but it is sizable even in the fields high in both status and income (see Figure 14.3). The fact that many individuals are not happy with career choices they have made raises an important question: Can anything be done to enhance the effectiveness of this process? In short, are there any steps individuals can take to increase the likelihood of making an appropriate selection? We believe there are. In the hope that this information will prove

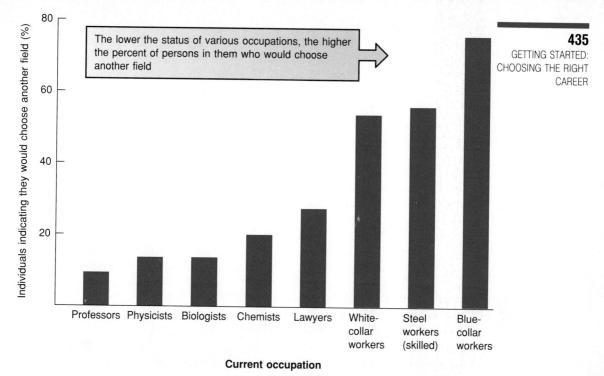

The lower the status of various occupations, the higher the percent of persons in them who would choose another field

FIGURE 14.3 Career Choice: Often It Goes Astray
Many individuals indicate that if given the chance to start over they would choose a different career. As you might expect, the lower the status of a given field the higher the percentage of individuals indicating that they would make another choice. *Source:* Based on data from Kahn (1972); see Note 5.

helpful to you, here are some recommendations for making an effective and successful career choice.

First, Know Yourself Before you choose an appropriate career, you need to know something about yourself. Ideally, you should understand your own interests, your major motives and goals, your abilities, and your central traits. This is essential for an obvious reason: Unless you possess the key characteristics required for a given job or field, you are unlikely to be either happy or successful in it. Thus you should begin by seeking to understand yourself.

At this point, you may be thinking something along these lines: "Well, at least *that's* pretty easy. All I have to do is think about myself for a while and the picture will become clear." This sounds reasonable enough, and most of us tend to accept it at face value. Actually, though, it can often be misleading. A large body of evidence indicates that in many cases, it is far more difficult to learn about ourselves by focusing inward than we might suspect.[6] As we noted in Chapter 5, many of our motives are hidden from view, locked in the unconscious. Similarly, we are often uncertain about some of our major traits and unaware of our impact

436

CHAPTER 14
CAREER CHOICE AND
DEVELOPMENT:
PLANNING FOR
SUCCESS

on others. Indeed, even our goals may be unclear and difficult to describe. For these reasons, the task of knowing ourselves is trickier than we think. Fortunately, though, there are other ways of gathering such knowledge apart from simply glancing inward. First, we can obtain it from others either directly, by asking them for their views, or indirectly by observing our effects on them or by comparing ourselves with these persons. This latter process, known as *social comparison,* is a key technique we use in learning about ourselves.[7] Second, and even better, we can obtain such information from persons specially trained in the task of measuring individual differences. Most schools have a career counseling office with one or more professionals (usually psychologists) who can test your abilities, measure your interests, and even help identify key aspects of your personality. More important, they can compare your standing on each of these dimensions with that of others, and so help to pinpoint both your strengths and your relative weaknesses. This is essential information for making an effective career choice, so if at all possible, you should seek the advice and guidance of these counselors at an early stage in the game. The benefits for your future can be substantial.

Second, Learn about the Requirements of Various Jobs   Once you know something about yourself, you can move on to the next step: finding out about various jobs. What you need to know, specifically, is what skills, abilities, traits, and interests they require. Some of this information is readily available. For example, you can find it in job descriptions, or in pamphlets about training programs for a given occupation. Since these sources are not designed to provide you with a complete picture of all the characteristics required by a particular career, you may want to turn to others as well. Individuals who can be helpful in this regard are career counselors and persons actually holding jobs of interest to you. Career counselors have access to profiles of different occupational groups, showing the traits possessed by successful persons in them. Obviously, such knowledge can be useful to you. Persons already occupying given jobs can call attention to aspects of their work you might otherwise miss and can offer views on exactly what it takes to succeed in their field. Whatever your sources of information, your overall goal should be to find out as much as possible about what the people in a given job really do, and what skills, abilities, interests, and traits seem most helpful to them.

FIGURE 14.4   Choosing the Right Career: An Overview
Effective career choice involves three major steps. First, we must understand our own interests, motives, skills, and goals. Second, we must comprehend the requirements of various jobs. Finally, we must seek a close match between these two groups of factors.

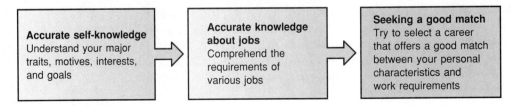

Accurate self-knowledge
Understand your major traits, motives, interests, and goals

Accurate knowledge about jobs
Comprehend the requirements of various jobs

Seeking a good match
Try to select a career that offers a good match between your personal characteristics and work requirements

Third. Seek a Match   By now, the final step in the process should be obvious: Seek a good match between your own strengths and the requirements of various jobs (see Figure 14.4). In other words, rule out careers for which you are clearly unsuited, no matter how prestigious or attractive they may be. And try, instead, to focus on ones that are consistent with your personal assets.

Unfortunately, this process can be quite painful. First, you are unlikely to find any one career for which you seem to be a perfect natural. Thus a considerable amount of flexibility and willingness to compromise are needed on your part. Second, attempting to match your personal assets to career requirements is certain to lead to the dashing of at least some of your childhood hopes; after all, you must (perhaps) face up to the fact that you are not cut out to be a surgeon, a great actress, or a Nobel-prize winning scientist. All the discomfort and effort are well worthwhile, however. To the extent you succeed in identifying a pool of careers for which you are well suited, and then select one of these, your chances of both success and personal satisfaction can be sharply enhanced. Who, we wonder, could ask for more? (Just what are you seeking in your career? Stability, achievement, development as a unique person? For some insight into this issue, see the **Human Relations in Action** on page 438.)

CAREER DEVELOPMENT: STAYING ON TRACK

Imagine that, for once, fate has smiled on you. After examining your own traits and interests, and studying the requirements of many different jobs, you have found one that seems just about perfect. Further, through hard work and careful preparation, you have actually landed such a position with an excellent, growing company. What happens next? How do you launch your career with a bang, and then ensure that it stays on track? Fortunately, there are many things you can do to accomplish these goals. Since some of these involve getting help from your company, while others center around steps you can take yourself, we will divide them into these two major categories here.

Getting Help from Your Company: Benefiting from Human Resource Planning

The world of the 1990s is a tough place for organizations as well as individuals. Increased competition, rapid changes in technology, rising energy costs—these are only a few of the problems currently challenging even successful companies. In their efforts to cope with such conditions, many organizations have directed careful attention to the management of their financial and physical resources— closer attention to these matters than was true in the past. But this is only part of the total picture. In addition, organizations have come to realize that human resources, too, are precious, and must be effectively managed.[9] The guiding principle behind this general approach—often known as **human resource planning**—

438

CHAPTER 14

CAREER CHOICE AND
DEVELOPMENT:
PLANNING FOR
SUCCESS

is this: In order to operate at peak efficiency, organizations must put their human resources to the best possible use. That is, they must ensure that they have the *right* people with the *right* skills in the *right* jobs. This, in turn, requires three basic conditions. First, they must succeed in attracting and retaining a core of talented, motivated employees. Second, they must be able to foresee future personnel needs and plan, as well as hire, accordingly. Third, they must ensure that persons within the organization do not stagnate. On the contrary, they must assist employees' growth so that their knowledge and skills keep pace with the demands of an everchanging and increasingly complex world.

As the importance of human resource planning has gained acceptance, a number of companies have developed special programs of career *management* or *development* for their employees. Such programs are designed to make remaining within the organization more attractive, and to assist individuals in acquiring new skills and competence. A wide range of specific techniques have been used for these purposes. For example, some organizations have provided employees with time off to attend college-level courses, and they have also paid any costs involved. Others have designed and conducted their own in-house training programs, often with the aid of outside consultants. By far the most popular techniques, however,

HUMAN RELATIONS IN ACTION

Up the Ladder, Round the Spiral, or Steady in Place? What Kind of Career Do You Want—and Why?

How do you see your future career unfolding? Will it involve steady progress through an orderly series of promotions? Large leaps from one function to another? Long periods in the same position? Which of these patterns do you prefer? To understand your own feelings about these issues, please answer the questions below. Simply insert a number from *1* to *5* in the blank next to each statement. Insert *1* if you agree strongly with the statement, *2* if you agree moderately, *3* if you are uncertain about whether you agree or disagree, *4* if you disagree moderately, and *5* if you disagree strongly.

_____ 1. My career will probably consist of a series of small steps up the organizational ladder.

_____ 2. During the course of my career, I expect to make major shifts from one kind of work or function to another.

_____ 3. I expect to have a lifelong commitment to my chosen job or field.

_____ 4. Although I will begin my career in one field, I fully expect to work in several different ones in the years ahead.

These questions are designed to measure distinct ways of viewing careers—contrasting *career concepts*. Specifically, they assess your acceptance of what have

have been those based on the use of detailed and constructive **performance appraisals.**[10] Such appraisals were once quite brief, consisting mainly of a few comments from a supervisor to the effect that an individual was doing a "good job" or, conversely, that he or she was in danger of losing his position. Within the last decade, however, informative appraisals have become widely viewed not simply as a means of letting employees know where they stand but also as a valuable tool for helping them develop in ways beneficial to both themselves and the company. Thus today's performance appraisals often include the following features: (1) detailed and highly specific feedback on various aspects of job performance; (2) identification of special strengths and weaknesses shown by a particular individual; (3) the establishment of concrete objectives to be attained by the employee during the next evaluation period; and (4) a statement of each employee's career goals, along with concrete steps for moving toward them. As you can readily see, information of this type can often be helpful to employees in planning their future development and growth.

In sum, recent emphasis on human resource planning has led many companies to recognize the value of assisting their employees in career development. Of course, not every organization has "seen the light" in this respect—far from it.

been termed a *linear, spiral, steady state,* and *transitory* concept of your career.[8] To the extent you agree with the first item, you tend to view your career as one consisting of orderly steps and promotions. This is the linear career concept. To the degree that you express agreement with the second question, you tend to see your career developing in a spiral pattern involving major shifts from one function to another (jumps from one spiral to another). If you agree with the third question, you have a more stable view of your career. You perceive it as a lifetime commitment to a particular job, field, or organization; this is the steady state concept. Finally, if you endorse the fourth item, you expect a high degree of mobility. In fact, you anticipate moves from one field to another at several points during your career. This is the transitory concept.

Some evidence suggests that these contrasting perspectives on one's future career are related to differences in career motivation. For example, persons who favor the linear concept tend to be high in need for achievement and power—they view their careers as ways of growing in these dimensions. Those who favor the spiral pattern are high in growth needs such as the ones discussed in Chapter 4. And those who expect a great deal of change (the transitory concept) are high sensation seekers, or persons with a high need for continued challenge. Now, consider your own views about your career. Do you see any link between these and your major career-related motives?

440

CHAPTER 14

CAREER CHOICE AND
DEVELOPMENT:
PLANNING FOR
SUCCESS

But if your organization (or one you join in the future) has such programs, try to take full advantage of them. Your participation will be duly noted and, one way or another, will contribute to your career.

Helping Yourself: Forming Your Own Plan for Career Development

Supposed that you interviewed one hundred individuals who had enjoyed outstanding careers and asked them to describe the factors that led to their success. Do you think you would uncover any common themes? The chances are excellent that you would. Further, we can even predict what the most important of these might be: self-knowledge, insight into one's organization, clearcut goals, and careful planning. Briefly, many of the individuals with whom you spoke would suggest that their success stemmed mainly from (1) knowledge of their own strengths, weaknesses, interests, and motives; (2) having a good grasp of the internal workings of their organizations; (3) having clear and obtainable goals; and (4) developing concrete plans for reaching these objectives. Can you apply these basic principles to your own career? We believe you can. In fact, growing evidence suggests that to the extent you do, your chances of attaining success may be measurably enhanced. Given such potential benefits, each of these points is certainly worthy of a closer look.

Self-Knowledge Revisited   We noted earlier that understanding yourself—knowing your own motives, interests, traits, and abilities—can be very helpful in choosing an appropriate career. Here, we wish to add that such knowledge can be beneficial in another way as well: It can help you to develop your career along highly positive lines. There are several reasons for this. First, unless you have a good grasp of your current strengths and weaknesses, it is difficult to know just where you need extra effort, or require additional training. Thus having an accurate grasp of where you stand right now is essential.

Second, consider this basic fact: Career development, by its very nature, suggests change and movement. It implies that a given individual is not standing still; rather, he or she is making progress, moving forward. But where, precisely, is this movement directed? The answer depends, to a large degree, on a person's basic motives—what he or she is seeking. As you already know, tremendous differences exist with respect to this dimension. Some desire status and power (see Figure 14.5), others focus on wealth, still others lust after fame, while many ask only security and stability. Which of these motives is central to you? In short, which form the core of your own *career motivation*.[11] Obviously, it is useful to know before setting out.

For these and several other reasons, accurate self-knowledge is a valuable "plus" from the point of view of effective career development. Thus an important step in this process—perhaps the first step you should perform—is to evaluate as many of your traits and characteristics as possible. This knowledge is sure to come in handy in many ways.

FIGURE 14.5 Careers: A Variety of Motives
Careers may be motivated by a variety of desires such as power, wealth, or security. Which of these motives is most important to you?

Know Your Organization Individuals who seem to possess every trait needed for success often fail to live up to their bright promise. Instead of rising like a rocket across the organizational sky, they fall flat on their faces, much to their own surprise and that of others around them. Many factors contribute to such disappointments. However, one of the most important is this: Such persons often lack what might be termed *career insight*.[12] Specifically, they do not seem to have a good grasp of what makes their organization tick—how it really operates, apart from what the formal organizational chart dictates. For example, they lack insight into **organizational politics**—who holds power and how they use it. Similarly, they do not grasp the nature of *informal networks of communication*. As a result,

442

CHAPTER 14

CAREER CHOICE AND
DEVELOPMENT:
PLANNING FOR
SUCCESS

they are often among the last to learn important information, and they fail to plug into one or more of the support groups that are essential to furthering their careers. They may be outstanding engineers, accountants, or programmers, but these technical skills do them little good. They simply don't know how to operate in the complex world of a modern organization.

Obviously, you want to do everything in your power to avoid sharing this fate. Thus second essential ingredient in your personal plan for success should be gaining good career insight. Unfortunately, we can't offer any simple guidelines for becoming skilled in this respect. In general, though, the best policy is to watch and listen as carefully as possible when you first join an organization. During the first few weeks or months, you will be given an opportunity to learn the ropes— to figure out how things should be done, what style is required, who really communicates with whom, and who really counts. Use this period of organizational socialization to maximum advantage.[13] That is, gather as much information as possible during this period and try to form the clearest picture you can of your department and organization. If you do your homework carefully in this general area, you will certainly help establish a firm base for your future career development. (For a concrete illustration of the problems that can arise when an individual lacks insights into the nature of his or her organization, see the **Case in Point** on page 444.)

Establish Clear-Cut Goals and Steps for Moving toward Them Now we come to the heart of any personal plan for career development. In essence, this consists of two major parts: (1) establishing clear-cut goals and (2) formulating concrete steps for their attainment. At first glance, these may seem like relatively simple tasks. Don't we all know what we want from our working lives? And isn't it clear how to get it? The answer on both counts is "no!" To see why this is so, let's take them in order, one at a time.

First, what about goals? In most cases, it appears, individuals have only vague and poorly defined career objectives. If asked what they are seeking, they reply "success," "happiness," or "personal fulfillment." Certainly, no one could argue with the desirability of such outcomes; but no one could describe them very clearly, either. And vague goals have serious drawbacks. Usually, it is impossible to tell when—or whether—they have been reached. It is also often difficult to know just how to approach them. For these reasons, it is usually preferable, in developing your own career plan, to try to formulate specific goals. For example, try to determine just what promotions or other accomplishments you want to achieve during a given time period. Establishing such goals is no guarantee that you'll reach them—many factors influence your progress. But at least once they are determined, you'll know just where you are going and can gauge your own progress.

Now, a related issue arises: In choosing such goals, how do you know which are appropriate? Certainly, you don't want to aim for goals that are too easy and pose no challenge. Similarly, you don't want to select those that are too difficult and impossible to reach—*that* can be downright demoralizing! So, how can you tell which ones are challenging but within your reach? This is a complex matter with no simple answers. In order to deal with it, you need certain information about your organization. For example, you must understand the nature of various *career lines*—what jobs or positions lie between an entry-level one and the top slot.[14] Similarly, you must know something about *transit time*—how long it usually takes for an individual to advance from one position to the next. And you need a grasp of level of *upward mobility* in your company—how many openings are likely to develop at higher levels and with what frequency? Only by taking these and related factors into account can you establish appropriate goals for your own career.

Setting the right goals, though, is only part of the process. In addition, you need to specify, as precisely and accurately as possible, just how to reach them. In short, you must outline a series of steps which, if carried out successfully, will lead you to your goals. Again, you need quite a bit of information about your organization and its policies to accomplish this task. For example, you must know precisely what accomplishments are needed to gain a specific promotion. You must understand the organizational politics of promotions and other benefits—who has input into the process, who makes the final decision, and so on. Obviously, the precise series of steps needed to reach different goals will vary with the nature of the goals themselves and with countless features of your organization. Regardless of these factors, your basic strategy should remain the same: Determine just what you have to do to move from Point A (where you are now) to Point B (where you want to get) and beyond.

Personal Career Development: Summing Up   Looking back over our comments in this section, you can probably see that the process we have described is almost like a personal program of *management by objectives*.[15] As we described in Chapter 5, you begin by figuring out who and where you are. Then, you select concrete goals you wish to attain, and devise specific steps for reaching them. And along the way, you continually gauge your progress and adjust the process to make sure you stay on track. (The major steps in this basic plan for career development are summarized in Figure 14.6.) Of course, we should hasten to add that even this

FIGURE 14.6   Personal Career Development: Summing Up
An effective approach to career development requires each of the steps outlined here.

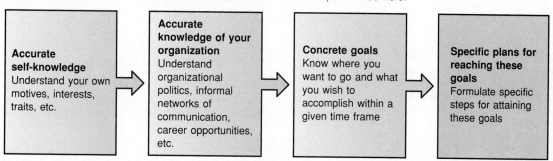

444

CHAPTER 14

CAREER CHOICE AND
DEVELOPMENT:
PLANNING FOR
SUCCESS

approach, as systematic and rational as it is, can offer no guarantee of ultimate success. There are simply too many personal, organizational, and external events that impinge on your career for this to be the case. The steps outlined here, however, will definitely accomplish one thing: They will get you thinking clearly and systematically about yourself, your organization, and your career. This in itself should give you an important edge, and at least get you moving in the right (constructive) directions.

CASE IN POINT

The "Star" that Didn't Shine

Sandy was good and she knew it. When she received her degree in business, she was at the very top of her class. Her professors viewed her as the most talented person to graduate from their program in many years. Job offers literally poured in, and when she accepted a position with TDI, a well-managed and highly profitable financial investment firm, Sandy looked forward to a bright future.

But now, four years later, Sandy realizes that something has gone wrong—seriously wrong. As far as she can tell, she has been doing good work; she certainly puts out the effort. And her performance appraisals have been uniformly positive. Yet, she has been passed over for promotions on three separate occasions. The most recent of these happened just this week and is the most painful yet. Julie Bishop, someone with far less talent than Sandy, and who has been with the company a year less than she has, got the nod. And now Sandy is both depressed and bewildered. After thinking things over for three days, she has decided to take a step she has never taken before. She will talk to Bob Bassett, the assistant director of her department, and try to find out what she's doing wrong. She doesn't really know Bob all that well—Sandy keeps pretty much to herself. But at least she's had a few conversations with him, which is more than she can say for anyone else. With a shaking hand, she knocks on his door. When Bob calls, "Come in," she enters.

"Hello, Bob," she stammers. "Do you have a minute?"

"Sure, Sandy," Bob replies. "What can I do for you?"

"Well, it's this promotion business," Sandy murmurs. "I'm really upset about it and I wondered whether you could sort of clear things up for me."

"You mean you want to know why Julie got it and you didn't, right?"

"Yes, that's it. Please tell me."

"Are you sure you want to know?" Bob asks, a serious look on his face.

"Oh, yes, please, please!" Sandy exclaims, the color rising to her cheeks.

"Okay, then *you* tell *me* something first: Who has the most input into these decisions?"

"Bill Thompson I suppose. I mean, he's the department head and all."

"Hmph!" Bob replies. "See there's part of your trouble right away. Don't

CAREERS: CHANGES OVER A LIFETIME

During their work years (which typically fill from forty to fifty years), most individuals experience major shifts with respect to their work. The tasks they perform, the status they enjoy, the roles they play, their geographic location, the compensation they receive—all these features of working life, plus many others,

you know it's really Helen Tarshes who controls these things? You should have been cultivating her all along."

"But . . . but . . ." Sandy stammers. "I had no idea."

"I'm sure you didn't," Bob answers coldly. "After all, it's not on the organizational chart. And that's a major part of your problem around here. I mean, you've been with the company four years and you don't even know a basic thing like that!"

"Well," Sandy answers weakly. "I usually keep my nose in my work—I'm so busy most of the time."

"So is everyone else," Bob answers, "and yet they still have time to find out how the company ticks. See, the way things work around here, you've got to have friends plugging for you if you want to get promoted. And let's face it—you don't. In fact, you're kind of isolated. You don't belong to any of the informal networks, and that really costs you."

"What do you mean?" Sandy asks, still bewildered.

"Here's an example. Remember when you gave that report last week? You came down strong in favor of the new Ampex 500's. Didn't you know that Herb Costman had already decided against them? That never would have happened if you were part of the grapevine. As it was, you looked pretty darn foolish and annoyed Herb to boot."

At these last words, Sandy shakes her head and groans. "I begin to see what you mean, Bob. Somehow I've really been left on the outside. No wonder I can't get promoted. There's really a lot more to getting ahead around here than doing good work—if only I'd realized sooner . . ."

Questions

1. Why do you think Sandy has been so isolated from members of her department? Is she basically unfriendly? Conceited? Lacking in social skills?

2. Do you think she can act on Bob's advice and finally learn the ropes of her company? Or is it too late no matter what she does?

3. Suppose Sandy does decide to move to another company. What steps can she take to ensure that the same situation doesn't develop again?

446

CHAPTER 14

CAREER CHOICE AND
DEVELOPMENT:
PLANNING FOR
SUCCESS

can alter radically as the decades slip by. As individuals move through various stages or portions of their careers, they are also moving from one stage of life to another. Youth is replaced by maturity, which gives way to middle-age, and so on. This movement through the lifespan, and the changes in family obligations and personal relationships it brings, is often closely linked to changes in individuals' careers. Thus it is impossible to consider one of these topics (careers) in isolation from the others (development during adult life). Recognizing this fact, we will call attention to links between careers and life events and change at several points.

Career Development and Life Stages

As careers develop, they seem to move through repeated cycles of stability and change.[16] After individuals have been hired or promoted to a new position, there is a stage of *career growth*. During these periods, individuals consolidate their recent gains by acquiring the new skills and information needed to perform their current job effectively. As this process is completed, they enter a stage of *stabilization*—one in which they are performing their job to their fullest capacity, and things are (temporarily) on an even keel. This is followed by a period of *transition*, in which individuals prepare themselves, psychologically, for their next move upward. During this period they anticipate the demands of their next career stage and get ready to meet these. When the expected promotion arrives, the cycle starts over again. In short, the careers of many individuals are marked by a process in which they grow into each new position, become acclimated to it, and then begin preparations for the next step on the ladder (see Figure 14.7).

Cross-cutting this cycle are important critical choice points most persons face in their career planning. These are age-related and occur for different individuals at different points on the cycle of growth, stabilization, and transition noted above. The twenties are a time of getting started—choosing a career, getting established in it, selecting a mate. For many persons, the thirties bring increasing family responsibilities, as they start or add to their families. The forties bring a mid-life crisis for at least some individuals, as they realize that they are now as close to the end as to the beginning and come to terms with the fact that they will never achieve many of their youthful dreams. And so the process continues: different concerns and problems during different decades of life. In a similar way, different stages of our careers are also marked by contrasting sets of issues. These are often divided into issues relating to early, middle, and late career stages (see Figure 14.8).

FIGURE 14.7 The Career Change Cycle
Careers often move through repeated cycles of career growth, stabilization, and transition.

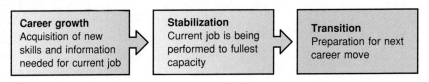

FIGURE 14.8 Different Career Stages: Different Career Issues
The people shown here are at different career stages (early, middle, and late) and are likely to
be facing rather different career issues.

Early Career Issues The main task we face during our early careers is *career planning*. At this time, we generally map the course of our future careers, deciding what types of jobs and activities we will pursue in the decades that follow. Although not all of us make such decisions in a rational way, most of us base them on **career anchors.**[17] According to Schein, these are self-perceptions of our job-related talents and abilities, needs and motives, and attitudes and values. These self-perceptions come to guide and stabilize our career, as we attempt to choose jobs and goals that are consistent with these basic characteristics. While everyone has such anchors, however, they take several distinct forms.

For some persons, such career anchors are *technical* or *functional* in nature. Their primary concern in making job decisions and mapping their future careers involves the *content* of work. They want to do certain things, and plan their

448

CHAPTER 14

CAREER CHOICE AND
DEVELOPMENT:
PLANNING FOR
SUCCESS

careers accordingly. For a second group, career anchors emphasize *managerial competence*. Persons in this category want to attain high-level management positions. They like to analyze and solve difficult business problems, enjoy influencing others, and like exercising power. They are likely to choose career paths that will lead them to such goals.

A third group is primarily concerned with *security* and *stability*. Their search for security often leads them to enter large, stable companies, and long-term employment with a single firm. A fourth group, in contrast, emphasizes *creativity* or *entrepreneurship* in career plans. Such persons want to build or create a product that is unique and of their own devising. They may be good at starting and running small companies. Finally, some individuals emphasize *autonomy* and *independence*. They want to be free of external constraints, and prefer to work at their own pace and set their own goals. Such persons often select careers in academia and professional writing, or prefer to run their own small businesses. (See Figure 14.9 for a summary of these different career anchors.)

While the task of identifying their own abilities, motives, and values is important, it is hardly the only issue individuals face during the early portion of their careers. In addition, they must confront relatively frequent job changes—changes stemming from transfers and promotions. While such changes can be beneficial to one's career, they involve considerable costs, both for organizations and the persons involved. Individuals who are transferred or promoted are expected to "hit the floor running"—to demonstrate high performance from the very start. Further, such demands occur just when individuals must establish new networks of social support, learn new skills, and eliminate old patterns of behavior and attitudes no longer appropriate to their new position. Clearly, this is an unsettling combination of events, but one that must be handled successfully if individuals are to stay on track with respect to their own career plans.

FIGURE 14.9 Contrasting Types of Career Anchors

Individuals' perceptions of their own abilities, motives, and values often serve as career anchors. Individuals then attempt to choose jobs and goals that are consistent with these characteristics. Such career anchors often emphasize one or more of the factors shown here. *Source:* Based on suggestions by Schein (1978); see Note 17.

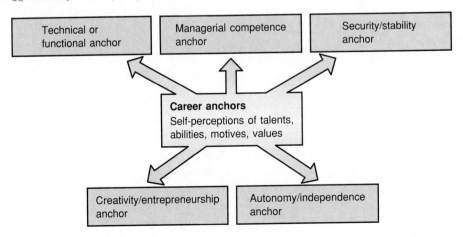

Middle Career Issues   As we noted earlier, age forty marks the end of the dream for many persons. It is at this point they realize they will never go as far as they had hoped and will never realize many of their fondest dreams.[18] Since they have already risen to fairly high-level positions within their organizations, there are fewer and fewer promotions available for them. On top of all this, there are many ambitious and well-trained younger employees eager to take over their positions. No wonder many persons find turning forty an unsettling experience (see Figure 14.10). They may become cynical or apathetic. Sometimes, they experience burnout and become liabilities to themselves and to their companies. Fortunately, however, they often resolve their mid-life dilemma in more constructive ways.

First, individuals can choose to become *mentors*. In fact, it is at this stage in their careers that they are expected to assume such a role in many organizations. As a mentor, the older and more experienced employee advises, counsels, and aids the development of younger employees. Second, individuals at this stage of their careers can remain active in their work but expand their interests so that they no longer focus exclusively on their jobs. This can involve a conscious decision to spend more time with one's family, the development of new hobbies, and related actions.

Another issue faced by many persons in mid-career is the discovery that they have reached a **career plateau**.[19] They find that they have arrived at a point from which they are unlikely to gain further promotions or be given increased responsibility and authority. In short, they are at a virtual dead-end in their careers. What leads to this state of affairs? Potentially, several factors. First, as noted earlier, some individuals consciously choose to put a brake on their own careers. They may not wish to take on added responsibility, or they may not want to leave a particular geographic region. For others, however, entry into a career plateau is less voluntary. They may have failed to keep up with developments in their field and so no longer possess the skills and knowledge required for further promotions.

Fortunately, involuntary career plateaus do not have to be permanent. By recognizing the need for change and taking such steps as seeking retraining, developing alternate roles within the organization (e.g., serving as a mentor), or

FIGURE 14.10   Middle Career Issues: Time for a Change?
The middle phase of a career can be a time when some people feel the need for a change. (Reprinted by permission Tribune Media Services.)

450

CHAPTER 14

CAREER CHOICE AND
DEVELOPMENT:
PLANNING FOR
SUCCESS

actually moving to another job, some persons, at least, can escape from such dead-ends and the malaise that often accompanies them.

With careers, as with almost anything else, what goes up usually, at some point, also comes down. This is the key issue faced by most individuals in the later years of their careers. Many find that they have indeed gone as far as they can go and have either accomplished key goals or will never be able to achieve them. They must also come to terms with the fact that, like their physical energies, their power and influence within the organization are beginning to wane.

Older employees are also increasingly becoming the subject of negative stereotypes. Typically, they are viewed as being less productive, efficient, motivated, and capable of working under pressure than younger persons.[20] Older workers (perhaps because of their greater experience) are actually *more* productive than younger ones![21] Still, the stereotypes remain and are a fact of life for many individuals as they approach the end of their careers.

Another issue faced by individuals late in their careers is coming to terms with their own retirement. This involves a gradual reorientation away from one's career and work, toward the leisure-time activities that will become dominant during retirement. In addition, it should involve careful planning to meet the special challenges faced by retired workers—a loss of social contact with many friends, reduced feelings of accomplishment, reduced earnings. Fortunately, growing evidence suggests that if individuals take the time to prepare for such factors, the end of their working years can be a beginning as well as an end. It can mark entry into a period of renewed personal growth and fulfillment, rather than merely a signal for inevitable decline.

ORGANIZATIONAL SOCIALIZATION: BECOMING PART OF AN ORGANIZATION

You have probably held a number of jobs in recent years. Can you recall your feelings and reactions during the first few days (or weeks) on each? You probably remember that these were uncomfortable periods. As a new employee, you were suddenly confronted with a work environment that was different, in many ways, from ones you had previously encountered. The people around you were unfamiliar, and you had to begin the process of getting to know them— and their many personal quirks. Unless your job was identical to one you had performed before, you also had to learn several new procedures, skills, and operations relating to it. It was necessary to become familiar with the policies, practices, and procedures of your new organization.

It is important for organizations that new employees quickly "learn the ropes." The process through which this task is accomplished is known as **organizational socialization,** or *the process through which individuals are transformed from outsiders to participating effective members of organizations.*[22]

In this section, we'll examine several features of this socialization. First, we'll describe the basic stages of socialization—steps through which most persons pass en route to becoming full members of their organization and work group. Then, we'll consider various techniques used by organizations to help smooth new employees' passage through this difficult process.

Major Phases in the Socialization Process

Organizational socialization is basically a continuous process—one that begins before an individual actually arrives on the scene and proceeds for weeks or months after their entry. However, it makes sense to divide it into three basic periods that are often marked by a specific event signifying their beginning and their end. These have been described as the stages of *getting in, breaking in,* and *settling in.*[23]

Getting In: Preliminary Socialization Before individuals actually join an organization, they usually know quite a bit about it. This information is the basis for expectations concerning what the organization and their specific jobs will be like and is obtained from several sources. It is often provided by friends or relatives already working for the organization. Sometimes information is obtained from professional journals, magazine and newspaper articles, annual reports, and other formal sources. Another important source of information is the organization's *recruitment procedures.* Since competition for good employees is often very keen, recruiters often describe their companies in glowing terms. As a result, potential employees receive an unrealistically positive impression about what working for a company will be like. When they actually arrive on the job and find that their expectations are not met, disappointment, dissatisfaction, and even resentment about being misled can follow. These reactions can result in high rates of turnover, low organizational commitment, and other negative outcomes.[24]

How can such reactions be avoided or reduced? One technique that seems quite useful is **realistic job previews**—providing job applicants with accurate descriptions of the jobs they will perform and the organizations they will enter.[25] Evidence suggests that persons exposed to such previews later report higher satisfaction and show lower turnover than those who receive glowing—but often misleading—information about the companies in question.[26]

Breaking In: The Encounter Stage The second major stage in organizational socialization begins when individuals actually take on their new duties. During this stage, they face several key tasks. First, they must master the skills required by their new job. Second, they must become oriented to the practices and procedures of the organization. Third, new members of an organization must establish good social relations with other members of their work group. They must get to know these people and gain their acceptance. Only then can they become full members of the team.

Settling In: The Metamorphosis Stage Some time after an individual enters an organization, he or she attains full member status. Depending on the type and length of the training program used, this entry may be marked by a formal ceremony (e.g., a dinner or reception) or may be quite informal (being invited to lunch by coworkers). Whatever form it takes, the settling in phase of social-

452
CHAPTER 14
CAREER CHOICE AND
DEVELOPMENT:
PLANNING FOR
SUCCESS

ization marks important shifts for both individuals and organizations. Employees now make permanent adjustments to their jobs (e.g., they resolve conflicting demands between their job and their personal life), and organizations now treat them as if they will be long-term members of the work team. (See Figure 14.11 for a summary of events and activities occurring during the three major stages of organizational socialization.)

Effective Socialization Programs: Some Basic Guidelines

While organizational socialization is a rather complex process, it basically involves the successful attainment of three major goals: (1) providing employees with the basic work skills and information needed for their jobs, (2) orienting them to practices, policies, and procedures of the organization, and (3) helping them adjust to membership in their new work groups. Below are some general guidelines that often prove useful in reaching each of these goals.

Training There are a variety of techniques for providing new skills and information. We will discuss three that are often used in organizations. In the *sink-or-swim* approach, recruits are simply placed in their new jobs and learn what they need from practical experience. Alternatively, in *job rotation,* they work in several different jobs in succession, thus acquiring a broad range of skills useful in different contexts. In contrast, in full-time *training,* they participate in training programs ranging from classroom instruction to detailed on-the-job training. Training programs should adopt the following principles in order to succeed:

1. Determine precisely what skills and information individuals need for their jobs; do *not* assume that their previous experience or professional training has armed them with these skills or information.

2. Provide individuals with feedback on their work and a sense of accomplishment about their growing expertise.

3. Design training programs for specific jobs; general training cannot be readily applied or transferred in many cases.

4. Evaluate the success of training programs on a regular basis; do not assume that they are succeeding.

FIGURE 14.11 Organizational Socialization: Its Major Phases
The process of organizational socialization is complex and involves many different activities. In general, however, it can be divided into the three major stages illustrated here.

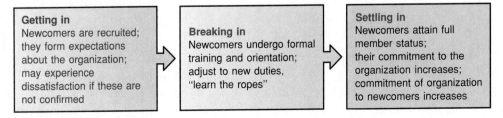

Getting in
Newcomers are recruited; they form expectations about the organization; may experience dissatisfaction if these are not confirmed

Breaking in
Newcomers undergo formal training and orientation; adjust to new duties, "learn the ropes"

Settling in
Newcomers attain full member status; their commitment to the organization increases; commitment of organization to newcomers increases

FIGURE 14.12 Orientation Programs: Part of Effective Socialization
Well-designed orientation programs are important for effective socialization in organizations. Here a group of newly hired employees are being briefed on company policies and procedures.

Orientation Orientation programs help individuals understand current organization practices, policies, and procedures. Most are fairly short-term, taking a few hours or a single day (see Figure 14.12). In order for such programs to succeed, they should use the following guidelines:

1. Avoid information overload; new employees cannot possibly absorb everything they need to know about the organization in a single day; this should be spread out over a longer period of time.

2. Don't overemphasize paperwork; it is impossible for individuals to gain an accurate overview of an organization and how it operates from a day spent filling out one form after another.

3. Avoid scare tactics, in which new employees are warned that their chances of success are quite low; also avoid focusing too heavily on praising the organization and its current practices.

4. Build in two-way communication so that new recruits do not merely receive information in a passive manner; they should have opportunities to raise questions and seek clarification.

SUMMARY

Individuals seem to choose their **careers** largely on the basis of personal interests, social influence from others, and accident. A better approach involves efforts to obtain thorough knowledge of one's own traits, interests, and motives, plus sys-

454

CHAPTER 14

CAREER CHOICE AND
DEVELOPMENT:
PLANNING FOR
SUCCESS

tematic information on the requirements of various jobs. A final step involves seeking a career that offers a good match between these two sets of factors.

In recent years, many companies have begun to appreciate the importance of effective *human resource planning*—efforts to make the best possible use of their employees' skills and talents. Consistent with this shift, some organizations have established special programs of career management/development. One feature of these programs is often the provision of detailed *performance appraisals* to employees. In addition to relying on such help from their companies, individuals can contribute to their own career development through several steps. These include (1) increasing their knowledge of their own strengths and weaknesses; (2) forming a clear picture of the functioning of their organization (including its internal politics); (3) establishing concrete goals; and (4) devising specific steps to reach these.

The sequence of occupations and jobs that individuals hold during their working lives constitutes their careers. Crucial points in career planning occur at key times during an individual's life—for example, at about age thirty, during the early forties, and again in the late fifties. Each career stage involves somewhat different issues. Important early career issues include the establishment of *career anchors*, and *job changes*. Middle career issues include coming to terms with the fact that all of one's hopes and dreams will not be realized, and the possibility of *career plateaus*. Late career issues include accepting reduced power and influence, choosing one's successors, and preparing for retirement.

The process through which newcomers learn the ropes in their organizations and become full-fledged members is known as **organizational socialization.** This process involves three distinct stages known as *getting in, breaking in,* and *settling in*. Various techniques for socializing new employees into an organization exist. The most useful of these tend to provide individuals with the skills they need for performing their jobs and with adequate orientation to the organization's policies and procedures.

KEY TERMS

career: The sequence of attitudes and behaviors associated with work-related activities experienced by individuals over the span of their working lives.

career anchors: Individuals' self-perceptions of their own abilities, motives, and values, and their efforts to choose jobs or careers consistent with these self-perceptions.

career development: The pattern of changes that occur during an individual's career.

career plateaus: Points in careers from which individuals are unlikely to gain further promotions or receive increased responsibility.

human resource planning: Efforts by organizations to make the best possible use of the skills, abilities, and talents of their employees.

organizational politics: The process through which power and influence are exercised within a given organization. A clear understanding of such politics is necessary for effective career development.

organizational socialization: The process through which newcomers to an organization are converted to full-fledged members who share its major values and understand its policies and procedures.

performance appraisal: Various steps undertaken by organizations to provide employees with feedback on their current performance. Detailed and constructive performance appraisals often form part of company-run programs of career management/career development.

realistic job previews: Accurate information concerning conditions within an organization that is provided to potential employees prior to their decision to join the organization.

social models: Individuals who affect the behavior or attitudes of others through their words or deeds, often without any conscious desire to produce such effects.

NOTES

1. Feldman, D.C. (1988). *Managing Careers in Organizations*. Glenview, Ill: Scott, Foresman.

2. Hall, D.T. (1987). *Careers and Organizations*. Pacific Palisades, Calif.: Goodyear Publishing.

3. Sonnenfeld, J. (1984). *Career Management: An Introduction to Self-Assessment, Career Development, and Career Systems*. Chicago: SRA.

4. Liebert, R.M., Sprafkin, J.N., & Davidson, E.S. (1982). *The Early Window: Effects of Television on Children and Youth*, 2d ed. New York: Pergamon.

5. Kahn, R.L. (1972). "The Meaning of Work: Interpretations and Proposals for Measurement." In A.A. Campbell and P.E. Converse, eds. *The Human Meaning of Social Change*. New York: Basic Books.

6. Baron, R.A., & Byrne, D. (1991). *Social Psychology: Understanding Human Interaction*, 6th ed. Boston: Allyn and Bacon.

7. Suls, J., & Miller, R.C. (1977). *Social Comparison Processes: Theoretical and Empirical Perspectives*. Washington, D.C.: Halsted-Wiley.

8. See Note 1.

9. Von Glinow, M.A., Driver, M.J., Brousseau, K., & Prince, J.B. (1983). "The Design of a Career Oriented Human Resource System." *Academy of Management Review, 8*, 23–32.

10. Baron, R.A., & Greenberg, J. (1990). *Behavior in Organizations*. Boston: Allyn & Bacon.

11. London, M. (1983). "Toward a Theory of Career Motivation." *Academy of Management Review, 8*, 620–30.

12. See Note 11.

13. Jones, G. (1983). "Psychological Orientation and the Process of Organizational Socialization: An Interactionist Perspective." *Academy of Management Review, 8*, 464–74.

14. Scholl, R.W. (1983). "Career Lines and Employment Stability." *Academy of Management Journal, 26*, 86–103.

15. Kondrasuk, J.N. (1981). "Studies in MBO Effectiveness." *Academy of Management Review, 6*, 419–30.

16. Levinson, D.J. (1986). "A Conception of Adult Development." *American Psychologist, 41*, 3–13.

17. Schein, E.H. (1978). *Career Dynamics: Matching Individual and Organizational Needs*. Reading, Mass.: Addison-Wesley.

18. Dalton, G.W., Thompson, P.H., & Price, R. (1977). "Career Stages: A Model of Professional Careers in Organizations." *Organizational Dynamics* (summer), pp. 19–42.

19. Ference, T.P., Stoner, J.A.F., & Warren, E.K. (1977). "Managing the Career Plateau." *Academy of Management Review, 2*, 602–12.

456

CHAPTER 14
CAREER CHOICE AND
DEVELOPMENT:
PLANNING FOR
SUCCESS

20. Rosen, B., & Jerdee, T.H. (1976). "The Nature of Job-Related Age Stereotypes." *Journal of Applied Psychology, 61,* 180–83.

21. Waldman, D.A., & Avolio, B.J. (1986). "A Meta-Analysis of Age Differences in Job Performance." *Journal of Applied Psychology, 71,* 33–38.

22. Feldman, J.C. (1976). "A Contingency Theory of Socialization." *Administrative Science Quarterly, 21,* 433–52.

23. Feldman, D.C. (1980). "A Socialization Process that Helps New Recruits Succeed." *Personnel, 57,* 11–23.

24. Wanous, J.P. (1981). *Organizational Entry.* Reading, Mass.: Addison-Wesley.

25. Wanous, J.P. (1983). "The Entry of Newcomers into Organizations." In J.R. Hackman, E.E. Lawler, & L.W. Porter, eds. *Perspectives and Behavior in Organizations,* 2d ed., pp. 126–35). New York: McGraw-Hill.

26. McEvoy, G.M., & Cascio, W.F. (1985). "Strategies for Reducing Employee Turnover: A Meta-Analysis." *Journal of Applied Psychology, 70,* 342–53.

ADDITIONAL CASES AND EXERCISES: APPLYING WHAT YOU'VE LEARNED

Jackson Design

Robert D. Goddard III
Associate Professor, Department of Management
Appalachian State University

Jim Jackson is a young man literally "on the way up." Jim graduated with a degree in accounting from the University of Colorado in June 1982, and went to work for an accounting firm in Denver. He had always been interested in rock climbing and mountaineering, and had been a member of the Rocky Mountain Climbers for three years while in college.

In September 1982, Jim purchased a commercial sewing machine and began to make mountain climbing accessories for himself. He knew what he wanted and found that none of the commercially available products suited his needs and tastes. Specifically, Jim wanted a backpack that was lightweight but sturdy enough to survive the rigors of rock climbing. He also wanted to make a series of "fanny packs" small pouches to wear around his waist to hold small items of climbing gear. Jim had ideas for other items for rock climbing such as cold-weather clothing that would also stand up to the heavy abrasion encountered during a climb.

Jim constructed the items he wanted and tested them out himself on the rock faces of the nearby mountains. His fellow climbers saw that Jim's climbing accessories were more suited to climbing than those they had purchased (at considerable expense) from the mountaineering stores in the area and from the traditional mail-order outlets. They simply worked better and lasted longer. Jim's friends wanted accessories like his for themselves.

At first, Jim was reluctant to comply with their requests for copies of his climbing accessories. After all, he had a new career as an accountant and that job required him to work long hours. If he spent his free time making climbing accessories for his friends, he would have no time for climbing himself, and he looked forward to getting out of the office and getting "on the rocks." However, he knew that his backpacks and fanny packs were better than those his friends were able to purchase, so he agreed to put together a few for his friends at night after work.

Like many good things, word soon got out in the climbing community of Colorado, and Jim was soon overwhelmed with requests for his climbing accessories. Jim, being the astute business school graduate that he was, saw that there was a need for a set of products that he could fill (Jim's marketing classes were not totally lost on him). He began to produce back and fanny packs and designed a single-page brochure describing his products and prices. This brochure was sent to mountaineering stores and climbing clubs in Colorado, and responses started to come in. Jim was really shocked when a large store in Boulder sent him a letter in November asking if he could produce 100 backpacks and 250 fanny packs

Source: This case was developed in 1989 by Robert D. Goddard, after seeing the film, "The Climber," a 1974 production of the General Motors Corporation, Detroit, Michigan. All rights reserved.

458

CHAPTER 14

CAREER CHOICE AND
DEVELOPMENT:
PLANNING FOR
SUCCESS

for shipment by January 1983. The largest order he had had up to then was a request for two backpacks for a couple in Colorado Springs.

Jim knew he was faced with a decision that would alter the course of his life. Should he quit his good job and become a manufacturer of climbing accessories, or should he give up on this crazy idea of being an entrepreneur? Jim chose the former option and resigned from his job. With a business plan and this large order in his hand, Jim went to a local bank and obtained financing for two more sewing machines. He rented space at a mini-warehouse, set up the three sewing machines, ordered materials, and hired two women on a part-time basis. Jim was in business.

It was a struggle at first. Jim claims now that he learned more in the first six months of business than he did in four years of business school. Of course, the training he received in school helped him understand the kinds of things he should do in order to survive and grow. And grow he did. Over the next two years, Jim moved twice, needing more space for additional sewing machines, storage, and employees. By the beginning of 1985, Jim had five full-time and three part-time employees, and his company, Jackson Design, had reached $225,000 in sales.

However, Jim felt that his sales were reaching a plateau in mountaineering products, and he was looking for additional types of products that could be made on his existing equipment. Since Jim had been raised on a dairy farm, he knew that there was a need for a product that could dispense insecticide, reducing the fly problem that led to diseases and infections in the cattle. After much thought, and a few design failures, Jim came up with a product that would dust the cattle with powdered insecticide as they entered and left the barn. Based on the materials Jim was using in his mountaineering accessories, this item gave Jackson Design a year-round product with wide acceptability. Jim was successful in obtaining a patent on his *cattle duster*.

This new product required Jim to take a hard look at his marketing efforts. The traditional promotional outlets for climbing and mountaineering accessories were not suitable for this new agricultural item. Additionally, it was expected that this and other products for the agricultural market would require yet more expansion. Up until this point in time, Jim had been intimately involved with product design, ordering, production, and marketing and sales for his mountaineering products. He had helped with everything from unloading trucks, running sewing machines, calling customers and prospects, handling the accounting and bookkeeping to sweeping the floors at night.

After promoting the cattle duster in publications aimed at the agricultural market (*Farm Bureau* magazine, rural electric cooperative magazines, etc.), Jackson Design found itself swamped with orders. Jim was forced to reassess his whole organization. He was faced with the prospect of moving again to larger quarters, hiring at least five more sewing machine operators, as well as additional people for the shipping and receiving area. He realized that he could no longer be as involved in the everyday aspects of the business, and that he and Jackson Design were going to have to become more specialized.

Problem: Jackson Design has grown from one employee, Jim Jackson, to a company employing 25 full- and part-time men and women. The product line has expanded from mountaineering and climbing accessories to include agricultural products. All of the business functions—research and product development, marketing, production, finance and accounting, distribution, and management—are currently being handled by Jim himself. The agricultural product line is expected to expand with the development of new items, while the mountaineering product line has probably reached its growth peak.

Design an organization chart that will fit the requirements of this expanding firm. Keep in mind that Jim Jackson has been a "hands-on" type of manager up to this point, but conditions may force him to reassess his function in the firm.

What Are Your Career Anchors?

Earlier in this chapter we discussed the role of career anchors in choosing a particular career. To check on your career anchors, fill out the scale below.

In choosing a job or making career decisions, how important are each of the following factors to you?

1. Content of the job/career: What I'll actually be doing in my daily work

Relatively unimportant						Very important
1	2	3	4	5	6	7

2. Development of my management skills/potential

Relatively unimportant						Very important
1	2	3	4	5	6	7

3. Security (stable, long-term employment; predictable career progress)

Relatively unimportant						Very important
1	2	3	4	5	6	7

4. Being able to create new products or services

Relatively unimportant						Very important
1	2	3	4	5	6	7

5. Being free of external constraints or constant supervision; being able to operate independently, make my own decisions, etc.

Relatively unimportant						Very important
1	2	3	4	5	6	7

Interpretation: If you circled 5 or higher on any of the above items, the career anchor it represents may be an influential factor in your career choices. What do you think your pattern of responses implies about the type of career that might be best for you? See pages 447–48 for a more detailed discussion of this issue.

CHAPTER

15

Changes in the Workplace: Coping with the Future

Learning Objectives

After reading this chapter,
you should be able to:

1. Describe several major causes of change
   in work settings.

2. Explain why individuals often resist
   change at work.

3. Discuss the organizational barriers to
   change.

4. Indicate the best way of introducing
   change into an organization.

5. Define organizational development, and
   outline several major techniques often
   used for this purpose.

veryone at the Downtown Herald was still buzzing about the news. They had been informed that morning that they had been bought by the media conglomerate headed by Peter Dermer. Dermer was one of the richest men in America and already had a large number of television stations and newspapers as part of his corporate empire. He was a dynamic and strong-willed individual who often made drastic changes at his new acquisitions. Jim Daniels and Carol Schein were sitting in the employee cafeteria sharing their feelings about the impending changes. Jim was a newly hired photographer; Carol had been a writer for the business section for five years.

Jim looked a little depressed. "I'm afraid I could lose my job if this guy comes in and makes a lot of changes. At least you've been here for a while and might be able to stick around."

Carol looked at Jim for a moment and shrugged her shoulders. "It's hard to know what to expect, really. Sometimes, he has left the operation fairly intact. At other times, he has made wholesale changes."

"I'm sure he'll make some changes here though," replied Jim. "Even though this area has grown, this paper has not increased in circulation at all. We probably need to take a fresh approach with our marketing and our presentation of the news. He'll probably want to bring in some new blood."

"If that's the case, they might even get rid of us more senior people," said Carol, a little more concerned than before. "He likes to give people what they want, even if it means watering down the editorial quality. His papers are high on local news and entertainment. He might downplay business and international news."

Jim and Carol sat quietly for a while as they finished their lunch. They looked around at the other people in the cafeteria and thought about the many friends they had made at the Downtown Herald. Both of them were filled with feelings of uncertainty and anxiety.

"Well," mused Jim, "If he does come in here and make wholesale changes, I hope that he'll at least take the time to get to know us and to get input from all of us."

"I hope so too," replied Carol. "But it's time to get back to work. We might as well enjoy our jobs, while we have them," she said with a slight smile.

"That's not funny, Carol!" said Jim as he slowly got up from the table.

This situation is faced by employees every day. Change seems to be inevitable in today's companies. To illustrate this basic fact, simply consider a few of the major shifts that have occurred in the world of work in recent decades: the information explosion, coupled with vastly increased use of computers; robotics and other types of automated production (see Figure 15.1); increased foreign competition and its impact on many industries. All of these trends have produced

FIGURE 15.1 Change: An Inevitable Process

In our workplaces, we have to cope with continual changes. Increased use of computers, automation, and robotics are just a few examples of this process. (Ziggy © Ziggy & Friends./Distributed by Universal Press Syndicate. Reprinted with permission. All rights reserved.)

major alterations in the work people do and the way they do it. Indeed, taken as a whole, these changes are so complex and varied that it is still too early to gauge their total impact. One point, though, is already clear: In the late twentieth century, change is a basic fact of life at work. In order to survive and prosper, both organizations and individuals need the ability to cope with it effectively. They must be able to react appropriately when change occurs. And, perhaps even more important, they must be able to see it developing, and prepare for its arrival in advance. Companies that do not change or adjust to new realities may not survive. However, changes are often disruptive to the personal and social lives of employees. So it is probably not surprising that change is often strongly resisted by employees and some organizations. In this chapter, we will explore the different forces that lie behind change, the factors that underlie resistance to change, and the various ways in which the process of change can be facilitated.

CHANGE: SOME BASIC CAUSES

"Business as usual." This old sentiment is still very much with us. What it suggests is this: Given their 'druthers, most organizations would prefer to continue with the same procedures and policies. Only if these no longer work will they seriously, if reluctantly, consider change. Unfortunately, this traditional stand-pat attitude is far from appropriate in the 1990s. In recent decades many forces have combined to render old approaches and methods unsuitable in many work settings. A large number of such forces exist—many more than we would hope to consider here. However, most center around changes in technology, shifts in social attitudes or values, and important alterations in the nature of competition or other economic factors.

Technology as a Source of Change

The space shuttle, genetic engineering, powerful microcomputers, wristwatch size televisions, artificial hearts—the flow (should we say flood?) of new technological marvels seems endless. Of course, all these advances are the "splashy" kind—the type journalists like to report on the evening news or in feature articles. Thousands of other advances are of less public interest and are largely unknown outside the industries in which they are applied. But they may still revolutionize the way many products are made and the basic ways many companies conduct their daily business.

The positive side of the coin, where technological advances are concerned, is easy to recognize. New products are developed, old ones are greatly improved, and many work tasks can be performed more rapidly and efficiently than ever before. Thus, in these respects, technological progress is certainly a force for positive change both in the world of work and in society generally. This can be seen from the development of communication systems. With today's sophisticated satellite transmission systems, fiber-optic cables crisscrossing the planet, fax machines, portable telephones, teleconferencing facilities and the like, it is easier than ever for businesses to communicate with each other and with their clients (see Figure 15.2). As such communication systems improve, opportunities for organizational growth and improvement immediately follow.[1]

The other and more negative side of the process, though, is also obvious—often painfully obvious! First, consider jobs. For every new technological breakthrough, thousands, or perhaps even hundreds of thousands, of persons find their jobs in jeopardy. New skills may be required; skills they do not now possess. Or, even worse, the jobs themselves may totally vanish into a kind of high-tech limbo. For example, when supermarkets and department stores install computerized cash registers, their need for stock clerks drops sharply; the computer can now keep track of every single purchase and return. Similarly, when robots are installed on production lines, the need for human employees decreases; after all, these devices can work tirelessly day and night, without rest and without demand for higher wages! One reply to the concerns often voiced over such shifts is that the same advances that eliminate old jobs tend to create new ones. This may well be true, but so far, the new industries created by high technology tend to be super-efficient, requiring far fewer workers than the older businesses they replace. For example, the use of robots has reportedly helped the General Electric Company produce 20 percent more dishwashers in 20 percent less floor space in its Louisville, Kentucky, plant. Robots have also helped the Walgreen's drugstore chain increase the rate of packing shipments from its distribution center.[2] Thus, at present, it remains unclear whether the current revolution in technology will result merely

FIGURE 15.2 Communication Systems: One Major Source of Change
New communication systems, such as fax machines, have drastically changed the way we
interact with each other. (Reprinted by permission of UFS, Inc.)

in shifts in the pattern of employment or in actual declines in the total number
of jobs.

Second, some technological advances carry with them new and previously
unknown dangers. You have probably read about fears relating to genetic engineering. The main concern is that some new microbe, specifically created for
industrial purposes, will mutate into something sinister that could threaten the
entire planet. Similarly, the concentration of huge amounts of information brought
about by the increased use of computers poses potential threats to the privacy of
individuals. It also makes businesses vulnerable to new kinds of assaults on their
assets. In sum, while technological advances have certainly yielded many benefits,
they do not appear to be a mixed blessing (see Figure 15.3).

Whatever its relative costs and benefits, high technology is certainly here to
stay. The race is on and, as always, victory will go to the swiftest. Today, though,
speed is measured in terms of technological progress rather than mere velocity.
Only companies that both develop and adapt to the new technology can remain
competitive.[3] So, look for more change—probably much more—in this regard
in the years ahead.

FIGURE 15.3 Computers: Both Benefits and Threats
Our heavy dependence on computers in the workplace has made us susceptible to a new set of
problems, such as threats to privacy and computer viruses. (Reprinted with special permission of
King Features Syndicate.)

Society and Change in the World of Work

Businesses and organizations do not exist in a social vacuum. Rather, they reflect—and are often strongly influenced by—trends in the societies around them. One major change has been in the composition of the work force. Consider these statistics.[4]

1. There are more women working now than ever before. By 1995, it is estimated that 60.3 percent of American women will be working and will be doing so at all stages of their lives.

2. Minority group representation in the labor force rose from 10.7 percent in 1954 to 12.8 percent in 1982. The figure is expected to rise to 14.5 percent by 1995.

3. Union affiliation has been declining steadily, from a peak of 35 percent in 1955 to less than 20 percent today.

4. American workers are now better educated than ever. The percentage of the labor force that completed four years of college rose from 14.7 percent in 1970 to 24.2 percent in 1983. Today's figures are even higher.

These are, of course, only some of the major demographic changes that have occurred in the labor force in recent years. If you think about it, it is not difficult to imagine how such shifting conditions force organizations to change in many varied and important ways. Baby boomers are becoming more of an economic force than ever—their high income and educational levels have forced manufacturers to make a wide variety of comfort and convenience items available (e.g., luxury cars, convenience foods, and microwave ovens in which to cook them).[5] With more female employees of child-bearing age in the work force than ever before, organizations have been forced to make child care facilities available, and to allow many employees to work on a part-time basis or to "share" jobs. As workers grow older, they will soon put an increasing burden on pension systems. If they live longer lives, and work farther into their lives, the drain on health insurance may become severe. Even if higher levels of affluence allow people to retire earlier than ever before, the lack of experienced personnel may pose a formidable organizational problem.[6] Scientists are just beginning to understand how the ever-changing composition of the work force is influenced by the operation of organizations. Although the exact nature of the changes forced by shifting demographics is complex and not yet fully understood, one thing is certain— changes in the composition of the work force demand corresponding changes in organizations.

Economic Causes of Change: The Role of Governmental Regulation and Mergers

One of the greatest challenges faced by an organization is responding to changes from the outside world over which it has little or no control. As the environment changes, organizations must follow suit. Research has shown that organizations that can best adapt to changing conditions are those that tend to survive.[7] Three of the most important unplanned external factors are governmental regulation, economic competition, and mergers.

Some of the most commonly witnessed unplanned organizational changes result from governmental regulations. In the late 1980s restaurant owners in the United States had to completely change the way they reported the income of waiters and waitresses to the federal government for purposes of collecting income taxes. Similarly, any change in the minimum wage law would greatly influence organizations, forcing them to revise the amount they pay their lowest-paid employees. In recent years the United States federal government has been involved in both imposing and eliminating regulations in industries such as commercial airlines (e.g., mandating inspection schedules but no longer controlling fares) and banks (e.g., restricting the amount of time checks can be held before clearing but no longer regulating interest rates). There can be little doubt that such activities have greatly influenced the way business is conducted in these industries.

Another fact of life that corporations face is that someone is always building a better mousetrap—or at least a cheaper one or one that is marketed more effectively. As a result, companies often have to fight to maintain their share of the market, advertise more effectively, and produce products more inexpensively. It is this kind of economic competition that not only forces organizations to change but demands that they change effectively if they are to survive.

Although competition has always been a crucial element in organizational success, today competition comes from all over the world. As it has become increasingly less expensive to transport materials around the world, industrialized nations such as the United States, Canada, Japan, and the nations of Western Europe have found themselves competing with each other for shares of the marketplace in nations all over the world. In other words, there is an ever-growing *global marketplace*. This situation is made more complex by the newly developing economic powers of the third world (e.g., Mexico, and South Korea). These nations are not only exploited by corporations from other nations for their vast natural resources and their pool of inexpensive labor but are also developing their own multinational corporate giants ready to take their place in the world's market.[8]

This extensive globalization of the economy presents a formidable challenge to all organizations who wish to throw their hats into the ring of the world's economic system. The primary challenge is to meet the ever-present need for change, to be innovative. As an example, just consider how the large American automobile manufacturers suffered by not being ready to meet the world's growing demand for small, high-quality cars—products their Japanese (and now, Korean) competitors were only too glad to supply to an eager marketplace. One thing is certain: As the stakes get higher and the number of players increases, the world marketplace becomes an arena where only the most adaptive organizations can survive.

A third important cause of change in the world of work—and one that usually strikes much closer to home—is the continuing trend toward "bigness" apparent during the past three decades. As you already know, large companies often seek to grow still bigger by acquiring control of smaller ones. There are many reasons behind this push toward mergers or takeovers. For example, by gaining control of the right businesses, a large corporation can substantially enhance its own profitability. Second, by purchasing companies that supply its needs, a large business can ensure its lines of supply at advantageous prices. Third, acquiring a strong competitor is one sure way of eliminating its impact on the corporate balance sheet! Whatever the specific reasons involved, the trend toward growing size has continued without pause for many years.

When one company acquires another, this is often the basis for substantial change. Usually, the acquiring firm soon installs its own people in key positions, and they may well differ greatly in style from the ones they replace. New goals and policies may quickly be established, with many effects on employees. And the entire climate of the organization may soon be altered as efforts to bring it into line with that of the parent company are instituted. Thus mergers, takeovers, and other reflections of the persistent trend toward bigness are often a major cause of change in work settings; indeed, in one sense, they may represent the most dramatic single cause of change (see Figure 15.4).

FIGURE 15.4 Mergers and Takeovers: A Source of Major Organizational Change
Takeovers and mergers are a major cause of change in corporate settings.

Business Day

The New York Times

NBC Alters Its Count Of Viewers

Network Joins ABC In Rebuffing Nielsen

By BILL CARTER

NBC announced yesterday that it would change the system it uses to account for the number of viewers its programs deliver to advertisers.

The network emphasized that it no longer considered the current A. C. Nielsen ratings system to be reliable.

NBC's approach differs from the one announced two weeks ago by ABC. Both networks will statistically adjust their ratings, starting in the fall television season, to include previous years' information.

But the NBC system will use information covering the Nielsen's overall viewing trends for the last eight television seasons to project the expected audience size for next season. ABC, meanwhile, will measure the audience against a three-year average.

The Established System

Both networks are trying to change the established system of using the current Nielsen rating information as the sole basis for documenting that a program has reached the number of viewers that its network had guaranteed to advertisers.

Advertising executives, who took their first look at the NBC system yesterday, described it as fundamentally similar to ABC's, but potentially more attractive to advertisers.

"Using an eight-year trend is not a bad idea," said Paul Schulman, whose agency buys commercial time for advertisers, "It seems to be fair. I think it's a little better than the ABC plan."

He said NBC would have an advantage by using a trend, which tracks the actual viewing level with a line on a graph, rather than using an average. "The trend over eight years is going to show viewing going down, where an audience average for three years will be higher," he said.

As a result, advertisers could possibly pay less for commercial time using NBC's method than ABC's method.

'That Is Unfair'

But Betsy Frank, senior vice president of Saatchi & Saatchi, said her advertising agency did not like either plan. "Conceptually, they are the same," she said. "Both of them require potentially adding in audience that the Nielsen system says isn't there. That is unfair."

Nielsen recently reported that overall television viewing has been declining. The major broadcast networks protested, arguing that steep declines in the first three months of this year were a result of faulty methodology in the Nielsen "people meter" system.

Viewers using people meters must push buttons each time they view television to record who is watching which show. Nielsen executives have said their methodology is valid.

Larry Hoffner, NBC's executive vice president of sales, said the unexpected declines in national television viewing in the first three months of the year had cost NBC $40 million. The network had to give advertisers

Continued on Page D9

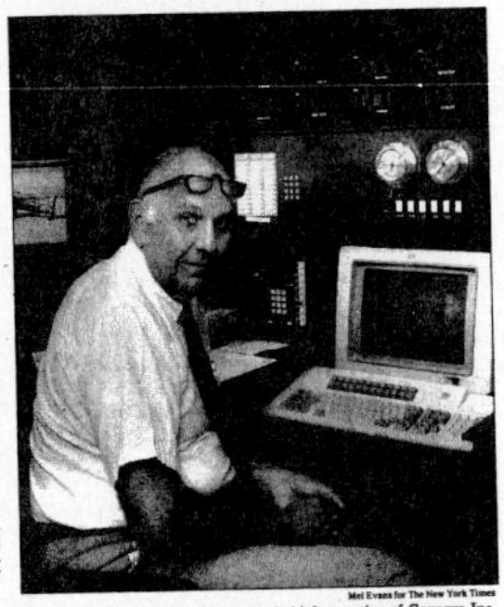

Mel Evans for The New York Times

Charles M. Harper, the chairman and chief executive of Conagra Inc. The Omaha-based company, which agreed to acquire Beatrice last week, is the nation's second-largest food company.

'Conagra Who?' Seeks Mainstream Success

By EBEN SHAPIRO

Special to The New York Times

CHICAGO, June 12 — With more than 100 acquisitions over the last 16 years, Conagra Inc. has changed itself from an obscure and troubled agricultural commodities business into one of the nation's largest companies. Now, with a $1.34 billion agreement last week to acquire the Beatrice Company, the executive behind the transformation, Charles M. Harper, is gambling that Conagra can stand up to the fierce marketing wars in the aisles of the nation's supermarkets.

Conagra's latest deal is expected to raise the Omaha-based company's sales in its current fiscal year above $20 billion. That size would easily place it among the nation's 20 largest industrial corporations, close to giants like the Procter & Gamble Company and the Boeing Company.

$16 Billion in Sales Seen

Conagra, the nation's second-largest food company, after the Kraft General Foods subsidiary of the Philip Morris Companies, is expected to report sales of about $16 billion for the fiscal year that ended on May 28.

The company is still so little known that it recently published a corporate history entitled "Conagra Who?" Yet it is now the only American business that operates across the entire food chain, Mr. Harper said. And it has been growing quickly not only in revenues but in return to its investors, far outpacing other food companies and the Standard & Poor's 500.

Conagra has thrived in meats and poultry, including the Monfort meatpacker and Country Pride chicken brands, and in frozen foods, primarily the Armour Classics, Banquet, Healthy Choice, Chun King, Patio and Morton brands. Together, those account for 62.5 percent of the company's sales.

The company also maintains its business in agricultural commodities like grains, which it mills and trades, accounting for 16.5 percent of its business. Almost all of the remaining 21 percent is in sales of pesticides and animal feed and in distributing fertilizers.

The addition of Beatrice's portfolio of well-known brands — including Hunt's tomato products, Wesson cooking oils, Orville Redenbacher's popcorn and Swiss Miss puddings and cocoa mixes — will give Conagra new strength in dry goods.

An acquisition brings strength and challenges.

But moving into the consumer-products mainstream presents some risks for Conagra, one analyst cautions. John M. McMillin of Prudential-Bache Securities Inc. said Conagra might find itself on dangerous and unfamilar ground.

"Deals go wrong when somebody tries to be something that they are not," Mr. McMillin said. "Conagra has had little experience being a marketing company. Now they are going

Continued on Page D2

CHANGE: WHY IT'S OFTEN RESISTED

Almost all of us want to think of ourselves as "modern" or "progressive." Thus, if you stopped fifty people on the street or interviewed fifty employees at almost any company and asked them how they felt about change, most would probably express positive views. "Change," they might say, "yep—it's good. Without it, we'd just sort of stagnate." On the basis of such sentiments, you might conclude that instituting change in work settings is a simple task. In fact, it is not. Contrary to what they may say, people often resist change and resist it vigorously. Thus there is often a sizable gap between their attitudes and their behavior in this regard. Why is this the case? Why do individuals and organizations so often seek to block change? Many factors seem to play a role in this respect.

Psychological Factors: Barriers to Change

There are a variety of psychological factors that make people resistant to change. You can probably come up with your own list quite easily. Obviously, people may become quite comfortable with the way things have been and may be afraid of bad consequences of change.

One major reason why people resist change can be stated in a single word: uncertainty. Will the proposed changes benefit them or make their lives unpleasant? Will changes help them perform their jobs, or get in the way? Often, it is impossible to tell in advance. And since the stakes are so high, many persons are reluctant to take the gamble and find out. Thus fear of the unknown—of the unpredictable effects that may result from change—often serves as a major barrier to the acceptance of new policies or procedures.

Researchers have found that a number of specific factors make people resistant to change in organizations.[9]

1. *Economic insecurity.* Any changes on the job have the potential of threatening one's livelihood or economic security—either loss of job or reduced pay, and some degree of resistance to change is inevitable unless job security can be ensured.

2. *Fear of the unknown.* Employees derive a sense of security out of doing things the same way, knowing with whom they are going to work, and to whom they're supposed to answer from day to day. Disrupting these well-established, comfortable, familiar patterns creates unfamiliar conditions, and a fear of the unknown, a state of affairs that is often rejected.

3. *Threats to social relationships.* As people continue to work within organizations, they form strong social bonds with their co-workers. Many organizational changes (e.g., the reassignment of job responsibilities) threaten the integrity of friendship groups that provide such an important source of social rewards for many employees.

4. *Habit.* Jobs that are well-learned and become habitual are easy to perform. The prospect of changing the way jobs are done challenges

workers to relearn their jobs and to develop new job skills. Doing this is clearly more difficult than continuing to perform the job as it was originally learned.

5. *Failure to recognize need for change.*   Unless employees can recognize and fully appreciate the need for changing things in organizations, any vested interests they may have in keeping things the same may easily overpower their willingness to accept change.

There can be little wonder, then, that many persons attempt to resist change with every trick and tactic at their disposal! Although most persons seem to dislike change, this is certainly not true of everyone. In fact, some people seem to seek it out and thrive on it. Where do you stand on this dimension? For an answer, please see the **Human Relations in Action** section below.

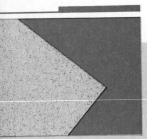

HUMAN RELATIONS IN ACTION

Change or Stability? Are You a High or Low Sensation Seeker?

Would you ever consider skydiving for the thrills and danger it produces? Do you like to gamble? Would you enjoy leading a life like that of Indiana Jones in the *Temple of Doom*? If so, you may be a **high sensation seeker**—the kind of person who enjoys excitement, danger, and unpredictability.[10,11] If, in contrast, the things we have just mentioned frighten you, and you prefer a life of calmness, order, and tranquility, you are probably a **low sensation seeker.** As you can readily guess, high and low sensation seekers also differ in their reactions to change. Persons high on this dimension tend to see change as a stimulating challenge— something to be sought out and savored. In contrast, low sensation seekers often view it as a potentially upsetting source of danger—something they would prefer to avoid if possible.

Where do you stand in this regard? Are you a high sensation seeker, a low sensation seeker, or somewhere in between? To find out, please answer the questions below. For each, simply circle the letter (A or B) next to the choice that best describes your likes or the way you feel.

1. *A*   I often wish I could be a mountain climber.
    B   I can't understand people who risk their necks climbing mountains.

2. *A*   A sensible person avoids activities that are dangerous.
    B   I sometimes like to do things that are a little frightening.

3. *A*   I would like to take up waterskiing.
    B   I would not like to take up waterskiing.

4. *A*   I would like to try surfboarding.
    B   I would not like to try surfboarding.

Organizational Factors: Social and Structural Barriers

It is probably obvious to you that we can't blame all the resistance to change on an individual. Many individuals may be more than willing to go along with sensible change. However, resistance to change can also come from several factors associated with the organization itself.[12]

1. *Structural inertia.* Organizations are designed to promote stability. To the extent that employees are carefully selected and trained to perform certain jobs, and rewarded for performing them, the forces acting on individuals to perform in certain ways are very powerfully determined—that is, jobs have structural inertia.[13] In other words, because jobs are designed to have stability, it is often difficult to overcome the resistance created by the many forces that create that stability.

5. A   I would not like to learn to fly an airplane.
   B   I would like to learn to fly an airplane.

6. A   I would like to go scuba diving.
   B   I prefer the surface of the water to the depths.

7. A   I would like to try parachute jumping.
   B   I would never want to try jumping out of a plane with a parachute.

8. A   I enjoy spending time in the familiar surroundings of home.
   B   I get very restless if I have to stay around home for any length of time.

9. A   Sailing long distances in small sailing crafts is foolhardy.
   B   I would like to sail a long distance in a small but seaworthy sailing craft.

10. A   Skiing fast down a high mountain slope is a good way to end up on crutches.
    B   I think I would enjoy the sensation of skiing very fast down a high mountain slope.

To obtain your score, give yourself one point for each of the following answers: (1) A, (2) B, (3) A, (4) A, (5) B, (6) A, (7) A, (8) B, (9) B, (10) B. If you attained a score of 7 or above, you are probably a high sensation seeker. If you attained a score of 3 or below, you are probably a low sensation seeker. By the way, note that there's ample room for both types in the world of work. For example, would you want to do business with a banker who was high in sensation seeking? Probably not—but you may well seek this quality in a salesperson or marketing expert. So, neither orientation is better; they are just different.

2. *Work group inertia.* Inertia to continue performing jobs in a specified way comes not only from the jobs themselves but from the social groups within which many employees work. Because of the development of strong social norms within work groups, potent pressures exist to perform jobs in certain ways, and at certain accepted rates. Introducing change causes disruption in these established normative expectations, which imposes formidable barriers to change.

3. *Threats to existing balance of power.* If changes are made with respect to who is in charge and how things are done, a shift in the balance of power between individuals and organizational subunits is likely to occur. Those units that now control the resources, have the expertise, and wield the power may fear losing their advantageous positions as a result of any organizational changes made.

4. *Previously unsuccessful change efforts.* Anyone who has lived through a disaster may be understandably reluctant to endure another attempt at the same thing. Similarly, groups or entire organizations that have been unsuccessful in introducing change in the past may be understandably reluctant to accept further attempts to introduce change in the system.

There are obviously many barriers to change in organizations. You may wonder how organizations can overcome these barriers. Fortunately, there are some techniques that are useful, and we'll discuss a number of these next.

OVERCOMING RESISTANCE TO CHANGE: SOME USEFUL TACTICS

By now it should be apparent that there are many reasons that most persons fail to greet change with open arms. Whatever its specific causes, resistance to change is a serious matter. As we have noted, the ability to adapt to, and even foresee, changing conditions is essential for survival in the 1990s. In view of this basic fact, an important question arises: Can anything be done to overcome such resistance—to encourage the acceptance of change in work settings? The answer, of course, is yes. Several techniques for reaching this goal exist which focus primarily on tactics for the introduction of change.[14,15]

Change: How to Introduce It

Imagine two companies faced with the necessity of change. In one, top management examines all existing options and then simply decrees major alterations in jobs, corporate structure, and procedures. No discussions of the proposed changes are held, and no one is told why they are viewed as necessary. Employees are simply expected to comply with management's decisions. In contrast, efforts are made in the second company to involve all of the people who will be affected in both the planning and implementation of change. Special meetings are held in which the necessity for change is discussed, and the benefits to be gained through its adoption are described. Then a plan acceptable to most persons involved is adopted. In which company would you expect more resistance to change? Obviously, in the first. And the reason for this, too, is apparent. Change is simply introduced in a more effective and appropriate manner in the second company. But what, precisely, does this mean? In essence, it involves attention to several factors that can strongly influence reactions to actual or potential change.

The first of these centers around the issue of *participation*. In order to maximize the acceptance of change, and to reduce resistance to it, it is essential that the persons affected by it (or at least their representatives) participate in its planning. When this principle is followed, employees may conclude that they have given their approval to change and have even helped shape its final form. However, when this principle is ignored, they may feel that it has been "shoved down their throats" over their protests. Under the latter conditions, of course, they may do their best to block its implementation through passive or active means.

Closely related to the principle of participation is the need for *clarity*. Briefly, persons affected by proposed change should be made aware of the necessity for its occurrence and the potential future benefits. When individuals do not understand the reasons behind change, they may view it as an unnecessary annoyance, dreamed up by managers just to complicate their lives, and they may see only the drawbacks associated with the change. Clearly, avoiding such reactions is important, and it makes the effort involved in explaining the necessity for change and its long-term benefits worthwhile.

Another rather obvious, and quite successful, mechanism for facilitating organizational change is rewarding people for behaving in the desired fashion. Changing organizational operations may necessitate a change in the kinds of behaviors that need to be rewarded by the organization. This is essential when an organization is in the transition period of introducing the change. For example, employees who are required to learn to use new equipment should be praised for their successful efforts. Feedback on how well they are doing not only provides a great deal of useful assurance to uncertain employees, but also goes a long way in shaping the desired behavior (see Chapter 4).

Finally, political variables are crucial when it comes to getting organizational changes accepted. Politically, resistance to change can be overcome by getting the support of the most powerful and influential individuals. Doing so builds a critical internal mass of support for change. Demonstrating clearly that key organizational leaders support the change is an effective way of getting others to go along with it—either because they share the leader's vision, or because they fear the leader's retaliation. Either way, political support for change will facilitate acceptance of change.

Through attention to these and several other factors (see Figure 15.5), resistance to change can often be held to a minimum. Thus careful consideration

CASE IN POINT

The Plan That Worked

For many years *Keeping Fit*, a magazine dealing with personal health, had been a small, sleepy affair. Issues were produced only once every three months, and total circulation remained stable at about 20,000. Then came the 1970s, with rising public interest in physical fitness. Circulation began a dramatic climb and soon topped 100,000. At that point, the magazine's owners, sensing a golden opportunity, decided to switch to a monthly format, and to greatly expand its length. These plans required major changes in the way *Keeping Fit* was put together. No longer could employees enjoy the luxury of a leisurely production schedule; instead, activities at the magazine's headquarters became frenzied. And the increased circulation altered every facet of its operations—from advertising through subscriptions. Despite the vast scope of these shifts, the magazine came through with flying colors. In fact, at present, *Keeping Fit* is viewed as a model of efficiency and success by other publishers. It is for this reason that Jane Cushing, editor of another small magazine on the verge of what appears to be major growth, has come for a visit. She hopes to discover the secret of *Keeping Fit*'s success in coping with major change so that she can bring it back to her own company. She has just completed a tour of the facilities with Clark Hammon, *Keeping Fit*'s top executive, and has returned to his office.

"Nice, very nice," Jane says with feeling. "You've certainly done a bang-up job of modernizing your equipment."

"Thanks," says Clark, motioning her to a seat. "We're all pretty proud of our operation. It really seems to be holding together well."

"Yes, Clark," Jane responds, "and that's why I'm here today. As you know, we're going to be facing some of the same changes you did—or, at least I hope that's the case! But I'm worried about it. We've already heard a lot of grumbling from our staff. Seems as though many of them enjoy the comfortable country club atmosphere we've developed over the years and are afraid of what's coming. In fact, there's even been some dark talk about sabotage. So tell me, how did you manage to do it so well? How did you avoid all these problems?"

Clark chuckles. Then, smiling, he begins. "I ought to say that's our secret! But really, there's no secret to tell. It all centered around planning. When we began to sense that a change was coming, we sat down and thought things through. One of the first points that occurred to us was this: People on the staff are going to be worried. After all, most of us are a little afraid of change, whatever we say about liking it. We don't know what it will bring, and that can be upsetting."

"Yes, I see," Jane comments. "But what did you do to handle those reactions?"

"Good question," Clark answers. "First off, we arranged a series of special meetings with everyone—from senior copy editor on up. We described what kind of changes were coming, and asked for suggestions on planning the whole thing. We tried to give everyone some say in how to proceed. But that's not all. We soon discovered that a lot of people couldn't see how they would benefit from a big rise in sales. They could grasp the costs, all right, but not what they had to gain."

"Ah!" Jane exclaims. "They knew there would be extra work, but didn't see what that would buy them."

"Right. That's when we decided to install our bonus plan—one that would let everyone share in the rewards if circulation and profits went up. That was really the turning point. As soon as people saw how they would benefit, they become downright enthusiastic."

"Good strategy," Jane states admiringly.

"Thanks. But we didn't stop there. We knew there were a number of popular people on the staff—you know, people everyone looked up to. Well, we made a real effort to win their support. That took some doing, but finally we got just about all of them on our side. Once they threw their weight behind us, it was smooth sailing."

"So, really, you didn't have a magic formula," says Jane. "It all sounds like good common sense to me. But still, it's the kind of common sense people often overlook. Thanks a lot, Clark. You've been a big help. If we follow in your footsteps, I don't see how we can go wrong."

Questions

1. What do you think were the major concerns among employees at *Keeping Fit* when they first learned about the coming changes?

2. Do you think that giving employees a chance to participate in planning these changes was a good idea? Why?

3. What other tactics might Jane use in her own company to increase the likelihood of smooth and orderly change?

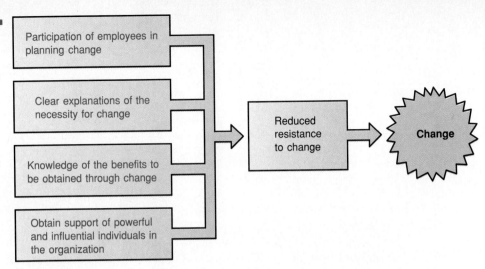

FIGURE 15.5 Overcoming Resistance to Change: Some Useful Tactics
Careful attention to the factors shown here can help minimize or surmount resistance to change.

of just how change is to be introduced into a specific work setting often yields handsome dividends in terms of its smooth and rapid acceptance. (For a concrete example of the successful introduction of change, see the **Case in Point** on page 474.)

CHANGE AND EFFECTIVENESS: TECHNIQUES OF ORGANIZATIONAL DEVELOPMENT

So far in our discussion of change we have adopted what might be termed an "external" orientation. That is, we have focused on change in response to shifting external conditions (e.g., advances in technology, increased competition). Often, though, change in work settings comes from another source: the quest, by an organization, for excellence and effectiveness. In short, organizations actively *seek* change as a means of improving the way in which they function. Such planned change is generally known as **organizational development,** and a number of techniques for achieving it exist. Here, we will briefly describe five of the most popular: *survey feedback, sensitivity training, team building, grid training,* and *quality of work life.* (We have already described an additional procedure for organizational development—management by objectives—in Chapter 4.)

Survey Feedback: Change through Information

Survey feedback, a widely used technique of organizational development, rests largely on the following principle: Before useful change can take place in an organization, the people in it must understand both its current strengths and its weaknesses. Flowing from this sound principle, survey feedback proceeds through three distinct steps.[16] First, groups of employees (or perhaps even all employees) respond to a carefully designed questionnaire. This survey is tailored to the specific organization in question, but it usually seeks information on such issues as the quality and style of leadership, current organizational climate, and employee satisfaction. The second major step involves reporting the information obtained through the questionnaire to employees, usually in group meetings. This step requires considerable skill, for such information is often complex and leaves plenty of room for misinterpretation. Also, since the survey is designed to pinpoint problems, much of the resulting feedback is negative (e.g., it may indicate that some persons within the organization are performing poorly). The consultants who present the results must therefore be skilled at minimizing anxiety and other negative reactions. Finally, in a third step, specific plans for dealing with and overcoming the problems identified by the survey are developed, again usually in sessions where open discussion is encouraged. (See Figure 15.6 for a summary of these steps.)

Survey feedback offers a number of major advantages. It often yields a large amount of useful information quickly. It is flexible and can be used in many different settings, and the information it provides is often helpful in developing concrete plans for change. Thus, when used with skill and care, it can be a valuable tool for assisting organizations toward enhanced effectiveness.

Sensitivity Training: Development of Insight

Sensitivity training is a method by which small, face-to-face group interaction experiences are used to give people insight into themselves (who they are, the way others respond to them, etc.). Developed in the 1940s, sensitivity training groups (also referred to as *encounter groups, laboratory groups,* or *T-groups*) were among the first organizational development techniques used in organizations.[17]

The premise behind sensitivity training is that people are usually not completely open and honest with each other, a condition that limits insights into oneself and others. However, when people are placed in special situations within

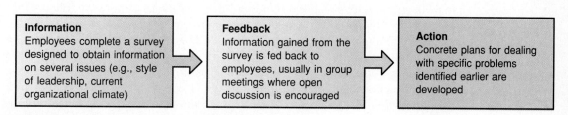

FIGURE 15.6 Survey Feedback: An Overview
As shown here, survey feedback often involves three major steps.

which open, honest communication is allowed and encouraged, such personal insights may be gained. To do this, employees are divided into small groups of about 8 to 15 people that arrange to meet away from the pressures of the job site for several days. An expert trainer (referred to as the *facilitator*) guides the group at all times, helping to ensure that the proper atmosphere is maintained.

The sessions themselves are completely open with respect to what is discussed. Often, to get the ball rolling, the facilitator will frustrate the group members by not getting involved at all, and appearing to be passively goofing off. As members sit around and engage in meaningless chit-chat, they begin to feel angry at the change agent for wasting their time. Once these expressions of anger begin to emerge, the change agent has created the important first step needed to make the session work—he or she has given the group a chance to focus on a current event. At this point, the discussion may be guided into how each of the group members expresses his or her anger toward each other. They are encouraged to continue discussing these themes openly and honestly, and not to hide their true feelings as they often do on the job. The rule is to openly and honestly share your feelings about others. So, for example, if a group member thinks someone is goofing off and relying too much on him or her, this is the time to say so. Participants are encouraged to respond by giving each other *immediate feedback* to what was said. By doing this people presumably will come to learn more about how they interrelate with others, and will become more skilled at interpersonal relations. These are among the major goals of sensitivity groups.

It probably comes as no surprise to you that the effectiveness of sensitivity training is difficult to assess. Even if interpersonal skills seem to be improved, it is not always the case that people will be able to successfully transfer their newly learned skills when they leave the artificial training atmosphere and return to their jobs.[18] As a result, sensitivity training tends not to be used extensively by itself but rather along with other organizational development techniques.

Team Building: Creating Effective Work Groups

Team building is a technique that developed in an attempt to apply the procedures and rationale of sensitivity training to work groups. The approach attempts to get members of a work group to diagnose how they work together, and to plan how this may be improved.[19] Given the importance of group efforts in effective organizational functioning, attempts at improving the effectiveness of work groups are likely to have significant effects on organizations. If one assumes that work groups are the basic building blocks of organizations, it follows that organizational change could emphasize changing groups instead of individuals.

Team building begins when members of a group admit that they have a problem and gather data to provide insight about it. The problems that are identified may come from sensitivity training sessions, or more sensitive sources, such as production figures or attitude surveys. These data are then shared, in a *diagnostic session,* to develop a consensus regarding the group's current strengths and weaknesses. For this, a list of desired changes is created, along with some plans for implementing these changes. In other words, an *action plan* is developed—some task-oriented approach to solving the group's diagnosed problems.

Following this step, the plan is carried out, and its progress is evaluated to determine whether the originally identified problems still remain. If the problems are solved, the process is completed, and the team may stop meeting. If not, the process should be restarted. (See Figure 15.7 for a summary of these steps.)

Work teams have been used effectively to combat a variety of important organizational problems.[20] For these efforts to be successful, however, all group members must participate in the gathering and evaluating of information as well as in the planning and implementing of action plans. Input from group members is also especially crucial in evaluating the effectiveness of the team building pro-

479
CHANGE AND
EFFECTIVENESS:
TECHNIQUES OF
ORGANIZATIONAL
DEVELOPMENT

FIGURE 15.7   Team Building: An Overview
Team building, a popular technique of organizational development, follows the steps outlined here.

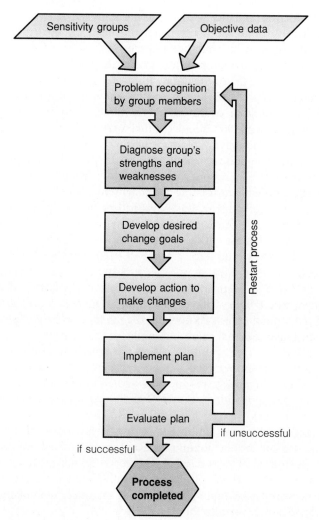

gram.[21] It is also important to keep in mind that because the team-building approach is highly task-oriented, interpersonal problems between group members may be disruptive and need to be neutralized by an outside party. With such interpersonal strain out of the way, the stage is set for groups to learn to effectively solve their own problems. However, this does not happen overnight. To be most effective, team building should not be approached as a one-time exercise undertaken during a few days away from the job. Rather, it should be thought of as an ongoing process that takes several months (or even years) to develop. Given the tremendous impact effective groups can have on organizational functioning, efforts at building effective work teams certainly seem to be quite worthwhile.

Grid Training: Managerial Style and Enhanced Effectiveness

In our discussion of leadership (Chapter 8), we noted that leaders vary greatly in terms of their position along two key dimensions: concern with people and concern with production. Further, we noted that many experts believe that leaders who are high on both dimensions are often the most effective. This reasonable suggestion lies at the heart of another popular technique of organizational development—**grid training.** This technique, originally proposed by Blake and Mouton, is designed to shift existing leaders within an organization toward the ideal pattern: high concern with *both* people and production.[22] In order to accomplish this goal, it follows a number of distinct steps. First, of course, it is necessary to determine just where managers stand on these two dimensions. This is accomplished through a special questionnaire. On the basis of their answers to this survey, managers are assigned two numbers—one representing their concern with production and the other their concern with people. Many different patterns are possible, and these reflect contrasting management styles. For example (as we noted in Chapter 8), a manager who shows little concern with both people and production would receive a score of 1,1. (This is often described as *impoverished management.*) A manager who shows a great deal of concern for production but little concern for people would earn a score of 9,1. (This is known as *task management.*) In contrast, one who shows the opposite pattern—high concern with people but little interest in production would receive a score of 1,9. (This is sometimes known as a *country club* style of management.) These patterns can be represented in the type of diagram known as the *managerial grid* (shown previously in Figure 8.7 on page 251).

Once a manager's current position within the grid is determined, training can begin. This involves a number of different steps. For example, managers themselves participate in designing plans for moving toward the preferred 9,9 pattern. In addition, they devise an ideal model of their organization—how they would like it to be—and steps for reaching this goal. Later in the process, progress toward these goals is assessed, and areas requiring further work are identified.

Grid training has been very popular in recent years. Indeed, more than 250,000 people have participated in it to date! And some research evidence suggests that it works—it helps managers adopt a more effective leadership style.[23] In sum, it appears to be a useful technique for instituting planned organizational change, and so for enhancing organizational effectiveness.

481
CHANGE AND
EFFECTIVENESS:
TECHNIQUES OF
ORGANIZATIONAL
DEVELOPMENT

FIGURE 15.8 Quality of Worklife: Important for Morale
How would you feel if you were regularly criticized by your boss in front of your fellow employees? You would probably feel as badly as the poor employee in this picture.

Quality of Work Life: Humanizing Work and Work Settings

How would you like to work for someone like the boss character in Figure 15.8? Your answer, we're sure, is "No way!" The reasons for this are clear: In an organization headed by someone with this style, employees are probably held in very low regard. Further, management would probably show little concern for their feelings or welfare. What do you think would be the result of such conditions? If you guessed "poor morale and motivation, plus a corresponding low level of organizational effectiveness," you are probably correct. Fortunately, during the 1960s and 1970s, a growing number of managers became aware of these facts. As they did, they sought techniques for changing this negative type of *organizational climate*—ways of humanizing work settings and making them more pleasant. The result of these efforts has been the emergence of yet another technique of organizational development—one that focuses primarily on the **quality of work life.**[24]

This approach is not as unified or systematic in nature as the others we have described. However, it usually focuses on several major goals. First, it seeks to create a climate of mutual respect between management and employees—the opposite of what is shown in Figure 15.8. Second, it often makes use of work *restructuring*—changing jobs to make them more interesting and varied. Third, it attempts to narrow the status gap between employees and supervisors. Finally, it usually recommends a *participative style of decision making*, one in which employees are asked for their input on new policies and procedures. The ultimate goal, of course is to attain a climate of partnership between managers and em-

FIGURE 15.9 Quality Circles: One Way to Increase Quality of Work Life
Quality control circles are very popular and have been introduced into a number of international companies like Hewlett-Packard. They appear to bring about some short-term improvement in quality of work life.

ployees, a sharp contrast to the standard pattern in which they view one another as natural enemies.

Another approach to improving the quality of work life, and an increasingly popular one in recent years, has been borrowed from Japan—**quality circles.** These are small groups of volunteers (usually, around ten) who meet regularly (usually weekly) to identify and solve problems related to (a) the quality of the work they perform, and (b) the conditions under which they do their jobs.[25] An organization may have several quality circles operating at once, each dealing with a particular work area about which it has the most expertise. To help them work effectively, the members of the circle usually receive some form of training in problem solving. Large companies such as Westinghouse, Hewlett-Packard, and Eastman Kodak, to name just a few, have used quality circles (see Figure 15.9).[26] Groups have deal with such issues as how to reduce vandalism, how to create safer and more comfortable work environments, and how to improve product quality. Research has shown that while quality circles are very effective at bringing about short-term improvements in quality of work life (i.e., those lasting up to eighteen months), they are less effective at creating more permanent changes.[27] As such, they may be recognized as useful temporary strategies for enhancing organizational effectiveness.

As you might imagine, there are a variety of benefits that might result from quality of work life programs. The most direct benefit is usually increased job satisfaction and organizational commitment among the work force. There can also be increased productivity and increased organizational effectiveness (e.g., profitability, goal attainment, etc.).[28]

483
CHANGE AND
EFFECTIVENESS:
TECHNIQUES OF
ORGANIZATIONAL
DEVELOPMENT

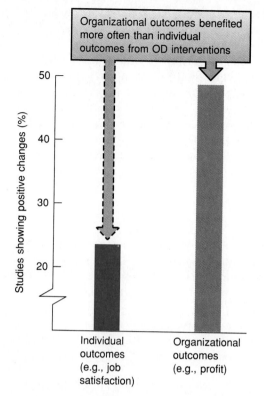

FIGURE 15.10 Organizational Development: Evidence of Its Effectiveness
It has been found that organizational outcomes (e.g., productivity) more often benefit from organizational development (OD) than individual outcomes (e.g., job satisfaction). *Source:* Based on data reported by Porras et al. (in press); see Note 29.

Achieving these benefits is not automatic, however. There are two major potential pitfalls that need to be avoided for quality of work life programs to be successfully implemented. First, it is essential that both management and labor cooperate in designing their program. If either side believes that the program is really just a method of gaining an advantage over the other, it is doomed to fail. Second, it is essential that the plan agreed to by all concerned parties be fully implemented. It is too easy for action plans developed in quality of work life groups to be forgotten and lost amidst the hectic pace of daily activities. It is the responsibility of employees at all levels—from the highest-ranking manager to the lowest-level laborer—to follow through on their part of the plan.

The Effectiveness of Organizational Development: How Well Does It Work?

Although the various organizational development techniques we have discussed are often used by corporations, are they worth the time, money, and effort involved? There does appear to be some evidence for beneficial effects. For example, one review of a wide variety of methods found that these techniques often benefited organizational outcomes such as profit and productivity but evidence for positive changes at the individual level (e.g., job satisfaction) was relatively weak[29] (see Figure 15.10). Organizational development also tends to be more effective with blue collar workers and when several techniques are used instead of only one.[30]

Organizational development has shown a lot of promise, but it is clear that additional research and refinements are required to increase the effectiveness of these techniques to provide long-lasting positive changes for both corporations and individual workers.

SUMMARY

In the 1990s, change is a fact of life in most work settings. Change arises from technological advances, shifts in social attitudes and values, and economic factors (e.g., foreign competition). Many persons resist change because of their fear of the unknown, concerns over loss of status, and the possibility that it will endanger their jobs.

A number of tactics for overcoming resistance to change exist. Several of these relate to the specific ways in which change is introduced. In general, acceptance of change is increased when the persons affected by it have had an opportunity to participate in its planning, when they understand the reasons it is necessary, and when they perceive the benefits it will yield.

While organizations often change in response to external pressures, they also actively seek change as a means of improving their own effectiveness. Several techniques for accomplishing such organizational development exist. Among these are survey feedback, sensitivity training, team building, grid training, and quality of work life programs.

KEY TERMS

grid training: A technique of organizational development designed to shift managers toward the preferred managerial style—one involving high concern with both people and production.

high sensation seekers: Individuals who enjoy, and actively seek, a high level of sensation. This often includes danger, risk, and a high degree of challenge.

low sensation seekers: Individuals who prefer a calm, ordered, stable lifestyle, free from danger and risk.

organizational development: Various techniques and procedures designed to produce planned change in an organization. Such change, in turn, is aimed at enhancing the organization's effectiveness and efficiency.

quality circles: An approach to improving the quality of work life in which small groups of volunteers meet regularly to identify and solve problems related to the work they perform and the conditions under which they work.

quality of work life: An organizational development technique designed to make work more interesting and rewarding, and work settings better places in which to function.

resistance to change: The tendency for employees to be unwilling to go along with organizational changes, either because of individual fears of the unknown, or organizational impediments (such as *structural inertia*).

sensitivity training: An organizational development technique that seeks to enhance employees' understanding of their own behavior and its impact on others. This understanding may reduce the interpersonal conflicts that interfere with organizational effectiveness.

structural inertia: The organizational forces acting on employees that encourage them to perform their jobs in certain ways (e.g., training, reward system), thereby making them resistant to change.

survey feedback: An organizational development technique in which information about an organization is fed back to employees, and plans for dealing with specific problems are formulated.

team building: An organizational development technique in which employees discuss problems related to their work group's performance. On the basis of these discussions, specific problems are identified and plans for solving them are devised and implemented.

NOTES

1. Keen, P.G.W. (1988). *Competing in Time: Using Telecommunications for Competitive Advantage* (rev. ed.). Cambridge, Mass.: Ballinger.

2. Foulkes, F.K., & Hirsch, J.L. (1984). "People Make Robots Work." *Harvard Business Review* (January-February): 94–102.

3. Ettlie, J.E. (1988). *Taking Charge of Manufacturing: How Companies Are Combining Technological and Organizational Innovations to Compete Successfully.* San Francisco: Jossey-Bass.

4. Best, F. (1985, January). "The Nature of Work in a Changing Society." *Personnel Journal*, 37–42.

5. Colvin, G. (1984). "What Baby Boomers Will Buy Next." *Fortune*, (October 15): 28–34.

6. Dennis, H. (1988). *Fourteen Steps in Managing an Aging Work Force.* Lexington, Mass.: Lexington Books.

7. Singh, J.V., House, R.J., & Tucker, D.J. (1986). "Organizational Change and Mortality." *Administrative Science Quarterly, 31,* 587–611.

8. Kilmann, R.H., & Covin, T.J. (1987). *Corporate Transformation: Revitalizing Organizations for a Competitive World.* San Francisco: Jossey-Bass.

9. Nadler, D.A. (1987). "The Effective Management of Organizational Change." In J.W. Lorsch, ed. *Handbook of Organizational Behavior*, pp. 358–69. Englewood Cliffs, N.J.: Prentice-Hall.

10. Zuckerman, M. (1979). *Sensation Seeking: Beyond the Optimal Level of Arousal.* Hillsdale, N.J.: Laurence Erlbaum Associates.

11. Goldman, D., Kohn, P.M., & Hunt, R.W. (1983). "Sensation Seeking, Augmenting-Reducing, and Absolute Auditory Threshold: A Strength-of-the-Nervous System Perspective." *Journal of Personality and Social Psychology, 45,* 405–11.

12. Katz, D., & Kahn, R.L. (1978). *The Social Psychology of Organizations* (2d ed.). New York: John Wiley.

13. Hannan, M.T., & Freeman, J. (1984). "Structural Inertia and Organizational Change." *American Sociological Review, 49,* 149–64.

14. Kotter, J.P., & Schlesinger, L.A. (1979). "Choosing Strategies for Change." *Harvard Business Review*, (March-April): 106–14.

15. See Note 9.

16. Huse, E.F., & Cummings, T.G. (1985). *Organizational Development and Change*, 3d ed. St. Paul, Minn.: West.

17. Golembiewski, R.T. (1972). *Renewing Organizations: A Laboratory Approach to Planned Change*. Itasca, Ill.: Peacock.

18. Campbell, J.P., & Dunnette, M.D. (1968). "Effectiveness of T-group Experience in Managerial Training and Development." *Psychological Bulletin, 70,* 73–104.

19. Beer, M. (1980). *Organizational Change and Development: A Systems View*. Glenview, Ill.: Scott, Foresman.

20. Beckhard, R. (1972). "Optimizing Team-Building Efforts." *Journal of Contemporary Business* (summer): 23–32.

21. Vicars, W.M., & Hartke, D.D. (1984). "Evaluating OD Evaluations: A Status Report." *Group and Organization Studies, 9,* 177–88.

22. Blake, R.R., & Mouton, J.S. (1978). *The Managerial Grid*. Houston: Gulf.

23. Porras, J.I., & Berg, P.O. (1978). "The Impact of Organization Development." *Academy of Management Review, 3,* 249–66.

24. Burke, W.W. (1982). *Organizational Development: Principles and Practices*. Boston: Little, Brown.

25. Munchus, G. (1983). "Employer-Employee Based Quality Circles in Japan: Human Resource Implications for American Firms." *Academy of Management Review, 8,* 255–61.

26. Meyer, G.W., & Scott, R.G. (1985, Spring). "Quality Circles: Panacea or Pandora's Box?" *Organizational Dynamics,* 34–50.

27. Griffin, R.W. (1988). "Consequences of Quality Circles in an Industrial Setting: A Longitudinal Assessment." *Academy of Management Journal, 31,* 338–58.

28. Suttle, J.L. (1977). "Improving Life at Work—Problems and Prospects." In J.R. Hackman, & J.L. Suttle, eds. *Improving Life at Work: Behavioral Science Approaches to Organizational Change*, pp. 1–29. Santa Monica, Calif.: Goodyear.

29. Porras, J.I., Robertson, P.J., & Goldman, L. (in press). "Organization Development: Theory, Practice, and Research." In M.D. Dunnette, ed. *Handbook of Industrial/Organizational Psychology*, 2d ed. Chicago: Rand McNally.

30. Nicholas, J.M. (1982). "The Comparative Impact of Organization Development Interventions on Hard Criteria Measures." *Academy of Management Review, 7,* 531–42.

ADDITIONAL CASES AND EXERCISES: APPLYING WHAT YOU'VE LEARNED

The Memo

Robert D. Goddard III
Associate Professor, Department of Management
Appalachian State University

The purpose of this exercise is to give you some first-hand experience in overcoming resistance to change. In preparing the memo described below, try to integrate one or more of the techniques for coping with resistance to change discussed in this chapter.

Susan West is facing one of the more difficult assignments in her career at Second City Bank. The Board of Directors has just voted to install second-generation automatic teller machines, announced by a major computer manufacturer just recently, in the home office location on a six-month trial basis. These new machines have a host of new features not found on the twenty-four hour bank machines that have been in use for years. The new machines can read signatures on checks, deposit them directly into a customer account, make change (coins and bills), issue traveler's checks, and speak to the customer. They even have a voice recognition feature that allows customers to talk to them, eliminating the need for complicated keyboards or buttons.

Sue realizes that these machines are going to cause problems for the tellers at Second City Bank. Not only can these new machines do what tellers can, they don't need lunch hours and time off for doctor's appointments, and they are never late for work. Tellers at Second City are not going to be happy to hear of the experiment. One of the major fears Sue will have to contend with is the apprehension about the tellers' future with Second City.

Sitting at her desk, Sue is pondering how to handle this delicate situation. The Board of Directors has confirmed that no one will lose his or her job because of these new machines, but that displaced workers will be either reassigned or retrained for other meaningful jobs at Second City. If workers elect to accept neither reassignment nor retraining, the Board assured Susan that every attempt would be made to place them with other financial institutions in the city.

Assignment: Place yourself in Susan West's shoes, and prepare a memorandum to the employees in the home office of Second City Bank. In the memo, you are to explain the Board's decision to introduce the new teller machines on a six-month trial basis, stressing the financial and service benefits to Second City's customers. Also include in the memo an explanation of the Board's policies of reassignment, retraining, and outplacement. Try to incorporate in your memo some of the tactics for overcoming resistance to change described in this chapter.

Optimism-Pessimism: An Important Dimension for Change

Our attitudes toward changes in our life may be related to some extent to our general degree of optimism and pessimism. To assess yourself on this dimension, fill out the scale below. Indicate the extent to which you agree or disagree with each of the statements listed below. (Circle one answer for each.)

1. I hardly ever expect things to go my way.

Strongly disagree	Disagree	Uncertain	Agree	Strongly agree
1	2	3	4	5

2. In unusual times, I generally expect the best.

Strongly disagree	Disagree	Uncertain	Agree	Strongly agree
1	2	3	4	5

3. I tend to worry about the possibility of failure.

Strongly disagree	Disagree	Uncertain	Agree	Strongly agree
1	2	3	4	5

4. I'm usually pretty certain that things will turn out well in the end.

Strongly disagree	Disagree	Uncertain	Agree	Strongly agree
1	2	3	4	5

5. Most difficulties can be overcome by hard work.

Strongly disagree	Disagree	Uncertain	Agree	Strongly agree
1	2	3	4	5

6. Very few people can be relied on or trusted.

Strongly disagree	Disagree	Uncertain	Agree	Strongly agree
1	2	3	4	5

7. When I face a difficult problem, I often try to avoid thinking about it.

Strongly disagree	Disagree	Uncertain	Agree	Strongly agree
1	2	3	4	5

Scoring: Items 1, 3, 6, and 7 are reversed, so you should change the scores as follows: 1 = 5, 2 = 4, 4 = 2, 5 = 1. Then add the scores for all of the items to obtain a total score. A score of 24 or higher indicates a high level of optimism, while a score of 14 or lower indicates a tendency toward pessimism. A score in between these two indicates that you have no strong tendency toward either optimism or pessimism. In general, it would be expected that optimists would handle change somewhat better than pessimists. You might take this factor into account when choosing a career path. Of course, you should not take the results of this scale too seriously since it is only designed to provide an informal assessment. To more precisely determine a person's personality would require detailed testing by a trained specialist.

Index

Proximity
    interpersonal attraction and, 181
    perceptual grouping and, 38, 39
    romance and, 191
Psychoanalytic theory, 141–143
Psychological needs, satisfied by groups, 272

Quality circles, 482
Quality of work life, 481–483

Reactance, failure of persuasion and, 213–214
Realistic conflict theory, 369
Reality principle, 142
Reciprocity
    cooperation and, 306–307
    interpersonal relationships and, 188
    organizational politics and, 227–228
Reference groups, job satisfaction and, 348–349
Referent power, 225
Relatedness needs, 110
Relaxation training, 420
Repression, 142
Research
    applied, 17
    case method and, 23
    correlational, 20–22
    experimental, 17, 19–20
    observations in, 17, 20–23
    theory and, 23–24
Responsibility
    for behavior, 44–45
    diffusion of, in groups, 275–280, 309
    as source of stress, 402–403
Reward(s)
    exchange theory and, 188–191
    introducing change and, 473
    linking to performance, 117
    power based on, 224
    social, affiliation and, 177, 178
    valence to employees, 117–118
Reward power, 224
Reward systems
    conflict and, 315
    job satisfaction and, 341
    stress management and, 421
Role(s)
    ambiguity of, 401
    conflict among, 399–401
    perceptions of, expectancy theory and, 115–116
    sex-role stereotypes and, 58–59, 375–376
Romance. *See also* Love
    in workplace, 191–197

Safety needs, 108, 109
Scalar chain of command, 73
Scientific management, 7–9
Selective perception, 35
Self-actualization needs, 109, 113
Self-concept, 162–167. *See also* Self-esteem
    accuracy of, 163–164
    development of, 162
    effects of, 164–166
Self-control, loss of, in groups, 276–277

Self-esteem. *See also* Self-concept
    internal and external causes and, 165–166
    job satisfaction and, 343
    self-serving bias and, 52–53
    stress and, 412
Self-esteem needs, job satisfaction and, 113
Self-perceptions, 447–448. *See also* Self-concept; Self-esteem
Self-presentation, 218, 221
Self-realization needs, 109
Self-serving bias, 52–53, 307
Sensation seeking, 470–471
Sensitivity training, 477–478
Sex-role stereotypes, 58–59, 375–376
Sexual harassment, 382–384
Similar-to-me effects, 54–55
Similarity
    compliance and, 217
    interpersonal attraction and, 182–183
    love and, 187
    perceived, in job interviews, 58
    perceptual grouping and, 38, 39
Situational approach, leadership and, 243–244
Situational control, leader effectiveness and, 254–255
Situational leadership theory, 260
Social categorization, prejudice and, 370–371
Social comparison, 177, 179–180, 288, 436
Social control, 161
Social facilitation, 280–283
Social influence, role in career choice, 433–434
Social learning, prejudice and discrimination and, 372, 384
Social loafing, 277–280
Social needs, 108, 109, 272
Social perception, 40–60. *See also* Discrimination; Prejudice
    attribution and. *See* Attribution
    contrast effects and, 55–56
    failures of, 49–56, 365
    halo effects and, 54
    impression formation and, 47–49
    in job interviews, 57–59
    self-serving bias and, 52–53, 307
    similar-to-me effects and, 54–55
    stereotypes and, 53–54, 58–59
Social skills, 160–162
Social support, 403–404, 409, 416–418
Social systems, work settings as, 9–12
Status, power and, 224, 225
Stereotypes, 53–54
    conflict and, 319–320
    of older employees, 450
    prejudice and, 365
    sex-role, 58–59, 375–376
Stress, 394–422
    alcohol and drug abuse and, 414–415
    behavior at work and, 412–414
    burnout and, 415–418
    health and, 406–407, 411
    life events and, 406–407
    managing, 419–421
    mental state and, 411–412
    nature of, 396–398